Research Anthology on Big Data Analytics, Architectures, and Applications

Information Resources Management Association
USA

Volume II

Published in the United States of America by
IGI Global
Engineering Science Reference (an imprint of IGI Global)
701 E. Chocolate Avenue
Hershey PA, USA 17033
Tel: 717-533-8845
Fax: 717-533-8661
E-mail: cust@igi-global.com
Web site: http://www.igi-global.com

Library of Congress Cataloging-in-Publication Data

Names: Information Resources Management Association, editor.
Title: Research anthology on big data analytics, architectures, and
  applications / Information Resources Management Association, editor.
Description: Hershey, PA : Engineering Science Reference, an imprint of IGI
  Global, [2022] | Includes bibliographical references and index. |
  Contents: Overview of big data and its visualization / Richard S.
  Segall, Arkansas State University, USA, Gao Niu, Bryant University, USA
  -- Big data analytics and visualization of performance of stock exchange
  companies based on balanced scorecard indicators / Iman Raeesi Vanani,
  Allameh Tabataba'i University, Iran, Maziar Shiraj Kheiri, Allameh
  Tabataba'i University, Iran. | Summary: "This complete reference source
  on big data analytics that offers the latest, innovative architectures
  and frameworks, as well as explores a variety of applications within
  various industries offering an international perspective on a variety of
  topics such as advertising curricula, driven supply chain, and smart
  cities"-- Provided by publisher.
Identifiers: LCCN 2021039213 (print) | LCCN 2021039214 (ebook) | ISBN
  9781668436622 (h/c) | ISBN 9781668436639 (eisbn)
Subjects: LCSH: Big data. | Quantitative research.
Classification: LCC QA76.9.B45 .R437 2022 (print) | LCC QA76.9.B45
  (ebook) | DDC 005.7--dc23/eng/20211019
LC record available at https://lccn.loc.gov/2021039213
LC ebook record available at https://lccn.loc.gov/2021039214

British Cataloguing in Publication Data
A Cataloguing in Publication record for this book is available from the British Library.

The views expressed in this book are those of the authors, but not necessarily of the publisher.

For electronic access to this publication, please contact: eresources@igi-global.com.

List of Contributors

Table of Contents

Section 4
Utilization and Applications

Volume IV

Section 5
Organizational and Social Implications

Section 6
Managerial Impact

Section 7
Critical Issues and Challenges

Preface

Society is now completely driven by data with many industries relying on data to conduct business or basic functions within the organization. With the efficiencies that big data bring to all institutions, data are continuously being collected and analyzed. However, data sets may be too complex for traditional data processing, and therefore, different strategies must evolve to solve the issue. For managers, data management can be particularly overwhelming as businesses sift through information and determine how to utilize it. Thus, investigating the current architectures and applications of data analytics is integral for achieving efficient and productive processes. The field of big data works as a valuable tool for many different industries.

Staying informed of the most up-to-date research trends and findings is of the utmost importance. That is why IGI Global is pleased to offer this four-volume reference collection of reprinted IGI Global book chapters and journal articles that have been handpicked by senior editorial staff. This collection will shed light on critical issues related to the trends, techniques, and uses of various applications by providing both broad and detailed perspectives on cutting-edge theories and developments. This collection is designed to act as a single reference source on conceptual, methodological, technical, and managerial issues, as well as to provide insight into emerging trends and future opportunities within the field.

The *Research Anthology on Big Data Analytics, Architectures, and Applications* is organized into seven distinct sections that provide comprehensive coverage of important topics. The sections are:

1. Fundamental Concepts and Theories;
2. Development and Design Methodologies;
3. Tools and Technologies;
4. Utilization and Applications;
5. Organizational and Social Implications;
6. Managerial Impact; and
7. Critical Issues and Challenges.

The following paragraphs provide a summary of what to expect from this invaluable reference tool.

Section 1, "Fundamental Concepts and Theories," serves as a foundation for this extensive reference tool by addressing crucial theories essential to understanding the concepts and uses of big data in multidisciplinary settings. Opening this reference book is the chapter "Understanding Big Data" by Profs. Naciye Güliz Uğur and Aykut Hamit Turan of Sakarya University, Turkey, which defines big data basically and provides an overview of big data in terms of status, organizational effects (technology, healthcare, education, etc.), implementation challenges, and big data projects. This first section ends with the chapter "A Brief Survey on Big Data in Healthcare" by Prof. Ebru Aydindag Bayrak of Istanbul University-Cerrahpaşa, Turkey and Prof. Pinar Kirci of Bursa Uludağ University, Turkey, which presents a brief introduction to big data and big data analytics and their roles in the healthcare system.

Section 2, "Development and Design Methodologies," presents in-depth coverage of the design and development of big data architectures for their use in different applications. This section starts with "Big Data Analytics and Models" by Prof. Ferdi Sönmez of Istanbul Arel University, Turkey; Prof. Ziya Nazım Perdahçı of Mimar Sinan Fine Arts University, Turkey; and Prof. Mehmet Nafiz Aydın of Kadir Has University, Turkey, which explores big data analytics as a comprehensive technique for processing large amounts of data to uncover insights. This section ends with the chapter "Big Data Analytics and Visualization for Food Health Status Determination Using Bigmart Data" by Profs. Sumit Arun Hirve and Pradeep Reddy C. H. of VIT-AP University, India, which elaborates on pre-processing a commercial market dataset using the R tool and its packages for information and visual analytics.

Section 3, "Tools and Technologies," explores the various tools and technologies used in the implementation of big data analytics for various uses. This section begins with "Big Data and Advance Analytics: Architecture, Techniques, Applications, and Challenges" by Prof. Surabhi Verma of National Institute of Industrial Engineering, Mumbai, India, which investigates the characteristics of big data, processes of data management, advance analytic techniques, applications across sectors, and issues that are related to their effective implementation and management within broader context of big data analytics. This section ends with the chapter "Big Data for Satellite Image Processing: Analytics, Tools, Modeling, and Challenges" by Prof. P. Swarnalatha of Vellore Institute of Technology, Vellore, India and Prof. Prabu Sevugan of VIT University, India, which presents an introduction to the basics in big data including architecture, modeling, and the tools used.

Section 4, "Utilization and Applications," describes how big data is used and applied in diverse industries for various technologies and applications. The opening chapter in this section, "An Analysis of Big Data Analytics," by Profs. Vijander Singh, Amit Kumar Bairwa and Deepak Sinwar of Manipal University Jaipur, India, explains that the immense measure of organized, unstructured, and semi-organized information is produced each second around the cyber world, which should be managed efficiently. This section ends with the chapter "Computational and Data Mining Perspectives on HIV/AIDS in Big Data Era: Opportunities, Challenges, and Future Directions" by Prof. Ali Al Mazari of Alfaisal University, Saudi Arabia, which provides a review on the computational and data mining perspectives on HIV/AIDS in big data era.

Section 5, "Organizational and Social Implications," includes chapters discussing the ways in which big data impacts society and shows the ways in which big data is used in different industries and how this impacts business. The chapter "Big Data and IoT Applications in Real Life Environment" by Prof. Anjali Chaudhary of Noida International University, India and Pradeep Tomar of Gautam Buddha University, India, discusses various applications of big data and IoT in detail and discusses how both the technologies are affecting our daily life and how it can make things better. This section ends with the chapter "Cloud Computing Big Data Adoption Impacts on Teaching and Learning in Higher Education: A Systematic Review" by Prof Fahad Nasser Alhazmi of King Abdulaziz University, Saudi Arabia, which evaluates and assesses the impact of big data and cloud computing in higher education.

Section 6, "Managerial Impact," presents coverage of academic and research perspectives on the way big data analytics affects management in the workplace. Starting this section is "Big Data Technologies and Management" by Profs. Jayashree K. and Abirami R. of Rajalakshmi Engineering College, India, which discusses the background of big data. It also discusses the various application of big data in detail. This section ends with the chapter "Exploring Big Data Analytic Approaches to Cancer Blog Text Analysis" by Prof. Viju Raghupathi of Koppelman School of Business, Brooklyn College of the City University of New York, Brooklyn, USA and Profs. Yilu Zhou and Wullianallur Raghupathi of Gabelli School of Business, Fordham University, New York, USA, which establishes an exploratory approach to involving big data analytics methods in developing text analytics applications for the analysis of cancer blogs.

Section 7, "Critical Issues and Challenges," highlights current problems within the field and offers solutions for future improvement. Opening this final section is the chapter "A Survey on Comparison of Performance Analysis on a Cloud-Based Big Data Framework" by Profs. Krishan Tuli and Amanpreet Kaur of Chandigarh University, India and Prof. Meenakshi Sharma of Galgotias University, India, which discusses the survey on the performance of the big data framework based on a cloud from various endeavors which assists ventures to pick a suitable framework for their work and get a desired outcome. This section ends with the chapter "How Big Data Transforms Manufacturing Industry: A Review Paper" by Profs. Victor I. C. Chang and Wanxuan Lin of Xi'an Jiaotong-Liverpool University, Suzhou, China, which defines what big data means for the manufacturing industry. It explains four advantages about big data analytics and their benefits to manufacturing.

Although the primary organization of the contents in this multi-volume work is based on its seven sections, offering a progression of coverage of the important concepts, methodologies, technologies, applications, social issues, and emerging trends, the reader can also identify specific contents by utilizing the extensive indexing system listed at the end of each volume. As a comprehensive collection of research on the latest findings related to big data, the *Research Anthology on Big Data Analytics, Architectures, and Applications* provides data scientists, data analysts, computer engineers, software engineers, technologists, government officials, managers, CEOs, professors, graduate students, researchers, and academicians with a complete understanding of the application and impact of big data. Given the vast number of issues concerning usage, failure, success, strategies, and applications of big data in modern technologies and processes, the *Research Anthology on Big Data Analytics, Architectures, and Applications* encompasses the most pertinent research on its uses and impact on global institutions.

Chapter 24
Building High Quality Big Data–Based Applications in Supply Chains

Kamalendu Pal

https://orcid.org/0000-0001-7158-6481

City, University of London, UK

ABSTRACT

Global retail business has become diverse and latest Information Technology (IT) advancements have created new possibilities for the management of the deluge of data generated by world-wide business operations of its supply chain. In this business, external data from social media and supplier networks provide a huge influx to augment existing data. This is combined with data from sensors and intelligent machines, commonly known as Internet of Things (IoT) data. This data, originating from the global retail supply chain, is simply known as Big Data - because of its enormous volume, the velocity with which it arrives in the global retail business environment, its veracity to quality related issues, and values it generates for the global supply chain. Many retail products manufacturing companies are trying to find ways to enhance their quality of operational performance while reducing business support costs. They do this primarily by improving defect tracking and better forecasting. These manufacturing and operational improvements along with a favorable customer experience remain crucil to thriving in global competition. In recent years, Big Data and its associated technologies are attracting huge research interest with academics, industry practitioners, and government agencies. Big Data-based software applications are widely used within retail supply chain management - in recommendation, prediction, and decision support systems. The spectacular growth of these software systems has enormous potential for improving the daily performance of retail product and service companies. However, there are increasingly data quality problems resulting in erroneous tesing costs in retail Supply Chain Management (SCM). The heavy investment made in Big Data-based software applications puts increasing pressure on management to justify the quality assurance in these software systems. This chapter discusses about data quality and the dimensions of data quality for Big Data applications. It also examines some of the challenges presented by managing the quality and governance of Big Data, and how those can be balanced with the need of delivery usable Big Data-based software systems. Finally, the chapter highlights the importance of data governance; and it also includes some of the Big Data managerial practice related issues and

DOI: 10.4018/978-1-6684-3662-2.ch024

their justifications for achieving application software quality assurance.

INTRODUCTION

The retail business world is grappling with major changes of new retail channels, increasing global customers, and growing complexity of supply chain operations. Customers are increasingly influencing how retail businesses design and set out their supply chain operations. These demanding customers can now do their shopping *anywhere* and *anytime*, and expect a more fulfilling experience from retailers. However, many retail businesses are dealing with how to find an innovative approach to sourcing, replenishment and distribution strategies to address these changes. Retail businesses are starting to consider seriously how best to optimize their supply chain operations to face fast-changing customer demand, while minimizing corporate expenditure and achieving healthy growth.

A retail supply chain consists of interconnected activities, and their associated business processes together to provide value-added service to its customers. Customer-engaged retail companies, from *automobile dealers* to highly attractive summer *beachwear makers*, always need different stakeholders' information for their supply chains. An entire network of manufacturers and distributors, transportation and logistics agencies, financial institutions, warehouses and freight-forwarders work together to make sure that the right goods and services are available at the right price, where and when the customers want them. Having supplied value-added services (e.g. products and associated customer services), the supply chain does not terminate. The retail supply chain is comprised of several steps from the front end, through the customer request, supply chain order processing initiation, quality assurance assessment for products and services, relevant training processes for staffs, customer support facilities, to maintenance and replacement facilities. Retailers are investing in *state-of-the-art* operational practices to optimize both cost and efficiency of their supply chain.

Figure 1. A schematic diagram of retail supply chain

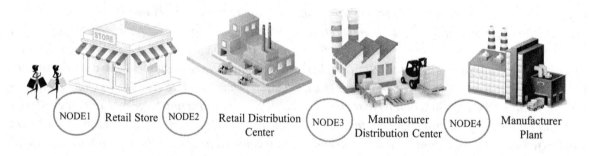

In a typical retail supply chain, raw materials are purchased from suppliers and products are manufactured at one or more manufacturing plants. Then they are transported to intermediate storage (e.g. warehouse, distribution center) for packaging and shipping to retailers or customers. The path from supplier to customer can include several intermediaries such as wholesalers, warehouse, and retailers, depending on the products and markets. In this way, supply chain management relates to business activities such as inbound and outbound transportation, warehousing, and inventory control. Importantly, it also embodies the information systems necessary to monitor these business activities. Figure 1 presents a simple diagrammatic representation of a retail supply chain, which consists of two separate legal entities, a retailer and a manufacturer. The retailer owns the first two nodes on the left-hand-side of the diagram, which consists of the retail store and the retail distribution center; and the manufacturer owns the last two nodes, the manufacturing distribution center and the plant.

Increased internationalization of retail industries is changing the operational practices of global retail supply chains, and many retailers have adopted new business models, either by outsourcing or by establishing business-alliances in other countries. Globalization has also led to changes in operational practices, where products are designed and manufactured in one part of the world and sold in another. The retail supply chain has become more global in its geographical scope; the international market is getting more competitive and customer demand oriented. Customers are looking for more variety as well as better *quality assured* products and services.

This evolution of many retail supply chain networks means that their members are working across different time zones, and bringing together many culturally diverse workforces. These teams are often quickly brought together and coordinated in nearly real-time to provide retail deliverables within short time spans and limited resources. In this way, collaboration and coordination among these teams plays a key role in delivering the ultimate customer experience; and it is also more information intensive. Under this working environment, nearly real-time collaboration between mobile and geographically distributed retail supply chain members is a very difficult task. It highlights the need for an efficient communication infrastructure that provides reliable on-demand access to supply process information accurately (Pal, 2016).

Information Systems (IS) play a significant role in coordination and decision-making for global retail supply chains. Recent development in IS, such as Enterprise Resource Planning (ERP), Material Requirement Planning (MRP), Customer Relationship Management (CRM), Vendor Managed Inventory Systems (VMIS), Warehouse Management Systems (WMS), Transportation Management Systems (TMS), marketing and collaborative planning, forecasting and procurement systems, help to make global retail supply chains more efficient. The generation of large volumes of supply chain data by these systems has provided an impetus for global retail supply chains to extract information from raw data to improve business performance.

More and more business activities are digitized and computerized; new sources of information and machineries with global retail supply chains bring new types of information. The amount of digital information pertaining to a specific retail supply chain fluctuates in real-time on different business topics, such as price, weight, packaging dimension, *carbon foot print* for consignments, weather forecast for consignments supply and delivery routes. Business practitioners get excited about 'Big Data' – the term *du jour* that describes the expanding universe of available data outside of that traditionally circulating in a retail company's CRM, ERP, or MRP systems stored for analysis. These new data sources originate in cyber-physical computing environments of global retail supply chains. For example, with every online survey from customers, Global Positioning System (GPS) signals from trucks or trains, tweets from the head of marketing, and every Radio-Frequency Identification Device (RFID) tagged package speeding off to the shrink-wrap station, retailers have more data than they know what to do with. Retail supply chain operations are hotbeds of data-inputs sought, captured, and reported. Some of this data produced within the global retail chain is unstructured and unwieldy – not suitable for applications based on standard relational database management systems. There is, however, a huge amount of unwanted noise in generated data simply waiting to be released into the operational environment. Intelligent business analysis brings rigorous data manipulating techniques with special purpose software, the *business analytic* platform, for timely decision making.

Retail supply chain mangers are increasingly seeking to *'win with data'*. They are reliant upon data to gain visibility into expenditure, looking for trends in corporate operational cost and related performance, and support process control, inventory monitoring, production optimization, and process improvement efforts. In fact, many retail businesses are awash in data, with many seeking to capture data analysis as a means for gaining a competitive advantage. In this way, appropriate data capture, data cleaning, and different data analysis techniques are each thought to be part of an emerging competitive area that will transform the way in which retail supply chains are designed and managed. In addition, due to the huge volume of generated data, the fast velocity of arriving data, and the large variety of heterogeneous data, the Big Data-based applications bring new challenges. It is a hard job to test the correctness of a Big Data-based software system due to its enormous size and timeliness. This is an important concern for Big Data-based software system practitioners who are motivated to come up with innovative ways of thinking about how data is produced, organized, and analyzed. Thus, Big Data-based systems quality assurance plays a crucial role.

The main objective of this chapter is to provide some perspectives on Big Data-based decision-making software applications and their quality related issues. The reminder of this chapter is organized as follows. Section 2 discusses basic concepts of Big Data and importance of business analytics; and the advantages of their use are highlighted in the context of retail supply chain management. Section 3 introduces a brief review of research in Big Data-based supply chain applications; and in particular it examines the influence of intelligent business software applications to modern supply chain management. Section 4 provides the fundamentals of data, data quality, and dimensions of data quality related issues. Section 5 highlights scope and process of data quality management. It also includes role of business teams in corporate data governance, and main advantages of seamless data governance. Section 6 examines some of the data quality monitoring facts. Finally, concluding remarks have been put forward in Section 7.

DATA EXPLOSION IN RETAIL SUPPLY CHAIN

In recent years due to increased automation of business activity planning and execution using a new generation of information systems (e.g. ERP, SCM, CRM), retail supply chains experience a deluge of data. Additional data is received by many sources, such as mobile devices, Radio Frequency Identification Device (RFID) sensors, robotic devices, and different online portal for global supply chain management. Such a *'data explosion'* has created issues on how to effectively and optimally manage copious amounts of data. There are also issues around how to identify innovative ways to analyses huge volumes of data to unlock information from it. Doing so would lead subsequently to crucial knowledge used to manage the retail supply chain.

As Big Data is one of the most *'hyped'* terms in the business information systems world now-a-days, there is no consensus as to how to define it. The term is often used synonymously with related concepts – such as Business Intelligence (BI) and data mining. This creates an interesting question about how these technical terms (i.e. Big Data, Business Intelligence, and Data Mining) are related. In a simplistic sense, all these terms are involved in analyzing data and may perform *advanced analytics*. However, Big Data is different from the two other concepts when data volumes, number of transactions and the number of data sources are so *huge* and *complex* that that they need *dedicated techniques* and *technical infrastructures* to produce meaningful outcomes out of it.

Figure 2. The typical types of Big Data application systems

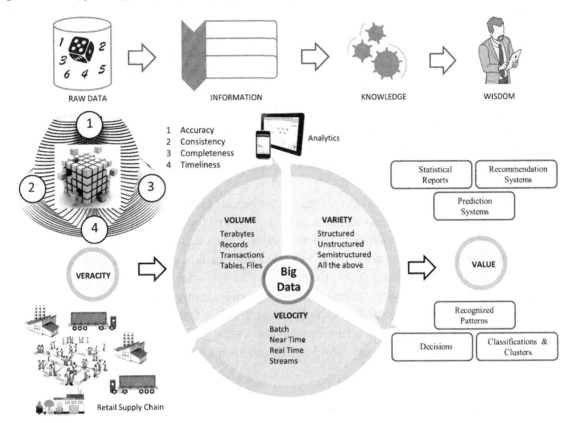

This also forms the basis for the most used definition of Big Data, the five V's: Volume, Velocity, Variety, Veracity, and Values as shown in Figure 2.

1. **Volume:** The sheer size of the data set (e.g. petabytes, exabytes or larger) in a transactional applications environment, of course, is a major challenge, and is the one that is most easily recognized. A petabyte is one quadrillion bytes, or the equivalent of about 20 million filing cabinets' worth of text. An extrabyte is 1,000 times that amount. However, availability of fine-grained raw data is not sufficient unless appropriate analyzing techniques are used for abstracting them in meaningful ways that are actionable. This characteristic, volume, bears demand on Big Data-based software application infrastructures.

2. **Velocity:** The velocity, with which data flows into the retail supply chain environment, or the expected response time to the data, is the second V-feature of Big Data. In several retail business applications, data continuously arrives at possible very high frequencies, resulting in continuous high-speed data streams. It is very important that the time needed to act on such data be very short. In this way, there is a huge shift in the data processing operation from batch processing to real time streaming. Big Data streams may arrive quickly in (near) real-time, requiring a timely response from the computing infrastructure to avoid data loss. Additionally, real-time or nearly real-time information makes it possible for a retail business to be much more *agile* than its competitors.

3. **Variety:** Data comes from different data sources. In other words, this characteristic refers to the fact that data comes in many formats: from structured data, organized according to some structures like the data record, to unstructured data, like image, sound, email text, social media (e.g. Facebook, Twitter) messages, which are much more difficult to search and analyses. Data streams can come from both internal and external sources within global retail businesses. Big Data may have diverse structures and forms, not conforming to the rigid relational structure of SQL (Standard Query Language) databases. In this way, Big Data-based software applications are using NoSQL database systems, which are useful for storing unstructured data such as sensor data, HTML documents, web pages, text, and e-mail message streams from data storage hardware and environment sensors, GPS (Global Positioning, System) data, click stream from web queries, social media updates, and so on).

4. **Veracity:** This feature is defined in relation to two aspects in a business environment: *data consistency* and *data trustworthiness*. Consistency demands that the data set must be statistically reliable; and data trustworthiness relates to a number of factors e.g. data origin, data collection and processing methods, facilities within Big Data-based information systems infrastructure. The data must be in a secure environment during the entirety of its lifecycle: beginning with collection from trusted sources to processing on trusted software systems infrastructure.

5. **Value:** The fourth V-feature for Big Data is value. The Big Data Value dimension denotes the potential value of Big Data which first requires processing, in order to make it useful for retail business decision making purposes. The Value feature bears special importance for retail supply chain design and management.

Big Data is changing the way resources are used within retail business environments. The managerial challenges are acknowledged within academic and practitioner circles; it is also highlighted that senior decision makers must embrace evidence-based decision-making. Detailed analysis and interpretation from Big Data can help those in global retail businesses make judicious decisions. In addition, it can help deepen customer engagement, optimize retail operational costs, enable business operational risks related warnings, facilitate resource management appropriately and capitalize on new sources of revenue. This extra demand on Big Data-based software applications for clear insights needs an innovative approach. An approach to find out meaningful value from Big Data-based software processing power as well as abilities to analyses the data (analytics) as well as appropriate skills.

In this way, data manipulation mechanisms transform data into information. Knowledge workers equipped with analytical tools identify patterns in the information and create rules and models, to be used to develop global retail business strategies. Retail enterprises gain wisdom by reviewing the impact of their strategies and repeating the cycle, as shown in Figure 3.

Value resides in Big Data, and the insights derived from the data can be leveraged for improved operational competitive advantage. Researchers and practitioners define analytics by three categories:

1. **Descriptive Analytics:** These types of analytics prepare and analyses historical data; they identify patterns from samples for reporting trends.

2. **Predictive Analytics:** These types of analytics predict future probabilities and trends; they find relationships in data that may not be clear with descriptive analysis.

3. **Prescriptive Analytics:** These types of analytics evaluate and use innovative ways to operate, consider business operational objectives, and try to mitigate all business constraints.

Figure 3. A diagrammatic representation of enterprise data transformation cycle

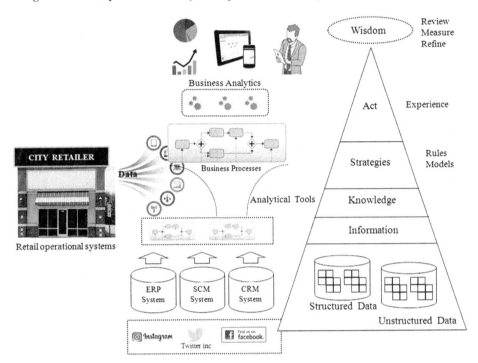

In addition, International Business Machines (IBM) Corporation provides the definition of Social Media Analytics and Entity Analytics. Social media analytics try to analyses data based on patterns embedded in it; and they use data classification and clustering mechanisms. The main characteristic of social media analytics is that data does not originate from within an enterprise; these are simply considered transactional data. Entity Analytics focus on sorting and grouping data belonging to the same entity. Modern computing power permits the analysis of data much more quickly, in a much more detailed fashion than ever before.

In a broad range of functional areas within the retail supply chain, data is being collected on an unprecedented scale. Decisions that previously were based on guesswork, or on painstakingly constructed models of reality, can now be made based on the data itself. Such Big Data analysis now drives nearly every aspect of global retail business. The promise of Big Data-driven decision-making is now being recognized broadly, and there is growing enthusiasm for this research challenges among academics and practitioners. While the potential advantages of Big Data are real and significant, and some initial successes have already been achieved, there remain many technical challenges that must be addressed to fully realize this potential.

RESEARCH IN BIG DATA-BASED SUPPLY CHAIN APPLICATIONS

In recent years Big Data and Business Analytics have attracted burgeoning interest among researchers due their potential in the business community (Waller & Fawcett, 2013). Particularly, research conducted by IBM Institute for Business Value in collaboration with MIT Sloan Review revealed the importance of

Big Data to business managers (LaValle et al, 2011). The subject has been embraced in special journals including Harvard Business Review (HBR, 2012), and some articles in MIT Sloan Management Review (LaValle et al, 2011) (Wixom & Ross, 2017). However, despite increasing contributions, Big Data-based software applications in supply chain management (SCM) are still in their infancy.

J R Stock (Stock, 2013) discusses Big Data driven supply chain management related issues in one of his recent publications. He also proposes that Big Data-based analytics for SCM will allow decision makers to make faster decisions. In an industry survey conducted by Mitsubishi Heavy Industries and consulting company Deloitte (Deloitte & MHI, 2014) supply chain executives were questioned about innovations that drive supply chains. The main objective was to get the views of business executives on emerging technology trends that could dramatically impact supply chains of the future. The survey also identified areas for analytics-based SCM. The Council for Supply Chain Management Consultants published a report on Big Data in SCM, based on interviews with supply chain managers. One of the objectives of this research was to find out best practices in using Big Data for better SCM performance. Many commercial Big Data applications related to SCM have attracted the attention of academics and practitioners (Watson et al, 2014) (Davenport, 2006) (Davenport & Harris, 2007) (McAfee & Brynjolfsson, 2012) (Deloitte & MHI, 2016). For example, some research work in corporate marketing management shows tremendous opportunity in Big Data-based business analytics (Svilar et al, 2013). The number of publications on supply chain network design using Big Data-based business analytics is also growing ceaselessly (Baesens, 2014) (Dietrich et al, 2014) (Sathi, 2012) (Siegel, 2013) (Watson et al, 2013).

It is evident from reviewing research literature that the critically important organizational functions of SCM will evolve and adapt to Big Data analytics. A particular industry report (Deloitte & MHI, 2016) expressed a view about the potential of supply chains to deliver massive economic and environmental rewards for society. However, to fulfill this potential, the report suggests technological innovation will need to play a crucial role. Big Data analytics can provide step-change improvements in supply chain visibility, cost savings, and customer service. The key is to not only generate insightful data analysis, but to share it between business partners along retail supply chain so that they can act on it.

To solve a problem, Big Data-based application used intelligent reasoning in automated software environment that helps users apply analytical and scientific methods to business decision making. The software applications that focus on the retail supply chain domain are referred to as retail decision support systems, providing Big Data-based tools to support a user for global supply chain related reasoning processes to come up with a solution to a problem. This type of reasoning can be considered an intellectual process by which retail managers use diverse types of artificial intelligence-based inference mechanisms (e.g. rule-based reasoning, case-based reasoning, model-based reasoning, and neutral network-based reasoning) to solve day-to-day operational problems.

Each of these approaches focuses on enriching some aspect of the traditional retail intelligent decision support systems. In addition, these automated software systems regularly make use of models that are expected to be reasonably accurate reflections of real-world work practices. In the term, *reasonably accurate*, one discovers the need of evaluation. The way these models are obtained and deployed across decision-making entities (i.e. *human* and *machine*) can introduce inconsistencies, incompleteness, redundancies, as well as problems in coordination. Consequently, there is a clear need for the evaluation of Big Data-based systems that are intended for serious business use.

Moreover, considering both the proliferation of Big Data-based analytics use for global retail business management and the fact that the data upon which these software applications (i.e. analytics) functions rely are often error-prone, there is an important need to assess the *data quality* as it pertains to the field of global retail management. As such, poor data quality can have a direct impact on retail supply chain operational decisions, and this will promote several tangible and intangible losses for global business. Retail operational managers are seeing the problems and impacts attributed to poor *data quality* growing in importance.

DATA QUALITY AND ITS RAMIFICATION TO BUSINESS ANALYTICS

In simple, pieces of data describe characteristics of retail supply chain day-to-day operations. Data is a formalized representation of the characteristics of business objects suitable for communication, interpretation, and processing. For example, the numeric value of price (e.g. 10 pounds sterling) and weight (e.g. 450 grams) of a commodity in a retail business represent some meaningful information. In this way, data are the building blocks of business information systems. When data is used within a context or when data is being processed, it turns into information. The value of data as an economic good depends on its quality. It is worth to note that poor data quality would impact setting strategy, its execution, ability to derive value from data, and ability to lead a retail business. It would also affect decision-making capability, trust between business partners, customer satisfaction, and employee morale.

Data quality is defined as a context dependent, multidimensional concept. Context dependency means that data quality is in the "eye of the beholder" (i.e. the user). Multidimensionality refers to the fact that there is no single criterion by which data quality can be fully ascertained. Therefore, data quality is often described as "*fitness for use*".

The term 'quality' is derived from the Latin (*qualitas*) and means characteristic, property, or condition. There are many definitions but the most commonly accepted definition of quality is "*The degree to which a set of inherent characteristics fulfills a requirement*". Quite simply, quality must be *defined* and *measured* if improvement is to be achieved. But one of the main problems in quality practice in the business world and its management is that quality is ambiguously defined such that it is commonly misunderstood. This confusion may be due to many reasons. First, quality is not a *single idea* but rather a *multidimensional* concept. The dimensions of quality include the *object of interest*, the viewpoint on that object, and the *quality attributes* of that object. Secondly, there are various levels of abstraction for any concept and when people discuss quality; one group could be referring to it in its broadest sense, whereas another group might be referring to its specific meaning. Thirdly, the term quality is used by ordinary people in their day-to-day communication. The popular views of the term may be totally and utterly different from its use in professions in which it is approached from the *manufacturing, or logistics management* perspective.

Popular Views of Quality

A 'popular view' of quality is that it is an *intangible trait*; it can be discussed, felt, and judged, but cannot be weighted or measured. For example, an important view of quality is based in luxury, class-based societies, and its testimony. Costly, big, and more complex items are regarded as offering a *higher level* of quality than their poor siblings. In this way, an Aston Martin is a quality car, but a Ford Fiesta is not, regardless of their actual reliability and logbook records (e.g. number of previous owners, accident history). In this view, quality is restricted to a small group of expensive products with supplicated functionality and items that have a brand name for *privileged groups*.

Professional Views of Quality

The misconceptions and vagueness of the popular views do not help the quality improvement effort in the commercial world. To that end, quality must be described and prescribed in a workable way. Several individuals made significant contributions to the professional world of quality, its measurement, and control. Edward Deming (Deming, 2000) defines quality as – "to create constancy of purpose for improvement of product and service"; Philip B Crosby (Crosby, 1995) presents quality as "conformance to requirements"; and Joseph M Juan and his colleague (Juan & Godfrey, 1999) define it as "fitness for use". These two definitions are interrelated and consistent with each other. These definitions of quality have been adopted and used among quality professionals (e.g. qualified industrial engineers, certified business engineers). These three definitions are interrelated and consistent with each other. These definitions of quality have been adopted and used among quality professionals.

"Conformance to requirements" implies that requirements must be clearly stated such that they cannot be misunderstood. Then in the development and production process, measurements are taken in pre-defined intervals to determine conformance to those requirements. The nonconformances are then regarded as defects – the absence of quality. For example, if an Aston Martin conforms to all the requirements of an Aston Martin, then it is a quality car. If a Ford Fiesta conforms to all the requirements of a Ford Fiesta, then it is also a quality car. The two cars may be very different in style, performance, and economy. But if both measure up to the standards set for them, then both are quality cars.

The 'fitness for use' definition considers customers' expectations and needs into account. Customers' expectations and needs involve where the products or services fit their uses. Since different customers may use the products in diverse ways, it means that products must possess multiple elements of fitness for use. According to quality management guru J. M. Juan (Juan, 1970), each of these elements is a quality characteristic and they can be classified into categories known as parameters for fitness for use. The two most important parameters are 'quality of design' and 'quality of conformance'.

Quality of design in popular terminology is known as grades or models, which are related to the spectrum of purchasing power. The differences between grades are the result of intended or designed differences. Using the example of cars again, all automobiles provide to the user the service of transportation. However, models differ in size, comfort, performance, style, economy, and status conferred. In contrast, quality of conformance is the extent to which the product conforms to the intent of the design. In other words, quality of design can be regarded as the determination of requirements and specifications and quality of conformance is conformance to requirements.

The two definitions of quality (conformance to requirements and fitness for use), therefore, are essentially similar. The difference is that the fitness for use concept implies a more significant role for customers' requirements and expectations.

To increase overall customer satisfaction as well as satisfaction towards various quality attributes, the quality attributes must be considered in the planning and design of the software. However, these quality attributes are not always congruous with each other. For example, the higher the functional complexity of the software, the harder it becomes to achieve maintainability. Depending on the type of software and customers, different weighting factors are needed for different quality attributes.

In view of these discussions, the updated definition of quality (i.e. conformance to customers' requirements), is specifically relevant to the software industry. It is not surprising that requirements errors constitute one of the major problem categories in software development. Particularly, Big Data-based application systems quality assurance is heavily dependent on data quality. To understand the data quality, one needs to appreciate the overview of data production process and related data quality issues.

Data Manufacturing Processes

Quality assurance has its roots in assuring the quality of a manufactured physical product; this is achieved by inspecting the product and evaluating its quality near its completion or at various stages of production. Data however is not as tangible as products that are more physical. Typically, a data product is its functionality and not its use. There is no physical data product to evaluate. This complex nature of data adds to the complications of assessing its quality.

Figure 4. Analogical comparison between engineering production and big data production

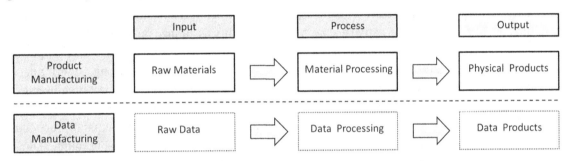

To understand data and its quality assurance related issues in Big Data-based software applications, one needs to pay a closer attention to data production processes in global retail supply chains. Various researchers and practitioners have tried to compare the similarities between engineering, product manufacturing, and data manufacturing processes (Emery, 1996; Arnold, 1992; Ballou et al, 1998; Huh et al, 1990; March & Heiner, 2007; Roner & Spiegler, 1991; Wang & Kong, 1993; Wang et al, 1995). Particularly, Wang and his fellow researchers (Wang et al, 1995) introduced a framework, as shown diagrammatically in Figure 4, to present the analogical similarities between these two manufacturing processes.

Moreover, Richard Wang (Wang, 1998) extended the previous analogical comparison between data and manufacturing processes by proposing data quality be addressed via a Total Data Quality Management (TDQM) cycle, which calls for continuously defining, measuring, analyzing, and improving data quality. This approach resembles Edward Deming's Total Quality Management cycle (Plan, Do, Check, and Act) and is analogous to the Define, Measure, Analyze, Improve, Control (DMAIC) cycle, as ascribed by Six Sigma (Smith, 1993), for data manufacturing processes. However, Allison Jones-Farmer and her colleagues (Jones-Farmer et al, 2013) pointed out that unlike the DMAIC cycle from Six Sigma, there is no control stage recommended in the TDQM cycle.

The analogy of data production process to a manufacturing process is, perhaps, one of the most widely accepted views in the business world. However, practitioners are putting forward some differentiating points, too. It is worth mentioning two of the most significant differences. In the manufacturing world, raw ingredients are input into engineering fabrication processes, and in the end the required output is produced. The raw ingredients are generally depleted as the items of interest are produced. However, in data production processes, the data represents the input into the data production process, and a transformed data product is the output of the production process. The data is generally not depleted through production. A bad batch of data in the data production process will remain until it is purposefully cleaned up. Perhaps the most pertinent, yet challenging, difference between a manufacturing and data production process relates to the difficulty in measuring the quality of intangible data. A very common phrase, of the quality controlling world, is "*you cannot improve that which you cannot measure*". Therefore, intentional attempts need to be made for defining and measuring data quality in Big Data-based applications. In order to do this, one needs to figure out the dimensions of data quality in a manufacturing supply chain.

Dimension of Data Quality

Dimensions of data quality are fundamental to understanding how to improve data. Data quality can be defined as "data that is fit for use by data consumers"; and *data quality dimension* can be defined as "a set of data quality attributes that represent a single aspect or construct of data quality". In this way, dimensions of data quality are already an active research area for quality assurance purposes. Practitioners and researchers suggest that data quality is comprised of several dimensions (Ballou & Pazer, 1985; Ballou et al, 1998; Pipino et al, 2002; Redman, 1996; Wand & Wang, 1996; Wang & Strong, 1996). Specifically, two research groups (Wang & Strong, 1996; Lee et al, 2002) categorized data quality dimensions into two distinct categories: *intrinsic* and *contextual*. Intrinsic data quality denotes that data has quality; understood largely as the extent to which data values are in conformance with the actual or true values. Intrinsically, useful data is accurate, correct, and objective, and comes from a reputable source. Dimensions include: *accuracy objectivity, believability*, and *reputation*. Contextual data quality points to the requirement that data quality must be considered within the context of the task at hand, understood largely as the extent to which data is applicable to the task of the data user. The focus of contextual data quality is the data consumer's task, not the context of representation itself. In this process - contextual dimensions consist of *relevancy, value-added, quality* (Wang & Strong, 1996), *believability, accessibility*, and *reputation of the data* (Lee et al, 2002; Lee et al, 2004). Identification and measurement of these dimensions have mainly been based on self-report surveys and user questionnaires, as they rely on subjective and contextual judgments of decision-markers' for quantification. But contextual dimensions of data quality put forward are inclined towards *information* as opposed to *data*. These dimensions are put forward by using data within a specific situation (Batini et al, 2009; Davenport & Prusak, 2000; Watts et al, 2009). The main consideration in this chapter is the quality of data, and concept of information creation out of raw data is irrelevant. The discussion is mainly focused to the intrinsic data and measurement of its quality related issues.

Intrinsic data quality has been consistently categorized along four dimensions: *accuracy, timeliness, consistency*, and *completeness* (Ballou & Pazer, 1985; Batini et al, 2009; Haug & Arlbjorn, 2011; Blake & Mangiamli, 2011; Haugh et al, 2009; Kahn et al, 2002; Lee et al, 2002; Passion, 2006; Canopies & Cataract, 2002; Wang & Strong, 1996; Zeithaml et al, 1990). The main concepts of these four dimensions are discussed below:

1. **Accuracy:** Accuracy indicates how close a measurement is to the accepted value. In the case of Big Data, the term "accuracy" means the degree to which the 'data' correctly presents the phenomena it was designed to measure. For example, a data record in a retailer's Supplier Relationship Management (SRM) system, where the postal address for a supplier in the system matches the

street address where the supplier is currently located. In this case, correctness of the street address value in the system could be assessed by validating the shipping address on the most recent material order. In this validation process, no problem context or value-judgment of the data is needed; it is either correct or incorrect.

2. **Timeliness:** Timeliness refers the temporal correctness of data values. Data values can be correctly inserted in a Big Data-based system, but is incorrect (out-of-date) if there is a change in the status of the object being represented between the times the data is inserted and when it is used. For some data, the concept of currency (the degree to which data value is up-to-date) is very important. For other data (which has got low volatility or representing '*permanent*' values), the concept of currency is not very crucial. For example, a floor manager in a retail business wants to keep track of inventory levels in real-time for effective operation management.

3. **Consistency:** This dimension of *data quality* refers to the extent to which data is presented in the same format. Consistency problems appear when datasets overlap and represent the same or similar concepts in a different manner, or when their specific content does not correspond. For example, in a retail supply chain information system's application all required delivery dates are entered in a DD/MM/YY (where DD is the day of the month between 01 and 31, MM is the month of the year between 01 [January] and 12 [December], and YY is the last two digits of the year in standard calendar) format to maintain system consistency.

4. **Completeness:** Completeness refers to the population of data fields. Incompleteness of any given field can have different effects on the quality of data. In other words, completeness refers to the degree to which data is full and complete in content, with no missing data. For example, if a supplier's address includes a name and high street address, but no county (or district), city, and postal code, then that record is considered incomplete. The minimum amount of data needed for a correct address is not present. A simple ratio of complete versus incomplete record can then form a potential measure of completeness.

Once data quality measures are understood, these quality measures can be monitored for improvement or adherence to standards. For example, data can be tagged as either accurate or not. Once tagged, there should be a method in place to monitor the long-term accuracy of the data. Combined with the measuring and monitoring the other three data quality dimensions, this helps to ensure that the records in the dataset are as accurate, timely, complete, and consistent.

Many of the issues in Big Data-based retail supply chain applications may not be new, but there is an evolving positive view of business analytics that is resulting in significant business transformations. The use of the term business analytics is now becoming standard to communicate the full life cycle of enhanced data-driven business decision making. Big data is the key ingredient in the computation of many analytical models in different areas of retail supply chain operations (e.g. demand forecasting, risk management, inventory planning).

In addition, the scale and scope of value that Big Data can bring is coming to an inflection point, set to expand greatly as the availability of Big Data converges with the ability to affordably harness it. Hidden in the immense volume, variety and velocity of data that is produced today is new information – facts, relationships, indicators and pointers that either could not be practically discovered in the past, or simply did not exist before. This new information, effectively captured, managed, and analyzed, has the power to change the retail supply chain management.

So, it is simple to become so focused on the anticipated business advantages of huge-scale data analytics that enterprises lose sight of the intricacy associated with data acquisition, preparation and quality assurance. In some ways, the clamoring demand for large-scale analysis only heightens the need for data governance and data quality assurance. And while there are some emerging challenges associated with managing Big Data quality, reviewing good data management practices will help to maximize data usability.

SCOPE AND PROCESS OF DATA QUALITY MANAGEMENT

The traditional prudence among conventional data quality professionals has evolved in recent years to advocate the application of manufacturing quality practices to Big Data management and its governance. With inferior quality data, a retail supply chain management system will fail to enhance its decision making. In general, Big Data-based application quality assurance refers to the study and use of different assurance processes, methods, standards, criteria, and systems to make sure the quality of Big Data-based systems in terms of a set of quality assessment criteria. The expectation of controlling the quality of Big Data must be viewed in reference to two aspects that increase the complexity of what one might call "*Big Data Quality*", namely:

1. **Widespread Repurposing:** One of the crucial properties of Big Data is the desire to use a wide collection of data sets, both *structured* and *unstructured*, for different user-group analyses. In the lack of proper data governance on reusing data sets means that each retail supply chain application must structure its data use in reference to the expected outcome. The result is that the same data sets are perceived to have different meanings in different references, creating technical questions about data *validity* and *consistency*.
2. **Data Restoration:** The assurance of being able to handle huge data sets creates the possibility of prolonging the lifetime of historical data that previously might have been demoted to near-line archival storage. The ability to access these older data sets and align them with data sets of more recent vintage implies the capability for enhancing *validation* and *governance* by controlling the information moves across the data life cycle into the Big Data-base retail business application systems.

These technical issues make Big Data quality assurance much more complex. The conjectural struggle posed when data sets are brought in from uncontrolled external sources is quickly being subsumed by the demand to make sure Big Data usability for the retail supply chain information consumers. The traditional method of attempting to govern the process of data creation and preventing errors is taking a back seat to pinpointing inconsistencies, standardizing data, and introducing improvements. In this way, realistic data quality techniques – including data profiling, data cleansing, entity recognition and identity resolution – are very important to assure the success of any Big Data-based system initiative.

The growing practice of Big Data, particularly about *business analytics,* pays much more attention to the aggregate outputs resulting from the accumulation and analysis of huge-size data sets, holding a variety of artifacts that are both structured and unstructured. This data variety, in conjunction with the fact that that data sets are likely to originate outside the retail business enterprise as opposed to inside,

Table 1. Some of the issues of data governance

Criteria	Description
Data Diagnosis	The hereditary meaning associated with data values that are originated from outside the retail enterprise may be slightly (or totally) different from the meaning of the internal business data.
Data Volume	The volumes of retail enterprise data may swamp the capability of existing data manipulation approaches (e.g. SQL queries or flat-file edits) to make sure there is conformance with anticipations.
Affirmative Management	There is very limited capability to manage the consistency of data sets that are produced outside retail business's administrative boundaries. For example, it would be very hard to try to make sure that Twitter feeds be free of spelling mistakes.
Keeping Consistency	In some cases, it is unwise to cleanse values in a procured source if the corrections would make the data inconsistent with the original source. This type of inconsistency can disallow traceability of application processes, and likely asking question about application outcomes.

complicates data governance and data quality assurance for many reasons. A summary of the problems and the corresponding description is presented in Table 1.

There is an expectation that to include data, originating from various sources (e.g. including emails, electronic documents, blog posts, text messages in social media and tweets) beyond retail business corporate boundaries needs guarantee *consistency* and *usability*. Big data quality managers generally try to inoculate the whole end-to-end data production flow against the introduction of data incorrectness, about design and development of Big Data-based analytics for supply chain management. Analytics developing software engineers are looking for trustworthy results, which can be achieved by using appropriate *data governance*.

In simple, governance is the means to infuse order, thereby mitigating conflict and realizing mutual gains (Williamson, 1996). Data governance is a framework of decision-making rights and responsibilities regarding the management and use of data, aiming at maximizing the value of data. Data governance is a crucial facet of delivering quality for business related analytical and corporate data integration projects. In doing this, data governance identifies the *relevant area* of business, *ownership* and meaning of information with efficient *procedures* and *corporate policies*. It also identifies *data infrastructure* and *processing capability* to meet demands of self-service data and accessibility while supporting compliance for *risk* and *security* requirements.

Retail organizations need to determine who should manage corporate Big Data resources. Data scientist roles have emerged to capitalize on the analytical opportunities of Big Data, but placing these specialists in retail operational business units without leadership at the organizational level might be insufficient to harness the full potential of Big Data and its software applications. To address the challenges and opportunities of Big Data, leading organizations have established a new breed of management role, the Chief Data Officer (CDO). One can describe the position of CDO as a *main data strategist* and this particular role will be responsible for business data management, data governance, use of data for corporate information systems (e.g. data warehousing, business intelligence, and business analytics), data quality assurance practices, metadata management related polices, and enterprise data management strategy formulation. In this way, to create appropriate collaborative data governance with business partners, it is important for CDOs to engage the proper teams within Data Governance Organization in order to align *corporate data governance* and *business objectives*. These teams are crucial to formulate strategic vision, identify data and their sources to be governed help the deployment of data governance policies, while proactively taking part in change management where it is necessary; and most importantly sup-

Figure 5. Role of business teams in data governance

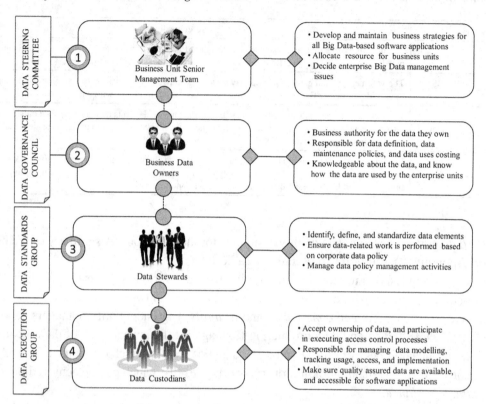

port the monitoring activities. Information and communication technology (ICT) teams are responsible for the management of data and measurement of data quality, and at the same time these teams collect and manage the overall business processes of *metadata* and *master data*. These teams also provide tools and technical provisions for data governance. Role of these business teams in a simple data governance environment is shown in Figure 5.

Under the right circumstances, applying proactive data quality monitoring, maintain Big Data-based software applications correctness, business users empowerment, and appropriate management of data and metadata can provide a motivating data governance environment.

Benefits of Seamless Data Governance Initiatives

Seamless data governance initiatives need to keep al the business partners engaged and makes sure proactive participation. It is also important to articulate the value created by data governance practices by using the correct enterprise data metrics. Business intelligence application software with proper graphical user interface facilities and relevant data metrics can be an appropriate tool to facilitate the impact of retail data governance initiatives. It can enhance business data quality parameters, and the capability to harmonize enterprise metrics to data definition standardization; and such software tools play crucial role in monitoring and managing the enterprise data governance policies.

Figure 6. Main advantages of seamless data governance

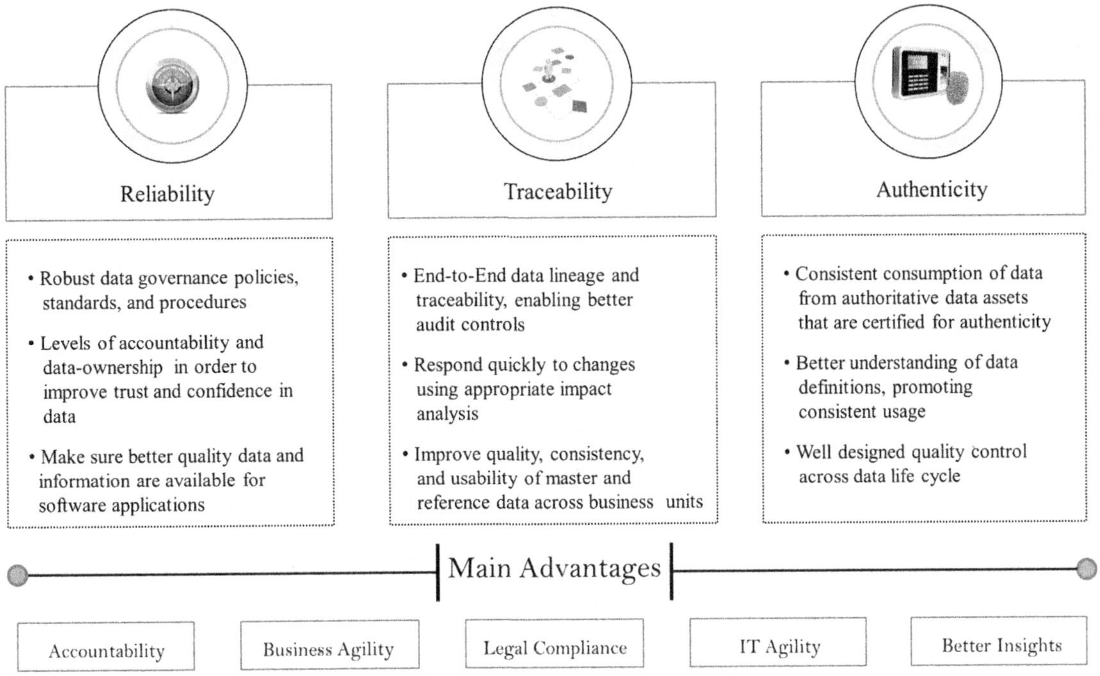

Reliability	Traceability	Authenticity
• Robust data governance policies, standards, and procedures • Levels of accountability and data-ownership in order to improve trust and confidence in data • Make sure better quality data and information are available for software applications	• End-to-End data lineage and traceability, enabling better audit controls • Respond quickly to changes using appropriate impact analysis • Improve quality, consistency, and usability of master and reference data across business units	• Consistent consumption of data from authoritative data assets that are certified for authenticity • Better understanding of data definitions, promoting consistent usage • Well designed quality control across data life cycle

Main Advantages

Accountability	Business Agility	Legal Compliance	IT Agility	Better Insights

The data governance plan consists of business operational rules for data quality management, corporate information systems master data management, metadata management, as well as the control the data access, use, and movement of data deemed sensitive by external regulations (e.g. HIPAA, and Basel II) or internal measures (e.g. the enterprise privacy policy). The deployment of each and every aspects of enterprise policies usher the intended advantages, as shown in Figure 6. However, enterprise data governance strategies and deployments, which enhance common objectives and integrate outcomes across these areas, enjoy advantages like improved reliability, traceability, and appropriate security of enterprise data. This will also create an appropriate communication platform for all the global business partners.

BIG DATA QUALITY MONITORING FACTORS

Digital technologies have a dual role – empowering, liberating, and transparent, yet also intrusive, restricting, and opaque. Big Data, as the embodiment of the latest advances in digital technologies, represents this dual character in a rigorous way, creating the tensions and dilemmas of modern technology savvy business world. Dilemmas, of course, do not easily lend themselves to solutions or resources. Nonetheless, they should not be understood as impediments to action. To go beyond dilemma, one needs to understand their conceptual origins, the dynamics of their development, the drivers of the dynamics, and the alternative motivating factors that they present. This tactic helps to trace out motivating factors for big data quality.

That suggests that under the right circumstances, applying proactive data quality methods such as profiling, standardization, cleansing, and record matching and linking can positively contribute to the ultimate business objectives. Introducing these techniques as part of a Big Data program is motivated by many key improvement factors, as shown in Figure 7, which will ultimately shape how those data quality management techniques need to be applied.

Figure 7. Big data quality motivating factors

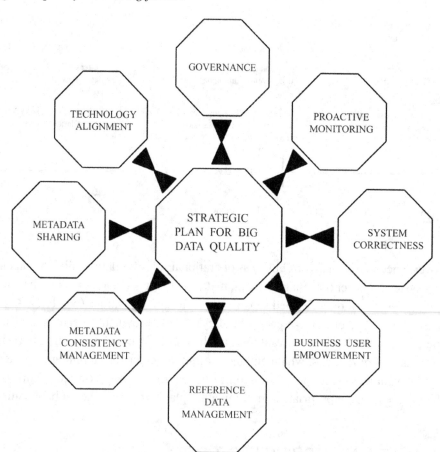

- **Proactive Monitoring:** The first step to proactive monitoring is to know the source of the data and how the data will be used. Data source is particularly important with inter / intra-enterprise monitoring as data formats are more likely to differ from source to source. Because a poor-quality data source will require more time and resources to resolve data issues, creating and using an excellent quality source should be the primary goal. When data errors are found to be contained with the data source, it is generally recommended that corrections be made to the data source. Proactive monitoring of most of important data quality dimensions can be used to signal data quality managers when data is not achieving expectations thus activating necessary business policy.
- **Business User Empowerment:** The incapability to impose management over the production of collected data sets is a naked truth that cannot be neglected. This conveys that the only policy for

data quality assurance is given out from the end-user group. Requesting data confidences from the users will structure the analysis and finally the assurance of data quality and usability. In addition, given the big data skills deficiency, reveling data quality processes to business users can serve to unburden IT and straightway engage relevant business users in the data quality process.

- **System Correctness:** Knowing the primary source of data and what happens to it as it moves through different systems across the enterprise is basic to enact confidence in the completeness and correctness of that data. Data validation and traceability is a crucial factor in business regulations (e.g. Sarbanes-Oxley Act, international customs and excise related regulations). These regulatory and compliance rules help to verify the accuracy, history and origin of the information. Global retail supply chains' data stewards promote this holistic system correctness culture within their business communities.

- **Reference Data Management:** Reference data is a special type of data. It is essentially code whose basic job is to turn other data into meaningful business information and to provide an informational context for the wider world in which the retail business functions. Even with a high numbers of data source, it is credible to put-together standards for commonly used reference data domains, particularly if those domains are to be used for monitoring data consistency and validity. Moreover, more data about individuals means that the need for entity recognition and record linkage will increase; similarity-assessment depends on good reference information for similarity scoring and linkage.

- **Metadata Consistency Management:** The data management office shall keep a data dictionary of key business terms. Data stewards shall be responsible for ensuring the correctness of data definitions within their subject areas. This makes sure appropriate reference data is a prelude to developing more general metadata standards. While the need may seem obvious for a variety of structured sets, consider that metadata definition is integral to any kind of examination of unstructured content, where it refers to the information about various images, graphics, videos or audio artifacts, or contributes to parsing content from freeform text documents.

- **Metadata Sharing:** Data stewards shall focus on customer, product, and vendor data as core subject areas. The data stewards for customer, product, and vendor areas will report into the sales, research and development, and supply chain groups, respectively. The data stewards will be responsible for ensuring the quality of the data within their respective subject areas. In this way, a different byproduct of the absence of source data semantics is the need for reinterpretation of meaning. The quality of data will reference how that information is used, and when data sets are used in diverse ways. There will be a requirement to collaborate on business terms that appear with frequency and what different users believe those terms to mean. Creating a participative view of metadata that urges collaboration and sharing will minimize the potential of sever inappropriate assessments.

- **Technology Alignment:** Data quality and data governance should not be counterproductive for the big data platform's performance. In this way, IT operational managers need to make sure that their data quality tools are adapted to execute within the Big Data environment appropriately.

- **Data Governance:** Data governance plays a crucial role in retail supply chain businesses. A well-defined catalog of information is required to align business and compliance requirements within enterprise and reference architectures. It is important to urge a standardized mechanism for information governance to lay structure and understanding within any retail business about data integration. This improves the value of information and empowers its usage.

CONCLUSION

One of the valuable assets within a retail company is its business-critical data regarding corporate partners, staff, products, financial information, and customers. Despite its importance, data is often replicated and scattered across business processes, systems, and applications throughout the company. Managing data effectively is a continuous activity, whereby retailers define the principles, policies, processes, business rules and matrices for fulfilling corporate strategic goals, by managing the quality of their data.

This chapter highlights the growing importance of Big Data-based trends that have the potential of changing and impacting the retail supply chain industry. Some of the sources of Big Data within retail business have been identified and discussed briefly. There are numerous examples of supply chain operations applying big data solutions which demonstrate the abundance of process improvement opportunities available through the effective use of data. The development of Big Data-based software applications has been proven useful in a diverse area of application for solving problems in global retail industry, for example – raw material procurement planning, marketing strategy formulation, logistics planning, and so on. The retail enterprises are leveraging the power of analytics in formulating business strategy in every facet of their operations to mitigate a healthy corporate growth. Nevertheless, there are increasing quality problems resulting in erroneous data costs in retail enterprises. This chapter provides informative discussions on Big Data-based systems; quality assurance related issues, including discussion about dimensions of data quality for Big Data, justify the reasons for approaches to proactive monitoring. It also discusses managing reference data and metadata, and sharing knowledge about interpreting data sets.

REFERENCES

Arnold, S. E. (1992). Information manufacturing: The road to database quality. *Database, 15*(5), 32–39.

Baesens, A. (2014). *Analytics in a big data world: The essential guide to data science and its applications*. Hoboken, NJ: John Wiley & Sons.

Ballou, D. P., & Pazer, H. L. (1985). Modeling data and process quality in multi-input, multi-output information systems. *Management Science, 31*(2), 150–162. doi:10.1287/mnsc.31.2.150

Ballou, D. P., Wang, R., & Pacer, H. (1998). Modeling information manufacturing systems to determine information product quality. *Management Science, 44*(4), 462–484. doi:10.1287/mnsc.44.4.462

Battani, C., Cappelli, C., Francians, C., & Maurino, A. (2009). Methodologies for data quality assessment and improvement. *Association for Computing Machinery Computing Surveys, 41*(3), 1–52.

Blake, R., & Mangiameli, P. (2011). The effects and interactions of data quality and problem complexity on classification. *Association for Computing Machinery Journal of Data and Information Quality, 2*(2), 1–28. doi:10.1145/1891879.1891881

Cooke, J. A. (2013). Three trends to watch in 2013, Perspective. *Supply Chain Quarterly, 1*, 11.

Crosby, P. (1995). *Philip Crosby's Reflections on Quality*. McGraw-Hill.

Davenport, T. H., Harris, J. G., & Morison, R. (2010). *Analytics at work – smart decisions, better results*. Boston: Harvard Business Press.

Davenport, T. H., & Prusiks, L. (2000). *Working knowledge: how organizations manage what they know*. Boston: Harvard Business Press.

Deloitte & MHI. (2014). *The 2014 MHI Annual Industry Report – Innovation the driven supply chain*. Charlotte, NC: MHI.

Deloitte & MHI. (2016). *The 2016 MHI Annual Industry Report – Accelerating change: How innovation is driving digital, always-on Supply Chains*. MHI.

Deming, W. E. (2000). The New Economics for Industry, Government, Education (2nd ed.). MIT Press.

Dietrich, B., Plachy, E. C., & Norton, M. F. (2014). *Analytics across the enterprise: How IBM realize business value from big data and analytics*. Boston: IBM Press Books.

Emery, J. C. (1969). *Organizational planning and control systems: Theory and management*. New York: Macmillan.

Haug, A., & Arlbjorn, J. S. (2011). Barriers to master data quality. *Journal of Enterprise Information Management, 24*(3), 288–303. doi:10.1108/17410391111122862

Hauge, A., Arlbjorn, J. S., & Pedersen, A. (2009). A classification model of ERP system data quality. *Industrial Management & Data Systems, 109*(8), 1053–1068. doi:10.1108/02635570910991292

HBR. (2012, Oct.). Getting Control of Big Data. *Harvard Business Review*.

Huh, Y. U., Keller, F. R., Redman, T. C., & Watkins, A. R. (1990). Data quality. *Information and Software Technology, 32*(8), 559–565. doi:10.1016/0950-5849(90)90146-I

Immonen, A., Paakkonen, P., & Ovaska, E. (2015, October 16). paracone, P., & vasa, E (2015). Evaluating the quality of social media data in big data architecture. *IEEE Access, 3*, 2028–2043. doi:10.1109/ACCESS.2015.2490723

Jones-Farmer, L. A., Ezell, J. D., & Hazen, B. T. (2013). *Applying control chart methods to enhance data quality*. Technimetrics.

Juran, J. M., & Godfrey, A. B. (1999). *Juran's Quality Handbook* (5th ed.). McGraw-Hill.

Kahan, B. K., Strong, D. M., & Wang, R. Y. (2002). Information quality benchmarks: Product and service performance. *Communications of the ACM, 45*(4), 184–192. doi:10.1145/505248.506007

Lee, Y. W., Pipino, L., Strong, D. M., & Wang, R. Y. (2004). Process-embedded data integrity. *Journal of Database Management, 15*(1), 87–103. doi:10.4018/jdm.2004010104

Lee, Y. W., Strong, D. M., Kahn, B. K., & Wang, R. Y. (2002). AIMQ: A methodology for information quality assessment. *Information & Management, 40*(2), 133–146. doi:10.1016/S0378-7206(02)00043-5

March, S. T., & Hevner, A. R. (2007). Integrated decision support systems: A data warehousing perspective. *Decision Support Systems, 43*(3), 1031–1043. doi:10.1016/j.dss.2005.05.029

McAfee, A., & Brynjolfsson, E. (2012). Big data: The management revolution. *Harvard Business Review, 90*(10), 61–68. PMID:23074865

Murphy, C., Kaiser, G., Hu, L., & Wu, L. (2008). Properties of machine learning applications for use in metamorphic testing, *Proceeding of the 20th Internal Conference on Software Engineering and Knowledge Engineering (SEKE)*, 867-872.

Pal, K. (2016). *Supply Chain Coordination Based on Web Service, Supply Chain Management in the Big Data Era*. IGI Global.

Parssian, A. (2006). Managerial decision support with knowledge of accuracy and completeness of the relational aggregate functions. *Decision Support Systems, 42*(3), 1494–1502. doi:10.1016/j.dss.2005.12.005

Pipino, L. L., Lee, Y. W., & Wang, R. Y. (2002). Data quality assessment. *Communications of the ACM, 45*(4), 211–218. doi:10.1145/505248.506010

Sathi, A. (2012). Big data analytics: Disruptive technologies for changing the game. MC Press Online, LLC.

Scannapieco, M., & Catarci, T. (2002). Data quality under a computer science perspective. *Archivi and Computer*, 21-15.

Siegel, E. (2013). *Predictive analytics: The power to predict who will click, buy, lie or die*. Hoboken, NJ: John Wiley & Sons Inc.

Stock, J. R. (2013). Supply chain management: A look back, a look ahead. *Supply Chain Quarterly, 2*, 22–26.

Svilvar, M., Charkraborty, A. & Kenora, A. (2013, Oct.). Big data analytics in marketing. *OR/MS Today*, 22-25.

Wang, R. Y., & Kon, H. B. (1993). Towards total data quality management (TDQM). In R. Y. Wanf (Ed.), *Information technology in action: Trends and perspectives*. Englewood Cliffs, NJ: Prentice-Hall.

Wang, R. Y., Storey, V. C., & Firth, C. P. (1995). A framework for analysis of data quality research. *IEEE Transactions on Knowledge and Data Engineering, 7*(4), 623–640. doi:10.1109/69.404034

Wang, R. Y., & Strong, D. M. (1996). Beyond Accuracy: What data quality means to data consumers. *Journal of Management Information Systems, 12*(4), 5–33. doi:10.1080/07421222.1996.11518099

Watson, M., Lewis, S., Cacioppi, P., & Jayaraman, J. (2013). *Supply chain network design – applying optimization and analytics to the global supply chain*. FT Press.

Watts, S., Shankaranarayanan, G., & Even, A. (2009). Data quality assessment in context: A cognitive perspective. *Decision Support Systems, 48*(1), 202–211. doi:10.1016/j.dss.2009.07.012

Williamson, O. (1996). *The Mechanisms of Governance*. New York: Oxford University Press.

Wixom, B. H., & Ross, J. W. (2017). How to Monetize Your Data, MIT Sloan Management Review. *Spring Issue, 58*(3), 10–13.

Zeithaml, V. A., Berry, L. L., & Parasuraman, A. (1990). *Delivering quality service: Balancing customer perceptions and expectations*. New York: Free Press.

KEY TERMS AND DEFINITIONS

Big Data Analytics: Analytics is the discovery, interpretation, and visualization of meaningful patterns in Big Data. To do this, analytics use data classification and clustering mechanisms.

Data Governance: Data governance is a crucial fact of delivering quality for business related analytical and corporate data integration projects. Simply put, data governance refers to the overall management of the availability, usability, integrity, and security of the data employed in an enterprise. A proper data governance strategy consists of a governing council, a defined set of policies (or procedures), and a plan to execute those procedures.

Decision Making Systems: A decision support system (DSS) is a computer-based information system that supports business or organizational decision-making activities, typically resulting in ranking, sorting, or choosing from among alternatives. DSSs serve the management, operations, and planning levels of an organization (usually mid and higher management) and help people make decisions about problems that may be rapidly changing and not easily specified in advance - i.e. unstructured and semi-structured decision problems. Decision support systems can be either fully computerized, human-powered or a combination of both.

Internet of Things: The Internet of things (IoT) is the inter-networking of physical devices, vehicles (also referred to as "connected devices" and "smart devices"), buildings, and other items; embedded with electronics, software, sensors, actuators, and network connectivity that enable these objects to collect and exchange data.

Neural Network: Neural network is an information processing paradigm that is inspired by the way biological nervous systems, such as brain, process information. It uses a classification mechanism that is modelled after the brain and operates by modifying the input through use of weights to determine what it should output.

Quality Assurance: Quality Assurance (QA) is a way of preventing mistakes or defects in manufactured products and avoiding problems when delivering solutions or services to customers; which ISO 9000 defines as "part of quality management focused on providing confidence that quality requirements will be fulfilled". This defect prevention in quality assurance differs subtly from defect detection and rejection in quality control.

Radio Frequency Identification (RFID): This is a wireless technology used to identify tagged objects in certain vicinities. Generally, it has three main components: a tag, a reader and a back-end. A tag uses the open air to transmit data via radio frequency (RF) signal. It is also weak in computational capability. RFID automates information collection regarding an individual object's location and actions.

Supply Chain Management: A supply chain consists of a network of key business processes and facilities, involving end users and suppliers that provide products, services and information. In this chain management, improving the efficiency of the overall chain is an influential factor; and it needs at least four important strategic issues to be considered: supply chain network design, capacity planning, risk assessment and management, and performances monitoring and measurement. Moreover, the details break down of these issues need to consider in the level of individual business processes and sub-processes; and the combined performance of this chain. The coordination of these huge business processes and their performance are of immense importance.

This research was previously published in Supply Chain Management Strategies and Risk Assessment in Retail Environments; pages 1-24, copyright year 2018 by Business Science Reference (an imprint of IGI Global).

Chapter 25
Big Data Analytics and Visualization for Food Health Status Determination Using Bigmart Data

Sumit Arun Hirve
VIT-AP University, India

Pradeep Reddy C. H.
VIT-AP University, India

ABSTRACT

Being premature, the traditional data visualization techniques suffer from several challenges and lack the ability to handle a huge amount of data, particularly in gigabytes and terabytes. In this research, we propose an R-tool and data analytics framework for handling a huge amount of commercial market stored data and discover knowledge patterns from the dataset for conveying the derived conclusion. In this chapter, we elaborate on pre-processing a commercial market dataset using the R tool and its packages for information and visual analytics. We suggest a recommendation system based on the data which identifies if the food entry inserted into the database is hygienic or non-hygienic based on the quality preserved attributes. For a precise recommendation system with strong predictive accuracy, we will put emphasis on Algorithms such as J48 or Naive Bayes and utilize the one who outclasses the comparison based on accuracy. Such a system, when combined with R language, can be potentially used for enhanced decision making.

DOI: 10.4018/978-1-6684-3662-2.ch025

INTRODUCTION

Classes of 'Big Data'

Big Data could be found in three structures: structured, unstructured, semi-structured.

Structured

Any information that can be put away got to and prepared as the settled configuration is named as a 'Structured' information. Over the timeframe, ability in software engineering has made more noteworthy progress in creating methods (Li, Wang, Lian et al., 2018) for working with such information (where the organization is outstanding ahead of time) and furthermore inferring an incentive out of it. In any case, presently days, we are predicting issues when the size of such information develops to an immense degree, normal sizes are being in the fury of a various zettabyte.

Unstructured

Any information with the obscure frame or the structure is delegated unstructured information. Notwithstanding the size being tremendous, un-organized information represents various difficulties as far as its preparing for inferring an incentive out of it. The regular case of unstructured information is a heterogeneous information source containing a blend of basic content records, pictures, recordings and so on (Anandakumar & Umamaheswari, 2018). Presently, multi-day associations have an abundance of information accessible with them yet sadly they don't realize how to determine an incentive out of it since this information is in its crude shape or unstructured arrangement.

Semi-structured

Semi-organized information can contain both types of information. We can see semi-organized information as a structured in frame however it is not characterized with for example a table definition in social DBMS. A case of semi-organized information is information spoken to in XML document.

Qualities of 'Big Data'

Volume

The name Big Data itself is identified with a size which is tremendous. Size of information assumes the extremely vital job in deciding an incentive out of information (Ahmed, 2019). Likewise, regardless of whether a specific information can be considered as a Big Data or not, it is an endless supply of information. Henceforth, 'Volume' is one trademark which should be considered while managing Big Data.

Variety

The following part of Big Data is its assortment (Lee, 2019). Assortment alludes to heterogeneous sources and the idea of information, both organized and unstructured. Amid prior days, spreadsheets and databases were the main wellsprings of information considered by the vast majority of the applications. Presently days, information as messages, photographs, recordings, checking gadgets, PDFs, sound, and so forth is additionally being considered in the examination applications. This assortment of unstructured information represents certain issues for capacity, mining and dissecting information.

Velocity

The term 'speed' alludes to the speed of age of information. How quick the information is created and handled to meet the requests, decides genuine potential in the information.

Enormous Data Velocity manages the speed at which information streams in from sources like business forms, application logs, systems, and web-based life locales, sensors, Mobile gadgets, and so on. The stream of information is huge and ceaseless (Anandakumar & Umamaheswari, 2017).

Variability

This alludes to the irregularity which can be appeared by the information on occasion, subsequently hampering the way toward having the capacity to deal with and deal with the info viably.

Advantages of Big Data Processing

Capacity to process 'Big Data' acquires numerous advantages, for example,

1. Businesses can use outside knowledge while taking choices
2. Access to social information from web crawlers and locales like Facebook and Twitter are empowering associations to calibrate their business systems.
3. Improved client benefit
4. Conventional client input frameworks are getting supplanted by new frameworks planned with Big Data advances. In these new frameworks, Big Data and normal dialect preparing innovations are being utilized to peruse and assess shopper reactions.
5. Early recognizable proof of hazard to the item/administrations, assuming any better operational effectiveness.
6. 'Big Data' innovations can be utilized for making organizing zone (Lv, Zhu, & Liu, 2019) or landing zone for new information before recognizing what information ought to be moved to the information stockroom. Such coordination of Big Data advances and information distribution center causes the association to offload inconsistently gotten to information.

Visualization of Big Data Analytics

Visualization has led to a rapid increase in the growth of innovations. The display can be categorized into analytical visualization and Information Visualization. When data is not directly processed and conveyed as information, then information Visualization is similar to Data Visualization. Information Visualization is used for visual analysis of public and private repositories such as business datasets, student datasets, medical datasets (Haldorai & Ramu, 2019) in their research article mentioned the use of visual analytics for information age-solving problems. People who access Social media sites such as

YouTube, Facebook, and Google leave their traces on social media and help other investigators to track them via social media datasets. Chen et al. mentioned the process of analytics of geo-sampled social media data along with the movement patterns and Visual Analytics of sampled trajectories.

What Is Business Intelligence?

The amazing quality the universe of information examination has seen is stunning, developing from spreadsheets to OLTP and OLAP frameworks and after that digging device for the procedure of choice making (Harerimana, Jang, Kim et al., 2018). "Business knowledge is intended to help the procedure of basic leadership." Arnott and Gibson characterize the job of business insight "to remove the data esteemed vital to the business, and to display or control that information into data that is helpful for administrative choice help." The authors noticed that business insight is "utilized to comprehend the capacities accessible in the firm; the condition of the workmanship, patterns, and future headings in the business sectors, the advances, and the administrative condition in which the firm contends; and the activities of contenders and the suggestions of these activities". Along these lines, Business knowledge (BI) is an umbrella term used to envelop the procedures, techniques, and estimations to effectively see, dissect and get it data significant to the history, current execution or future projections for a business.

What Is Business Intelligence?

The transcendence the world of data analysis has seen is staggering, growing from spreadsheets to OLTP and OLAP systems and then mining tools for the process of decision making. "Business intelligence is designed to support the process of decision-making." Arnott and Gibson define the role of business intelligence "to extract the information deemed central to the business, and to present or manipulate that data into information that is useful for managerial decision support." (Haldorai & Kandaswamy, 2019) notes that business intelligence is "used to understand the capabilities available in the firm; the state of the art, trends, and future directions in the markets, the technologies, and the regulatory environment in which the firm competes; and the actions of competitors and the implications of these actions." Thus, business intelligence (BI) is an umbrella term used to encompass the processes, methods, and measurements to easily view, analyze and understand information relevant to the history, current performance or future projections for a business.

Big Data

Data nowadays is flowing in from all directions be it a multimedia website, a sensor or RFID panel to support the internet of things or mobile applications the term Big Data is ominously causing the most turbulences. According to McKinsey, Big Data refers to datasets whose size are beyond the ability of typical database software tools to capture, store, manage and analyze. The exact grain size of the data set in case of big data cannot be defined explicitly (Mokhtari, Anvari-Moghaddam, & Zhang, 2019). Thus, big data forms the basis of data analysis of larger size that may be structured, semi structured or unstructured. According to O'Reilly, "Big data is data that exceeds the processing capacity of conventional database systems. The data is too big, moves too fast, or does not fit the structures of existing database architectures. To gain value from these data, there must be an alternative way to process it."

Business Intelligence Tools

Business intelligence tools (BI tools) act as a mechanism for companies to monitor data and generate business insights that are necessary components in making smarter, better decisions that drive results. But once research into BI is done a realization is observed that there are many types, from analytics and big data statistics to reporting tools and dashboards that offer at-a-glance information across indicators. When choosing the right business intelligence tools for an organization, consideration is given to the company, its employees, departments and teams – and the success factors that drive the process of decision-making. What isn't working currently, and what factors would benefit from improvement (Salloum, Huang, He, & Chen, 2019).

The goal thus is to make fact-based and insightful decisions that will improve company performance. BI Tools can range from simple MS-Excel spreadsheets to querying and reporting software, OLAP as well as data mining tools. But it may be conclusively reported that business intelligence tools can be categorized into generalized or tools that function on normal data sets, of smaller size, in structured or semi-structured format and big data-specific tools that utilize the big data, i.e., data large enough but of no explicit size and that too in any structural format be it structured, semi-structured or unstructured.

PHASES OF DATA ANALYTICS

The sort of systematic process picked is reliant on the client's utility and mastery. The client may shift from business examiners, engineers, end-client, researcher that require to work upon data, separated from information (Xiao, Li, Zhang, Liu, & Bergmann, 2018). The undertaking which is performed on information can be from basic information questions to information mining, algorithmic preparing, content recovery, and information explanation.

Planning Phase

In the readiness stage the information is being arranged, gathered, what's more, chose for further preparing or examination — the planning stage experiences following advances viz information arranging, information accumulation, highlight age, information determination. Here accumulation of information should be possible either by the review of information or utilizing existing information, and consequently, the information is chosen for the second stage preparing.

Pre-Processing Phase

The pre-handling stage bargains for the most part with sentence structure examination and remedy of information. After the readiness of information, the information is prepared for starting handling. This stage incorporates the information cleaning process, separating of information, the fruition of information, information revision, institutionalization, and change (Jang, Park, Lee, & Hahn, 2018).

Investigation Phase

After the pre-preparing stage, there is the investigation stage where the characterization and gathering of information are done in a way that information with comparative examples is united. The examination stages experience the accompanying advances viz representation, connection, relapse, estimating, arrangement and bunching.

Post-Processing Phase

The post handling stage is the last phase of information investigation. The post preparing stage incorporates the information understanding, documentation of information and assessment of information.

TYPES OF DATA ANALYTICS

Prescriptive analytics is valuable, but largely not used. Where big data analytics in general sheds light on a subject, prescriptive analytics gives you a laser-like focus to answer specific questions. For example, in the health care industry, you can better manage the patient population by using prescriptive analytics to measure the number of patients who are clinically obese, then add filters for factors like diabetes and LDL cholesterol levels to determine where to focus treatment (Haldorai & Kandaswamy, 2019).

The same prescriptive model can be applied to almost any industry target group or problem. Predictive analytics use big data to identify past patterns to predict the future. For example, some companies are using predictive analytics for sales lead scoring. Some companies have gone one step further use predictive analytics for the entire sales process, analyzing lead source, number of communications, types of communications, social media, documents, CRM data, etc. Properly tuned predictive analytics can be used to support sales, marketing, or for other types of complex forecasts. Demonstrative investigation is utilized for disclosure or to decide why something occurred. For instance, for a web-based life promoting the effort, you can utilize distinct investigation to survey the number of posts, specifies, supporters, fans, online visits, audits, pins, and so forth. There can be a great many online notices that can be refined into a solitary view to perceive what worked in your past crusades and what didn't. Spellbinding investigation or information mining is at the base of the huge information esteem chain, yet they can be significant for revealing examples that offer knowledge. A straightforward case of spellbinding examination would evaluate credit hazard; utilizing past budgetary execution to anticipate a client's imaginable money related execution. The expressive investigation can be valuable in the business cycle, for instance, to order clients by their presumable item inclinations and deals cycle (She, Liu, Wan, Xiong, & Fan, 2019).

Illustrative Analytics

As the name infers, elucidating investigation or insights can outline crude information and convert it into a frame that can be effectively comprehended by people. They can depict in insight concerning an occasion that has happened previously. This sort of investigation is useful in inferring any example if any from past occasions or drawing translations from them so better techniques for the future can be encircled. This is the most much of the time utilized kind of examination crosswise over associations. It's essential in uncovering the key measurements and measures inside any business.

illustrative analytics examines "what has occurred?" This is a straight forward methodology way to deal with assessing and that reduce the huge information into confined or little scale accommodating information chunks. The dominant part of the ventures keeps an eye on this application. As it's the perfect or plain procedure, a large portion of the online life patterns are found through this office. The brilliant component of this system is that it considers constant information gathering with vital information understanding which advantages to orchestrate approaches to the future (Haldorai & Kandaswamy, 2019).

Symptomatic Analytics

The conspicuous successor to elucidating examination is a symptomatic investigation. Indicative logical instruments help an expert to dive further into an issue within reach so they can touch base at the wellspring of an issue. In an organized business condition, devices for both distinct and indicative examination go connected at the hip!

Prescient Analytics

Any business that is seeking after progress ought to have a premonition. Prescient investigation causes organizations to gauge patterns dependent on recent developments. Regardless of whether it's foreseeing the likelihood of an occasion occurring in future or assessing the precise time it will happen would all be able to be resolved with the assistance of prescient systematic models. Generally, various yet mutually dependent factors are broken down to foresee a pattern in this kind of investigation. For instance, in the human services area, planned wellbeing dangers can be anticipated dependent on a person's propensities/diet/hereditary piece. In this way, these models are the most essential crosswise over different fields.

Prescriptive Analytics

This sort of examination clarifies the well-ordered process in a circumstance. For example, a prescriptive investigation is a thing that becomes possibly the most important factor when your Uber driver gets the less demanding course from G-maps. The best course was picked by considering the separation of each accessible course from your get course to the goal and the traffic imperatives on every street. An information expert would need to apply at least one of the above examination forms as an aspect of his responsibilities. In the wake of perusing the above post, are you left considering how to end up an information examiner, at that point If you are pondering about the extent of information examination in India, If you are excited about seeking after a profession in the field of information investigation, you can apply for these courses offered by Availed. On fruition of these courses, you would be qualified for probably the most difficult jobs in the area. A prescriptive examination can be named as a mix of upsurge reproduction which is the main methodology. It additionally benefits in producing the FICO rating to reason business establishments. By prescriptive investigation, Aurora Health Care spared $6 million yearly to lessen readmission rates by 10%.

Figure 1. Phases of Data Analytics

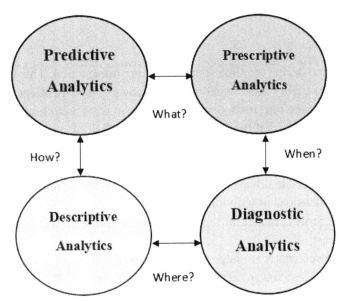

METHODOLOGY

The examination system of the investigation comprised of a contextual analysis of 5 associations in the wellbeing division, browsed Big Data Analytics pioneers headquartered in New York City and featured in driving professional distributions in the July – December 2014 period. The wellbeing segment was picked by the creators as the segment connected to the main division of concentrate in their fixation educational modules for Big Data Analytics at the Seidenberg School of Computer Science and Information Systems of Pace University– vitality, stimulation, monetary and retailing areas will be contemplated in the 2016 – 2019 period. The activities in the five associations in the wellbeing area were assessed by the first and third creators from an agenda definition instrument of the overview of the 41 previously mentioned Big Data Analytics components of the system program, in January – April 2015 period. The variables were assessed on proof of commitment to Big Data Analytics venture achievement, on a 6-point Likert-like rating scale: - (5) Very High in Contribution to Project Success; - (4) High in Contribution; - (3) Intermediate in Contribution; - (2) Low in Contribution; - (1) Very Low in Contribution; and - (0) No Contribution to Success. The assessments were established on inside and out perception of mid-administration venture individuals in the associations, averaging 3 – 5 staff in the associations; educated impression of perception basis by the third creator, a specialist of 35+ years; and research audits of optional investigations by the principal creator. The agenda instrument of the examination was checked with regards to develop, substance and face legitimacy and substance legitimacy, estimated in test legitimacy, continuously creator. The strategy was predictable in respectability and demonstrated unwavering quality with before concentrates by the creators on distributed computing and benefit arranged design (SOA) innovation. The information from the assessments was deciphered in the MATLAB 7.10.0 Statistics Toolbox continuously creator, in the May – June 2015 period, for the accompanying segment and the tables in the Appendix.

Approach and Solution to break in Top 20 of Big Mart Sales expectation

Hypothesis Generation

This is an essential advance during the time spent dissecting information. This includes understanding the issue and making some theory about what could conceivably goodly affect the result. This is done BEFORE taking a gander at the information, and we end up making a clothing rundown of the distinctive analysis which we can perform if the information is accessible.

Store Level Hypotheses:

- **City Type**: Stores situated in urban or Tier 1 urban communities ought to have higher deals due to the higher salary dimensions of individuals there.
- **Populace Density**: Stores situated in thickly populated zones ought to have higher deals on account of more interest.
- **Store Capacity:** Stores which are huge ought to have higher deals as they act as one-stop-shops and individuals would lean toward getting everything from one place
- **Contenders**: Stores were having comparative foundations close-by should have fewer deals on account of more challenge.
- **Showcasing**: Stores which have a decent promoting division ought to have higher deals as it will probably pull in clients through the correct offers and publicizing.
- **Area**: Stores situated inside well-known commercial centers ought to have higher sales because of better access to clients.
- **Client Behavior**: Stores keeping the correct arrangement of products to meet the neighborhood needs of clients will have higher deals.
- **Vibe**: Stores which are very much kept up and overseen by respectful and humble individuals are relied upon to have higher footfall and in this manner higher deals.

Product Level Hypotheses

Brand: Branded products should have higher deals given higher trust in the client.

- **Bundling**: Products with great bundling can pull in clients and move more.
- **Utility**: Daily use items ought to have a higher inclination to offer when contrasted with the particular use items.
- **Show Area**: Products which are given greater retires in the store are probably going to get consideration first and move more.
- **Visibility in Store:** The area of item in a store will affect deals. Ones which are comfortable will grab the attention of client first as opposed to the ones toward the rear.
- **Promoting**: Better publicizing of items in the store will should higher sales much of the time.
- **Limited Time Offers:** Products went with appealing offers and limits will move more.

These are only some essential 15 speculations I have made. However, you can think further and make your very own portion. Keep in mind that the information probably won't be adequate to test these, however, framing these gives us a superior comprehension of the problem and we can even search for open source data if accessible.

Data Exploration

We will be playing out some essential information investigation here and think of a few deductions about the information. We will endeavor to make sense of a few inconsistencies and address them in the following segment.

The initial step is to take a gander at the information and endeavor to distinguish the data which we conjectured versus the accessible information. An examination between the information lexicon on the challenge page and out speculations appears as follows:

Table 1. Data Exploration Values

	Item_MRP	**Item_Outlet_Sales**	**Item_Visibility**	**Item_Weight**	**Outlet_Establishment_Year**
Count	14204.000000	8523.000000	14204.000000	11765.000000	14204.000000
Mean	141.004977	2191.288914	0.065953	12.792854	1997.830681
Std.	62.086938	1706.499616	0.051459	4.652502	8.371664
Min	31.290000	33.290000	0.000000	4.555000	1985.000000
25%	94.012000	834.247400	0.027036	8.710000	1987.000000
50%	142.247000	1794.331000	0.054021	12.600000	1999.000000
75%	185.855600	3101.296400	0.094037	16.750000	2004.000000
Max	266.888400	13086.964800	0.328391	21.350000	2009.000000

Data Cleaning

This progression normally includes crediting missing qualities and treating exceptions. Even though anomaly evacuation is critical in relapse methods, propelled tree based calculations are impenetrable to anomalies.

PROPOSED SYSTEM

The proposed framework will defeat the constraints of the current frameworks. This framework will foresee the wellbeing remainder of the client dependent on the way of life he/she lives for example how much solid an individual is as of now and what the illnesses he/she can get are in not so distant future if the client keeps on carrying on with a similar kind of way of life. A portion of the explanations behind any client falling sick is the way of life the individual lives, the sustenance and the planning of having nourishment, not doing any activity, not taking enough rest and not taking breaks from work for unwinding. This framework will likewise recommend maintaining a strategic distance from those maladies. Recommendations of sustenance to have and way of life to adjust to have a sound existence. This framework will likewise give proposals of specialists whenever required. This framework will likewise demonstrate its client's late headways in the field of medicinal sciences.

Information Analysis Module will comprise of the expectation module planned in R. The model is planned to utilize Naive Bayes characterization algorithm. The characterization calculation is connected to the information present in the database.

COMPARISON OF VISUALIZATION TOOLS

The visualization tools have been analyzed and assessed on the premise of their highlights, support, attributes, and offices gave. A few datasets with size fluctuating Densities were tried on every one of these devices, and Google Charts and Apache Zeppelin were considered on needs as they outflanked the examination test. Scene: As examined in the writing review, Tableau is a Visualization device which is utilized in numerous corporate ventures and territories of the building. Its primary reason for existing is utilized to make outlines, pie charts and maps for graphical examination. Discussing cost, Tableau is available for $200 every year for a solitary client get to. Combination Charts XL is the new e-outlines created utilizing JavaScript for web and portable by Infosoft Global private constrained offer an incredible component of similarity with web programs (Mozilla Firefox, Google Chrome, and Safari).

Additionally, this enables the delicate mapped code to prepare methods, for example, outlines, line charts, pie diagrams, and others. Numerous social associations, for example, Facebook, Twitter, and other colossal associations use Data Wrapper apparatuses for reportage and Analytics. It has an intuitive GUI and is Easy to utilize, requires right around zero Coding. Google Charts is an API made by Google which is anything but difficult to learn and envision information. Takes a shot at all cutting-edge programs and can peruse information from MySQL, Big Data's HDFS and exceed expectations spreadsheet. The main drawback of Google graphs is that it re-quires a system association with showcase the pictured substance. This representation technique would be a perfect skill to use in the proposed idea as the API is suitable to coordinate with an incorporated advancement Environment (IDE, for example, Eclipse. The information created in SQL can be transported into Eclipse utilizing modules and .container records availability strategies. The information can be installed in the API code and displayed on the web interface in the 2D frame. Ying Zhu in the year 2012 featured the ideas of Google maps and instruments utilized for Visualization. The proposed hypothesis turned out to be entirely noteworthy for understudies seeking after investigations of significance.

NOURISHMENT QUALITY

Quality incorporates positive and negative traits that impact an item's incentive to the purchaser. Positive properties that show great quality might be the inception, shading, flavor, surface and handling strategy for the sustenance, while negative traits might be unmistakable deterioration, sullying with foulness, discoloration, or terrible smells or tastes. Anyway, not every perilous nourishment may show terrible quality, that is, hazardous sustenance may have all the earmarks of being of good quality, for example, spoiled meat camouflaged utilizing dye or solid flavors. This qualification among security and quality has suggestions for open arrangement and impacts the nature and substance of the sustenance control framework most suited to meet foreordained national destinations.

How Is Nourishment Quality Assessed?

Customarily, characteristics of sustenance are assessed by our tactile organs – our eyes, nose or mouth or, all the more as of late, by the utilization of instruments. Tangible assessment is normally drilled by sustenance administrative specialists who comprise of deciding the nature of nourishment by a board of judges. The assessment manages to estimate, assessing, dissecting and deciphering the characteristics of sustenance as they are seen by the faculties of sight, taste, contact, and hearing.

Watchful inspecting of the nourishment is important for tangible assessment. It is not constantly conceivable to recognize with tactile strategies alone the defilement of sustenance by pesticides, veterinary medication deposits and contaminated. Target assessment is done which incorporates compound, physiochemical, microbial and physical techniques for examination. Compound techniques incorporate the assurance of nutritive estimation of nourishments when cooking, and to distinguish the results of disintegration and adulterants in sustenance's. The most generally utilized target assessment is the estimation of physical properties by the utilization of instruments. Estimations of the appearance and volume of nourishments are additionally vital.

What Is Sustenance Wellbeing?

Sustenance wellbeing alludes to constraining the nearness of those perils whether endless or intense, that may make nourishment harmful to the soundness of the purchaser. Sustenance wellbeing is tied in with creating, taking care of, putting away and planning nourishment to anticipate disease and defilement in the sustenance generation chain and to help guarantee that nourishment quality and healthiness are kept up to advance great wellbeing.

How Protected Is Natural or Privately Created Nourishment?

Natural and privately created sustenance's may have ecological advantages, for example, utilizing fewer pesticides or composts. These sustenance's, similar to other people, can be presented to destructive microbes amid the developing and collecting process. It is vital for agriculturists and merchants to utilize great clean practices to limit nourishment defilement. Purchasers ought to dependably plan and cook sustenance appropriately, regardless of where it is from.

What Is the Hazard Analysis of Critical Control Point Framework (HACCP) and How Does HACCP Work in Sustenance Generation

HACCP, or the Hazard Analysis Critical Control Point framework, is a procedure control framework that distinguishes where risks may happen in the nourishment generation process and institute stringent activities to keep the dangers from happening. By entirely observing and controlling each progression of the procedure, there is less shot for perils to happen. HACCP is an essential piece of the current sustenance industry used to distinguish and control real nourishment dangers, for example, microbiological, compound and physical contaminants. Shoppers can actualize HACCP-like practices in the home by following appropriate capacity, taking care of, cooking and cleaning systems. The presentation of preventive methodologies, for example, HACCP, have brought about industry assuming more noteworthy liability for and control of sustenance dangers. Such an incorporated methodology encourages enhanced shopper assurance, successfully invigorates horticulture and the nourishment handling industry, and advances residential and global sustenance exchange.

What Are Sustenance Security Issues Identified With Fish and Fish?

Fish and fish can wind up tainted with pathogens, for example, vibrio cholera, salmonella, e. coli, shigella, listeria because of human action or poor cleanliness and sanitation amid nourishment creation and preparing. There have been flare-ups of foodborne diseases and diseases connected to the utilization of polluted fish and fish. Likewise, methyl mercury is framed by bacterial activity in an amphibian domain from the dumping of mechanical mercury just as regular wellsprings of basic mercury. Testing of fish against methyl mercury is requested by most bringing in nations. Certain parasite hatchlings can be available in fish, which is the reason most fish ought to be cooked all together.

What Is Nourishment Sullying and What Might Be Potential Reasons for Tainting?

Nourishment contaminants are any substances not purposefully added to sustenance, which are available in such nourishment because of the creation (counting tasks completed in harvest cultivating, creature farming and aquaculture), make, handling, arrangement, treatment, pressing, bundling, transport or holding of such sustenance or because of ecological sullying. Nourishment sullying alludes to the nearness of destructive synthetic substances or miniaturized scale creatures in sustenance, which can cause a few weakening diseases whenever devoured. The unexpected pollution may happen amid creation, handling, stockpiling and showcasing. Palatable oil might be debased amid handling because of spillage of mineral oil underway line.

Sustenance sullying is a significantly greater danger in nations of the South-East Asia area because of the absence of delivering collecting standards, nourishment dealing with models, and natural directions.

What Is Being Done to Lessen the Introduction to Pesticides?

It is generally realized that pesticides/bug sprays and herbicides/fungicides are utilized for nuisance and weed/deterioration control. These agrochemicals are accessible over the counter; ranchers may utilize them without legitimate comprehension or supervision. These synthetic concoctions can be perilous, and there is dependably an opportunity of tainting of farming produce with deposits of these synthetic compounds. Considering the conceivable wellbeing peril of dietary admission of buildups of these synthetic substances, the Joint FAO/WHO Meetings on Pesticide Residues gives free logical master guidance on pesticide deposits, remaining cutoff points and the adequate most extreme dietary admission (ADI) and greatest lingering limit (MRL) based on proof-based data and hazard appraisal.

What Is Satisfactory Day by Day Allow (ADI) and the Greatest Lingering Limit (MRL)?

Adequate every day consumption (ADI) of a substance is the day by day allow which, amid a whole lifetime, gives off an impression of being without apparent hazard to the wellbeing of the buyer based on all the well-established actualities at the season of the assessment of the synthetic by the Joint FAO/

WHO Meeting on Pesticide Residues (JMPR). It is communicated in milligrams of the substance per kilogram of body weight. Greatest lingering limit (MRL) is the most extreme convergence of a pesticide buildup (communicated as mg/kg), prescribed by the Codex Alimentarius Commission to be legitimately allowed in nourishment items and creature bolsters. Particular MRLs are proposed to be toxicologically worthy. MRLs which are principally expected to apply in universal exchange are gotten from estimations made by the JMPR following both:

1. Toxicological evaluation of the pesticide and its buildup
2. Review of buildup information from administered preliminaries and managed utilizes including those reflecting national sustenance farming practices. Information from directed preliminaries led at the most noteworthy broadly prescribed, approved, or enlisted utilizes are incorporated into the audit. To suit varieties in national bug control necessities, ADI and MRLs are likewise decided for veterinary medication deposits and antimicrobial substances as these synthetic concoctions are utilized for development advancement and creature illness avoidance and control.

Instances of Data

Practically all product programs expect information to do anything valuable. For instance, if you are altering an archive in a word processor, for example, Microsoft Word, the report you are dealing with is the information. The word-preparing programming can control the information: make another report, copy an archive, or alter a record. Some different instances of information are an MP3 music document, a video record, a spreadsheet, a site page, and a digital book. Now and again, for example, with a digital book, you may just be able to peruse the information.

Data Types

When characterizing the fields in a database table, we should give each handle an information type. For instance, the field Birth Year is a year, so it will be a number, while the First Name will be content. Most current databases take into account a few unique information types to be put away. A portion of the more typical information types are recorded here:

1. **Text:** For putting away non-numeric information that is brief, by and large under 256 characters. The database fashioner can distinguish the greatest length of the content.
2. **Number:** For putting away numbers. There are generally a couple of various number sorts that can be chosen, contingent upon how extensive the biggest number will be.
3. **Yes/No:** A unique type of the number information type that is (typically) one byte long, with a 0 for "No" or "False" and a 1 for "Yes" or "Genuine."
4. **Date/Time:** An extraordinary type of the number information type that can be deciphered as a number or a period.
5. **Currency:** An extraordinary type of number information type that arranges all qualities with a money maker and two decimal spots.
6. **Paragraph Text:** This information type considers message longer than 256 characters.
7. **Object:** This information type takes into consideration the capacity of information that can't be entered employing console, for example, a picture or a music record.

There are two imperative reasons that we should legitimately characterize the information kind of a field. Initial, an information type tells the database what capacities can be performed with the information. For instance, on the off chance that we wish to perform scientific capacities with one of the fields, we should make certain to tell the database that the field is a number information type. So, on the off chance that we have, say, a field putting away a birth year, we can subtract the number put away in that field from the present year to get age. The second essential motivation to characterize information type is with the goal that the correct measure of the storage room is designated for our information. For instance, if the First Name field is characterized as a text (50) information type, this implies fifty characters are selected for every first name we need to store. In any case, regardless of whether the primary name is just five characters in length, fifty characters (bytes) will be designated. While this may not appear to be a major ordeal, if our table winds up holding 50,000 names, we are dispensing $50 * 50,000 = 2,500,000$ bytes for the capacity of these qualities. It might be reasonable to lessen the span of the field, so we don't squander the storage room.

CASES ANALYSIS

Notwithstanding being such a popular expression as of late, huge information is as yet an entirely shapeless term. While datasets have dependably existed, with late advances in innovation, we have more routes than any time in recent memory to catch immense measures of information, (for example, through implanted frameworks like sensors) and better approaches to store them. Enormous information likewise incorporates the procedures and devices used to dissect, envision, and use this tremendous volume of information to tackle it and help individuals settle on better choices.

The prescient investigation is another word that is frequently observed with enormous information. Fundamentally, prescient investigation alludes to the utilization of verifiable information and measurable procedures, for example, machine figuring out how to make forecasts about what's to come. A precedent may be how Netflix recognizes what you need to watch (forecasts) before you do, in light of your past survey propensities (authentic information). It is likewise imperative to take note of that information doesn't such allude to lines and segments in a spreadsheet, yet additionally increasingly complex information records, for example, recordings, pictures, sensor information, etc.

The best way to see how big data applies to our food is through an example from my own life. It's no secret that I love Stacy's Pita Chips. Despite so, it was a surprise when I opened up my Kroger app the other day and found a digital coupon for these pita chips staring straight back at me. How did they know what I was thinking? Was it just a happy coincidence? Kroger was one of the first food retailers in the US to jump onto big data analytics bandwagon, by using previously collected consumer data to generate personalized offers as well as tailored pricing for its consumers. They were also the first to use infrared body-heat sensors combined with a computer algorithm to track how customers were moving through the store, and accordingly, predict how many cashiers to deploy, thus shortening check-out time for shoppers.

From the first look, it gives the idea that information examination utilized in the sustenance business is frequently based on store network the board, operational effectiveness and marketing1, for example, mining buyer information to comprehend their conduct, or making sense of how to stock items at the perfect time to give organizations a focused edge. Be that as it may, enormous information is likewise a noteworthy player in nourishment quality and wellbeing, however, isn't frequently discussed. This specific article centers around four more contextual investigations in which huge information examination are utilized for propelling nourishment wellbeing.

Chicago's Sanitation Inspections

In the city of Chicago, there are just 32 auditors in charge of the sterile examinations of more than 15,000 sustenance foundations in the city of Chicago, which comes down to approximately 470 foundations for every reviewer. Basic infringement of the sanitation code can prompt the spread of foodborne diseases, in this way getting eateries with infringement at an early stage is principal.

The program examines 10 years of verifiable information utilizing 13 primary indicators, (for example, close-by refuse objections) to recognize the high-chance foundations, with the objective of occupying valuable assets (overseers for this situation) to the more hazardous sustenance foundations so any basic infringement can be immediately distinguished and corrected before they make anybody debilitated.

Given results from the examination, a 2-month test case program in which controllers were all the more effectively apportioned was launched10. By and large, foundations with infringement were discovered 7.5 days sooner than when the monitors worked as usual11. Need to know the best part? The logical code utilized for gauging nourishment investigations is composed on an open-source programming dialect and accessible for nothing on Github, enabling clients to constantly enhance the calculation.

Whole Genome Sequencing

The approach of reasonable and quick entire genome sequencing is creating an abundance of high-goals genomic information. At the essential dimension, entire genome sequencing can separate practically any strain of pathogens, something that past systems, for example, beat field gel electrophoresis (PFGE) was not able to do. At the more elevated amount, genomic information is being created in enough high-goals to track and follow foodborne diseases crosswise over various sustenance sources, nourishment fabricating offices and clinical cases.

The FDA is likewise fronting a global exertion called the GenomeTrakr to organize, where research facilities around the globe are sequencing pathogens segregated from debased sustenance, natural sources and foodborne outbreaks12. This exertion comes full circle in a worldwide database where general wellbeing authorities can rapidly survey for data when required. Theoretically, if a nourishment episode happens, the pathogen can be secluded from the culpable sustenance, its genome sequenced and after that immediately contrasted with the database. Since the genomic information of a specific animal category or strain of foodborne pathogen is not quite the same as one geographic region to another, knowing the geographic zone of the obscure pathogen can be instrumental in deciding the root wellspring of sullying.

Given our inexorably worldwide sustenance supply and the way that nourishment items are regularly multi-fixing, this will be a vigorous instrument for following sustenance pollution rapidly and expelling any debased nourishment items from the sustenance supply.

What's Next?

Foodborne ailments slaughter practically a large portion of a million people for each year13, with a lot more hospitalized, and even a lot more who are influenced however did not report their side effects. Given late advancements in our capacity to catch, store and process information, the nourishment business is exceptionally situated to take measures to lessen foodborne sicknesses. The contextual investigations here are disengaged to give a case of what prescient examination and enormous information can mean for nourishment wellbeing. It isn't just about what specific innovation, sensor, or calculation that can do something amazing, however it is likewise about the collection of extensive, apparently random datasets, can uncover examples and help us inventively enhance nourishment wellbeing.

Encouraging the selection of information driven culture in sustenance science and security requires the help of the scholarly world as well as contributing to the administration and industry. There are numerous energetic scholastic establishments and network software engineers who are eager to help. Work that should be possible today incorporates building up the enormous information framework, preparing and mindfulness for future nourishment experts.

What Is R?

R is a coordinated suite of programming offices for information control, estimation and graphical show. In addition to other things it has

1. A compelling information taking care of and storeroom,
2. A suite of administrators for estimations on exhibits, specifically networks,
3. A substantial, reasonable, coordinated gathering of moderate devices for information investigation,
4. Graphical offices for information investigation and show either straightforwardly at the PC or on the printed version, and
5. A very much created, straightforward and viable programming dialect (called 'S') which incorporates conditionals, circles, client characterized recursive capacities and info and yield offices. (Surely the vast majority of the framework provided capacities are themselves written in the S dialect.)

The expression "condition" is expected to describe it as a completely arranged and rational framework, as opposed to a steady, gradual addition of unmistakable and firm devices, as is every now and again the case with other information investigation programming.

R is particularly a vehicle for recently creating techniques for intuitive information investigation. It has grown quickly and has been reached out by a substantial accumulation of bundles. Notwithstanding, most programs written in R are transient, composed for a solitary bit of information examination.

Basic Features of R

In the good old days, a key element of R was that its language structure is fundamentally the same as S, making it simple for S-PLUS clients to switch over. While the R's sentence structure is about indistinguishable to that of S's, R's semantics, while externally like S, is very extraordinary. Indeed, R is a lot nearer to the Scheme dialect than it is to the first S dialect with regards to how R functions in the engine.

Today R keeps running on practically any standard registering stage and working framework. Its open source nature implies that anybody is allowed to adjust the product to whatever stage they pick. For sure, R has been accounted for to keep running on current tablets, telephones, PDAs, and diversion supports.

One decent component that R imparts to numerous mainstream open source ventures is visited discharges. These days there is a noteworthy yearly discharge, normally in October, where major new highlights are consolidated what's more, discharged to people in general. Consistently, littler scale bugfix discharges will be made as required. The successive discharges and normal discharge cycle demonstrates dynamic improvement of the product and guarantees that bugs will be tended to in an auspicious way. While the center designers control the essential source tree for R, numerous individuals around the globe make commitments as new include, bug fixes, or both. Another key preferred standpoint that R has over numerous other factual bundles (even today) is its advanced designs abilities. R's capacity to make "distribution quality" illustrations has existed since the earliest reference point and has for the most part been exceptional than contending bundles. Today, with some more perception bundles accessible than previously, that slant proceeds. R's base designs framework permits for fine power over basically every part of a plot or chart. Other more up to date illustrations frameworks, like cross section and ggplot2 consider perplexing and advanced representations of high-dimensional information.

R has kept up the first S theory, which is that it gives a dialect that is both helpful for intelligent work yet contains an amazing programming dialect for growing new instruments. This permits the client, who takes existing instruments and applies them to information, to gradually yet without a doubt turn into a designer who is making new instruments.

At last, one of the delights of utilizing R has nothing to do with the dialect itself, yet rather with the dynamic and energetic client network. From numerous points of view, a dialect is fruitful see that it makes a stage with which numerous individuals can make new things. R is that stage, and a large number of individuals around the globe have met up to make commitments to R, to create bundles, and help each other use R for a wide range of utilizations. The R-help and R-devel mailing records have been very dynamic for over ten years now, and there is significant movement on sites like Stack Overflow.

Limitations of R

No programming dialect or factual investigation framework is flawless. R has various disadvantages. First of all, R is founded on very nearly multi-year-old innovation, returning to the unique S framework created at Bell Labs. There was initially minimal worked in help for dynamic or 3-D illustrations (yet things have enhanced enormously since the "days of yore"). Another ordinarily referred to the impedi-ment of R is that objects should, for the most part, be put away in physical memory. This is to a limited extent because of the perusing standards of the dialect, yet R by and large is, even more, a memory hoard than other measurable bundles. Be that as it may, there have been various headways to manage this, both in the R center and furthermore in various bundles created by benefactors. Additionally, figuring power and limit has kept on developing after some time and measure of physical memory that can be introduced on even a buyer level workstation is generous. While we will probably never have enough physical memory on a PC to deal with the undeniably substantial datasets that are being produced, the circumstance has gotten significantly less demanding after some time. At a larger amount one "impedi-ment" of R is that its usefulness depends on customer request and (willful) client commitments. On the off chance that nobody has a craving for actualizing your most loved technique, it's your employment to execute it (or you have to pay somebody to do it) — the abilities of the R framework for the most part mirror the interests of the R client network. As the network has expanded in size over the past ten years, the abilities have correspondingly expanded. When I previously began utilizing R, there was practically nothing in the method for usefulness for the physical sciences (material science, stargazing, and so on.). Be that as it may, presently a few of those networks have embraced R, and we are seeing more code be-ing composed for those sorts of applications.

SUMMARY

The imminent value of Big Data Analytics has been proved profoundly as global wide business opportunities have opened up ensuring new future and also thereby assuring a great deal of security too. The knowledge that has been revealed through big data has proven to easily convert into valuable busi- ness. Decisions that are highly effectual could be made with the available data analysis techniques and tactical data administration by the corporate organizations. The recent emergence of Big Data Analytics is seen to be replacing these old methods and puts on a fresh face to the situation with more productive and effective results. The commercial market dataset used for our proposed research is passed under several contingencies tests using R-studio and R-programming language. The predictive accuracies will be combined and used for future predictions of healthy and unhealthy food for unknown food records. The decision tree suggested for this experiment will be J48 and Random Forest. Ctree and RPART are old fashion and does not give sufficient results for predictions with a dull classification model. The future scope for our research can be widely expanded to huge market company's dataset and prevention of illness by classifying the food products even before they are revealed to the buyers or customers in the stores.

REFERENCES

Ahmed, M. (2019). Intelligent Big Data Summarization for Rare Anomaly Detection. *IEEE Access: Practical Innovations, Open Solutions*, 7, 68669–68677. doi:10.1109/ACCESS.2019.2918364

Anandakumar, H., & Umamaheswari, K. (2017). Supervised machine learning techniques in cognitive radio networks during cooperative spectrum handovers. *Cluster Computing*, 20(2), 1505–1515. doi:10.100710586-017-0798-3

Anandakumar, H., & Umamaheswari, K. (2018). A bio-inspired swarm intelligence technique for social aware cognitive radio handovers. *Computers & Electrical Engineering*, 71, 925–937. doi:10.1016/j.compeleceng.2017.09.016

Haldorai, A., & Kandaswamy, U. (2019). Energy Efficient Network Selection for Cognitive Spectrum Handovers. In *Intelligent Spectrum Handovers in Cognitive Radio Networks* (pp. 41–64). Springer; doi:10.1007/978-3-030-15416-5_3

Haldorai, A., & Kandaswamy, U. (2019). Software Radio Architecture: A Mathematical Perspective. In Intelligent Spectrum Handovers in Cognitive Radio Networks (pp. 65-86). Springer.

Haldorai, A., & Ramu, A. (Eds.). (2019). Cognitive Social Mining Applications in Data Analytics and Forensics. Hershey, PA: IGI Global. doi:10.4018/978-1-5225-7522-1

Haldorai, A., & Kandaswamy, U. (2019). Intelligent Spectrum Handovers in Cognitive Radio Networks. Springer International Publishing. doi:10.1007/978-3-030-15416-5

Harerimana, G., Jang, B., Kim, J. W., & Park, H. K. (2018). Health Big Data Analytics: A Technology Survey. *IEEE Access*, 6, 65661–65678. doi:10.1109/ACCESS.2018.2878254

Jang, B., Park, S., Lee, J., & Hahn, S.-G. (2018). Three Hierarchical Levels of Big-Data Market Model Over Multiple Data Sources for Internet of Things. *IEEE Access*, *6*, 31269–31280. doi:10.1109/ACCESS.2018.2845105

Lee, D. (2019). Big Data Quality Assurance Through Data Traceability: A Case Study of the National Standard Reference Data Program of Korea. *IEEE Access*, *7*, 36294–36299. doi:10.1109/ACCESS.2019.2904286

Li, X., Wang, L., Lian, Z., & Qin, X. (2018). Migration-Based Online CPSCN Big Data Analysis in Data Centers. *IEEE Access: Practical Innovations, Open Solutions*, *6*, 19270–19277. doi:10.1109/ACCESS.2018.2810255

Lv, D., Zhu, S., & Liu, R. (2019). Research on Big Data Security Storage Based on Compressed Sensing. *IEEE Access*, *7*, 3810–3825. doi:10.1109/ACCESS.2018.2889716

Mokhtari, G., Anvari-Moghaddam, A., & Zhang, Q. (2019). A New Layered Architecture for Future Big Data-Driven Smart Homes. *IEEE Access*, *7*, 19002–19012. doi:10.1109/ACCESS.2019.2896403

Salloum, S., Huang, J. Z., He, Y., & Chen, X. (2019). An Asymptotic Ensemble Learning Framework for Big Data Analysis. *IEEE Access*, *7*, 3675–3693. doi:10.1109/ACCESS.2018.2889355

She, R., Liu, S., Wan, S., Xiong, K., & Fan, P. (2019). Importance of Small Probability Events in Big Data: Information Measures, Applications, and Challenges. *IEEE Access*. doi:10.1109/access.2019.2926518

Xiao, C., Li, P., Zhang, L., Liu, W., & Bergmann, N. (2018). ACA-SDS: Adaptive Crypto Acceleration for Secure Data Storage in Big Data. *IEEE Access*, *6*, 44494–44505. doi:10.1109/ACCESS.2018.2862425

This research was previously published in Big Data Analytics for Sustainable Computing; pages 179-205, copyright year 2020 by Engineering Science Reference (an imprint of IGI Global).

Section 3
Tools and Technologies

Chapter 26
Big Data and Advance Analytics: Architecture, Techniques, Applications, and Challenges

Surabhi Verma

National Institute of Industrial Engineering, Mumbai, India

ABSTRACT

The insights that firms gain from big data analytics (BDA) in real time is used to direct, automate and optimize the decision making to successfully achieve their organizational goals. Data management (DM) and advance analytics (AA) tools and techniques are some of the key contributors to making BDA possible. This paper aims to investigate the characteristics of BD, processes of data management, AA techniques, applications across sectors and issues that are related to their effective implementation and management within broader context of BDA. A range of recently published literature on the characteristics of BD, DM processes, AA techniques are reviewed to explore their current state, applications, issues and challenges learned from their practice. The finding discusses different characteristics of BD, a framework for BDA using data management processes and AA techniques. It also discusses the opportunities/applications and challenges managers dealing with these technologies face for gaining competitive advantages in businesses. The study findings are intended to assist academicians and managers in effectively quantifying the data available in an organization into BD by understanding its properties, understanding the emerging technologies, applications and issues behind BDA implementation.

INTRODUCTION

In today's highly competitive markets enterprises are differentiated by their ability to make timely, accurate, and effective decisions at all levels – strategic, tactical, and operational – to address different business processes and performance (Tien, 2013). Increasingly, companies in almost every industries around the world are analyzing Big Data (BD) (both structured and unstructured) to create and capture value through real-time decision-making (Amankwah-Amoah, 2015). BD is defined as high volume, high velocity or/and high variety information assets which require new forms of processing to enable

DOI: 10.4018/978-1-6684-3662-2.ch026

enhanced insight discovery, decision-making, and process optimization (Gartner, 2001; Kshetri, 2014). More specifically, a data set is called BD if it is difficult to capture, store, analyze and visualize using existing technologies in enterprises (Halaweh, 2015). To capitalize advantages from BD, a firm needs Advanced Analytics (AA) techniques and technology to capture, curate, analyze and visualize ever-growing data sets (Gandomi and Haider, 2015). This integration of BD with AA is collectively known as Big Data Analytics (BDA) (Mcneely and Hahm, 2014). BDA is used to describe the data sets that is so large (from terabytes to exabytes) and complex (from social media data to the sensor and mobile data) that they require advanced data storage, management, analytical and visualization techniques and technologies (Chen et al. 2012). It helps in combining historical data with present events and projected future actions (Chen and Zhang, 2014). To uncover the value from BD, it needs to be tapped, analyzed and used for decision making (Kimble and Milolidakis, 2015).

BDA is the subject of attention for business managers, researchers, and government, and to some extent, challenge (Bihl et al., 2016). The exponential rise of BDA in very short period left firms unprepared to handle BD (Bendler et al., 2014). In the past, the rise of new technologies concepts was first discussed in technical and academic publications. The fast evolution of BDA technologies and extremely competitive business environment left little time for the discourse to develop and mature in the academic domain (Bhimani, 2015). There are several articles, industrial reports and books on BDA, including Big Data@ work, but not enough fundamental discourse in academic publications (Kwon et al., 2015). This lagging of academic literature in BDA context implies that a coherent understanding of this emerging technology and its applications in different areas is yet to be developed. For instance, there is little consensus on the fundamental question of what quantify BD (Gu and Zhang, 2015), which type of data and AA techniques is suitable in a particular context (Tan et al., 2015) and how the information extracted after analysis of BD could be used across industries and for public welfare by the government (Vera-Baquero et al., 2015). Thus, there is need to extend the academic literature of BD and AA concepts, techniques, benefits, and challenges.

Many academic studies on BDA have discussed different tools and techniques to analyze BD (Gandomi and Haider, 2015; Goth, 2015), none of them have discussed which type of structured and unstructured data is suitable in a particular situation and how this tremendous data could be leveraged to create value across industries (Vera-Baquero, 2015). Therefore, this paper aims to: investigate the current state of big data, review different process and advance analytics tools and techniques utilized for leveraging big data; provide a concise summary of applications of big data across sectors; and identify challenges which need to overcome before implementing big data. In this process, a wide range of articles is reviewed which discussed various tools and techniques, applications and challenges of big data. In order to understand the process of leveraging big data, a wide range of tools and techniques are reviewed which can manipulate big data. This paper also presents the review of applications of big data differentiated by sectors (i.e., retail, oil and gas, manufacturing and more).

The reminder of this research paper is as follows. This study starts with understanding the current state of BD. In section 3, a holistic framework of BDA is discussed which covers all the steps involved in leveraging the BDA (i.e. from data acquisition to decision making based on information extracted from various analysis). In the same section, different techniques and tools of AA are discussed. In section 4 various challenges faced by an organization to adopt BDA are discussed in detail. The discussion has remained focused on usage of BD at various level and factors that are used to evaluate BDA software suite.

CURRENT STATE OF BIG DATA

Increasingly digital devices, the development and deployment of business-related data standards, electronic data interchange (EDI) formats, databases and information technologies are facilitating business data creation and utilization (Kwon et al., 2014; Chen et al., 2012). A prodigious amount of web-based, sensor and mobile generated, highly detailed and contextualized data arriving at a terabyte, petabyte and even exabyte scale, are used by business and organizations for new discovery and insights (Chen and Zhang, 2014). Although, lot of population in the developing world has no access to digital devices and internet and they are not yet part of BD (Taylor et al., 2014). However, sooner or later, they will and BD management issues will only get worse, if not considered seriously today (Chen and Zhang, 2014). BD have become the part of everyone's lives and BD hides in it the solutions to many real life problems.

BD can play an important role to understand human and machines as both are the data agents (Honavar, 2014). It is identified as one of the current and future research frontiers. Gartner listed BD in both the "Top 10 Critical Tech Trends For the Next Five Years" (Savitz, 2012a) and "Top 10 Strategic Technology Trends For 2013" (Savitz, 2012b). BD is produced every time from all corners of the world. It is a lot wiser to make intelligence and value out of it (Huberty, 2015). Therefore, it is important to understand the characteristics of BD before leveraging it in various context. Understanding, analyzing and discussing various V's discussed by different authors in the academic papers will open doors towards understanding the data and finding the true value of BD. Laney characterized the concept of BD by, volume, velocity, and variety, known as 3V's (Laney, 2001). IBM added another V to describe BD called veracity (Schroeck et al., 2012). Demchenko et al., (2013), Gandomi and Haider (2014) and more have discussed 'value' as another V of BD. Khan et al., (2014) added validity and volatility to define BD. Vera-Baquero (2015) and Katal et al. (2013) and more have added variability as another V's of BD. Therefore, several academic research articles are reviewed to understand the views of different authors about the characteristics of BD. Although this search is not exhaustive, it serves as a comprehensive base for understanding the characteristics/V's of BD. From the literature review, BD characteristics are summarized in 8 V's (Table 1) and quantified in Figure 1. All tables are in the Appendix.

Volume

Data volume (terabytes and petabytes of data) is the primary attribute of BD. BD is also quantified by counting transactions, tables, records, or files (Bendler et al., 2014). Some enterprises found it more useful to quantify BD in terms of time (Erevelles, 2016). The scope of BD is also affecting its quantification (Adolph, 2014). For example, the data collected by many organizations, for general data warehouses differs from data collected for analytics (Jukić et al., 2015). Each of these quantifications of BD is growing continuously and becoming tough to quantify for analytics.

Variety

Enterprises are collecting data from a greater variety of new sources than ever before (Manyika et al., 2011). For example, web data from clickstreams, logs, and social media, text data from call centre applications, RFID data from supply chain applications, geospatial data in logistics and semi-structured data from various business-to-business processes (Opresnik and Taisch, 2015). Few data are hard to categorize, as it comes from video, audio and other devices (Slinger and Morrison, 2014). Also, multidimensional

Figure 1. Characteristics of big data

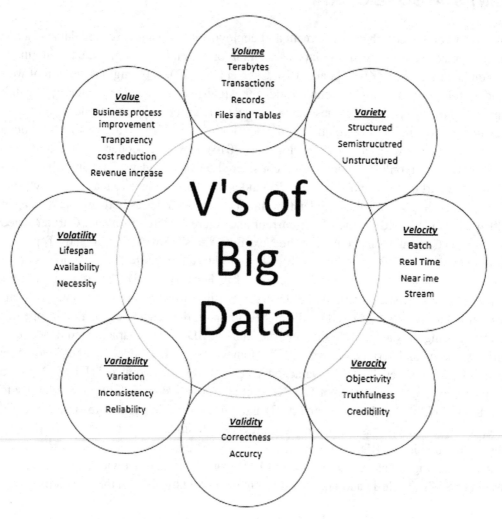

data are drawn from data warehouses to add historic context to BD. But most of this untapped BD is only collected and hoarded by organizations (Kimble and Milolidakis, 2015). Analysis of these eclectic data types from different sources can lead to better insights and decision-making (LaValle, 2013). Therefore, a variety of BD is as huge as volume, and tend to fuel each other.

Velocity

Data feed velocity became the defining attribute of BD. BD velocity or speed is quantified by the frequency of data generation or frequency of data delivery, generated by sensors or machines (Ularu et al., 2012). For example, video analytics for a specific face in the crowd, audio analytics for listening the movement in the secure area, thermometer sensing temperature, robotic manufacturing machine and more. The collection of BD in real time isn't new, as many enterprises are collecting clickstream data from websites from a long time ago (Opresnik and Taisch, 2015). But the main challenge is to analyse the streaming data in real time to make sense from data and take actions such as purchase recommendations to web visitors (Wielki, 2013).

Veracity

BD has biases, ambiguities and inaccuracies, depending on its origin, data processing technologies and data collection methodologies (Lukoianova and Rubin, 2014). Therefore, there is a need to identify biases and ambiguities to reduce inference errors and improve the accuracy of generated insights (Oliver and Vayre, 2015). Veracity is defined as the level of reliability associated with certain types of data including precision correctness, truthfulness or accuracy (IBM, 2013; Schroeck et al., 2012). The veracity of BD is recognized as a necessary property for the BD utilization and complementing the other three quality dimensions of BD (Du et al., 2015).

Validity

Refers to correctness and accuracy of data with regard to the intended usage (Khan et al., 2014). The validity of data may sound similar to the veracity of data, but, they are not the same concepts. When the data moves from exploratory to actionable, data must be validated. A data set may not have any veracity issues but may not be valid if not properly understood (Henry and Venkatraman, 2015). This characteristic of BD is important to find the existence of hidden relationships between elements within massive BD sources (Dubey et al., 2015). The Same set of data may be valid for one application or usage and then invalid for another applications/usage. The validity of BD sources and subsequent analysis must be accurate if the results are going to be used for decision making.

Variability

Refers to the variation in the data flow rates (Katal et al., 2013). Often, BD velocity is not consistent with time. Data flows are highly inconsistent with periodic peaks and troughs. This refers to the inconsistency which can be shown by the data at times, which hampers the process of being reliable to handle and manage the data effectively (Gandomi and Haider, 2014). Daily, seasonal and event-triggered peak structured and unstructured data loads are challenging to those who manage and analyze the BD (Jukić et al., 2015).

Volatility

Due to the volume, variety, and velocity of BD, there is a need to understand volatility. BD volatility refers to how long is data valid and how long should be stored (Khan et al., 2014). In this world of real-time data, there is a need to determine at what point is data no longer relevant to the current analysis. For some sources, the data will always be there, for others, this is not the case. Therefore, there is a need to understand the availability, requirements and lifespan of data (van de Pas and van Bussel, 2015). In a standard data setting, data are kept for decades to build an understanding of the importance of data. In the case of BD, where data is vastly growing every second, there is a need to establish rules for data currency and availability that map to enterprises work processes.

Value

Unlike other V's of big data, this V is the desired outcome of BD processing. Firms are always interested in extracting maximum value from any data set available to them (Roth and Milkau, 2015). That is, the data received in the original form usually has a low value relative to its volume. However, a high value can be obtained by analyzing large volumes of such data (Oracle). According to Jukić et al. (2015): big data can generate values by improving value chain of an organization: for example, transparency and access to information at higher frequency, detailed information about transactional data, customer segments and better management decisions, the foundation for sophisticated analytics to improve decision making and development of next generation products and services. This can improve customer experience, sales and marketing (Spiess et al., 2014).

BIG DATA ANALYTICS (BDA)

BDA is defined as suite or cluster of technologies (e.g. data mining tools and database) and techniques (e.g. analytical methods) that an enterprise employs to analyze sheer quantity of complex data from various applications anticipated to predict and optimize firm performance in several dimensions (Kwon et al., 2014) (Figure 2). The implementation technologies of BDA include a wide portfolio of databases, algorithms, AA tools and visualization techniques to produce accurate business models in real time basis (Labrinidis and Jagadish, 2012) (Figure 3). Traditional relational databases are more prone to incomplete, inconsistent and noisy data (Chen and Zhang et al., 2014). BD must be well-constructed and pre-processed before data analysis, to improve the data quality and analysis results. Therefore, firms need different data pre-processing tools and techniques. The overall process of extracting insights from BDA can be broken down into five stages (Bihl et al., 2016). These five stages involve BD acquisition and recording of data, information extraction, cleaning and analysis of BD, then visualizing the information into a readable form and finally interpreting the information extracted from BD. A framework for BDA depicting the whole process from identifying the BD present in an industry is summarized in Figure 4. Table 2 gives an overview of BDA tools which are used for efficient and precise analysis and management of BD. After data processing, data is used for data analysis using various techniques such as text analytics, sentiment analytics, fraud analytics and more depending on their needs. In the following subsections, the sub process of BDA has been discussed.

Figure 2. Big data analytics (An integration of Big Data with Advanced Analytics)

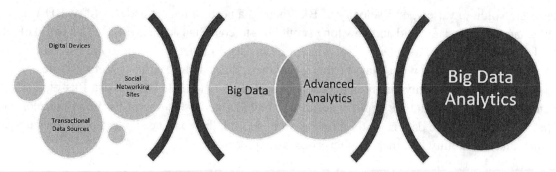

Figure 3. Big data analysis tools

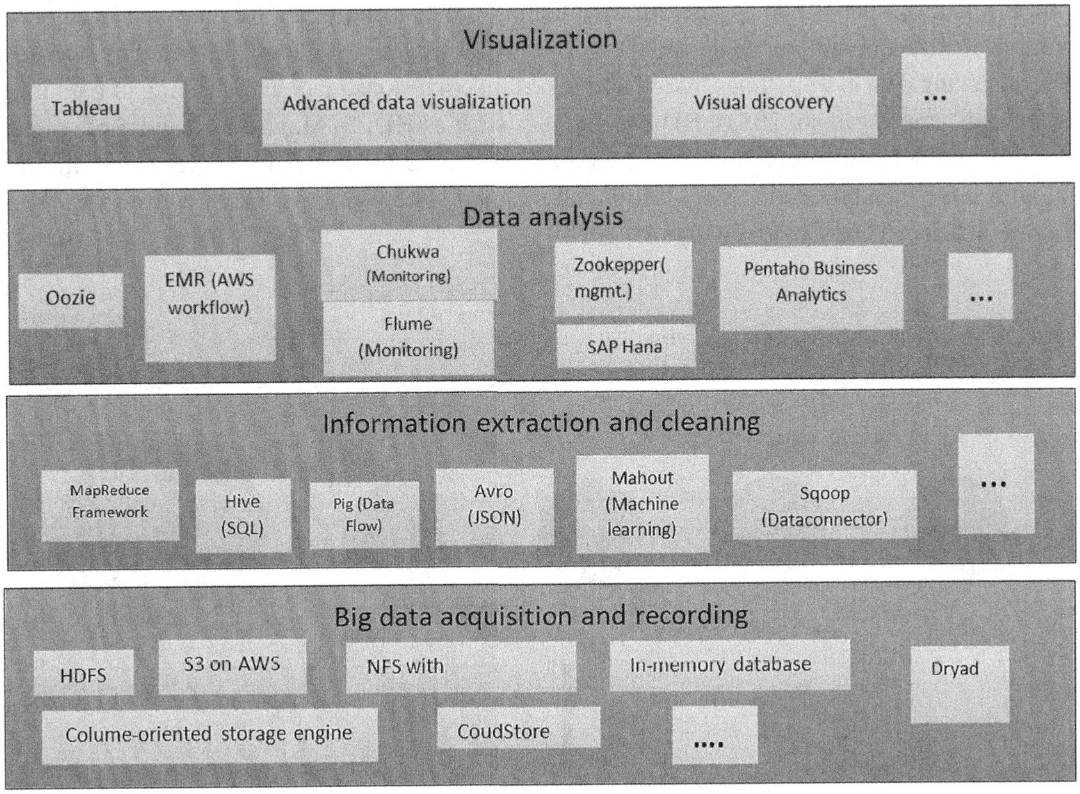

Data Acquisition and Recording

BDA is changing the way of capturing and storing data including data storage architecture, data storage devices and data access mechanism (Brennan et al., 2014; Katal et al., 2013). BDA technologies such as Apache Hadoop, Dryad, Talend Open Studio, In-memory database, Private and public cloud, Column-oriented storage engine and more handle high volume of data in a distributed environment and support flexible and dynamic data structure (Hashem et al., 2015; Russom, 2011; Chen and Zhang et al., 2014). Much of this data is not important, and it could be filtered and compressed by orders of magnitude (Zezula, 2014). One challenge is to define filters in such a way that they do not discard useful information (Bhat and Quadri, 2015). The second challenge is to generate metadata automatically to describe what and how data is recorded and measured (Menchen-Trevino, 2013; Labrinidis and Jagadish, 2012). Recording information about the data at its birth is not useful unless this information could be interpreted and carried along through the data analysis pipeline (Rahm, 2014).

Information Extraction and Cleaning

Acquisition data are in wide forms and the information collected are not in a format ready for analysis (Hill, 2012). Also, a large volume of heterogeneous data has high probability of inconsistencies and data errors while sourcing. Analyzing untimely and inaccurate data leads to erroneous results (Katal et al.,

2013). Therefore, the sourced data should be expressed in structured form and appropriate extraction and cleaning mechanisms should be applied for maintaining the quality of data for analysis. Doing correct and complete extraction and cleaning of BD is a technical challenge (Zezula, 2014). The instruments used for capturing data is sometimes biased under certain conditions made the cleaning of data imperative (Labrinidis and Jagadish, 2012). BDA techniques such as HDFS, MapReduce and more organize, process and manipulate data in the original location to save time and cost, support very high throughput to deal with large data processing steps and handle a huge variety of data formats, from structured to unstructured (Jaseena and David, 2014).

Figure 4. Framework for big data analytics

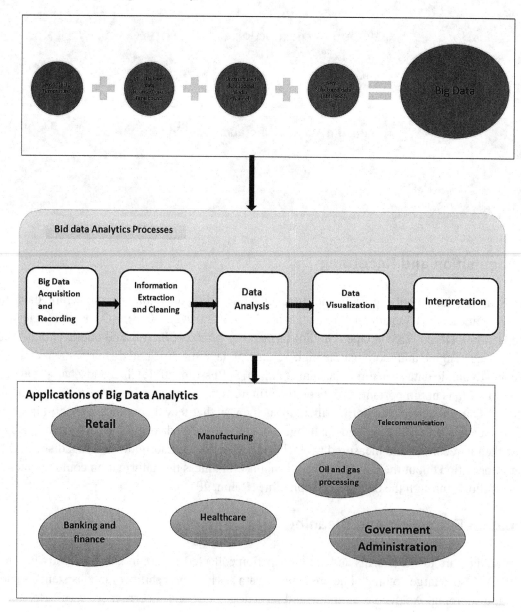

Data Analysis

In this sub-process, techniques such as data mining, machine learning algorithms, statistical analysis are used on a huge data sets with a wider variety of data types stored in distributed system (Chen and Zhang, 2014). AA emerge as processing techniques, which have capabilities to discover the valuable knowledge from the massive volume of data in real time (Gandomi and Haider, 2015). AA tapes and join BD from various sources, for example, structured data has been now joined with semi-structured (RSS feeds, XML) and unstructured data (human and text language). These AA techniques help in reducing the response time driven by changes in behavior and automating decisions based on the analytical model. To utilize the new insights from BD within the context of traditional problems, BDA must be able to integrate analysis on the combination of BD with traditional enterprise data (Chen et al., 2012). In the following sections, several AA techniques for analyzing structured and unstructured data are briefly reviewed. Given the breadth of the AA techniques, an exhaustive list of AA techniques is beyond the scope of a single paper. Thus, the following AA techniques represent a relevant subset of the tools available for analyzing structured and unstructured data like audio, video and social media in real or near real time.

Fraud Analytics (FA)

FA is a combination of analytical technologies and techniques to detect potential improper transactions (Chen et al., 2012) (Table 3). The insights from fraud analytics allow an organization to manage potential threats before they occur as well as develop a proactive fraud and/or bribery detection environment (Abdelhafez, 2014). FA pull data from enterprises into one central platform, helping in creating a true, enterprise-wide approach (Mantelero, 2014). It incorporates unsupervised or non-rules-based analytics technologies to uncover new patterns, trends, fraudulent schemes, and scenarios that traditional analaytics miss (Galbraith, 2014).

Sentiment Analysis (SA)

SA refers the techniques that analyze customers' opinionated text (Durahim and Coskun, 2015) (Table 4). Businesses are increasingly capturing more data about their customers' sentiments toward entities such as products, organizations, individuals, and events (Liu, 2010). Social sciences, marketing, finance, and political campaign are the major application areas of sentiment analysis (Davenport, 2014). Sentiment analysis techniques are further divided into three sub-groups, namely document-level, sentence-level, and aspect based (Feldman, 2013). Document-level techniques determine whether the whole document expresses a positive or a negative sentiment. While, sentence-level techniques attempt to define the polarity of a single sentiment about a known entity expressed in a single sentence. This technique distinguishes subjective sentences from objective ones. Aspect-based techniques are used to recognize all sentiments within a document and identify the aspects of the entity to which each sentiment refers. For instance, using this technique, the vendor could obtain valuable information about different features of the product depending upon the aspect of a consumer.

Digital Analytics (DA)

DA is defined as the analysis of quantitative and qualitative data from business and competition to drive a continual improvement of the online experience that customers or potential customers have which translate to desired outcome (both online and offline) (Kaushik, 2010). With DA the size and location of online consumers and performance of online marketing are determined (Mahrt and Scharkow, 2013). DA tools help in keeping the track of customer engagement or touch points such as mobile applications, CRM systems, and cloud-connected point of sales systems, video game consoles and more (Spiess et al., 2014). It can also provide valuable information about user's experience by analyzing qualitative data, such as users intended task completion feedback (Table 5). DA help in determining and measuring business objectives or outcomes. For example, personalized marketing actions in real time, increased revenues by targeting prospective customers with significant content across digital channels (Abdelhafez, 2014). It also helps firms to improve visitor reacquisition and retention rates, multichannel strategy formation and implementation and optimize the budget allocation and marketing mix, including display advertising, mobile marketing, email marketing and social media marketing (Oliver and Vayre, 2015; Wiren, 2013).

Audio Analytics

This technique is used to analyze and extract information from unstructured audio data (Dubey et al., 2015). It is also known as speech analytics when applied to human spoken language (Ramasamy, 2015). Healthcare and customer call centers are using this technique to analyze thousands or even millions of hours of recorded calls (Habte et al., 2015). Audio analytics helps in improving customer experience by gaining insight into customer behavior, enhance sales turnover rates, evaluate agent performance, monitor compliance with different policies (e.g., privacy and security policies), and identify product or service issues and more. (Hirschberg et al., 2010) (Table 6).

Video Analytics (VA)

It involves a variety of techniques to monitor, analyze, and extract meaningful information from video streams data (Panigrahi et al, 2010) (Table 7). The increasing prevalence of closed circuit television (CCTV) cameras and video-sharing websites are lead contributors to the growth of computerized video analysis (Nunan and Domenico, 2013). The main application of VA is to automate security and surveillance systems. (e.g., Hakeem et al., 2012). The emergence of offline and online videos highlights the need to index multi-media content for easy search and retrieval (Abdelhafez, 2014). Therefore, another domain of video analytics applications includes automatic video indexing and retrieval constitutes.

Social Media Analytics

It refers the analysis of unstructured and structured data from social media channels (Gupta and Gupta, 2016; Marine-Roig and Anton Clavé, 2015). Social media encompasses a variety of online platforms that allow consumers to create and exchange content (Table 8). Barbier and Liu (2011) and Gundecha and Liu, (2012) categorizes social media into following types: social networks, social news, social bookmarking, media sharing, blogs, microblogs, wikis, question-and-answer sites and review sites. Marketing has been the primary application of social media analytics (Gupta and Gupta, 2016).

In-Database Analytics

It is the technologies that allow conduction of data processing within the database of an enterprise by building analytic logic into the database itself (Joydeep, 2010) (Table 9). It consists of an Enterprise Data Warehouse (EDW) built on an analytic database platform. This integration eliminates the time and effort required to transform data back and forth between a database and a separate analytics application (Zhang et al., 2015). In these techniques, data retrieval and analysis are much faster and corporate information is more secure because it doesn't leave the EDW (Bärenfänger et al., 2014). This approach is useful for helping banks in identifying trends, spot anomalies and make better predictions about future business risks and opportunities (Bärenfänger et al., 2014).

Data Visualization

Data visualization main objective is to represent knowledge more effectively and intuitively by using different graphs (Simoff, 2008; Keim, 2004). It helps in conveying information to managers by providing knowledge hidden in the large and complex data sets. Data visualization techniques such as Tableau, Advanced data visualization, Visual discovery provides information in an aesthetic form or intuitive pictures which are abstracted in some schematic forms, including variables and attributes for a unit of information (Henry and Venkatraman, 2015).

Interpretation

The ability of analyzing BD using AA would have limited value if users cannot understand the result from analysis (Sanghvi; 2012). Finally, decision-makers have to interpret the results of analytics. Usually, the interpretation of results involves the investigation of all the assumptions and retracting the analysis (Zezula, 2014). Furthermore, the results are erroneous as the computer system have bugs, or data are incorrect (Labrinidis and Jagadish, 2012). For all these reasons, decision makers could not cede the authority of automatic decision making to algorithms, especially with BD due to its complexity.

A successful BDA infrastructure must be able to transform the huge volume of disparate data into an efficient information, analyze BD with different AA to deliver insights in real time for effective decision-making for competitive advantage across the firm (Gandomi and Haider, 2015). A comprehensive BDA architecture must be able to access internal and external data of firms of any format and analyze it in (near) real-time (Sakr et al., 2013). Therefore, BDA should transform the unstructured and semi-structured data into the required format, store it, analyze it thoroughly in (near) real-time and disseminate information through familiar interfaces for decision-making in firms.

APPLICATIONS OF BIG DATA ANALYTICS

This section identifies and discusses some of the opportunities in business and commerce and public welfare in current technology penetration and future adoption of BDA.

BDA in Retail

The disparity between consumer sentiment spreading across social networks and limits to track these sentiments puts retailers at risk of losing the loyalty of customers, control of the brand, revenue and margins and market shares (Ramsey & Bapna, 2016; Durahim and Coskun, 2015). Therefore, the understanding of two capabilities- supply and apply- of BDA in retail is needed (Girard, 2012). The supply side capabilities include IT assets which encompass the hardware and software that integrate, manage, organize, analyze and visualize data (Henten and Windekilde, 2016). While the applied side of BDA competence includes the decision management framework, business processes and role and organizational constructs by which a firm consumes BDA insights to control and optimize its strategic, tactic and operational decisions to achieve its business objectives (Narayanan, 2015). BDA provides actionable insights to firms including marketing campaigns, new product development and introduction, store operations and design, product design and quality, pricing, promotions, and personalization, assortment localization, crisis management, selling techniques, and store associate management, and competitive intelligence and differentiation (Girard, 2012; Donnelly et al., 2015; Jun et al., 2015). An automatic integration of BDA into various retail business processes enables retailers to understand, react and engage their customers which can help in earning customer loyalty, innovations of new products to market, collaborate through supply chains with business partners and reduce risk (Ramsey & Bapna, 2016; Armstrong et al., 2015).

BDA in Manufacturing

In the manufacturing sector, exponential data is generated from a multitude of sources including supply chain management systems, production machinery, performance monitoring systems of products, collaborative product development systems and more (Zhou & Ji, 2015). This sector can leverage BDA for operational improvement that increases the efficiency of manufacturing processes and quality improvements of the products manufactured (Mathai, 2011; Dubey et al., 2015). Usage of BDA in manufacturing can offer opportunities to accelerate product development and minimize production and development costs based on customer insights (Opresnik & Taisch, 2015; Papanagnou, 2014). Fast-moving consumer goods (FMCG) manufacturers can improve their supply chain planning and demand forecasting by integrating data from other sources including data from retailers such as launch data (e.g. items listed/delisted), promotion data (e.g, prices, items, sales) and inventory data (e.g., sales per store, stock level per warehouse) (Weckman, 2016; Agarwal, 2014; Nedelcu, 2013). The increasing deployment of the Internet of Things (IoT) allows a manufacturer to optimize operations for reducing waste and maximizing throughput, by embedding highly granular real-time data from networked sensors in the production processes and supply chain (Zhou & Ji, 2015; Zhong et al., 2015; Nedelcu, 2013). Leveraging BDA in the manufacturing sector can facilitate mass customization, increase energy efficiency, shift to lean manufacturing, simulate new manufacturing processes, and improve marketing, sales and after-sales services activities (Zhou & Ji, 2015; Li et al., 2015; Papanagnou, 2014).

BDA in Banking and Finance

In order to reduce net interest income and fee income, with capital requirements increasing, bank and financial companies are undergoing a paradigm shift to build new revenue sources, improve customer experience, predict and mitigate fraud and risk and enhance operational efficiency more efficiently

(Turner et al., 2013; Bedeley and Iyer, 2014). BDA can refocus IT implementations to address these challenges by offering insights to improve performance management, CRM and risk management (Roth and Milkau, 2015). BDA is also helping banks and financial companies to identify opportunities for business development, enhancement of employee and processes and customer retention (Versace, 2012; Zhu and Huang, 2014). They can access the social media information of customers over the stored data in CRM systems (Turner et al., 2013). Integration of information extracted from unstructured external data to specific transactions or to specific customer data from in-branch face-to-face interactions, mobile banking or net-banking, can help banks to improve their CRM (Versace, 2012; Roth and Milkau, 2015). Also, BDA can help to trace credit card and other defaulters by tracking the social media footprint of defaulters (Turner et al., 2013).

BDA in Healthcare

In healthcare, BDA supports a wide range of medical and healthcare functions, including disease surveillance, clinical decision support and population health management in (near) real-time (Cohen et al., 2014; Burghard, 2012; Dembosky, 2012 and Feldman et al., 2012). According to Bates et al., 2014 and Raghupathi and Ragupathi (2014), the main sources of data in healthcare included patient data in electronic patient records (EPRs), clinical data from clinical decision support systems, machine/sensor generated data, and social media posts and other platforms. Potential benefits of digitizing, combining and effectively using BDA in healthcare firms includes clinical operations improvement by detecting diseases at earlier stages, managing individual and population health and detecting healthcare fraud quickly and efficiently at lower cost (Berg and Black, 2014; Groves et al., 2013). The actionable information provided by BDA helps in identifying needs, provide services, and predict and prevent the crisis of populations (Bates et al., 2014). In addition, BDA in healthcare also contributes to evidence-based medicine by combining and analyzing different format of BD, to match treatments with outcomes, predict patients at risk for disease or readmission and provide more efficient care (Fleurence et al, 2014). It also reduces fraud, waste and abuse by analyzing a large number of claim request (Phillips et al., 2014).

BDA in Telecommunication

BDA offers telecommunication operators a real business opportunity to gain a much more transparent, holistic and end-to-end view of their customers and operations, and to advance their innovation efforts by finding correlations and connections from internal and external data (Zhou, 2015; Prescott, 2013). BDA can improve the efficiency and profitability across the entire telecommunication value chain by optimizing route and quality of services by analyzing network traffic in real time (Fox et al., 2013). It can also help in identifying fraudulent behavior in real time by analyzing call data records immediately (Hirsch, 2013). Other advantages of BDA in telecommunication includes flexible and profitable subscriber calling plans in real time, targeted marketing campaign using location-based and social networking technologies and new products and services development via insights from customer behaviour and usage (Ramsey & Bapna, 2016; Li et al., 2015; Fox et al., 2013). BD can also open a new source of revenue to telecommunication enterprises, by selling insights about customers to third parties (Acker et al., 2013).

BDA in Oil and Gas Processing

Analyzing the data across disciplines in oil and gas industry (geology and geophysics, production engineering, reservoir engineering, etc.) can improve operations and enhance production, reduces risk especially in the area of safety, health and environment and finally reduces cost (Perrons and Jensen, 2015). BDA in upstream oil and gas have potential to improve seismic drilling and production, deliver benefits in development, drilling, exploration, maintenance and production operations (Feblowitz, 2012; Davenport, 2014). BDA can also collect and analyze pressure, volume and temperature data in upstream and compare it with past history of equipment failure to predict potential failure (Hems et al., 2013; Perrons and McAuley; 2014). Another application of BDA is in performing social business scans in the service of recruitment (Halaweh, 2015).

BDA in the Public Sector

Across the public sector, an extraordinary quantity of data is amassed while running public services- tax, election, National Health Service, passport issue, welfare payments and more (Chen and Hsieh, 2014). BDA enable a government to link data available in different departments which can be used to streamline transactions – reducing the scope for errors and avoiding asking people to provide the same information multiple times (White and Breckenridge, 2014). BDA empowers an organization with astonishing capabilities such as forecasting specific needs of citizens or individual users with a very high degree of precision (Jun and Chung, 2015). In the welfare arena, better personalization and segmentation helps in identifying the support that unemployed people need and get them into long-term work (Lavertu, 2014). At a macro level, there is scope to accelerate efforts to reduce fraud and error, to make further inroads into the tax gap and to improve the overall efficiency of government operations (Lee et al., 2014; Cumbley and Church, 2013; Yiu, 2012). BDA also facilitates advanced crime prevention, personalized and detailed tax and benefits statements for household and individual, and accelerate smart grid investments to increase the overall efficiency of energy usage by businesses and households (Lavertu, 2014).

CHALLENGES WITH BIG DATA ANALYTICS

Recent research has recognized that technological factors are not the only key to the effectiveness of BDA implementations. There is also a need to understand the impact of human and organizational factors for effective implementation of IT in organizations (McAfee and Brynjolfsson, 2012). Technological aspects involve technical solutions such as protocols and applications (Davenport et al., 2014). Human aspects are related to cognition at the individual level, as well as culture and interaction with other people (Russom, 2011). Organizational aspects are related to the structure of the organization, including size and managerial decisions around BDA implementation (LaValle et al., 2013). A variety of factors is discussed by different researchers which made the implementation of BDA difficult in organizations. These challenges are classified as technological, human and organizational using the definitions described above. Given that some challenges are multi-dimensional and could be classified in different ways depending on the particular interpretation of the authors, the emphasis is on understanding the different types of challenges that affect the implementation of BDA. Table 10 provides a summary of these challenges discussed by various authors. The key challenges encountered in BDA adoption and usage are identified and summarized below.

Technological Factors

Managing large and rapidly increasing volume of data is one the challenging issues to enterprises these days (Labrinidis and Jagadish, 2012). Some incompleteness and error in data are likely to remain, even after data cleaning and error correction. This incompleteness and error must be managed before data analysis (Katal et al., 2013). In the course of data analysis, the search of data meeting a specified criterion likely to occurred repeatedly. The repetitive scanning of such a large data requires a lot of time. Therefore, indexing of data is required to permit the finding of qualifying data quickly (Dutta and Bose, 2015). Another technical challenge is to manage real-time data which is not static and gets larger and changes over time (Davenport, 2014). The privacy of data is another huge concern in the context of BDA (Manyika et al., 2011). It is difficult to share private data while limiting disclosure and ensuring sufficient shared data utility. The security for information sharing and linking of private data in BD use cases is also identified as one of the technical challenge (Lafuente, 2015).

Human Factors

From the human point of view, adoption of BDA poses several challenges for BDA practitioners. Lack of BDA skills is a common challenge (McAfee and Brynjolfsson, 2012). Specifically, it is found to be difficult to implement BDA techniques when people do not have enough orientation or education about best analytics practices (Kwon et al., 2015). In organizations, the lack of skills exists related both to IT professionals able to implement and maintain BDA and analysts who can interpret the data and generate actionable information for creating value to businesses (Kim et al., 2014). Since BDA is an emerging technology and at its nascent stage, it needs to attract organizations and people with diverse new skill sets (Davenport, 2014). It needs data scientist and other professionals like analytical, interpretive skilled people who can handle huge quantities of information (McAfee and Brynjolfsson, 2012). Other than statistical knowledge, skills in cleaning and organizing large data sets and handling visualization tools and techniques are also required (Chen and Zhang, 2014). Expertise in the design of experiments can help to cross the gap between correlation and causation. But people with these skills are hard to find and in great demand. Therefore, IT professionals need to be trained in specialized areas. Also, the universities need to introduce curriculum on BDA to produce skilled employees in this expertise.

Lack of trust in the data collected and results of the analysis is a barrier to BDA adoption (Katal et al., 2013). Data-drove organizations should be more data-oriented for decisions making rather than acting solely on instinct and hunches. Organizations need to develop an analytical mind-set that supports the usage of data and analytics across a wide range of corporate activities (Rahm, 2014). They should lean to view data as a core asset and open to new ways of thinking. Analytical insights should be part of the organizational culture and should be utilized in strategic, tactic and operational decision making.

Organizational Factors

To succeed in BDA, enterprises not only need data but also need the support of leaders to set clear goals, visions or insights (McAfee and Brynjolfsson, 2012). Organizational leaders should have the vision to exploit their growing data and computational power to get smart and innovative than their competitors (Davenport, 2014). BDA's power does not erase the need for human vision and insights (Davenport, 2014). The successful companies' leaders can change the way their organizations make decisions. The main challenge for leaders of companies is to identify where their organization stands with BD and what are their responsibility. Organizations leaders are still learning the BDA or are unaware of it (Ularu et al., 2012). In organizations ambiguity still exists regarding clear responsibility between Chief Information Officer, Chief Technology Officer, Head of Analytics, Chief Data Officer, or other personnel in the implementation of BDA (Labrinidis and Jagadish, 2012). Lack of regulations, policies and standards about BDA are another critical challenge to leaders of companies (LaValle et al., 2013).

DISCUSSION

BDA is forming the basis of rapidly growing tools in management decision making (Agrawal, 2014). BDA support executives at all levels – strategic, tactical, and operational – for their decision-making needs (Tien, 2013). Strategic managers use them for identifying market opportunities, competitive intelligence, new products and services launch decisions and product positioning (Bhimani, 2015). Tactical managers use BDA to make decisions in the areas of direct marketing, customer acquisition, retention and extension purposes, targeted marketing campaign and sales forecasting (Taylor et al., 2014). Operational managers use them for decisions involving better supply chain management or utilization of facilities (Dubey et al., 2015). BDA techniques identify patterns which help managers in better and real-time decision making. Using BDA, firms can increase the profitability from customers' interactions, fraud detection, and risk management improvement (Henry and Venkatraman, 2015).

Table 11 lists the steps one goes through to use BDA. Each of these steps is interactive and iterative. Technological advances in storage and computations are enabling enterprises to capture the informational value of BD in a cost-effective and timely manner (Fulgoni, 2013). This advancement in technologies helps in acquiring data from multiple internal and external sources. These data are extracted and cleaned to make it in the suitable format before analysis. After data transformation, various analytical techniques are used for getting the desired outcome, depending upon the needs of enterprises. For instance, sentiment analysis is used to glean useful insights from millions of consumer opinions shared on social media (Feldman, 2013). Although major innovations in AA techniques for BD are yet to take place, one anticipates the emergence of new AA in the near future. For instance, real-time analytics will likely become a prolific field of research in BDA because of the growth in mobile apps and location-aware social media (Labrinidis and Jagadish, 2012).

Since BD are unreliable, noisy and highly interrelated, it will likely lead to the development of statistical techniques more readily apt for mining BD while remaining sensitive to the unique characteristics. The implementation of BDA could be done within a range of technology infrastructure. Therefore, before adopting the BDA technologies, managers of enterprises should have a clear understanding of their internal needs of BDA. The factors that are typically used to evaluate BDA software suite includes:

- The ability to handle vast amount of data with maximum number of tables/rows/attributes allowed
- Ability to access a wide variety of data sources
- Ability to access data both internal and external data
- Ease of learning
- Ease of use and effectiveness

Therefore, the BDA vendors should provide an integrated environment and holistic solutions for AA, optimization, forecasting, simulation and more for informed and guided decision making for managers.

CONCLUSION

The objective of this paper describes review and reflect on characteristics, processes, applications and challenges of BDA. The paper's focus is also on analytics to gain valid and valuable insights from BDA. BDA is identified as the next frontier for innovation, productivity, and competition. The better analysis of the large volumes of data in (near) real time have the potential for making faster advances in many disciplines and improving the profitability and success of many enterprises. By understanding 8 V's (i.e. properties of available BD), firms and government can utilize their data to optimize available resources for gaining competitive advantage and solving real world problems. In this research paper, BDA problems are discussed briefly, including BDA processes, opportunities and challenges, current techniques and technologies. Different analytics techniques for structured data, text, and social media data, audio and video data are reviewed in this paper. As BDA is still in the initial stage of development, the existing techniques and tools of BDA are very limited to solve the real BDA problems completely. Therefore, more investments should be dispensed into different processes of BDA to capture huge values from BDA. From data capture, storage, analysis to interpretation, there is an immediate requirement of advanced storage and input-output techniques, more efficient data-intensive techniques, more favorable computer architectures, and more progressive technologies like BD platforms with comprehensive architecture, infrastructure, approach, and properties. The viable list of BDA tools and applicable areas discussed in this study can benefit practitioners and researchers by enabling them to choose a BDA tool and/or technique according to their need.

However, the technical, human and organizational challenges described in this paper must be addressed before this potential can be realized fully. The technical challenges include heterogeneity, lack of structure, timeliness, scale, error-handling, privacy, provenance, and visualization, at all stages of the analysis pipeline from data acquisition to result from interpretation. These technical challenges are common across a large variety of application domains, and therefore not cost-effective to address in the context of one domain alone. The human challenges include lack of skills, lack of trust in data and results of analysis and lack of data-driven organizational culture. The organizational challenges include lack of leadership and lack of regulations, policies, and standards of BDA. Furthermore, these challenges will require transformative solutions, and will not be addressed naturally by the next generation of industrial products. Therefore, there is a need to support and encourage fundamental research towards addressing these technical challenges, to achieve the promised benefits of BD. After studying literature about BDA research and current state of art and then summarizing ideas in this paper, in future there is need of developing algorithms to utilize 8 V's of BD for more accurate results and developing holistic solutions to utilize the BD in order to improve business processes, increase revenues and reduce costs to specific industries.

REFRENCES

Abdelhafez, H. A. (2014). Big data technologies and analytics: A review of emerging solutions. *International Journal of Business Analytics, 1*(2), 1–17. doi:10.4018/ijban.2014040101

Abraham, A., & Das, S. (Eds.). (2010). *Computational intelligence in power engineering.* Springer.

Acker, O., Blockus, A., & Pötscher, F. (2013). Benefiting from big data: A new approach for the telecom industry. *Strategy&, Analysis Report.*

Adolph, M. (2014). Big data, its enablers and standards. *PIK-Praxis der Information's verarbeitung und Kommunikation, 37*(3), 197-204.

Agrawal, D. (2014). Analytics based decision making. *Journal of Indian Business Research, 6*(4), 332–340. doi:10.1108/JIBR-09-2014-0062

Alhabashneh, O., Iqbal, R., Shah, N., Amin, S., & James, A. (2011). Towards the development of an integrated framework for enhancing enterprise search using latent semantic indexing. In *Conceptual Structures for Discovering Knowledge* (pp. 346-352). Springer Berlin Heidelberg.

Amankwah-Amoah, J. (2015). Safety or no safety in numbers? Governments, big data and public policy formulation. *Industrial Management & Data Systems, 115*(9), 1596–1603. doi:10.1108/IMDS-04-2015-0158

Barbier, G., & Liu, H. (2011). Data mining in social media. In Social network data analytics (pp. 327-352). Springer US.

Bärenfänger, R., Otto, B., & Österle, H. (2014). Business value of in-memory technology–multiple-case study insights. *Industrial Management & Data Systems, 114*(9), 1396–1414. doi:10.1108/IMDS-07-2014-0212

Bates, D. W., Saria, S., Ohno-Machado, L., Shah, A., & Escobar, G. (2014). Big data in health care: Using analytics to identify and manage high-risk and high-cost patients. *Health Affairs, 33*(7), 1123–1131. doi:10.1377/hlthaff.2014.0041 PMID:25006137

Bedeley, R. T., & Iyer, L. S. (2014). Big Data Opportunities and Challenges: The Case of Banking Industry. *Proceedings of the Southern Association for Information Systems Conference.*

Bendler, J., Wagner, S., Brandt, D. V. T., & Neumann, D. (2014). Taming uncertainty in big data. *Business & Information Systems Engineering, 6*(5), 279–288. doi:10.100712599-014-0342-4

Bhat, W. A., & Quadri, S. M. K. (2015). Big Data promises value: Is hardware technology taken on-board? *Industrial Management & Data Systems, 115*(9), 1577–1595. doi:10.1108/IMDS-04-2015-0160

Bhimani, A. (2015). Exploring big datas strategic consequences. *Journal of Information Technology, 30*(1), 66–69. doi:10.1057/jit.2014.29

Bihl, T. J., Young, W. A. II, & Weckman, G. R. (2016). Defining, Understanding, and Addressing Big Data. *International Journal of Business Analytics, 3*(2), 1–32. doi:10.4018/IJBAN.2016040101

Bizer, C., Boncz, P., Brodie, M. L., & Erling, O. (2012). The meaningful use of big data: Four perspectives-four challenges. *SIGMOD Record, 40*(4), 56–60. doi:10.1145/2094114.2094129

Brook Wu, Y. F., Li, Q., Bot, R. S., & Chen, X. (2006). Finding nuggets in documents: A machine learning approach. *Journal of the American Society for Information Science and Technology, 57*(6), 740–752. doi:10.1002/asi.20341

Buell Hirsch, P. (2013). Corporate reputation in the age of data nudity. *The Journal of Business Strategy, 34*(6), 36–39. doi:10.1108/JBS-07-2013-0063

Burghard, C. (2012). Big Data and Analytics Key to Accountable Care Success. *IDC Health Insights.*

Che, D., Safran, M., & Peng, Z. (2013, January). From big data to big data mining: challenges, issues, and opportunities. In *Database Systems for Advanced Applications* (pp. 1-15). Springer Berlin Heidelberg.

Chen, C. P., & Zhang, C. Y. (2014). Data-intensive applications, challenges, techniques and technologies: A survey on Big Data. *Information Sciences, 275*, 314–347. doi:10.1016/j.ins.2014.01.015

Chen, H., Chiang, R. H., & Storey, V. C. (2012). Business Intelligence and Analytics: From Big Data to Big Impact. *Management Information Systems Quarterly, 36*(4), 1165–1188.

Chen, Y. C., & Hsieh, T. C. (2014). Big Data for Digital Government: Opportunities, Challenges, and Strategies. *International Journal of Public Administration in the Digital Age, 1*(1), 1–14. doi:10.4018/ijpada.2014010101

Clifton, B. (2012). *Advanced web metrics with Google Analytics.* John Wiley & Sons.

Cohen, I. G., Amarasingham, R., Shah, A., Xie, B., & Lo, B. (2014). The legal and ethical concerns that arise from using complex predictive analytics in health care. *Health Affairs, 33*(7), 1139–1147. doi:10.1377/hlthaff.2014.0048 PMID:25006139

Cumbley, R., & Church, P. (2013). Is Big Data creepy? *Computer Law & Security Report, 29*(5), 601–609. doi:10.1016/j.clsr.2013.07.007

Davenport, T. (2014). How strategists use big data to support internal business decisions, discovery and production. *Strategy and Leadership, 42*(4), 45–50. doi:10.1108/SL-05-2014-0034

Davenport, T. (2014). *Big data at work: dispelling the myths, uncovering the opportunities.* Harvard Business Review Press. doi:10.15358/9783800648153

Davenport, T. H., & Patil, D. J. (2012). Data scientist. *Harvard Business Review, 90*, 70–76. PMID:23074866

Dembosky, A. (2012). Data prescription for better healthcare. *Financial Times, 11*(12), 2012.

Du, D., Li, A., Zhang, L., & Li, H. (2014). Review on the Applications and the Handling Techniques of Big Data in Chinese Realty Enterprises. *Annals of Data Science, 1*(3-4), 339–357. doi:10.100740745-014-0025-5

Dubey, R., Gunasekaran, A., Childe, S. J., Wamba, S. F., & Papadopoulos, T. (2015). The impact of big data on world-class sustainable manufacturing. *International Journal of Advanced Manufacturing Technology.*

Durahim, A. O., & Coşkun, M. (2015). # iamhappybecause: Gross National Happiness through Twitter analysis and big data. *Technological Forecasting and Social Change*, *99*, 92–105. doi:10.1016/j.techfore.2015.06.035

Dutta, D., & Bose, I. (2015). Managing a big data project: The case of ramco cements limited. *International Journal of Production Economics*, *165*, 293–306. doi:10.1016/j.ijpe.2014.12.032

Erevelles, S., Fukawa, N., & Swayne, L. (2016). Big Data consumer analytics and the transformation of marketing. *Journal of Business Research*, *69*(2), 897–904. doi:10.1016/j.jbusres.2015.07.001

Feblowitz, J. (2012). *The big deal about big data in upstream oil and gas. Paper & presentation.* IDC Energy Insights.

Feldman, R. (2013). Techniques and applications for sentiment analysis. *Communications of the ACM*, *56*(4), 82–89. doi:10.1145/2436256.2436274

Fels, G., Lanquillon, C., Mallow, H., Schinkel, F., & Schulmeyer, C. (2015). Technik. In *Praxishandbuch Big Data* (pp. 255-330). Springer Fachmedien Wiesbaden.

Fleurence, R. L., Beal, A. C., Sheridan, S. E., Johnson, L. B., & Selby, J. V. (2014). Patient-powered research networks aim to improve patient care and health research. *Health Affairs*, *33*(7), 1212–1219. doi:10.1377/hlthaff.2014.0113 PMID:25006148

Fulgoni, G. (2013). Big Data: Friend or Foe of Digital Advertising? *Journal of Advertising Research*, *53*(4), 372–376. doi:10.2501/JAR-53-4-372-376

Galbraith, J. R. (2014). Organizational design challenges resulting from big data. *Journal of Organization Design*, *3*(1), 2–13. doi:10.7146/jod.8856

Gandomi, A., & Haider, M. (2015). Beyond the hype: Big data concepts, methods, and analytics. *International Journal of Information Management*, *35*(2), 137–144. doi:10.1016/j.ijinfomgt.2014.10.007

Gates, A. F., Natkovich, O., Chopra, S., Kamath, P., Narayanamurthy, S. M., Olston, C., ... Srivastava, U. (2009). Building a high-level dataflow system on top of Map-Reduce: The Pig experience. *Proceedings of the VLDB Endowment*, *2*(2), 1414–1425. doi:10.14778/1687553.1687568

Gundecha, P., & Liu, H. (2012). Mining social media: a brief introduction. *Tutorials in Operations Research*, *1*(4).

Gupta, V., & Gupta, M. (2016). Social Media Mining: A New Framework and Literature Review. *International Journal of Business Analytics*, *3*(1), 58–68. doi:10.4018/IJBAN.2016010104

Hakeem, A., Gupta, H., Kanaujia, A., Choe, T. E., Gunda, K., Scanlon, A., . . . Haering, N. (2012). Video analytics for business intelligence. In Video Analytics for Business Intelligence. 309-354. Springer Berlin Heidelberg. doi:10.1007/978-3-642-28598-1_10

Halaweh, M., & Massry, A. E. (2015). Conceptual Model for Successful Implementation of Big Data in Organizations. *Journal of International Technology and Information Management*, *24*(2), 2.

Hashem, I. A. T., Yaqoob, I., Anuar, N. B., Mokhtar, S., Gani, A., & Khan, S. U. (2015). The rise of big data on cloud computing: Review and open research issues. *Information Systems*, *47*, 98–115. doi:10.1016/j.is.2014.07.006

Hellerstein, J. M., Ré, C., Schoppmann, F., Wang, D. Z., Fratkin, E., Gorajek, A., & Kumar, A. (2012). The MADlib analytics library: Or MAD skills, the SQL. *Proceedings of the VLDB Endowment*, *5*(12), 17001711. doi:10.14778/2367502.2367510

Henry, R., & Venkatraman, S. (2015). Big Data Analytics the Next Big Learning Opportunity. *Journal of Management Information and Decision Sciences*, *18*(2), 17.

Henten, A. H., & Windekilde, I. M. (2016). Transaction costs and the sharing economy. *info, 18*(1), 1-15.

Hirschberg, J., Hjalmarsson, A., & Elhadad, N. (2010). "You're as Sick as You Sound": Using Computational Approaches for Modeling Speaker State to Gauge Illness and Recovery. In Advances in Speech Recognition (pp. 305-322). Springer US.

Honavar, V. G. (2014). The promise and potential of big data: A case for discovery informatics. *Review of Policy Research*, *31*(4), 326–330. doi:10.1111/ropr.12080

Huberty, M. (2015). Awaiting the second big data revolution: From digital noise to value creation. *Journal of Industry, Competition and Trade*, *15*(1), 35–47. doi:10.100710842-014-0190-4

Jukić, N., Sharma, A., Nestorov, S., & Jukić, B. (2015). Augmenting Data Warehouses with Big Data. *Information Systems Management*, *32*(3), 200–209. doi:10.1080/10580530.2015.1044338

Katal, A., Wazid, M., & Goudar, R. H. (2013, August). Big data: Issues, challenges, tools and Good practices. *Proceedings of the 2013 Sixth International Conference on IEEE Contemporary Computing (IC3)* (pp. 404-409). IEEE.

Keim, D., Panse, C., Sips, M., & North, S. C. (2004). Visual data mining in large geospatial point sets. *Computer Graphics and Applications, IEEE, 24*(5), 36–44. doi:10.1109/MCG.2004.41 PMID:15628099

Kim, B. G., Park, S. C., & Lee, K. J. (2008). A structural equation modeling of the Internet acceptance in Korea. *Electronic Commerce Research and Applications, 6*(4), 425–432. doi:10.1016/j.elerap.2006.08.005

Kimble, C., & Milolidakis, G. (2015). Big data and business intelligence: Debunking the myths. *Global Business and Organizational Excellence*, *35*(1), 23–34. doi:10.1002/joe.21642

King, D. L. (2015). Analytics, Goals, and Strategy for Social Media. *Library Technology Reports*, *51*(1), 26–32.

Knapp, S. (2009). Ooyala–Accelerating the evolution of online video–An Interview with Sean Knapp of online video publishing. *Journal of Digital Asset Management, 5*(5), 264–273. doi:10.1057/dam.2009.23

Kshetri, N. (2014). Big data's impact on privacy, security and consumer welfare. *Telecommunications Policy, 38*(11), 1134–1145. doi:10.1016/j.telpol.2014.10.002

Kwon, O., Lee, N., & Shin, B. (2014). Data quality management, data usage experience and acquisition intention of big data analytics. *International Journal of Information Management, 34*(3), 387–394. doi:10.1016/j.ijinfomgt.2014.02.002

Kwon, T. H., Kwak, J. H., & Kim, K. (2015). A study on the establishment of policies for the activation of a big data industry and prioritization of policies: Lessons from Korea. *Technological Forecasting and Social Change, 96*, 144–152. doi:10.1016/j.techfore.2015.03.017

Labrinidis, A., & Jagadish, H. V. (2012). Challenges and opportunities with big data. *Proceedings of the VLDB Endowment., 5*(12), 2032–2033. doi:10.14778/2367502.2367572

Lafuente, G. (2015). The big data security challenge. *Network Security, 2015*(1), 12–14. doi:10.1016/S1353-4858(15)70009-7

Laney, D. (2001). 3D data management: Controlling data volume, velocity and variety. *META Group Research Note, 6*, 70.

LaValle, S., Lesser, E., Shockley, R., Hopkins, M. S., & Kruschwitz, N. (2013). Big data, analytics and the path from insights to value. *MIT sloan management review, 21*.

Lee, Y. M., An, L., Liu, F., Horesh, R., Chae, Y. T., & Zhang, R. (2014). Analytics for Smarter Buildings. *International Journal of Business Analytics, 1*(1), 1–15. doi:10.4018/ijban.2014010101

Leventhal, B. (2010). An introduction to data mining and other techniques for advanced analytics. *Journal of Direct. Data and Digital Marketing Practice, 12*(2), 137–153. doi:10.1057/dddmp.2010.35

Litt, M. (2014). How online video is changing the way B2B marketers engage and convert prospects. *Journal of Brand Strategy, 3*(2), 129–134.

Liu, B. (2010). Sentiment analysis and subjectivity. In Handbook of natural language processing (Vol. 2, pp. 627-666).

Loganathan, A., Sinha, A., Muthuramakrishnan, V., & Natarajan, S. (2014). A Systematic Approach to Big Data. *International Journal of Information & Computation Technology, 4*(09), 869–878.

Lukoianova, T., & Rubin, V. L. (2014). Veracity roadmap: Is big data objective, truthful and credible? *Advances in Classification Research Online, 24*(1), 4–15. doi:10.7152/acro.v24i1.14671

Mahrt, M., & Scharkow, M. (2013). The value of big data in digital media research. *Journal of Broadcasting & Electronic Media, 57*(1), 20–33. doi:10.1080/08838151.2012.761700

Mantelero, A. (2014). Social control, transparency, and participation in the Big Data world. *Journal of Internet Law, 17*(10), 23–29.

Marine-Roig, E., & Clavé, S. A. (2015). Tourism analytics with massive user-generated content: A case study of Barcelona. *Journal of Destination Marketing & Management, 4*(3), 162–172. doi:10.1016/j.jdmm.2015.06.004

McAfee, A., Brynjolfsson, E., Davenport, T. H., Patil, D. J., & Barton, D. (2012). Big data. *The management revolution. Harvard Business Review, 90*(10), 61–67. PMID:23074865

McAfee, A., Brynjolfsson, E., Davenport, T. H., Patil, D. J., & Barton, D. (2012). Big data. *The management revolution. Harvard Business Review, 90*(10), 61–67. PMID:23074865

McNeely, C. L., & Hahm, J. O. (2014). The big (data) bang: Policy, prospects, and challenges. *Review of Policy Research*, *31*(4), 304–310. doi:10.1111/ropr.12082

Menchen-Trevino, E. (2013). Collecting vertical trace data: Big possibilities and big challenges for multi-method research. *Policy & Internet*, *5*(3), 328–339. doi:10.1002/1944-2866.POI336

Michael, K., & Miller, K. (2013). Big data: New opportunities and new challenges [guest editors' introduction]. *Computer*, *46*(6), 22–24. doi:10.1109/MC.2013.196

Mikami, S., Ohta, K., & Tatebe, O. (2011, September). Using the Gfarm File System as a POSIX compatible storage platform for Hadoop MapReduce applications. *Proceedings of the 2011 IEEE/ACM 12th International Conference on Grid Computing* (pp. 181-189). 10.1109/Grid.2011.31

Milakovich, M. E. (2012). *Anticipatory Government: Integrating Big Data for Smaller Government.*

Mohanty, S., Jagadeesh, M., & Srivatsa, H. (2013). Extracting value from big data: In-memory solutions, real time analytics, and recommendation systems. In Big Data Imperatives (pp. 221-250).

Narayanan, V. K. (2015). Customer-focused IT: A process of continuous value innovation. *Strategy and Leadership*, *43*(4), 11–17. doi:10.1108/SL-05-2015-0037

Nedelcu, B. (2013). About Big Data and its Challenges and Benefits in Manufacturing. *Database Systems Journal*, *4*(3), 10–19.

Nunan, D., & Di Domenico, M. (2013). Market research and the ethics of big data. *International Journal of Market Research*, *55*(4), 2–13. doi:10.2501/IJMR-2013-015

Opresnik, D., & Taisch, M. (2015). The value of Big Data in servitization. *International Journal of Production Economics*, *165*, 174–184. doi:10.1016/j.ijpe.2014.12.036

Perera, R. D., Anand, S., Subbalakshmi, K. P., & Chandramouli, R. (2010, October). Twitter analytics: Architecture, tools and analysis. *Proceedings of the IEEE Military communications conference* (pp. 2186-2191).

Perrons, R. K., & Jensen, J. W. (2015). Data as an asset: What the oil and gas sector can learn from other industries about Big Data. *Energy Policy*, *81*, 117–121. doi:10.1016/j.enpol.2015.02.020

Phillips, K. A., Trosman, J. R., Kelley, R. K., Pletcher, M. J., Douglas, M. P., & Weldon, C. B. (2014). Genomic sequencing: Assessing the health care system, policy, and big-data implications. *Health Affairs*, *33*(7), 1246–1253. doi:10.1377/hlthaff.2014.0020 PMID:25006153

Pop, D. (2012). Machine learning and cloud computing: Survey of distributed and saas solutions (tech. report 1). *Institute e-Austria Timisoara.*

Rackley, J. (2015). Tools and Technologies. In Marketing Analytics Roadmap (pp. 103-117). doi:10.1007/978-1-4842-0259-3_8

Raghupathi, W., & Raghupathi, V. (2014). Big data analytics in healthcare: Promise and potential. *Health Information Science and Systems*, *2*(1), 3. doi:10.1186/2047-2501-2-3 PMID:25825667

Rahm, E. (2014). Discovering product counterfeits in online shops: A big data integration challenge. *Journal of Data and Information Quality*, 5(1-2), 3. doi:10.1145/2629605

Ramasamy, R. (2015). The production of salary profiles of ICT professionals: Moving from structured database to big data analytics. *Statistical Journal of the IAOS*, 31(2), 177–191. doi:10.3233ji-150891

Ramsey, G., & Bapna, S. (2016). Text Mining to Identify Customers Likely to Respond to Cross-Selling Campaigns: Reading Notes from Your Customers. *International Journal of Business Analytics*, 3(2), 33–49. doi:10.4018/IJBAN.2016040102

Russom, P. (2011). *Big data analytics*. TDWI Best Practices Report, Fourth Quarter.

Sakr, S., Liu, A., & Fayoumi, A. G. (2013). The family of MapReduce and large-scale data processing systems. [CSUR]. *ACM Computing Surveys*, 46(1), 11. doi:10.1145/2522968.2522979

Saluja, P., Rao, P., Mittal, A., & Ahmad, R. (2012, January). CDAC Scientific Cloud: On Demand Provisioning of Resources for Scientific Applications. *Proceedings of 18th international conferences PDPTA* (pp. 16-19).

Sarumathi, S., Shanthi, N., & Sharmila, S. V. M. (2014). A Review: Comparative Study of Diverse Collection of Data Mining Tools. *International Journal of Computer, Information, Systems and Control Engineering*, 8(6).

Sawant, N., & Shah, H. (2013). *Resources, References, and Tools*. In Big Data Application Architecture Q & A (pp. 127–136).

Simoff, S., Böhlen, M. H., & Mazeika, A. (Eds.). (2008). Visual data mining: theory, techniques and tools for visual analytics. Springer Science & Business Media.

Slinger, G., & Morrison, R. (2014). Will Organization Design Be Affected By Big Data? *Journal of Organization Design.*, 3(3), 17–26. doi:10.7146/jod.9729

Spiess, J., TJoens, Y., Dragnea, R., Spencer, P., & Philippart, L. (2014). Using big data to improve customer experience and business performance. *Bell Labs Technical Journal*, 18(4), 3–17. doi:10.1002/bltj.21642

Tan, K. H., Zhan, Y., Ji, G., Ye, F., & Chang, C. (2015). Harvesting big data to enhance supply chain innovation capabilities: An analytic infrastructure based on deduction graph. *International Journal of Production Economics*, 165, 223–233. doi:10.1016/j.ijpe.2014.12.034

Taylor, L., Cowls, J., Schroeder, R., & Meyer, E. T. (2014). Big data and positive change in the developing world. *Policy & Internet*, 6(4), 418–444. doi:10.1002/1944-2866.POI378

Taylor, R. C. (2010). An overview of the Hadoop/MapReduce/HBase framework and its current applications in bioinformatics. *BMC Bioinformatics*, 11. PMID:21210976

Tien, J. M. (2013). Big data: Unleashing information. *Journal of Systems Science and Systems Engineering*, 22(2), 127–151. doi:10.100711518-013-5219-4

Topps, D., Helmer, J., & Ellaway, R. (2013). YouTube as a platform for publishing clinical skills training videos. *Academic Medicine*, 88(2), 192–197. doi:10.1097/ACM.0b013e31827c5352 PMID:23269305

Ularu, E. G., Puican, F. C., Apostu, A., & Velicanu, M. (2012). Perspectives on Big Data and Big Data Analytics. *Database Systems Journal, 3*(4), 3–14.

van de Pas, J., & van Bussel, G. J. (2015). *'Privacy Lost-and Found?' The information value chain as a model to meet citizens' concerns.* Electronic Journal Information Systems Evaluation, 18, 2.

Vera-Baquero, A., Colomo Palacios, R., Stantchev, V., & Molloy, O. (2015). Leveraging big-data for business process analytics. *The Learning Organization, 22*(4), 215–228. doi:10.1108/TLO-05-2014-0023

Webb, H., & Laing, K. (2015). Engaging with Social Media: The Emily Carr University of Art and Design Library Experience. *Art Documentation, 34*(1), 137–151.

Weckman, G. R., Dravenstott, R. W., Young, W. A. II, Ardjmand, E., Millie, D. F., & Snow, A. P. (2016). A Prescriptive Stock Market Investment Strategy for the Restaurant Industry using an Artificial Neural Network Methodology. *International Journal of Business Analytics, 3*(1), 1–21. doi:10.4018/IJBAN.2016010101

White, P., & Breckenridge, R. S. (2014). Trade-Offs, Limitations, and Promises of Big Data in Social Science Research. *Review of Policy Research, 31*(4), 331–338. doi:10.1111/ropr.12078

Wielki, J. (2013). Implementation of the big data concept in organizations-possibilities, impediments and challenges. *Proceedings of the IEEE Computer Science and Information Systems (FedCSIS)* (pp. 985-989).

Wu, X., Zhu, X., Wu, G. Q., & Ding, W. (2014). Data mining with big data. *IEEE Transactions on Knowledge and Data Engineering, 26*(1), 97–107.

Xin, R. S., Rosen, J., Zaharia, M., Franklin, M. J., Shenker, S., & Stoica, I. (2013, June). Shark: SQL and rich analytics at scale. *Proceedings of the 2013 ACM SIGMOD International Conference on Management of data* (pp. 13-24). 10.1145/2463676.2465288

Zezula, P. (2015). Similarity Searching for the Big Data. *Mobile Networks and Applications, 20*(4), 487–496. doi:10.100711036-014-0547-2

Zhou, L. (2015). D2D Communication Meets Big Data: From Theory to Application. *Mobile Networks and Applications, 20*(6), 783–792. doi:10.100711036-015-0637-9

Zhou, S. B., & Ji, F. X. (2015). Impact of Lean Supply Chain Management on Operational Performance: A Study of Small Manufacturing Companies. *International Journal of Business Analytics, 2*(3), 1–19.

Živković, R., Njeguš, A., Zlatanović, M., Gajić, J., & Brdar, I. (2015). Comparative Analysis of Facebook and Communication Activities of the Mountain Hotels in Stara Planina, Kopaonik and Zlatibor/Uporedna Analiza. *The European Journal of Applied Economics, 12*(1), 26–36. doi:10.5937/ejae12-8159

This research was previously published in the International Journal of Business Analytics (IJBAN), 4(4); pages 21-47, copyright year 2017 by IGI Publishing (an imprint of IGI Global).

APPENDIX

Table 1. Characteristics of big data

Authors(year)	Volume	Variety	Velocity	Veracity	Value	Validity	Volatility	Variability
McAfee and Brynjolfsson (2012)	✓	✓	✓					
Sagiroglu and Sinanc (2013)	✓	✓	✓					
Nunan and Domenico (2013)	✓	✓	✓					
Ularu et al., 2012	✓	✓	✓	✓				
Raghupathi and Raghupathi V. (2014)	✓	✓	✓	✓				
Jagadish et al., (2014)	✓	✓	✓	✓				
Narasimhan and Bhuvaneshwari (2014)	✓	✓	✓	✓	✓			
Demchenko et al., (2013)	✓	✓	✓	✓	✓			
Thirunarayan and Sheth (2013)	✓	✓	✓	✓	✓			
Fan and Bifet (2013)	✓	✓	✓		✓			✓
Katal et al., 2013	✓	✓	✓		✓			✓
Gandomi and Haider (2014)	✓	✓	✓	✓	✓			✓
Khan et al. (2014)	✓	✓	✓	✓	✓	✓	✓	

Table 2. Big data tools and techniques

Product category/name	Features	Authors (years)
Big Data Analysis Platforms and Tools		
Hadoop	Store and distribute very large data sets across servers that operate in parallel.	
MapReduce	Process huge volume of data in parallel on large clusters of compute nodes.	Shukla et al. (2015); Jain and Kumar; Van et al. (2015); Mohanty et al., (2013)
GridGain	In-memory processing	
Storm	Distributed real-time computation capabilities.	
Databases/Data Warehouses		
Cassandra; Hypertable; OrientDB	NoSQL database	
Redis	In-memory key-value storage	
Hive	Provide easy data summarization and ad-hoc queries	Shukla et al. (2015); Selmer (2012); Fermigier (2011); Conesa (2014)
CouchDB	Online distributed scaling with fault-tolerant storage.	
MongoDB	NoSQL database with index support	
HBase	Non-relational data storage for Hadoop	
Business Intelligence (BI) suite		
Jaspersoft	Flexible, cost effective BI software.	

Product category/name	Features	Authors (years)
Konstanz Information Miner (KNIME)	Offers data integration, processing, analysis, and exploration tools.	Azarmi (2014); Damiani et al. (2009); Livinus ; Bulusu (2012);
Talend	Data integration tools	
Data Mining		
Mahout	Machine learning library	
R Analytical Tool To Learn Easily (Rattle)	R language graphical interface	Sarumathi et al., (2014); Shukla et al., (2015)
Knowledge Extraction based on Evolutionary Learning (KEEL)	Collection of evolutionary algorithms	
File Systems		
Hadoop Distributed File System (HDFS)	Replicates data onto several nodes in a cluster	Mikami (2011); Saluja (2012); Verkuil (2013)
Gluster	Unified file and object storage for very large datasets.	
Programming Languages		
R	Manipulate data, perform calculations and generate charts and graphs.	Taylor (2010); Gates et al., (2009)
Pig/Pig Latin	Produce sequences of Map-Reduce programs in parallel.	
Big Data Search		
Solr	Platform for improving an enterprise search capabilities	Alhabashneh et al., (2011); Goll et al., (2010)
Lucene	Indexing and searching for very large datasets.	
Data Aggregation and Transfer		
Chukwa	Display and analyse data from distributed system	Sawant and Shah (2013); Loganathan et al., (2014); Shukla et al., (2015)
Sqoop	Transfers data between Hadoop, relational databases and warehouses.	
Flume	Collects, aggregates and transfers log data	
Miscellaneous Big Data Tools		
Zookeeper	Maintain configuration information and distributed synchronization.	Shukla et al., (2015); Livinus (2014);Fels (2015);
Terracotta	Store and manage BD in server memory.	
Oozie	Coordinate the scheduling.	
Avro	Data serialization	

Table 3. Big data tools for fraud analytics

Tools	Advantages	Authors (year)
TransactionGuard; RiskTracker; Compliancy+ Corporate	Real-time monitoring of transactions and fraudulent activities	Albrecht et al., (2008); Monica and Cuza
SVAT; PATRIOT OFFICER	Discover links and money flow	
Reputation Manager 360	Cyber fraud detection	
preCharge Fraud Screening	In-depth fraud scoring and customer verification	
Fractals; ZoiD; minFraud	Card payment fraud detection and prevention	
Oracle Bharosa	Risk-analysis and strong authentication solution	
Kount Complete	SaaS solution for fraud management	
ThreatMetrix	Online fraud prevention solution	
NetReveal	Fraud, risk and compliance solution suite for financial services and government clients	
Signifyd	Fraud detection solution for e-commerce businesses.	
AssetArchive	Examine and audit loan trends	

Table 4. Big data tools for sentiment analytics

Tools	Advantages	Authors (year)
Google Alerts	Track content marketing, influencers, trends and competitors.	Live (2011); Pelser (2012); Ray (2013); Tips and S Tips (2014)
Meltwater	Assess commentary as a proxy for brand reputation.	
Social Mention	Track mentions for identified keywords in comments, news, Q&A, hash tags, blogs, video, events, and audio media.	
Marketing Grader	Calculate grade by looking at customer's updates on social media.	
Facebook Insights	Analyse daily active users, new Likes/Unlikes, number of fans, demographics and more	
Google Analytics	Create custom reports; advanced segments to breakdown visitor data.	
Pagelever	Measure content consumption shared on the Facebook platform.	

Table 5. Big data tools for digital analytics

Tools	Advantages	Authors (year)
IBM Watson Analytics	Create infographics	Herschel et al., (2014); Rackley (2015); Pelser (2012); Alacot (2014)
Tableau Software	Share analytics in cloud to create custom charts.	
MixPanel	Platform for mobile and web to measure engagement metrics	
Cyfe All-In-One Dashboard	Monitor all the business's data	
KeenIO	Analyse cloud data to strengthen the network	

Table 6. Big data tools for audio analytics

Tools	Advantages	Authors (year)
Qfiniti Explore; Eureka Enterprise; Behavioral Analytics Service	Analyses customer interactions across multiple communication channels and languages,	Khan et al. (2014); Blair and Keenan (2010);
Praetorian Voice Recorder	Recording functionality for quality monitoring.	
Interaction Recorder	Track script adherence, compliance, workplace performance and customer satisfaction.	
Harmony Suite	Advanced Speech Analyser modules for call monitoring and reporting	
NICE Interaction Analytics	Provides in-depth information based on keywords, call flow and emotional parameters	
RealCall; Language Assessor	Training platform for call centre agents	
VirtualMonitor	Virtual recording and monitoring pay based service	

Table 7. Big data tools for video analytics

Tools	Advantages	Authors (year)
Vidyard	Solution for custom video player and real-time analytics	Litt (2014); Clifton (2012); Topps et al., (2013); Agneeswaran (2014); Knapp (2009)
Google Analytics	Event Tracking by categorising the video and actions and label name.	
YouTube Analytics; Vimeo Analytics	An analytics suite to find total views, number of comments, likes and dislikes based on channel subscriber changes and demographics.	
Ooyala	Provide asset performance, social sharing, video engagement and custom analytics	

Table 8. Big data tools for social media analytics

Tools	Advantages	Authors (year)
Google+ Insights	Show visibility, engagement, and audience overviews.	Gupta & Gupta (2016); Russell (2013); Choudhury and Pulipati (2012); Perera et al., (2010); Hess (2013); Živković (2015) Webb and Laing (2015); King (2015)
Facebook Insights	Show the full stats behind posts, fans, and reach.	
LinkedIn analytics for businesses	Provide an overview of all the posts on business page	
Twitter analytics	Provides a 28-day overview of how tweets have performed	
LinkedIn analytics for individuals	Show how views have changed over time.	
Pinterest analytics	The dashboard shows growth in impressions and followers	
Rival IQ	Track a number of different companies and compare performance.	
Moz Pro	Track network size, engagement, and traffic breakdowns per network.	
Social Report	Provides an overview of activities on social networks and measure ROI	
Iconosquare	Instagram management tool	

Table 9. Big data tools for in-database analytics

Tools	Advantages	Authors (year)
Teradata In-Database Analytics ; IBM Netezza	Platform that prepare the data, develop and score data models in the data warehouse.	Xin et al., (2013); Hellerstein et al., (2012); Leventhal (2010); Pop (2012)
MonetDB	Reduce the data loading and processing time	
SAS IN-Database Analytics	Minimize data preparation; accelerate data discovery; reduce data movement; improve data integrity; enable data governance; minimize information latency	

Table 10. Challenges with big data analytics

Factors	Challenges	Authors (year)
Technological factors	• Managing large volume of data • Incompleteness and error in data • Searching of data. • Manage real time data • Sharing private data • Security for information sharing	Che et al., (2013); Sagiroglu and Sinanc (2013); Michael and Miller (2013); Bizer (2012)
Human factors	• Orientation or education about best analytics practices. • Analysts to interpret the data • Data scientist and other professionals • Trust in results of analysis. • Data-driven organizational culture.	Yan (2013); McAfee et al., (2012); Davenport and Patil (2012)
Organizational factors	• Support of leaders • Responsibilities of management • Regulations, policies and standards • Support of leaders • Responsibilities of management • Regulations, policies and standards	Wu et al., (2014); LaValle et al., (2013); Labrinidis and Jagadish (2012); Villars (2011) Wu et al., (2014); LaValle et al., (2013); Labrinidis and Jagadish (2012); Villars (2011)

Table 11. Steps showing how to use BDA

Steps involved in using advanced analytics
1. Developing an understanding of the application domain and the goals of BDA process
2. Acquiring or selecting a target BD set
3. Integrating and checking the BD set
4. Data cleaning, pre-processing, and transformation
5. Choosing suitable analytics for BD
6. Result visualization
7. Interpretation
8. Developing an understanding of the application domain and the goals of BDA process
9. Acquiring or selecting a target BD set
10. Integrating and checking the BD set
11. Data cleaning, pre-processing, and transformation
12. Choosing suitable analytics for BD
13. Result visualization
14. Interpretation

Chapter 27
Big Data and Digital Analytics

Sumathi Doraikannan
Malla Reddy Engineering College (Autonomous), India

Prabha Selvaraj
Malla Reddy Institute of Engineering and Technology, India

ABSTRACT

Data becomes big data when then the size of data exceeds the ability of our IT systems in terms of 3Vs (volume, velocity, and variety). When the data sets are large and complex, it becomes a great difficult task for handling such voluminous data. This chapter will provide a detailed knowledge of the major concepts and components of big data and also the transformation of big data in to business operations. Collection and storage of big data will not help out in creation of business values. Values and importance are created once when the action starts on data by performing an analysis. Hence, this chapter provides a view on various kinds of analysis that can be done with big data and also the differences between traditional analytics and big data analytics. The transformation of digital data into business values could be in terms of reports, research analyses, recommendations, predictions, and optimizations. In addition to the concept of big data, this chapter discuss about the basic concepts of digital analytics, methods, and techniques for digital analysis.

BIG DATA: INTRODUCTION

Big data owns 3 V's (Volume, Velocity and Variety). It is defined as the data that appears to be in huge volume of different data that travels with right speed and reaches the destination within the stipulated time frame so that the data could be used for real-time analysis and further reaction. The structure of big data could be structured or unstructured data that could be in any form such as text files, multimedia files, financial data etc. Data comes from several data sources in order to form data inundation. Data sources could be categorized as electronic gadgets like mobile sensors, medical imaging, smart grids, video surveillance, social media video rendering and genetic engineering etc. so as to form data surge. The fastest- growing sources of big data are social media and genetic engineering. Big data might possess data that contains data structures such as structured, unstructured, semi structured and quasi structured.

DOI: 10.4018/978-1-6684-3662-2.ch027

The configuration of structured data includes reports, contracts, email and other communications. Structured data displays the information in the form of text files. The information is displayed in columns and rows. Furthermore, it could be easily organized and processed with the help of data mining tools. This could be envisaged as a perfectly organized filing cabinet in which identification, labeling is a simple task and it is easy to access.

Most of the organizations might like to be familiar with this type of data and it is used in an effective and efficient manner. Data does not have any intrinsic structure. It is available in the form of complex data sources such as email, multimedia content, web logs, sales automation and social media data as denoted by Marcos et al (2015). As per Holzinger et al (2013), unstructured information may account for more than 70% to 80% of all data in organizations. Semi structured data does not match with the prescribed structure of data models in the perspective of relationships. Examples of semi structured data could be XML, JSON, MongoDB that stores data in JSON. Quasi structured data is defined as the textual data with inconsistent data formats that could be formatted with effort and time. For example, quasi structured data refer to the click stream data that might consist of inconsistent data values and formats. Few organizations, definite methods must be extended so that it has to manage the huge volume of data. The below Table 1 illustrates the generation of data that occurred in several organizations.

Table 1. Growth of unstructured data

Organizations	Generation
Wordpress (Nawsher Khan et al., 2014)	It is a free open source content management system in which nearly 350 new blogs per minute are published by bloggers
LinkedIn (Nawsher Khan et al., 2014)	A business and employment-oriented social networking service. Through this 2.1 million groups have been created
Apple (Nawsher Khan et al., 2014)	Around 47000 applications are downloaded per minute
Facebook	34,722 likes are registered in each and every minute 47% of Facebook users only access the platform through mobile Users generate 4 million likes every minute More than 250 billion photos have been uploaded to Facebook This equates to 350 million photos per day
YouTube	300 hours of video are uploaded to YouTube every minute! Almost 5 billion videos are watched on Youtube every single day. YouTube gets over 30 million visitors per day In an average month, 8 out of 10 18-49 year-olds watch YouTube.
Twitter	Barack Obama's victory tweet was the most retweeted tweet ever with over 800K retweets Top 3 countries on Twitter are the USA at 107 million, Brazil 33 million and Japan at nearly 30 million The average Twitter user has tweeted 307 times

Components of Big Data

As the name implies, big data contributes much for business applications and it has produced a noteworthy impact in various fields that includes the social media, satellite imaging, banking transactions and healthcare machines. S. Hendrickson (2010) noted that information increase takes place in a rapid manner at the rate of 10x every five years. It was found that the capacity for storage in general-purpose computers was 2.9×1020 bytes and that for communication was 2.0×1021 bytes. From Hilbert & Lopez (2011), it is understood that these computers could also perform 6.4×1018 instructions per second. Yet, there is a tremendous increase in the computing size of general-purpose computers and it is found to be at the rate of 58%. In computational sciences, big data is treated as a critical issue. It cannot be processed with the help of conventional methods and existing technologies. As a result of this, the production of immense data from several fields like business, society and science is a global issue that has to be addressed. Procedures and standard tools have not been designed to search and analyze large data sets as suggested by Bhadani and Jothimani (2016). Hence few organizations come across challenges in the creation and manipulation of large data sets. The data type that is been collected is considered as unstructured data. It is described by human information such as photos, high-definition videos, movies, financial transactions, geospatial maps, email, sensor data, medical records, weather records and tweets etc. Industrial Development Corporation (IDC) and EMC Corporation stated the amount of data generated in 2020 will be 44 times greater [40 zettabytes (ZB)] than in 2009. This rate of increase is expected to persist at 50% to 60% annually.

A suitable environment has to be created in order to support big data. Therefore, one has to follow good design principles that might have an opportunity to deal with storage, reporting analytics or applications. Certain considerations must be included for setting up hardware, software, management software, operational software and well-defined application programming interfaces. The Figure 1 illustrates some common components of Big Data analytical heaps and their amalgamation with each other as suggested by Gupta and Shilpi (2016).

Figure 1. Components of big data

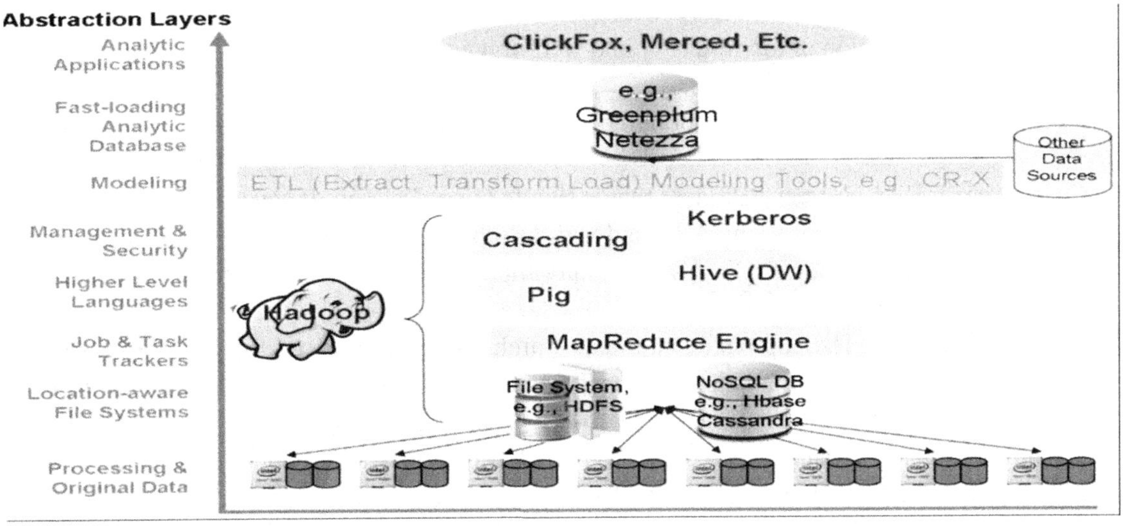

The data has to get processed in the physical infrastructure which is situated at the lowest level of the stack. The requirements have to be examined on a layer-by layer basis in order to assure that the implementation has to be performed and it has to be scaled according to the business demands. The data is conventionally stored in relational database. At certain circumstances, there is a need for the data that has to be extracted periodically from the operational database. These data are transformed and loaded into data warehouse for further reporting and analysis. To handle high-value transactional data which is already a structured data, a massive parallel relational platform is required, and it needs to support a large amount of user and applications that enquired about the known data with performance and enterprise level security. The components of big data are represented in the Figure 1 are described as follows:

- A storage system might comprise any one of the following:
  - **Hadoop Distributed File System(HDFS):** It is the storage layer which deals with the storage of data and metadata;
  - NOSQL also could be used like HBase or key-value based columnar. Cassandra also could be used.
- Computation is required, and this could be any one of the following:
  - **MapReduce:** It is an amalgamation of two processes. It consists of a mapper and reducer. The role of the mapper is that it first gets executed and the raw dataset is transformed into another key-value data. The reducer accepts the map that has been created by the mapper as an input, collects the input and converges it into a smaller dataset.
  - **Pig:** A platform which is required has to be situated on top of Hadoop. This tool is used in conjunction with or as a substitute for MapReduce. Pig is a high level language and it is mainly used to create processing components that are utilized to analyze very large datasets. The main feature of this language is the adaptability of its structure to various degrees of parallelism. It owns a compiler which is used to translate pig scripts to MapReduce jobs. This language is commonly used because of the following advantages such as:
    - Programming is very easy;
    - It is extendible;
    - Optimization of jobs are easy and well-organized.

Next comes the interaction or application logic. It could be any one taken from the list given below:

- **Cascading:** It is an abstract API layer that is situated over Hadoop. It acts as a framework which depicts the set of data processing APIs and various other components are used in data processing execution over the Hadoop/Big data stack. Many applications have been developed due to its easiness, job scheduling and job creation.
- **Hive:** On top of the Hadoop platform, a data warehousing layer (Hive) is built. HDFS data are analyzed, processed with the help of hive. It acts like SQL. It plays a vital role in the RDBMS world since it makes the job of Hadoop in an easy way.
- Specialized analytics data bases could be used. Various analytics models require fast data ingestion, refresh and scaling out facility. This could be done with databases such as Netezza or Greenplum.

Traditional Analytics vs. Big Data Analytics

Analytics is defined as the process of detecting and communicating the patterns that are found to be meaningful in data. It helps to optimize roles, functions and key processes.

Difference between the traditional analytics and big data analytics is given in the Table 2.

Table 2. Traditional analytics vs. big data analytics

Traditional Analytics	Big Data Analytics
Data sets are condensed, structured and highly rich featured.	Tools are used in organizations so as to construct a framework. This is mainly used to retrieve the features from the large dataset in order to model the data.
Sliced data could be used. Part of the database could be made visible.	Data is productized and shared across the enterprise.
Well-developed traditional data analytics methods were used widely to analyze structured data and to limit extend the semi-structured data. This involves further processing over heads.	Analytics is the process of extracting useful information by analyzing different types of big data sets. Big data analytics is used to discover hidden patterns, market trends and consumer preferences, for the benefit of organizational decision making.
Normally traditional data analysis methods are not designed for large-scale and complex data. It is also impossible to analyze the big data.	They are mainly designed for large scale data.
Traditional analytics methods find that the impact of learning is on one or two real-world metrics	Big data analytics look at the unanticipated impact of learning
Processing time for traditional analytics is 1-2 days	Processing time for big data analytics is 1-5 seconds
Traditional analytics is built on relational data models	Big data comes in various form and formats from multiple disconnected systems.
It mainly focus on descriptive and diagnosis analytics	This main focus is on predictive analytics and data science

TAXONOMY OF BIG DATA

Several elements of big data taxonomy are shown in the Figure 2. Big data dimensions: volume, velocity, variety, veracity, validity, value, variability, vagueness, and vocabulary could be considered to characterize the quality of the data.

Figure 2. Taxonomy of big data

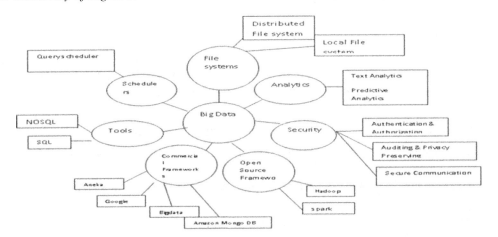

Analytics: Big Data Techniques

Traditional analytics are used to explore dissimilar data when it is present in huge amount. Some examples are given below:

- **Slicing and Dicing:** This is the process of breaking data into small groups of data so that it could be very easy to explore.
- **Basic Monitoring:** It is the process of monitoring large volumes of data in real time.
- **Anomaly Identification:** Anomalies are identified in this process.
- **Advanced Analytics:** This is used to do complex analysis of either structured or unstructured data. It consists of several machine learning, neural networks, sophisticated statistical models and other advanced data mining techniques. Decision making process is considered as a part of advanced analytics due to the vast increase in computational power, new developments in the algorithms that are used to solve real time problems, latest data infrastructure and huge amount of data. Some of the examples of advanced data analytics are:
  - **Text Analytics:** It is used in all sorts of analysis and in social media analytics so as to identify frauds. The unstructured text is analyzed, the relevant information is extracted and transformed into structured information.
  - **Predictive Modeling:** It is a statistical model or data-mining solution that consists of techniques or algorithms that could be used on both structured and unstructured data in order to identify future outcomes.
  - **Other Data Mining and Statistical Algorithms:** This includes optimization, cluster analysis for segmentation or affinity analysis.

Different approaches are required for analyzing big data. Approaches might be traditional or advanced since it depends on the problem that has to be solved. To manage big data, different approaches are required in order to help the business to successfully plan for the near future. Several features of big data are massive, complex, incomplete, unstructured, incomplete, noisy and erroneous.

Technologies

This could be mainly categorized into three parts known as i) file system – this is used to organize the data ii) computing frameworks and iii) tools for analytics.They are described as given below:

- **File System:** This represents the way of naming,sharing,organizing, storing and protecting files.
  - **Distributed Access and Location Transparency:** During the file access, clients are unaware about the location of the file they try to access.
  - **Heterogeneity:** File services could be made available across the several operating system platforms and different hardware resources.
  - **Failure Handling:** It could be achieved with some level of redundancy and replication. The client and application programs handle the failures in the system.
  - **Support Fine-Grained Distribution of Data:** Individual objects could be located in order to optmize performance.

- **Tolerance for Network Partitioning:** The file system shouldbe able to handle the situations and the appropriate synchronization mechanisms could be applied. Certain segments of the entire network might be unavailable to a client during certain periods.
- **Computing Frameworks:** This could be categorized as open source frameworks and commercial frameworks.
  - **Spark:** This is a fast and general engine for large-scale data processing. It could run on Hadoop YARN ncluster manager and could read any existing Hadoop data.
  - **Apache Hadoop:** Distributed processing of large-scale data sets across clusters of computers could be done through this open-source reliable,scalable and sitributed computing platform.
  - **Hadoop:** Hadoop cluster is used for big data analysis and NoSQL supports columnar database with the help of DynamoDB. Rackspace offers Horton Hadoop framework on Openstack platform. .NET – based desktop MapReduce platform and other enterprise frameworks based on open-source Hadoop are Horton and Cloudera are been offered by Aneka.
- **Tools for Analytics:** Several big data tools that are described are as follows:
  - **Graph Database:** This is useful for dealing out complex many-to-many connections such as social networks and for traversing large-scale multi-level relationship. A graph could be captured by a table store and this supports recursive joins such as Cassandra and big table. Graph structures are used to store data and semantic query on the data. Every entity consists of direct pointers to its adjacent element, and index lookups are not required. Graph database is used since large-scale multi-level relationship traversals are common in processing social networks. Examples of graph databases are infintegraph from objectivity and Neo4j open-source graph database.
  - **Column Family/Big Table Database:** Key values are grouped in order to create the composite data. Each column contains the equivalent row number as key and the data as value. Data that comes from various streams such as web logs, time series that occurs from sensors are stored in this database. Examples are HBase and Google big table.
  - **Document-Oriented Database:** This is mainly used for storing semi-structured data. In this, contents are encapsulated or encoded in some standard format. Examples are MongoDB, and CouchDB.
  - **Big Table Database/Column Family:** In this database, the column contains the row number as key and the data as value. This database is applicable for storing weblogs, time series data coming from several devices and sensors. Examples are HBase and Google big table.

Programming Models

Several programming models such as Map Reduce, Aneka, Mahout, and Google have been discussed.

- **Map Reduce:** This is a data-intensive programming model which comprises of Map and Reduce functions in the cluster of distributed compute and storage nodes as referred by M. Ghazi & D. Gangodkar (2015). Certain operations like sorting and filtering are done by Map function and the role of reduce function aggregates the output that has been obtained from the map function and the final result is generated. With the help of this recursive programming model, similar logic operations are operated on multiple distributed data sets. Examples are Apache Spark and Aneka MapReduce.

- **Aneka:** This is considered as a thread programming model which is used for high-performance applications. It is also known as task programming model. It is used for work flow programming model.
- **Machine Learning Tools:** These are mainly used for decision-making. Few tools such as Hadoop and Mahout are used.
- **Big Query Languages:** This language is used for searching texts, words and their occurrences. The study of the data available in the web is known as web log mining. Google big query platform is used to search for the words and their frequencies. This is an example for web log mining.

Big Data Security

Data sharing must be done based on the authenticity of the user. Several methods were used for resolving the issues related with security when the data scales in large-scale high-volume. Conventional methods of computing and data security mechanisms are not adequate when the data volumes and infrastructures are very large. There is a possibility of attacks as the cloud infrastructures grow in size and when software platforms spread across the large networks of computers. Certain issues related to big data security are given below:

- **End Points:** Authentication must be done at the end points by extracting logs from endpoints.
- **Storage:** High priority data or confidential data must be stored on flash media. Hence, locking the storage would create a tier-conscious method. Usually in the big data architecture, data is stored on multiple layers. This type of data storage depends on the business needs.
- **Real-Time Security/Compliance Tools:** These tools are used to produce a huge amount of information. The main feature is to identify a method to overlook false positives. Hence, finding the true breaches could be made easier by humans.
- **Non-Relational Data Stores:** NOSQL databases lack security.
- **Distributed Frameworks:** Jobs that possess huge processing power are distributed among many systems for rapid analysis. Distributed processing refers to the processing of data by more number of systems which might leads to security issues.
- **Granular Auditing:** This is used to identify the attacks that have been missed, check out the consequences of these attacks and ensure to follow the guidelines that could be done in the future.
- **Data Provenance:** It briefly explains about the origin of data, the owner of data and other information about the data. This meta-data information accessibility must be done with an incomparable speed so as to reduce the time in which a security breach is found to be active. Users could be given certain privileges for continuous monitoring and examining the network to identify the violations that might happen. This activity needs great attention since the users might become a threat to their own big data.
- **Access Controls:** This refers to the process of issuing rights to the users to do the process such as read, write and view etc the data.
- **Data Mining Solutions:** These solutions are treated as the heart of many big data environments. It is ensured that more security has been provided not only against external threats, but also against the users those who exploit network privileges in order to achieve sensitive and confidential information.

Tools for Analyzing Big Data

To analyze big data, there are five mechanisms:

- **BI Tools:** These tools are essential for analysis, reporting and performance management. The inputs for BI tools deal mostly with data that originates from data warehouses and production information systems. In addition, a wide-ranging facility for performance management and business intelligence includes dashboards, scorecards, enterprise report creation, ad-hoc analysis and what-if scenario analysis on an incorporated enterprise scale platform.
- **In-Database Analytics:** Patterns and relationships about the data could be found with a variety of techniques James Taylor (2013). Information cycle time could be accelerated, and total cost of ownership could be reduced and also the data movement is eliminated, if the techniques are applied within the database.
- **Decision Management:** Predictive modeling, business rules and self-learning to decide based on the current context are included in the decision management. Individual recommendations posted by the customer are also considered for analysis and thus the value of the customer interaction is augmented. Oracle Advanced Analytics scores could be included to use complex predictive analytic models and real-time decision processes are created.
- **Discovery Tools:** Thorough investigation and analysis of information from both structured and unstructured sources could be retrieved with the help of these tools. These tools are used for analysis besides traditional Business Intelligence source systems since there is no necessity for up-front modeling, users derive conclusions which could be useful, and users could draw new insights and formulate informed decisions in a rapid manner.
- **Hadoop:** Data pre-processing is done in order to find out macro trends or to discover chunks of information such as out-of-range values. In addition, the impending value from new data has been facilitated. This tool is used by the organizations as a forerunner of advanced analytics tool.

Solutions/Proposals to Address Big Data Security and Privacy Challenges

When data grows in huge amount, certain operations such as masking, tokenization and encryption are applied for protecting the sensitive data. Due to the characteristics of big data such as the creators of data, data originates from different sources and data might be accessed by several users a complete focus is required for providing security. Proper classification of data must be done in order to identify the nature of the data and the location where it has to be placed. It must be ensured that the certain access policies and data handling policies must be framed and aligned with the organization. Several security mechanisms must be framed to provide security to the data at its source and to the data itself. In addition, different control and prevention strategies also must be implemented on data archiving, data leakage prevention and access control.

The most important challenge for big data security and privacy is to deal with the storage and processing of encrypted data. The basic security requirement for secure bigdata is a challenging task. When a query is posted, certain difficulties that have to be examined are:

- Whether the database is encrypted with single or multiple keys?
- Which user has the permission to decrypt the database?

- Is it necessary to decrypt the database before executing the query?

There might be a possibility of two types of adversaries in the case of unauthorized access:

- An adversary who might be involved in accessing the raw data to facilitate the compromising feature of interpretation/analysis process. For example, a false data might be injected into the raw data, or a large volume of data which is considered as sensitive might be stolen.
- Different data sets that have been already analyzed could be prone to attacks by the adversaries. In addition, they might extract the required information. This is possible by the intelligence legitimate analysts.

Violation of data privacy (Gabroit, 2007) could be done by the adversaries either with the help of software or hardware design flaws in the infrastructures.

As a result of this, more focus should be given at the infrastructure that includes data centers and cloud platforms since confidential raw data and contingent knowledge are stored in this place. This could be solved by providing encryption, access control and data anonymization. On the other hand, critical data that resides in big data infrastructures are stored without encryption. When several data protection mechanisms are deployed, data controllers usually depend on either encryption mechanisms or coarse-grained access control models that avoid further processing of the data.

Data Quality/Integrity and Provenance Issues

Certain mechanisms could be followed to check on the quality and integrity of the data. In addition, focus is also on to capture the details of the data and data from where it has been derived. Big data analysts find the difficulty in managing the huge amount of data. This also deals with the analysis of data and the way of interpreting the results of the analysis particularly in context-sensitive settings such as data dependency analysis, crucial and deliberate decision optimization within organizations, and malevolent/illegal behavior detection by law enforcement authorities.

Unwanted Data Correlation and Inferences

Data that originates from various sources might increase the risk of re-identification/de-anonymization. But, analysts could intentionally or fortuitously, categorize new inferences or determine new sets of confidential information the data subject has not agreed to share. The process of correlating hypothetically de-identified data sets with publicly or privately available data sets.

A solution that has been suggested by people at MIT is CryptDB. This allows the users to execute queries over the encrypted data. CryptDB proxy resides between the database and application. It takes care of the process of rewriting the query in a particular way such that they could be executed against the encrypted database. Trustworthy applications that need the data pass the query to the CryptDB. The results that are encrypted are sent back to the proxy. Using the master key, the results are decrypted, and the final answer is sent back to the application. Various encryption strategies have been developed for supporting different types of operations on data in CryptDB. Encrypted big queries enable SQL-like queries against append-only tables with the processing power of Google's infrastructure. The most important security practice is to security controls at the boundary of the networks. If an attacker violates the security perimeter, all the data that resides in it would be accessed. Hence, more focus should be given to the data. To improve the security of the data that resides in the infrastructure and controls the existing security solutions.

Applications of Bigdata

Due to the advent of big data, many applications including biomedical, traditional manufacturing, business and other applications.

Business Applications

Big data intelligent analysis technology is used to discover fraud risk, trends and patterns throughout the structured and unstructured data. Big data addresses the issues such as crime detection, crime prevention and financial analysis etc.

Manufacturing

Certain emerging technologies such as physical network and advanced analysis are used by the manufactures in order to compete with in the recent revolution manufacturing industry. During the process of automated production, big data is used to manage costs and reduce effects. Data collection such as storing the detail of the product, sales history of the product etc at all stages helps the manufacturers to find out better solutions.

Bio Medical Industry

Big Data analysis is carried out in the fields like angiography, magnetic resonance imaging or computed tomography and echocardiography to form cardiac imaging. New imminent information about the disease treatment and interventions are also made possible with the big data. With the help of Bioinformatics analysis and immune genomics disease etiology, information about variations in genetics, immune function and regulation could be easily understood. Personal health of the patients could be more benefitted due to the development in biomedical technology.

Importance of Digital Analytics

With the advent of cloud computing – infinite computing power that has been connected through real-time communication networks made the data collection more affordable. Recently the world gets connected always with the help of connected devices such as smart phones, tablets and other digitally connected devices. This enables the people to monitor, collect and present the information to the customers based on their needs. The data that has been collected from various sources like websites, mobile devices are considered to be the digital data. It is a paradigm of the big data. Digital data are exemplified by:

- Flow of information is not always clearly combined;
- There are many variables for each activity;
- Millions of activities per day;

- There is high cardinality of the variables.

The data thus collected needs a clear analysis which describes the behavior of customers. This process of analyzing digital data is known as digital analytics as mentioned in Philips (2014). It helps the organizations to provide a better online experience to its clients as well as potential customers that progressively results in the attainment of desired goals. The main advantage of digital analytics is that business could be developed in many ways. The two ultimate goals of digital analytics are:

- Value has been created by generating profitable revenue;
- Less cost.

Apart from these goals, various business objectives that evolve for digital analytics are:

- The ultimate goal of content publishers is to encourage commitment and regular manifestation.
- The main intention of branding is to coerce awareness, engagement and fidelity.
- Information about the financial leads of products has to be collected and the same must be displayed in the web sites to attract customers.
- Especially, e-commerce sites are developed to sell products or services.
- Users get the information at the right time due to its availability in online.

Common terminologies used in digital analytics are described as given below:

- **Cookies:** It is defined as the text that gets stored on a user's system with the help of a web browser. Information such as user preferences, the identifier for a server-based session, shopping cart contents, or other data used by websites to identify visitors are stored. These cookies are used for the identification of mechanics and technicalities of how visitors and visits are counted by both audience measurement tools and analytics tools.
- **Entry Page:** The first web page that is been accessed during the visit to a particular website.
- **Exit Page:** This page represents the last web page during the visit to a website. The page that is visited at last by the visitor could be identified as the final page in a tabbed or multi-window browser environment.
- **Direct Traffic:** Visitors those who visit the corresponding website in any of the following ways.
  ◦ The corresponding site URL could be types in the web browser.
  ◦ Mark the site as the bookmark and clicking on the corresponding bookmark to enter into the website.
- This also includes visitors those who are recruited through offline campaigns.
- **New Visitor:** A visitor who has cleared browser cookies before the recorded visit or who has never visited the website.
- **Returning Visitor:** When a visitor returns to the website again, then he/she is treated as the returning visitor.
- **Page View:** It is termed as the frequency of the webpage that was viewed during the visit.
- **Visit:** This is defined as the communication that occurs between the individual and the website that consists of one or more requests for a unit of content. If a person stays on the site for more

that the particular time period, then the visit session gets terminated and the second visit might be recorded.

- **Visitor:** It is possible for the individual to make multiple visits and the identification of that corresponding person depends on the visitor's computer. Through the cookies, it is easy to identify whether the visitor is new or returning back to the website.
- **Landing Page:** When a visitor identifies that the web site entered gives the needed information after clicking on it, then it is known as the landing page. This is identified as the entry page for the site. The main intention is to observe the behavior of the visitor for the targeted content.
- **Referring Sites:** There is a possibility of traffic generation due to the diversion of other websites to the corresponding website which user is visiting at present.
- **Search Engine:** It is defined as the web-based program that explores web pages and documents for the specified keywords and returns the list of web pages and/or documents based on the keywords.
- **Bounce Rate:** It is denoted as the percentage of entrances on a web page that results in an immediate exit from the website.

Search Analytics

This is considered to be an area where many people have come in and provided counsel to companies. Search analytics is broken up into two categories namely organic searches and paid searches.

Organic searches: The results that occur due to this search are the listings on search engine result pages that might appear due to the specific relevance to search terms. Metrics that are used by the communicators are given below:

- Known and unknown branded words: Communicators must be able to identify the words that are specific to their brands and they must know about the frequency of the words.
- Known and unknown keywords: This metric is used to identify the possible keywords that might drive the people to the corresponding website. A list which consists of known and unknown keywords could be prepared. In addition, it is obvious that the unknown keywords might also be unknown to the competitors. Communicators might look for the opportunity to optimize the content based on those unknown keywords.
- Average search position: This is considered as the vital factor since it identifies the rank in search engine results page based on the known, unknown, branded and unbranded keywords.
- Total visits: This refers to the number of total visits to the corresponding website in the web analytics platform.
- Total conversions from known keywords: Conversions could be either a dollar figure, downloads, signing up for a newsletter and etc. when the content is being optimized properly based on the known keywords that are used by the people, and then an uptick in conversion could be visualized.
- Paid searches: This refers to any form of online advertising that attach an advertisement to a specific keyword-based search request. Some of the most popular paid search metrics are:
  - **Cost Per Click (CPC):** It is the average amount an advertiser would pay for a click.
  - **Impression Share:** This is the ratio of the impressions the advertisement received to the possible impressions it could have received. This is similar to the share of conversation in social media analytics.

- ○ **Impressions:** An impression happens when a paid search advertisement appears on the search engine results page. This metric counts the number of such impressions.
- ○ **Sales or Revenue Per Click:** This is the amount of money generated per click received on an advertisement.
- ○ **CTR (Clickthrough Rate):** It is expressed as the ratio of the number of clicks an advertisement receives to the number of impressions received.
- ○ Average Position: This is used to measure the position of the advertisement on the search engine results page.
- Digital Analytics for Social Media: Social Media Analytics (SMA) is a type of digital analytics. SMA symbolizes a change in the way people use the Internet and how digital data is measured. SMA generates economic value through analysis of the significant and appropriate signals in social media data. Social media has become pervasive and persuasive during the last several years. It refers to the enormous directional impact across the world. In addition, it refers to the people those who create, produce, edit share, exchange and consume information.

Vocabulary that are used in the social media analytics are:

- **Lurking:** This refers to the viewing of social media content and just identify the information that has been said and not about any other thing or participating.
- **Participating:** During the start and stop of business or shifting of social media strategies, channel gets switched and would not be constant. This is considered to an action of mere participation.
- **Engagement:** This is an active participation process since communication takes place continuously among the social media channels. Promotions on social media, advertisement regarding the new products, replying to criticisms posted by people, informal participation during the conversation with customers refers to the process of engagement. This process is considered to be planned and strategic.
- **Listening:** An active monitoring about the brands, consumers, and business activities is done with the help of social media tool or technology. This is used to identify the products/consumers/brands that might be general or specific. This process might be considered as a complex since there is a need of automatic classification of huge volumes of incoming, text-based social media from several sites into various categories using text and sentiment analysis.
- **Virality:** This refers to the sudden and noteworthy impact while the content is viewed in a short period of time. It means that the content has been hastily communicated across the distances that help to understand the meaning of vitality.
- **Social Sharing:** This is enabled when the digital content gets shared among the users. Sharing is made possible with the help of story tools on various sites such as like on Facebook, or post on Reddit. Users could post their pictures during their vacation and it could be shared among their friends.
- **Privacy:** Global governments, businesses and consumers think and reply to questions about the effect of social media on privacy are the important factors for social media analytics.
- **Copyright Laws:** This is considered as the significant factor during the sharing of digital content. Consumers might not be aware of copyrights during their sharing. Therefore, the region, country, local and jurisdiction laws and rules that direct and frame the sale and sharing of digital content are the important factors for social media analytics.

- **Influencers:** The opinion posted by influencers has a value. People those who have a great influence on the acuity of any brand, products or service care are treated as influencers. They have the ability to create an impact on the business either positively or negatively due to their posting of views.
- **Social Networking:** A group of activities across social media that includes social sharing, engaging, bookmarking, linking and transacting that is been done across various social media platforms and the measurement is done through social media tools.
- **Social Applications:** To create a social experience, data inputs might be social experience or some behavioral features. Certain mobile applications that are mostly based on social and online collaboration over mobile devices despite the consequences of physical location, which are also GPS location aware, are referred as social applications. Macro conversions are identified as the main actions on any website or applications that developed for mobile that bind with the business objectives. Micro conversions are termed as the person might receive an email coupon or a new product notification. Both these conversions must be measured in order to achieve the right outcomes of any website.

Digital Analytics Tools

The main notion behind the digital analytics tool is to facilitate companies to track the behavior of customers those who prevail in digital channels. In addition, it is also used to assess the responses posted by the customer against the marketing stimuli. These types of tools are used by marketers in order to compute the efficiency of marketing activities, check the corresponding tactics for certain customer segments and then later optimize future actions.

Several marketing automation tools Jarvinen Joel (2016) those are available in the market for various reasons:

- **Meltwater:** Used to track news and discussions that are online.
- **SAS Text Miner:** This is a text mining tool which is used to mine information from text sources.
- **iPerceptions:** This is a website survey tools to get customer feedback.
- **Oracle Eloqua:** Personalize marketing content and manage sales leads.
- **Hitwise:** An online panel to increase the perception of target audience behavior on web.
- **SimplyMeasured:** An online intelligence tool is used to track competitor performance.

Certain digital analytics tools are customized for a specific platform while others are developed and designed for a specific activity. Tools are available for identification of search rankings, analyzing keywords, nurturing link building, crawling and auditing the website to identify the issues related to search engine optimization. Few factors have been identified are considered as the power of digital analytics. They are described as follows:

- More detailed information on the customer's behavior has been offered as the clickstream data records all the actions performed by the customers in the digital environment whereas the traditional analytics records only the transactions. The main features of digital analytics are digital analytics metrics and business goals are interdependent since it helps the marketers to investigate and exhibit the activities of digital marketing that might support the attainment of business goals.

The identified metrics must be structured and prioritized under the framework and the interrelationships augment the actionability of the metrics system. Mobilizing digital analytics data needs a systematic approach with clearly allocated responsibilities in terms of data collection, reporting and analysis.

- Surveys and interviews have been done to collect customers' preferences and intentions.
- From this, it is easy to predict genuine behavior and expressions of opinions in users' natural environment.
- Users' behavior has been tracked with the help of digital analytics tools.
- Location information is used to make the progress of personalized and contextual marketing messages.
- Offline settings could be provided by digital analytics tools.

Benefits of Using Digital Analytics

To increase the budget for digital marketing and to improve the standing of marketers within a company, the digital analytics is mainly used to compute and display the financial outcomes of digital marketing.

Interaction could be improved much more between the company and potential customers due to the awareness of the digital marketing channels and tactics. Due to this, a better understanding about the types of marketing content could be improved. It is also used to assess the behavior of the customer by tracking. As a result of this, a buzz is been created in social media. It also assists in framing the linkage between behavioral metrics and financial outcomes due to the tracking of the customers' behavior. Hence, due to this activity, the customers those who visit the websites are identified as the first task. Next, digital analytics identifies the nature of the customer. The corresponding customer after been attracted by the website might be intended to buy the product or service. The decision taken by the customer is easily predicted with the help of digital analytics tool. The behavioral metrics provided by digital analytics could be credibly linked with financial outcomes. When compared with the traditional measurement tools, digital analytics plays the vital role in prediction of the customer's behavior due to its genuine nature. Digitization increases the significance of the objective metrics and it could be made out even at the same cost of subjective metrics. The need for subjective metrics will not be eliminated since the customers behavior is tracked, whereas offline behaviors as well as thoughts and feelings remain uncaptured. As a result of this, to achieve the complete information about the marketing impacts, behavioral metrics must be harmonized with subjective metrics. Digital analytics monitors the regular activities of customer right from the initial step till the sales deal closing period. This in fact identifies the customers' interest and provides the information according to their needs and as well predicts their relative contributions to sales impact. Thus, the customers could be valued accordingly by the marketers. This tool is also able to track the priority of digital marketing activities and the decisions made by the customer. Purchasing a product could be based on both through the information displayed on the sites and as well as the information received through emails. Hence, the email alone could not be considered as the reason that accounts for the customer's purchase decision. This is a remarkable constraint on the use of digital analytics that must be often ignored when computing the productivity of marketing activities. It is understood that the digital analytics could only overcome the challenges of marketing performance measurement up to some extent since data have two important restrictions:

- Data is restricted to the digital footprint left in the firm's own media space, whereas not much information could be known about the customers those who work offline or in other digital channels.
- The behavioral dimension of the customer impact is possible with the digital analytics.

Role of big data in marketing:

- **Semantic Search:** Searching the natural language terms is denoted as semantic search. Machine learning together with the big data makes it easy for the search engines to identify what the user is searching for and the marketers those who really act as smart implement this special feature into their site search functionality. As a result of this, the user experience for the visitors those who visit the site could be improved.
- **Related Information:** Publishers will be able to provide the content to their visitors by identifying the wealth of data to decide the content liked by the people. Content marketers will be capable of getting job and digital marketers must make their site as a dynamic site.
- **Targeted Advertising:** Facebook and Google provide the details through advertising and attract the users.
- **Machine Powered Analytics:** When there is huge amount of data, digital marketers face the difficulty in deciding. Hence, machine learning is used to analyze data and decisions could be made accordingly.
- **More Conclusive Testing:** Analyzing the huge amount of data enables to perform more decisive testing that might include various other factors such as prior histories so that the results that are obtained will be more accurate and certain.

CONCLUSION

Big Data growth can be accredited to three market forces: trendy consumers, product and process automation, and data monetization. In particular, parallel platform provide abilities for data storage, integration and analytics. Decision making in the business world is mainly driven by the usage of data and analytics. This chapter discussed the major concepts, components of big data and also the big data transformation. In addition, the evolution of digital analytics and its importance is also explored. Moreover, it also gives an overview of several digital analytics tools that are available in the market.

FUTURE RESEARCH DIRECTIONS AND CHALLENGES

There is a need to know the importance of the technology since it yields results rapidly. Large scale data guides people in the field of invasive marketing and privacy incursions. Data analytics also analyze the online behavior, communities and political movements. The life cycle of the data has to be defined and this in turn creates a value for the data. The data that is been stored has to be made available and reliable at all times when there is a need for the usage of the data.

REFERENCES

Assunção, M. D., Calheiros, R. N., Bianchi, S., Netto, M. A. S., & Buyya, R. (2015). Big Data computing and clouds: Trends and future directions. *Journal of Parallel and Distributed Computing*.

Bhadani, J. D (2016). Big data: Challenges, opportunities and realities. In Effective Big Data Management and Opportunities for Implementation (pp. 1-24). IGI Global.

Decandia, G., Hastorun, D., Jampani, M., Kakulapati, G., Lakshman, A., Pilchin, A., ... Vogels, W. (2007). Dynamo: Amazon's Highly Available Key -value Store. *Proceedings of the 21st ACM Symposium on Operating Systems Principles (SOSP 2007)*. 10.1145/1294261.1294281

Gaborit, P., & Girault, M. (2007). Lightweight code-based identification and signature. *2007 IEEE International Symposium on Information Theory*, 191-195. 10.1109/ISIT.2007.4557225

Gantz, J., & Reinsel, D. (2012). *The Digital Universe in 2020: Big Data, Bigger Digital Shadows, and Biggest Growth in the Far East*. Retrieved from www.emc.com/leadership/digital-universe/index.htm

Ghazi, M., & Gangodkar, D. (2015). Hadoop, MapReduce and HDFS: A Developers Perspective. *International Conference on Intelligent Computing, Communication & Convergence*, 45-50. 10.1016/j.procs.2015.04.108

Gupta, S. (2016). Real time big data Analytics. Packet Publishing Ltd.

Hendrickson, S. (2010). *Getting Started with Hadoop with Amazon's Elastic MapReduce*. EMR.

Hilbert, M., & Lopez, P. (2011). The world's Technological Capacity´ to store, communicate, and compute information. *Science*, *332*(6025), 60–65. doi:10.1126cience.1200970 PMID:21310967

Holzinger, A., Stocker, C., Ofner, B., Prohaska, G., Brabenetz, A., & Hofmann-Wellenhof, R. (2013). Combining HCI, natural language processing, and knowledge discovery—potential of IBM content analytics as an assistive technology in the biomedical field. In Lecture Notes in Computer Science: Vol. 7947. Human-Computer Interaction and Knowledge Discovery in Complex, Unstructured, Big Data (pp. 13–24). Springer. doi:10.1007/978-3-642-39146-0_2

Jarvinen, J. (2016). *The use of digital analytics for measuring and optimizing digital marketing Performance*. Retrieved from https://jyx.jyu.fi/dspace/bitstream/handle/123456789/51512/978-951-39-6777-2_vaitos21102016.pdf?sequence=1

Judah Philips. (2014). *Digital analytics primer*. Pearson Education, Inc.

Khan, N., Yaqoob, I., Ibrahim, A. T. H., Inayat, Z., Waleed, K. M. A., Alam, M., ... Gani, A. (2014). Big Data: Survey, Technologies, Opportunities, and Challenges. *The Scientific World Journal*, *2014*, 712826. doi:10.1155/2014/712826 PMID:25136682

Lee, J., Lapira, E., Bagheri, B., & Kao, H. A. (2013). *Recent Advances and Trends in Predictive Manufacturing Systems. Big Data Environment Manufacturing Letters*, *1*, 38–41. doi:10.1016/j.mfglet.2013.09.005

Narula, J. (2013). Are We Upto Speed? From Big Data to Rich Insights in CV Imaging for a hyper connected World JACC. *Cardiovascular Imaging*, *6*, 1222–1224. doi:10.1016/j.jcmg.2013.09.007 PMID:24229779

Soares, S. (2012). A Framework That Focuses on the Data in Big Data Governance. *IBM Data Management*, *13*(June). Retrieved from http://ibmdatamag.com/2012/06/a-frameworkthat-focuses-on-the-data-in-big-data-governance

Taylor, J. (2013). *In Database Analytics*. Decision Management Solutions.

KEY TERMS AND DEFINITIONS

Aneka: A framework which is used for constructing applications that are customized and it could be used further by deploying it on private or public clouds.

Anonymization: It is defined as the masking of personal information of a user which is been used in the process of transaction.

Business Intelligence Tools: Unstructured data from various resources such as documents, email, video, health records, etc. are collected and processed.

Crawling: The process of identifying web pages and downloading is termed as crawling.

JSON: Java script object notation. It is defined in terms of text format and it is language independent.

Mahout: An open source project and it is mainly used for producing scalable machine learning algorithms. Applications that are developed using Mahout are used to investigate large data sets effectively and it takes less time for analysis.

Social Media Analytics: It uses algorithms in order to endow the public with critical intelligence.

Chapter 28
Big Data Visualization Tools and Techniques

Obinna Chimaobi Okechukwu
Arkansas State University, USA

ABSTRACT

In this chapter, a discussion is presented on the latest tools and techniques available for Big Data Visualization. These tools, techniques and methods need to be understood appropriately to analyze Big Data. Big Data is a whole new paradigm where huge sets of data are generated and analyzed based on volume, velocity and variety. Conventional data analysis methods are incapable of processing data of this dimension; hence, it is fundamentally important to be familiar with new tools and techniques capable of processing these datasets. This chapter will illustrate tools available for analysts to process and present Big Data sets in ways that can be used to make appropriate decisions. Some of these tools (e.g., Tableau, RapidMiner, R Studio, etc.) have phenomenal capabilities to visualize processed data in ways traditional tools cannot. The chapter will also aim to explain the differences between these tools and their utilities based on scenarios.

INTRODUCTION

Business decisions have always been reliant on available information. Without the right type of information at the right time, business decisions can be flawed and in some cases catastrophic. Managers and top line executives alike rely on data, facts and historical records to be able to take actions that would solve a problem, avoid a potential business problem or even create new business opportunities. In a recent research study conducted among 600 medium sized British firms, insufficient information and information barriers are accounted as one of the biggest constraints to management efficiency (Bloom, Lemos, Qi, Sadun, & Reenen, 2011).

It is argued that the visual representation of data (data visualization) is perhaps one of the most important aspects of data analysis. Decision makers can relate better with a visual reference to information that is given to them as opposed to textual information. Through visual perceptions and cognitive processes, data can be made easier to understand and better business insight can be obtained from the data. Let us consider an example.

DOI: 10.4018/978-1-6684-3662-2.ch028

Figure 1. Visual navigation map showing vehicular route from Hauppauge to Long Island (Google, 2015)

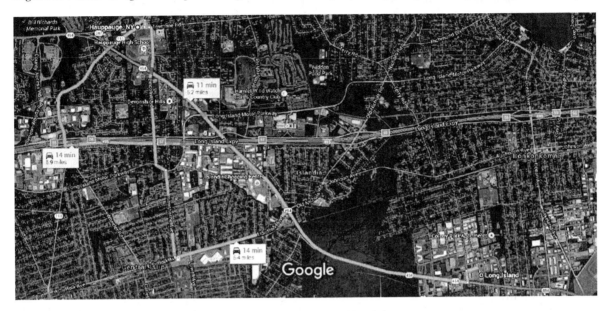

Figure 2. Textual description of the vehicular route from Hauppauge to Long Island. (Google, 2015)

Hauppauge, NY

Take Lincoln Blvd to NY-454 E in Islip

3 min (0.7 mi)

1. Head west toward Hauppauge Blvd

0.1 mi

2. Turn right onto Hauppauge Blvd

348 ft

3. Turn left onto Smithtown Islip Townline Rd/Townline Rd

285 ft

4. Turn right onto Lincoln Blvd

0.5 mi

5. Turn left onto NY-454 E

8 min (4.1 mi)

Continue on 5th Ave to your destination in Ronkonkoma

2 min (0.4 mi)

6. Turn left onto 5th Ave

0.1 mi

7. Turn right

0.2 mi

8. Turn right

400 ft

Long Island

In the example above, an illustration of how graphical visualization can provide better information than textual information is shown. Suppose an individual wants to determine the relative geographic position of Hauppauge from Long Island. Figure 1 will better provide that individual with information on the relative positions of both locations than Figure 2 would. This illustrates the effectiveness of visual data presentation over textual data.

VISUALIZATION TECHNIQUES

In every business organization – *and even in people's personal lives* – there is a constant flow of data visualization. These come in several forms such as bar charts, pie charts, line graphs, scatter plots, etc. However, not every graph or chart can be used to display the result of every type of data. There are several parameters or factors that determines what sort of visual reporting tool is most appropriate for reporting the results of a given set of data. Some of these parameters are:

- The characteristics of the data set: numeric, alphanumeric, graphical, etc.
- The volume of the data: few records of data or large records of data.
- The dimension of the data: few data attributes or large number of data attributes.
- The relationship between the attributes of the data.
- The number of variables in the data set: univariate, bivariate or multivariate.
- The data source, etc.

Other factors that can affect what reporting tool should be used is the data type. A set of data can be discrete or continuous in nature (Soukup & Davidson, 2002). These data types are referred to as *discrete variables* and *continuous variables* respectively. Discrete variables can be:

1. **Nominal:** These are finite variables with multiple categories that are not in any specific order. An example of this would be cities in the state of Colorado. While there are multiple cities, there is no intrinsic order to the cities in the state.
2. **Dichotomous:** These are finite variables with only 2 levels of categories. A good example of this would be gender (male or female).
3. **Ordinal:** These are finite variables with multiple categories that are in a specific order. An example of this would be the stages in education (Elementary, High school, Some college, College, etc.) As you would observe in the example, there is an inherent order in the categories.

On the other hand, continuous variables can be classified as:

1. **Interval:** These are typically numeric variables that have a continuum of values with equal intervals between each succeeding value. For example, temperature values. Temperature values have equidistant intervals between each value.
2. **Ratio:** These are variables that group or classify other intervals of values. An example of this would be a height of 8 feet is double that of 4 feet.

Understanding the differences in these data types will help you figure out the best technique to use in representing your analyzed data set visually. It is often noted that timely and accurate information which is not well understood is equivalent to no information at all (Laerd Statistics, 2016). This underscores the need to use the right tool when attempting to present information resulting from an analysis. Let us look at some of the common analysis techniques.

Series Charts

Series charts, also commonly referred to as time series graphs are a type of chart that utilizes a set of data points known as markers to plot a connecting line typically across an x-axis. The main purpose of line graphs is to show a continuous trend of data over a period of time. These sort of analyses are known as trend-based analysis or time-series data analysis. Most times this would be used to show historical trend of a given variable over a period of time or the forecast of possible values of a given variable over a projected period of time.

Time series charts are often mathematically expressed through a linear equation. This simply means that the line can be expressed in form of a mathematical expression that would determine elements of the graph such as: the y-intercept, the gradient of the line, the x-axis value for every y-axis value and vice versa. The equation is given as:

$y = ax + b$ (Wikipedia, 2016)

where;
y = y-axis value
a = gradient of the line (also referred to as the 'rise over run')
x = x-axis value and
b = y-intercept value (where the line intercepts the y-axis)

An example of a time series graph is a graph showing the time-based index values of 3 variables as seen in Figure 3.

As mentioned above, series charts are particularly useful for displaying information on the state of values of a parameter or variable over a period of time. Trend charts utilize one or more variables that have contiguous values and plots a connecting line horizontally to display the values in a time period. A classic example of this is the time series chart shown below. This is an example of hardware sales forecast over a given period.

Treemaps

Treemaps show hierarchical (tree-structured) data as a set of nested rectangular blocks. The data blocks within a dataset are assigned to a tiled square or rectangle. The rectangle can be embedded into smaller branches which represents sub-branches of the data set. To show differences in the data dimensions, the rectangles have different colors to show differences in the data dimensions (Bruls, Huizing, & Wijk, 2015).

The colors and sizes of the rectangles indicates that the dimensions are correlated in some way with the tree structure. The color and size differences help the data interpreters visually recognize the patterns that exist within the data set and can help in easy interpretation of the information being presented.

Figure 3. State index values of 3 variables (RapidMiner, 2015)

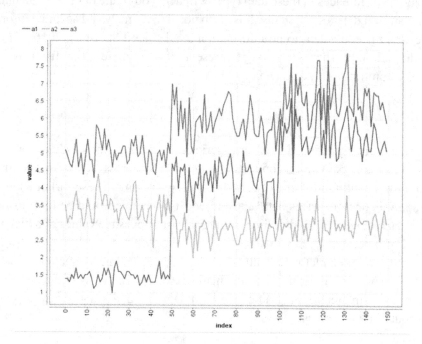

Figure 4. Sales forecast for hardware equipment (Designed by the author)

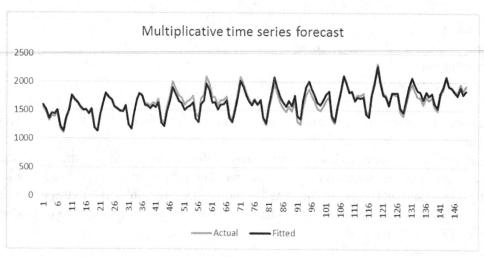

This makes data interpretation a much easier process because the color similarities and contrasts can adequately show the relationships between the data points in the entire data set.

Another advantage treemaps has is that it makes use of space very efficiently due to its form of construction. This makes it relatively easy for huge amounts of data items to be visually represented at the same time. This is particularly good for hierarchical structured data sets which need to be efficiently represented.

Figure 5. Treemap data representation of population and birth rate among selected countries (Tableau, 2016)

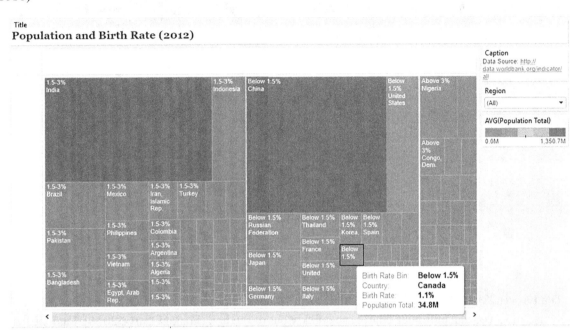

In the course of this chapter there will be more evaluation of tree maps using one of the many functional analytics tools in the market.

DATA VISUALIZATION TOOLS

There are a number of Big Data analytics tools in the market. Some of them are free or relatively inexpensive while others are quite costly and are designed to address large corporations that process significantly huge datasets per second.

However, working with visualization tools require some skillset and knowledge on how to process different data structures and present the right type of results. Imagine allowing a 9-year-old being allowed to take the steering wheel of a car. No matter how functional the car is, if the driver of the car is not skilled at driving, the results could be less than desirable. The same is true with data analytics tools, the user needs to be able to understand what insight is required and the nature and structure of the data being analyzed.

The chapter will highlight some of the common data analytics and visualization tools in the market and then there will be a review of some analytical procedures using a few of them to illustrate how they deal with visualization processes.

FusionCharts

Arguably one of the most versatile data analytics software in the market for visualization, FusionCharts supports a whole lot of visualization techniques and presents them in a graphically appealing manner.

Figure 6. FusionCharts analytics software (FusionCharts, 2016)

The FusionCharts Suite XT supports more than 90 chart types and over 1000 chart maps making it really useful as you can pull out a chart type quickly out of the box (FusionCharts, 2016). FusionCharts is a developer-oriented software allowing developers to embed the charts into their programs. It supports the JSON (JavaScript Object Notation) and XML (Extensible Markup Language) data formats, reports can be exported in formats of: PNG (Portable Network Graphics), JPEG (Joint Photographic Experts Group), SVG (Scalable Vector Graphics), or PDF (Portable Document Format). Their charts and maps are compatible across all devices and platforms.

Google Charts

Google Charts is a developer based charting engine that provides APIs for developers to embed visualization tools into their programs. It supports a host of charts from simple line charts to complex hierarchical tree maps, the chart gallery provides a large number of ready-to-use chart types (Google, 2016).

It renders the charts in HTML5 which enables it to display charts and graphs on websites and mobile devices. The large chart gallery allows users to select a lot of options depending on the analysis that is being performed.

RStudio

The RStudio is undoubtedly one of the most powerful analytics and visualization engines available. It is multi-functional and able to support most visualization techniques available. Some of the interesting features of this tool is its flexibility and ability to allow users import or directly input data, perform data cleaning and massaging operations and then draw several types of charts to visually represent the results of the analysis.

Figure 7. Google charts (Google, 2016)

Figure 8. RStudio analytics interface (RStudio, 2015)

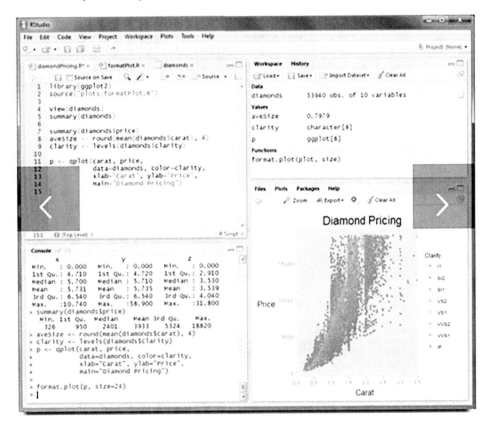

Some of the important features of this product is the availability of a console with a syntax-highlighting editor that supports direct code execution as well as tools for plotting, history, debugging and workspace management (RStudio, 2015). The RStudio program works very efficiently for analytics and visual data representation. It can be used on small projects or large projects. It has the capacity to connect to external data sources or direct data imports.

IBM SPSS Modeler

The IBM SPSS Modeler is one of the most complex and powerful data analytics and visualization tool available today. It is the tool of choice for a majority of enterprises, research labs, educational institutions and government agencies. It supports a significantly huge set of functions and can be used to model just about any type of data. (SPSS (Hong Kong), 2015).

This tool is considered to be a versatile analytics platform designed to bring the potential of predictive intelligence to decisions made by individuals or organizations. It provides a range of algorithms and techniques which include text analytics, decision management and optimization to name a few. The SPSS Modeler is also scalable and can be deployed from desktop deployments to integration within operational systems (IBM Software, 2015).

Figure 9. IBM SPSS Modeler for data analytics (SPSS (Hong Kong), 2015)

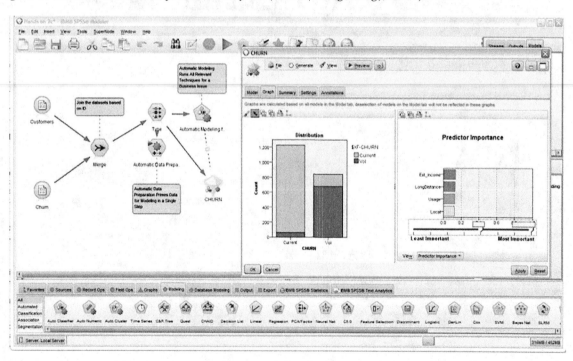

SAS

SAS has been a leading provider of data analytics software for decades. They currently command the largest share in the advanced analytics market according to a research by IDC (SAS Institute Inc., 2014). The success of the SAS product is largely due to its versatility in working with huge sets of data. The interactive nature of the product helps companies to identify insights into their data and discover new relationships in their data.

The tool allows users to perform business intelligence, data exploration and analytics in simple ways without the user needing to have any coding knowledge. Some of the other very useful features that SAS has is text sentiment analysis, mobile business intelligence, dashboards and reporting. The SAS software is certainly a great tool that can be used to manipulate huge amounts of data (which is one of the characteristics of a Big Data processing software).

Figure 10. SAS Studio for data analytics and visualization (SAS Institute Inc., 2016)

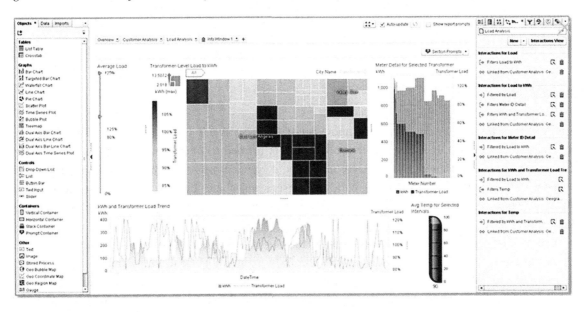

Tableau

Tableau software is a very flexible and robust analytics platform. It is a growing contender for being the most sought after data analytics and visualization tool in the market. As of 2015, Tableau was voted at #1 market leader in the Gartner 2015 Magic Quadrant for Business Intelligence and Analytics Platforms. It held a strong position in the 'Completeness of Vision' and 'Ability to Execute' criteria (Sallam, et al., 2015). This is a commendable achievement for the tool.

The Tableau software features visual analysis capabilities, deep statistical analysis, metadata management and mapping capabilities. The new version also supports mobile portability. Some of the visualization techniques Tableau supports are Tree maps, Bubble charts, Stock charts, Area charts, etc.

Figure 11. Tableau integrated data analytics dashboard (Tableau, 2016)

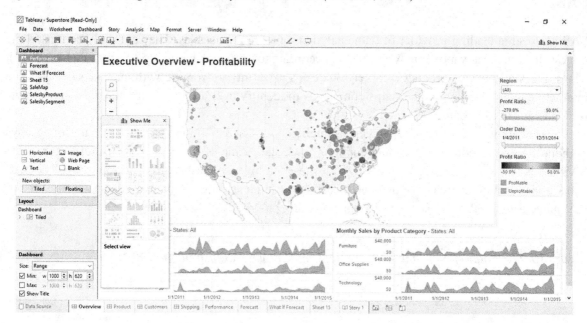

RapidMiner

RapidMiner is a cutting edge analytics and visualization software that has redefined analytics and visualization techniques. It is a versatile product that is primed to meet the requirements of Big Data analysis. Not only is it an agile platform for analytics, it also features a community based collaborative ecosystem that allows users to interact with other users and share ideas or get solutions to problems they may be encountering. This is accomplished through the 'Wisdom of Crowds' feature in the product (RapidMiner, 2015).

The RapidMiner studio supports some statistical programming languages such as R and Python that help modelers build and develop specific analytical algorithms that deal with complex scenarios and problems. It also supports open and extensible sources that aid in data modeling, visualization, data loading and transformation from a host of databases. The RapidMiner can handle scaling very efficiently which makes it easy for analysts to progress from relatively small data sets to extensively large datasets. It can also be run from any of the major operating system platforms.

In the next section a review of a few of these tools will be made along with examples of how they are used.

BIG DATA ANALYTICS WITH RAPIDMINER

In recent times text mining has increasingly gotten more attention as it evolves. Text mining involves utilizing exploratory methods and techniques to extract some meaningful information from unstructured text-based data. This is chiefly done by identifying patterns from the extracted data (Mooney & Nahm, 2002). There has been great advancement in the process of text mining and there can be significant busi-

Figure 12. RapidMiner analytics software (RapidMiner, 2015)

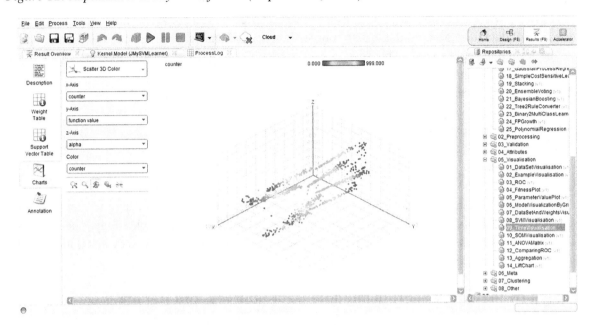

ness insight obtained from processing textual data to discover new data relationships which eventually lead to smarter decision making.

To illustrate how text mining can help decision processes, let us consider an example. A company may intend to find out why it is having a huge churn rate of its clients. It may have noticed that a lot of its customers are not only disengaging from its services but more of those customers are signing up to its competitors. To find out why this 'migration' is occurring, the company may decide to review online reviews of its services from its customers or the general public. But with hundreds of thousands of reviews and comments from people online, it may be very difficult for the company to read every single online review to assess the sentiment of customers to its business. This is where text mining can become an incredibly useful tool to work with.

Using text mining techniques, the company can extract valuable insight from the relatively large set of unstructured textual information extracted from the online resource to try to find insights on what the feelings of the customers are to its services. Certain words or phrases can be identified and a strong pattern can be discovered. Let us say most customers are dissatisfied with the price point for the company's services some of the words and phrases that would have a high hit ratio in the customer reviews will be *'expensive', 'high cost', 'too costly', 'pricey', 'highly priced', 'costly'*, etc. If such words or phrases seem to have a relatively larger frequency, then the company may have discovered some insight. But this is only the start. There is need to find out what the customers seem to be referring to when they write about cost. Is there a specific element of the company's services that customers are saying are costly? Or is it the entire service? Or are the customers in fact referring to the reason they engaged in the company's services in the first place (due to high cost from other competitors)? To mine meaningful information from the data, there are techniques in text mining that can be performed.

RapidMiner is a great tool for text mining and has been used by some of the world's most influential companies to derive insight from their data. This chapter will look at a few techniques that can be used to process text-based data and derive meaningful insight from the data. There are a set of steps that are required to process data from a large body of text (also referred to as a *corpus*). These steps vary based on the type of data to be processed, the data source, the intended analysis on the data, the volume of the data, the format of the data, etc. This section assesses an example using RapidMiner to extract some meaningful value from a corpus of text.

Let us perform a text mining exercise. In this exercise the following tasks will be performed:

- Loading textual data into RapidMiner analytics software
- Preprocess the loaded data
- Learn the classification model based on the data

This example will show how to process data based on users' comments online about the evolution of technology in the areas of Voice Recognition, Healthcare and Automobile Technology. The objective of this is to identify what users are saying about these topics and if there is any relevant relationship to these three subject areas.

Loading of Textual Data From Multiple Data Sources Into RapidMiner

In the first step, the data is loaded by selecting the directory paths(s) where the data source is located. Data has been extracted as textual comments into CSV files and have been saved in the 'Healthcare' directory (for comments on Healthcare), 'Voice Recognition' directory (for the comments on Voice Recognition) and 'Technology' directory (for the comments on Automobile Technology).

Once the data has been loaded or imported into the workspace and an instance of the data is created, the next step is to run a set of preprocessing activities to prepare the data for analysis. The next section shows a walk-through of how preprocessing can be conducted.

Figure 13. Importing data into a RapidMiner process (Designed by the author)

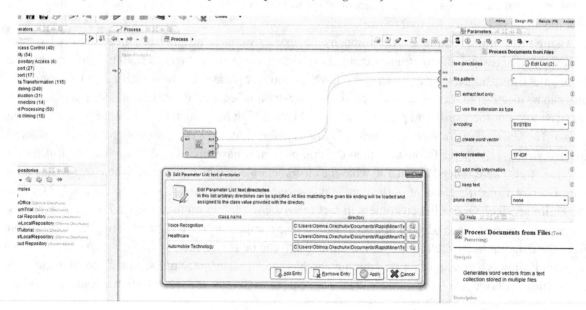

Preprocessing the Data for Analysis by RapidMiner

After having selected the directory paths for the CSV files, the next step is to define the weighting scheme so when the unstructured text is processed it is transformed into an ordered list of words which is known as the document vector model. The document is presented in a way so that each section of the document represents a fixed word over the entire document corpus, this is sort of an indexing process of the text in the document.

Figure 14. Word vector options (Designed by the author)

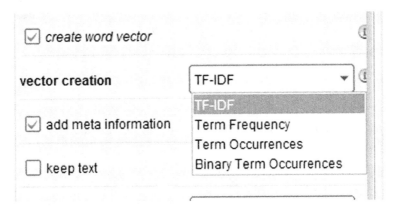

The vector options that can be selected in RapidMiner could be;

- **Binary Term Occurrences:** This option just lets the user know if a specific word (term) occurs in a corpus of text. It returns a true or false value.
- **Term Occurrences:** This option is used to let a user know how many times a word (term) occurs in a corpus of text, in other words the frequency of a given word. It returns a count of the word frequency.
- **Term Frequency:** This option returns a relative frequency of the occurrence of a particular text in relation with the entire corpus of text. This tells us how much of the document was occupied by a given term.
- **Term Frequency/Inverse Document Frequency:** This option is based on the ratio of which a term occurs in a document with relative reference to the terms in that document and it also compares the number of times a word occurs across several documents.

The next step in the process is to tokenize the document. Tokenization refers to the process of splitting the body of text into separate individual words. The tokenizing parameter can be defined based on spaces between the words or specific characters or special characters. In this example words would be tokenized based on spaces between each individual word.

The next step is to filter the document by removing words that may not have useful analytical values, these could include pronouns, conjunctions, articles, etc. This filtering process is performed using the *Filter Stopwords* function.

Figure 15. Tokenizing the document (Designed by the author)

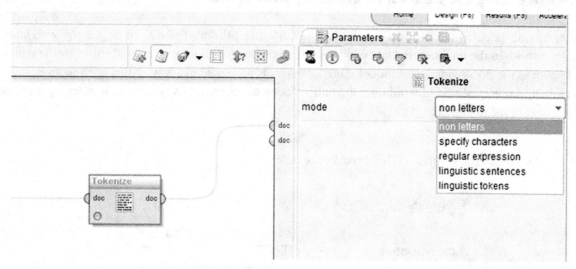

Figure 16. Inclusion of the Filter Stopwords function to remove non analytical words (Designed by the author)

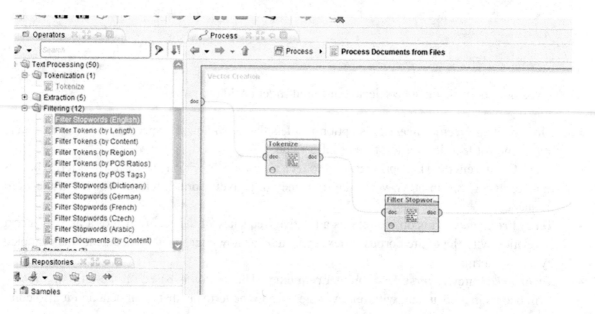

The extraction, tokenization and filtration process can now be executed in order to view the result of the process thus far.

In the image above, the upper section comprises of the text in one of the documents. The altering colors show the succession of words. The software does this in order to show the separation of words from the original document(s). The section just below that of the colored words shows a snapshot of the original document. Each document can be viewed by clicking on the execute button at the top (in the toolbar area).

Figure 17. Extraction, tokenization and filtration. (Designed by the author)

The software also gives us an initial analysis of the word frequencies in both documents as can be seen in the image below:

Figure 18. Frequency occurrences of words in both documents (Designed by the author)

Learning the Data Using the Naïve Bayes Classification Model With RapidMiner

The next step in the processing is learning the data using the Naïve Bayes classification model. The classification model uses the frequency of independent words or predictors in the corpus to try to predict a certain outcome. It is based on the Bayes model but expands on it using a naïve computation of the likelihood of the occurrence of predictors in the corpus.

In Figure 19, the simple distribution results of the Naïve Bayes classification on the corpus of data being worked on can be seen.

Figure 19. Results of the distribution of words from the different data sources (Designed by the author)

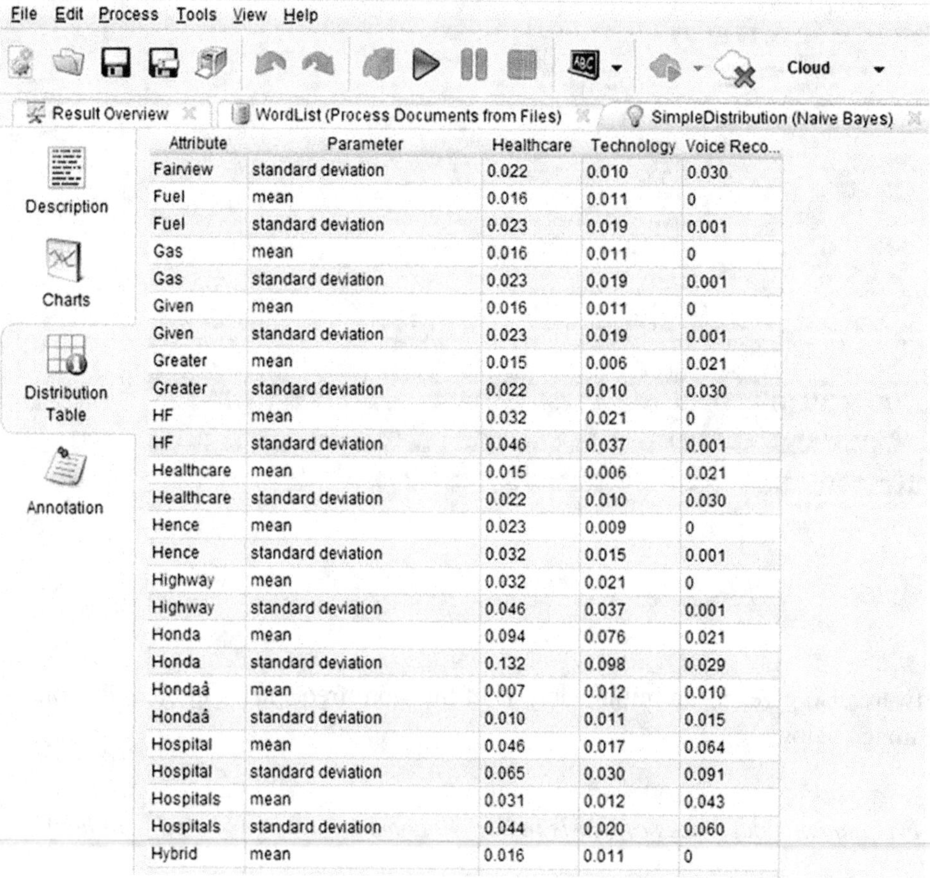

Attribute	Parameter	Healthcare	Technology	Voice Reco...
Fairview	standard deviation	0.022	0.010	0.030
Fuel	mean	0.016	0.011	0
Fuel	standard deviation	0.023	0.019	0.001
Gas	mean	0.016	0.011	0
Gas	standard deviation	0.023	0.019	0.001
Given	mean	0.016	0.011	0
Given	standard deviation	0.023	0.019	0.001
Greater	mean	0.015	0.006	0.021
Greater	standard deviation	0.022	0.010	0.030
HF	mean	0.032	0.021	0
HF	standard deviation	0.046	0.037	0.001
Healthcare	mean	0.015	0.006	0.021
Healthcare	standard deviation	0.022	0.010	0.030
Hence	mean	0.023	0.009	0
Hence	standard deviation	0.032	0.015	0.001
Highway	mean	0.032	0.021	0
Highway	standard deviation	0.046	0.037	0.001
Honda	mean	0.094	0.076	0.021
Honda	standard deviation	0.132	0.098	0.029
Hondaå	mean	0.007	0.012	0.010
Hondaå	standard deviation	0.010	0.011	0.015
Hospital	mean	0.046	0.017	0.064
Hospital	standard deviation	0.065	0.030	0.091
Hospitals	mean	0.031	0.012	0.043
Hospitals	standard deviation	0.044	0.020	0.060
Hybrid	mean	0.016	0.011	0

With RapidMiner users can look at a chart of the relative word density of the textual results of the Naïve Bayes classification process. In the example shown in Figure 20, there is a normal *'bell-shaped'* distribution graphs that depict the likelihood of certain words occurring within the text-based sources.

As can be seen, the word 'health' has a higher density reading on the 'Voice Recognition' data source than in either the 'Technology' or 'Healthcare' data sources. But from the relationship, it is safe to say that people discussed and are very likely to talk about health matters in each of the subject areas. This means that health is of concern not only in healthcare topics but also in automobile and voice recognition technologies. The next step would be to further drill down and identify what people are actually saying about health in each of these subject areas. RapidMiner also has tools that can achieve more advanced Big Data analytical structures such as sentiment analysis.

DATA PROCESSING USING RSTUDIO

RStudio is a very powerful, yet flexible software that enables data analysts to perform different sorts of analysis based on their business needs. The program allows users to run different statistical processes with significant ease. The RStudio supports the R programming language, a high level programming language that is easy to learn with simple syntax that can be learned. There are readily available libraries developed by a huge community of developers which users can utilize for their statistical processes. The programming interface is also well laid out to help users access frequently used tools.

Figure 20. Word density chart based on the Naive Bayes classification results (Designed by the author)

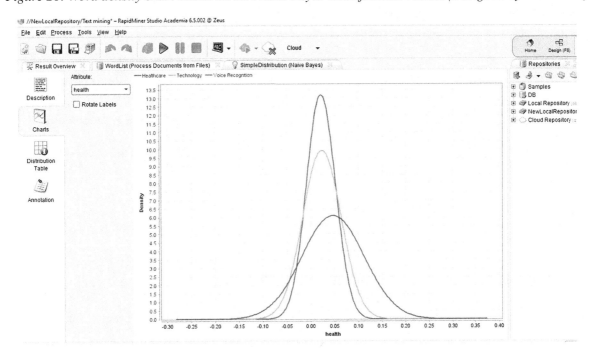

Some examples of using the RStudio will be shown next. In the first example a simple linear regression analysis using data based on the automotive industry will be performed. The objective of the example is to investigate the relationship between the sales of Automobile manufacturing equipment to the index of car prices, the index of engine prices and the prevailing interest rates. Our aim is to identify if there is any relationship between the purchase of car manufacturing equipment to any of the other variables. The *dependent variable* is the manufacturing equipment while the *explanatory variables* are the index of car prices, the index of engine prices and the prevailing interest rate.

Loading the Data Into RStudio

The first step in our process is to load the data from the data source. RStudio provides an easy syntax for loading data into the workspace before the data is processed.

Data can be loaded from different sources. These could be CSV files, spreadsheets, tables, delimited tab files, etc. Once the data is loaded, use the *Attach (<datafilename>)* command to attach the imported data to the instance so as to maintain a copy of the data in memory for processing.

Figure 21. Importing data from a CSV data source into Rstudio (Designed by the author)

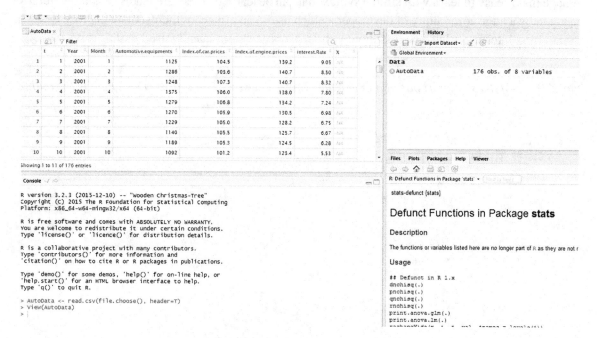

Creating a Linear Regression Model Using RStudio

A set of commands as seen in Figure 22 below can be issued in order to create a regression model of the data.

Figure 22. Plotting a scatterplot of the dependent and explanatory variables in our data (Designed by the author)

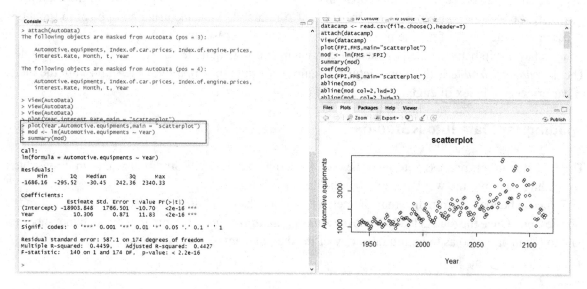

In the console, you can see the following command was issued:

```
plot(Year, Automotive.equipments,main = "scatterplot")
mod <- lm(Automotive.equipments ~ Year)
summary(mod)
```

What this command does is to plot the scatter plot seen at the right section of the image. Using the lm command a user can create a linear model of automotive equipment (dependent variable) against the various years (independent variable). After that, the user can obtain a summary of the linear model and the results are displayed with statistical information on the data.

Another option is to proceed to generate the Pearson's correlation value to identify the strength of the relationship between the automotive equipment and both the engine price index and car price index. As can be observed, the relationships are relatively strong based on a moderate Pearson's value.

Figure 23. Computation of the Pearson's correlation value (Designed by the author)

```
Coefficients:
               Estimate Std. Error t value Pr(>|t|)
(Intercept) -18903.848    1766.501  -10.70   <2e-16 ***
Year             10.306       0.871   11.83   <2e-16 ***
---
Signif. codes:  0 '***' 0.001 '**' 0.01 '*' 0.05 '.' 0.1 ' ' 1

Residual standard error: 587.1 on 174 degrees of freedom
Multiple R-squared:  0.4459,    Adjusted R-squared:  0.4427
F-statistic:   140 on 1 and 174 DF,   p-value: < 2.2e-16

> cor(Automotive.equipments,Index.of.engine.prices)
[1] 0.6576863
> cor(Automotive.equipments,Index.of.car.prices)
[1] 0.7285197
>
```

A regression line can be drawn by issuing the command:

```
abline(mod, col=2, lwd=3)
```

This produces the Figure 24.

RStudio allows us to define the regression line using whatever parameters is chosen by only having to enter the y-intercept value for the '*a*' parameter and the slope or gradient of the line for the '*b*' parameter using the *abline* function.

If the objective is to investigate the relationship between the residual values (deviation of observed value from a predicted value) and the fitted values (the set of predicted values), this can be done by calling the plot(mod) command in our scenario.

Figure 24. Regression line on the analyzed data (Designed by the author)

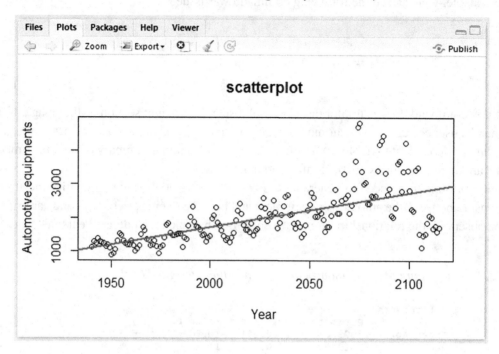

Figure 25. Residual vs. Fitted plot (Designed by the author)

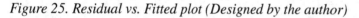

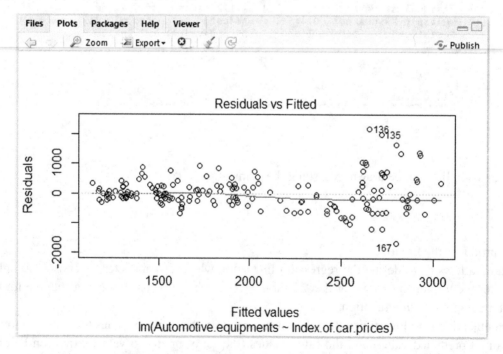

From the data it can be seen clearly that our prediction of automotive equipment sales is not 100% accurate (and typically will never be in any statistical analysis). However, note that the variance in predicted values increases as the mean value increases as can be seen by the relation of the data points to the line on the graph.

There are a host of other statistical methods and techniques that can be performed within the RStudio platform.

VISUALIZATION USING TABLEAU

The Tableau platform is capable of processing various analytical tasks. These can range from statistical computing tasks to other modeling tasks such as predictive analytics, sentiment analysis, etc. It is also able to integrate with external systems for machine learning and it can even integrate with the Hadoop framework.

In the example this section will be looking at in Tableau using data collected on a retail store with different products and customers. The various dimensions of the data include the products on sale, the operational segments of the store, the customers of the store and the store's locations. Using some analytics tools there will be a review of Product drilldown data, Customer analysis, Shipping trends and Sales forecast information.

Viewing the Various Data Dimensions Using Tableau

From our data source, the information on product sales over a period of time is given in Figure 26.

Figure 26. Product drilldown (Tableau, 2016)

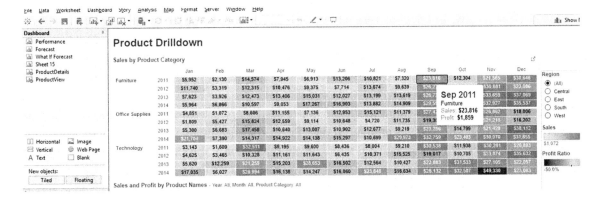

As can be observed, a mouse over on each cell will reveal other data dimensions of the cell. In our example, the sales value of furniture in September, 2011 is USD $23,816 and the profit for the same period is USD $1,859. The color scale of each cell also indicates the relative value of sales for that period, a darker shade of blue indicates higher sales figure while a lighter shade of blue indicates lower sales for that period.

Figure 27. Sales and Profit by products (Tableau, 2016)

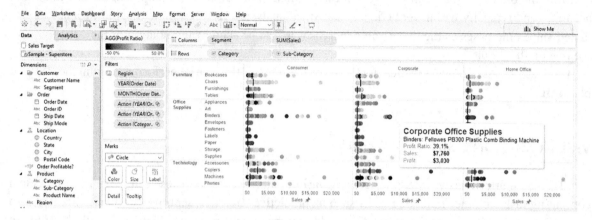

Figure 27 shows an analysis of each product categorized by product line (e.g. furniture, office supplies, technology, etc.). The graph indicates the sales value and the profit margin for that product. This then gives us an idea of the profit ratio which in this case is computed as:

$$\left(\frac{Profit}{Sales}\right)*100 \text{ (Accounting for Management, 2016)}$$

The color of the bubbles indicate the profit ratio and the relative values are indicated on the legend on the card named *'AGG (Profit Ratio)'*.

A look at customer related information gives us an insight into the company's customer profile showing us how each of the individual customers are performing relative to sales purchases. One of the performance measures is the profit ratio of that customer.

Tableau gives us different data representation techniques to show different data dimensions. In the charts above, an analysis of customer activities by region can be seen. Some of the grouping dimensions are: number of customers by region, sales by region, quantity by region, profit by region, etc. With this sort of data, a decision maker can easily assess what the revenue sales and profit potential are based on different criteria.

Next, a scatter diagram representing the dispersion of customers based on the profit ratio each customer possesses is observed. The bubbles are placed on a Profit-to-Sales graph which depicts the customers' positions on the graph. This information is supplemented by a bar graph showing the customer ranking. The ranking information is obtained by computing each customer's sales volume and contributory profit margin. The length of the bar indicates the relative sales value and the color of the bar represents the profit ratio. So for example 'Sean Miller' who generates the most sales is one of the few customers who in fact generates a loss in profit for the retail company!

The Chart Area is yet another powerful visualization format available for analytics in Tableau. In this data dimension of the retail company, there will be a review of the shipping trends of the products to customers.

Figure 28. Customer profiling using Tableau's charting techniques (Tableau, 2016)

Figure 29. Shipping trends using a stacked area chart (Tableau, 2016)

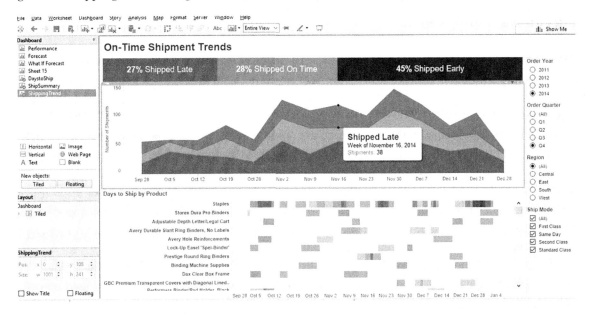

The area chart is stacked in categories of early, on-time or late shipping. A mouse hover on any section reveals the week of the shipment and an analyst can view the relative volume of early, on-time and late shipments. A further drill down analysis can be performed.

In Figure 30, the analyst can view the actual products that shipped on the specific week of interest. This provides users of Tableau great access to the insight within the data that is presented.

Figure 30. Shipment trends drilldown (Tableau, 2016)

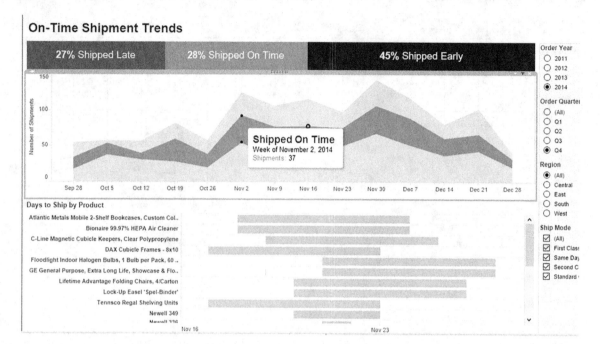

Data Analysis With Tableau

In this next section, a review of some sales forecast analysis is performed using defined dimensions, parameters and measures. Tableau allows the user to define analytical components called measures. These measures can be any sort of quantity, grouping or aggregation of data to summarize or give other perspectives to the data.

For the store sample data being used, there are some dimensions and measures that the company may wish to use to project a forecast for sales of the different business segments. To generate the right forecast, the company may want to know what the *total sales* is over a period of time (in *months*) for a particular market *segment*. In the data that is obtained, there is sales information over a set of prior periods. Using analytical algorithms, the company can learn the data and identify a pattern in sales over recurring periods, for instance seasonal sales of commodities. This allows the company to project or forecast plausible sales outcome over a future period.

In Figure 31, the months (by order date) are displayed at the columnar level while the segment and the sales volumes are displayed at the row level. A trend line chart can then be plotted using the data that has been analyzed.

The forecast data shows us order of dates by month on the x-axis and the forecasted sales values on the y-axis for each of the categorized segments. The unshaded lines depict data that has been collected over a 4-year period. The shaded line section represents the forecasted data for the next year. This is based on the learned data from the historical sales activity.

Figure 31. Trend line chart showing sales forecast for 3 market segments (Tableau, 2016)

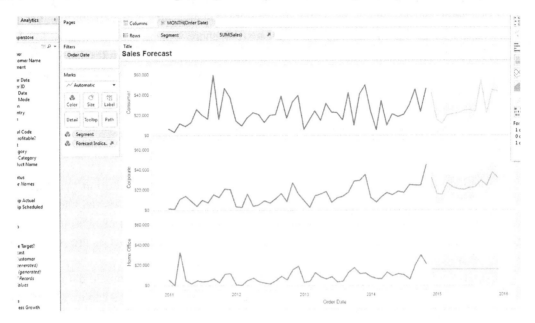

Information can also be rendered using an area chart. The area chart gives a visual rendering of the volume of data representative of the sales for the period that is being measured. The chart below shows an area chart for each of the market segments. The blue area charts shows the historical information collected on sales activities for the various segments while the orange areas charts show the forecasted trends for the segments in the data.

Figure 32. Area chart showing sales forecast for 3 market segments (Tableau, 2016)

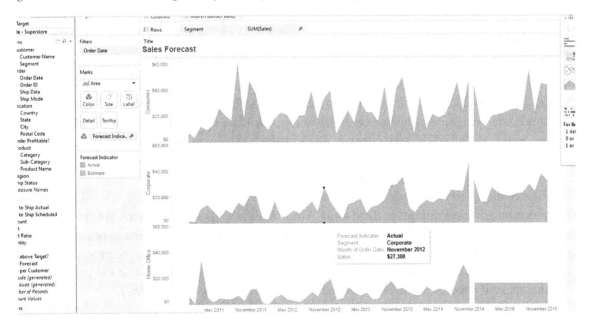

As can be seen from the visual representations shown in the images, it is clear that displaying analyzed information in graphically as opposed to textual information can give substantial meaning or perspective to the data. If the information shown above was all textual, there will be some challenge for decision makers to utilize the data in the most efficient manner. When the data is shown textually, it introduces value and newer dimensions to the information that makes it easier for the data to be understood and more precise decisions to be made.

CONCLUSION

Data is the lifeblood of almost all institutions in the world. There is no institution, whether government, profit oriented or even non-profit oriented that doesn't rely extensively on data and information to make critical (or non-critical) tactical or strategic business. All organizations need data to exist! It is a well-researched fact that Big Data has had an influence in the way businesses are run all over the globe (Halevi & Moed, 2012).

Big Data analytics has tremendously helped businesses capture opportunities in data links and patterns that previously may not have been captured if those relationships had to be captured using manual means. The ability to capture causal links in huge data sets by trying to figure out relationships through manual processes would be almost impossible to achieve but using dynamic and evolving data analytics techniques it has become a more feasible task (Lane, 2012).

There is still a lot to be discovered in this evolving trend called Big Data and where it would lead in the future but it is generally accepted that it has potentially greater implications in the way people interact with information. Years into the future there will be newer data dimensions and a whole new way data is consumed (Snijders, Matzat, & Reips, 2012). These new data dimensions would impact all of the activities people engage in individually, as a group or as an organizational entity. The important underlying theme should be finding newer and more effective ways of analyzing our data so institutions can get the best value out of the data.

FUTURE RESEARCH DIRECTIONS

With the increase in the use of data and the growing importance of how information is retrieved from databases, there is well researched information that suggests that the tools available for data representation will become even more efficient and easier to use. Tools will no longer just connect to traditional databases or directly linked data sets but they would also be able to process data from remote locations and port to data sources such as cloud services. The challenge here is to find out a way to standardize the extraction, transformation and loading processes across different platforms.

Another challenge (which adequate research may be able to provide some answers to) is the segregation of processing responsibilities of these tools. Most of these tools will have to be able to let business users stay focused on the high level questions that address the analyses they intend to process while the tool takes care of the internal business logic that provides the right results from the processed data. In essence, users should be able to stay within their strategic thinking mindset while the tools build the blocks that make it possible to provide decisional information for business strategy.

There is also the opportunity to research on newer techniques of visualization. Because visualization primarily appeals to the visual sensory perception, newer tools and techniques will have to identify efficient and effective ways to visually communicate data or information to individuals. This is a hard task due to the fact that visual representation of data can be subjective and may be interpreted differently by different people. However, greater research is being conducted to identify newer ways information can be communicated to people for decision purposes using visual reference.

It is almost impossible to predict how visualization will change in the years to come but there is a firm certainty that it will definitely grow due to the fact that all aspects of human endeavor demands and increased generation and use of data. This guarantees that Big Data visualization will only become more prominent as data use increases.

REFERENCES

Accounting for Management. (2016). *Gross profit ratio (GP ratio) - Formula, Example, interpretation | Explanation | Accounting For Management*. Retrieved May 2, 2016 from Accounting for Management: http://www.accountingformanagement.org/gross-profit-ratio/

Bloom, N., Lemos, R., Qi, M., Sadun, R., & Van Reenen, J. (2011). *Constraints on Developing UK Management Practices*. BIS Research Paper No 58, November 2011, Department of Business Innovation & Skills (BIS). Retrieved on July 19, 2017 from https://www.gov.uk/government/publications/barriers-to-developing-strong-management-skills-in-the-uk

Bruls, M., Huizing, K., & Wijk, J. J. (2015). *Squarified Treemaps. Technical Report of Dept. of Mathematics and Computer Science*. Eindhoven, The Netherlands: Eindhoven University of Technology.

Cisco. (2016). *IP Addressing and Subnetting for New Users - Cisco*. Retrieved May 2, 2016 from Cisco website: http://www.cisco.com/c/en/us/support/docs/ip/routing-information-protocol-rip/13788-3.html

Eckerson, W., & Hammond, M. (2011). *Visual Reporting And Analysis: Seeing Is Knowing*. Retrieved on May 2, 2016 from http://www.datavisualization.fr/files/tdwi_bpreport_q111_vra_web.pdf

FusionCharts. (2016). *Chart Gallery - FusionCharts Suite XT*. Retrieved on May 2, 2016 from FusionCharts Web site: http://www.fusioncharts.com/charts/

Garcia, J. (2014). *Data Visualization: When Data Speaks Business*. Retrieved on May 19, 2016 from http://www.prolifics.com/sites/default/files/resource/1.%20Data%20Viz%20Product%20Analysis%20report.PDF

Google. (2016). *Chart Gallery | Charts*. Retrieved on May 22, 2016 from Google Charts web site: https://developers.google.com/chart/interactive/docs/gallery

Google. (2015, August 4). *Hauppauge, NY to Long Island*. Retrieved on August 4, 2015 from https://www.google.com/maps/dir/Hauppauge,+NY/Long+Island/@40.8073496,-73.2039712,13z/data=!3m1!4b1!4m14!4m13!1m5!1m1!1s0x89e830ea942b213d:0x191010fed8f3db56!2m2!1d-73.2026138!2d40.8256536!1m5!1m1!1s0x89e84454e1eea5cb:0x1df7f96186940d18!2m2!1d-73.134961!2d40.789142!3e0

IBM Software. (2015). *IBM - SPSS Modeler*. Retrieved on May 2, 2016 from IBM Software Web site: http://www-03.ibm.com/software/products/en/spss-modeler

Kandel, S., Paepcke, A., Hellerstein, J. M., & Heer, J. (2016). *Enterprise Data Analysis and Visualization: An Interview Study*. Retrieved on February 19, 2016 from http://vis.stanford.edu/files/2012-EnterpriseAnalysisInterviews-VAST.pdf

Keim, D. A., & Kriegel, H. P. (1996). *Visualization Techniques for Mining Large Databases: A Comparison*. Retrieved on February 15, 2016 from https://bib.dbvis.de/uploadedFiles/365.pdf

Kohavi, R. (2016). *Data Mining and Visualization*. Retrieved on February 19, 2016 from http://robotics.stanford.edu/~ronnyk/naeMining.pdf

Laerd Statistics. (2016). *Types of Variables*. Retrieved on May 12, 2016 from Laerd Statistics web site: https://statistics.laerd.com/statistical-guides/types-of-variable.php

Microsoft Corporation. (2016). *Address Classes*. Retrieved on May 2, 2016 from Microsoft Technet: https://technet.microsoft.com/en-us/library/cc940018.aspx

Mooney, R. J., & Nahm, U. Y. (2002). *Text Mining with Information Extraction*. AAAI Technical Report SS-02-06. Retrieved on March 15, 2016 from http://www.cs.utexas.edu/~ml/papers/discotex-melm-03.pdf

Panko, R. R., & Panko, J. L. (2014). *Business Data Networks and Security*. Pearson Education.

RStudio. (2015). *RStudio Web site*. Retrieved on June 15, 2016 from RStudio | RStudio: https://www.rstudio.com/products/rstudio/

Sallam, R. L., Hostmann, B., Schlegel, K., Tapadinhas, J., Parenteau, J., & Oestreich, T. W. (2015). *Magic Quadrant for Business Intelligence and Analytics Platforms*. Retrieved on June 17, 2016 from Gartner Web site: http://www.gartner.com/technology/reprints.do?id=1-2ACLP1P&ct=150220&st=sb

SAS Institute Inc. (2014). *SAS ranked No. 1 advanced and predictive analytics provider by industry research firm*. Retrieved on July 17, 2017 from SAS Institute Inc. Web site: https://www.sas.com/en_th/news/press-releases/2014/july/sas-number-1-advanced-and-predictive-analytics.html

Soukup, T., & Davidson, I. (2002). *Techniques and Tools for Data Visualization and Mining*. Danvers: John Wiley & Sons, Inc.

SPSS (Hong Kong). (2015). *IBM SPSS Modeler - Data mining, text mining, predictive analysis*. Retrieved on May 5, 2016 from SPSS (Hong Kong) Web site: http://www.spss.com.hk/software/modeler/

Tableau. (2016). *Population and Birth Rate*. Seattle, WA: Tableau Inc. Retrieved on May 2, 2016 from https://public.tableau.com/en-us/s/resources

Tableau. (2016). *Top 10 Trends for 2016 Business Intelligence*. Retrieved on February 6, 2016 from http://www.tableau.com/sites/default/files/media/top10bitrends2016_final_gs.pdf

Trifunovic, N., Milutinovic, V., Salom, J., & Kos, A. (2016). *Paradigm Shift in Big Data SuperComputing: DataFlow vs. ControlFlow*. Retrieved on February 19, 2016 from https://journalofbigdata.springeropen.com/articles/10.1186/s40537-014-0010-z

Wikipedia. (2016). *Linear Equation*. Retrieved on May 20, 2016 from Wikipedia: https://en.wikipedia.org/wiki/Linear_equation

Wikipedia. (2016). *Wikipedia (computer graphics)*. Retrieved on May 19, 2016 from Wikipedia: https://en.wikipedia.org/wiki/Visualization_(computer_graphics)

ADDITIONAL READING

Datameer. (2016). *Big Data Visualization, Hadoop Data Visualization*. Retrieved on July 15, 2016 from Datameer: http://www.datameer.com/product/big-data-visualization/

Davenport, T. H. (2014). *A Predictive Analytics Primer*. Boston: Harvard Business Review.

Declara, D. H. (2012). *What Does Big Data Look Like? Visualization Is Key for Humans*. Retrieved on July 15, 2016 from Wired: http://www.wired.com/insights/2014/01/big-data-look-like-visualization-key-humans/

IBM. (2012). *Predicting the future, Part 2: Predictive modeling techniques*. Retrieved on July 15, 2016 from IBM: http://www.ibm.com/developerworks/library/ba-predictive-analytics2/

Intel. (2016). *How IT managers can leverage visualization-based data discovery tools for valuable insight*. Retrieved on July 15, 2016 from Intel: http://www.intel.com/content/www/us/en/big-data/big-data-visualization-turning-big-data-into-big-insights.html

John, B. (2013). *6 Practical Predictive Analytics Tools*. Retrieved on July 15, 2016 from CIO: http://www.cio.com/article/2385497/data-management/6-practical-predictive-analytics-tools.html

L'Astorina, E. (2015). *Big Data Visualization: Review of the 20 Best Tools*. Retrieved on July 15, 2016 from BluFrame: http://inspire.blufra.me/big-data-visualization-review-of-the-20-best-tools/

Marvin, R. (2016). *Predictive Analytics, Big Data, and How to Make Them Work for You*. Retrieved on July 15, 2016 from PC Mag: http://www.pcmag.com/article/345858/predictive-analytics-big-data-and-how-to-make-them-work-fo

Open Data Tools. (2016). *Tools to Explore, Publish and Share Datasets*. Retrieved on July 15, 2016 from Open Data Tools: http://opendata-tools.org/en/visualization/

Oracle. (2010). *Predictive Analytics: Bringing The Tools To The Data*. Redwood Shores: Oracle. Retrieved on July 15, 2016 from http://www.oracle.com/us/products/middleware/bus-int/crystalball/riskmgmt-analysis-wp-326822.pdf

Pentaho. (2016). *Big Data Analytics tool*. Retrieved on July 15, 2016 from Pentaho: http://www.pentaho.com/product/big-data-analytics

Practical Analytics. (2016). *Predictive Analytics 101*. Retrieved on July 15, 2016 from Practical Analytics: https://practicalanalytics.co/predictive-analytics-101/

Predictive Analytics Today. (2016). *Top 33 Predictive Analytics Software*. Retrieved on July 15, 2016 from Predictive Analytics Today: http://www.predictiveanalyticstoday.com/top-predictive-analytics-software/

SAS. (2013). *How does data visualization fit into the predictive analytics process?* Cary: SAS.

SAS. (2016). *Predictive Analytics*. Retrieved on July 15, 2016 from SAS: http://www.sas.com/en_sg/insights/analytics/predictive-analytics.html

Search Business Analytics. (2016). *Dashboard development and data visualization tools for effective BI*. Retrieved on July 15, 2016 from TechTarget: http://searchbusinessanalytics.techtarget.com/essentialguide/Dashboard-development-and-data-visualization-tools-for-effective-BI

Sharma, N. (2015). *The 14 best data visualization tools*. Retrieved on July 15, 2016 from The Next Web: http://thenextweb.com/dd/2015/04/21/the-14-best-data-visualization-tools/#gref

Sparks, S. (2011). *Schools Find Uses for Predictive Data Techniques*. Retrieved on July 15, 2016 from Education Week: http://www.edweek.org/ew/articles/2011/06/22/36analytics.h30.html

Spencer, J. (2015). *4 Marketing Analytics Tools That Are Shaping the Industry*. Retrieved on July 15, 2016 from Entrepreneur: https://www.entrepreneur.com/article/241534

Suda, B. (2016). *The 38 best tools for data visualization*. Retrieved on July 15, 2016 from CB Creative Bloq: http://www.creativebloq.com/design-tools/data-visualization-712402

Tiwari, N. (2015). *8 excellent open source data visualization tools*. Retrieved on July 15, 2016 from Opensource.com: https://opensource.com/life/15/6/eight-open-source-data-visualization-tools

Voorhees, C. (2016). *Predictive analytics tools point to better business actions*. Retrieved on July 15, 2016 from TechTarget: http://searchbusinessanalytics.techtarget.com/feature/Predictive-analytics-tools-point-way-to-better-business-decisions

Wang, D. (2016). *Big Data Visualization tools, software and techniques*. Retrieved on July 15, 2016 from DataInformed: http://data-informed.com/big-data-visualization/

Washtell, J. (2016). *The Single Best Predictive Modeling Technique. Seriously*. Retrieved on July 15, 2016 from Predictive Analytics Times: http://www.predictiveanalyticsworld.com/patimes/single-best-predictive-modeling-technique-seriously/4257/

What is Predictive Analytics? (2016). Retrieved on July 15, 2016 from Predictive Analytics Today: http://www.predictiveanalyticstoday.com/what-is-predictive-analytics/

KEY TERMS AND DEFINITIONS

Corpus: A collection of written texts, literary works or aggregated data on a particular subject matter or the entire textual aggregation of works by a specific author.

Linear Regression: A modeling approach for determining the relationship between a scalar variable and one or more explanatory variables. It is a statistical technique frequently used in determining variable relationships.

Naïve Bayes Classification Model: A probabilistic model that is based on applying the Bayes' theorem with significant independent assumptions between features.

Pearson's Correlation: Is a measure of the linear correlation between two variables AandB which is widely used as a measure of the degree of linear dependence between two variables.

Series Charts: Also known commonly as time series graphs are a type of chart that utilizes a set of data points known as markers to plot a connecting line typically across an x-axis. The main purpose of line graphs is to show a continuous trend of data over a period of time.

Term Frequency/Inverse Document Frequency: Is a numerical statistic that is aimed at indicating how important a word is to a document or a corpus of text. It is mostly used as a critical indication factor in information retrieval.

Tokenization: This is the process of breaking strings of text into smaller pieces. These pieces of text are referred to as tokens. One other key task in the process of tokenization is discarding characters that may not provide valuable information such as punctuations.

Treemaps: A chart style that depicts the hierarchical data relationships of data subsets as a set of nested rectangular graphical blocks.

Visualization: Visualization is any technique for creating images, diagrams or animations to communicate a message. Visualization through visual imagery has been an effective way to communicate both abstract and concrete ideas since the dawn of mankind (Wikipedia, 2016).

This research was previously published in the Handbook of Research on Big Data Storage and Visualization Techniques; pages 465-496, copyright year 2018 by Engineering Science Reference (an imprint of IGI Global).

Chapter 29
Big Data Analytics Tools and Platform in Big Data Landscape

Mohd Imran
Aligarh Muslim University, India

Mohd Vasim Ahamad
Aligarh Muslim University, India

Misbahul Haque
Aligarh Muslim University, India

Mohd Shoaib
Aligarh Muslim University, India

ABSTRACT

The term big data analytics refers to mining and analyzing of the voluminous amount of data in big data by using various tools and platforms. Some of the popular tools are Apache Hadoop, Apache Spark, HBase, Storm, Grid Gain, HPCC, Casandra, Pig, Hive, and No SQL, etc. These tools are used depending on the parameter taken for big data analysis. So, we need a comparative analysis of such analytical tools to choose best and simpler way of analysis to gain more optimal throughput and efficient mining. This chapter contributes to a comparative study of big data analytics tools based on different aspects such as their functionality, pros, and cons based on characteristics that can be used to determine the best and most efficient among them. Through the comparative study, people are capable of using such tools in a more efficient way.

INTRODUCTION

Big data technology is a revolutionary technology which is currently adapted by all scale organization varying from small private industries to large government organization. It is now agreeable among all academicians and entrepreneurs that big data is having some game changer capabilities which makes the big data analytics a great and powerful tool for market research. Now at these times, most of the

DOI: 10.4018/978-1-6684-3662-2.ch029

business hubs as well as small organizations are coming forward to opt the big data analytics tool to dig up their strategy of marketing and produce maximum output from same; despite of having their forefront challenges of investment and cost of marinating stabilization. Another benefit which business organizations are looking into consists of a well new customer experience, more reliable and efficient goal and a better look up of organization from a completely different perspective. The extensive use of this technology is in educational purpose as well as in health care organization. Research, which is augmented educational wing uses the tools of big data analytics at various level, and for numerous applications (Samiya, kashish & Alam, 2016). According to study, educational as well as healthcare sector is generating huge amount of data which make it a potential source for big data analytics but to make it happen all the data must be refined, recorded and managed. Big data analytics also have its security concern and challenges (Jayasingh et. al). The analytics tools used in big data for security must have their encrypting capabilities to protect large exploding amount of data at every level from system to forensic level. To enhance the performance, reliability, and accuracy of system, people should know the environment where the analytics tool is most suited. The Apache Hadoop is one the revolutionary platform that provides various remarkable analytics tool to manage processing and handling. Some of these are suitable for collaborative distributed computing, some are well adopted for real time streaming and likewise some are popular for their graph representing capability. Apache Hadoop consists of various tools which can be categorized as Business tools, data Science tool, Interaction tool, Sql/NoSql tool, Cognition, conversion, security, search and storage tool. Apache Spark is another add on for big data application which provides processing speed faster than Hadoop is nearly hundred times faster. It is a remarkable analytical tool, well known for its distributed computing and graph computational analytics. There are some other analytical tools are available like Hive, Pig, HBase, Cassandra, Storm, HPCC which are handy. In order to exploit feature of these tools, we have to learn a comparative analysis, by exposing them in different factors and parameters. By learning this, People are capable of using them in more simplified manner.

BACKGROUND AND MAIN FOCUS

The Big data analytics is new trending analytical standard used to fetch previously collected data which is generated by numerous applications for pattern searching that cannot be examined, processed, managed and categorized by any other existing tools or technologies (Yadav, Verma, and Kaushik, 2015).Hence new technology or tools must be adapted which can handle vast datasets generated from commodity servers which are distributed all across the globe. It is a technique of extracting useful correlated informations form massive dataset. Big data can be categorized in structured, Semi and Unstructured format. Mining of these structured, unstructured, and unrelated information collected from vast corporations, research, and healthcare organizations and make it useful by managing, structuring, controlling is main objective of big data analytics. Together, Big data analytics (BDA) is information managing tool that uncover the hidden pattern, correlated from vast big data set to make a decision control for large organization for optimized performance. The main focus is to deploy big data analytics tool in different sector of market, in order to obtain various pattern of market research.

- **Big Data in Healthcare Sector:** The health sectors are applying the big data analytics for determining the pattern of disease in various patients as well as in demographic variations. The digital image processing and communication medicine (DICOM) (D. K. Thara, B. G. Premasudha, V. R. Ram and R. Suma, 2016), HATS (HIV/ AIDS Tuberculosis and Silicosis) division are the perfect example of health sectors which uses analytics tool for premature or initial detection of disease and for prevention method (Tiwari et al., in press). According to (Groves P et. al, 2013) and (Hermon R., 2014), the utility of data analytics in health sector can be characterized in these major parts: Delivery & administration, decision support and clinical information, consumer/ behaviour market analysis and concrete analysis of gathered data from patient worldwide.

- **Big Data in Politics:** Big data analytics also emerged as one of the strongest tool in election. In prime minister election of india 2014, Big data was used to determine the flow of thought for candidate. In various district of india, various survey has been conducted, and then it is fed to big data tool to determine the strong and potential candidature of PM. Similarly US Presidential election (Plumer & Brad, 2012) was also follow the same practice and that had produced a magnificent and revolutionary change in election campaign.

- **Big Data in Social Networking:** Social Activities and Blogging also produces a large amount of data on the internet in daily basis. In today's digital era, people present their consent and opinion via social media. Twitter is the most popular platform (Arias,M., Arratia,A. and Xuriguera,R, 2014) chosen by people all around the world. Hence comes the concept of mining these opinion in order for determining likes and dislikes of people. Sometime these method is also called as sentiment analysis or opinion mining (Tan, S., Li, Y., Sun, H.,Guan∗,Z.,Yan, X., 2012). These models are generally used by product website, Stock market analysis (Bollen, J., 2010), Movie rating website as well as blog.

- **Big Data in Education Sector:** Another prime and major use of big data is in education sector. Research section of education is well growing in India. The Indian government is also empowering the research and attracting bright researchers to pursue their career in this stream by providing numerous funds for full time as well as part time. so it is also mandatory to maintain the data of all post graduate students all over India. Big data is playing a vital role in this arena. By using big data analytics, it is easy and possible to extrapolate students by filtering their research field and highlighting their achievements and ensuring that they are capable of performing satisfactory work throughout project and hence ensuring the grants are not wasted.

BIG DATA ANALYTICS TOOLS

There are numerous tools of big data analytics such as Hadoop (Bhosale & P. Gadekar, 2014), apache spark, Hbase, Storm, Grid Gain, HPCC, Casandra, Pig, Hive, and No SQL etc. It is used to improve the various factors in the development of big data and functionality of a computer system. The main concern of exploitation of these tools is to form the people virtuoso with additional analytical initiative and to urge more awareness within the areas of technologies and development. These tools are extremely most popular within the space of Business Intelligence to develop the prevailing business to larger extent and increase the economy of the company and also satisfy the business goals of the corporate. According to (Wu and Zhang, 2003; Wu, et al, 2005; Su et al, 2006) there exist a local pattern analysis model which which enhanced the knowledge mining just not in full manner but also globally.

1. **Hadoop:** Hadoop is tool based on java framework that supports the processing, managing and storage of extremely extensive dataset in an environment of distributive computing (Chawada & Thakur, 2016). It is an open source platform developed by apache software foundation as a sponsored project of apache. (Mujawar & Aishwarya Joshi, 2015). This project is designed as a storage platform which manages and processes vast datasets across hundreds to thousands of terminals operating in parallel mode. It offers a cost beneficial storage solution for all recurring data generated in voluminous amount from numerous private as well as government organization, from private business sector to healthcare and research organizations. In the Heart of Hadoop, there is MapReduce programming paradigm which offers extensive scalability. MapReduce is actually composed from the two task performed by Hadoop; first is it maps all the unrelated and structured or unstructured data (Gahi et.al.) collected from various recorded source and then reduce it with no format requirements. Hadoop consists of two main components namely HDFS and YARN.

Figure 1. HDOOP platform and its components

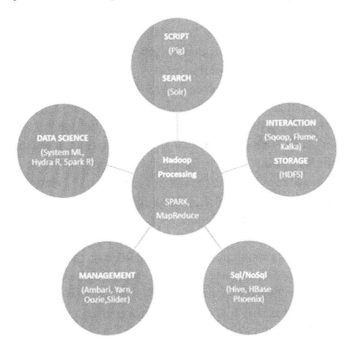

2. **HPCC (High Performance Computing Cluster):** This is an open source solution available as an alternative to Hadoop. It is a supercomputing platform developed by LexisNexis Risk Solutions in order to enhance the capability of system. This tool is useful for both batch as well as parallel processing of applications.
3. **Spark:** Apache spark is marvelous analytic tool for streaming, predictive and graph computational analytics. It is an open source engine packaged with advanced analytics tools which provide efficiency and advancement to application. Its processing speed is measured hundred times faster than MapReduce as it provide immediate data reuse in memory. Many research organizations uses both Hadoop and spark together although it is designed as an alternative of Hadoop. In fact both

are complementary framework of big data, together they make an extremely powerful machine from batch processing using HDFS for speed analysis to streaming and in-memory distributive processing in real time.

4. **Storm:** This analytics tool is widely applicable and preferable for real time system in more reliable manner for analysis of unbounded streaming data that can be developed in any programming language. The speed of the processing is millions of tuples per second per node. The feature of this analytical tool are free, open source, fault tolerant, and real time computing system.

5. **Grid Gain:** Based on Java platform and being open source, this tools gains it popularity in commercial applications. It is also employed in many other sectors like health sector, finance, education, and retail applications. Due to its real time distributed architecture, it works fast and acts as an alternative to the MapReduce of Hadoop.

6. **HBase:** It is also an open source tool. Combined together with Hadoop, It enhances the processing speed of cluster based system accommodated with Hadoop as well as its functionality in a measurable amount. It is one of the distributed database and non-relational tool in open source environment developed after Google`s Bigtable. Its core shell is written in java funded by apache software foundation and natively integrated with Hadoop. It perform the mapping on large data and map it into number of datasets, each of which is slated into n-tuple. This is performed as a separate task for the reduction part of output and after that it merge all of them into original one.

7. **Pig:** It is one of the popular big data tool that reflects the abstraction over MapReduce of Hadoop. Based on a high level platform, it creates the program that run on apache Hadoop. The functionality of Pig tool comprises of analyzing larger datasets consisting of high level language and express them into data flow. It is one of the important key component of Hadoop ecosystem similar to hive. It was initially developed by Yahoo Company in year 2006 to provide abstraction over the complex syntax of program for MapReduce. It provide an ease in writing small program running on a high level data flow system and uses Pig latin to manipulate queries. It is multi query approach, easy to read & write, simple to understand as SQL, and equipped with nested data types like Maps, tuples that are not featured by Hadoop`s MapReduce.

8. **Hive:** In Ecosystem of Hadoop, Hive also play a vital role as analytics tool. It functionality is similar to Pig. It can be seen as a data warehouse package mounted on the top layer of Hadoop ecosystem for managing and processing huge amount of data generated. It is featured with simple interface using SQL. Hence user don't need to bother about MapReduce complex program. Hive worked to access the data set stored at Hbase. It is can be summarized as:
    a. Data Warehouse Infrastructure
    b. Definer of a Query Language popularly known as HiveQL (similar to SQL)
    c. Provides us with various tools for easy extraction, transformation and loading of data.
    d. Hive allows its users to embed customized mappers and reducers.

9. **Cassandra:** Cassandra is a scalable, highly enhanced performance distributed architecture database capable of handling vast amount of structures data generated over a number of servers. Based on NoSql database, it is highly reliable and open source software by apache with no single point of failure. The main noted feature of this tool is its elasticity depending upon requirements it can support addition of multiple hardware servicing more customer at single instance. Increasing number of servers doesn't have any adverse effects on its throughput, in fact it is increased stabilizing the response time. It is flexible on distribution wherever and whenever it is needed to replicate data across distributed data centers, reflecting no point of failure over critical business transaction

application, hence it is more reliable than any other tools offered by apache. Since it have NoSql database, it reflects ACID (Atomicity, Consistency, Isolation and durability) property and capable of storing huge data gathered from multiple points without affecting the reading efficiency of distributed system.

10. **Phoenix:** It is a SQL skin for HBase. Being open source software, it provides massive parallelism on handling larger relational databases. It has support over online transaction processing OLTP making it real good one. It has enhanced the performance of Hadoop`s Hbase due to its added functionality over SQL.

Table 1. Comparison table between Pig and Hive

Characteristics	Pig	Hive
Language Name	Pig Latin	HiveQL
Developed By	Yahoo	Facebook
Type of Language	Dataflow	Declarative (SQL Dialect)
Data Structures Supported	Nested and Complex	---
Relational Complete	YES	YES
Turing Complete	YES	YES
Schema Optional	YES	NO

Comparison of Big Data Analytics Tools

The main focus on studying the different big data tools is to understand different features and functionalities provided by them so that user can easily use it depending upon need. Its study makes people who are engaged in companies, more skillful and knowledgeable about usability of these in more enhanced, simpler and more convenient way. When these tools are subjected to numerous factors and parameters, it yields their pros and cons in different environment. The importance of big data tools can be acknowledged by grouping it into 3 categories;

1. Comparison of 3 V`s (Velocity, variety, & Volume) (Shuijing, 2016)
2. Comparison of 4 C`s (Conversion, Cyber, Cognition, and Configuration
3. Basic parameters

Table 2. Comparison of Big Data Tools W.R.T Basic important Factors

Characteristics / Big Data Tools	Volume	Velocity	Variety
Hadoop	250 PB	Structured, Semi and Unstructured Data	Fast Consumption, Collection and processing of Data
Storm	One million 100 bytes	Cluster of Data	High Velocity
HPCC	Petabytes	Data Centric & Query Processing	Faster than Hadoop
HBase	Petabyte	Task & Node processing	Complex processing of datasets
Grid Gain	Terabyte to Petabyte	Memory Processing	High Speed and Fast Processing

Table 3. Comparison of Big Data Analytics W.R.T 4`Cs

Characteristics Big Data Tools	Conversion	Cognition	Cyber	Configuration
Hadoop	Type Conversion, Apache Avro to Parquet format, PDI Data Type Conversion, Elastic Search	Big Data + Analysis, Saffron, Cognitive Computing, Cognitive Clouds	Cloud era, Big Yellow Elephant, Primer, MapR	Apache Hadoop 2.4.1 API, Apache Hadoop 2.7.0 API, Apache Hadoop 1.0.4 API
Storm	Batch processing and Streaming	Burgeoning Cognitive Systems, Irving WladaWsky Berger	Masergy, Beating Back Cyber Attacks, Horton Works	Apache Spark. Storm Cluster,Spout, Azura dArk Lake
HPCC	String to parse out Substring, ASCII to EBCDIC conversion, Typecasting, C++, ECL Plugins, Mainframe Binary format, ABO type Conversion	HPC, Sci Tech Daresbury, Human 00 cognition	HPC Asia, Cyber Security, White papers, Scientific Computing	Data Analytics, Tyrome, and Thor & Roxie Clusters
HBase	One text to Composite String, Stream of Binary Data, Sorting, Queries, MR Integration	Data Intensive Text processing, Apache Mahout, Cognitive Analytics, Saffron Big data	Cyber Warfare, Harnessing Big Data, Aster HBase	MATLAB using MR, Pentaho MR, Hadoop Clusters
Grid Gain	Implicit Conversion, Grid Projection type, Scalar type, Grid Cache Projection, Media Types	Rapid Cognition, Cognitive Neurodynamics, cognitive Computing	In Memory Data Fabric, Cyber Dust Leverages	Data Grid Configuration, Grid Configuration, Gridgain 6.5.0, Gridgain API

Table 4. Comparison of Big Data Analytics W.R.T Basic Performance parameters

Characteristics Big Data Tools	Performance	Simplicity	Type of Software	Extensibility
Hadoop	Boosted	Easy	Open Source	DFS to Teradata
Storm	Accustomed Performance	Difficult	Open Source	OLA application
HPCC	High	Flexible	Open Source	Extensible to ML Platform
HBase	Efficient	Uncomplicated	Freeware	Processing of Big Data
Grid Gain	Vary	Effortless	Trail ware	Application scaling

FUTURE PERSPECTIVE AND OPPORTUNITIES

Big data is considered as a biggest transition in recent advancement of technology. It has major opportunities in various sector of society. Most of the sector has been changed due to application of analytical tools while still there are some which are untouched. We need to focus on that area, where maximum utilization of analytical tools can be possible. There are various challenges in big data which are listed below:

1. Visualization of data
2. Privacy

3. Extraction of rightful data
4. Retails and logistics
5. Data Integration and cleaning
6. Small business
7. Market evaluation
8. Web crawling (Mohd Shoaib, 2014)

CONCLUSION

In this chapter we have described about basics of big data which a tremendous and revolutionary landscape in pattern searching and data mining. We have also seen different type of data analytics tools like PIG, hive, Cassandra in Apache Hadoop ecosystem as well as their pros & cons, and features. We also have categorized the big data tool in different fields. By exposing these data analytics tools to different parameters and factors, we have represented a comparative survey where a person can easily and effectively learn that in which conditions, what tools is most suited to application. By learning these comparative analysis, people belonging to numerous sectors like healthcare, retail, finance, education and research can become capable of enhancing their performance of system in a good proportion. In brief his whole chapter describe big data both in tabulation and in well expressed and detailed manner which help people to make them more skillful and productive.

REFERENCES

Choi, T. M., Chan, H. K., & Yue, X. (2016). Recent Development in Big Data Analytics for Business Operations and Risk Management. *IEEE Transactions on Cybernetics*, *47*(1), 81–92. doi:10.1109/TCYB.2015.2507599 PMID:26766385

Wu, X., Zhu, X., Wu, G. Q., & Ding, W. (2014). Data Mining with Big data. *IEEE Transactions on Knowledge and Data Engineering*, *26*(1), 97–107. doi:10.1109/TKDE.2013.109

Mishra, A. D., & Singh, Y. B. (2016). Big Data Analytics for Security and Privacy Challenges. *Int. Conf. Computing, Communication, and Automation ICCCA*, 50-53 10.1109/CCAA.2016.7813688

Khan, S., Shakil, K. A., & Alam, M. (2016). Educational Intelligence: Applying Cloud based big data analytics to Indian education sector. *Int. IEEE Conf. Contemporary Computing and Informatics IC3I*, 29-34 10.1109/IC3I.2016.7917930

Jayasingh, B. B., Patra, M. R., & Mahesh, D. (2016). Security Issues and Challenges of big data analytics and visualization. *Proc. Int. IEEE Conf. Contemporary Computing and Informatics IC3I*, 204-208 10.1109/IC3I.2016.7917961

Yadav, V., Verma, M., & Kaushik, V. D. (2015, October). Big data analytics for health systems. In *Green Computing and Internet of Things (ICGCIoT), 2015 International Conference on* (pp. 253-258). IEEE. 10.1109/ICGCIoT.2015.7380468

Thara, D. K., Premasudha, B. G., Ram, V. R., & Suma, R. (2016). Impact of big data in healthcare: A survey. *2nd International Conference on Contemporary Computing and Informatics (IC3I)*, 729-735. 10.1109/IC3I.2016.7918057

Groves, P., Kayyali, B., Knot, D., & Van Kuiken, S. (2013). *The Big Data revolution in healthcare, Accelerating value and innovation.* McKinsey & Company.

Hermon & Williams. (2014). Big data in healthcare: HAT is used for SRI security research institute. Edith Cowan University.

Plumer, B. (2012, November 5). Pundit Accountability: The Official 2012 Election Prediction Thread, WONKBLOG. *The Washington Post.*

Tiwari, V., Thakur, R. S., Tiwari, B., & Choube, M. (in press). Optimization of EHR data flow towards healthcare analytics. In *International Conference on Recent Advancement in Computer and Communication (IC-RAC-2017).* Springer.

Arias, M., Arratia, A., & Xuriguera, R. (2014). Forecasting with twitter data. *ACM Trans. Intel. Syst. Technol., 5*(1).

Bollen, J., Mao, H., & Zeng, X.-J. (2010). Twitter mood predicts the stock market. *Journal of Computational Science, 2*, 8.

Wu, X., & Zhang, S. (2003). Synthesizing High-Frequency Rules from Different Data Sources. *IEEE Transactions on Knowledge and Data Engineering, 15*(2), 353–367.

Bhosale, H. S., & Gadekar, D. P. (2014). A Review Paper on Big Data and Hadoop. *International Journal of Scientific and research Publication, 4*(10).

Chawada, R. K., & Thakur, G. (2016). Big Data and Advanced Analytics Tools. *Proc. of Int. Symposium on Colossal Data Analysis and Networking CDAN*, 1-8.

Mujawar, S., & Joshi, A. (2015). Data Analytics Types, Tools and their Comparison. *IIJARCE, 4*(2), 488–491.

Gahi, Y., Guennoun, M., & Mouftah, H. T. (2016). Big Data Analytics: Security and Privacy Challenges. *Proc. Of Int. Symposium on Computer and Communication ISCC*, 952-957 10.1109/ISCC.2016.7543859

Shuijing, H. (2016). Big Data Analytics: Key Technologies and Challenges. *Proc. Int. Conf. on Robots & Intelligent Systems*, 141-145. 10.1109/ICRIS.2016.30

Shoaib, M., & Maurya, A. K. (2014, August). URL ordering based performance evaluation of Web crawler. In *Advances in Engineering and Technology Research (ICAETR), 2014 International Conference on* (pp. 1-7). IEEE. 10.1109/ICAETR.2014.7012962

KEY TERMS AND DEFINITIONS

Batch Processing: It is defined as the processing of all collected jobs/batch which are same in nature.

Data Grid: An architecture or in other word batch of services which provides a solution to individuals or bunch of users the ability to manipulate, access and transfer voluminous amount of data that is distributed geographically and intend to be used for research purposes.

Digital Image Processing and Communication Device: It is one of the standard procedures for integration of imaging devices like scanners, printers, network hardware, and servers that enables storage and communication of the medical images online.

Hadoop: Open source software that stores and analyzes massive unstructured data sets.

HATS: HATS is a HIV and AIDS testing software developed by doctor for the diagnosis of symptoms. It diagnoses and providse a quick report of patient who is tested and it can be shareable on the internet.

Hive: SQL programming framework that allows a programmer to use the MapReduce algorithm via a SQL type programming language.

MapReduce: Algorithm that is used to split massive data sets among many commodity hardware pieces in an effort to reduce computing time.

OLAP: Online analytical application processing is used in applications for analytical processing.

Opinion Mining: This is method of collecting opinions of different people on website in documented format.

Structured Query Language (SQL): Is a programming language that is specifically designed for managing data sets in a relational database management system.

Text-Processing: Refers to the discipline of mechanizing the creation or manipulation of electronic text.

This research was previously published in the Handbook of Research on Pattern Engineering System Development for Big Data Analytics; pages 80-89, copyright year 2018 by Engineering Science Reference (an imprint of IGI Global).

Chapter 30
Statistical and Computational Needs for Big Data Challenges

Soraya Sedkaoui

Khemis Miliana University, Algeria & SRY Consulting Montpellier, France

ABSTRACT

The traditional way of formatting information from transactional systems to make them available for "statistical processing" does not work in a situation where data is arriving in huge volumes from diverse sources, and where even the formats could be changing. Faced with this volume and diversification, it is essential to develop techniques to make best use of all of these stocks in order to extract the maximum amount of information and knowledge. Traditional analysis methods have been based largely on the assumption that statisticians can work with data within the confines of their own computing environment. But the growth of the amounts of data is changing that paradigm, especially which ride of the progress in computational data analysis. This chapter builds upon sources but also goes further in the examination to answer this question: What needs to be done in this area to deal with big data challenges?

INTRODUCTION

With the advent of digital technology and smart devices, a large amount of digital data is being generated every day. Individuals are putting more and more publicly available data on the web. Many companies collect information on their clients and their respective behavior. As such, many industrial and commercial processes are being controlled by computers. The results of medical tests are also being retained for analysis. Financial institutions, companies, and health service providers, administrations generate large quantities of data through their interactions with suppliers, patients, customers, and employees. Beyond those interactions, large volumes of data are created through Internet searches, social networks, GPS systems, and stock market transactions.

This brings us to think about the legend of the wise 'Sissa' in India. When King 'Belkib' asked about the reward he desired, after his invention, he asked to receive a grain of rice for the first square, two grains for the second, four grains for the third and so on. The king agreed, but he didn't know that on the last square of the board he should drop 2^{63} grains, or more than 700 billion tons. In their book

DOI: 10.4018/978-1-6684-3662-2.ch030

"Race Against the Machine," Brynjolfsson and Mcaffee (2011) referenced the fable of the chess and rice grains to make the point that "exponential increases initially look a lot like linear, but they are not. As time goes by – as the world move into the second half of the chessboard – exponential growth confounds our intuition and expectation".

Thus currently, not only is the quantity of digitally stored data much larger, but the type of data is also very varied, thanks to the various new technologies (Sedkaoui & Monino, 2016). Data volume will continue to grow and in a very real way, the data produced, as well as other data accumulated, constitutes a constant source of knowledge. This widespread production of data has resulted in the 'data revolution' or the age of 'big data'. Big data gets global attention and can be best described using the three Vs: volume, variety and velocity. These three dimensions often are employed to describe the phenomenon. Each dimension presents both challenges for data management and opportunities to advance decision-making. In another way, every data tells a story and data analytics, in particular the statistical methods coupled with the development of IT tools, piece together that story's reveal the underlying message.

This 3 V's provide a challenge associated with working with big data. The volume put the accent on the storage, memory and computes capacity of a computing system and requires access to a computing cloud. Velocity stresses the rate at which data can be absorbed and meaningful answers produced. The variety makes it difficult to develop algorithms and tools that can address that large variety of input data. So, there are still many difficulties and challenges in the use of big data technologies. And, if decision-makers can't understand the power of data processing and analytics, they may be, in some ways, the "Belkibs" of big data value. The key is applying proper analytics and statistics methods to the data. Thus, from this data companies derive information and then producing knowledge, or which it called the target paradigm of "knowledge discovery", described as a "knowledge pyramid" where data lays at the base. To advance successfully the paradigm effectiveness data analysis is needed.

The analysis of big data involves multiple distinct phases which include data acquisition and recording, information extraction and cleaning, data integration, aggregation and representation, query processing, data modeling and analysis and interpretation. These all are the methods of modern statistical analysis necessary for dealing with big data challenges. But, each of these phases introduces other challenges: Heterogeneity, scale, timeliness, complexity, quality, security...

Modern data analysis is very different from other methods which existed prior. Also, data is very different from data which existed before. In another word, the nature of modern data (greatest dimension, diverse types, mass of data) does not authorize the use of most conventional statistical methods (tests, regression, classification). Indeed, these methods are not adapted to these specific conditions of application and in particular suffer from the scourge of dimension. These issues should be seriously considered in big data analytics and in the development of statistical procedures.

Consider a simple example to explain a quantitative variable Y through a set $\{X1, ... Xp\}$ of quantitative variables: $Y = f(X1, ... Xp) + \varepsilon, [(yi, xi), i = 1,..., n]$

If the function is assumed to be linear and p is small, on the order of ten; the problem is well known and widely discussed in the literature. In the case where the function f is not exactly linear and n is large, it is possible to accurately estimate a larger number of parameters and therefore to envisage more sophisticated models. Keeping to the usual Gaussian model, even the simplest case of a polynomial model quickly becomes problematic. Indeed, when the function is linear, take $p = 10$, the model selection procedure is facing a group of 2^{10} possible models and shrewd algorithms allow to cope.

However, consider to estimate f, a simple polynomial of second or third degree, with all its interactions, leads us to consider a large number of parameters and thus, by combinatorial explosion, an astronomical number of possible models. Other methods must then be considered taking into account necessarily the algorithmic computational complexity. This explains the involvement of another discipline, computing. The concern of computability outweighs the mathematical definition of the problem comes down to optimizing a criterion adjustment of the function f over a set of more or less rich solutions.

These methods have often been developed in another disciplinary environment: computers, artificial intelligence, K-means, neural networks, decision trees… support vector machines become credible alternatives since the number of observations is sufficient or the number of variables is very important.

Development of new statistical methods is an interdisciplinary field that draws on computer sciences, artificial intelligence, machine learning, and visualization models etc. So, two technical entities have come together. First, there is big data for massive amounts of data. Second, there is advanced analytics, which is actually a collection of different tool types, including those based on predictive analytics, data mining, statistics, clustering, data visualization, text analytics, artificial intelligence, and so on (Shroff, 2013; Siegel, 2016).

Current technologies software tries to overcome the challenges that "V's" raises. One of these is Apache Hadoop, which is open source software that its main goal is to handle large amounts of data in a reasonable time. While one major aspect of big data is the computational handling of network induced data, another is the proper application of data analytic and statistical tools for large scale use in business and commercial contexts. Cukier and Mayer-Schoenberger (2013a; 2013b, p.29) see a paradigmatic change in the statistical handling of large data:

Using great volumes of information … require three profound changes in how we approach data. The first is to collect and use a lot of data rather than settle for small amounts or samples as statisticians have done for well over a century. The second is to shed our preference for highly curated and pristine data and accept messiness: in an increasing number of situations, a bit of inaccuracy can be tolerated, because the benefits of using vastly more data of variable quality outweigh the costs of using smaller amounts of very exact data. Third, in many instances, we will need to give up our quest to discover the cause of things, in return for accepting correlations. With big data, instead of trying to understand precisely why an engine breaks down or why a drug's side effect disappears, researchers can instead collect and analyze massive quantities of information about such events and everything that is associated with them, looking for patterns that might help predict future occurrences. Big data helps answer what, not why, and often that's good enough.

Big data deals with unconventional, unstructured databases, which can reach petabytes, exabytes or zetabytes, and require specific treatments for their needs, either in terms of storage or processing/display (Vermesan and al, 2014). The challenges include not just the obvious issues of scale, but also heterogeneity, lack of structure, error-handling, timeliness, provenance, and visualization, at all stages of the analysis driving from data acquisition to result interpretation. The ultimate goal is not only to collect, combine, or process all data, but also to increase its value and efficiency. This means that it must evolve from big data to 'smart data', since the effectiveness of companies' strategies now depends on the quality of data. Which should be kept in mind as the analysis unfolds.

It would require tailored statistical methods and data quality control to superimpose on large data streams to make sense of the data and use them for statistical inference and decisions. More frequently than not also good theoretic insights and models of the subject discipline would be helpful to identify the 'payoff relevance' of data for predictive purposes (Harford, 2014). This explains the formation of handling data through scalable tools as developed in econometrics, psychometrics, technometrics etc.

The goal of this chapter is to show what is specifically the power of 'data'? And why it is so important for companies? And how big data can benefit from the mixture of two fields: 'computer science' and 'statistics' in order to make the inquiry from data a more successful endeavor, rather than dwelling on theoretical issues of dubious value. This chapter presents the main statistical computing issues and challenges in the age of data deluge, and examines whether traditional statistical approach and methods substantially differ from the new trend of big data analytics. In another word, the objective writing this chapter is to present and explain the important role of computing statistical methods in data analysis and knowledge extraction, and the necessity of developing such methods.

To show that the challenges around the era of "data revolution" focus on data uses, Author will firstlyl describe, review, and reflect on big data, by defining what is it meant in order to consolidate the divergent discourse on it and presenting its various dimensions and challenges. Also, in this chapter one section will be dedicate for introducing knowledge discovery from data and the interest of searching new analytics methods for efficiently obtain the potential value from the massive data. Then, author will explain and present how the most basic of statistical methodologies has developed to create very flexible tools, and how statistics and computational tools should act together to better analyze big data in order to extract value.

BIG DATA: THE BIGGEST GAME-CHANGING OPPORTUNITY

Nowadays, an increasing number of data silos are created across the world, which means that this growth will never stop. This data is not only voluminous; it is also continuous, streaming, real time, dynamic and volatile. This is generally described by what it called the phenomenon of "3 Vs", or "big data". Businesses can exploit big data to extract valuable information. Such information can help decision makers to enhance their strategies and optimize their plans. But, what really is subsumed under big data?

Big data qualifies under a few main characteristics: (i) It is primarily network generated on a large scale volume, by variety and velocity and comprises large amounts of information at the enterprise and public level, in the categories of terabytes (10^{13} bytes), petabytes (10^{15}) and beyond of online data. (ii) It consists of a variety and diversity of data types and formats, many of them dynamic, unstructured or semi-structured and hard to handle by conventional statistical methods. (iii) Big data is generated by disparate sources as in interactive application through IoT from wireless devices, sensors, streaming communication generated by machine-to-machine interactions (Sedkaoui, 2017).

Big data nowadays has become one of the biggest concepts in the world of IT especially with the rapid development of IoT driving the increase of data. It also brings new opportunities for the discovery of new values that are temporarily hidden. The success of large companies such as Amazon, Google, Facebook, Twitter etc. proves the emergence of a factor in the development of today's hyper-connected world. The companies, increasingly aware of the importance of data and information, which represents the result of data processing and it is in the heart of decision-making (see next section), throng to reflect on the way to "manage" to enrich and benefit. Henceforth, this gives new properties to data, as they are Meta tagged piecemeal, produced in real time, and arrive in continuous streams from multiple sources.

In addition, data is now abundant resources in many circumstances, thus data can pile-up or "many managers find themselves drowning in data" (Mann, 2004). Companies are leveraging these and many other sources of data to achieve a better understanding of their customers, employees, partners and operations, with an eye towards improving every aspect of business. But it must first of all understand the rich ecosystem and extended big data. Inside this ecosystem some phases and processes can be identified, such as: (i) Data Collection: which implies the proper use of Networks, Infrastructure, and data centers in order to access and analyze a particular set of dynamic data. (ii) Data Processing: this is influenced directly by the technologies used for the storage and database management. (iii) Data Analysis: data analytics is gaining increasing attention in business and consequently also Data-Driven Decision-making (DDD), which refers to the practice of basing decisions on the analysis of data.

Big data applications are numerous and constitute a factor in strengthening the capacity for innovation within companies. Innovation certainly comes from crosses and treatments that have not been thought originally. But nothing better than good examples to understand how big data transformed the business.

An extremely popular example is Hadoop, an Open Source framework in this field that allows applications to work with huge repositories of data and thousands of nodes. These have been inspired by Google tools such as the MapReduce and Google File system, or NoSQL systems, which in many cases do not comply with the ACID (atomicity, consistency, isolation, durability) characteristics of conventional databases.

Spotify, an on-demand music service, uses Hadoop big data analytics, to collect data from its millions of users worldwide and then uses the analyzed data to give informed music recommendations to individual users.

The American company 'Harrah's' has made progress in sales of 8 to 10 percent by analyzing customer segmentation data, while Amazon stated that 30 percent of its turnover came from its engine analytical recommendations (McKinsey, 2011, 2013). With massive production of online data Google, in 2009, was able to predict the timely spread of influenza through simple correlation (Foster et al., 2017, Chap. 1). In the same spirit, the United Nations has developed a program anticipating epidemics and reversals of economic conditions through keywords exchanged on Twitter.

Such examples, and many others, share common principles: extreme digitalization of their process leads to extensive use of data to experiment with new business models, beyond their original boundaries. IDC (2011) describes big data technologies as a new generation of technologies and architectures, designed to economically extract value from very large volumes of a wide variety of data, by enabling high-velocity capture, discovery, and/or analysis. Technologies for big data harvesting from multiple resources have been fast growing in the forms of data mining systems; search engines; query languages; filtering systems; cloud services, etc.

Big data will fundamentally change the way businesses compete and operate. Companies that invest in and successfully derive value from their data will have a distinct advantage over their competitors (McKinsey Global Institute, 2011). It is difficult to identify the all issues brought about by big data, but there is now increasing opportunity to capitalize on the approach. The question continues as to how companies can maintain and improve our knowledge store over time.

TURN DATA INTO KNOWLEDGE FOR SUPPORTING DECISION

The explosion of data volumes will gradually increase as the Internet of Things (IoT) develops. Data volume will continue to grow and in a very real way constitutes a constant source of knowledge. The difficulty of transforming big data into value or knowledge is related to its complexity, the essence of which is broadly captured by the three Vs. Volume, Variety and Velocity are used to define the term big data. Each of these dimensions presents both challenges for data management and opportunities to advance decision-making.

Traditionally, the decision-making process is shaped on the model of limited rationality by Herbert Simon (1977): Intelligence, modelling, choice and control. The intelligence phase is all about finding the occasions over which a decision should be made (Simon, 1997). "The major role of the intelligence stage is to identify the problem and collect relevant information" (Turban et al., 2011) which would be used later in the next stages of the decision-making process.

However, with the exploitation of big data this process is being complicated and has to improve. Organizations need to use a structured view of data to improve their decision-making process. Big data has the potential to aid in identifying opportunities related to decision in the intelligence phase of Simon's model, where the term of "intelligence" refers to knowledge discovery. To achieve this structured view, they have to collect and store data, perform an analysis, and transform the results into useful and valuable information, and then it's essentially about discovering new knowledge.

In relating these three concepts: "Data, Information and Knowledge", a hierarchy can be suggested, which suggest in turn that one can be changed into other. This model is often used in the literature relating to the information and knowledge management. Several studies claim that the first appearance of knowledge hierarchy is in T.S Elliot's poem "The Rock" in 1934. In recent literature, many authors refer to the publication "From data to wisdom" of R.L Ackoff published in 1989 as a source of knowledge hierarchy.

Many other authors (Zeleny, 1987; Cleveland, 1982) have also proposed extensions of the hierarchy; Ackoff includes understanding (and some use intelligence) as its own level before attaining wisdom.

The relationship between these three words can be represented as a pyramid where knowledge occupies the highest place to highlight the fact that many data are necessary for the acquisition of knowledge.

The knowledge pyramid is by nature a multidisciplinary endeavor (Piegorsch, 2015): computer scientists construct algorithms to manipulate and organize the data, aided by statisticians and mathematicians who instruct on development and application of quantitative methodology. Then, database expert collect and warehouse the data, software designers write programs that apply the analytics algorithms to the data, engineers build electronics and hardware to implement the programming, and subject-matter/domain experts – that is, biologists, chemists, economists, and social scientists – interpret the finding.

The most important asset of large volumes of data has to do with the fact that they make it possible to apply knowledge and create considerable value. Combined with advanced analysis methods, new explanations can be provided for several phenomena. There are two ways to transforms data into a valuable contribution to a company (Sedkaoui, 2016):

- Transforming data into information is one of the stages of data value production, which is exploited in order to obtain useful information and to successfully carry out company strategies. This automatically involves database information in company decision making processes;
- Transforming data into products or processes adds value to companies. This is produced when data analysis must be implemented in the physical world.

Before one attempts to extract useful knowledge from data, it is important to understand the overall approach or the process that leads to finding new knowledge. The process defines a sequence of steps (with eventual feedback) that should be followed to discover knowledge in data. To advance successfully each step, effective data collection must be applied, description, analysis and interpretation (Walter, 2015, Chapter 1). Each step is usually realized with the help of available software tools. Data mining is a particular step in this process – application of specific algorithms for extracting models from data. The additional steps in the process, such as data preparation, data selection, data cleaning, incorporation of appropriate prior knowledge, and proper interpretation of the results of mining ensure that useful knowledge is derived from the data.

There is, however, a serious challenge in making good use of such massive datasets and trying to learn new knowledge of the system or phenomenon that created these data. Knowledge extraction from data volumes of ever increasing size requires ever more flexible tools to facilitate interactive query. Today's applications are therefore required to extract knowledge from large, often distributed, repositories of text, multimedia or hybrid content. A new generation of computational techniques and tools is required to support the extraction of useful knowledge from the rapidly growing volumes of data. The nature of this quest makes it impossible to use traditional computing techniques. Instead, various soft computing techniques are employed to meet the challenge for more sophisticated solutions in knowledge discovery.

Knowledge discovery process is an automatic, exploratory analysis and modeling of large data for understandable patterns from large and complex datasets. It's focused on the development of methodologies and techniques that 'make sense' out of data, i.e. for extracting relevant and non-trivial information from data. So, data are a set of facts i.e. cases in a database, while a pattern is an expression in some language describing a subset of the data or a model applicable to the subset. Knowledge discovery process is thus a sequence of steps that, starting from rough data, leads to the discovery of knowledge. This is particularly so where the use of data for decision-making and knowledge discovery is novel.

It may be observed that the knowledge discovery process is reminiscent of the real beginnings of statistics. However, it's not only using statistics, but also contributing to statistics. The need for effective tools for knowledge discovery and mining is large especially as a crucial component of data-warehouses. Indeed, harnessing data may also require the complete overhaul of the businesses to create structures and processes that can respond to any information gleaned in a short timeframe, potentially even in real-time.

The value of a given piece of data increases in time and depends on the variety of uses it is given. In this sense, companies must possess the capacity to absorb the entirety of data available, which allows them to assimilate and reproduce knowledge. This capacity requires specific skills familiar with statistical data analytics which becomes a fundamental skill for any scientist dealing with big data. Since statistical methods are applied at the base of the pyramid (data), the data process guided knowledge discovery will entail an integrated plan of descriptive analysis and predictive modeling.

But, examining the current state of big data use in business, as well as the main opportunities many challenges are presented. Typically, a variety of some major challenges will be discussed in the next section. These challenges are regarded mostly as internal and reflect procedural problems in collecting, archiving and handling data.

BIG DATA CHALLENGES BEYOND 3Vs

Some analysts suggest that the world is entering the 'Industrial Revolution of Data' where the amount of data will be generated not only by people and companies but also by machines and interactive devices. The dimension related to the variety involves several different issues. First of all, data – especially in an industrial environment – can be presented in several different ways, such as texts, functions, curves, images, and graphs, or a combination of these elements. On the other hand, this data shows great variety, which often reflects the complexity of the studied phenomenon.

So data complexity is growing with the increase of its quantity its velocity and diversification of its types and sources. Variety usually means heterogeneity of data types, representation, and semantic interpretation. However, velocity means both the rate at which data arrive and the time in which it must be acted upon. There are also wider challenges relating to the use of big data within society-at-large, which have been widely discussed in the literature (Boyd & Crawford, 2012; Ekbia et al., 2015).

As previously stated, big data analytics involves multiple distinct and each of them introduces challenges. The problems start right away during data acquisition, when the data deluge requires us to make decisions, currently in an ad hoc manner, about what data to keep and what to discard, and how to store what is keeping reliably with the right data. In this section author gives a broad overview of the challenges that need to be addressed in order to build capabilities in big data analytics.

The 3 V's provide a challenge associated with working with big data. The volume put the accent on the storage, memory and computes capacity of a computing system and requires access to a computing cloud. Velocity stresses the rate at which data can be absorbed and meaningful answers produced. The variety makes it difficult to develop algorithms and tools that can address that large variety of input data.

However, many technical challenges must be addressed before this potential can be realized fully. The challenges include not just the obvious issues of scale, but also heterogeneity, quality, timeliness …, at all stages of the analysis driving from data acquisition to result interpretation. Security and privacy are also a big concern, especially when considering that the linking of databases can disclose information that was meant to remain anonymous (Sedkaoui, 2017).

Heterogeneity

Data can be both structured and unstructured. They are highly dynamic and does not have particular format. It may exists in the form of email attachments, images, pdf documents, medical records, graphics, video, audio etc. and they cannot be stored in row/column format as structured data. Transforming this data to structured format for later analysis is a major challenge in big data analytics. However, machine analysis algorithms expect homogeneous data, and cannot understand nuance. In consequence, data must be carefully structured as a first step in data analysis.

- **Scale:** Managing large and rapidly increasing volumes of data has been a challenging issue for many decades. In the past, this challenge was mitigated by processors getting faster, following Moore's law, to provide us with the resources needed to cope with increasing volumes of data. The difficulties of BD analysis derive from its large scale as well as the presence of mixed data based on different patterns or rules (heterogeneous mixture data) in the collected and stored data (heterogeneous mixture data issue). Especially, in the case of complicated heterogeneous mixture data, the data has not only several patterns and rules but characteristically, the properties of the patterns vary greatly (Fujimaki & Morinaga, 2012).

Timeliness

As the size of the data sets to be processed increases, it will take more time to analyse. In some situations results of the analysis is required immediately. So businesses need to develop partial results in advance so that a small amount of incremental computation with new data can be used to arrive at a quick determination. In BD the realization time to information is critical to extract value from various data sources, including mobile devices, radio frequency identification, the web and a growing list of automated sensory technologies.

Complexity

Complexity measures the degree of interconnectedness and interdependence in big data structures such that a small change in one or a few elements can yield very large changes or a small change that ripple across or cascade through the system and substantially affect its behavior, or no change at all (Katal and al 2013). Traditional software tools are not enough for managing the increasing volumes of data. Data analysis, organization, retrieval and modeling are also challenges due to scalability and complexity of data that needs to be analyzed.

Quality

Big data processing requires an investment in computing architecture to store, manage, analyze, and visualize an enormous amount of data. It is the indispensable raw material of one of the new century's most important activities. But it is important to be prudent in our analysis and predictions because a lot of data is not yet "the right data". There is, therefore, underlying difficulty behind big data, since more data is not necessarily better data.

Security

The vast majority of data comes from the many devices and machines reporting to each other and to those running them. From the assembly line at the manufacturing plant to the passenger jet in flight, millions of bytes of data are generated and then analyzed. Some of captured data is personal information, and as such, both cutting-edge security and responsible stewardship models must be used to make sure this information is safe and correctly used.

Privacy

The advance in big data analytics brought us tools extract and correlates this data which would make data violation much easier. That makes developing the big data applications a must without forgetting the needs of privacy principles and recommendations. The lawsuit following the Netflix Challenge is a striking example of that where linking the provided data to the IMDB movie reviews allowed to identify some users.

To make the most out of big data, the issue is not limited to the "simple" technical issues of collection, storage and processing speed. The use of big data requires rethinking the process of collecting, processing and the management of data. It's the "analysis" that will be applied to data which will justify big data, not the collection of data itself. What is truly necessary are excellent analytic skills, a capacity to understand and manipulate large sets of data, and the capacity to interpret and apply the results. The need to analyze and use enormous amounts of data more efficiently drives companies towards "data science" in the hope of unlocking the power of big data analytics.

THE NEED FOR NEW ANALYTICS METHODS

The rise of big data reflects the growing awareness of the "power" behind data, and of the need to enhance gathering, exploitation, sharing and processing. The process of gathering, processing, and interpreting data is not limited to defining ideas, but also consists of materializing them in order to ensure improved knowledge production that leads to innovation. It is the use of data that empowers decision-making. In another word, it's the "analysis" that will be applied to data which will justify big data, not the collection of data itself.

Data analysis came in in the 20th century when the information age really began. Zhang have mentioned in his book "data analytics" published in 2017, that the first real data processing machine came during the Second World War. But, the advent of the internet was sparked the true revolution in data analysis. The importance of data analysis started in the late 1960 when researchers begin to speak about databases as repositories of data. E.F. Codd (Codd, 1970) and his research group at IBM labs applied some mathematical principles and predicate logic to the field of data modelling.

Since then, data bases and their evolutions have been used as a source of information to query and manipulate data. In 1974, still at IBM labs, the first language for database was developed. SEQUEL (Structured English Query Language) (Chamberlin and Boyce, 1974), later called SQL for copyright issues, was the forerunner of all the query languages becoming the standard for relational database. In the 1970s and 1980s, computers could process information, but they were too large and too costly. Only large firms could hope to analyze data with them. Edgar F. Codd was the first to work on data organization by designing database management systems (DBMSs), in particular of relational databases.

In recent years, with the advent of Web 2.0 and the semantic Web era, data analysis have become very important, replacing the traditional storing systems in many applications. They represent now the new technology for knowledge representation, data storage and information sharing. Even with big data, data collection and analysis will become more and more important. Then, it's then necessary to adapt new approaches, new methods, new knowledge and new ways of working, resulting in new properties and new challenges, as logic referencing must be created and implemented. But, before breaking down the process of data analytics and in order to understand this process, author will define what data analytics is?

Data analytics is a process of inspecting, cleansing, transforming, and modeling data with the goal of discovering useful information, suggesting conclusions, and supporting decision-making. It focuses on knowledge discovery for predictive ad descriptive purposes, to discover new ideas or to confirm existing ideas.

It can be seen from the above definition that data analysis is a primordial step in the process of knowledge discovery in databases (KDD). This step involves the application of specific algorithms for extracting patterns (models) from data. The additional steps are data preparation, data selection, data cleaning, incorporation of appropriate prior knowledge, and proper interpretation of the results of mining (Mitra and al, 2002).

Data processing and analysis, in the present day, are brought together under the notion of "Business Intelligence" (BI), due especially to computers' increased processing capabilities. Powerful analytics tools can then be used to process the information gathered in large sets of structured and unstructured data. However, there are many technical challenges that must be addressed to realize the full potential of big data. Jagadish and al (2012) provide a comprehensive discussion of such challenges based on the notion of data analysis pipeline:

- **Data Acquisition and Recording:** It is critical to capture the context into which data has been generated, to be able to filter out non-relevant data and to compress data, to automatically generate metadata supporting rich data description and to track and record provenance.
- **Information Extraction and Cleaning:** Data may have to be transformed in order to extract information from it and express this information in a form that is suitable for analysis. Data may also be of poor quality and/or uncertain. Data cleaning and data quality verification are thus critical.
- **Data Integration, Aggregation, and Representation:** Data can be very heterogeneous and may have different metadata. Data integration, even in more conventional cases, requires huge human efforts. Novel approaches that can improve the automation of data integration are critical as manual approaches will not scale to what is required for big data. Also different data aggregation and representation strategies may be needed for different data analysis tasks.
- **Query Processing, and Analysis:** Methods suitable for big data need to be able to deal with noisy, dynamic, heterogeneous, untrustworthy data and data characterized by complex relations. However despite these difficulties, big data even if noisy and uncertain can be more valuable for identifying more reliable hidden patterns and knowledge compared to tiny samples of good data. Also the (often redundant) relationships existing among data can represent an opportunity for cross-checking data and thus improve data trustworthiness. Supporting query processing and data analysis requires scalable mining algorithms and powerful computing infrastructures.
- **Interpretation:** Analysis results extracted from big data needs to be interpreted by decision makers and this may require the users to be able to analyze the assumptions at each stage of data processing and possibly re-tracing the analysis. Rich provenance is critical in this respect.

Big data analysis are essential when organizations want to engage in predictive analysis, natural language processing, image analysis or advanced statistical techniques such as discrete choice modeling and mathematical optimization, or even if they want to mash up unstructured content and analyze it with their BI. Companies will be able to suggest data management for decision-making. The new analytical power is seen as an opportunity to invent and explore new methods which are able to detect correlations between the quantities of available data.

For example, the e-commerce giant Amazon recommends products to customers based on their browsing and purchasing habits. The "ad-tech" companies such as RocketFuel apply statistical and optimization techniques to determine which banner ads to display. Thus, devices such as "Fitbit" that the recording and monitoring of our physical activities, and their integration with other applications, allows individuals to obtain information on calories burned and food consumed. This allows a creation of new models which sell this information to insurance companies to better calculate risks.

The case of these companies in various fields illustrates the power that brings analytics for management of the proposed services and applications available. To capitalize on its potential, companies must put data analytics at the center of their strategy. That is truly necessary are excellent analytic skills, a capacity to understand and manipulate large sets of data, and the capacity to interpret and apply the results.

But, they need also to establish clear guidelines for data integrity and security, as digital ecosystems can only function efficiently if all parties involved can trust in the security of their data and communication. The analysis of big data is not only a matter of solving computational problems, even if those working on big data come from the natural sciences or computational fields. Rather, expertly analyzing big data also requires thoughtful measurement (Patty & Penn 2015), careful research design, and the creative deployment of statistical techniques.

Indeed, massive datasets will require the full range of statistical methodology to be brought to bear in order for assertions of knowledge on the basis of massive data analysis to be reliable. Following a period when the main issue is how to organize and structure databases? The question now is what to do? What analyzes developed to value and support decision-making? In another term, how should statistical procedures be designed so as to be scalable computationally to the massive datasets? These issues should be seriously considered in big data analysis and in the development of statistical procedures.

HOW ARE COMPUTATIONAL TOOLS SUPPORTING STATISTICAL METHOD TO DEAL WITH BIG DATA?

During the time of applying methods of statistical inference and statistical decisions some 70 years ago, information derived from data collection was considered costly. Models were built where information was linked to payoff relevance of a decision-making criterion (utility or payoff function), therefore statistical information was handled to satisfy these criteria. Now as masses of data are produced at relatively low costs all these data could be quickly aggregated. Statisticians have coined a term, 'value of perfect information', which is set up to integrate data points, collection and analysis through statistical inferential models i.e., exploratory data analysis (EDA) or through statistical decision models (Piegorsch, 2015). For example, achieving this goal is quite challenging to gather all the data for perfect information.

In traditional statistics, there are limited amounts of data, and it must get as much information as possible out of it. In the big data age, there is a limited amount of computational power, and companies need to make the best decision. Big data pose new challenges to statisticians both in terms of theory and application. Some of the challenges include: Size, scalability of statistical computation methods, non-random data, assessing uncertainty, sampling, modelling relationships, mixture data, real-time analysis on streaming data, statistical analysis with multiple kinds of data, data quality and complexity, protecting, privacy and confidentiality, high dimensional data …

There are several methods that are recently developed and feasible for statistical inference of big data and workable on parallel machines, including the bag of little bootstraps, aggregated estimation equation, and so on. Each method was being developed to find and design tools that explicitly reveal tradeoffs relating complexity, risk, and time.

Statistics is the traditional field that deals with the quantification, collection, analysis, interpretation, and drawing conclusions from data. Development of new statistical methods is an interdisciplinary field that draws on computer sciences, artificial intelligence, machine learning, and visualization models and so on.

Concerning statistical methods literature summarizes the change in two points (Sedkaoui, 2017):

- *The new approaches are on the crossroads of IT tools and statistics.* it's concerning Machine Learning, where algorithms generate alone, more or less models on large amounts of data;
- *These methods are not new because machine learning dated from 1960s.* this return to the center stage is due to the fact that these techniques work especially well on high amounts of information.

The applied statistics and machine learning community have been quite concerned with identifying ways to cross-validate predictions produced by these techniques, and avoid simply capitalizing on chance by overfitting their data (James and al, 2014). But, it's necessary to point that there are two computational barriers for big data analysis: the first concerns the data that can be too big to hold in a computer's memory; while the second is related to the computing task that can take too long to wait for the results. These barriers can be approached either with newly developed statistical methodologies and/ or computational methodologies (Wang and al, 2015).

From an IT point of view, knowledge of Hadoop is highly desirable. It allows the creation of distributed applications and "scalable" on thousands of nodes to manage petabytes of data. The principle is to split and parallelize (distribution) data batch task to linearly reduce the computation time (scalable) depending on the number of nodes. Hadoop becomes the mining web reference tool and e-commerce.

From a statistical point of view the new challenge is both the functional representation of bases of construction and relevant models to address and take into account the complex data structures: geolocation on graphs, real-time signal, 3D images, sequences... Every problem, especially industrial, requires a specific approach after a search that a conventional engineering development. In the case of data streams, the decision support becomes adaptive or sequential. The computational tools that often are associated with the analysis of big data also can help scholars who are designing experiments or making causal inferences from observational data.

Besides the aforementioned advantages, the heterogeneity of big data also poses significant challenges to statistical inference. The model is also changing; reason why data were collected to feed statistical models but now models reinventing or adapting to best exploit available data. Processing big data, in turn, puts demand on computational frameworks and models that need to be fault tolerant, flexible and light weight; example by supporting iterative and stream computing, as well as local processing of data.

Computing and storage solutions form basis for advanced data analysis, including machine learning and statistical modeling. For example, Imai and Ratkovic (2013) extended variable selection methods to estimate treatment-effect heterogeneity, whereas Green and Kern (2012) used Bayesian additive regression trees to capture systematic heterogeneity in treatment effects.

The scalability of statistical methods also poses a major challenge. When data becomes big, the possible number of simultaneous hypotheses, as well as data points, can be on the order of millions (American Statistical Association, 2015). Data sets derived from big data sources are not necessarily random samples of the target population.

The big data introduce unique computational and statistical challenges, including scalability and storage bottleneck, noise accumulation, spurious correlation and measurement errors. These challenges are distinguished and require new computational and statistical paradigm. In order to confront the challenges mentioned above statistical methods will need to be modernized. More application is needed to overcome the methodological difficulties impeding the exploitation of big data sources.

Big data are characterized by high dimensionality and large sample size. These two features raise three unique challenges:

- High dimensionality brings noise accumulation, spurious correlations and incidental homogeneity;
- High dimensionality combined with large sample size creates issues such as heavy computational cost and algorithmic instability;
- The massive samples in big data are typically aggregated from multiple sources at different time points using different technologies (Fan and al, 2014).

Another important point, which represents an often issue in data mining and analytics, is the need for sufficiently high quality in the database. Once the implementation of the first data warehouse in the 1990s the question of the quality of the data was a major issue. In the US, the theorem 'garbage in, garbage out', or the "GIGO" principal, was immediately widespread. So there is nothing new about this description: only data quality will help produce an event, a forecast or strategic information and define an action lever. Therefore, the volume of data is of little importance, since internal data must be combined with external data in order for a company to obtain the most out of its data. The reconciliation of internal and external data has always been a challenge.

It is possible to obtain better results by making better use of available data. When researchers encounter a set of data, they need to understand not only the limits of the available set of data, but also the limits of the questions that it can respond to, as well as the range of possible appropriate interpretations. Data analysis, when it is not preceded by the word 'Big', refers to the development and sharing of useful and effective models.

Currently, one of the innovations that make it possible to share and store large volumes of data is Cloud Computing. The 'Cloud' allows access to shared computing resources through an on-demand telecommunication network or self-service modules. The cloud transforms storage infrastructure and computing power into services through the intermediary of companies that possess servers and rent out their capacities. This approach makes it possible to share costs and to provide greater data storage and processing flexibility for users. The volume of data generated and stored by enterprises made a new step. As already indicated in previous sections, this new step creates new approaches for both architectures databases, the parallelization of computations as for algorithms and methods used.

While the parallel and distributed architectures present new capabilities for storage and manipulation of data, from an inferential point of view, it is unclear how the current statistical methodology can be transported to the paradigm of big data. Cutting-edge data management, querying, and analysis techniques in computer science must be linked with fundamental approaches in statistics and machine learning to create data systems that are flexible, responsive, and predictive. Computer-science techniques need to incorporate more statistical approaches, while statistical techniques need to develop approaches for trading off statistical power and computational complexity (it will be discussed in the next section). The need to analyze and use enormous amounts of data more efficiently drives companies towards "data science" in the hope of unlocking the power of big data.

SOME NEW METHODS DEVELOPED (ALGORITHMS) FOR MASSIVE DATASETS ANALYSIS

The transformation of big data into knowledge is by no means an easy task. Therefore, it is challenging for businesses to analyze and extract knowledge from a universe due to lack of computing resources available. This section is about methods which ride of the progress in computational data analysis. Sound statistical methods that are scalable computationally to massive datasets have been proposed. From a computational perspective, much effort has been put into the most active, open source statistical environment. Software review focuses on the open source R and R packages, covering recent tools that help break the barriers of computer memory and computing power. Statistician R developers are relentless in their drive to extend the reach of R into big data. The statistical methodologies for big data can be grouped as follow:

Subsampling-Based

This means that a subsample from the original dataset is taking with respect to a carefully designed probability distribution, and uses this sample as a surrogate for the original dataset to do model estimation, prediction as well as statistical inference.

1. **The Big Data Bootstrap:** Traditionally, subsampling has been used to refer to "m-out-of-n" bootstrap, whose primary motivation is to make approximate inference owing to the difficulty or intractability in deriving analytical expressions (Efron, 1979; Jackknife, 1989). In the massive data setting, there is a serious problem: each bootstrap resample is itself massive. However, in settings involving large datasets, the computation of bootstrap-based quantities can be prohibitively demanding. A new procedure which incorporates features of both the bootstrap and subsampling is known as the Bag of Little Bootstraps (BLB), to obtain a robust, computationally efficient means of assessing estimator quality. This method, proposed by Kleiner and al. (2014), is a combination of subsampling (Politis and al., 1999), the m-out-of-n bootstrap (Bickel and al., 1997), and the bootstrap to achieve computational efficiency. The development of BLB was motivated by the computational imperative; it can be viewed as a novel statistical procedure to be compared to the bootstrap and subsampling according to more classical criteria.

2. **Leveraging:** Leveraging methods are designed under a subsampling framework, in which one samples a small proportion of the data (subsample) from the full sample, and then performs intended computations for the full sample using the small subsample as a surrogate. Ma and Sun (2014) proposed to use leveraging to facilitate scientific discoveries from big data using limited computing resources. The key to success of the leveraging methods is to construct the weights, the nonuniform sampling probabilities, so that influential data points are sampled with high probabilities.

3. **Mean Log-Likelihood:** Liang and al. (2013) proposed a new parameter estimator, maximum mean log-likelihood estimator, for big data problems, and a resampling-based stochastic approximation method for obtaining such an estimator. The method uses Monte Carlo averages calculated from subsamples to approximate the quantities needed for the full data. Motivated from minimizing the Kullback–Leibler (KL) divergence, they approximate the KL divergence by averages calculated from subsamples. The solution to the mean score equation is obtained from a stochastic approximation procedure, where at each iteration; the current estimate is updated based on a subsample of size m drawn from the full data. As m is much smaller than n, the method is scalable to big data. Liang and al. (2013) established the consistency and asymptotic normality of the resulting estimator under mild conditions.

Divide and Conquer Method

The divide and conquer method solves big data problems in the following manner. First, the original massive dataset is divided into K small blocks that are manageable to the current computing facility unit. Then, the intended statistical analysis is performed on each small block. Finally, an appropriate strategy will be used to combine the results from these K blocks. As a result, the computation for the divide and conquer method can easily be done in parallel.

This is trivial for some models, like linear models or generalized linear models, for which the estimation procedures are linear by construction. More specifically, the estimating equations for the full data themselves can be written as a summation of all smaller blocks. The readers are referred to for more detailed discussion and theoretical properties for resulting estimators for a single parameter case.

1. **Aggregated Estimating Equations:** In recent years, there have been active researches on developing compression and aggregation schemes to support fast online analytical processing (OLAP) of various statistical analyses, such as linear regression, general multiple linear regression, logistic regression analysis… However, many advanced statistical analyses are nonlinear and thus most of the current OLAP tools cannot be used to support these advanced analyses. Aggregated estimating equations develop a computation and storage efficient algorithm for estimating equation (EE) estimation in massive data sets using a divide and conquer strategy. In each partition of the data set, the raw data is compressing into some low dimensional statistics and then discard the raw data. Results an approximation to the EE estimator, the AEE estimator, by solving an equation aggregated from the saved low dimensional statistics in all partitions. Such low dimensional statistics are taken as the EE estimates and first-order derivatives of the estimating equations in each partition. For general nonlinear assessment equations were offered a linear approximation of the estimating equations with the Taylor expansion at the solution in each block. Lin & Xi (2011) showed that the aggregated estimator has the same limit as the estimator from the full data.

2. **Parallel MCMC:** Computational intensity and sequential nature of estimation techniques for Bayesian methods in statistics and machine learning, combined with their increasing applications for big data analytics, necessitate both the identification of potential opportunities to parallelize techniques such as Monte Carlo Markov Chain (MCMC) sampling. In the Bayesian framework, it is natural to partition the data into k subsets and run parallel MCMC on each one of them. The prior distribution for each subset is often obtained by taking a power 1/k of the prior distribution for whole data in order to preserve the total amount of prior information. Neiswanger and al. (2013) proposed to use kernel density estimators of the posterior density for each data subset, and estimate the full data posterior by multiplying the subset posterior densities together. This method is asymptotically exact in the sense of being converging in the number of MCMC iterations. Wang and al (2015) replaced the kernel estimator of Neiswanger and al. (2013) with a random partition tree histogram, which uses the same block partition across all terms in the product representation of the posterior to control the number of terms in the approximation such that it does not explode with m. Scott and al. (2013) proposed a consensus Monte Carlo algorithm, which produces the approximated full data posterior using weighted averages over the subset MCMC samples.

Divide-and-conquer is a natural computational paradigm for approaching big data problems, particularly given recent developments in distributed and parallel computing, but some interesting challenges arise when applying divide-and-conquer algorithms to statistical inference problems. One interesting issue is that of obtaining confidence intervals in massive datasets.

Massive Time-Series Datasets

The detection and analysis of events within massive collections of time-series has become an extremely important task. In particular, many scientific investigations (e.g. the analysis of microlensing and other transients) begin with the detection of events in irregularly-sampled series with both non-linear trends and non-Gaussian noise. This approach harnesses the power of Bayesian modeling while maintaining much of the speed and scalability of more ad-hoc machine learning approaches.

Coarse-to-Fine Method

Another surprising yet proved to be effective idea proposed much recently is the coarse-to-fine method. In order to make intended algorithms for the massive dataset scalable, statisticians introduced a simple solution: rounding parameters. Hence the continuous real numbers of data are simply rounded from higher decimal places to lower decimal places. A substantial number of observations are degenerated to be identical. This idea was successfully applied to the functional data analysis using smoothing spline ANOVA models (Helwig and Ma, 2016). Indeed, in recent years slanted plane methods that jointly reason about stereo/flow and super pixels have been proposed (Yamaguchi and al, 2013). While they perform very well in challenging scenarios they are however computationally very expensive, limiting their applicability to real-wold applications such as autonomous driving.

Algorithm Weakening

In the case of BLB the flexibility inheres in the choice of m (the subsample size) and in the case of Divide-Factor-Combine (DFC) it is the choice of l (the submatrix dimension). Chandrasekaran and Jordan (2013) define a notion of "algorithmic weakening," in which a hierarchy of algorithms is ordered by both computational efficiency and statistical efficiency.

The problem that they address is to develop a quantitative relationship among three quantities: the number of data points, the runtime and the statistical risk. Chandrasekaran and Jordan (2013) focus on the denoising problem, an important theoretical testbed in the study of high-dimensional inference. General framework for algorithm weakening based on relaxations of convex sets.

Convex optimization methods offer a powerful framework for statistical inference due to the broad class of estimators that can be effectively modeled as convex programs. Further the theory of convex analysis is useful both for characterizing the statistical properties of convex programming based estimators as well as for developing methods to compute such estimators efficiently.

Online Updating Approaches

Motivated from a Bayesian inference perspective, Schifano and al. (2015) extends the work of Lin and Xi (2011) in a few important ways. First, they introduce divide-and-conquer-type variance estimates of regression parameters in the linear model and estimating equation settings. Then, they develop iterative estimating algorithms and statistical inferences for linear models and estimating equations that update as new data arrive. After that, they address the issue of possible rank deficiencies when dealing with blocks of data, and the uniqueness properties of the combined and cumulative estimators when using a generalized inverse.

Instead, they propose outlier tests relying on predictive residuals, which are based on the predictive values computed from the cumulative estimate of the regression coefficients attained at the previous accumulation point. In addition, a new online-updated estimator of the regression coefficients corresponding estimator of the standard error in the estimating equation setting which takes advantage of information from the previous data are introduced by authors.

CONCLUSION

With the developing of the IoT and the coming the semantic web, new methods for representing, storing and sharing information are going to replace the traditional systems. Offering to businesses and decision-makers, unprecedented opportunities to tackle much larger and more complex big data challenges. This chapter has dealt with the issue of extraction of knowledge from data driven by statistics and computing in order to deal big data challenges. Such as: (i) the complexity of data (collected from different sources and different formats). (ii) Noisy data challenge: big data generally include different kinds of measurement errors, outliers and missing values. (iii) Dependent data challenge: in varied types of current data, such as financial time series and so on.

To handle the challenges of big data, new statistical thinking and computational methods are needed. Because, classical statistical methods are often unsuited for big data purposes, which can be linked to a lack of flexibility in existing methods, but also to the assumptions that are typically made for mathematical convenience, and the particular way of drawing inference from data.

For example, many traditional methods that perform well for moderate sample size do not scale to massive data. Similarly, many statistical methods that perform well for low-dimensional data are facing significant challenges in analyzing high-dimensional data. In terms of statistical methods, dimension reduction and variable selection play pivotal roles in analyzing high-dimensional data. New statistical procedures with these issues in mind are crucially needed.

With the challenges and opportunities of big data and necessity of turning data into knowledge, statistics is an essential scientific discipline because of its sophisticated methods for statistical inference, prediction, quantification of uncertainty, and experimental design. Statistics is closely related to machine-learning and knowledge discovery, and depends heavily on data-visualization techniques. And knowledge discovery is on the interface of computing and statistics, and the main issues faced were to find a point of contact between the two disciplines already explored, statistics and computing science.

The collaboration between statistics and computer science is needed to control runtimes that will maintain the statistical procedures usable on large-scale data while ensuring good statistical properties. Then, analysis of the data is application oriented and driven by computation. In case of data analytics, companies analyzed requirements regarding (i) Data: types, structure, format and sources and (ii) data Processing: operations, performance and conditions.

Obviously, more can be done, following either the undertaken direction or exploring new solutions. This include the ever-changing landscape of data and their associated characteristics, evolving data analysis paradigms, challenges of computational infrastructure, data sharing and data access, and – crucially – our ability to integrate data sets and their analysis toward an improved understanding. Moreover the type of analysis which is needed to be done on the data depends highly on the results to be obtained through decision making. This can be done to (i) incorporate massive data volumes in analysis or (ii) determine upfront which big data is relevant (quality). So, the biggest challenge of the zetabytes age will not be storing all that data, it will be figuring out how to make sense of it.

ACKNOWLEDGMENT

I would like to gratefully and sincerely thank Professor H.W Gottinger for his guidance, understanding, in the planning and preparation of this chapter, and most importantly, his friendship. I must express my very profound gratitude to my mother and to my sisters and brother for providing me with unfailing support and continuous encouragement throughout my years of study and through the process of researching and writing this chapter. This accomplishment would not have been possible without them. Thank you.

REFERENCES

Ackoff, R. L. (1989). From data to wisdom. *Journal of Applied Systems Analysis*, *15*, 3–9.

American Statistical Association. (2015). *Discovery with Data: Leveraging Statistics with Computer Science to Transform Science and Society, Web. 3.0*. Retrieved from http://www.amstat.org/policy/pdfs/BigDataStatisticsJune2014.pdf

Bickel, P., Gotze, F., & Van Zwet, W. (1997). Resampling fewer than n observations: Gains, losses and remedies for losses. *Statistica Sinica*, *7*, 1–31.

Boyd, D., & Crawford, K. (2012). Critical questions for big data: Provocations for a cultural, technological, and scholarly phenomenon. *Information Communication and Society*, *15*(5), 662–679. doi:10.1080/1369118X.2012.678878

Brynjolfsson, E., & McAfee, A. (2011). *Race Against the Machine: How the Digital Revolution is Accelerating Innovation, Driving Productivity, and Irreversibly Transforming Employment and the Economy*. Lexington, MA: Digital Frontier Press.

Chamberlin, D. D., & Boyce, R. F. (1974, April). SEQUEL: A structured English query language. *Proc. 1974 ACM SIGFIDET Workshop*, 249-264.

Chandrasekaran, V., & Jordan, M. (2013). Computational and statistical tradeoffs via convex relaxation. *Proceedings of the National Academy of Sciences of the United States of America*, *13*(13), 1181–1190. doi:10.1073/pnas.1302293110 PMID:23479655

Cleveland, H. (1982, December). Information as Resource. *The Futurist*, 34–39.

Codd, E. F. (1970, June). A relational model of data for large shared data banks. *Communications of the ACM*, *13*(6), 377–387.

Cukier, K., & Mayer-Schoenberger, V. (2013b). The Rise of Big Data. *Foreign Affairs*, *92*(3), 28–40.

Cukier, K., & Mayer-Schonberger, V. (2013a). *Big Data: A Revolution That Will Transform How We Live, Work and Think*. Boston, MA: Houghton Mifflin Harcourt.

Efron, B. (1979). Bootstrap methods: Another look at the jackknife. *Annals of Statistics*, *7*(1), 1–26. doi:10.1214/aos/1176344552

Ekbia, H., Mattioli, M., Kouper, I., Arave, G., Ghazinejad, A., Bowman, T., ... Sugimoto, C. R. (2015). Big data, bigger dilemmas: A critical review. *Journal of the Association for Information Science and Technology*, *66*(8), 1523–1545. doi:10.1002/asi.23294

Eliot, T. S. (1934). *The rock*. Faber & Faber. Available at: http://www.wisdomportal.com/Technology/TSEliot-TheRock.html

Fan, J., Han, F., & Liu, H. (2014). Challenges of Big Data analysis. *National Science Review, 1*(2), 293–314. doi:10.1093/nsr/nwt032 PMID:25419469

Foster, I., Ghani, R., Jarmin, R. S., Kreuer, F., & Lane, J. (2017). *Big Data and Social Science*. Boca Raton, FL: CRC Press.

Fujimaki, R., & Morinaga, S. (2012). The Most Advanced Data Mining of the Big Data Era. *Advanced Technologies to Support Big Data Processing, 7*(2).

Green, D. P., & Holger, L. K. (2012). Modeling Heterogeneous Treatment Effects in Survey Experiments with Bayesian Additive Regression Trees. *Public Opinion Quarterly, 76*(3), 491–511. doi:10.1093/poq/nfs036

Harford, T. (2014). Big Data: A Big Mistake. *Significance, 11*(5), 14–19. doi:10.1111/j.1740-9713.2014.00778.x

Helwig, N. E., & Ma, P. (2016). Smoothing spline ANOVA for super-large samples: Scalable computation via rounding parameters. *Statistics and Its Interface, 9*(4), 433–444. doi:10.4310/SII.2016.v9.n4.a3

IDC. (2011). *World's data will grow by 50X in next decade*. IDC Study.

Imai, K., & Ratkovic, M. (2013). Estimating Treatment Effect Heterogeneity, *Randomized Program Evaluation. The Annals of Applied Statistics, 7*(1), 443–470. doi:10.1214/12-AOAS593

Jagadish, S. V. K., Septiningsih, E. M., Kohli, A., Thomson, M. J., Ye, C., Redoña, E., ... Singh, R. K. (2012). Genetic advances in adapting rice to a rapidly changing climate. *Journal Agronomy & Crop Science, 198*(5), 360–373. doi:10.1111/j.1439-037X.2012.00525.x

James, G., Witten, D., Hastie, T., & Tibshirani, R. (2014). *An introduction to statistical learning with applications in R*. New York: Springer.

Katal, A., Wazid, M., & Goudar, R. H. (2013). Big Data: Issues, Challenges, Tools and Good Practices. *IEEE Spectrum*, 404–409.

Kleiner, A., Talwalkar, A., Sarkar, P., & Jordan, M. I. (2014). A scalable bootstrap for massive data. *Journal of the Royal Statistical Society. Series B, Statistical Methodology, 76*(4), 795–816. doi:10.1111/rssb.12050

Liang, F., Cheng, Y., Song, Q., Park, J., & Yang, P. (2013). A resampling-based stochastic approximation method for analysis of large geostatistical data. *Journal of the American Statistical Association, 108*(501), 325–339. doi:10.1080/01621459.2012.746061

Liang, F., & Kim J., (2013). *A bootstrap Metropolis–Hastings algorithm for Bayesian analysis of big data*. Tech. rep., Department of Statistics, Texas A & M University.

Lin, N., & Xi, R. (2011). Aggregated estimating equation estimation. *Statistics and Its Interface, 4*(1), 73–83. doi:10.4310/SII.2011.v4.n1.a8

Ma, P., & Sun, X. (2014). *Leveraging for big data regression*. WIREs Computational Statistics.

Mann, D. (2004). *Hands-on Systematic Innovation for Business*. CREAX Press.

McKinsey. (2011). *Internet matters: The Net's sweeping impact on growth, jobs, and prosperity*. Author.

McKinsey. (2013). *Big Data, Analytics and the Future of Marketing and Sales*. New York: McKinsey.

Mitra, S., Pal, S. K., & Mitra, P. (2002). Data mining in soft computing framework: A survey. *IEEE Transactions on Neural Networks*, *13*(1), 3–14. doi:10.1109/72.977258 PMID:18244404

Neiswanger, W., Wang, C., & Xing, E. (2013). *Asymptotically exact, embarrassingly parallel MCMC*. arXiv preprint arXiv: 1311-4780

Patty, J., & Penn, E. M. (2015). Analyzing Big Data: Social Choice and Measurement. *PS, Political Science & Politics*, *48*(1), 95–101. doi:10.1017/S1049096514001814

Piegorsch, W. W. (2015). *Statistical Data Analytics*. New York: Wiley.

Politis, D. N., Romano, J. P., & Wolf, M. (1999). Subsampling. New York: Springer.

Schifano, E. D., Wu, J., Wang, C., Yan, J., & Chen, M.-H. (2015). Online Updating of Statistical Inference in the Big Data Setting. *Technometrics*. PMID:28018007

Scott, S.L., Blocker, A.W., Bonassi, F.V., Chipman, H., George, E., & McCulloch, R. (2013). Bayes and Big Data: The Consensus Monte Carlo Algorithm. *EFaBBayes 250 Conference*, 16.

Sedkaoui, S. (2017). The Internet, Data Analytics and Big Data. In Internet Economics: Models, Mechanisms and Management (pp. 185-210). Bentham Science.

Sedkaoui, S., & Monino, J. L. (2016). *Big data, Open Data and Data Development*. New York: ISTE-Wiley.

Shroff, G. (2013). *The Intelligent Web, Search, Smart Algorithms and Big Data*. Oxford, UK: Oxford Univ. Press.

Siegel, E. (2016). *Predictive Analytics*. New York: Wiley.

Turban, E. (2011). *Business Intelligence: A Managerial Approach* (2nd ed.). Upper Saddle River, NJ: Prentice Hall.

Vermesan, D., Prejbeanu, R., Laitin, R., Georgianu, V., Haragus, H., & Nitescu, S. (2014). Meniscal tears left in situ during anatomic single bundle anterior cruciate ligament reconstruction. *European Review for Medical and Pharmacological Sciences*, *18*(2), 252–256. PMID:24488916

Wang, X., Guo, F., Heller, K. A., & Dunson, D. B. (2015). *Parallelizing MCMC with Random Partition Trees*. arXiv preprint arXiv: 1506-03164

Wu, C. F. J. (1989). Bootstrap and other resampling methods in regression analysis. *Ann Stat*, *14*, 1261–1295.

Yamaguchi, K., Hazan, T., McAllester, D., & Urtasun, R. (2013). *Robustmonocular epipolar flow estimation*. CVPR.

Zeleny, M. (1987). Management Support Systems: Towards Integrated Knowledge Management. *Human Systems Management*, *7*(1), 59–70.

Zhang, A. (2017). *Data analytics: Practical guide to leveraging the power of Algorithms, data science, data mining, statistics, big data, and predictive analysis to improve business, work, and life.* Kindle Edition.

KEY TERMS AND DEFINITIONS

Analytics: Has emerged as a catch-all term for a variety of different business intelligence (BI)- and application-related initiatives. For some, it is the process of analyzing information from a particular domain, such as website analytics. For others, it is applying the breadth of BI capabilities to a specific content area (for example, sales, service, supply chain, and so on). In particular, BI vendors use the "analytics" moniker to differentiate their products from the competition. Increasingly, "analytics" is used to describe statistical and mathematical data analysis that clusters, segments, scores, and predicts what scenarios are most likely to happen. Whatever the use cases, "analytics" has moved deeper into the business vernacular. Analytics has garnered a burgeoning interest from business and IT professionals looking to exploit huge mounds of internally generated and externally available data.

Big Data: The term big data is used when the amount of data that an organization has to manage reaches a critical volume that requires new technological approaches in terms of storage, processing, and usage. Volume, velocity, and variety are usually the three criteria used to qualify a database as "big data."

Business Intelligence (BI): An umbrella term that includes the applications, infrastructure and tools, and best practices that enable access to and analysis of information to improve and optimize decisions and performance.

Data: This term comprises facts, observations, and raw information. Data itself has little meaning if it is not processed.

Data Analysis: A class of statistical methods that makes it possible to process a very large volume of data and identify the most interesting aspects of its structure. Some methods help to extract relations between different sets of data, and thus, draw statistical information that makes it possible describe the most important information contained in the data in the most succinct manner possible. Other techniques make it possible to group data in order to identify its common denominators clearly, and thereby understand them better.

Data Mining: This practice consists of extracting information from data as the objective of drawing knowledge from large quantities of data through automatic or semi-automatic methods. Data mining uses algorithms drawn from disciplines as diverse as statistics, artificial intelligence, and computer science in order to develop models from data; that is, in order to find interesting structures or recurrent themes according to criteria determined beforehand, and to extract the largest possible amount of knowledge useful to companies. It groups together all technologies capable of analyzing database information in order to find useful information and possible significant and useful relationships within the data.

Data Science: A new discipline that combines elements of mathematics, statistics, computer science, and data visualization. The objective is to extract information from data sources. In this sense, data science is devoted to database exploration and analysis. This discipline has recently received much attention due to the growing interest in big data.

Exploratory Data Analysis (EDA): In statistics, EDA is an approach to analyzing data sets to summarize their main characteristics, often with visual methods.

Garbage In, Garbage Out (GIGO): In the field of computer science or information and communications technology refers to the fact that computers, since they operate by logical processes, will unquestioningly process unintended, even nonsensical, input data ("garbage in") and produce undesired, often nonsensical, output ("garbage out"). The principle applies to other fields as well.

Hadoop: Big data software infrastructure that includes a storage system and a distributed processing tool.

Information: Consists of interpreted data, and has discernible meaning. It is lies in descriptions and answers questions like "Who?" "What?" "When?" and "How many?"

Knowledge: A type of know-how that makes it possible to transform information into instructions. Knowledge can either be obtained through transmission from those who possess it, or by extraction from experience.

Machine-to-Machine (M2M): Communications is used for automated data transmission and measurement between mechanical or electronic devices. The key components of an M2M system are field-deployed wireless devices with embedded sensors or RFID-wireless communication networks with complementary wireline access including but not limited to cellular communication, Wi-Fi, ZigBee, WiMAX, wireless LAN (WLAN), generic DSL (xDSL), and fiber to the x (FTTx).

MapReduce: A programming model or algorithm for the processing of data using a parallel programming implementation and was originally used for academic purposes associated with parallel programming techniques.

Scalability: The measure of a system's ability to increase or decrease in performance and cost in response to changes in application and system processing demands. Enterprises that are growing rapidly should pay special attention to scalability when evaluating hardware and software.

Semantic Web: (Also known as the Web 3.0) This is a network that allows machines to understand semantics, which is to say the meaning of information published online. It expands the network of web pages understandable by humans by adding metadata that is understandable by a machine and that creates links between content and different pages, which in turn allows automatic agents to access the web in a more intelligent manner and to carry out some tasks in the place of users.

Smart Data: The flood of data encountered by ordinary users and economic actors will bring about changes in behavior, as well as the development of new services and value creation. This data must be processed and developed in order to become "smart data." Smart data is the result of analysis and interpretation of raw data, which makes it possible to effectively draw value from it. It is, therefore, important to know how to work with the existing data in order to create value.

Statistical Inference: The process of deducing properties of an underlying distribution by analysis of data. Inferential statistical analysis infers properties about a population. This includes testing hypotheses and deriving estimates. The population is assumed to be larger than the observed data set; in other words, the observed data is assumed to be sampled from a larger population.

Web 2.0: The set of techniques, functions, and uses of the world wide web that have followed the original format of the web. It concerns, in particular, interfaces that allow users with little technical training to appropriate new web functions. Internet users can contribute to information exchanges and interact (share, exchange, etc.) in a simple manner.

This research was previously published in Big Data Analytics in HIV/AIDS Research; pages 21-53, copyright year 2018 by Medical Information Science Reference (an imprint of IGI Global).

Chapter 31
A Survey of Big Data Analytics Using Machine Learning Algorithms

Usha Moorthy
Vellore Institute of Technology, India

Usha Devi Gandhi
Vellore Institute of Technology, India

ABSTRACT

Big data is information management system through the integration of various traditional data techniques. Big data usually contains high volume of personal and authenticated information which makes privacy as a major concern. To provide security and effective processing of collected data various techniques are evolved. Machine Learning (ML) is considered as one of the data technology which handles one of the central and hidden parts of collected data. Same like ML algorithm Deep Learning (DL) algorithm learn program automatically from the data it is considered to enhance the performance and security of the collected massive data. This paper reviewed security issues in big data and evaluated the performance of ML and DL in a critical environment. At first, this paper reviewed about the ML and DL algorithm. Next, the study focuses towards issues and challenges of ML and their remedies. Following, the study continues to investigate DL concepts in big data. At last, the study figures out methods adopted in recent research trends and conclude with a future scope.

1. INTRODUCTION

Big data analytics is the vast level investigation and preparing of data in dynamic utilize in a few fields and, as of late, has pulled in light of a legitimate concern for the security group for its guaranteed capacity to dissect and correspond security related data effectively and at phenomenal scale (Shirudkar et al., 2015). Separating between customary data examination and enormous data investigation for security is, in any case, not clear (Imperva, 2015). All things considered, the data security group has been utilizing

DOI: 10.4018/978-1-6684-3662-2.ch031

the investigation of system movement, framework logs, and other data sources to recognize dangers and identify noxious exercises for over 10 years, and it's not clear how these customary methodologies vary from big data (Mulanee et al., 2015). "Big Data Analytics for Security Intelligence," concentrates on big data's part insecurity (Raja et al., 2014). In advanced world, data are produced from different sources and the quick move from computerized innovations has prompted the development of enormous data (Suryawanshi et al., 2015). It gives transformative leaps forward in numerous fields with an accumulation of vast datasets. When all is said in done, it alludes to the accumulation of extensive and complex datasets which are hard to process utilizing customary database administration instruments or data handling applications (UK Data Archive, 2011). These are accessible in the organized, semi-organized, and unstructured organization in peta bytes and past (Tsai et al., 2015). Some of these extraction strategies for acquiring accommodating data were examined by Gandomi and Haider (Gandomi et al., 2015). The, however, correct definition for big data is not characterized, and there is trusted that it is issue particular. This will help us in getting upgraded basic leadership, knowledge disclosure, and advancement while being inventive and financially savvy (Kaur and Kaur, 2016). Extensive scale data sets are gathered and examined in various spaces, from designing sciences to interpersonal organizations, trade, bimolecular examination, and security (Tsai et al., 2015). Especially, advanced data produced from an assortment of computerized gadgets, and are developing at amazing rates. As per Gandomi and Haider (2015), in 2011, computerized data is grown nine times in volume in only 5years, and its sum on the planet will be reached 35 trillion gigabytes by 2020 (Lynch, 2008). In this manner, the expression "Enormous Data" was begotten to catch the significant importance of this data blast pattern (Qiu et al., 2016).

The aim of Machine Learning (ML) is to empower a framework to gain from the past or present and utilize that data to settle on expectations or choices with respect to obscure future occasions (Rajkumar et al., 2016). In the broadest terms, the work process for an administered ML errand comprises of three stages: manufacture the model, assess and tune the model, and afterward put the model into creation (Natarajan et al., 2012). The multiplication of big data has constrained us to reexamine data preparing systems, as well as usage of ML algorithms too. Picking the fitting apparatuses for a specific errand or environment can overwhelm for two reasons. To start with, the expanding multifaceted nature of ML venture necessities and additionally of the data itself may require distinctive sorts of arrangements. Second, frequently engineers will discover the determination of devices accessible to be unsuitable; however, as opposed to adding to existing open source ventures, they start one of their own (Mani et al., 1998). This has prompted a lot of discontinuity among existing big data stages (Kashyap et al., 2014). Both of these issues can add to the trouble of building a learning situation, the same number of alternatives have covering use cases, yet separate in imperative regions. Since there is no single device or system that covers all or even the larger part of normal assignments, one must consider the exchange offs that exist between ease of use, execution, and calculation choice while inspecting diverse arrangements. There is an absence of extensive examination of a large number of them, in spite of being generally utilized on an undertaking level and there is no present industry standard (Landset et al., 2015).

2.1 Review of Big Data Processing

In recent world processing of a large amount of data is difficult task which makes big data processing more complex. This section provides a detailed review of challenges facing by various big data processing mechanisms.

2.1.1. Learning of Large Scale Data

- The solution to overcoming the learning of large data set is considering alternating direction method (ADMM) of multipliers which serves as computing framework (Hu et al., 2014)
- This framework is used to develop convex optimizing, scalable and distributed algorithms in both distributed and parallel data processing.
- ADMM has capacity to part or decouple numerous variables in improvement issues, which empowers individual, discover an answer for an extensive scale worldwide advancement issue by organizing answers for littler sub-issues.
- For the most part, ADMM is united for raised enhancement, yet it is the absence of a meeting, and hypothetical execution ensures for non-convex improvement. It is immeasurable trial proof in the writing bolsters experimental merging and great execution of ADM (Boyd et al., 2010).

2.1.2. Learning of Different Types of Data

- The effective key to concentrate on the problem of data integration is to obtain a proper data representation since the one to present in the data source.
- These data sources are then integrated to various features from the different levels (Hinton, 2012). and hence learning is considered to this problem
- In Wu (2013), the authors proposed a data combination hypothesis given actual learning for the 2D range different data. Moreover, Deep Learning (DL) strategies have likewise been appeared to be extremely compelling in incorporating data from various sources.

2.1.3. Learning for High-Speed Streaming Data

- Online learning approach is considered as one of the optimal solutions for the problem of learning such as very high velocity of data
- Online learning (Shalev-Shwartz, 2011; Wang et al., 2014; Bilenko et al., 2005) is a created learning worldview whose methodology is learning a example at once, rather than in a disconnected or bunch learning design, which needs to gather the full data of preparing data.
- This chronological learning instrument functions admirably for enormous data as present machines can't hold the whole dataset in process.
- To speed up adapting, as of late, a fresh algorithm for single concealed layer sustain forward neural systems (SLFNs) named amazing learning machine (ELM) (Huang et al., 2006) was proposed.
- ELM gives amazingly speedier learning speed, better speculation execution, and with slightest human intercession than some other customary learning calculations (Ding et al., 2014) Hence, ELM has solid preferences in managing the high speed of data.

2.1.4. Learning for Uncertain and Incomplete Data

- Uncertainty data are a unique sort of data reality where data readings and accumulations are no more deterministic however are liable to some arbitrary or likelihood disseminations.
- In numerous applications, data instability is basic. For instance, in remote systems, some range data are. Naturally, indeterminate came about because of omnipresent commotion, blurring, and

shadowing, and the innovation obstruction of the GPS sensor hardware additionally confines the exactness of the data to specific levels.

- For indeterminate data, the significant test is that the data highlight or property is caught not by a solitary point esteem but rather spoke to as test disseminations (Wu et al., 2014). A basic approach to handling data instability is to apply synopsis insights, for example, means and differences to extract test appropriations.

- Another methodology is to use the complete data conveyed by the likelihood dispersions to develop a choice tree, which is called dissemination based methodology in (Tsang et al., 2011).

2.1.5. Learning for Data With Low-Value Density and Meaning Diversity

- To handle the problem the solution that used is data mining technologies and knowledge discovery in databases (KDD) (Wu et al., Fayyad et al., 1996; Tsai et al., 2014), this provides a solution with data hidden in the massive data.

- In Tsai et al., the authors looked into studies on applying data mining and KDD innovations to the IoT. Especially, using grouping, characterization, and continuous examples innovations to mine quality from enormous data in IoT, from bases and the viewpoint of administrations were talked about in subtle element.

- In Wu et al., Wu et al. described the components of the big data transformation and proposed big data preparing techniques with ML and data mining calculations.

Table 1. ML and data types

ML Technique	Data Type
Alternating Direction Method (ADMM)	Large Scale Data
Data combination hypothesis for two-dimensional range heterogeneous data	Different Data Type
Sustain forward neural systems (SLFNs)	High-speed streaming data
Knowledge discovery in databases (KDD)	Data with low-value density and meaning diversity

3.0. OVERVIEW OF ML

ML could be a field of examination that formally concentrates on the hypothesis, execution, and properties of learning frameworks and algorithms (Domingos, 2012). It is an exceptionally interdisciplinary field expanding upon thoughts from various sorts of fields of research (Pawlak, 1982; Molodtsov 1999; Peters, 2007; Wille, 2005). Due to its execution in an extensive variety of utilizations, ML has secured practically every logical area, that has brought incredible effect on the science and society (Jolliffe, 2002). It has been utilized on an assortment of issues, including suggestion motors, acknowledgment frameworks, informatics and data mining, and self-governing control frameworks (Al-Jarrah et al., 2015).

For the most part, the area of ML has three subdomains: managed learning, unsupervised learning, and support learning (Changwon et al., 2014). Quickly, directed learning needs preparing with named data which has independent variables whereas craved yields. Interestingly with the directed learning, unsupervised learning doesn't need marked preparing data and nature just gives inputs without fancied targets (Bengio et al., 2014). Fortification taking in empowers gaining from input got through connections with an outer situation. Given these three crucial learning ideal models, a great deal of hypothesis components and application administrations have been proposed for managing data undertakings (Singh et al., 2014; Jacob et al., 2009; Zhu et al., 2015). For instance, in (Singh, 2014), Google implements ML algorithms to monstrous lumps of muddled data got since the Internet for Google's interpreter, Google's road view, Android's voice acknowledgment, and picture web crawler. The "Data Processing Tasks" segment of the table provides the issues that should be understood, and the "Learning Algorithms" segment depicts the techniques which might be utilized. A rundown, since data preparing point of view, directed learning and unsupervised adapting, for the most part, concentrate on data investigation while support learning is favored for basic leadership issues (Alsheikh 2014). An additional point, is that most conventional machine-learning based frameworks are planned with the suspicion that all the gathered data would be totally stacked into memory for incorporated handling (Nithya, 2016). In any case, as the data continues getting greater and greater, the current ML systems experience incredible troubles when they are needed to hold the phenomenal quantity of data. These days, an awesome necessitate to create productively and practicality learning strategies to adapt to expectations data handling requests (Setia, 2008).

In the common emphasis of ML is the illustration of the info data and speculation of the educated examples for utilize on expectations concealed data. The integrity of the data representation largely affects the execution of machine learners on the data: a poor data representation is prone to diminish the execution of even a propelled, complex machine learner, while a decent data representation can prompt superior for a moderately less complex machine learner. Along these lines, highlight building, which concentrates on developing components and data representations from crude data (Domingos, 2012), is a critical component of ML. Highlight designing devours an expensive bit of the exertion in a ML assignment, and is ordinarily very space particular and includes extensive human info (Najafabadi, 2015).

3.1. Various ML Algorithms

Several algorithms were differentiated before in the assessment of the extensive data set experience the diverse work done to hold Big Data. Before all else diverse Decision Tree Learning was used before to divide the big data. This section provides extensive analysis of existing ML algorithm for data processing in the cloud. In work done by Hall et al. (Hall, 1998), there is characterized a methodology for shaping taking in the standards of the substantial arrangement of preparing data. The methodology is to have a solitary choice framework produced from an extensive and free n subset of data. Patil et al., utilizes a cross breed approach joining both hereditary calculation and choice tree to make a streamlined choice tree in this manner enhancing proficiency and execution of calculation (Patil, 2006). At that point, bunching systems appeared. Distinctive grouping procedures were being utilized to dissect the data sets.

The above Table 2 describes various ML types and its corresponding functionality on collected big data for analysis. The observed ML techniques are used in the second stage of the hierarchical method of data processing as defined in Figure 2. Another calculation called GLC++ was created for substantially blended data set not at all like calculation which manages Whereas Koyuturk et al. Characterized another procedure PROXIMUS for the pressure of exchange sets, quickens the affiliation mining guideline, and a proficient strategy for bunching and the revelation of examples in a substantial dataset (Koyuturk et al., 2005).With the developing learning in the field of enormous data, the different strategies for data investigation auxiliary coding, frequencies, co-event and diagram hypothesis, data diminishment systems, progressive bunching procedures, multidimensional scaling were characterized in Data Reduction Techniques for Large Qualitative Data Sets. It depicted that the requirement for the specific methodology emerge with the kind of dataset and the way the example is to be broke down (Namey et al., 2007).

Table 2. ML types and functionality

ML Types [6]	Functionality
Representation Learning	• Feature Selection • Feature Extraction • Dimensionality Reduction
DL	• Learning Deep Architectures
Distributed and Parallel Learning	• Parallel and Distributed Computing • Scalable Learning
Transfer Learning	• Knowledge Transfer • Multi-domain Learning
Active Learning	• Query Strategies and resampling • Labeling Patterns
Kernel-based learning	• Nonlinear data processing • High-dimensional mapping
Online Learning	• Streaming Processing • Sequential Learning
Extreme Learning Machine	• Fast Learning Speed • Good Generalization Performance • Less human intervention

Table 3. Impact of big data challenges

Big Data Challenges (UK Data Archive, 2011)	Impact
Volume	Large Scale
Variety	Heterogeneous, High-Dimensional, Nonlinear
Velocity	Real Time, Streams, High Speed
Veracity	Uncertain and Incomplete
Value	Low value density, Diverse data mining

Through the analysis of existing research articles related to ML approaches certain drawbacks challenges has been identified. The Table 2 defines challenges that exist in big data (UK Data Archive, 2011) and its impacts like insufficient volume for a large dataset, lack of variety identification regarding nonlinear, high-dimensional and heterogeneous data. Due to lack of incomplete and uncertainty veracity is also exists in cloud data and other problems like value get reduced for diverse data (Dragicevic et al., 2015)

The review of traditional researches related to ML provides certain limitation and drawbacks as stated in Table 2 also due to structural drawback it faces certain drawbacks. Due to drawbacks in existing traditional approaches Advanced Streaming Hierarchical Clustering for Concept Mining has been characterized for semantic substance from the expansive dataset (Looks et al., 2007).. The calculation was intended to be actualized in equipment, to handle data at high ingestion rates (Looks et al., 2007). In thecase of Hierarchical Artificial Neural Networks for Recognizing High Similar Large Data Sets., portrayed the procedures of SOM (self-arranging highlight map) system and learning vector quantization (LVQ) systems for regulated learning. It classifies vast data set into smaller in this way enhancing the general calculation time expected to prepare the extensive dataset (Lu et al., 2007). At that point change in the methodology for mining online data originates from Archana et al. suggested that the web mining affiliation tenets were characterized to mine the data to evacuate the excess principles. The result appeared through a diagram that the quantity of hubs in this chart is less as contrasted and the grid (Singh, 2014]. Figure 1 pictorially illustrates various types of ML methods and their technique for data processing. In same Figure 1 data security challenges observed from existing research articles.

Figure 1.

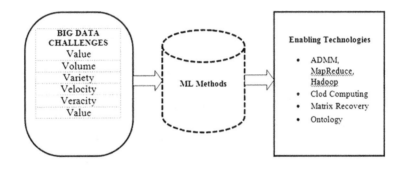

Figure 2.

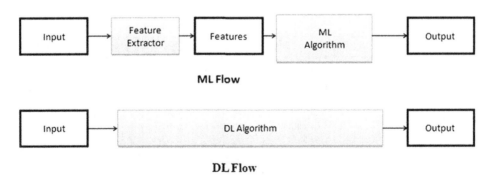

At that point after the procedures of the choice tree and grouping, there came a strategy of maximal data coefficient (MIC) was characterized, which is maximal reliance between the pair of variables of different non-direct connections of data (Reshef et al., 2015). Advancement of different methodologies through hierarchical framework discovered more productive in distinguishing the reliance and affiliation (Dong et al., 2016; Vadivel et al., 2014). But developed faces certain limitations like it has low power and accordingly as a result of it doesn't fulfill the property of evenhandedness for substantial dataset (Reshef et al., 2011). At that point Wang (2012) utilizes the idea of Physical Science, the Data field to produce collaboration between among articles and after that gathering them into bunches. This calculation was contrasted and K-Means, CURE, BIRCH, and CHAMELEON and was observed to be a great deal more productive than them (Wang et al., 2011). To overcome existing challenges in data mining, various technologies are evolved stated in Table 3 like cloud computing, ADMM, cognition, and matrix recovery as stated below.

Table 4. Emerging technologies and its function

Enabling Technologies	Functionality
ADMM, MapReduce, Hadoop	• Distributed Theoretical Framework • Parallel Programming Platform
Cloud Computing	• Efficient Storage • Effective Computation
Matrix Recovery or Completion	• Uncertainty • Incomplete Data Processing
Cognition, Ontology, and Semantic	• Intelligent Techniques • Context-aware Techniques

To Investigate big biological datasets with affiliation system" to change numerical and ostensible data gathered in tables, data processing was carried out through study structures, polls or sort esteem explanation records into systems of affiliations (ANets) and afterward producing Association manages (A Rules) (Kalanat et al, 2015). After processing of data through A Netsany perception or grouping calculation can be connected to them. It experienced the downside that the configuration of the dataset ought to be linguistically and semantically right to get the outcome (Karpinets et al., 2012).

Table 5. Review of ML methodology

Author	Method	Advantages	Research Gap
Hall, 1998	Creation of large dataset using Clustering	Proposed framework is most extensive and free n subset of data	This research does not concentrate on non-stationary datasets
Patil et al., 2007	Cross breed approach	The incorporation of Cross breed approach enhances the proficiency and execution of calculation in the cloud data.	The evaluation is not examined for particular data applications
Koyuturk et al., 2005	PROXIMUS for the pressure of exchange sets	Quickens the affiliation mining guideline, and a proficient strategy for bunching and the revelation for datasets.	This research does not focus on computational time.
Looks et al., 2015	Streaming Hierarchical Clustering	The calculation was intended to be actualized in equipment, to handle data at high ingestion rates	The computational complexity of the proposed approach is not examined.
Lu & Fahn, 2014	SOM (self-arranging highlight map) system and learning vector quantization (LVQ) systems	It classifies vast data set into littler in this way enhancing the general calculation time expected to prepare the extensive dataset.	Computational time is high
Reshef et al., 2014	Maximal data coefficient (MIC)	Methodologies were discovered more productive in distinguishing the reliance and affiliation.	The proposed approach is not examined for specific data set applications.

Later, in Survey of Different Issues of Different Clustering Algorithms utilized as a part of Large Data Sets groups distinctive DL algorithms and gives a review of various grouping calculation utilized as a part of extensive datasets (Vijayalakshmi, 2012)

3.2 Relationship Between ML and DL Techniques

The principle idea in DL algorithms is mechanizing the extraction of representations (deliberations) from the data (Le Callet et al., 2006; Wu et al., 2016; Ali et al., 2016). DL algorithms utilize a major measure of unsupervised data to consequently extricate complex representation. These algorithms are to a great extent persuaded in the field of computerized reasoning, which has the general objective of copying the human cerebrum's capacity to watch, dissect, learn, and decide, particularly for to a great degree complex issues. Work relating to this mind-boggling challenges have been a key inspiration driving DL algorithms which endeavor to imitate the progressive learning methodology of the human cerebrum. Interestingly, DL designs contain the ability, to sum up in non-nearby and worldwide ways, producing learning examples whereas connections past quick neighbors in the data (Bengio et al., 2013).

A key idea is hidden DL strategies is conveyed representation of the data, in which countless designs of the dynamic components of the info data are possible, taking into consideration (Fent, 2015).Taking note of that the watched data was created through connections of a few known/obscure components, and in this manner when a data example is acquired through a few designs of learned variables, extra (concealed) data examples can likely be depicted through new arrangements of the learned elements (Le Callet et al., 2006; Wu et al., 2016). This algorithm may lead to abstract samples of more dynamic representations are regularly developed in light of less conceptual ones (Najafabadi et al., 2015). An imperative favorable position of more theoretical representations is that they can be invariant to the neighborhood changes in the data. The genuine data utilized as a part of AI-related errands, for the most part, emerge from confounded connections of numerous sources. For instance, a picture is made out of various wellsprings of varieties such as light, protest shapes, and question materials. The dynamic representations gave by profound learning algorithms can isolate the diverse wellsprings of varieties in data (Goodfellow et al., 2015).

The DL algorithm is deep structures of back to back layers. Every layer applies a non-linear change in its data whereas gives a sample in its yield (Sivarajah et al., 2016). The goal is to take in a confounded and theoretical sample of the data in a progressive way by going the data through various change levels. The tangible data which means pixels in a picture is sustained to the principal level. Therefore, the yield of every level is given as a contribution to its next level (Najafabadi et al., 2015). The principle contrast between ML and profound learning calculations is in the element building. In ML calculations, we have to hand-make the components. By difference, in DL calculations, highlight building is done consequently by the calculation. Highlight building is troublesome, tedious and requires space mastery. The guarantee of profound learning is more exact ML calculations contrasted with ML with less or no component building.

4.0. ML APPROACH THROUGH DL PROCESSING

The framework can prepare 1 billion framework systems on only 3 machines in a few days, and it can scale to systems with more than 11 billion frameworks utilizing only 16 machines and where the adaptability

Table 6. Review of DL approach

Authors	Learning Approach	Outcome	Problem Identified
Zhou et al., 2012	DL technique using autoencoders	In a denoising autoencoder, there is one concealed layer which removes highlights, with the quantity of hubs in this shrouded layer at first being the same as the quantity of elements that would be separated.	Not Identified
Calandra et al., 2012	DL for online non-stationary and spilling data	The approaching this research specimen and examined tests are utilized to take in the new Deep convection system which has adjusted to the recently watched data.	Developed have a drawback of a versatile Deep convection system is the prerequisite for consistent memory utilization.
Chen et al., n. d.	Minimized stacked denoising autoencoders (mSDAs)	Methodology framed in this research underestimates clamor in SDA and generates stochastic slope for other improved algorithms to learn parameters.	The capacity of the proposed approach is not sufficient for the vast amount of data for ML and data mining approach.
Coates and Ng, 2011	Commodity-Off-The-Shelf High Performance Computing (COTS HPC)	The framework can prepare 1 billion parameter systems on only 3 machines in a few days, and it can scale to systems with more than 11 billion parameters utilizing only 16 machines using DistBelief.	This proposed framework COTS HPC is accessible to a bigger gathering of people alone which means for huge dataset,

is equivalent to that of DistBelief. In contrast with the manipulational assets utilized by DistBelief, the circulated framework system given COTS HPC is all the more for the most part accessible to a bigger gathering of people, making it a sensible option for other DL specialists investigating extensive scale models. Overall review of DL algorithm and it methodologiesare tabulated in Table 5.

4.1 Application of ANN in DL Algorithm

Artificial neural systems (ANNs) are a group of ML models motivated by natural neural systems. Natural Neurons are the center parts of the human cerebrum. A neuron comprises a cell body, dendrites, and an axon. It forms and transmitsdata to different neurons by radiating electrical signs. Every neuron gets info signals from its dendrites and produces yield signals along its axon. The axon branches out and interfaces using neurotransmitters to dendrites of different neurons as described in Figure 3. Counterfeit neurons are enlivened by Biological neurons, and attempt to define the model clarified above in a computational structure. An Artifical neuron has a limited number of inputs with weights related to them, and an initiation capacity (likewise called exchange capacity).

Feedforward Neural Networks are the most straightforward type of Artificial Neural Networks graphically illustrated in Figure 4. These systems have 3 sorts of layers: anInput layer, shrouded layer, and yield layer (Yu et al., 2011). In these systems, data moves from the info layer through the shrouded hubs (assuming any) and to the yield hubs. The following is a case of a completely associated feedforward neural system with 2shrouded layers. "Completely associated" implies that every hubis associated with every one of the hubs in the following layer. Note that, the quantity of shrouded layers and their size are the main free parameters. The bigger and more profound the shrouded layers, the more perplexing examples we can demonstrate in principle (Arel, 2010).

Figure 3.

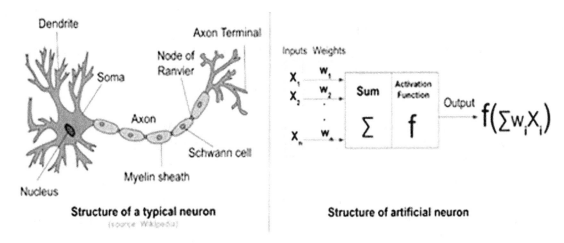

Figure 4.

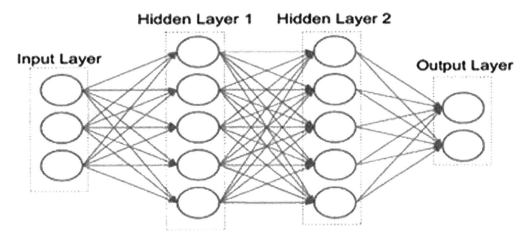

4.1.1 Implementation Challenges in DL

Now a days, there is most likely profound learning is one of the most blazing examination patterns in ML field. DL technique utilizes regulated and unsupervised procedures in profound designs to naturally learn various leveled representations (Bengio, et al., 2009). DL designs can regularly catch more confused, progressively propelled measurable examples of inputs for accomplishing to be versatile to new zones than conventional learning techniques and frequently beat best in class accomplished by hand-made elements (Collobert et al., 2011). DL based network(DBNs) (Bengio 2009; Le Callet et al., 2006) and Convolutional Neural Systems (CNNs) (Chen et al., 2014; Dahl et al., 2012) are two standard profound learning methodologies and exploration headings proposed over the previous decade, which have been settled in the profound learning field and demonstrated extraordinary guarantee for future work (Hinton et al., 2012)

Because of the best in class execution of DL, it has pulled in much consideration among research group for group discourse acknowledgment, PC vision, dialect handling, and data recovery (Bengio, 2009; Ciresan et al., 2010; Jones, 2014; Wange t al, 2011). DL technique assumes that huge data sets expanded preparing power and the advances in illustrations processors (Hinton et al 2012).. For instance, IBM's cerebrum like PC (Bengio et al., 2007; Baker, 2016) and Microsoft's continuous dialect interpretation in Bing's voice seek (Baker 2016) have utilized strategies like DL out how to influence big data for theupper hand.

DL algorithms utilizea gigantic measure of unsupervised data to consequently separate complex representation. These algorithms are to a great extent inspired by the field of computerized reasoning. Conversely, DL designs have the capacity, to sum up in non-nearby and worldwide ways, creating learning examples and connections past quick neighbors in the data (Bengio et al., 2013). DL is, indeed, a critical stride toward computerized reasoning. It not just gives complex representations of data which are appropriate for AI assignments additionally makes the machines free of human learning which is a definitive objective of AI. It removes representations specifically from unsupervised data without human obstruction.DL alludes to a class of Artifical Neural Systems (ANNs) made out of numerous handling layers (Bengio et al., 2013). ANNs existed for a long time, yet endeavors at preparing profound designs of ANNs fizzled until Geoffrey Hinton's leap forward work of the mid-2000s. Notwithstanding algorithmic advancements, the expansion in processing abilities utilizing GPUs and the gathering of bigger datasets are all figures that helped the late surge of profound learning (Wadhwa et al., 2014).

4.2 Application of DL in Big Data

As expressed already, DL algorithms remove significant dynamic representations of the crude data using a progressive multi-level learning approach. While DL can be connected to gain from named data on the off chance that it is accessible inadequately substantial sums, it is principally alluring for gaining a lot of unlabeled/unsupervised data (Bengio et al., 2013; Wu et al., 2016; Ali et al., 2016)., making it appealing for removing significant representations and examples from Big Data. DL algorithms are appeared to perform better at removing non-nearby and worldwide connections, and examples in the data, contrasted with generally shallow learning models (Bengio et al., 2014). Other helpful qualities of the learnt conceptual representations by DL include:

1. Generally basic straight models can work viably with the data acquired from the more mind boggling and more theoretical data representations,
2. Expanded computerization of data representation extraction from unsupervised data empowers its wide application to various data sorts.,
3. Social and semantic learning can be gotten at the more elevated amounts of reflection and representation of the crude data.

Considering each of the four Vs. of Big Data attributes, i.e., Volume, Variety, Velocity, and Veracity, DL algorithms and models are all the more apropos suited to deliver issues identified with Volume and Variety of Big Data Analytics (Deng, 2915). DL characteristically abuses the accessibility of enormous measures of data, i.e. Volume in Big Data, where algorithms with shallow learning chains of importance neglect to investigate and comprehend the higher complexities of data examples. Besides, since DL manages data reflection and representations, it is entirely likely suited for investigating crude data displayed in various arrangements and/or from various sources, i.e. Assortment in Big Data, and may minimize the requirement for contribution from human specialists to concentrate highlights from each new data sort saw in Big Data (Abdarbo et al., 2016). While displaying distinctive difficulties for more traditional data investigation approaches, Big Data Analytics presents an essential open door for creating novel algorithms and models to deliver particular issues identified with Big Data. For instance, the removed representations by DL can be considered as a pragmatic wellspring of data for basic leadership, semantic indexing, data recovery, and for different purposes in Big Data Analytics, and furthermore, straightforward, direct displaying procedures can be considered for Big Data Analytics when complex data is spoken to in higher types of deliberation (Najafabadi et al., 2015).

5.0 CHALLENGING IN MACHINE LEARNING WITH CORRESPONDING TO BIG DATA

In this present section, we present discussion about the issues of ML approaches with corresponding for the five different perspective (Hu et al., 2015) which has been explained in Figure 5 that includes learning of large-scale data, learning of different data types, learning of high-speed data streaming, learning of incomplete and uncertain data and learning of extracting the data that are valuable from the amount of data set.

Figure 5.

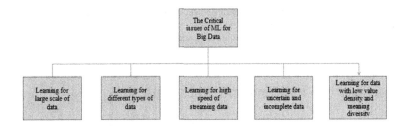

The Table 6 defines challenges that are related to big data analytics that observed from the existing literature. Through the observation of existing literatures challenges like processing of large datasets, uncertain datasets, high dimensional data, non-stationary difficulties are identified.

5.2. Implementation Challenge of DL in Big Data

This segment exhibits a few ranges of Big Data where DL needs encourage investigation, particularly, learning with spilling data, managing high-dimensional data, the versatility of models, and dispersed processing (Huang et al., 2006). The major challenges of the DL are (Ding et al., 2014)

- Incremental learning for non-stationary data
- High-dimensional data
- Large-scale models

Table 7. Challenges in big data analytics

Critical Parameters	Author Name	Drawbacks
Large Dataset (2015)	Wang et al., 2015	Taking just the computerized data as an example, consistently, Google alone needs to prepare around 24 petabytes. Also, on the off chance, it encourages other data sources, the data scale will turn out to be much greater.
Different data type (2011)	UK Archive, 2011	The tremendous assortment of data is the second measurement that makes enormous data both intriguing and testing. Learning with such a dataset, the colossal test is detectable, and the level of intricacy is not in any case believable before we profoundly arrive
High-speed streaming data (2015)	Gandomi and Haider, 2015	For huge dataset rate or learning rate or speed truly matters, which is another rising test for learning. The preparing results turn out to be less profitable or even useless. In these time-touchy cases, the potential estimation of data relies on upon data freshness that should be handled in a continuous way.
Learning for Uncertain and incomplete data	UK Archive, 2011	ML algorithms were regularly encouraged with generally exact data from surely understood and very restricted sources, so the learning results have a tendency to be unerring. The significance of tending to and dealing with the vulnerability and inadequacy on data quality.
Data with low-value density and meaning diversity	Wang et al., 2015; Vincent et al., 2010	Abusing an assortment of learning techniques to investigate enormous datasets, the last design is to concentrate significant data from monstrous measures of data as profound understanding or business advantages.
Incremental learning for non-stationary data	Vadivel et al., 2014; Reshef et al., 2011; Wang et al., 2011	This incremental component learning and mapping can enhance the discriminative or generative target capacity; be that as it may, monotonically adding elements can prompt having a considerable measure of excess elements and overfitting of data.
High-dimensional data	Kalanat et al., 2015	The utilization of DL algorithms for Big Data Analytics including high dimensional data remains to a great extent unexplored, and warrants advancement of DL based arrangements that either adjust approaches like the ones introduced above or create novel answers for tending to the high-dimensionality found in some Big Data areas.
Large-scale models	Coates, 2011	The system bolsters model parallelism both inside a machine (by means of multi-threading), and crosswise over machines (through message going), with the points of interest of parallelism, synchronization, and correspondence oversaw by DistBelief.

5.2.1. Incremental Learning for Non-Stationary Data

One of the testing perspectives in Big Data Analytics is managing spilling and quick moving info data. Such data investigation is valuable in observing errands, for example, extortion location. It is imperative to adjust DL to handle gushing data, as there is a requirement for algorithms that can manage a lot of nonstop info data. In this area, we talk about a few works connected with DL and spilling data, including incremental element learning and extraction (Shou et al., 2012), denoising autoencoders (Vincent et al., 2008), and profound conviction systems (Chen et al., n. d.). Zhou et al. (2012) portray how a DL calculation can be utilized for incremental component learning on big datasets, utilizing denoising autoencoders (Vincent et al., 2008). Denoising Autoencoders are a variation of autoencoders which extricate highlights from adulterated info, where the separated components are powerful to boisterous data and useful for order purposes. Zhou et al. show that the incremental element learning strategy rapidly localizes to the ideal number of components in a substantial scale web setting. This sort of incremental component extraction is helpful in applications where the conveyance of data changes as for time in monstrous online data streams. Incremental element learning and extraction can be summed up for other DL algorithms, for example, RBM (Wu et al., 2014), and makes it conceivable to adjust to anew approaching stream of online expansive scale data. In addition, it maintains a strategic distance from costly cross-acceptance investigation in selecting the quantity of components in expansive scale datasets. Calandra et al. (2012) present versatile profound conviction systems which exhibit how DL can be summed up to gain from online non-stationary and gushing data (Chen, n. d.). Their study abuses the generative property of profound conviction systems to emulate the specimens from the first data, where these examples and the new watched tests are utilized to take in the new profound conviction system which has adjusted to the recently watched data. Be that as it may, a drawback of a versatile profound conviction system is the prerequisite for consistent memory utilization.

5.2.2. High-Dimensional Data

Some DL algorithms can turn out to be restrictively computationally-costly when managing high-dimensional data, for example, pictures, likely because of the frequently moderate learning process connected with a profoundly layered chain of command of taking in data deliberations and representations from a lower-level layer to a more elevated amount layer. That is to say; these DL algorithms can be hindered when working with Big Data that shows big Volume, one of the four Vs connected with Big Data Analytics. A high-dimensional data source contributes intensely to the volume of the crude data, notwithstanding entangling gaining from the data. Chen et al. (nd) present minimized stacked denoising autoencoders (mSDAs) which scale successfully for high-dimensional data and is computationally quicker than standard stacked denoising autoencoders (SDAs). The quick preparing time, the capacity to scale to expansive scale and high dimensional data, and execution effortlessness make mSDA a promising technique with speak to a substantial group of onlookers in data mining and ML.

CNNs are another strategy which scales up adequately on high dimensional data. Analysts have taken preferences of CNNs on Image Net dataset with 256×256 RGB pictures to accomplish best in class results (Tsang et al., 2011; Fayyad et al., 1996). In CNNs, the neurons in the concealed layers units don't should be associated with the greater part of the hubs in the past layer, however just to the neurons that are in the same spatial zone. The utilization of DL algorithms for Big Data Analytics including high dimensional data remains to a great extent unexplored, and warrants advancement of DL based arrangements that either adjust approaches like the ones introduced above or create novel answers for tending to the high-dimensionality found out some Big Data areas.

5.2.3. Large-Scale Models

Dean et al. (2012) consider the issue of preparing a DL neural system with billions of parameters utilizing countless CPU centers, with regards to discourse acknowledgment and PC vision. A product system, DistBelief, is created that can use figuring bunches with a big number of machines to prepare extensive scale models. The system bolsters model parallelism both inside a machine (by means of multi-threading), and crosswise over machines (through message going), with the points of interest of parallelism, synchronization, and correspondence oversaw by DistBelief. What's more, the system additionally bolsters data parallelism, where numerous copies of a model are utilized to enhance a solitary goal (Hu, 2015). With a specific end goal to make vast scale appropriated preparing conceivable an offbeat SGD and additionally a dispersed cluster improvement methodology is produced that incorporates a disseminated usage of L-BFGS (Limited-memory Broyden-Fletcher-GoldfarbShanno, a semi Newton technique for unconstrained advancement). Coates et al. (2013) influence the moderately modest registering force of a bunch of GPU servers. All the more particularly, they build up their own particular framework (utilizing neural systems) taking into account Commodity-Off-The-Shelf High Performance Computing (COTS HPC) Innovation and present a fast correspondence foundation to arrange appropriated algorithms. The framework can prepare 1 billion parameter systems on only 3 machines in a few days, and it can scale to systems with more than 11 billion parameters utilizing only 16 machines and where the versatility is practically identical to that of DistBelief (Lopez-Moreno, 2016). In contrast with the computational assets utilized by DistBelief, the appropriated framework system taking into account COTS HPC is all the more for the most part accessible to a bigger group of onlookers, making it a sensible option for other DL specialists investigating extensive scale models.

Same like ML approach certain DL mechanisms were examined for its own functionality to its corresponding data type. The table 8 provides types of DL techniques and its corresponding supportable data type for analysis of data. From the review, it is observed that DDM technique will be applicable for high-dimensional dataset and large scale data will be analyzed using deep scaling models.

6. CONCLUSION

ML and DL has the leverage of possibly giving an answer for the location the data investigation and learning issues found in gigantic volumes of data. Both ML and DL techniques help in consequently extricating difficult data representations from vast volumes of unsupervised data. This makes it a significant instrument for big data analytics, which includes data examination from huge accumulations of crude data that is, for the most part, unsupervised and unsorted. The present study began to explain with a description of ML algorithm followed by issues faced in the ML algorithm and its possible remedies. Then it discusses the DL relationship between DL and ML and deep applications with that of the big data. At last, the challenges faced by the DL in the research trends have been discussed. Also, the present study aimed to implement a solution for particular issue i.e. Uncertain and incomplete dataset using the solution learning of uncertain and incomplete dataset with the use of Parkinson telecommunication dataset. In future, it would be more interesting in concentrating towards the trend one or a greater amount of these issues frequently seen in big data, hence accumulation the DL and big data analytics research corpus.

7. FUTURE SCOPE

This review article provides the detailed description of the application of ML approach to big data analytics. Specifically, this research concentrates on DL algorithm implementation in big data analytics. Further, this research provides implementation difficulties of the machine and DL algorithm in big data analytics. This research suggested that ML through DL approach enhances to medical data processing where it is described as Parkinson dataset. Usually, Parkinson dataset contains a large number of medical records which can be examined using Hadoop platform in future.

REFERENCES

Aakash, P. K., & Pushpalatha, S. (2016). A Survey on Applications of Artificial Neural Networks in Data Mining, Int. *J. Sci. Eng. Technol. Res.*, *5*, 1470–1473.

Abdrabo, M., Elmogy, M., Eltaweel, G., & Barakat, S., & (2016Enhancing Big Data Value Using Knowledge Discovery Techniques, I.*J. Inf. Technol. Comput. Sci.*, *8*, 1–12. Retrieved from http://www.mecs-press.org/ijitcs/ijitcs-v8-n8/IJITCS-V8-N8-1.pdf

Al-Jarrah, O. Y., Yoo, P. D., Muhaidat, S., Karagiannidis, G. K., & Taha, K. (2015). Efficient ML for Big Data: A Review. *Big Data Res.*, *2*(3), 87–93. doi:10.1016/j.bdr.2015.04.001

Ali, A., Qadir, J., Rasool, R., Sathiaseelan, A., Zwitter, A., & Crowcroft, J. (2016). Big data for development: Applications and techniques. *Big Data Anal.*, *1*(1), 2. doi:10.118641044-016-0002-4

Alsheikh, M. A., Lin, S., Niyato, D., & Tan, H.-P. (2014). ML in Wireless Sensor Networks: Algorithms, Strategies, and Applica. *IEEE Communications Surveys and Tutorials*, *16*(4), 1996–2018. doi:10.1109/COMST.2014.2320099

Arel, I., Rose, D., & Karnowski, T. (2010). Deep ML-A new frontier in artificial intelligence research. *IEEE Computational Intelligence Magazine*, *5*(4), 13–18. doi:10.1109/MCI.2010.938364

Baker, J. (2016). Artificial Neural Networks and DL, Lancaster. Retrieved September 27, 2016 from http://www.lancaster.ac.uk/pg/bakerj1/pdfs/ANNs/Artificial_neural_networks-poster.pdf

Bengio, Y. (2009). Learning Deep Architectures for AI, Found. Trends. *Machine Learning*, *2*(1), 1–127. doi:10.1561/2200000006

Bengio, Y., Courville, A., & Vincent, P. (2013). Representation learning: A review and new perspectives. *IEEE Transactions on Pattern Analysis and Machine Intelligence*, *35*(8), 1798–1828. doi:10.1109/TPAMI.2013.50 PMID:23787338

Bengio, Y., Courville, A., & Vincent, P. (2014). Representation Learning: A Review and New Perspectives. *IEEE Transactions on Pattern Analysis and Machine Intelligence*, *35*(8), 1798–1828. doi:10.1109/TPAMI.2013.50 PMID:23787338

Bengio, Y., & LeCun, Y. (2007). Scaling learning algorithms towards. In S. K. M. Large (Ed.), *L. Bottou, O. Chapelle, D. DeCoste, J. Weston* (pp. 321–360). Cambridge, MA: MIT Press.

Bengio Y. (2013) Deep Learning of Representations: Looking Forward. In A.H. Dediu, C. Martín-Vide, R. Mitkov et al., (Eds.), Statistical Language and Speech Processing, LNCS (Vol. 7978). Springer. doi:10.1007/978-3-642-39593-2_1

Boyd, S., Parikh, N., Chu, E., Peleato, B., & Eckstein, J. (2010). Distributed Optimization and Statistical Learning via the Alternating Direction Method of Multipliers, Found. *Machine Learning*, *3*(1), 1–122. doi:10.1561/2200000016

Calandra, R., Raiko, T., Deisenroth, M. P., & Pouzols, F. M. (2012). Learning deep belief networks from non-stationary streams. In Artificial Neural Networks and Machine Learning–ICANN 2012, LNCS (Vol. 7553, pp. 379–386). doi:10.1007/978-3-642-33266-1_47

Changwon, Y., & Ramirez, L. (2014). Juan. Liuzzi, Big data analysis using modern statistical and ML methods in medicine. *Int. Neurourol. J.*, *18*, 50–57. doi:10.5213/inj.2014.18.2.50 PMID:24987556

M. Chen, Z. Xu, K. Weinberger, F. Sha, Marginalized denoising autoencoders for domain

Chen, X., & Lin, X. (2014). Big Data Deep Learning: Challenges and Perspectives. *IEEE Access*, *2*, 514–525. doi:10.1109/ACCESS.2014.2325029 PMID:24963700

Ciresan, D. C., Meier, U., Gambardella, L. M., & Schmidhuber, J. (2010). Deep Big Simple Neural Nets Excel on Handwritten Digit Recognition. *Neural Computation*, *22*(12), 1–14. doi:10.1162/NECO_a_00052 PMID:19842986

Coates, A., Huval, B., Wang, T., Wu, D. J., Ng, A. Y., & Catanzaro, B. (2013). DL with COTS HPC systems. In Proc. of the 30th Int. Conf. Mach. Learn., Atlanta, Georgia. Retrieved from http://www.jmlr.org/proceedings/papers/v28/coates13.pdf

Coates, A., & Ng, A. (2011). The importance of encoding versus training with sparse coding and vector quantization. In *Proc. of the 28th Int. Conf. Mach. Learn* (pp. 921–928). Omnipress.

Collobert, R., Weston, J., Bottou, L., Karlen, M., Kavukcuoglu, K., & Kuksa, P. (2011). Natural language processing (almost) from scratch. *Journal of Machine Learning Research*, *12*(August), 2493–2537.

Dahl, G. E., Yu, D., Deng, L., & Acero, A. (2012). Context-dependent pre-trained deep neural networks for large-vocabulary speech recognition. *IEEE Trans. Audio, Speech Lang. Process.*, *20*(1), 30–42. doi:10.1109/TASL.2011.2134090

Dean, J., Corrado, G., Monga, R., Chen, K., Devin, M., Le, Q., & … . (2012). In P. Bartlett, F. Pereira, C. Burges, L. Bottou, & K. Weinberger (Eds.), *Large scale distributed deep network* (pp. 1232–1240). Retrieved from http://papers.nips.cc/book/advances-in-neural-information-processing-systems-25-2012

Deng, L., & Togneri, R. (2015). Deep Dynamic Models for Learning Hidden Representations of Speech Features. In Speech Audio Process. Coding, Enhanc. Recognit. (pp. 153–195). Springer. doi:10.1007/978-1-4939-1456-2_6

Ding, S. F., Xu, X. Z., & Nie, R. (2014). Extreme learning machine and its applications. *Neural Computing & Applications*, *25*(3-4), 549–556. doi:10.100700521-013-1522-8

Domingos, P. (2012). A few useful things to know about ML. *Communications of the ACM*, *55*(10), 78–87. doi:10.1145/2347736.2347755

Dong, L., Lin, Z., Liang, Y., He, L., Zhang, N., Chen, Q., & … (2016). A Hierarchical Distributed Processing Framework for Big Image Data. *J. Latex Cl. Files.*, *20*, 1–13.

Fayyad, U., Piatetsky-Shapiro, G., & Smyth, P. (1996). From Data Mining to Knowledge Discovery in Databases. *AI Magazine*, *17*, 37–54. doi:10.1609/aimag.v17i3.1230

Feng, J., & Darrell, T. (2015). Learning the Structure of Deep Convolutional Networks. In *Proceedings of the 2015 IEEE Int. Conf. Comput. Vis.* (pp. 2749–2757). 10.1109/ICCV.2015.315

Gandomi, A., & Haider, M. (2015). Beyond the hype: Big data concepts, methods, and analytics. *International Journal of Information Management*, *35*(2), 137–144. doi:10.1016/j.ijinfomgt.2014.10.007

Goodfellow, I. J., Erhan, D., Luc Carrier, P., Courville, A., Mirza, M., Hamner, B., ... Bengio, Y. (2015). Challenges in representation learning: A report on three ML contests. *Neural Networks*, *64*, 59–63. doi:10.1016/j.neunet.2014.09.005 PMID:25613956

Heger, D. A. (n. d.). An Introduction to Artificial Neural Networks (ANN) - Methods, Abstraction, and Usage. Retrieved from http://www.dhtusa.com/media/NeuralNetworkIntro.pdf

Hinton, G., Deng, L., Yu, D., Dahl, G., Mohamed, A. R., Jaitly, N., ... Kingsbury, B. (2012). Deep neural networks for acoustic modeling in speech recognition: The shared views of four research groups. *IEEE Signal Processing Magazine*, *29*(6), 82–97. doi:10.1109/MSP.2012.2205597

Hinton, G. E., Osindero, S., & Teh, Y.-W. Y. (2006). A fast learning algorithm for deep belief nets. *Neural Computation*, *18*(7), 1527–1554. doi:10.1162/neco.2006.18.7.1527 PMID:16764513

Hu, W., Qian, Y., Soong, F. K., & Wang, Y. (2015). Improved mispronunciation detection with deep neural network trained acoustic models and transfer learning based logistic regression classifiers. *Speech Communication*, *67*, 154–166. doi:10.1016/j.specom.2014.12.008

Huang, G.-B., Zhu, Q., & Siew, C. (2006). Extreme learning machine: Theory and applications. *Neurocomputing*, *70*(1-3), 489–501. doi:10.1016/j.neucom.2005.12.126

Imperva. (2015). Top Ten Database Threats. Retrieved from https://www.imperva.com/docs/gated/WP_TopTen_Database_Threats.pdf

Jacob, A. (2009). The pathologies of big data. *Communications of the ACM*, *52*(8), 36–44. doi:10.1145/1536616.1536632

Jolliffe, I. T. (2002). *Principal Component Analysis*. New York: Springer.

Jones, N. (2014). The learning machines. *Nature*, *505*(7482), 146–148. doi:10.1038/505146a PMID:24402264

Kalanat, N., & Kangavari, M. R. (2015). Data Mining Methods for Rule Designing and Rule Triggering in Active Database Systems. *Int. J. Database Theory Appl.*, *8*(1), 39–44. doi:10.14257/ijdta.2015.8.1.05

Karpinets, T. V., Park, B. H., & Uberbacher, E. C. (2012). Analyzing large biological datasets with association networks. *Nucleic Acids Research*, *40*(17), e131. doi:10.1093/nar/gks403 PMID:22638576

Kashyap, H., Ahmed, H. A., Hoque, N., Roy, S., & Bhattacharyya, D. K. (2014). Big Data Analytics in Bioinformatics: A ML Perspective. *J. LATEX Cl. FILES.*, *13*, 1–20.

Kaur, P., & Kaur, P. (2016). A Review on Cloud Computing: Backbone Technologies, Fundaments & Challenges. *Int. J. Eng. Appl. Sci. Technol.*, *1*, 123–129.

Koyuturk, M., Grama, A., & Ramakrishnan, N. (2005). Compression, clustering, and pattern discovery in very high-dimensional discrete-attribute data sets. *IEEE Transactions on Knowledge and Data Engineering*, *17*(4), 447–461. doi:10.1109/TKDE.2005.55

L. 0. Hall, N. Chawla, K.W. Bowyer, Decision Tree Learning on Very Large Data Sets, IEEE, 1998.

Landset, S., Khoshgoftaar, T. M., Richter, A. N., & Hasanin, T. (2015). A survey of open source tools for ML with big data in the Hadoop ecosystem. *J. Big Data.*, *2*(1), 24. doi:10.118640537-015-0032-1

Le Callet, P., Viard-Gaudin, C., & Barba, D. (2006). A convolutional neural network approach for objective video quality assessment. *IEEE Transactions on Neural Networks*, *17*(5), 1316–1327. doi:10.1109/TNN.2006.879766 PMID:17001990

Li, S., Dragicevic, S., Anton, F., Sester, M., Winter, S., Coltekin, A., ... (2015). Geospatial Big Data Handling Theory and Methods: A Review and Research Challenges. Retrieved from https://arxiv.org/ftp/arxiv/papers/1511/1511.03010.pdf

Looks, M., Levine, A., Covington, G. A., Loui, R. P., Lockwood, J. W., & Cho, Y. H. (2007). *Streaming Hierarchical Clustering for Concept Mining. In Proceedings of the 2007 IEEE Aerosp. Conf.* (pp. 1–12). IEEE. doi:10.1109/AERO.2007.352792

Lopez-Moreno, I., Gonzalez-Dominguez, J., Martinez, D., Plchot, O., Gonzalez-Rodriguez, J., & Moreno, P. J. (2016). On the use of deep feedforward neural networks for automatic language identification. *Computer Speech & Language*, *40*, 46–59. doi:10.1016/j.csl.2016.03.001

Lu, Y.-L., & Fahn, C.-S. (2007). Hierarchical Artificial Neural Networks for Recognizing High Similar Large Data Sets. In *Proceedings of the 2007 Int. Conf. Mach. Learn. Cybern.* (pp. 1930–1935). 10.1109/ICMLC.2007.4370463

Lynch, C. (2008). Big data: How do your data grow? *Nature*, *455*(7209), 28–29. doi:10.1038/455028a PMID:18769419

Mani, S., Shankle, W. R., Dick, M. B., & Pazzani, M. J. (1998). Two-Stage ML Model for Guideline Development. Retrieved from http://www.ics.uci.edu/~pazzani/Publications/two_stage_ml.pdf

Molodtsov, D. (1999). Soft set theory—First results. *Computers & Mathematics with Applications (Oxford, England)*, *37*(4-5), 19–31. doi:10.1016/S0898-1221(99)00056-5

Moujahid, A. (2016). A Practical Introduction to DL with Caffe and Python. Retrieved August 27, 2016 from http://adilmoujahid.com/posts/2016/06/introduction-deep-learning-python-caffe/

Mulanee, A., Shaikh, A., Dhavale, H., Lambate, S., & Teke, A. R. (2015). Database Security Against Intrusion. *Int. J. Adv. Eng. Glob. Technol.*, *3*, 560–566. http://ijaegt.com/wp-content/uploads/2014/12/409440-pp-560-566-shaik.pdf

Najafabadi, M. M., Villanustre, F., Khoshgoftaar, T. M., Seliya, N., Wald, R., & Muharemagic, E. (2015). DL applications and challenges in big data analytics. *J. Big Data.*, *2*(1), 1–21. doi:10.118640537-014-0007-7

Namey, E., Guest, G., Thairu, L., & Johnson, L. (2007). Data Reduction Techniques for Large Qualitative Data Sets. In G. Guest & K. M. MacQueen (Eds.), *Handbook for team-based qualitative research* (pp. 137–163). Rowman Altamira, United kingdom: Team-Based Qual. Res.

Natarajan, S., Joshi, S., Saha, B., Edwards, A., Khot, T., Moody, E., ... (2012). A ML Pipeline for Three-way Classification of Alzheimer Patients from Structural Magnetic Resonance Images of the Brain. *Int. J. Mach. Learn. Cybern.*, *5*, 659–669. Retrieved from http://pages.cs.wisc.edu/~tushar/papers/icmla12.pdf

Nithya, B. (2016). An Analysis on Applications of ML Tools, Techniques and Practices in Health Care System. *Int. J. Adv. Res. Comput. Sci. Softw. Eng.*, *6*(6), 1–8.

Patil, D. V., & Bichkar, R. S. (2006). A Hybrid Evolutionary Approach To Construct Optimal Decision Trees With Large Data Sets. In *Proceedings of the 2006 IEEE Int. Conf. Ind. Technol.* (pp. 429–433). 10.1109/ICIT.2006.372250

Pawlak, Z. (1982). Rough sets. *Int. J. Comput. Inf. Sci.*, *11*(5), 341–356. doi:10.1007/BF01001956

Peters, J. F. (2007). Near Sets. General Theory About Nearness of Objects. *Appl. Math. Sci.*, *1*, 2609–2629.

Qiu, J., Wu, Q., Ding, G., Xu, Y., & Feng, S. (2016). A survey of ML for big data processing. doi:. doi:10.1186/s13634-016-0355-x

Raja, C., & Rabbani, M. A. (2014). Big Data Analytics Security Issues in Data Driven Information System. *Int. J. Innov. Res. Comput. Commun. Eng.*, *2*, 6132–6135.

Rajkumar, D., & Usha, S. (2016). A Survey on Big Data Mining Platforms, Algorithms and Handling Techniques. Int. J. Res. Emerg. Sci. Technol., 3, 50–55. Retrieved from http://ijrest.net/downloads/volume-3/special-issue/ncrtct-16/pid-ijrest-3s1ncrtct2016018.pdf

Reshef, Y. A., Reshef, D. N., Sabeti, P. C., & Mitzenmacher, M. (2015). Theoretical Foundations of Equitability and the Maximal Information Coefficient. Retrieved from https://arxiv.org/pdf/1408.4908.pdf

Reshef, D. N., Reshef, Y. A., Finucane, H. K., Grossman, S. R., McVean, G., Turnbaugh, P. J., ... & Sabeti, P. C. (2011). Detecting novel associations in large data sets. *science*, *334*(6062), 1518-1524. doi:. doi:10.1126/science.1205438

Setia, L. (2008). Strategies for Content Based Image Retrieval. Albert-Ludwigs-University. Retrieved from https://www.freidok.uni-freiburg.de/fedora/objects/freidok:6150/datastreams/FILE1/content

Shirudkar, K., & Motwani, D. (2015). Big-Data Security. *Int. J. Adv. Res. Comput. Sci. Softw. Eng.*, *5*, 1100–1109.

Singh, A., Chaudhary, M., Rana, A., & Dubey, G. (2011). Online Mining of data to generate association rule mining in large databases. In *Proceedings of the 2011 Int. Conf. Recent Trends Inf. Syst.* (pp. 126–131). 10.1109/ReTIS.2011.6146853

Singh, P., & Suri, B. (2014). Quality assessment of data using statistical and ML methods. In L. C. Jain, H. S. Behera, J. K. Mandal, & D. P. Mohapatra (Eds.), *Comput* (2nd ed., pp. 89–97). Intell. Data Min.

Sivarajah, U., Kamal, M. M., Irani, Z., & Weerakkody, V. (2016). Critical analysis of Big Data challenges and analytical methods. *Journal of Business Research*. doi:10.1016/j.jbusres.2016.08.001

Suryawanshi, S. S., Mulani, T., Zanjurne, S., Inarkar, K., & Jambhulkar, A. (2015). Database Intrusion Detection and Protection System Using Log Mining and Forensic Analysis. *Int. J. Comput. Sci. Inf. Technol.*, *6*, 5059–5061.

Tsai, C., Lai, C., Chiang, M., & Yang, L. (2014). Data mining for internet of things: A survey. *IEEE Communications Surveys and Tutorials*, *16*(1), 77–97. doi:10.1109/SURV.2013.103013.00206

Tsai, C. W., La, C. F., Chao, H. C., & Vasilakos, A. V. (2015). Big data analytics: A survey. *J. Big Data.*, *2*(1), 1–32. doi:10.118640537-015-0030-3 PMID:26191487

Tsang, S., Kao, B., Yip, K. Y., Ho, W. S., & Lee, S. D. (2011). Decision trees for uncertain data. *Knowl. Data Eng. IEEE Trans.*, *23*(1), 64–78. doi:10.1109/TKDE.2009.175

Tulasi, B., Wagh, R. S., & Balaji, S. (2015). High Performance Computing and Big Data Analytics – Paradigms and Challenges. *International Journal of Computers and Applications*, *116*(2), 28–33. doi:10.5120/20311-2356

UK Data Archive. (2011). Managing and Sharing Data. Retrieved from http://www.data-archive.ac.uk/media/2894/managingsharing.pdf

Vadivel, M., & Raghunath, V. (2014). Enhancing Map-Reduce Framework for Bigdata with Hierarchical Clustering. *Int. J. Innov. Res. Comput. Commun. Eng.*, *2*, 490–498.

Vijayalakshmi, M., & Devi, M. R. (2012). A Survey of Different Issue of Different clustering Algorithms Used in Large Data sets. *Int. J. Adv. Res. Comput. Sci. Softw. Eng.*, *2*(3), 304–307. Retrieved fromhttp://www.ijarcsse.com/docs/papers/March2012/volume_2_Issue_3/V2I300137.pdf

Vincent, P., Larochelle, H., Bengio, Y., & Manzagol, P.-A. (2008). Extracting and composing robust features with denoising autoencoders. In Proc. of the 25th Int. Conf. Mach. Learn. ICML '08 (pp. 1096–1103). New York, NY: ACM. 10.1145/1390156.1390294

Wadhwa, A., & Madhow, U. (2014). Bottom-up DL using the Hebbian Principle. Retrieved from http://www.ece.ucsb.edu/wcsl/people/aseem/Aseem_stuff/hebbian_preprint.pdf

Wang, L., Wang, G., & Sng, D. (2015). DL Algorithms with Applications to Video Analytics for A Smart City: A Survey.

Wang, S., Gan, W., Li, D., & Li, D. (2011). Data Field for Hierarchical Clustering. *International Journal of Data Warehousing and Mining*, *7*(4), 43–63. doi:10.4018/jdwm.2011100103

Wang, Y., Yu, D., Ju, Y., & Acero, A. (2011). Voice search. In *Lang. Underst. Syst. Extr. Semant. Inf. from Speech*. New York: Wiley. doi:10.1002/9781119992691.ch5

Wille, R. (2005). Formal concept analysis as mathematical theory of concept and concept hierarchies. In Form. Concept Anal. Springer. doi:10.1007/11528784_1

Wu, C., Buyya, R., & Ramamohanarao, K. (2016). Big Data Analytics = ML + Cloud Computing. Retrieved from https://arxiv.org/ftp/arxiv/papers/1601/1601.03115.pdf

Wu, Q., Ding, G., Wang, J., & Yao, Y. D. (2013). Spatial-temporal opportunity detection for spectrum-heterogeneous cognitive radio networks: Two-dimensional sensing. *IEEE Transactions on Wireless Communications*, *12*(2), 516–526. doi:10.1109/TWC.2012.122212.111638

Wu, X., Zhu, X., Wu, G. Q., & Ding, W. (2014). Data mining with big data. *IEEE Transactions on Knowledge and Data Engineering*, *26*(1), 97–107. doi:10.1109/TKDE.2013.109

Yu, D., & Deng, L. (2011). DL and Its Applications to Signal and Information Processing. *IEEE Signal Processing Magazine*, *28*, 145–150. doi:10.1109/MSP.2010.939038

Zhou, G., Sohn, K., & Lee, H. (2012). Online incremental feature learning with denoising autoencoders. In Proceedings of the *Int. Conf. Artif. Intell. Stat.* (pp. 1453–1461).

Zhu, H., Xu, Z., & Huang, Y. (2015). Research on the security technology of big data information. In *Proceedings of the Int. Conf. Inf. Technol. Manag. Innov.* (pp. 1041–1044).

Chapter 32
Big Data Analytics With Machine Learning and Deep Learning Methods for Detection of Anomalies in Network Traffic

Valliammal Narayan

Avinashilingam Institute for Home Science and Higher Education for Women, India

Shanmugapriya D.

Avinashilingam Institute for Home Science and Higher Education for Women, India

ABSTRACT

Information is vital for any organization to communicate through any network. The growth of internet utilization and the web users increased the cyber threats. Cyber-attacks in the network change the traffic flow of each system. Anomaly detection techniques have been developed for different types of cyber-attack or anomaly strategies. Conventional ADS protect information transferred through the network or cyber attackers. The stable prevention of anomalies by machine and deep-learning algorithms are applied for cyber-security. Big data solutions handle voluminous data in a short span of time. Big data management is the organization and manipulation of huge volumes of structured data, semi-structured data and unstructured data, but it does not handle a data imbalance problem during the training process. Big data-based machine and deep-learning algorithms for anomaly detection involve the classification of decision boundary between normal traffic flow and anomaly traffic flow. The performance of anomaly detection is efficiently increased by different algorithms.

INTRODUCTION

Over the past decades, the significance of cyber-security has increased and developed as a general branch of an individual life that is associated with a computer or a mobile phone. When a person submits his/ her information via online, it becomes susceptible to cyber-attacks or cyber-crimes like hijacking or

DOI: 10.4018/978-1-6684-3662-2.ch032

unauthorized access, injection of virus, malware, etc. As a result, authorized access via web services is offered by cyber-security. This chapter summarizes the significance of cyber-security, how it can be developed and the considered key points during the selection of a cyber-security service provider.

The cyber world is expanding rapidly day by day and more and more people are getting connected to this world, resulting in generation of a large amount of data called Big Data. Big data is large in both quantity and quality and can be efficiently used to analyze certain patterns and behaviour anomalies which can help us prevent or be prepared for the thread or any upcoming attack. This proactive and analytical approach will help us greatly reduce the rate of Cyber Crimes and also get the knowledge out of that data which was not previously observable. Big Data analytics using machine learning techniques have a major and evolving role to play in cyber security (M.D. Anto Praveena, 2017) as in Figure 1 The cyber security problems can now impact every aspect of modern society, from hospitals, banks, and telecoms to governments and individuals.

Figure 1. Overview of the Big Data Analytics for Cyber Security

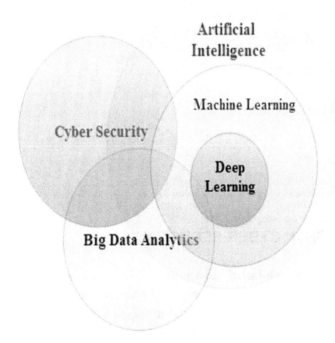

The battle against cyber security breaches is fought along the four dimensions of Prevention, Preparation, Detection, and Response. Over the last decade, the security industry seems to have largely given up on Prevention, but that is a topic for another day. It is in the dimensions of Preparation and Detection that Big Data Analytics capabilities are being used to identify anomalous patterns and to connect the dots across diverse systems and data sets. The data may be categorized into transaction and interaction data, entity data, systems operations data, reference data, and activity logs data. Big Data analytics using artificial intelligence techniques will self-learn normal patterns by observing a data flows under normal operations (Sebestyen.G, 2017).

CYBER SECURITY

Several aspects of human survival rely on the computer networks including interactions, transportation, administration, economics, medication and academic. Cyber-security, also known as computer security or Information Technology (IT) security involves the prevention of those systems from thievery or damage to their components or electronic data. There are different cyber-security standards or techniques available to protect the cyber environment of a user or organization. The major goal is reducing the threats by preventing or mitigating the cyber attacks from unintended or unauthorized access (Craigen, 2014). Due to this, authorized access and a secure data transmission are provided to the user.

Principles of Cyber-Security

The core principles of cyber-security are:

- SECRECY: The secrecy level of sensitive data is unchanged and shared only with authorized users.
- Reliability: Data should maintain its reliability and not be changed from its original state.
- Accessibility: Systems and data should be accessible to those who want it.

Cyber-Security Techniques

- Access Control and password security
- Authentication of data
- Malware scanners
- Firewalls
- Anti-virus software

ANOMALY DETECTION IN CYBER SECURITY

Anomaly detection considers that a hijacker can acquire access to his/her required targets and is powerful in infringing a given security policy. While unwanted activities occur during the data transmission without any interference, anomaly or intrusion detection takes place to offer warning information that something went mistaken and to respond in a suitable manner. The existence of a security policy that declares which activities are assumed malicious and must be protected is an indispensable for an anomaly/intrusion detection system. Infringes may only be identified while activities are compared against given rules (Ahmed, 2014b).

Mostly, Anomaly Detection Systems (ADS) are designed for detecting anomalies or intrusions against a target network satisfying the following requirements:

- Accuracy
- Performance
- Completeness
- Fault tolerance

- Scalability

WHY ANOMALY DETECTION FOR CYBER SECURITY IS IMPORTANT?

The increasing amount and complexity of cyber security risks including aiming phishing scams, information thievery and other web susceptibilities insist that people remain attention about protecting their computers and data. A typical vulnerable system linked to the network can be compromised in moments (Balabine, 2018). Each and every day, thousands of spoiled web pages are being exposed and billions of files have been involved in information infringes. New attack models are launched endlessly. Below Figure 2 shows the top 20 countries with appropriate percentage levels of cyber-crime.

Figure 2. Cyber-Crime: Top 20 Countries

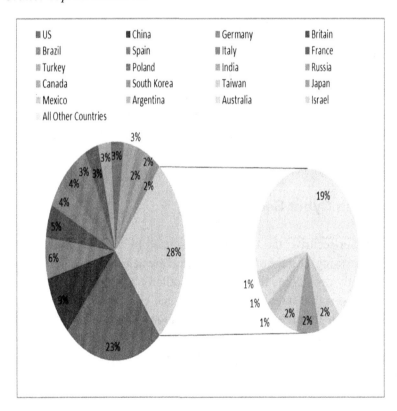

Anomaly Detection Methods

In a networked atmosphere, information security has been a foremost concern for network manager and security personnel who has the complete responsibility for network security, since the networks are under risk by adversaries. Creation of new information from previous information becomes more crucial when data from multiple sources are integrated. An anomaly may get access to significant information and they may share or steal the information, causing harm to the network and applications operating on the database. Several methods and techniques have been considered for securing the data from one place to another (Deljac, 2015). Some methods include:

- **Authentication:** Technology that requires user authentication before using the system or network. There are different levels of authentication like verifying the user with one-factor authentication (user id and password), two-factor authentication (security token) or three-factor authentication (fingerprint).
- **Packet Inspection:** It analyzes the data of a bundle as it passes an investigation point, hunting down convention rebelliousness, infections, spam, oddities or characterized criteria for choosing whether the parcel may pass or in the event that it requires to be directed to an alternate goal or for the utilization of gathering the measurable data.
- **Signature Detection:** It screens the packets in the system and contrasts them and pre-designed and pre-decided assault designs.

Fundamental Methodology of ADS

- **Parameterization***:* Information is pre-processed to get pre-established formats such that it is suitable or along with the targeted system's behaviour.
- **Training phase:** A model is constructed based on the normal or abnormal behaviour of a system. Depending on the considered type of anomaly detection, different ways of training are chosen. It can be both automatic and manual.
- **Detection phase:** Once the model for the system is constructed, it is compared with the observed traffic. If the observed variance exceeds from a fixed threshold, then a warning will be triggered.

Anomaly Detection in Cyber Security

In networks used for cyber-security, the traffic is dominated by periodical data flows. Normally, the data acquisition, pre-processing, storage and visualization are achieved in a periodical way and thus the traffic related to these activities adopts the similar periodicity. Moreover, the order of the activities is somehow stable. This quasi-stable state may change if a malicious code tries to penetrate in the system or if few types of physical malfunction occurred and the system reacts with some countermeasures. These both cases may be classified as anomalies (Ahmed, 2015). According to these observations, an anomaly discriminator is defined as an important change in the pattern of the packets transmitted on the network. The pattern may be detected through the following characteristics:

- Frequencies of different types of packets
- Order of different types of packets
- Lengths of different packet types
- Delays between different packets

In the training phase, the program may recognize the types of packets transferred via the network, their periodicity, the typical length and the order of the packets by using a network sniffer component. Occasionally, these data are a-priori recognized by the physical system's designer or by the control systems developer. Likewise, in some industrial networks, the traffic pattern is set in the configuration phase and it is firmly forced via a MAC protocol. Any change in this pattern is called as an anomaly.

In less restricted networks, few pattern characteristics can still be identified and converted into anomaly detection rules. In a training phase, a sniffer program may decide all the package types transmitted through the network, their length interval and recurrence frequency. Any major variation from normal values is considered as a candidate for an anomaly. Sporadic packets do not have a normal repetition time, but even in this case, a minimum frequency may be estimated from the physical phenomena or component that initiated it. For example, in a CAN network (i.e., car), the frequency of packets transmitted by the rotation sensor located on the engine cannot exceed the maximum rotation frequency of that engine. Multiple detection points should be established in a regular way, in different points of the network structure.

The cyber security breaches include external attacks and internal attacks. The reason for abnormality might be a pernicious action or some sort of interruption as shown in Figure 3. This abnormal behaviour found in the dataset is interesting to the analyst and this is the most important feature for anomaly detection. In this system, to detect the anomaly by solely monitor its cyber system footprint in network. Thus, we focus on monitoring applications network behaviour and aim to detect unexplained changes any time they occur.

Figure 3. Anomaly Detection in cyber Security

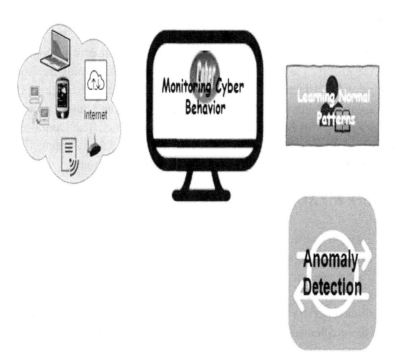

Motivation for Anomaly Detection

The aim of anomaly detection technique is their probable to detect previously unseen anomalies events. The security breaks are exceptionally basic now in the general public and associations neglect to take viable measures. Today digital assaults are regular in the general population managing an account area, wellbeing associations, protection, and administration division, so associations are have to give preparing and rules, approach changes, venturing up mindfulness programs. So our point is to plan for successful answers for maintain a strategic distance from the digital lawbreakers, infections, malware, etc.

Types of Anomalies

An anomaly may be classified into the following types:

- **Point Anomaly***:* When specific information is varied from the normal pattern of the data, it may be known as a point anomaly. For instance, if a normal car fuel usage is six litres per day but if it becomes sixty litres in any random day, then it is a point anomaly. Example of this anomaly is Remote-to-User (R2U) and User-to-Root (U2R) since these are condition specific and sophisticated.
- **Contextual Anomaly:** When information acts anomalously in a specific context, it is known as a contextual or conditional anomaly. For instance, expenses on a credit card during festivals are normally higher than during the remaining days. Though it may be high, it may not be anomalous since high expenditures are contextually normal in nature. Conversely, an equally high expense during a non-festive day could be believed as a contextual anomaly. Probe attacks are considered as a contextual anomaly since these are based on the particular intention for attaining information and exploration.
- **Collective Anomaly:** When a collection of similar information acts anomalously with respect to the entire data, the group of information is called a collective anomaly as shown in Figure 4. For instance, in an individual Electro Cardiogram (ECG) output, the existence of low values for a long duration indicates an outlying phenomenon corresponding to an abnormal premature contraction, whereas one low value by itself is not considered as anomalous. The Denial-of-Service (DoS) attacks are categorized under collective anomaly. In DoS attack, many connection requests to a web server is a collective anomaly; however, a single request is legitimate.

General Framework for ADS

Figure 5 shows the general framework for ADS or network anomaly detection. The input data requires processing since the data or packets are different types. For instance, the IP addresses are hierarchical whereas the protocols are categorical and port numbers are statistical in nature. Data processing techniques are performed based on the anomaly detection techniques which are classified into two types, namely supervised and unsupervised. To evaluate the output, either scores or labels are used.

The following are the challenges addressed in anomaly detection techniques:

- A lack of generally applicable anomaly detection technique; for instance, an anomaly detection technique in a wired network may be of modest utilization in a wireless network.
- The information contains noise which tends to be a genuine anomaly and therefore is complex for segregation.
- A lack of widely accessible labelled dataset to be used for anomaly detection.

Figure 4. Types of Anomaly

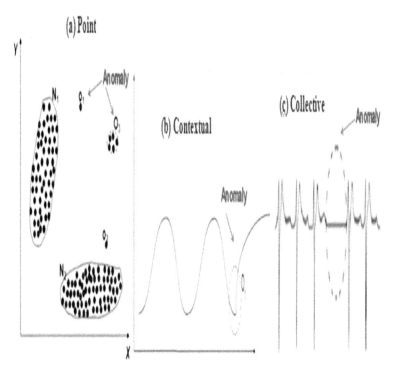

Figure 5. General Framework for ADS

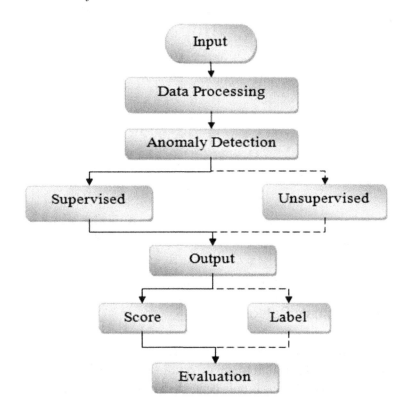

- As normal characteristics are frequently evolving and may not be normal, existing anomaly detection techniques may not be practical in the prospect [8]. A need for novel and more sophisticated techniques has been increased since the impostors are alert of the general techniques.

Classification of Anomaly Detection Techniques

Figure 6 illustrates the taxonomy of anomaly detection techniques. The detection of anomalies includes:

- Classification-based techniques
- Statistical-based techniques
- Clustering-based techniques
- Information theory techniques

Figure 6. Taxonomy of Anomaly Detection Techniques

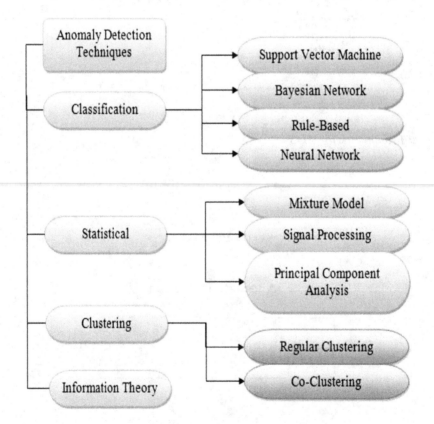

Classification-Based Anomaly Detection

These techniques rely on expert's general information of the network attacks behaviours. When a network expert provides characteristics information to the detection system, an attack with a known pattern is identified as soon as it is established. This is only dependent on the attack's signature as a system which is able to detect an attack solely if its signature has been provided prior by a network expert. This concludes a system which can identify only what it knows is susceptible to new attacks which are always emerging in different versions and more surreptitiously established. Even if a novel attack's signature is generated and incorporated in the system, the primary loss is unique and the restore process is particularly high-priced.

Classification-based techniques rely on the normal traffic activities that construct the knowledge base and consider the activities diverge from baseline characteristics as anomalous. The benefit lies in their ability to identify the attacks which are fully new, considering that they reveal sufficient divergences from the normal characteristics. Also, when normal attack not incorporated in the knowledge base is assumed as an attack, there will be unintentional false alarms. As a result, training is needed for anomaly detection techniques for constructing normal activity characteristics which are time-consuming and also depends on the availability of fully normal traffic database. Besides, it is very complex for maintaining a normal characteristic up-to-date due to modern dynamic network atmospheres (A. Meshram, 2017). Four major clustering-based techniques are:

- Support Vector Machine (SVM)
- Bayesian Network
- Neural Network
- Rule-Based

Statistical-Based Anomaly Detection

Some anomaly detection techniques have been designed by using statistical theories. For instance, a chi-square theory is used for detecting an anomaly. Based on this technique, a profile of normal events in a given system is generated. The fundamental concept of this technique is detecting a large departure of events from a normal as anomalous and intrusions. The anomaly is detected based on the following three major features:

- Type of request
- Length of request
- Payload distribution

Three main types of statistical-based anomaly detection techniques include:

- Mixture Model
- Signal processing technique
- Principal Component Analysis (PCA)

Information-Theory-Based Anomaly Detection

Information-theoretic measures such as entropy, conditional entropy, relative entropy, information gain and information cost are also used for detecting anomalies by describing the characteristics of a given dataset. According to these measures, suitable anomaly detection models have been constructed. Supervised anomaly detection techniques need a training dataset followed by test data for evaluating the accuracy of a model. In this case, information-theoretic measures are initially used for computing whether a model is suitable for testing the new dataset.

Clustering-Based Anomaly Detection

Typically, clustering is an unsupervised learning algorithm that does not need pre-labelled data for extracting the rules to combine similar information. This technique is mainly classified as regular and co-clustering. The major difference between these two clustering is the processing of rows and columns. Regular clustering technique such as k-means is used to cluster the data considering the rows of the dataset whereas the co-clustering considers both rows and columns of the dataset simultaneously for creating clusters (Ahmed, 2014a). The following three key statements are prepared while clustering-based techniques are used for detecting anomalies:

- **Statement 1:** Since clusters of only normal data are created, some following new data that do not robust with existing clusters of normal data are considered as anomalies. For instance, noise is considered as anomalous as density-based clustering algorithms do not contain noise inside the clusters.
- **Statement 2:** While a cluster has both normal and anomalous information, it has been discovered that the normal information lies near to the closest clusters centroid, but anomalies are far away from the centroids. Under this statement, anomalous events are identified by using a distance score.
- **Statement 3:** In a clustering with clusters of different sizes, a smaller and sparser may be considered as anomalous whereas a thicker is normal. Instances belonging to the clusters of sizes or densities below than a threshold are considered as anomalous.

Two main types of clustering-based anomaly detection techniques follow:

- **Regular Clustering:** This is the simplest technique to detect anomalous information. Mostly, k-means clustering is used for generating the normal and anomalous clusters. After generating the clusters, these are analyzed by using the above-mentioned statements. In Syarif et al. [21], different clustering algorithms were investigated while they have been applied for detecting anomalies through the network.
- **Co-clustering:** It is used to generate the clusters of both rows and columns simultaneously. Initially, a clustering criterion is defined and then it is optimized. It simultaneously discovers the subsets of rows and columns of a data matrix by using a particular criterion. The advantages of this technique over regular clustering are the following:
  - The simultaneous combination of both rows and columns may provide a more compressed representation and it maintains information enclosed in the original data.
  - It may be assumed as a dimensionality reduction technique and it is most suitable to create novel features.
- A considerable reduction in computational complexity. Such as, k-means clustering algorithm has a computational complexity as $O(mnk)$ where m is the number of rows, n is the number of columns and k refers to the number of clusters. However, the co-clustering algorithm has a computational complexity as $O(mkl+nkl)$ wherein l refers to the number of column clusters.

The comparison of these techniques shown in Table 1 is evaluated based on the following criteria:

- Computational complexity: Linear, quadratic and exceptional
- Preference of attack detection: DoS, Probe, R2U and U2R
- Output: Label and score

Table 1. Comparison of Anomaly Detection Techniques

Technique	Output	Attack Priority	Complexity
Classification-based	Label, score	DoS	Quadratic
Statistical-based	Label, score	R2U, U2R	Linear
Clustering-based	Label	DoS	Quadratic
Information Theory-based	Label	Neutral	Exponential

From this comparison in Table 1, the anomaly detection techniques which only have the labelled output are more efficient than the score-based outputs. In this analysis, clustering and information theory-based techniques are improved than the classification and statistical-based techniques. When the priority of attack detection is concerned, the classification and clustering-based techniques are more involved in identifying the DoS attacks. The reasons behind why clustering and classification-based techniques have the quadratic complexity are:

- Clustering techniques have need of pair wise distance computation.
- Classification techniques require quadratic optimization for separating two or more classes.

The information theory based techniques have exponential complexity due to the computation of the measurements such as entropy, relative uncertainty, etc. As well, these techniques require dual optimization to minimize the subset size and simultaneously reduce the complexity in the dataset. From this analysis, it is concluded that these techniques cannot be applied to data streams which are evolving and need to be mined in a single iteration. Above all, these anomaly detection techniques are used for monitoring a single system or network by carrying out local analysis for attacks. Hybrid techniques based on big data analytics are very essential which consist of different sensors for collecting data.

BIG DATA ANALYTICS

The term Big Data is characterized for the informational collections that are extremely expansive or complex that customary informational index handling application programming is deficient or can't manage these intricate or substantial informational indexes. The significant contrast between custom and huge information is as far as volume, velocity, and variation. For better understanding, these are outlined as in Figure 7.

Figure 7. Five V's of Big Data

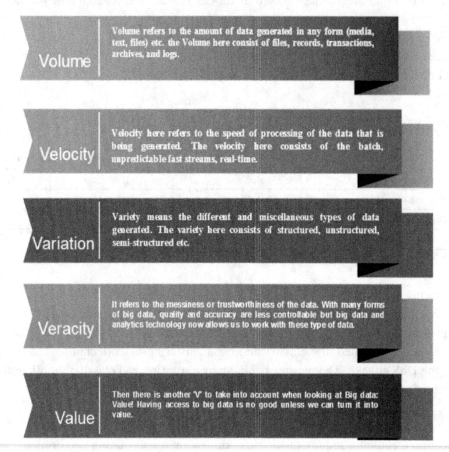

Big Data analysis need to store efficient data and to query large data sets, thus the techniques which make complete data sets instead of sampling are focused. These implications are in areas like machine learning, deep learning etc.

Data Availability

Today data is generated and stored in various sectors. That data may be video, image, audio and text files. Data availability in different sectors are listed as follows,

- Banking
- Social Networks & Smart phones
- Communication & Media
- Legacy Documents
- Education
- Resource Industries

Security Analysis for Big Data

The security of Big Data has also become one of the most challenging factors. As the data sets are increasing dramatically the storage and analysis also increases and because of that security should be increased as an unauthorized person can also download the data of a particular person and can harm him. Different surveillance tools and trackers are used to track the attacker but as the data is increasing the security also should increased. Overall, collection, storage, analysis and usage of personal data are now part of our everyday life at all levels of security. A solution for this problem can be data hiding. In this, the data can be hiding in the form of a pattern which only the analyst can decode. These data sets should also not be recognizable by the data collector otherwise the data can be leaked to the unauthorized party. But it is a difficult for large number of data sets. Big Data Analytics in cyber security includes the capacity to accumulate a huge measure of computerized data to investigate, picture and draw knowledge that can make it conceivable to foresee and stop digital assaults. The focus is on learning the cyber attack patterns both known and unknown so that the data can be more authenticated and secure. Theft of information, disruption of services, and unauthorized disclosures are believed to be the most serious cyber security threats. To reduce these risks the detection of anomaly and different attacks are taken into concerned. The big data sources are to be taken into considerations so that the security analysis can be more secure. Table 2 shows the sources of big data.

Table 2. Big data sources for security analysis

S.NO	Types of Data	Data sources
1	System-Based Data	IP Locations, Keyboard typing/Mouse click stream patterns etc
2	Mobile-Based Data	GPS Locations, Network Locations etc
3	Travel Data	Travel patterns, Sources, Destinations etc
4	Credential Data	User name & Password
5	OTP	One Time Passwords which are used for online access
6	Digital Certificates	Used for the authentication
7	Biometric Identification Data	Fingerprints, Iris, Speech Recognitions
8	Social Media Data	Face book, Google Drive, Twitter etc
9	Human Resource data	Organizational role and privilege of the user.

The focus is on learning the cyber attack patterns both known and unknown so that the data can be more authenticated and secure. Some examples of how to make big data secure are given as follows which can increase the efficiency of data. These are used for detecting and analyzing abnormal patterns related to server manipulations.

- **Network Traffic**: Detecting and analyzing the network traffic for the suspicious sources and destinations and unauthorized accesses of third party users with abnormal traffic patterns.
- **Network Sources**: Detecting and predicting abnormal user patterns from the sources the data is transmitting.

- **User Credentials**: Detecting anomalies with respect to a user, or a group of users of their transmission or access time.
- **Network Servers**: A Network Server is a computer system which is used as a central repository or data and various programs that are shared within a network.

Big Data Analytics Layers

Big data analytics has the following four layers for superior performance,

- **Data Layer:** This layer has RDBMS based structured data, Semi-structured and unstructured based data. NoSQL databases are used to store the unstructured data. For instance, MongoDB and Cassandra are the NoSQL databases. Streaming data from the web world, social media domain, data from IoT sensors and operational systems are the examples to unstructured and semi-structured data. Software tools such as HBase, Hive, HBase, Spark and Storm are also sitting at this layer. Hadoop and Map Reduce also support this layer.
- **Analytics Layer:** Analytics layer has the environment to implement the dynamic data analytics and deploy the real time values. It has building models developing environment and modify the local data in regular interval. This also improves the performance of the analytical engine.
- **Integration Layer:** This layer integrates the end user applications and analytical engine. This includes usually a rules engine and an API for dynamic data analytics.
- **Decision Layer:** This layer is where the end product hits the market. It includes applications of end user such as mobile app, desktop applications, interactive web applications and business intelligence software. This is the layer where people interact with the system. Each and every layer described above is associated with different sets of end users in real time and enables a crucial phase of real time data analytics implementation.

Types of Data Analytics Approaches

- **Descriptive Analytics**: Descriptive analytics can be said to be the starting stage of data processing which does a summarization of historical data to get out useful information.
- **Diagnostic Analytics**: Diagnostic analytics is type of advanced analytics which gets to the root of the notion why certain thing happened with techniques like drill down, data discovery etc.
- **Predictive Analytics:** This analytics procedure is used to determine or predict the future events on the basis of previous behaviors, by the techniques of data mining, modeling etc.
- **Prescriptive Analytics**: This analytics approach deals with finding of best course of action to take after certain situation. This in layman's terms is the remedy to take in consideration after certain situations.

Big Data Analytics Procedure

- **Collection of data from many sources:** In this step, the collection of data takes places from different sources. This collected data has variety of nature, some might be structured some might be unstructured. This collected data also needs to be stored for further processing.

- **Maintaining the data consistency**: In this step, the different nature data is taken and then pre-processing (the process of transforming raw data into understandable format) is done on it to make that data even. Different techniques of data pre-processing are shown in Table 3.

Table 3. Data pre-processing

Data Cleaning	It is the process of filling out unavailable information, removing noise from data and deleting unwanted value.
Data Integration	Data is taken and put together with different representation to resolve the conflicts within the data sets.
Data Transformation	The data is normalized i.e. the redundancy from the data is removed and is generalized
Data Reduction	After the data is pre-processed it is then reduce so that it can be integrate into the data warehousing where the analytical process will take place on this data

- **Perform Correlation**: In this process after the data is entered into the data warehouse the correlation and dependencies of one data set is checked with other data set to possibly find out that to which extent those sets fluctuate together.
- **Positive Correlation:** If the correlation between the data sets comes out to be positive then we can get the extent of those data sets decrease or increase in parallel i.e. they are directly proportional to each other.
- **Negative Correlation:** If the correlation between the data sets comes out to be negative then we can make out to the extent to which one data set increases as other decreases i.e. they are inversely proportional to each other.

The Role of Big Data Analytics in Cyber Security

In this modern era, cyber security has come into the big data analytics. The emergence of big data not only modifies the human lifestyle and effort, but also inherently modifies the research mode. Due to the rapid development of information technology, i.e., networking, the applications of big data have become an essential part in human's life. Conversely, as increasingly valuable information can be acquired, security issues fix huge awareness. The cyber security or network security has huge challenges due to the complexity of increased networks. Commonly, big data cannot be solved by conventional techniques in a specific time due to the complexity of network traffic and attack patterns; therefore novel techniques must be provided to deal with big data, namely machine learning and deep learning algorithms.

Generally, big data analytics can incorporate methods and techniques, hardware and software to gather, handle and analyze a large-scale structured and unstructured data in real-time. Nowadays, big data analytics provides a number of solutions in different ways and few of them are follows:

- It offers end-to-end visibility.
- It permits self-organization among network functions and entities.
- It allows evaluation of long-term dynamics of the network
- It constructs faster and proactive network.
- It facilitates energy efficient network functions.
- It enables a unified performance evaluation.

BIG DATA AND MACHINE LEARNING IN CYBER SECURITY

Machine learning algorithms can gather, analyze and process the information. In case of cyber security, these algorithms help for analyzing previous cyber-attacks efficiently and providing respective defence responses. Primarily, this approach enables an automated cyber defence system with a minimum-skilled cyber security power. When distributed by Google, 50-70% of emails on Gmail are spam. With the aid of these algorithms, Google makes it feasible to block those superfluous communications with the highest accuracy. Likewise, Apple takes benefit of these algorithms for protecting its user's private information and confidentiality [9].

With the use of machine learning algorithms, ADS can be automated and even deployed in real-time to detect malfunctions before any harm is achieved. For instance, a well-trained machine learning model will have the ability for detecting an abnormal traffic pattern on the network and removing these links as occurs. In addition to this, it also has the capability to detect the new samples of anomaly that may evade human generated signatures and maybe quarantine these samples before they may even execute. Also, a machine learning model trained on the common operating system of a given endpoint can able to detect when the endpoint itself is engaging in odd activities, maybe at the request of a malicious insider trying to thieve or destroy the susceptible information. Most of the machine learning algorithms in cyber security acts as warning or alerting system. They frequently require an individual in the loop for making the final decision with sufficient accuracy (Lee.B, 2018).

The rapid growth of internet usage includes a huge amount of data transmitting on the web or internet. It is not possible to analyze big data directly for individuals. The detection of events which have malicious activities becomes more challenging with increasing amount of data or traffic flow on the network. So, cyber security domain wants to strengthen their infrastructure by using machine learning algorithms. Therefore, combined these algorithms with big data analytics helps to increase the ability to perform previously impractical computations. Big data and machine learning are two modules which are balancing each other. Machine learning and data analytics will include significance to both government administrations and private organizations in supporting them battle cyber threats. Meanwhile, they must construct defense system that can tolerate more and more sophisticated cyber-attacks. Therefore, with increasing number of cyber-attacks from intruders, advances in big data and machine learning algorithms are more essential than ever. The classification of machine learning algorithms for cyber security applications is shown in following figure.

The advantages and disadvantages of using machine learning algorithms using big data for cyber security are summarized in Table 4.

ML and Big Data Analytics Methods for Cyber Security

This section describes a machine learning (ML) and big data analytics (BDA) methods for cyber security in support of anomaly detection. As cyber threats continue to evolve, combining BDA and ML capabilities as part of a more powerful approach to cyber security. Cyber assaults are expanding at a fast pace and are currently methodically focused towards defenceless nations. The developing number of online clients and their information is further compounding the circumstance (Alexandra L Heureux, 2017). What's more, there is an interconnection between advanced utilization and the clients in basic business parts, for example, keeping the money, which is offering ascend to cyber wrongdoings like never before previously.

Figure 8. Classification of machine Learning Algorithms for Cyber Security

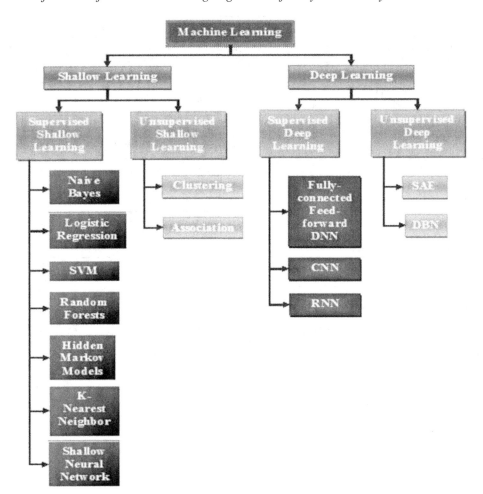

Datasets

The cyber security data sets for BDA and ML are given below:

- Packet Level Data
- Net flow Data
- Public Data Sets

Packet Level Data

Protocols are used for transmission of packet through network. The network packets are transmitted and received at the physical interface.

- Packets are captured by API in computers called as pcap.
- For Linux it is Libpcap and for windows it is WinPCap.

Table 4. Comparison of Machine Learning Algorithms with Big Data Analytics in Anomaly Detection.

Methods	Merits	Demerits
SVM	Insensitivity to input data dimension. High training rate and decision rate. Better learning ability for small data samples.	Inadequate to binary classifiers which cannot provide additional data about detected attack type. Longer training time.
DT	High detection accuracy. Operates better with large-scale datasets.	Computationally demanding to construct the trees.
LR	Linear models can be updated simply by means of new data. It is easy to understand and explain how decisions are made. It can be regularized for avoiding over fitting problem. More robust.	Its performance is poor when there are multiple or non-linear decision boundaries. Inflexible to obtain more complex patterns and high time consumption.
NB	It can integrate both prior knowledge and data. It can determine probabilistic relationships among the variables of interest.	It is not consider as a better classifier while the prior knowledge is inaccurate. Inflexible to manage continuous features.
RF	They can able to deal with unbalanced and missing data. Runtime is quite fast. Better performance on several problems including non-linear. Less computation cost for training process.	They may over-fit data that are specifically includes noise. No interpretability. Need to select the number of trees.
K-means	It is the most popular since its easiness. Flexible to pre-processed data and meaningful features.	The user should specify the number of clusters. It generates poor clusters if the true underlying clusters in the data are not spherical.

- Ethernet port have payload called as IP payload

Major Steps in ML Net Flow Data

It is introduced as a router feature by Cisco. Version 5 defines unidirectional flow of packets.

- The packet attributes: ingress interface, source IP address, destination IP address, IP protocol, source port, destination port and type of services.
- Net flow includes compressed and preprocessed packets.

ML is a data analysis method that automates building of an analytical model using algorithms that learn from data which can be easily automated, and find insights in the data without being explicit programming as to where to look. Machine Language is a computer program that learns from experience with respect to some class of task and performance measure. ML has three phases such as training, validation, and testing. To decide which best model of the alternatives is, the selection should be based on the performance of the model against validation data and not on the accuracy on test data set. The following steps are performed:

- Identify the features from training data.
- Identify the subset of attributes necessary for classification.

- Learn model using training data.
- Use trained model to classify unknown data and predict result accurately.

ML/BDA Framework

In this system, the idea is to deploy a platform that aggregates and manages big data, and to combine this with a machine learning algorithm that analyzes this data to uncover hidden patterns and detect anomalies. As cyber security methodologies advance to ensure against programmers, programmers are growing progressively complex systems to sidestep these assurances. Utilizing machine figuring out how to computerize their assaults, programmers are making breaks increasingly more hard to identify. Malignant performing artists can utilize machine figuring out how to robotize the determination of the exploited people most defenceless against their dangers. They can likewise utilize machine figuring out how to discover feeble purposes of digital protection frameworks or to grow new advancements that sidestep security programming. Here, the fundamental element for machine learning is big data analytics. Machine learning analyzes this information to find patterns, correlations, and anomalies within the big data. It means processing massive amounts of security data and distilling it into something more readable for security teams (Hirak Kashyap, 2014). So, the simple detection of security events isn't useful unless it's understandable to human beings. When machine learning technology processes and organizes data, security teams are able to assess anomalies within the vast amount of data as in Figure 9.

BDA and ML are part of a single architecture, a powerful duo that together can protect against even the most complex anomalies. A solid cyber security stage requires inbuilt information the board stage that gathers and sorts out huge information, in the mix with machine learning calculations that examine this information, react to assaults, and counteract against new assaults. Without big data analytics and machine learning, it would be impossible for security professionals to gather and organize the heaps of security events and to interpret all potential attacks. While security experts will dependably have an imperative task to carry out in choosing the proper behaviour on these occasions, the job of machine learning is to distil the lot of information into data. Using machine learning for automate anomaly detection and response to produce quick and robust cyber defense system. There are three main types of ML/BDA approaches:

- Unsupervised
- Semi-supervised
- Supervised

Computational Complexity of ML and BDA Methods

Factors that determine performance of ML and BDA methods in cyber security are as below:

- Accuracy
- Time for training a model
- Time for classifying unknown
- Instance of trained model
- Readability of final solution

Figure 9. ML/BDA framework for anomaly detection in cyber security system

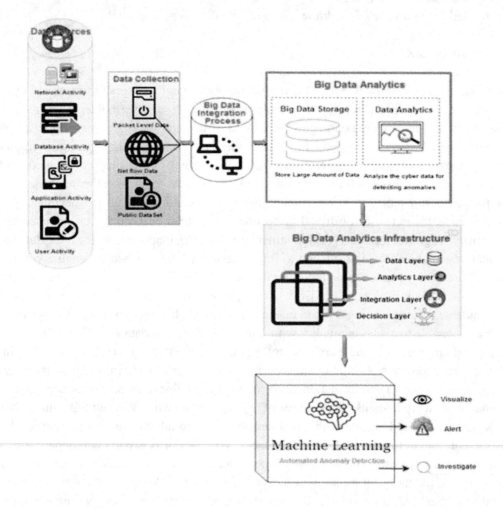

If one were to compare the accuracy of several ML/BDA methods, those methods should be trained on exactly the same training data and tested on exactly the same testing data. Unfortunately, even in the studies that used the same data set, when they compared their results with the best methods from the big data, they did so in an imperfect fashion. It used a subset of the big data set, but not necessarily the same subset that the other method used. So, the accuracy of these outcomes is not equivalent. The time for training a model is an important factor due to ever changing cyber-attack types and features. Indeed, even abnormality indicators should be prepared as often as possible, maybe gradually, with crisp anomaly signature refreshes.

Time for classifying a new instance is an important factor that reflects the reaction time and the packet processing power of the intrusion detection system. Understand ability or readability of the classification model is a means to help the administrators examine the model features easily in order to patch their systems more quickly. This information (such as packet type, port number, or some other high level network packet feature that reflects the cyber-attack footpath) will be available through the feature vectors that are tagged by the classifier as an anomaly category.

There are some peculiarities of the cyber problem that make ML and BDA methods more difficult to use. They are especially related to how often the model needs to be retrained. A fertile area of research would be to investigate the methods of fast incremental learning that could be used for daily updates of models for anomaly detection. In order to stay ahead, cyber defence systems need to deploy deep learning algorithms that are just as or even more powerful and complex.

BIG DATA AND DEEP LEARNING IN CYBER SECURITY

Large-scale organizations such as Google, Microsoft and Amazon are analyzing a huge amount of data for business analysis and decisions, forcing conventional and advanced technology. Likewise, social media organizations such as Facebook, Twitter and YouTube have billions of users that frequently generate an extremely high quality of data. Mining and extracting consequential patterns from huge input data for decision-making and prediction is at the core of big data analytics (C. L. Philip Chen, 2016). Big data analytics poses distinctive challenges for machine learning and data analysis including highly distributed input sources, noisy and poor quality data, high dimensionality data reduction, scalability, imbalanced input data, inadequate supervised/labeled data, unsupervised and uncategorized data, parallel and distributed computing, integration of heterogeneous data, innovating novel models for big data analysis, etc. As a result, big data and deep learning are two high-focus of cyber security in upcoming years. Deep learning algorithms known Deep Neural Network (DNN) can extract high-level and complex abstractions as data representations by means of a hierarchical learning process. Complex deliberations are scholarly at a given dimension dependent on to some degree simpler reflections detailed in the learning of tremendous measure of unsupervised information, making it a valuable device for big data analytics where raw data is mostly unlabeled and uncategorized.

Deep learning algorithms are one promising opportunity of research into an automated removal of complex data representations at high levels of abstraction. Such algorithms build a layered, hierarchical architecture of learning and representing data where higher-level features are defined in terms of lower-level features. The hierarchical learning architecture of deep learning algorithm is encouraged by artificial intelligence emulating the deep, layered learning process of the main sensorial regions of the neocortex in the human mind which naturally removes highlights and reflections from the basic information. Deep learning algorithms are relatively valuable for extracting the meaningful representations and patterns from big data while dealing with learning from huge number of unsupervised data and normally learn data representations in a greedy layer-wise manner (Anna L, 2016).

Once the hierarchical data abstractions are learnt from unsupervised data with deep learning, several traditional discriminative models can be trained with the help of comparatively smaller number of supervised or labeled data points where the labeled data is usually discovered via human or expert input. Mainly, deep learning algorithms have better performance to extract non-local and global relationships and patterns in the data compared to the shallow learning manner. When there are other helpful features of deep learning based representations of data, the most specific features of the learnt abstract representations by deep learning and big data analytics comprise:

- Comparatively uncomplicated linear models may perform efficiently with the knowledge attained from the more complex and more abstract data representations.

- Improved automation of data representation and extraction from unsupervised data may facilitate its broad application to different data types such as image, textual, audio, etc.
- Relational and semantic knowledge may be acquired at higher-levels of abstraction and representation of the raw data.

The advantages and disadvantages (Maryam M Najafabadi, 2015) of using deep learning algorithms using big data for cyber security are summarized in Table 5.

Table 5. Comparison of Deep Learning Algorithms with Big Data Analytics in Anomaly Detection.

Methods	Merits	Demerits
DBN	Supervised learning method with unlabelled data iteratively for significant feature or attribute representations	High computational cost due to extensive initialization process by huge number of parameter.
CNN	Robust supervised deep learning with high competitive performance Scalability is increased and the training time complexity is reduced with new features of CNN. Automatically learn features from security raw data	High computational cost. Challenge: Implementation on resource-constrained systems to support on-board security systems.
RNN	Better performance using sequential data	Key disadvantage: the problem of diminishing or exploding gradients.

In the broader field of machine learning, the recent years have witnessed proliferation of deep neural networks, with unprecedented results across various application domains (Bilal Jan, 2017). Deep learning is subset of machine discovering that accomplishes great execution and adaptability by figuring out how to speak to the information as settled progression of ideas inside layers of neural system. Deep learning is the element of artificial neural networks and related machine learning algorithms that contain more than one hidden layer.

Deep learning is a piece of a more extensive group of machine learning strategies dependent on learning portrayals of information. One of the guarantees of profound learning is supplanting carefully assembled highlights with proficient calculations for unsupervised or semi-directed element learning and progressive element extraction. Profound learning beats the customary machine learning as the size of information increments as shown in Figure 10. In recent years, deep learning-based anomaly detection algorithms have become increasingly popular and have been applied for diverse set of tasks. Therefore, the following figure has shown that deep learning completely surpasses traditional methods.

Motivation for DL/BDA Anomaly Detection System in Cyber Security

Performance of traditional algorithms in detecting anomalies is sub-optimal on complex cyber security data sets. As the volume of dataset increases, it becomes nearly impossible for the traditional methods to scale such large scale data. Deep anomaly detection techniques learn hierarchical discriminative features from data. This automatic feature learning capability reduces the need of feature engineering process in machine leaning system. Therefore, this lack of well defined challenges is resolved by DL/BDA algorithms in cyber security.

Figure 10. Performance Comparisons of Deep learning Vs Traditional Algorithms

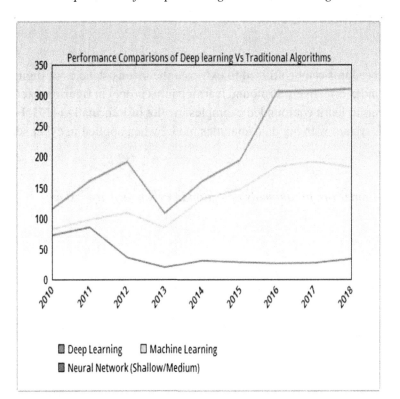

DL/BDA Framework

In order to protect legitimate users from anomaly, machine learning based efficient anomaly detection methods are developed. In the classical machine learning methods, the process of anomaly detection is usually divided into two stages: *feature extraction and classification/clustering*. The performance of traditional detection approaches critically depend on the extracted features and the methods for classification/clustering. The challenge associated in anomaly detection problems is the sheer scale of data, for instance considering data as bytes a certain sequence classification problem could be of the order of two million time steps. Furthermore the anomaly is very adaptive in nature, wherein the attackers would use advanced techniques to hide the anomaly behavior. Deep learning techniques address these challenges effectively and detect anomaly in greater approach.

The substantial advances are made by deep learning methods then compared to many machine learning problems. In recent years a number of new deep learning based anomaly detection techniques with greatly reduced computational requirements have been developed. Based on training objectives employed and availability of labels, deep learning-based anomaly detection techniques can be categorized into supervised, unsupervised, hybrid, and one-class neural network. For each category of techniques are described as follows,

- Supervised deep anomaly detection
- Semi-supervised deep anomaly detection

- Unsupervised deep anomaly detection
- One class neural network (OC-NN).
- Hybrid Models

Deep learning procedures can be utilized to extricate the inconsistencies of digital security in enormous informational index effectively. Profound learning joins propel in figuring force and extraordinary sorts of neural systems to learn confounded examples in a lot of information [17]. Figure 11 shows the generalization of DL system with big data analytics model when applied in cyber security for anomaly detection.

Figure 11. DL/BDA framework for anomaly detection in cyber security system.

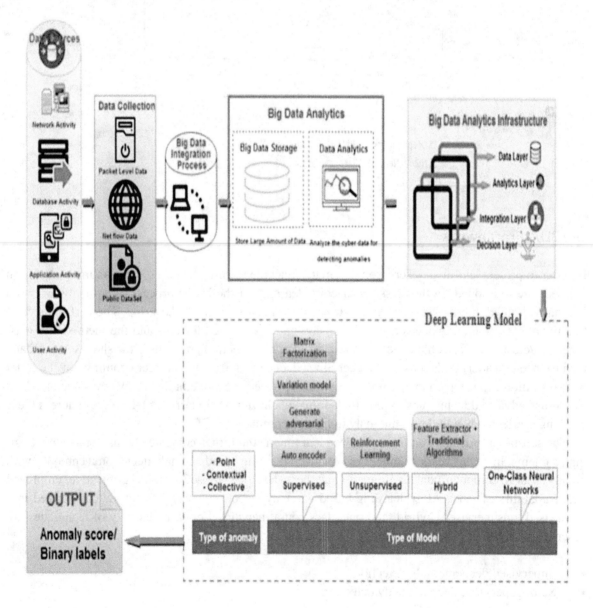

Big data technologies help enhance cyber security by improving the maintenance, storage, and analysis of security data. Anomaly occurs in the cyber space. Big Data analytics grants positive aspects of handle and process the large amount of data in efficient way. In response, DL needs to reinvent itself for big data analytics.

Output of DL/BDA Techniques

A critical aspect for anomaly detection methods is the way in which the anomalies are identified. In general, the outputs produced by anomaly detection techniques classified as follows,

- **Anomaly Score:** Anomaly score describes the level of outliers for each data point. The data instances may be ranked according to anomalous score, and a domain specific threshold (commonly known as decision score) will be selected by subject matter expert to identify the anomalies.
- **Binary Labels:** Instead of assigning scores, some techniques may assign a category label as normal or anomalous to each data in-stance. Unsupervised anomaly detection techniques using auto encoders measure the magnitude of residual vector (i,e reconstruction error) for obtaining anomaly scores, later on the reconstruction errors are either ranked or threshold by domain experts to label data instances.

ANOMALY DETECTION DATASETS AND ISSUES

Few openly available network traffic datasets for anomaly detection are mainly based on the modern operating systems and hardware. On the other hand, various researches committed to the improvement of benchmark anomaly detection evaluation datasets are presently being undertaken (Chen X-W, 2015). Some of the datasets are listed in below:

- PREDICT: Protected Repository for the Defence of Infrastructure against Cyber Threats (PREDICT) is a US-based commune of creators of security-relevant network functions data and consists of researchers of networking and data security. This dataset is useful for developers and evaluators by providing frequently updated network data related to the cyber-security research.
- CAIDA: It offers fundamental confined network traces, yet it is not labelled and requires multiple-attack scenarios (Ozlem Yavanoglu, 2017).
- Internet Traffic Archive: It is a repository to support common access to traces of network traffic and is supported by ACM SIGCOMM. Nonetheless, it undergoes from deep anonymization, requires the required packet information which is not labeled and has no multiple-attack scenarios (M. Bhuyan, 2014).
- DEFCON: It is entirely conflicting from real network traffic and consists mostly of anomaly traffic and commonly used for the alert correlation technique.
- ADFA Intrusion Detection Datasets: It encloses both Linux and Windows that are designed for the evaluation by a system call-based host-based ADS.
- NSL-KDD: It is a dataset suggested to solve few inherent issues of the KDD dataset stated in testing intrusion detection systems.
- KYOTO: It has traffic data from Kyoto University's Honeypots.

- ISCX 2012: It is designed by Information Security Centre of Excellence at University of New Brunswick. It includes seven days captured traffic with overall 2450324 flows with DoS attacks (Donghwoon Kwon, 2017).
- ICS Attack: Oak Ridge National Laboratories (ORNL) have generated three datasets which consist of measurements relevant to electronic transmission system normal, disturbance, control and cyber attack characteristics.

PERFORMANCE METRICS

Typically, the analysis of ADS performance using the various machine and deep learning algorithms with big data analytics is carried out based on the confusion matrix that defines the relationship between the actual data and predicted data of anomalies. During the detection process, each predicted data will belong to one of the four following possible outcomes that evaluate the accuracy of each algorithm:

- True Positive (TP) is actual positive data which are exactly detected as positives.
- True Negative (TN) is the actual negative data which are detected exactly as negatives.
- False Positive (FP) is known negative data which are wrongly predicted as positives.
- False Negative (FN) is known positive data which are wrongly predicted as negatives.

Table 6. Primary Metrics for Anomaly Detection.

Metric	Formula
Accuracy	$\dfrac{TP + TN}{TP + FP + FN + TN}$
Recall/Sensitivity	$\dfrac{TP}{TP + FN}$
Specificity	$\dfrac{TN}{TN + FP}$
Precision	$\dfrac{TP}{TP + FP}$
F-measure	$2 \times \dfrac{Precision \times Recall}{Precision + Recall}$
G-Mean	$\sqrt{Sensitivity * Specificity}$
AUC	$\dfrac{1 + TP - FP}{2}$

Likewise, the Receiver Operating Curve (ROC) also used for analyzing the efficiency of anomaly detection algorithms. Usually, ROC is the variation between accuracy on positive data and inaccuracy on negative data. As well, Area Under the Curve (AUC) performance differs between 0 and 1; the worst performance is indicated by 0 and the best performance is indicated by 1. The primary metrics used for anomaly detection are listed in Table 6.

The complexities of conventional anomaly detection techniques are addressed. To overcome such complexities, machine and deep learning with big data analytics to handle the numerous amounts of data while detecting the anomalies through the network. From Table 3 and 4, the advantages and disadvantages including their effectiveness of both machine and deep learning with big data analytics for cyber-security are discussed, respectively. It is concluded that big data deep learning algorithms achieve higher performance than the big data machine learning algorithms since these do not have the capability of solving the data imbalance issue due to high-dimensional large-scale datasets. As well, deep learning algorithms simplify the big data analytics process by automatically extracting the complex data representations from numerous amounts of unsupervised and un-categorized raw data.

CONCLUSION AND FUTURE SCOPE

With the advancement of the Internet, attacks are changing quickly and the cyber security circumstance isn't hopeful. Since machine learning techniques can gradually achieve human-like learning, it is becoming tightly associated with big data analytics.

Datasets for cyber security are very important for training and testing systems. The ML and DL methods do not work without representative data, and obtaining such a dataset is difficult and time-consuming. However, there are many problems with the existing public dataset, such as uneven data, outdated content and the like. Big Data analytics has become the greatest assets in the current scenario to handling this kind of difficult task. It has powerful techniques to make large set of data retrieval, management and storage in a great way. Deep Learning is an area of Machine Learning which applies neuron like mathematical structures for learning tasks.

A great deal of attention has been given to machine learning over the past several years. Nowadays, new deep learning techniques are emerging with improved functionality. Many computer applications actively utilize such deep learning algorithms and report enhanced performance through them. In this chapter, we present an overview of machine and deep learning methodologies, including big data analytics relevant to anomaly detection in cyber security. From this analysis, Deep learning is discovered and proves the best technique with state-of-the-art performances.

In the future, the vision of cyber-security involves the technologies which may be implemented along with the advanced hybrid algorithms applied by the security experts. These suggest near-term detections based on novel innovations and a number of logical evolutionary patterns. Generally, this logical evolution is a bottom-up process wherein the features are detected across a specific application and then verified for synergistic impacts. Moreover, quantum computing will establish to increase the computing speed directly as twice as conventional computing speed. Further, dynamic networks will apply to support higher levels of automation, self-healing, reconfigurability and performance. More significantly, the new cyber-security experts will be trained to explain cross domain crises and problems. Novel tools will support them.

REFERENCES

Ahmed, M., & Mahmood, A. N. (2014). Clustering based semantic data summarization technique: a new approach. *2014 IEEE 9th Conference on Industrial Electronics and Applications (ICIEA),* 1780-1785. 10.1109/ICIEA.2014.6931456

Ahmed, M., & Mahmood, A. N. (2014a). Network traffic analysis based on collective anomaly detection. *2014 IEEE 9th Conference on Industrial electronics and applications (ICIEA),* 1141-1146. 10.1109/ICIEA.2014.6931337

Ahmed, M., & Mahmood, A. N. (2014b). Network traffic pattern analysis using improved information theoretic co-clustering based collective anomaly detection. In *International Conference on Security and Privacy in Communication Systems,* (pp. 204-219). Cham, Switzerland: Springer.

Ahmed, M., & Mahmood, A. N. (2015). Novel approach for network traffic pattern analysis using clustering-based collective anomaly detection. *Annals of Data Science, 2*(1), 111–130. doi:10.100740745-015-0035-y

Balabine, I., & Velednitsky, A. (2018). *Method and system for confident anomaly detection in computer traffic.* Google Patents.

Bhuyan, M., Bhattacharyya, D., & Kalita, J. (2014). Network anomaly detection: Methods, systems and tools. IEEE Commun. Surv. Tuts., 16(1), 303–336.

Buczak, A. L., & Guven, E. (2016). A Survey of Data Mining and Machine Learning Methods for Cyber Security Intrusion Detection. IEEE Communications Surveys & Tutorials, 18(2).

Chen, C. L. P. (2016). Big Data Challenges, Techniques, Technologies, and Applications and How Deep Learning can be Used. *Proceedings of IEEE 20th international conference on Computer supported cooperative work in design.*

Chen, X.-W., Lin, X. (2014). Big data deep learning: challenges and perspectives. *IEEE Access, 2,* 514–525.

Craigen, D., Diakun-Thibault, N., & Purse, R. (2014). Defining cyber security. *Technology Innovation Management Review, 4*(10).

Deljac, Ž., Randić, M., & Krčelić, G. (2015). Early detection of network element outages based on customer trouble calls. *Decision Support Systems, 73,* 57–73. doi:10.1016/j.dss.2015.02.014

Jan, B., Farman, H., Khan, M., Imran, M., Islam, I. U., Ahmad, A., ... Jeon, G. (2017). Deep learning in big data Analytics: A comparative study. *Computers and Electrical Engineering.*

Najafabadi, M. M., Villanustre, F., Khoshgoftaar, T. M., Seliya, N., Wald, R., & Muharemagic, E. (2015). Deep learning applications and challenges in big data analytics *Journal of Big Data 2*(1), 1. doi:10.118640537-014-0007-7

Kashyap, H., Ahmed, H. A., Hoque, N., Roy, S., & Bhattacharyya, D. K. (2014). Big Data Analytics in Bioinformatics: A Machine Learning Perspective, *Journal of Latex Class Files, 13*(9). Retrieved from https://data-flair.training/blogs/deep-learning-vs-machine-learning/

Kwon, D., Kim, H., Kim, J., Suh, S. C., Kim, I., & Kim, K. J. (2017, September). A survey of deep learning-based network anomaly detection. *Cluster Computing,* 1–13.

L'heureux, A., Grolinger, K., Elyamany, H. F., & Capretz, M. M. (2017). Machine learning with big data: Challenges and approaches. (Vol. 5). IEEE.

Lee, B., Amaresh, S., Green, C., & Engels, D. (2018). Comparative Study of Deep Learning Models for Network Intrusion Detection. *SMU Data Science Review, 1*(1), 8.

Meshram, A., & Haas, C. (2017). *Anomaly detection in industrial networks using machine learning: a roadmap.* In *Machine Learning for Cyber Physical Systems.* Berlin, Germany: Springer. doi:10.1007/978-3-662-53806-7_8

Praveena, M. A., & Bharathi, B. (2017, February). A survey paper on big data analytics. In *2017 International Conference on Information Communication and Embedded Systems (ICICES)*(pp. 1-9). IEEE.

Sebestyen, G., & Hangan, A. (2017). Anomaly detection techniques in cyber-physical systems. *Acta Universitatis Sapientiae Informatica, 9*(2), 101–118.

Wang, J., & Paschalidis, I. C. (2017). Botnet detection based on anomaly and community detection. *IEEE Transactions on Control of Network Systems 4*(2), 392-404.

Yavanoglu, O., & Aydos, M. (2017). A review on cyber security datasets for machine learning algorithms. *IEEE International Conference on Big Data.* 10.1109/BigData.2017.8258167

This research was previously published in the Handbook of Research on Machine and Deep Learning Applications for Cyber Security; pages 317-346, copyright year 2020 by Information Science Reference (an imprint of IGI Global).

Chapter 33
Big Data Analytics and Mining for Knowledge Discovery

Carson K. Leung
https://orcid.org/0000-0002-7541-9127
University of Manitoba, Canada

ABSTRACT

Big data analytics and mining aims to discover implicit, previously unknown, and potentially useful information and knowledge from big data sets that contain huge volumes of valuable veracious data collected or generated at a high velocity from a wide variety of rich data sources. Among different big data analytic and mining tasks, this chapter focuses on frequent pattern mining. By relying on the MapReduce programming model, researchers only need to specify the "map" and "reduce" functions to discover (organizational) knowledge from (i) big data sets of precise data in a breadth-first manner or depth-first manner and/or from (ii) big data sets of uncertain data. Such a big data analytics process can be sped up by focusing the mining according to the user-specified constraints that express the user interests. The resulting (constrained or unconstrained) frequent patterns mined from big data sets provide users with new insights and a sound understanding of users' patterns. Such (organizational) knowledge is useful is many real-life information science and technology applications.

INTRODUCTION

Progresses in information science and technology have enabled the collection and generation of huge volumes of valuable data—such as streams of banking, financial, marketing, organizational, and transactional data—at a high velocity from a wide variety of rich data source in various real-life business, engineering, education, healthcare, hospitality and tourism, scientific, as well as social applications and services in government, organizations and society. These *big data* (Madden, 2012; Leung, 2015; Bellatreche et al., 2019) may be of different levels of veracities (e.g., precise data, imprecise and uncertain data) and/or of a variety of types or formats (e.g., structured data in relational databases; semi-structured data in extensible markup language (XML) or JavaScript object notion (JSON) format stored in document-oriented or graph databases; unstructured data in images, audios and videos). Embedded in the big data

DOI: 10.4018/978-1-6684-3662-2.ch033

is implicit, previously unknown, and potentially useful information and knowledge. However, the big data come with volumes beyond the ability of commonly-used software to capture, manage, and process within a tolerable elapsed time. Hence, new forms of information science and technology—such as *big data analytics and mining for knowledge discovery*—are needed to process and analyze the big data so to as enable the enhanced decision making, insight, and process optimization. For instance, the discovery of organizational knowledge (e.g., common customer complaints, main causes of employee turnover, sets of popular merchandise items in shopping carts)—via techniques like big data analysis, statistics, and business analytics—helps reveal important patterns about an organization. This organizational knowledge helps executive and management teams of the organization to get a better understanding of the organization so that they could make better use of human resources and technology, focus more on education and growth, keep customers top of mind, and further improve quality of services and products. To a further extent, the discovery of organizational knowledge and its subsequent actions help the organization to meet goals, gain competitive advantage, and ultimately ensure sustainability, organizational growth and development.

Over the past two decades, algorithms have been proposed for various big data analytics, mining and knowledge discovery—including clustering (which groups similar data together), classification (which categorizes groups of similar data), outlier detection (which identifies anomalies), and frequent pattern mining (which discovers interesting knowledge in the forms of frequently occurring sets of merchandise items or events). Many of these algorithms use the *MapReduce* model—which mines the search space with distributed or parallel computing (Shim, 2012). Among different big data analytics and mining tasks, this chapter focuses on applying the MapReduce model to big (organizational) data for the discovery of frequent patterns.

BACKGROUND

Since the introduction of the research problem of *frequent pattern mining* (Agrawal, Imieliński, & Swami, 1993), numerous algorithms have been proposed (Hipp, Güntzer, & Nakhaeizadeh, 2000; Ullman, 2000; Ceglar & Roddick, 2006; Aggarwal, Bhuiyan, & Al Hasan, 2014; Leung et al., 2017c). Notable ones include the classical Apriori algorithm (Agrawal & Srikant, 1994) and its variants such as the Partition algorithm (Savasere, Omiecinski, & Navathe, 1995). The Apriori algorithm uses a level-wise breadth-first bottom-up approach with a candidate generate-and-test paradigm to mine frequent patterns from transactional databases of precise data. The Partition algorithm divides the databases into several partitions and applies the Apriori algorithm to each partition to obtain patterns that are locally frequent in the partition. As being locally frequent is a necessary condition for a pattern to be globally frequent, these locally frequent patterns are tested to see if they are globally frequent in the databases. To avoid the candidate generate-and-test paradigm, the tree-based FP-growth algorithm (Han, Pei, & Yin, 2000) was proposed. It uses a depth-first pattern-growth (i.e., divide-and-conquer) approach to mine frequent patterns using a tree structure that captures the contents of the databases. Specifically, the algorithm recursively extracts appropriate tree paths to form projected databases containing relevant transactions and to discover frequent patterns from these projected databases.

In various real-life business, engineering, healthcare, scientific, and social applications and services in modern organizations and society, the available data are not necessarily *precise* but *imprecise or uncertain* (Leung, 2014; Leung, MacKinnon, & Tanbeer, 2014; Cheng et al., 2019; Rahman, Ahmed, &

Leung, 2019; Titarenko et al., 2019). Examples include sensor data and privacy-preserving data (Leung et al., 2018; Chen et al., 2019; Leung, Braun, & Cuzzocrea, 2019; Li & Xu, 2019). Over the past decade, several algorithms have been proposed to mine and analyze these uncertain data. The tree-based UF-growth algorithm (Leung, Mateo, & Brajczuk, 2008) is an example.

With huge volumes of big data, it is not unusual for users to have some phenomenon in mind. For example, a manager in an organization is interested in some promotional items. Hence, it would be more desirable if data mining algorithms return only those patterns containing the promotional items rather than returning all frequent patterns, out of which many may be uninteresting to the manager. It leads to *constrained mining*, in which users can express their interests by specifying constraints and the mining algorithm can reduce the computational effort by focusing on mining those patterns that are interesting to the users.

Besides the aforementioned algorithms discover frequent patterns *in serial*, there are also *parallel and distributed* frequent pattern mining algorithms (Zaki, 1999). For example, the Count Distribution algorithm (Agrawal & Shafer, 1996) is a parallelization of the Apriori algorithm. It divides transactional databases of precise data and assigns them to parallel processors. Each processor counts the frequency of patterns assigned to it and exchanges this frequency information with other processors. This counting and information exchange process is repeated for each pass/database scan.

As we are moving into the new era of big data, more efficient mining algorithms are needed because these data are wide varieties of valuable data of different veracities with volumes beyond the ability of commonly-used algorithms for mining and analyzing within a tolerable elapsed time. To handle big data, researchers proposed the use of the *MapReduce programming model*.

BIG DATA ANALYTICS AND MINING FOR FREQUENT PATTERNS

The MapReduce Programming Model

MapReduce (Dean & Ghemawat, 2004, 2010) is a high-level programming model for processing huge volumes of data. It uses parallel and distributed computing on large clusters or grids of nodes (i.e., commodity machines), which consist of a master node and multiple worker nodes. As implied by its name, MapReduce involves two key functions:

1. the "map" function, and
2. the "reduce" function.

To solve a problem using MapReduce, the master node reads and divides input big data into several partitions (sub-problems), and then assigns them to different worker nodes. Each worker node executes the *map function* on each partition (sub-problem). The map function takes a pair of ⟨key, value⟩ and returns a list of ⟨key, value⟩ pairs as an intermediate result:

- map: $\langle key_1, value_1 \rangle \mapsto$ list of $\langle key_2, value_2 \rangle$,

where:

1. key_1 & key_2 are keys in the same or different domains, and
2. $value_1$ & $value_2$ are the corresponding values in some domains.

The pairs in the list of ⟨key, value⟩ pairs for this intermediate result are then shuffled and sorted. Each worker node then executes the *reduce function* on:

1.   a single key from this intermediate result, and
2.   the list of all values that appear with this key in the intermediate result.

The reduce function "reduces"—by combining, aggregating, summarizing, filtering, and/or transforming—the list of values associated with a given key (for all k keys) in worker nodes and returns a single (aggregated or summarized) value:

- reduce: ⟨key_2, list of $value_2$⟩ ↦ a single $value_3$,

where:

1. key_2 is a key in some domains, and
2. $value_2$ & $value_3$ are the corresponding values in some domains.

Besides a single $value_3$, alternative output could be a list of ⟨key_3, $value_3$⟩-pairs or a list of $value_3$ (where key_3 is a key in some domains).

By using the MapReduce model, users only need to focus on (and specify) the map and reduce functions, without worrying about implementation details for partitioning the input data, scheduling and executing the program across multiple machines, handling machine failures, or managing inter-machine communication.

Earlier works on MapReduce mainly focused on data processing in big databases (Dean & Ghemawat, 2004, 2010) or some big data mining tasks other than frequent pattern mining. Examples of big data processing with MapReduce include the construction of inverted indexes, the evaluation of queries involving joins or selection, the elimination of duplicates, text processing tasks (Lin & Dyer, 2010; Jiang & Leung, 2015) like the word counting of documents, and the processing of data cubes (Lee & Kim, 2016). Examples of big data mining with MapReduce include classification (Arias, Gámez, & Puerta, 2017), clustering and outlier detection (Ceccarello, Pietracaprina & Pucci, 2019).

Apriori-Based MapReduce Algorithms: SPC, FPC, and DPC

To mine frequent patterns from big databases of precise data with MapReduce, Lin, Lee, & Hsueh (2012) proposed three algorithms—namely, the Single Pass Counting (SPC), Fixed Passes Combined-counting (FPC), and Dynamic Passes Combined-counting (DPC) algorithms—based on both the Apriori and the Count Distribution algorithms. SPC first divides the databases into partitions, and then executes map and reduce functions in each pass k to generate candidate k-itemsets (i.e., candidate patterns each consisting of k items) and count their support/frequency. More specifically, SPC executes the following map and reduce functions in Pass 1:

- map: $\langle$ID of transaction $t_j \in$ partition P_i, contents of $t_j\rangle \mapsto$ list of $\langle$item $x \in t_j$, 1$\rangle$, and
- reduce: $\langle x$, list of 1's$\rangle \mapsto$ list of $\langle$frequent 1-itemset $\{x\}$, $sup(\{x\}) =$ sum of 1's in the list for $x\rangle$.

Here, the worker node corresponding to each partition P_i of the big databases executes the map function by outputting $\langle x, 1\rangle$ (which represents the support of candidate 1-itemset $\{x\}$ in $t_j = 1$) for every item x in transaction $t_j \in P_i$. After grouping all the 1's for each x to form $\langle x$, list of 1's$\rangle$, the reduce function is then executed by summing all the 1's in the list for each x to compute its support $sup(\{x\})$, and outputting $\langle\{x\}, sup(\{x\})\rangle$ (which represents a frequent 1-itemset $\{x\}$ and its frequency) if $sup(\{x\}) \geq$ a user-specific *minsup* threshold.

In each subsequent pass $k \geq 2$, SPC generates candidate k-itemsets from frequent $(k–1)$-itemsets. The worker node corresponding to each partition P_i then outputs $\langle X, 1\rangle$ for every candidate k-itemset X that exists in some transaction $t_j \in P_i$. Afterwards, the reduce function sums all the 1's for each X to compute its support $sup(X)$, and output $\langle X, sup(X)\rangle$ (which represents a frequent k-itemset X and its frequency) if $sup(X) \geq minsup$. In other words, SPC executes the following map and reduce functions in Pass k (for every $k \geq 2$):

- map: $\langle$ID of $t_j \in P_i$, contents of $t_j\rangle \mapsto$ list of $\langle$candidate k-itemset $X \subseteq t_j$, 1$\rangle$, and
- reduce: $\langle X$, list of 1's$\rangle \mapsto$ list of $\langle$frequent k-itemset X, $sup(X) =$ sum of 1's in the list for $X\rangle$.

The three algorithms (SPC, FPC and DPC) are similar except that both FPC and DPC apply the *pass bundling* technique to reduce the number of passes/database scans in each P_i when generating candidate itemsets (for Pass $k \geq 3$). For instance, FPC statistically bundles a fixed number of passes (e.g., three passes) to generate all candidate k-, $(k+1)$-, and $(k+2)$-itemsets from frequent $(k–1)$-itemsets. In contrast, DPC dynamically bundles several passes (depending on the number of generated candidates in these bundled passes).

Partition-Based MapReduce Algorithm

On the one hand, the use of the pass bundling technique reduces the number of passes/database scans in each partition P_i. On the other hand, the Apriori-based SPC, FPC and DPC algorithms still require multiple passes/database scans when mining frequent patterns from big data. In contrast, the MapReduce version of the Partition algorithm—presented by Leskovec, Rajaraman, & Ullman (2020)—requires only two passes/database scans. Hence, the Partition-based MapReduce algorithm uses two sets of "map" and "reduce" functions. Specifically, the master node reads and divides big databases of precise data into partitions. The worker node corresponding to each partition P_i then outputs $\langle X, 1\rangle$ for every candidate pattern X (of any cardinality) that exists in some transaction $t_j \in P_i$. The reduce function then sums all the 1's for each X to find patterns that are locally frequent in P_i. Taking the union of these locally frequent patterns forms global candidate patterns. To summarize, the first set of "map" and "reduce" functions can be expressed as follows:

- map: $\langle$ID of transaction $t_j \in P_i$, contents of $t_j\rangle \mapsto$ list of $\langle$itemset $X \subseteq t_j$, 1$\rangle$, and
- reduce: $\langle X$, list of 1's$\rangle \mapsto$ list of $\langle$locally frequent itemset X, NULL$\rangle$.

Afterwards, the worker node corresponding to each partition P_i outputs $\langle X, 1 \rangle$ for every global candidate pattern X that exists in some transaction $t_j \in P_i$. Then, the reduce function sums all the 1's for each X to compute its support $sup(X)$, and outputs $\langle X, sup(X) \rangle$ (which represents a globally frequent pattern X and its frequency) if $sup(X) \geq minsup$. To summarize, the second set of "map" and "reduce" functions can be expressed as follows:

- map: $\langle$ ID of $t_j \in P_i$, contents of $t_j \rangle \mapsto$ list of $\langle$ global candidate pattern $X \subseteq t_j, 1 \rangle$, and
- reduce: $\langle X,$ list of 1's $\rangle \mapsto$ list of $\langle$ globally frequent pattern $X, sup(X) \rangle$.

Tree-Based MapReduce Algorithm for Precise Data: PFP

Given that tree-based algorithms avoid the candidate generate-and-test paradigm of Apriori-based algorithms, Li et al. (2008) proposed the Parallel FP-growth (PFP) algorithm for query recommendation. PFP uses MapReduce to parallelize the tree-based FP-growth algorithm by first reading and dividing big databases of precise data into several partitions. The worker node corresponding to each partition P_i then outputs $\langle \{x\}, 1 \rangle$ for every item x in transaction $t_j \in P_i$. The reduce function then sums all the 1's for each x to compute its support $sup(\{x\})$, and outputs $\langle \{x\}, sup(\{x\}) \rangle$ (which represents a frequent 1-itemset $\{x\}$ and its frequency) if $sup(\{x\}) \geq minsup$. In other words, PFP first executes the following set of "map" and "reduce" functions:

- map: $\langle$ ID of transaction $t_j \in$ database partition P_i, contents of $t_j \rangle \mapsto$ list of $\langle$ item $x \in t_j, 1 \rangle$, and
- reduce: $\langle x,$ list of 1's $\rangle \mapsto$ list of $\langle$ frequent 1-itemset $\{x\}, sup(\{x\}) =$ sum of 1's in the list for $x \rangle$.

Afterwards, PFP reads the big databases a second time to form an $\{x\}$-projected database (i.e., a collection of transactions containing x) for each item x in the list produced from the first reduce function (i.e., for each frequent 1-itemset $\{x\}$). The worker node corresponding to each projected database then performs the following:

1. builds appropriate local FP-trees (based on the projected database assigned to the node) to mine frequent k-itemsets (for $k \geq 2$), and
2. outputs $\langle X, sup(X) \rangle$ (which represents a frequent k-itemset X and its frequency) if $sup(X) \geq minsup$.

To summarize, PFP executes the second set of "map" and "reduce" functions as follows:

- map: $\langle$ ID of transaction $t_j \in P_i$, contents of $t_j \rangle \mapsto$ list of $\langle \{x\}, \{x\}$-projected database $\rangle$, and
- reduce: $\langle \{x\}, \{x\}$-projected database $\rangle \mapsto$ list of $\langle$ frequent itemset $X, sup(X) \rangle$.

As PFP was designed for query recommendation, it usually takes a third set of "map" and "reduce" functions to aggregate and rank the list of frequent itemsets for the top-K frequent patterns to facilitate recommendations.

Tree-Based MapReduce Algorithm for Uncertain Data: MR-Growth

Characteristics of big data can be described by at least 5Vs: volume, value, velocity, variety, and veracity. Among the 5Vs, veracity focuses on the quality of data (e.g., precision, uncertainty, messiness, or trustworthiness of data). In many real-life applications, available data can be *uncertain*. Uncertainty of the data may partially be caused by various factors such as imprecision or limitation of measuring instruments, as well as intentional blurring of data for privacy-preserving data. Hence, in these applications, users may be uncertain about the presence or absence of some merchandise items or events. For example, a manager may highly suspect (but cannot guarantee) that a customer is interested in certain products without explicitly asking the customer. The uncertainty of such suspicion can be expressed in terms of existential probability. Hence, to handle uncertain data, each item x in the transaction t_j is associated with an existential probability $P(x, t_j)$ expressing the likelihood of the presence of that item or event. With this notion, each item in a transactional database of precise data can be viewed as an item with a 100% likelihood of being present in the transaction.

When using probabilistic-based mining with the "possible world" interpretation (Leung, 2014), a pattern is considered *frequent* if its expected support is no less than the user-specified *minsup* threshold. When items within a pattern X are independent, the *expected support* of X in the database can be computed by summing (over all transactions) the product (of existential probabilities within X):

$$expSup(X) = \sum_{tj} \left(\prod_{x \in X} P(x, t_j) \right),$$

where $P(x, t_j)$ is the existential probability of item x in transaction t_j.

Leung & Hayduk (2013) presented the MR-growth algorithm, which uses MapReduce to mine frequent patterns from *uncertain* data in a tree-based pattern-growth fashion for big data mining. Again, MR-growth uses two sets of the "map" and "reduce" functions. Specifically, the master node reads and divides uncertain data into partitions. The worker node corresponding to each partition P_i then outputs $\langle \{x\}, P(x, t_j) \rangle$ for every item x in transaction $t_j \in P_i$. Note that, unlike the map functions for the aforementioned algorithms (which output $\langle \{x\}, 1 \rangle$ for representing the actual support of x in $t_j = 1$, i.e., x appears 1 time in t_j), the map function for MR-growth outputs $\langle \{x\}, P(x, t_j) \rangle$ (where $P(x, t_j)$ indicates the expected support of x in t_j, which means x has a probability of $P(x, t_j)$ to appear in t_j):

- map: $\langle$ID of transaction $t_j \in$ database partition P_i, contents of $t_j\rangle \mapsto$ list of $\langle$item $x \in t_j, P(x, t_j)\rangle$.

Then, the reduce function sums all the $P(x, t_j)$'s for each x to compute its expected support $expSup(\{x\})$, and outputs $\langle \{x\}, expSup(\{x\}) \rangle$ (representing a frequent 1-itemset $\{x\}$ and its expected support) if $expSup(\{x\}) \geq minsup$:

- reduce: $\langle x$, list of $P(x, t_j)$'s$\rangle \mapsto$ list of $\langle$frequent 1-itemset $\{x\}, expSup(\{x\})$,

where $expSup(\{x\}) =$ sum of $P(x, t_j)$ in the list for x. Notice that, when handling precise data, the actual support of $\{x\}$ is its frequency. In contrast, when handling uncertain data, the expected support of $\{x\}$ may not be the same as its frequency. For instance, consider an item b with existential probability of 0.9 that appears only in transaction t_1. Its expected support may be higher than item c that appears seven times but with an existential probability of 0.1 in each appearance. Then, $expSup(\{b\}) = 0.9 > 0.7 = expSup(\{c\})$.

Afterwards, MR-growth rereads the big databases to form an $\{x\}$-projected database (i.e., a collection of transactions containing x) for each item x in the list produced from the first reduce function (i.e., for each frequent 1-itemset x). The worker node corresponding to each projected database then performs the following:

1. builds appropriate local UF-trees (based on the projected database assigned to the node) to mine frequent k-itemsets (for $k \geq 2$), and
2. outputs $\langle X, expSup(X) \rangle$ (which represents a frequent k-itemset X and its expected support) if $expSup(X) \geq minsup$.

To summarize, MR-growth executes the second set of "map" and "reduce" functions as follows:

*   map: $\langle$ID of transaction $t_j \in P_i$, contents of $t_j\rangle \mapsto$ list of $\langle\{x\}, \{x\}$-projected database$\rangle$, and
*   reduce: $\langle\{x\}, \{x\}$-projected database$\rangle \mapsto$ list of $\langle$frequent itemset X, $expSup(X)\rangle$.

Constraint-Based MapReduce Algorithm: BigAnt and BigSAM

When mining and analyzing huge-volume big data, it is not uncommon that users may be interested in only some subsets of these big data in many real-life situations. This leads to *constraint-based mining* (Bonchi, 2009; Leung, 2009; Leung, 2018a), with which users can focus the mining on certain subsets of the big data by freely specifying some constraints to express their interest. For example, users can express their interests in finding a collection X of merchandise items having a total price of less than \$100 by specifying a constraint "sum($X.Price$) < \$100". Similarly users can also express their interests in finding a set Y of branches with a minimum GPS coordinate (latitude) of 49°N by specifying a constraint "min($Y.GPSCoordinate$) = 49°N".

To handle these constraints and to focus the mining on those subsets of big data that are interesting to users, Leung & Jiang (2014) proposed the BigAnt algorithm to handle the user-specified anti-monotonic constraints by exploring the anti-monotonicity of the constraints, which states that "if a pattern satisfies an anti-monotonic constraint, then so do all its subsets". In other words, if a pattern violates the anti-monotonic constraints, it can be pruned as any of its supersets is guaranteed to violate the constraints. For instance, if sum($Z.Price$) $\geq$ \$100 for some pattern Z, then sum($Z'.Price$) $\geq$ \$100 for any superset Z' of Z. So, the BigAnt algorithm also uses two sets of the "map" and "reduce" functions. The master node reads and divides uncertain data into partitions. The worker node corresponding to each partition P_i then performs constraint checking and outputs $\langle\{x\}, P(x, t_j)\rangle$ for every *valid* item x in transaction $t_j \in P_i$ (when $\{x\}$ satisfies the constraints):

*   map: $\langle$ID of transaction $t_j \in$ partition P_i, contents of $t_j\rangle \mapsto$ list of $\langle$valid item $x \in t_j$, $P(x, t_j)\rangle$.

Then, the reduce function sums all the $P(x, t_j)$'s for each valid x to compute its expected support $expSup(\{x\})$, and outputs $\langle\{x\}, expSup(\{x\})\rangle$ (representing a valid frequent 1-itemset $\{x\}$ and its expected support) if $expSup(\{x\}) \geq minsup$:

- reduce: ⟨valid x, list of P(x, t_j)'s⟩ ↦ list of ⟨valid frequent 1-itemset {x}, $expSup$({x}),

where $expSup$({x}) = sum of P(x, t_j) in the list for x. Afterwards, BigAnt rereads the big databases to form an {x}-projected database (i.e., a collection of transactions containing x) for each *valid* item x in the list produced from the first reduce function (i.e., for each valid frequent 1-itemset x). The worker node corresponding to each projected database then performs the following:

1. builds appropriate local UF-trees (based on the projected database assigned to the node) to mine frequent k-itemsets (for $k \geq 2$), (ii) performs constraint checking to find valid ones from these mined frequent k-itemsets, and (iii) outputs ⟨valid X, $expSup(X)$⟩ (which represents a valid frequent k-itemset X and its expected support) if $expSup(X) \geq minsup$ and X is valid with respect to the user-specified constraints. To summarize, BigAnt executes the second set of "map" and "reduce" functions as follows:
    - map: ⟨ID of transaction $t_j \in P_i$, contents of t_j⟩ ↦ list of ⟨valid {x}, {x}-projected database⟩, and
    - reduce: ⟨valid {x}, {x}-projected database⟩ ↦ list of ⟨valid frequent itemset X, $expSup(X)$⟩.

Note that BigAnt pushes the user-specified anti-monotonic constraints into the big data mining process so that it directly discovers frequent patterns that satisfy the constraints.

To a further extent, Jiang, Leung, & MacKinnon (2014) proposed the BigSAM algorithm to explore additional property of some anti-monotonic constraints. Specifically, BigSAM explores the succinctness of the constraints, which reveals that all and only those itemsets satisfying the succinct anti-monotonic (SAM) constraints can be explicitly and precisely generated using only individual items that satisfy the SAM constraints. For instance, any set Y of branches with min($Y.GPSCoordinate$) = 49°N must consist of only branches with GPS coordinate of 49°N. Hence, the BigSAM only needs to perform constraint checking in the first—but not the second—map function.

FUTURE RESEARCH DIRECTIONS

Besides the MapReduce model in Apache Hadoop, alternative approaches include the use of Apache Spark (which relies on the concept of resilient distributed dataset), edge computing, and fog computing (Zaharia et al., 2010; Garcia Lopez et al., 2015; Yi et al., 2015). Hence, a logic future research direction is to adapt and perform *big data analytics and mining for knowledge discovery* (e.g., constrained or unconstrained frequent patterns about an organization) *in Spark, edges, or fogs* (Leung et al., 2017b; Sarumi, Leung, & Adetunmbi, 2018; Braun et al., 2019).

Due to the popularity of Web-based communities and social networking sites, huge volumes of big social media data (including those Facebook, Instagram and Twitter data about an organization) are available. Embedded in these big data are rich sets of meaningful knowledge about the social networks (e.g., social networks within an organization, among different organizations). Hence, a second future research direction is to apply *social media mining and social network analysis* (Leung, Medina, & Tanbeer, 2013; Xu & Li, 2013; Leung et al., 2016; Jiang et al., 2018; Leung, 2018b) to social media data for discovery of rich sets of meaningful knowledge from these big data.

Many existing big data mining algorithms return the mined results in a textual form—e.g., a *textual list* of all (constrained or unconstrained) frequent patterns. As "a picture is worth a thousand words", visual representation of the mining results is usually easier to comprehend for users than its equivalent textual representation. Thus, it is desirable to show the mining results interactively by applying the concepts of visual analytics. As such, to enhance user experience in exploring big data, a third future research direction is to incorporate *visual analytics and interactive technologies* (Zhang, Segall, & Cao, 2011; Leung et al., 2017a; Jentner & Keim, 2019; Leung & Zhang, 2019) into big data mining so that the (constrained or unconstrained) frequent patterns mined from big data are returned to the users in visual forms.

CONCLUSION

Big data analytics and mining aims to discover implicit, previously unknown, and potentially useful information and knowledge from big databases that contain huge volumes of valuable veracious data collected or generated at a high velocity from a wide variety of data sources. Among different big data mining tasks, this chapter focuses on *big data analytics and mining for knowledge discovery*. By relying on the MapReduce programming model, researchers only need to specify the "map" and "reduce" functions to discover frequent patterns from:

1. big databases of precise data in a breadth-first manner (e.g., by using the SPC, FPC, and DPC algorithms) or in a depth-first manner (e.g., by using the PFP algorithm), and/or
2. big databases of uncertain data (e.g., by using the MR-growth algorithm).

Such a big data analytic and mining process can be sped up (e.g., by using the BigAnt and BigSAM algorithms, which focus the mining according to the user-specified constraints that express the user interests). The resulting (constrained or unconstrained) frequent patterns mined from big data provide users (e.g., executive and management teams of an organization) with new insights and a sound understanding of users' patterns about the organization. Such knowledge is useful is many real-life information science and technology, as well as organizational, applications.

REFERENCES

Aggarwal, C. C., Bhuiyan, M. A., & Al Hasan, M. (2014). Frequent pattern mining algorithms: a survey. In C.C. Aggarwal & J. Han (Eds.), *Frequent pattern mining*, (pp. 19-64). doi:10.1007/978-3-319-07821-2_2

Agrawal, R., Imieliński, T., & Swami, A. (1993) Mining association rules between sets of items in large databases. *Proceedings of ACM SIGMOD 1993*, 207-216. 10.1145/170035.170072

Agrawal, R., & Shafer, J. C. (1996). Parallel mining of association rules. *IEEE Transactions on Knowledge and Data Engineering*, 8(6), 962–969. doi:10.1109/69.553164

Agrawal, R., & Srikant, R. (1994). Fast algorithms for mining association rules in large databases. *Proceedings of VLDB, 1994*, 487–499.

Arias, J., Gámez, J. A., & Puerta, J. M. (2017). Learning distributed discrete Bayesian network classifiers under MapReduce with Apache Spark. *Knowledge-Based Systems*, *117*, 16–26. doi:10.1016/j.knosys.2016.06.013

Bellatreche, L., Leung, C.K., Xia, Y., & Elbaz, D. (2019) Advances in cloud and big data computing. *Concurrency and Computation: Practice and Experience, 31*(2), e5053:1-e5053:3. doi:10.1002/cpe.5053

Bonchi, F. (2009). Constraint-based pattern discovery. In J. Wang (Ed.), *Encyclopedia of data warehousing and mining* (2nd ed., pp. 313–319). doi:10.4018/978-1-60566-010-3.ch050

Braun, P., Cuzzocrea, A., Leung, C. K., Pazdor, A. G. M., Souza, J., & Tanbeer, S. K. (2019) Pattern mining from big IoT data with fog computing: models, issues, and research perspectives. *Proceedings of IEEE/ACM CCGrid 2019*, 854-891. 10.1109/CCGRID.2019.00075

Ceccarello, M., Pietracaprina, A., & Pucci, G. (2019). Solving *k*-center clustering (with outliers) in mapreduce and streaming, almost as accurately as sequentially. *PVLDB*, *12*(7), 766–778. doi:10.14778/3317315.3317319

Ceglar, A. & Roddick, J.F. (2006) Association mining. *ACM Computing Surveys, 38*(2), 5:1-5:42. doi:10.1145/1132956.1132958

Chen, R., Jankovic, F., Marinsek, N., Foschini, L., Kourtis, L., Signorini, A., Pugh, M., Shen, J., Yaari, R., Maljkovic, V., Sunga, M., Song, H. H., Jung, H. J., Tseng, B., & Trister, A. (2019). Developing measures of cognitive impairment in the real world from consumer-grade multimodal sensor streams. *Proceedings of ACM KDD 2019*, 2145-2155. 10.1145/3292500.3330690

Cheng, J., Yan, D., Hao, X., & Ng, W. (2019) Mining order-preserving submatrices under data uncertainty: a possible-world approach. *Proceedings of IEEE ICDE 2019*, 1154-1165. 10.1109/ICDE.2019.00106

Dean, J., & Ghemawat, S. (2004) MapReduce: simplified data processing on large clusters. *Proceedings of OSDI 2004*, 137-149.

Dean, J., & Ghemawat, S. (2010). MapReduce: A flexible data processing tool. *Communications of the ACM*, *53*(1), 72–77. doi:10.1145/1629175.1629198

Garcia Lopez, P., Montresor, A., Epema, D., Datta, A., Higashino, T., Iamnitchi, A., Barcellos, M., Felber, P., & Riviere, E. (2015). Edge-centric computing. *Computer Communication Review*, *45*(5), 37–42. doi:10.1145/2831347.2831354

Han, J., Pei, J., & Yin, Y. (2000) Mining frequent patterns without candidate generation. *Proceedings of ACM SIGMOD 2000*, 1-12. doi:10.1145/342009.335372

Hipp, J., Güntzer, U., & Nakhaeizadeh, G. (2000). Algorithms for association rule mining – a general survey and comparison. *SIGKDD Explorations*, *2*(1), 58–64. doi:10.1145/360402.360421

Jentner, W., & Keim, D. A. (2019). Visualization and visual analytic techniques for patterns. In P. Fournier-Viger, J. C. Lin, R. Nkambou, B. Vo, & V. S. Tseng (Eds.), High-utility pattern mining (pp. 303–337). doi:10.1007/978-3-030-04921-8_12

Jiang, F., & Leung, C. K. (2015). A data analytic algorithm for managing, querying, and processing uncertain big data in cloud environments. *Algorithms*, *8*(4), 1175–1194. doi:10.3390/a8041175

Jiang, F., Leung, C. K., & MacKinnon, R. K. (2014) BigSAM: mining interesting patterns from probabilistic databases of uncertain big data. *Proceedings of PAKDD Workshops 2014*, 780-792. 10.1007/978-3-319-13186-3_70

Jiang, F., Leung, C. K., Middleton, R., & Pazdor, A. G. M. (2018). Big social data mining in a cloud computing environment. *Proceedings of ICCBB*, *2018*, 58–65. doi:10.1109/ICCBB.2018.8756461

Lee, S., & Kim, J. (2016) Performance evaluation of MRDataCube for data cube computation algorithm using MapReduce. *Proceedings of BigComp 2016*, 325-328. 10.1109/BIGCOMP.2016.7425939

Leskovec, J., Rajaraman, A., & Ullman, J. D. (2020). Mining of massive datasets (3rd ed.). Cambridge University Press., doi:10.1017/9781108684163 doi:10.1017/CBO9781139924801

Leung, C. K. (2009). Constraint-based association rule mining. In J. Wang (Ed.), *Encyclopedia of data warehousing and mining* (2nd ed., pp. 307–312)., doi:10.4018/978-1-60566-010-3.ch049

Leung, C. K. (2014) Uncertain frequent pattern mining. In C.C. Aggarwal & J. Han (Eds.), *Frequent pattern mining*, (pp. 339-367). doi:10.1007/978-3-319-07821-2_14

Leung, C. K. (2015). Big data mining applications and services. *Proceedings of BigDAS*, *2015*, 1–8. doi:10.1145/2837060.2837076

Leung, C. K. (2018a). Frequent itemset mining with constraints. In L. Liu & M. T. Özsu (Eds.), *Encyclopedia of database systems* (2nd ed., pp. 1531–1536). doi:10.1007/978-1-4614-8265-9_170

Leung, C. K. (2018b). Mathematical model for propagation of influence in a social network. In R. Alhajj (Ed.), *Encyclopedia of Social Network Analysis and Mining* (2nd ed., pp. 1261–1269). doi:10.1007/978-1-4939-7131-2_110201

Leung, C.K., Braun, P., & Cuzzocrea, A. (2019) AI-based sensor information fusion for supporting deep supervised learning. *Sensors, 19*(6), 1345:1-1345:12. doi:10.3390/s19061345

Leung, C. K., Carmichael, C. L., Johnstone, P., Xing, R. R., & Yuen, D. S. H. (2017a). Interactive visual analytics of big data. In J. Lu (Ed.), *Ontologies and Big Data Considerations for Effective Intelligence*, (pp. 1-26). doi:10.4018/978-1-5225-2058-0.ch001

Leung, C. K., Deng, D., Hoi, C. S. H., & Lee, W. (2017b) Constrained big data mining in an edge computing environment. *Big Data Applications and Services 2017*, 61-68. doi:10.1007/978-981-13-0695-2_8

Leung, C. K., & Hayduk, Y. (2013) Mining frequent patterns from uncertain data with MapReduce for big data analytics. *Proceedings of DASFAA 2013, Part I*, 440-455. 10.1007/978-3-642-37487-6_33

Leung, C. K., Hoi, C. S. H., Pazdor, A. G. M., Wodi, B. H., & Cuzzocrea, A. (2018). Privacy-preserving frequent pattern mining from big uncertain data. *Proceedings of IEEE BigData*, *2018*, 5101–5110. doi:10.1109/BigData.2018.8622260

Leung, C. K., & Jiang, F. (2014). A data science solution for mining interesting patterns from uncertain big data. *Proceedings of IEEE BDCloud*, *2014*, 235–242. doi:10.1109/BDCloud.2014.136

Leung, C. K., Jiang, F., Dela Cruz, E. M., & Elango, V. S. (2017c) Association rule mining in collaborative filtering. *Collaborative Filtering Using Data Mining and Analysis*, 159-179. doi:10.4018/978-1-5225-0489-4.ch009

Leung, C. K., Jiang, F., Pazdor, A. G. M., & Peddle, A. M. (2016). Parallel social network mining for interesting 'following' patterns. *Concurrency and Computation*, *28*(15), 3994–4012. doi:10.1002/cpe.3773

Leung, C. K., MacKinnon, R. K., & Tanbeer, S. K. (2014) Fast algorithms for frequent itemset mining from uncertain data. *Proceedings of IEEE ICDM 2014*, 893-898. 10.1109/ICDM.2014.146

Leung, C. K., Mateo, M. A. F., & Brajczuk, D. A. (2008). A tree-based approach for frequent pattern mining from uncertain data. *Proceedings of PAKDD*, *2008*, 653–661. doi:10.1007/978-3-540-68125-0_61

Leung, C. K., Medina, I. J. M., & Tanbeer, S. K. (2013). Analyzing social networks to mine important friends. In G. Xu & L. Li (Eds.), *Social media mining and social network analysis: Emerging research*, (pp. 90-104). doi:10.4018/978-1-4666-2806-9.ch006

Leung, C.K., & Zhang, Y. (2019) An HSV-based visual analytic system for data science on music and beyond. *International Journal of Art, Culture and Design Technologies*, *8*(1), 68-83. doi:10.4018/IJACDT.2019010105

Li, H., Wang, Y., Zhang, D., Zhang, M., & Chang, E. Y. (2008) PFP: Parallel FP-growth for query recommendation. *Proceedings of ACM RecSys 2008*, 107-114. doi:10.1145/1454008.1454027

Li, Y., & Xu, W. (2019) PrivPy: general and scalable privacy-preserving data mining. *Proceedings of ACM KDD 2019*, 1299-1307. 10.1145/3292500.3330920

Lin, J., & Dyer, C. (2010). *Data-intensive text processing with MapReduce*. doi:10.2200/S00274ED-1V01Y201006HLT007

Lin, M., Lee, P., & Hsueh, S. (2012). Apriori-based frequent itemset mining algorithms on MapReduce. *Proceedings of ICUIMC*, *2012*, 76. doi:10.1145/2184751.2184842

Madden, S. (2012). From databases to big data. *IEEE Internet Computing*, *16*(3), 4–6. doi:10.1109/MIC.2012.50

Rahman, M. M., Ahmed, C. F., & Leung, C. K. (2019). Mining weighted frequent sequences in uncertain databases. *Information Sciences*, *479*, 76–100. doi:10.1016/j.ins.2018.11.026

Sarumi, O. A., Leung, C. K., & Adetunmbi, A. O. (2018). Spark-based data analytics of sequence motifs in large omics data. *Procedia Computer Science*, *126*, 596–605. doi:10.1016/j.procs.2018.07.294

Savasere, A., Omiecinski, E., & Navathe, S. (1995). An efficient algorithm for mining association rules in large databases. *Proceedings of VLDB*, *1995*, 432–444.

Shim, K. (2012). MapReduce algorithms for big data analysis. *PVLDB*, *5*(12), 2016–2017. doi:10.14778/2367502.2367563

Titarenko, S.S., Titarenko, V.N., Aivaliotis, G., & Palczewski, J. (2019) Fast implementation of pattern mining algorithms with time stamp uncertainties and temporal constraints. *Journal of Big Data*, *6*, 37:1-37:34. doi:10.1186/s40537-019-0200-9

Ullman, J. D. (2000). A survey of association-rule mining. *Proceedings of DS*, *2000*, 1–14. doi:10.1007/3-540-44418-1_1

Xu, G., & Li, L. (Eds.). (2013). *Social media mining and social network analysis: emerging research.* doi:10.4018/978-1-4666-2806-9

Yi, S., Hao, Z., Qin, Z., & Li, Q. (2015). Fog computing: Platform and applications. *Proceedings of IEEE HotWeb*, *2015*, 73–78. doi:10.1109/HotWeb.2015.22

Zaharia, M., Chowdhury, M., Franklin, M. J., Shenker, S., & Stoica, I. (2010) Spark: cluster computing with working sets. *Proceedings of USENIX HotCloud 2010*, 10:1-10:7.

Zaki, M. J. (1999). Parallel and distributed association mining: A survey. *IEEE Concurrency*, *7*(4), 14–25. doi:10.1109/4434.806975

Zhang, Q., Segall, R. S., & Cao, M. (Eds.). (2011). *Visual analytics and interactive technologies: data, text and web mining applications.* doi:10.4018/978-1-60960-102-7

KEY TERMS AND DEFINITIONS

Anti-Monotonic Constraint: A constraint C such that, if an itemset S satisfying C, then any subset of S also satisfies C.

Big Data: High-velocity, valuable, and/or multi-variety data with volumes beyond the ability of commonly-used software to capture, manage, and process within a tolerable elapsed time. These Big data necessitate new forms of processing to deliver high veracity (& low vulnerability) and to enable enhanced decision making, insight, knowledge discovery, and process optimization.

Data Mining: Non-trivial extraction of implicit, previously unknown and potentially useful information from data.

Frequent Pattern (or Frequent Itemset): An itemset or a pattern with its actual support (or expected support) exceeds or equals the user-specified minimum support threshold.

Frequent Pattern Mining: A search and analysis of huge volumes of valuable data for implicit, previously unknown, and potentially useful patterns consisting of frequently co-occurring events or objects. It helps discover frequently co-located trade fairs and frequently purchased bundles of merchandise items.

Itemset: A set of items.

MapReduce: A high-level programming model, which uses the "map" and "reduce" functions, for processing huge volumes of data.

Succinct Constraint: A constraint C such that all itemsets satisfying C can be expressed in terms of powersets of a fixed number of succinct sets using the set union and/or set difference operators. A succinct set is an itemset, in which items are selected from the domain using the usual Structured Query Language (SQL) selection operator. In simple terms, a constraint C is succinct meaning that all and only those itemsets satisfying C can be explicitly and precisely generated using some precise "formula".

This research was previously published in the Encyclopedia of Organizational Knowledge, Administration, and Technology; pages 1817-1830, copyright year 2021 by Business Science Reference (an imprint of IGI Global).

Chapter 34
Distributed Streaming Big Data Analytics for Internet of Things (IoT)

Sornalakshmi Krishnan
SRM University, India

Kayalvizhi Jayavel
SRM University, India

ABSTRACT

In this chapter, a discussion on the integration of distributed streaming Big Data Analytics with the Internet of Things is presented. The chapter begins with the introduction of these two technologies by discussing their features and characteristics. Discussion on how the integration of these two technologies benefit in efficient processing of IoT device generated sensor data follows next. Such data centric processing of IoT data powered by cloud, services and other enablers will be the architecture of most of the realtime systems involving sensors and real-time monitoring and actuation. The Volume, Variety and Velocity of sensor generated data make it a Big Data scenario. In addition, the data is real time and requires decisions or actuations immediately. This chapter discusses how IoT data can be processed using distributed, scalable stream processing systems. The chapter is concluded with future directions of such real time Big Data Analytics in IoT.

INTRODUCTION

Internet of Things has been identified as an emerging technology that will transform our environment to a more connected and smarter world. Cisco predicts that over the next five years, global IP networks will support up to 10 billion new devices and connections increasing from 16.3 billion in 2015 to 26.3 billion by 2020. The projection is 3.4 devices and connections per capita by 2020—up from 2.2 per capita in 2015. And if clearly observed, every company have ventured to IoT relevant to their sector. Cisco,

DOI: 10.4018/978-1-6684-3662-2.ch034

Juniper and other networking based companies have started talking about Edge, Mist Fog Analytics as next futuristic technologies for IoT.

MathWorks have acquired ThingSpeak which is a cloud based company and MathWorks have developed extensive toolbox for Internet of Things. It comprises of many open source hardware support, to name a few Raspberry Pi, Arduino and many more. IBM has come up with BluemixCloud, Google with its OS for Internet of Things, Brillo. Internet of Things allows envisaging the evolution of internet as a huge network of connected intelligent devices. These ubiquitous connected things not only sense, but also process, analyze real physical events ranging from simpler to complex and triggers actions as the need demands.

As the number of affiliated devices increases, the rate at which the data is generated and processed also increases. This requirement has led to the employment of technical advancements like Cloud, Software Oriented Architectural models, Software Defined Networks, Machine Learning, Artificial Intelligence and many more for making the things around us smarter, faster and dynamically intelligent.

In such a connected environment, the enormous amount of data generated by networked devices has to be processed in both real time as well as batch basis. The data generated by IoT devices possess the characteristics of Big Data in terms of Volume, Velocity, Variety and Value. The heterogeneous devices when connected together produce huge amounts of data from which useful inferences or decisions have to be drawn.

The powerful paradigm of MapReduce along with the implementing frameworks like Hadoop has made Big Data processing easier. The sub area of Big Data is Streaming Analytics which analyzes huge amounts of data that arrives with huge velocity and expects the actuation or decision in real time with low latency in terms of seconds. With the number of devices connecting to internet and the need for real time decision, making intelligent applications like self-driving is gaining importance. The frameworks for Streaming Analytics should possess the basic characteristics of Fault Tolerance, high availability, low Latency and Scalability. According to the requirement of application, processing can either follow the store-process-react or process-react-optional store style.

Cloud along with its different flavors and characteristics like Elasticity, Pay as per service and Scalability provides the best performance for centralized Storage, Analytics and Visualization in IoT. Cloud Services are available and provisioned without any human intervention and follow the pay-as-you-go model. Also, while utilizing cloud, the problems of over provisioning or under provisioning found in static fixed provisioning environments do not exist. Scalability and Load Balancing can help maintain the Quality of Service promised to the customers. By offering most of the components as a service, cloud environment is taking away most of the complexities handled at the user level. This enables the users to concentrate on the business processing rather than infrastructure.

Service science is an emerging companion to Streaming Analytics in cloud where there are numerous research areas such as Service Discovery, Composition and Orchestration. The service-oriented Cloud Computing is a supporting framework for cohesive set of cloud components. The big streaming data as opposed to the traditional services data is not structured or similar between services. There are a huge variety of sources in the IoT context like Wireless Sensor Network monitoring forest fire or a Weather station or Pollution monitoring or Home automation which vary exorbitantly unimaginable in the data formats. The data exchange needed before or after Data Analytics will be taken care by services.

The IoT paradigm along with Big Data, Cloud and Service Science promises revolutionary architecture which will be suitable for most of the critical IT applications ranging from smart grids to smart connected communities (Sun, Song, Jara & Bie, 2016).

In this chapter, the focus is on how Distributed Analytics will be done in the context of IoT. Such real time continuous data has to be processed on the fly for real time intelligent decision making. This Sensor-Actuator-Internet technology comprises of below main aspects:

- Heterogeneous Device Virtualization
- Data Fusion and Integration
- Dynamic Resource Provisioning
- Task Orchestration
- Cloud Analytics and Storage Platform
- High level Programming Model for SOA based applications
- Service Management

INTRODUCTION TO BIG DATA

The data is being generated in a multi folded exponential fashion. Such data possess huge amounts of information which has to be tapped and utilized for productive insights in business. Such data were initially handled by methods like relational database, distributed systems, etc. But the data that cannot be handled by such traditional methods due to its attributes like Volume, Velocity, Variety, etc. are termed as Big Data. With the Big Data that is generated and shared in social media, mobile phones, sensors, etc. we can arrive at an improved living environment with data driven solutions deployed everywhere. Big Data Analytics also includes several challenges like heterogeneity, noise, integrity of sources, relation to historical data which was recorded during a completely different period of time in terms of digital advancement, application and fine tuning of existing robust Machine Learning approaches to Big Data in a distributed and scalable way.

INTRODUCTION TO INTERNET OF THINGS (IoT)

Every technology that evolves has a legacy behind it and adds on new features as need demands. The Web which began its journey through Tim Bernesse Lee in 1990's is not the same now. It has taken huge leaps from Web1.0, Web2.0 and Web3.0 and now with IoT, people are tempted to call it the Web4.0 technology. Sometimes, they take completely new dimension or form which once was not the part of its fundamental dimension. It is human tendency to always understand new concepts with their previous knowledge. So, you will better understand about this new hyped technology the "Internet of Things" with the already known ones.

Wireless Sensor Networks (WSN) was known to all of us for a quite a long time. And the basic characteristics of Wireless Sensor Networks are data centric, (most of the time sleepy to save power) low power, application specific and in most cases proprietary solutions. People had their own wireless sensor networks to cater their needs. No one ever realized this simple technology will revolutionize this big. Though there were convincing reasons for wireless sensor networks to have long lifetimes especially when deployed in harsh environments, there are few questions to ponder up on. Are we really exploiting the level it can be? Not really, in the name of power consumption, truly speaking we are underexploiting it. So, few proactive people analyzed it from the angle of re-usability of these small networks. So, the thought of interconnecting these pervasively distributed wireless network came up and the idea is to make them speak to each other. That is alright, but how to do it????

There were different ways by which the researchers approached it. These ways include creating new communication means suitable for these low power networks. This idea was knocked for two reasons: the enormous cost it will consume and the wastage of already existing infrastructure. Hence, researchers started working on twists and tweaks of existing technology to support the current needs. The already existing best model on earth is INTERNET which rules the globe with its revolutionary technique to interconnect people. It all started with www, the web1 (Read Only Web) and then evolved to the web2 (Read-Write Web), and then the web3 (Semantic Web), the ubiquitous computing with concept of semantic and now web 4.0 (IoT Web) adding crown to the already irreplaceable technology.

Researchers have decided the backbone of IoT as Internet. Is it that all comes with ready to eat well wrapped pack which you open and use it right away? No, there need to be made a huge compromise, miniaturization, cut downs, translations, etc. at all levels. When it is said all levels, it is at Hardware, System Software, Protocols, Application Software and many more.

This leads to the creation of new architecture, protocols and application software for IoT. Yes, of course, the root is still the technologies and software which long existed in traditional networks. Thus, 8 bit-Microcontrollers, Arduino Boards, Rapberry Pi, Intel Edision, Intel Galileo, BeagleBone decorated the device layer or so called physical layer. Bluetooth, Zigbee, Z-wave, Wi-Fi, Cellular, NFC, Lora, 6TiSCH, etc. are the underlying communications for the physical layer. Then comes networking layer where there are protocols like 6LowPAN (Adaptation layer for traditional IPv6), RPL, etc. Application Layer protocols are MQTT, XMPP, DDS, AMQP, Restful Services, Web Sockets, etc. Sincere efforts are being taken to gradually increase the depth of intake. So, at any point of the chapter you should not feel burdened or overfed.

A quick recap: WSN was once data centric and people wanted to connect and achieve reusability which made them adopt Internet as their backbone but came across lot of hurdles and hence they modified, added, deleted to fit to the need which paved the way for connecting anything, anytime, anywhere. Though every minute IoT is evolving, newer definitions crawl up. But, this is ultimate as it actually adds a third dimension "Any device" to the already existing definition for Internet which makes the "Any time", "Anywhere" Internet to Internet of Things (Any-time Any-where of Things (Any-thing)). IoT is a new dimension aiming for "Devices Internet" as against the usual "People's Internet". The benefits are enormous and will at its best unveil a new era of free information for anyone, anytime, anywhere.

This will undoubtedly take all of our lives to such an elevated state which humans would have never ever dreamt anything near to it. Web 4.0 will no more be just about people's connection, it will be inclusive of these intelligent devices connection, the real M2M with no man in between literally. It is meant device-centric internet for people as against people-centric internet by the people which was the usual norm.

IoT should address these 5S: Specific, Speed, Space, Scale and Support. Specific because all needs are unique and hence the solution has to be tailored against generic universal solutions for all. Are you ready to listen to an interesting analogy? We heard the "YES" which you uttered now. Here we go. In the earlier days, there was a general physician who treated all people and in the later years, there came specialist (Do not get shocked if very soon you hear something like right eye specialist, Left Leg specialist..). Likewise, earlier it was only "Light Control" now it is "Mood Light Control". Speed because somewhere my system detects a fire, if it reports after few minutes, it would have been ashes by that time. Space because few deploy these systems or devices as wearable on human body. Hence, they should be portable and of small size. Scale because currently there are 100 sensor nodes but few months down the line 100 more can be added. Is our system still stable and reliable? Support because all that everyone does is to help humans, to make his or her life comfortable and to live with ease. Hence, the ultimate goal of any IoT system will be to support human lives and to enrich them.

IoT, can it exist as a separate entity? We see your head nodding in disagreement, you are right for obvious reasons, it is born to co-exist, interconnect in order to achieve bigger goals.

IoT is "Who's" Call?

If you are a networking expert with specialization in Ad Hoc, Mobile, Wireless or Wireless Sensor, by this time you would have understood it is your call, your area. Yes it is yours. If a Web Service, Cloud or Virtualization expert have read this, they would undoubtedly feel that they too form a core part to disseminate all that networks sense. If you are a database engineer, Big Data enthusiast or a Data Scientist, you will understand that IoT game is all about data and data processing, analysis and delivery. If you are a Hardware expert or an embedded engineer, all the micro controllers or nodes which IoT will use is all yours. Hence, IoT is an era of collaboration, culmination of various disciplines and it is the era for team up and grow up.

The relationship is deep that sometimes people directly equate IoT as physical internet, Ubiquitous Computing, Ambient Intelligence, Machine to Machine (M2M), Industrial Internet, Web of Things, Connected Environments, Smart Cities, Spimes, Everyware, Pervasive Internet, Connected World, Wireless Sensor Networks (Wikipedia, 2017c), Situated Computing, Future Internet and Physical Computing.

What Gartner Says About IoT?

The *Hype Cycle* is a branded graphical presentation developed and used by American Information Technology (IT) research and advisory firm Gartner for representing the maturity, adoption and social application of specific technologies (Wikipedia, 2017b). IoT platform is in its innovation trigger region.

Definition of IoT

There is no fixed definition for IoT but would like to share with, as what great organizations talk about IoT.

The Internet of Things(IoT) is the network of physical objects—devices, vehicles, buildings and other items—embedded with electronics, software, sensors, and network connectivity that enables these objects to collect and exchange data (Internet of Things Global Standards, 2013)

IoT starts with Intel inside (Intel, 2016)

The IoT links smart objects to the Internet. It can enable an exchange of data never available before, and bring users information in a more secure way. Cisco estimates the IoT will consist of 50 billion devices connected to the Internet by 2020 (Papke, 2016)

A global network infrastructure, linking physical and virtual objects through the exploitation of data capture and communication capabilities. This infrastructure includes existing and evolving Internet and network developments. It will offer specific object-identification, sensor and connection capability as the basis for the development of independent cooperative services and applications. These will be characterised by a high degree of autonomous data capture, event transfer, network connectivity and interoperability. (Minerva, 2014)

The Internet of Things (IoT) describes the revolution already under way that is seeing a growing number of internet enabled devices that can network and communicate with each other and with other web-enabled gadgets. IoT refers to a state where Things (e.g. objects, environments, vehicles and clothing) will have more and more information associated with them and may have the ability to sense, communicate, network and produce new information, becoming an integral part of the Internet. (Technology Strategy Board, Driving Innovation, 2011)

FEATURES OF IoT

Internet of Things (Mondal, Rao & Madria, 2016) have very interesting features when compared to other counterparts which took their places in Gartner's prediction like Big Data, Cloud, Quantum Computing, Smart Robots. The reason why it is said that this is all the above-mentioned technologies have clearly defined boundaries. But Internet of Things has spread its wings so wide and deep, so no technological area is spared. Thus, one would find overlapping features and every domain expert would feel at home when he or she enters the realm of IoT. However, our method has enough efforts to provide an agreeable list of features for IoT.

Sensing and Actuating

Sensors, Actuators are the prime ingredients of Internet of Things. The environment is sensed for the need of various parameters be it Temperature, Pressure, Humidity, Noise or polluting gases and the data measured is used to take various actions using appropriate actuators. The actuation can be as simple as switch on or off a LED or to a complex job as a robot performing extremely intelligent task.

Communication

The data measured by sensors can be processed locally or at intermediate entities or communicated to remote destinations. This clearly confirms the need for transportation of data. This can be achieved through various communication technologies like Wi-Fi, Bluetooth, Zigbee, Lora and many more.

Processing, Assimilation and Decision Making

As mentioned above, the data measured by sensors before communication can be processed at possibly three locations based on the scenario. The data can be processed at the device itself and the decision is made right there. This is technically called as Edge Computing. The data can travel one level up and the processing may happen at a gateway level, assimilated as needed and the decision is given back to the device level. This is Fog Computing. It gets the name Fog because it is one level down to Cloud which is well analogous to literal "Fog" and "Cloud" in sky. The final step could be the data can travel all the way to cloud and does the needed chores. This is Cloud Computing. You will see there is a deep link and a great relevance to the context introduced here with the Big Data, Data Analytics and Streaming Analytics which will be explored in later sections.

Storage

Storage can also take three levels as mentioned above - The Device, Gateway (Workstation) or Cloud (Khorshed, Sharma, Kumar, Prasad, Ali & Xiang, 2015). The choice of where to store is decided based on the emergency and nature of data. For instance, if it is temperature data, then it is enough to store once every 10 minutes or only when there is change in the reading to the cloud. During the first 10 minutes, the data can reside locally or at intermediate locations.

Analytics

The data from different sensors have to be filtered for noise and it would need different fusion techniques to be converted to acceptable formats. The fusion of data generated from heterogeneous sources would result in a pre-processed data for analytics. Later, advanced Machine Learning and Analytics Algorithms can be applied on these pre-processed data to arrive at real time insights.

Characteristics of IoT

As it is already discussed, name any domain or technology, there will be a role and relationship to IoT. Hence, it becomes extremely difficult to set clear boundaries and define its characteristics. However, we have attempted to do justice by categorizing few of them based on its priorities leaving the less frequent ones.

Heterogeneity

The kind of hardware and software IoT employs, be it sensors or actuators or the underlying micro-controller or the code which runs on it, all of these are extremely varied in its make, use and constraints. Hence, it becomes inevitable for an IoT based system to work with all odds. (Saini, 2016)

Dynamicity

Internet of Things can be synonymous to smartness. Thereby, it becomes unavoidable that the system in place needs to be dynamic, react and respond to events that trigger based on various environmental happenings.

Scalability

The architecture of Internet of Things should be so that any device that dies out of power or for any new addition to an existing infrastructure, the system should handle it gracefully with least time lapse possible. Thus, it is very vital to support scalability.

Interoperability

Having justified the need for heterogeneity, interoperability is a close ally that without any doubt qualifies its need to co-exist. Interoperability can be achieved through standardization on data formats and protocols for IoT. But our understanding as of now is, IoT being in the peak of inflated expectations, it might take few years of revision before it settles down to a rigid standard. So, as of now this would be handled by adaptation layers or middleware or conversion software.

Energy Requirements

Most of the Internet of Things application qualifies in the realm of wearable or portable systems. Having said this, energy constraint will be the greatest threat to the lifetime of these devices. Some devices may be installed in remote areas void of human inhabitants like forests or in volcanoes, hence it is call of the hour to explore on energy harvesting techniques to be part of the IoT systems.

Smartness

As already quoted, IoT is synonymous to Smartness. Every IoT system will have a default prefix smart to it, smart "X". X may be Smart House, Smart City, Smart Traffic Management, Smart Vehicular System and many more. So, the question is how to add the smartness quotient to these dumb devices. Researchers from Artificial Intelligence, Machine Learning, and DeepLearning are breaking their heads to add intelligence to the software and firmware that run on these IoT systems.

Standardization

It is a future call. As of now, it is too early to talk about standardized hardware, standardized software, standardized protocol or anything for that matter. Many researchers and big companies are working in their own fields to create their version of IoT enabled entities.

Data Centric cum Address Centric

Traditional internet enabled devices like PC's and desktops are viewed as mere IP centric systems, to reach a PC you need to provide its address, i.e. address specific. Though it is agreed that devices in IoT also need to identify as in conventional IP based systems, we believe IoT would also need to be data centric at times based on application in hand. So, IoT needs to be data-centric network as well as Address-centric, as applications are more specifically based on what user demands. For instance, sometimes the user may be interested to know the temperature of the room and never bothers of which Arduino Digital Humidity Temperature Sensor (DHT11) or Arduino Linear Monolithic (LM35) Temperature Sensor provides it. But, in some cases the same user would be interested to update a new firmware.

Connectivity and Availability

The Connectivity should be such that Availability becomes 24x7. So, IoT systems should be well connected with sufficient Fault Tolerance, Resilience and to some extent Redundancy.

Ease of Use

At the end of the day all that one does should be useful to human fraternity. If the system at use has a huge learning curve, difficult steps to operate and a clumsy UI, the system becomes a failure. Thus, IoT systems have to take enough attention in their design, look and feel and the UI.

Security

Having said all of the above, if the security is compromised, it could be highly dangerous and fatal as well. Thus, Security should be given extreme importance and care at all levels of design and implementation of an IoT system. Various security attacks possible can be at device level (Virus, Worm, Trojan, Root kit, etc.), Workstation or Gateway or Server level (Denial of Service attacks) or Cloud based attacks. It is paramount importance to defer hacking at every level possible. There are numerous challenges that exist as the existing Security Algorithms and Encryption Algorithms are heavy (computationally intensive). Hence, it becomes want of the minute to tailor, make it, in order to meet the needs of constrained environment which prevails in almost every IoT system.

INTRODUCTION TO OTHER ENABLING TECHNOLOGIES LIKE CLOUD, SOA AND SEMANTIC WEB

The integration of Big Data Streaming Analytics and IoT becomes more powerful and interesting with other supporting technologies like Cloud, Service Science and Semantic Web. Cloud Computing is the method of providing a set of shared computing resources which is the exact need of distributed stream processing systems for IoT data. The deployment models of cloud (Public, Private, Community and Hybrid) along with the delivery models of (PaaS, IaaS, SaaS, XaaS) gives the advantages of Scalability, Elasticity, Dynamic Resource Pooling, Self Service, low upfront costs and Fault Tolerance. Cloud Computing technologies plays an important role in development and management of IoT systems at a bulky scale. But the integration of IoT and Cloud brings along with it few challenges.

Among many other challenges like diversified systems, complex and dynamic scaling systems, programming the IoT applications on cloud gains paramount importance. Many researchers are working in this direction to provide programming models by abstracting most of the details and handling complexity, diversity and scaling of IoT systems swiftly (Nastic, Sehic, Vogler, Truong & Dustdar, 2013). Service Science is an emerging area which offers all applications as a service that could talk to each other on common platforms like Enterprise Service Bus (ESB) (Wikipedia, 2017e). Big Data technologies can make generating metadata and analyzing relationships in Semantic Web faster, straightforward and efficient. Linked Big Data as a service in the future will provide more meaningful strategies for governments where huge amount of data is held in silos among departments.

DISTRIBUTED STREAM PROCESSING

Most of the Big Data applications have the need to process data in real time and act according to the result of analytics. Roots of Stream Processing arise from the needs of business and scientific applications like Stock Exchange, Jet Propulsion Control, Call Detail Records Monitoring. The processing of such fast moving streams of data introduces significant additional attributes to be taken care of like Latency, Fault Tolerance, integration with existing historical data, integration with Batch Processing systems. Distributed Stream Processing systems form a section of Big Data processing where the data is moving in fast streams instead of static stored data on disk. It is highly time bound and sensitive to delays caused by analytics. This is a lively area of academic and industrial research, commercial products and open-source development.

Characteristics of Distributed Stream Processing

Below are the significant characteristics of Stream Processing systems (Ellis, 2014):

Fault Tolerance

The input streams out of sensors are generated on events or changes. So, the system should be on and available for processing always. The system should be robust and tolerant to failure. So, when a node or data failure occurs, the recovery procedures should be intact. Work should be distributed and when a node fails, others should be able to take up the work. Similarly, proper Replication and Storage procedures should be in place so that when the data fails, the system must be able to detect, do a replay and proceed further.

Low Latency

The time to process is referred to as the time when the input tuple enters the system and is made available in the delivery end. There has to be a trade-off between Latency, Security, Replication, Distribution and correct processing. The limits of latency have to be defined by the end users of system. This Service Level Agreement (SLA) has to be met by dynamically adjusting other processes.

Scalability

As the data size grows unexpectedly, the system must be able to process the same without any visible fluctuations to the user. There are two ways in which systems could scale – horizontal and vertical. Vertical Scaling was the predominant option in the recent past which refers to adding more resources in terms of RAM, processors to the same single server. With the advances and affordability in commodity hardware, Horizontal Scaling proves to be more efficient than Vertical Scaling. Horizontal Scaling does not burden a single server but adds more servers to the cluster. But in such cases, a Cluster Co-ordination service such as Zookeeper is essential.

Terminologies in Stream Processing

The different terminologies used in Stream Processing Graph are shown in Figure 1.

Data Source

This component is the producer of streaming data e.g. Sensors, Mobile Apps

Data Sink

This component consumes the result of Stream Processing result tuples.

Tuples

The individual data items produced by the source that can be consumed e.g. sensor readings at a time interval

Graph

Every stream processing engine converts the code of an application into a directed acyclic graph where the streams generated by sources are processed by multiple operators and finally routed to sinks as shown in the diagram below.

Processing Elements/Operators

These are the basic functional units that performs the tasks of Filtering, Aggregation, Grouping, Sorting, Applying Analytics, etc. on the incoming tuples.

Topology

A fixed or dynamic arrangement of sources, sinks, operators and flow.

Figure 1. Stream processing graph (Designed by the authors, 2017)

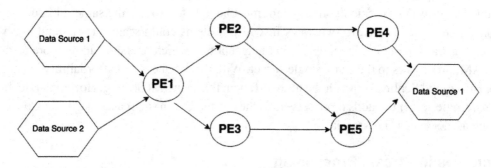

Work Flow of Streaming Analytics Engines

The stream processing systems have the below components as part of its workflow as shown in Figure 2.

Collection

This phase involves the collection of streaming data from different sources. This could be via subscribed services delivering sensor data, periodically monitoring push messages from mobile phones, etc. The format of data could be in JSON (Wikipedia, 2017g), micro text messages, etc. JSON proves to be a flexible and powerful format of data exchange in device to stream processing systems environment.

Flow

There are two main points to be considered in Information Flow Design in a Stream Processing engine. First, the flow should address how the data is going to be delivered to the processing elements from the sources. Second, after the data enters from the sources into the Stream Processing system, how is it going to flow between processing elements. Such internal flow is also important because the arrangement of operators could be static or dynamic depending on the volume of input.

Processing

Main operations such as Filtering, Dimensionality Reduction, Grouping, applying Machine Learning Algorithms, etc. is done in this phase.

Delivery

The output could be alerts, answers to tweets, triggers to actuators, to a UI Visualization dashboard or to another system.

Storage

Storage is done after Processing to avoid Latency. But Storage is essential for replay purpose on failure or inconsistency and historical analysis. NoSQL Storage systems provide excellent support for unstructured or semi structured data and when the dimension of every tuple is not fixed.

Figure 2. Stream processing workflow (Designed by the authors, 2017)

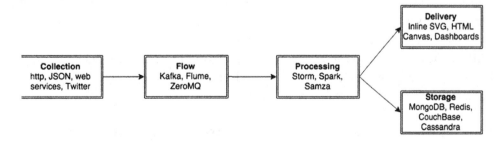

Architecture of Existing Stream Processing Engines

Apache Storm

Apache Storm (Apache Storm, 2016) is an Open Source Distributed, Scalable Stream Processing System. It can be used with a wide array of programming languages. It seamlessly integrates with the queuing technologies which are critical for IoT and Stream Processing integration. Storm has the components – Nimbus, Supervisor, Bolts and Spouts. Nimbus is the ring master, responsible for distributing code, assigning tasks, monitoring for breakdown. Supervisors are the worker nodes. Storm follows Master-Slave architecture. All the communication between the Master node (Nimbus) and the Slaves are done through a Cluster Management tool called Zookeeper. Storm does not support state handling at Master and Slave levels. The state is maintained in disks by zookeeper. A topology is a graph of computation having bolts and spouts. A topology can expand along different worker nodes. Spouts are sources of data and bolts are processing elements. Storm allows the user to control the level of parallelism allowed at each node level and spawns threads accordingly.

Apache Spark Streaming

Apache Spark Streaming (Apache Spark, 2016) can ingest data from different types of sources, process and apply algorithms and then deliver the results. The incoming data streams are divided into small batches of data with an abstraction called DStreams or Discritized Streams. DStreams (Zaharia, 2013) is a group of Resilient Distributed Datasets (RDDs) (Zaharia, 2012) which is composed of input tuples in a time interval. Various built in transformation operations like Reduce, Count, Comap, etc. are available in addition to provision for applying Machine Learning and Graph Algorithms from the built-in libraries. It supports windowed operations via Sliding Window operations by specifying the window length and sliding interval in terms of time. It provides options to persist data to disk or custom code could be written for persisting to NoSQL data stores. To ensure Fault Tolerance, it provides two levels of Checkpointing namely the metadata checkpointing and data check pointing.

Apache Samza

Apache Samza (Apache Samza, 2016) is a Distributed Stream Processing framework using Apache Kafka for its messaging and Apache YARN for Resource Management. Input streams here enter into a Samza job, processed and output streams are delivered. Streams are broken into partitions. Each partition has a sequence of messages. Each message in a partition has an identifier assigned to it called as Offset which denotes its relative position from the start of partition. Similarly, each Samza job is broken down to tasks. YARN Scheduler is responsible for assigning partitions to tasks. Jobs and Partitions are logical entities of Samza. Samza heavily relies on YARN and Kafka for stage wise scalable Stream Processing unlike the above two frameworks which have their own components.

Differences Between Streaming and Batch Processing of Big Data

In Batch Processing like Hadoop, the data is Static, stored on File System. The size of data is almost known and the processing is distributed among worker nodes that perform the same task on different chunks of data which are then consolidated to interpret the final result. But this sort of store-then-process style is not suitable for streaming data since data here is in motion. The data has to be analyzed in real time and the actions or results have to be published with fraction of a second latency. The other main challenges over here are Fault Tolerance – how to handle data or worker loss without compromising Latency and unpredictable highly fluctuating volume of input tuples.

Storage Options for Streaming Data

As discussed before, Stream Processing does not work well with the store-then-analyze model. However, data streams are stored for historical analysis, Fault Tolerance and Data Integrity purposes. The emerging class of non-relational not only SQL databases called as NoSQL databases are the best match for storing heterogeneous stream data. In general, they (Wikipedia, 2017f) share the common characteristics of Scalability, Query Support and Fast Persistence through support for In Memory Computing. The types include Key Value, Document, Spatial, Graph and so on.

MongoDB

(MongoDB, 2016) is composed of databases containing Collections. A Collection is in turn composed of documents which further is constructed using fields. A Collection can be indexed. It supports JSON and BSON formats of Data Storage. It has a Grid based File System enabling Storage of large objects divided between multiple documents. The databases are always on and are highly available which is the key requirement of Stream Processing Systems since the data is in motion and generated throughout.

The document model of MongoDB is highly flexible and supports all type of documents from flat to rich ones. MongoDB does not fix any Schema and the Schema is dynamically created depending on the document structure. While this offers a lot of flexibility, certain measures have to be taken to ensure Data Quality. MongoDB automatically distributes data across multiple physical partitions to address hardware limitations. This feature is called Sharding and does not have any effect on the application in terms of querying. The ACID properties are maintained at document level. The number of replications to be made is configurable and In-Memory Computing advantage can be utilized.

CouchBase Server

(CouchBase Server, 2016) is a Distributed Open Source Database. There are multiple storage engines and it can be used as a document database. The documents are stored in JSON format and they dynamically get their schema from the structure of the JSON object. So, in contrast to the traditional database where a fixed schema is defined and applications have to write code to fit to that scheme, CouchBase allows dynamic schema definition for each application. Users have to arrive at a compromise between having fewer richer documents or large number of smaller documents depending on the application needs.

Redis

(RedisLabs, 2016) is an Open Source, in-memory data structure store. It can be used for multiple purposes like Cache, Database and Message Broker. It has a huge variety of data structures ranging from

Strings, Hashes to more complicated Geospatial Indices. It supports publish subscribe type of messaging and supports Lua scripting.

INTEGRATION OF IoT, BIG DATA AND STREAM ANALYTICS

Data Generation and Flow in an IoT System

Internet of Things mostly generates data that is unstructured and has extremely varied message formats as they are collected from multitude of sensors and devices. The most popular IoT applications which pump a huge amount of data may be from sources that include Connected Homes, Smart Grids, Manufacturing, Healthcare, Fitness Trackers, Mobile Devices, Connected Vehicles and more. Thus, the challenges that unfold are really complex and time consuming to handle (Walker, Krishnan, Sivakumar & Al-Anbuky, 2017). The challenges arise due to the following characteristics of IoT data namely

1. Unstructured
2. Raw Form
3. No predefined Schema exists
4. Dynamic and self-describing

Adding to the existing challenges like Heterogeneity, Dynamicity and Storage, the complexity in analyzing them becomes even more difficult due to the nature of data which may be proprietary or privacy data. The need of the hour is to find solution by taking into consideration all of the given challenges and complexities. Few findings and proposals have been put forth by researchers from all over the world. The consolidated knowledge is provided here that is gathered from various sources and experimented thereafter.

Data Generation

The Data Generation can be addressed in two dimensions, the source of the Data Generation and the form of data generated. The primary source of data generated in an IoT system is Sensors. Though it looks as simple at first sight to find just one source to exist, but the variants which it holds under the umbrella word "Sensors" is so varied in its breadth and width. The Sensors can be analog or digital, the parameters they measure ranges from Temperature, Pressure, Humidity, Noise, Gas, Smoke to Sensing very complex in cars and nuclear reactors. The IoT data generated are from extremely heterogeneous sources that are not only noisy but also large-scale; this presents a major challenge to the process of Cleaning, Integrating and Processing the data. The data generated when collected for months together may result in large volumes of data which makes the existing traditional database Storage and data processing tools inadequate. The probable IoT applications capable of generating such huge volumes of data may be from Weather Station, Industrial Automation Hub, Wearable Devices, Driverless Cars, Logistics, Vehicle Tracking Systems and many more.

Assume that there are 100 sensors and each sensor reading is represented in 32 bits and the rate at which the sensor is sampled is every 60 minutes. Given these statistics, if done a simple calculation using the metric that is used to calculate the size of data it boils down to 192,000 bits/hour (32*100*60) i.e.

24,000 bytes/hour which will exponentially grow with time. A point not to forget is this calculation is made neglecting the Latency involved in transmitting the data from the Source Point to Sink which may have the database to store the same which if included may add up to few more bytes. Hence, it becomes extremely important to consider Big Data Analytics tools on Big Data Storage as against traditional methods which would fail for the reasons stated earlier.

Data Flow

The data generated at the lowest level of architecture has to travel all the way to the application layer via middleware i.e. the data generated at the sensors has to reach the applications intended to display the values to the users or perform Data Analysis or future Prediction Analysis or Storage at a database or Cloud or Server. And all this data from Sensors to Application Layer will traverse via gateway. The data generated at the sensors can be transported through radio transmission which is considered popular, apart from other transmission techniques like Wi-Fi or Internet available. Moreover, the way the data is transferred also gains sufficient importance as it contributes to major cause of Power Drain when compared to the energy needed to process.

The data from various sensors can be aggregated as a single data packet or each sensor data can be sent separately. Each of these methods has their own merits and demerits. The first model though seems to be appealing at the first glance; it fails to prove effective when data values of few sensors do not change for a considerable amount of time. Even if there is change in a single sensor, the whole set has to be resent. But the later scores in this scenario where one needs to send only when there is change in specific sensor reading. And also, the rate at which the sensor readings are sensed are completely application specific. For instance, polling a dairy factory very frequently may affect the quality of the product deliberately as it may be exposed to sensing procedures. So, care needs to be taken and decided accordingly to sense every minute or hour or alternative days.

The data transmission can be in Round Robin or in Arbitration Fashion. Appropriately, techniques like CSMA/CA (Carrier Sense Multiple Access/Collision Avoidance) or TDMA can be employed. Some kind of Data Compression is also recommended before the data leaves the device level to the application level. This provides good savings in energy during transmission and reduces considerable space in Storage. The reduction in space indirectly helps to save energy as size of the database is directly proportional to the search time.

Once the data generated from the sensors is ready to leave the device, it can be routed to the real time Streaming Analytics layer. In doing so, the options would be to use the device server IoTBroker Protocol like MQTT or Messaging Brokers like Kafka, Flume and ZeroMQ, etc.

High Level Architecture of IoT and Streaming Analytics

As Internet of Things is evolving, there exists no standard architecture as of now. Still there is some popular architecture proposed which sounds very convincing as shown in Figure 3.

The above Figure provides the abstract architecture of IoT. The physical layer is comprised of Sensors and Actuators. The Data Link and the Networking Layer are capable of performing Pre-processing, Filtering and Aggregation before sending to the above layers. The transportation layer can be TCP or UDP based on the application in hand. The Communication Protocols again are dependent on the application under consideration. The Gateway symbolically represents a Middleware or a Server or an extension to

Cloud which is capable of Data Storage and Complex Analytics. The Application Layer comprises of users from various walks of life who can access the data via their laptop or mobile browser.

Figure 3. IoT architecture (Designed by the authors, 2017)

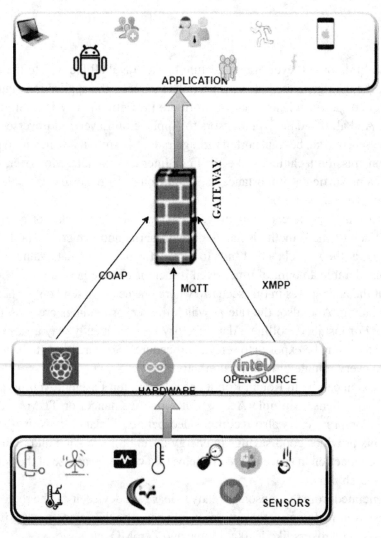

Application Domains of the Integration of Internet of Things and Big Data Analytics

The Application Domain of IoT is every exhaustive. As we have already discussed, few applications would qualify to be called as Internet of Things with Big Data, recalling it as Weather Station, Industrial Automation Hub, Wearable Devices, Driverless Cars, Logistics, and Vehicle Tracking Systems. Figure 4 provides the broad picture of all the application domains of IoT. IoT applications generate data that are of large volumes, great velocity and abundant variety. The case study which is considered is of Autonomous Cars, the vehicle which is capable of movement by sensing environment without human intervention.

Figure 4. IoT and streaming analytics application domains (Designed by the authors, 2017)

In 2015, Tesla Motors rolled out automobiles that included Tesla Autopilot capability. In 2012, Google announced its Driverless Car (Wikipedia, 2017g). There are huge advancements till 2016 after which both of these companies had a setback because of fatality that occurred due to the lack of proper decision and execution by the machines and they failed to apply breaks when needed. Having all that aside, humans would never surrender to failures and the urge to go beyond will exist beyond ages. This is an apt example of an IoT system which will employ Streaming Data and Analysis thereby.

The fact that "Cars having Sensors" is not something new. Every car has around 100 to 200 Sensors serving various purposes but what was not there is their connection to Cloud. The cars of this era comprise of Sensors, Mobile, Big Data and Cloud. Technologists convey there is around 1 GB of data every 90 minutes, having assumed if there exist 10 million cars, you can imagine the massive data in order of sextillions it would pump, which needs huge computational power cycles for that heavy Number Crunching application. Hence, there is a dire need for cloud to do that part of the logic for Data Storage and real time Predictive Analysis.

And coming to the protocols that will be used, one may think HTTP as the popular choice, but the heaviness, lack of QoS and Reliability Metrics makes it quite an alien to IoT based Big Data scenarios. Most popularly used protocol as of now is MQTT (Message Queuing Telemetry and Transport) (Banks & Gupta, 2014) a M2M protocol engineered for very small footprint, low power and less bandwidth usage, which also follows Publish-Subscribe Model with Cars subscribed to a central MQTT Broker which receives the real-time data published by the Sensors on board. Interestingly, Facebook Messenger also uses MQTT as its underlying protocol as it is extremely lightweight and compared to HTTP in a cellular 3G network, it provides 93 times faster throughput, uses 1/8th of Network Overhead and 1/11th of battery power to send (IBM Big Data & Analytics Hub, 2016).

The lightweight nature can be better understood with the MQTT data format. The MQTT command messages may use Fixed Header or Variable Header, a Payload and Message Identifiers.

Table 1. MQTT header (Designed by the authors, 2017)

Bit	7	6	5	4	3	2	1	0
Byte 1	Message Type				DUP	QoS		Retain
Byte 2	Remaining Length							

Table 1 shows the Fixed Header of MQTT. It follows Big-Endian Notation (MSB prefixes LSB). The bits 7-4 is used to indicate the message type which has values enumerated from 0-15. Few enumerated values like 0, 2, 8 indicates Reserved, Connect Acknowledge and Subscribe respectively. DUP indicated Duplicate Delivery. This flag is set when the Client or Server attempts to re-deliver a PUBLISH, PUBREL, SUBSCRIBE or UNSUBSCRIBE message. The QoS flag indicates the level of assurance for delivery of a PUBLISH message. The QoS values 0, 1, 2, 3 indicates Fire and Forget, Acknowledged Delivery, Assured Delivery and Reserved.

Table 2. QoS values (Designed by the authors, 2017)

QoS Value	Bit 2	Bit 1		Description
0	0	0	At most once	Fire and Forget
1	0	1	At least once	Acknowledged delivery
2	1	0	Exactly once	Assured delivery
3	1	1	Reserved	

Retain flag is used only by PUBLISH messages. This informs server to retain messages even after delivery and it will be cleared after receiving a zero length payload and Retain flag set on the same topic. MQTT broker identifies events that are published and subscribed using concept called as Topic. A Topic would look like this home/kitchen/+. "+" here indicates "all the topics under home/kitchen/ e.g.: home/kitchen/temperature, /home/kitchen/humidity are valid matches and home/bedroom/temperature, business/kitchen/humidity are invalid matches.

The variable header as shown in Table 2 comprises of Protocol Version, Connect Flags, Username and Password Flags, Keep Alive Timer, Connect Return Code and Topic Name. The Payload contains application specific data. The message commands like CONNECT, SUBSCRIBE, SUBACK have payloads. The Message ID is a 16-bit unsigned integer that must be unique. A client will maintain its own list of Message IDs separate to the Message IDs used by the server it is connected to. It is possible for a client to send a PUBLISH with Message ID 1 at the same time as receiving a PUBLISH with Message ID 1. (MQTT Wikipedia, 2017d). Though, there is simplicity maintained at almost all levels of communication but what makes things more complicated in autonomous cars is the data stream which it needs to handle. Streams are high speed data which needs real time decision. MQTT based integration with Stream Processing is shown in Figure 5.

Figure 5. MQTT based integration (Designed by the authors, 2017)

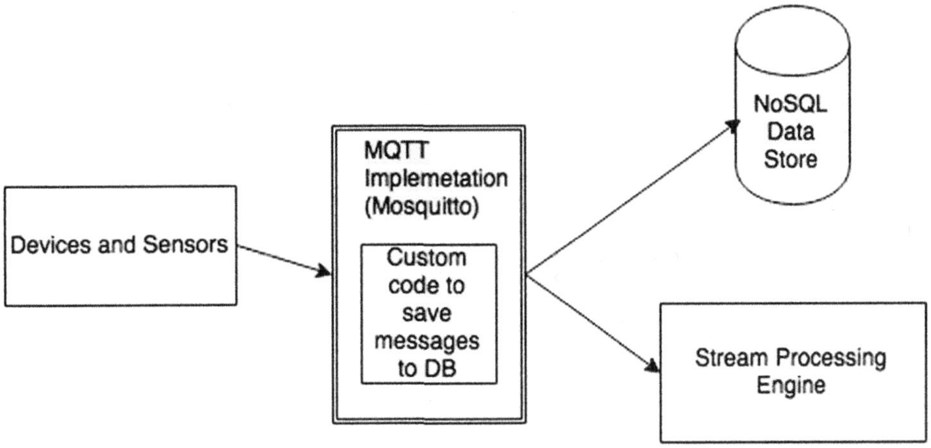

Suitability of Existing Stream Processing Engines for IoT Generated Data Analytics

There is huge amounts of data generated every hour as we have already discussed. But what makes IoT important and interesting is not the data by itself, but the analytics that is performed on it to create a meaningful information be it a Traffic Pattern Prediction, Weather Forecasting or whatever for that matter. Thus, it gains paramount importance to understand the analytical engines suitable for IoTData Analytics. The Stream Analytics engines help to develop and deploy solutions by performing Stream Processing in the Cloud using the data collected from Sensors, Devices and Applications thereby providing real time results. And it is particularly important for Internet of Things which are primarily event driven systems which stream in order of trillions of events every hour. And these systems demand High Performance, Reliability and would require real time dashboards to visualize and generate alerts when data is received from Sensors or Services.

There are so many Open Source Stream Analytics Platforms like Apache Flink, Spark Streaming, Apache Samza, Apache Storm and commercial tools like Azure Streaming Stream Analytics, Cisco Connected Stream Analytics, Informatica and many more. The real Data Generation and Analytics is what is highlighted in this chapter but there are some areas of research which would need large data than what can be produced at real time. In those cases, researchers have worked on synthesizing large amounts of data (Anderson, Kennedy, Ngo, Luckow & Apon, 2015) to facilitate analytics for research purposes. Interested readers are directed to refer the full paper as this is not in the scope of this chapter.

The data from IoT devices are sent to a Server/Gateway via various Device to Server (D2S) protocols like MQTT (Message Queuing and Telemetry Transport), CoAP (Constrained Application Protocol), XMPP (Extensible Messaging and Presence Protocol). As it is out of the scope to discuss about these protocols, we will not go in detail. But one thing to make it clear is, if your need is Client to Broker Application, then the simplest and easiest choice would be to go with MQTT and Mosquito, an Open Source MQTT Broker. The data thus received would be sent to an Analytics System. It is always a good practice to store the data, to achieve redundancy and reliability, in cases of faults or replay before transformation. The data can be stored in File Systems like HDFS or NoSQL Storage Systems like MongoDB and Couchbase. As the Protocol Broker is not capable of pushing the data, we need to write a custom code and attach it to the IoT Protocol Broker (Mosquito) which is shown in the below Figure.

Figure 6. Information flow in an IoT and streaming analytics integrated system
(Designed by the authors, 2017)

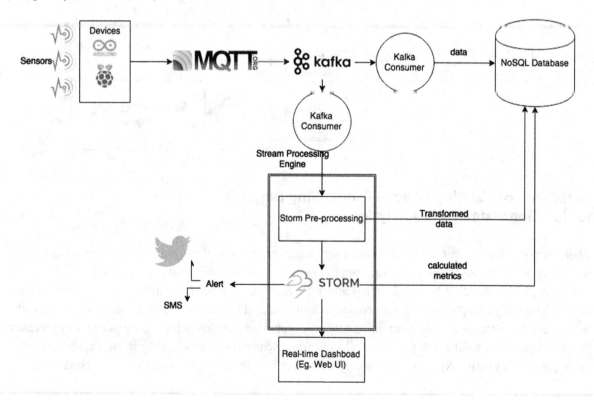

The alternative approach is to use Messaging Brokers like Apache Kafka, Apache Flume or ZeroMQ in place of the Custom Code. Message Brokers were traditionally used for delivery of messages and now have many advanced applications including Decoupling, Queuing and Buffering. There exist alternatives to this as well, instead of Messaging Brokers, we can have a separate operator in the directed acyclic graph to persist the input tuples. The second type of model discussed above (IoT Analytics Solution with Big data, 2015) with Kafka and Storm is shown in the diagram below Figure 6.

The raw data achieved may not be suitable to perform analytics, so it is recommended we do Pre-processing to achieve Enrichment and Transformation (during representation of values in other forms). The Transformation can be achieved using custom user defined functions like Pig in case of storing data in Hadoop (Batch Mode Analysis). The Stream Processing engines like Apache Spark, Storm and Samza can also serve better since they all aim at Scalable Distributed Streaming Analytics. The high-level principles of Big Data and IoT integration is shown in the diagram below Figure 7.

Figure 7. Big Data streaming analytics and IoT integration (Designed by the authors, 2017)

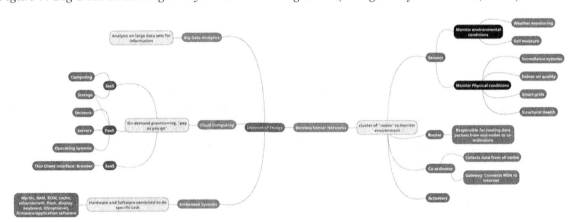

VISUALIZATION TECHNIQUES FOR REAL TIME DISTRIBUTED STREAMING DATA

The practice of using pictorial representation for viewing and analyzing data with maps and graphs has been around for years. The way in which human brain processes pictorial representation is much faster and efficient than going through text or spreadsheets. With the traditional data, earlier Visualization techniques used were 2D or 3D Graphs, Scatter Plots, and Box Plots and so on.

With the growth of data volume and dynamic structure of Big Data, there arises a necessity to find meaningful representation of the huge voluminous data in a holistic Visualization platform for business users to comprehend. Apart from the volume of data, the real-time data from sensors and other sources have to be visualized in near real time for analysis and interpretation. The Visualization of Big Data has to address many problems like the following:

- Prevent loss of information
- Appreciate the context of data relationships and patterns

- Handle dirty data
- Provide consequential pictorial representation
- Ingest data from different types of sources
- Choosing the type of visual to be used
- Aggregate, display and update in a timely manner with reduced latency.

Data Exploration is used by data scientists to understand the inherent relationships and structure in data. The graph types used for exploration might be more technical in nature. The non-technical end users or stakeholders prefer more simple graphs which clearly convey the messages rather than the structure of data. So, the graph type has to be chosen with much care depending on the problem. Though statistical analysis of data is done, Visualization before analysis communicates the differences in structure of distribution of data more effectively than statistical test result numbers.

TYPES OF GRAPHS

Map Markers

Maps are used to depict Geo-Coded data. Examples include flu trends in a country by density in different regions which would quickly enable planning and action for the most affected areas and proximal areas. Many different types of charts like Bubble, Density and Bullet can be laid on top of maps for additional effects. The map shown in Figure 8 shows a SIMILIE Widget Bubble Plot laid on top of United States map to demonstrate the population in US cities. The size of the bubble corresponds to the density of

Figure 8. Map markers showing US cities by population (Designed by Massachusetts Institute of Technology, 2009)

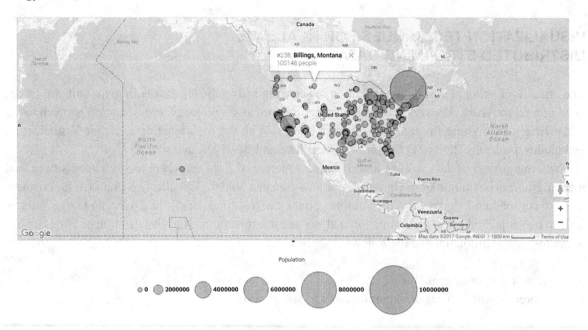

population in cities. Such maps can also be used for clustering regions based on attributes (Massachusetts Institute of Technology, 2009).

Box and Whisker Plots

These plots are used to visualize distribution of continuous data over discrete variables. These plots are very useful in quick understanding of the structure, finding if the data is skewed and for detecting outliers. This plot is based on IQR (Inter Quartile Range). A sample Box and Whisker Plot (Capitula, 2014a) is shown in Figure 9 which demonstrates the 40-yard dash times (speed) from the 2014 NFL Scouting combined with respect to different positions. Each box represents the speed with respect to different positions. The upper hinge of the box represents first quartile (slower players) and the lower hinge (faster players), the third quartile. The line inside the box represents the median value. Two outlier data points in the graph can also be seen.

Figure 9. Box and whisker plot (Designed by Capitula, 2014a)

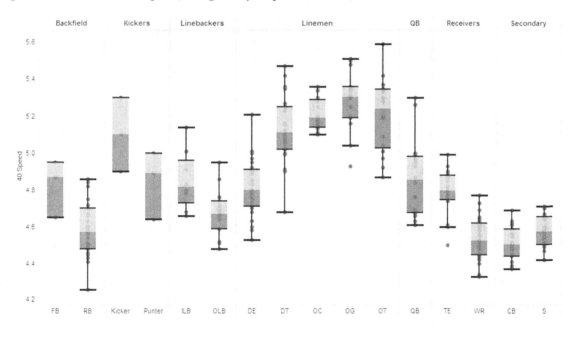

Word Clouds

This is a Visualization technique that displays how frequently words appear in a body of text as in Figure 10 (Digital SAP, 2014). The size of the word is proportionate to the frequency. The words in a word cloud could have metadata associated with it apart from frequency, say a word cloud with all country names and population assigned to the word size. The Word Clouds are generally used to understand the trending topics or terms and cannot be used where numerical insights are needed. Colors on a Word Cloud can be used for aesthetic purpose or could be used to add another dimension to Visualization.

Figure 10. Word cloud (Designed by Digital SAP, 2014)

Network Visualization

Many graphs such as Node-Link graphs, Matrix, Alluvial Diagram, Circular Hierarchy, Hive plot are used to show relationships, data flow and structural changes in a network of entities. A Node-Link Tree diagram is shown in the sample in Figure 11. (Bostock, 2010) depicts the entities as nodes and relationships as vertices. The Tree layout implements the Reingold-Tilford Algorithm for efficient, tidy arrangement of layered nodes. The depth of nodes is computed by distance from the root leading to a ragged appearance.

Time Series Plots

These plots are used when temporal data is available for display. The below Figure 12 (Myers, 2015) shows data with respect to date and time window. The concept of brush allows users to select a window and summarize the data.

Figure 11. Node link tree (Designed by Protovis, 2011)

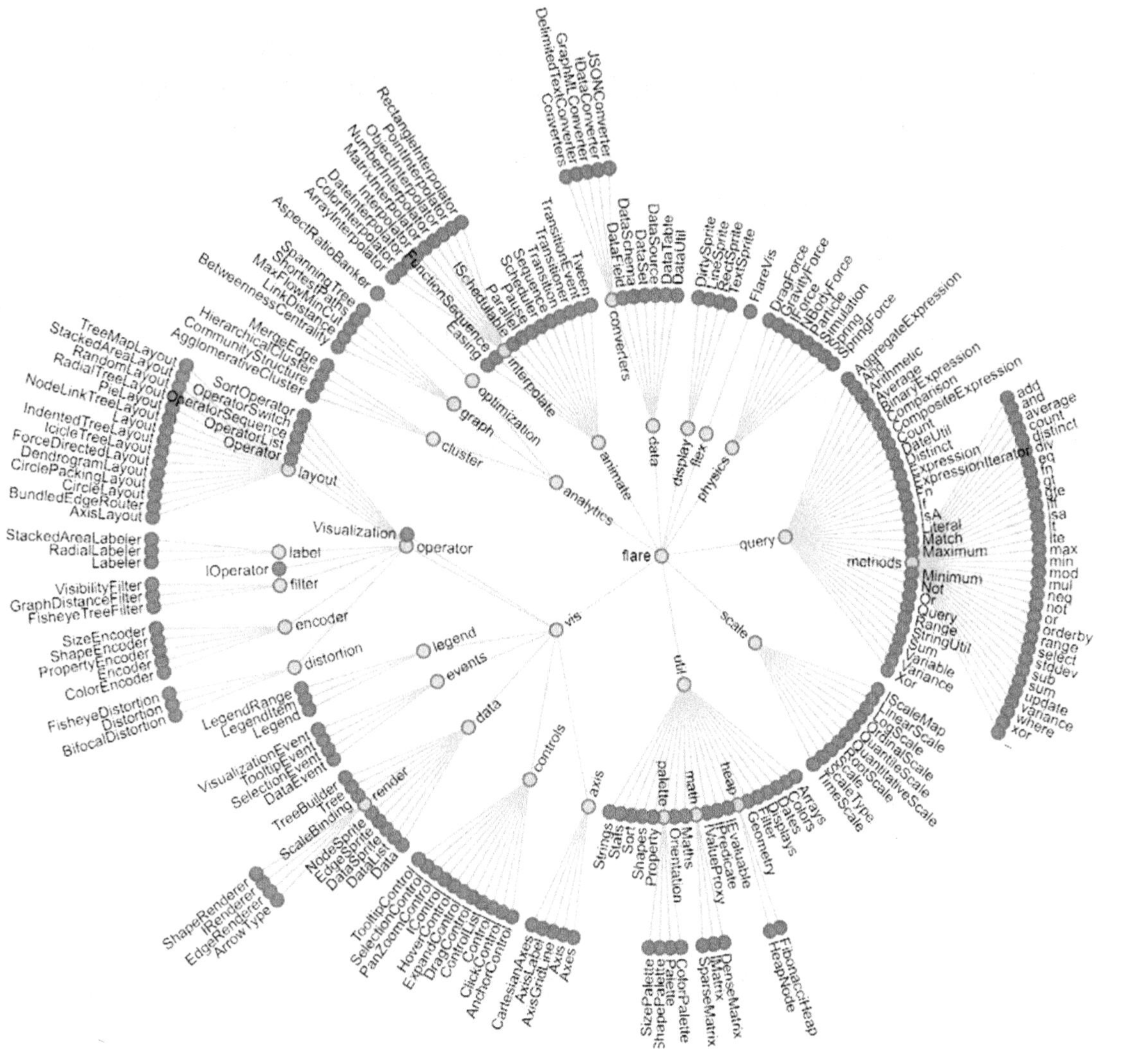

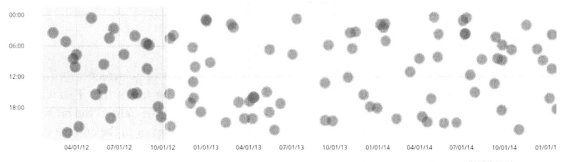

Figure 12. D3.js time series data (Designed by Myers, 2015)

Heat Map

This type of Visualization is used to compare categories using color. The below Heat Map in Figure 13 (Capitula, 2014b) shows the performance by global region for different product lines of a fictional company. The size of the square indicates volume of sales. The color indicates another attribute namely the Profit Margin. The product line performing beneath a certain threshold (50%) is highlighted in red. Profitable regions are coded in increasing shades of green. The darker the green, the more profitable the product category is in that region.

Figure 13. Tableau heat map (Designed by Capitula, 2014b)

TECHNIQUES USED FOR VISUALIZATION

HTML5 Canvas

The Canvas element added from HTML 5 can be used to draw Graphics on to screen with JavaScript. The Canvas tag is similar to any other tag except that it is rendered using JavaScript. This technology is building up as the best possible alternative to Flash. The latest versions of most of the browsers support the Canvas element. The real content of Canvas is not in its attributes or in the content of the tag. It is created using the associated Canvas Context object which is the powerful concept behind Canvas tag. The Canvas element is resolution dependent and is used to render graphics on the fly. It is faster to render and modify the image pixel by pixel if possible. But since it draws pixels, reacting to events and changes to existing drawings are not possible. Images may lose quality when enlarged.

Inline Support Vector Graphics (SVG)

Inline Support Vector Graphics (SVG) uses a DOM (Document Object Model) to define the image to be rendered. Inline SVG is resolution independent and hence preserves quality and clarity when enlarged or scaled on touch based devices. SVG images can be searched, indexed, styled and compressed. Also, HTML Canvas is not suitable for accessibility since it just draws the pixels and does not store it as an internal mode. Also, HTML Canvas works purely with JavaScript whereas for SVG, JavaScript is not mandatory. SVG results in Slow Rendering because of its document complexity since it maintains an internal model.

Server Sent Events (SSEs) and Web Sockets

Both of these technologies are used to push data to browsers. The main difference is that Web Sockets are bi-directional and full duplex. These can send/receive data to/from browsers. The common example for Web Sockets is a chat application where data is sent from the Application to Server and vice versa. In SSEs, the connections can push data from server to the browsers. Example usage of SSEs could be News Feeds, Stock Tickers, Twitter Feed Updates, etc. It might seem like Web Sockets can do everything that a SSE connection can do. Even this might be the reason behind Web Sockets gaining popularity and being supported by most browsers. But choosing Web Sockets for an application that only allows message flow from server to browser would be an overhead. SSEs are simpler and use existing HTTP protocol which is ideal for the above scenario.

VISUALIZATION TOOLS

Tableau

Tableau (Tableau Software Inc., 2017) is a tool for performing complicated, dynamic visualization of data. By complex visualizations we mean Dynamic Dashboards, Stories, Heat Map Visualizations, etc. It comes in different flavors like Desktop and Server. This provides a way in which your graph could interact with your data. The other main advantage of Tableau is the speed with which it analyzes and visualizes real time data. The flow for working with Tableau is – Connect to Data Source, Drag and Drop Data Fields and Customize. The basic style components like Data Panes, Shelves and Cards help for effective quick Visualization of the data.

D3.js

D3 stands for Data Driven Documents (Bostock, 2015). This is a JavaScript library for visualizing data dynamically with the use of HTML, CSS and SVG. It focuses on binding data to a Document Object Model (DOM). It is written using JavaScript in functional style which allows extensive code reuse and customization. The best part of D3.js is, it tries to fully employ the power of modern browsers and avoid using proprietary frameworks for Visualization.

Gephi

It is an Open Source Network Visualization Tool written in Java (Bastian, Heymann & Jacomy, 2009). It is interactive and best suited for exploring and comprehending networks and hierarchical graphs. It helps the data scientists to discover patterns, singularities and hidden structures in graphs. It supports a variety of formats including Graph Exchange XML Format (GEFX) and Geography Markup Language (GML). It allows modifying the visual aspects of graph and provides basic functionalities like Filtering, Aggregates, Query, Regular Expressions, etc.

SIMILIE Widgets

These are Widgets for different purposes created for a large-scale web project at MIT (SIMILIE Widgets, 2014). There are a group of widgets for different purposes like Diversified Data Sources, Time Series, Rich Visualizations, Map Markers, etc.

CONCLUSION

In this chapter, the characteristics and technologies of Distributed Big Data Stream Processing Systems and Internet of Things (IoT) and their integration are explored which is going to be the case with most of the applications in the future connected environment. The design of applications and supporting technologies will strive for the seamless integration of the above two driving forces. The Distributed Real Time Processing of Device Data, Correlation or Analytics with data from other devices or historical static stored data is of principal importance. The Middleware layer which pushes data from Sensor Actuator environments to the Stream Processing engines requires more Customization and Bridging. This combination attracts more research and commercial work due to its scale of application in near future.

FUTURE RESEARCH WORK AND DIRECTIONS

Other emerging technologies like Fog, Mist or Edge Computing where some level of computation is done at lower levels instead of a single centralized cloud level is gaining popularity and this feature could further augment the principles of Scalable, Distributed Stream Processing of real time IoT generated data. The computing power of Collection and Aggregation devices like Mobile Phones and Routers are also used for some level of Processing and are forwarded to a more centralized layer like Cloud that has a bigger picture. More efficient Algorithms for Dynamic Scaling and Optimizing of Stream Processing Operations depending on the volume and nature of device data on the fly can be analyzed to improvise on Latency. Virtualization of Sensors and Devices, efficient Algorithms for Data Fusion from heterogeneous sensing environments are also the other research areas.

REFERENCES

Apache Software Foundation. (2016a). *Apache Samza - What is Samza?* Retrieved March 4, 2017 from http://samza.apache.org

Apache Software Foundation. (2016b). *Apache Spark Streaming-Spark Streaming makes it easy to build scalable fault-tolerant streaming applications.* Retrieved January 3, 2017 from http://spark.apache.org/streaming/

Apache Software Foundation. (2016c). *Apache Storm.* Retrieved January 2, 2017 from http://storm.apache.org/

Banks, A., & Gupta, R. (2014). *Oasis, MQTT Version 3.1.1,* OASIS Committee Specification Draft 02 / Public Review Draft 02. *IBM.* Retrieved January 7, 2017 from http://docs.oasis-open.org/mqtt/mqtt/v3.1.1/csprd02/mqtt-v3.1.1-csprd02.html

Bastian, M., Heymann, S., & Jacomy, M. (2009). Gephi: An Open Source Software for Exploring and Manipulating Networks. In *Proceedings of the Third International AAAI Conference on Weblogs and Social Media ICWSM '09* (pp. 361-362). Retrieved March 4, 2017 from http://www.aaai.org/ocs/index.php/ICWSM/09/paper/view/154

Bostock, M. (2010). *Protovis, Node-Link Trees.* Protovis: *A Graphical Toolkit for Visualization.* Stanford Visualization Group. Retrieved January 8, 2017 from http://mbostock.github.io/protovis/ex/tree.html

Bostock, M. (2017). Data Driven Documents (D3). Retrieved January 3, 2017 from https://d3js.org/

Capitula, C. (2014a). *Tableau Essentials: Chart Types - Box-and-Whisker Plot.* Interworks Inc. Retrieved January 4, 2017 from https://www.interworks.com/blog/ccapitula/2014/12/09/tableau-essentials-chart-types-box-and-whisker-plot

Capitula, C. (2014b). *Tableau Essentials: Chart Types - Heat Map.* Interworks Inc. Retrieved January 4, 2017 from https://www.interworks.com/blog/ccapitula/2014/08/06/tableau-essentials-chart-types-heat-map

Cisco Inc. (2016). *IoT: Driving Digital Transformation, Connected Machines Case Study.* Retrieved December 12, 2016 from http://www.audentia-gestion.fr/cisco/case-study-c36-737400.pdf

CouchBaseServer. (2016). Developer Portal - *CouchbaseServer.* CouchbaseInc, couchbase.com. Retrieved January 3, 2017 from https://developer.couchbase.com

Ellis, B. (2014). *Real-Time Analytics: Techniques to Analyze and Visualize Streaming Data.* Hoboken, New Jersey: John Wiley & Sons, Inc. Retrieved May 7, 2017 from http://pdf.th7.cn/down/files/1411/Real-Time%20Analytics.pdf

Grance, T., & Mell, P. (2011). *The NIST Definition of Cloud Computing, Recommendations of the National Institute of Standards and Technology.* National Institute of Standards and Technology, U.S. Department of Commerce. Retrieved January 7, 2017 from http://nvlpubs.nist.gov/nistpubs/Legacy/SP/nistspecialpublication800-145.pdf

IBM Big Data & Analytics Hub. (2014). *Connected car powered by streaming analytics*. Video Retrieved January 7, 2017 from http://www.ibmbigdatahub.com/video/connected-car-powered-streaming-analytics

Intel (2017). *The Internet of Things (IoT) Starts with Intel Inside*. Retrieved December 13, 2016 from http://www.intel.in/content/www/in/en/internet-of-things/overview.html

IoT-GSI. (2017). *Internet of Things Global Standards Initiative*. (IoT-GSI). ITU. Retrieved January 3, 2017 from http://www.itu.int/en/ITU-T/gsi/iot/Pages/default.aspx

Massachusetts Institute of Technology. (2009). *SIMILIE Widgets, Free Open-Source Data Visualization Web Widgets, and More*. Retrieved January 12, 2017 from http://www.simile-widgets.org

Minerva, R. (2014). *From M2M to Virtual Continuum. Telecom Italia*. Presentation at IEEE Internet of Things. Retrieved January 5, 2017 from http://iot-360.eu/2014/wp-content/uploads/2014/10/Roberto_Minerva.pdf

MongoDB Inc. (2017). *MongoDB Atlas Database as a Service*. Retrieved March 4, 2017 from https://www.mongodb.com

Myers, B. (2015). *D3 Timeseries with Brush*. Machine Learning Visualization Lab (MLVZ). Retrieved January 3, 2017 from http://mlvl.github.io/timeseries/

Redis Labs. (2016). *Redis*. Retrieved December 10, 2016 from https://redis.io

Rhodes, P. (2015). Build an IoT analytics solution with big data tools. InfoWorld from IDG Communications Inc. Retrieved March 4, 2017 from http://www.infoworld.com/article/2876247/application-development/building-an-iot-analytics-solution-with-big-data-tools.html

SAP.com (2014). *Word Cloud*. Retrieved January 3, 2017 from https://digital.sap.com/word-cloud/

Tableau Software Inc. (2017). Make your data make an impact. Retrieved January 12, 2017 from https://www.tableau.com/

Technology Strategy Board. Driving Innovation (2011). *Internet of Things convergence: Competition for Funding of Preparatory Studies*. Retrieved January 4, 2017 from http://webarchive.nationalarchives.gov.uk/20130221185318/www.innovateuk.org/_assets/0511/tsb_internetofthingsconvergencecompflyert11-043_final_dh.pdf

Walker, C., Sivakumar, S., & Al-Anbuky, A. (2015). Data Flow and Management for an IoT Based WSN. In *Proceedings of 8th 2015 IEEE International Conference on Data Science and Data Intensive Systems (DSDIS)*, Sydney, NSW, Australia (pp. 624-631). Retrieved May 7, 2017 from http://ieeexplore.ieee.org/document/7396566/?denied

Wikipedia. (2017a). *Internet of Things*. Retrieved January 7, 2017 from https://en.wikipedia.org/wiki/Internet_of_things

Wikipedia. (2017b). *Gartner*. Retrieved January 7, 2017 from https://en.wikipedia.org/wiki/Gartner

Wikipedia. (2017c). *WSN (Wireless Sensor Networks)*. Retrieved January 7, 2017 from https://en.wikipedia.org/wiki/Wireless_sensor_network

Wikipedia. (2017d). *MQTT (Message Queue Telemetry Transport)*. Retrieved January 7, 2017 from https://en.wikipedia.org/wiki/MQTT

Wikipedia. (2017e). *Enterprise Service Bus*. Retrieved January 7, 2017 from https://en.wikipedia.org/wiki/Enterprise_service_bus

Wikipedia. (2017f). *NoSQL*. Retrieved January 7, 2017 from https://en.wikipedia.org/wiki/NoSQL

Wikipedia. (2017g). *JSON*. Retrieved January 7, 2017 from https://en.wikipedia.org/wiki/JSON

Wikipedia. (2017h). *Autonomous Car*. Retrieved January 7, 2017 from https://en.wikipedia.org/wiki/Autonomous_car

Zaharia, M., Choudhury, M., Das, T., Dave, A., Ma, J., McCauley, M., . . . Stoica, I. (2012). Resilient Distributed Datasets: A Fault-Tolerant Abstraction for In-Memory Cluster Computing. In *Proceedings of the 9th USENIX conference on Networked Systems Design and Implementation NSDI '12*. New York, NY: ACM. Retrieved May 7, 2017 from https://www.usenix.org/system/files/conference/nsdi12/nsdi12-final138.pdf

Zaharia, M., Das, T., Li, H., Hunter, T., Shenker, S., & Stoica, I. (2013). Discretized Streams: Fault-Tolerant Streaming Computation at Scale. In *Proceedings of the Twenty-Fourth ACM Symposium on Operating Systems Principles - SOSP '13* (pp. 423-438). San Jose, CA: University of California, Berkeley Press. Retrieved May 7, 2017 from https://people.csail.mit.edu/matei/papers/2013/sosp_spark_streaming.pdf

ADDITIONAL READING

Anderson, J. W., Kennedy, K. E., Ngo, L. B., Luckow, A., & Apon, A. W. (2014). Synthetic Data Generation for the Internet of Things. In *Proceedings of 2014 IEEE International Conference on Big Data* (pp. 171–176). New York, NY: IEEE. Retrieved from https://www.academia.edu/8810726/Synthetic_Data_Generation_for_the_Internet_of_Things

Andrade, H. C. M., Morgan, J. P., Gedik, B., & Turaga, D. S. (2014). *Fundamentals of Stream Processing, Application Design, Systems and Analytics*. Cambridge, UK: Cambridge Press. Retrieved from https://pdfs.semanticscholar.org/44d0/e6515ea555c4411e63f4d8a14a63d9083b8c.pdf

Borgia, E., Gomes, D. G., Lagesse, B., Lea, R., & Puccinelli, D. (2016). Special issue on "Internet of Things: Research challenges and Solutions". *Computer Communications*, *89-90*, 1–4. Retrieved from https://iths.pure.elsevier.com/en/publications/special-issue-on-internet-of-things-research-challenges-and-solut doi:10.1016/j.comcom.2016.04.024

Catarinucci, L., de Donno, D., Mainetti, L., Palano, L., Patrono, L., Stefanizzi, M. L., & Tarricone, L. (2015). An IoT- Aware Architecture for Smart Healthcare Systems. *IEEE Internet of Things Journal*, *2*(6), 515-526. Retrieved from https://www.researchgate.net/publication/277606319_An_IoT-Aware_Architecture_for_Smart_Healthcare_Systems

Cecchinel, C., Jimenez, M., Mosser, S., & Riveill, M. (2014). An Architecture to Support the Collection of Big Data in the Internet of Things. In *Proceedings of the 2014 IEEE World Congress on Services SERVICES '14* (pp. 442-449). New York, NY: ACM. Retrieved from http://dl.acm.org/citation.cfm?id=2673472

Chiang, M., & Zhang, T. (2014). Research Directions for the Internet of Things. *IEEE Internet of Things Journal, 1*(1), 3-9. Retrieved from http://web.eecs.umich.edu/~prabal/teaching/resources/eecs582/stankovic14iot.pdf

Cugola, G., & Margara, A. (2012). Processing flows of information: From data stream to complex event processing. In *Journal ACM Computing Surveys (CSUR), 44*(3), 1-62. Retrieved from http://dl.acm.org/citation.cfm?id=2187677

Damji, J. S. (2014). Real World Examples: Real Time Data from The Internet of Things (IoT). *Horton Works*. Retrieved from http://hortonworks.com/blog/real-world-examples-real-time-data-internet-things/

Din, S., Ghayvat, H., Paul, A., Ahmad, A., Rathore, M. M., & Shafi, I. (2015). An architecture to analyze big data in the Internet of Things. In *Proceedings of 2015 9th International Conference on Sensing Technology (ICST)* (pp. 677–682). New York, NY: IEEE. Retrieved from http://ieeexplore.ieee.org/document/7438483/

DT Editorial Services. (2015). *Big Data, Black Book*. New York, NY: Wiley Publishers. Retrieved from https://wdn2.ipublishcentral.com//wiley_publisher/viewinsidehtml/500218191202421

Gubbi, J., Buyya, R., Marusic, S., & Palaniswami, M. (2013). Internet of Things (IoT): A vision, architectural elements, and future directions. *Future Generation Computer Systems, 29*(7), 1645–1660. Retrieved from http://www.parkjonghyuk.net/lecture/2014-2nd-lecture/ubiquitous/salahe.pdf doi:10.1016/j.future.2013.01.010

Hashem, I. A. T., Yaqoob, I., Anuar, N. B., Mokhtar, S., Gani, A., & Khan, S. U. (2015). The rise of "big data" on cloud computing: Review and open research issues. *Information Systems, 47*, 98–115. Retrieved from http://www.sciencedirect.com/science/article/pii/S0306437914001288 doi:10.1016/j.is.2014.07.006

Holmes, A. (Ed.). (2012). *Hadoop in practice*. Greenwich, CT: Manning Publications. Retrieved from http://barbie.uta.edu/~jli/Resources/MapReduce&Hadoop/Hadoop%20in%20Practice%202012.pdf

Hurwitz, J., Nugent, A., Halper, F., & Kaufman, M. (Eds.). (2013). *Big Data ForDummies*. Hoboken, NJ: John Wiley & Sons, Inc. Retrieved from http://eecs.wsu.edu/~yinghui/mat/courses/fall%202015/resources/Big%20data%20for%20dummies.pdf

Khorshed, M. T., Sharma, N. A., Kumar, K., & Xiang, Y. (2015). Integrating Internet-of-Things with the power of Cloud Computing and the intelligence of Big Data analytics — A three layered approach. In *Proceedings of 2015 2nd Asia-Pacific World Congress on Computer Science and Engineering (APWC on CSE) (pp. 1-8)*. New York, NY: IEEE. Retrieved from http://ieeexplore.ieee.org/document/7476124/?denied

Laney, D. (2001). *3D Data Management: Controlling Data Volume, Variety and Velocity*. META Group Inc. Retrieved from https://blogs.gartner.com/doug-laney/files/2012/01/ad949-3D-Data-Management-Controlling-Data-Volume-Velocity-and-Variety.pdf

Lee, C. K. M., Yeung, C. L., & Cheng, M. N. (2015). Research on IoT based Cyber Physical System for Industrial big data Analytics. In *Proceedings of 2015 IEEE International Conference on Industrial Engineering and Engineering Management (IEEM)* (pp. 1855-1859). Retrieved from https://www. researchgate.net/publication/302480177_Research_on_IoT_based_Cyber_Physical_System_for_Industrial_big_data_Analytics

Marz, N., & Warren, J. (2015). Big *Data: Principles and Best Practices of Scalable Real-time Data Systems*. Greenwich, Connecticut: Manning Publications. Retrieved from http://www.datascienceassn. org/sites/default/files/Big%20Data%20Principles%20and%20Best%20Practices.pdf

Mondal, A., Rao, P., & Madria, S. K. (2016). Mobile Computing, Internet of Things, and Big Data for Urban Informatics. *Presentation at 17th IEEE International Conference on Mobile Data Management (MDM)*. Retrieved from https://www.slideshare.net/PraveenRao48/mobile-computing-internet-of-things-and-big-data-for-urban-informatics

Nastic, S., Sehic, S., Vogler, M., Truong, H. L., & Dustdar, S. (2013). PatRICIA-A Novel Programming Model for IoT Applications on Cloud Platforms. In *Proceedings of 2013 IEEE 6th International Conference on Service-Oriented Computing and Applications* (SOCA) (pp. 53 – 60). Retrieved from http:// www.infosys.tuwien.ac.at/staff/ssehic/papers/SOCA13-Nastic.pdf

Saini, N. K. (2016). Trust factor and reliability-over-a-period-of-time as key differentiators in IoT enabled services. In *Proceedings of International Conference on Internet of Things and Applications (IOTA)* (pp. 411-414). New York, NY: IEEE. Retrieved from http://ieeexplore.ieee.org/document/7562762/

Satyanarayanan, M., Simoens, P., Xiao, Y., Pillai, P., Chen, Z., Ha, K., ... Amos, B. (2015). Edge Analytics in the Internet of Things. *IEEE Pervasive Computing, 14*(2), 24–31. Retrieved from https://www. cs.cmu.edu/~satya/docdir/satya-edge2015.pdf doi:10.1109/MPRV.2015.32

Schneider, S. (2013). Understanding the protocols behind the Internet of Things. *Electronic Design, Penton*. Retrieved from http://electronicdesign.com/iot/understanding-protocols-behind-internet-things

Stankovic, J. (2016). Fog and IoT: An Overview of Research Opportunities. *IEEE Internet of Things Journal, 3*(6), 854-864. doi:. Retrieved from http://www.download-paper.com/wp-content/uploads/2017/01/2016-ieee-Fog-and-IoT-An-Overview-of-Research-Opportunities.pdf doi:10.1109/JIOT.2016.2584538

Sun, Y., Song, H., Jara, A. J., & Bie, R. (2016). Internet of Things and Big Data Analytics for Smart and Connected Communities. *IEEE Access, 4,* 766-773. Retrieved from http://ieeexplore.ieee.org/stamp/ stamp.jsp?arnumber=7406686

Yang, C., Liu, X., Zhang, X., Nepal, S., & Chen, J. (2015). A Time Efficient Approach for Detecting Errors in Big Sensor Data on Cloud. *IEEE Transactions on Parallel and Distributed Systems, 26*(2), 329–339. Retrieved from http://www.chennaisunday.com/2015DOTNET/A%20Time%20Efficient%20 Approach%20for%20Detecting%20Errors.pdf doi:10.1109/TPDS.2013.2295810

KEY TERMS AND DEFINITIONS

Discretized Streams (DStreams): A Discretized Stream or D-Stream groups together a series of RDDs and lets the user manipulate them through various operators. D-Streams provide both stateless operators such as map which act independently on each time interval and stateful operators such as aggregation over a Sliding Window which operate on multiple intervals and may produce intermediate RDDs as state. (Zaharia, 2013)

Enterprise Service Bus (ESB): An Enterprise Service Bus (ESB) is implementing a communication system between mutually interacting software applications in a Service-Oriented Architecture (SOA). It implements a software architecture as depicted on the right. As it implements a software architecture for Distributed Computing, it implements a special variant of the more general Client-Server model also whereas in general any application using ESB can behave as Server or Client in turn. ESB promotes agility and flexibility with regards to high protocol-level communication between applications. The primary goal of high protocol-level communication is Enterprise Application Integration (EAI) of heterogeneous and complex landscapes. (Wikipedia, 2017e)

Gartner: An American research and advisory firm providing Information Technology related insight for IT and other business leaders located across the world. Its headquarters are in Stamford, Connecticut, United States. It was known as Gartner Group, Inc. until 2000 when it was then changed to Gartner. (Wikipedia, 2017b)

Infrastructure as a Service (IaaS): The capability provided to the consumer is to provision Processing, Storage, Networks and other fundamental computing resources where the consumer is able to deploy and run arbitrary software which can include Operating Systems and applications. The consumer does not manage or control the underlying Cloud infrastructure but has control over Operating Systems, Storage and Deployed Applications; and possibly limited control of selected networking components (o.g., host firewalls). (Moll &Grance, 2011c)

Internet of Things (IoT): The internetworking of physical devices, vehicles (also referred to as "connected devices" and "smart devices"), buildings and other items embedded with Electronics, Softwares, Sensors, Actuators and Network Connectivity that enable these objects to collect and exchange data. (Wikipedia, 2017a)

JSON (JavaScript Object Notation): JSON is an open-standard format that uses human-readable text to transmit data objects consisting of attribute–value pairs. It is the most common data format used for asynchronous browser/server communication, largely replacing XML which is used by Ajax. JSON is a language independent data format. It derives from JavaScript but as of 2016 many programming languages include code to generate and parse JSON formatted data. The official Internet media type for JSON is application/json. JSON filenames use the extension.json. (Wikipedia, 2017g)

MQTT (Message Queueing Telemetry and Transport): MQTT (MQ Telemetry Transport) is an ISO standard (ISO/IEC PRF 20922) Publish-Subscribe based "lightweight" Messaging Protocol for use on top of the TCP/IP protocol. It is designed for connections with remote locations where a "small code footprint" is required or the Network Bandwidth is limited. (Wikipedia, 2017d)

NoSQL: A NoSQL (originally referring to "non SQL", "non-relational" or "not only SQL") database provides a mechanism for storage and retrieval of data which is modeled in means other than the tabular relations used in relational databases. The data structures used by NoSQL databases (e.g. Key-Value, Wide Column, Graph or Document) are different from those used by default in relational databases making some operations faster in NoSQL. (Wikipedia, 2017f)

Platform as a Service (PaaS): The capability provided to the consumer is to deploy onto the cloud infrastructure consumer-created or acquired applications created using Programming Languages, Libraries, Services and Tools supported by the provider. The consumer does not manage or control the underlying Cloud infrastructure including Network, Servers, Operating Systems or Storage but has control over the deployed applications and possibly configuration settings for the application hosting environment. (Mell &Grance, 2011)

Resilient Distributed Datasets (RDDs): Resilient Distributed Datasets (RDDs) are a distributed memory abstraction that lets programmers perform In-Memory Computations on large clusters in a Fault Tolerant manner. RDDs are motivated by two types of applications that current computing frameworks handle inefficiently: Iterative Algorithms and Interactive Data Mining Tools. Formally, an RDD is a read-only, partitioned collection of records. RDDs can only be created through deterministic operations on either (1) data in Stable Storage or (2) other RDDs. (Zaharia, 2012)

Software as a Service (SaaS): The capability provided to the consumer is to use the provider's applications running on a cloud infrastructure. The applications are accessible from various client devices through either a thin client interface such as a web browser (e.g., web-based email) or a program interface. The consumer does not manage or control the underlying cloud infrastructure including Network, Servers, Operating Systems, Storage or even individual application capabilities with the possible exception of limited user specific application configuration settings. (Mell &Grance, 2011)

WSN (Wireless Sensor Networks): Wireless Sensor Networks (WSN), sometimes called Wireless Sensor and Actuator Networks (WSAN) are spatially distributed autonomous sensors to monitor physical or environmental conditions such as Temperature, Sound, Pressure, etc. and to cooperatively pass their data through the network to a main location. (Wikipedia, 2017c)

Chapter 35
Statistical Visualization of Big Data Through Hadoop Streaming in RStudio

Chitresh Verma

Amity University, India

Rajiv Pandey

Amity University, India

ABSTRACT

Data Visualization enables visual representation of the data set for interpretation of data in a meaningful manner from human perspective. The Statistical visualization calls for various tools, algorithms and techniques that can support and render graphical modeling. This chapter shall explore on the detailed features R and RStudio. The combination of Hadoop and R for the Big Data Analytics and its data visualization shall be demonstrated through appropriate code snippets. The integration perspective of R and Hadoop is explained in detail with the help of a utility called Hadoop streaming jar. The various R packages and their integration with Hadoop operations in the R environment are explained through suitable examples. The process of data streaming is provided using different readers of Hadoop streaming package. A case based statistical project is considered in which the data set is visualized after dual execution using the Hadoop MapReduce and R script.

INTRODUCTION

This chapter highlights the points related to data visualization and its steps involved in the process. Use of R programming language and RStudio as an integrated development environment will be highlighted. R language statistical feature is commonly used for data analytics and visualization with active support of RStudio or Rattle for user friendly graphical environment.

DOI: 10.4018/978-1-6684-3662-2.ch035

Traditional system of data analytics is not able to meet the demands of the "Big Data Analytics". The term "Big Data" can trace its origin to data mining which is referred by statisticians. It attempts to extract information from the data set which is not support by the traditional systems. It involves construction of statistical data model which can be visualized with underlying data pattern that lays down the idea.

The reader of this chapter is assumed to have all the basic knowledge of Hadoop and its components. It is expected that he knows the Hadoop framework setup and its operations in profundity. Therefore only R and its data visualization part of Big Data Analytics will be explored in depth.

The amalgamation of "R" programming language and Hadoop framework had developed as a solution for Big Data Analytics. The recording of unstructured data collection by various industries and institutes has led to the employment of Hadoop framework. This framework is used for storing and data computation of the records. The conjugation of R and Hadoop system appears as the ideal solution for Big Data Analytics. R and Hadoop are open source solutions available on the web and both are data driven technologies. Usage of R and Hadoop in tandem has some fundamental problems. These problems and their solutions are discussed in the upcoming sections of this chapter.

DATA VISUALIZATION

Data visualization is not only done by standard charts and graphs but also by technologically more advanced ways such as info-graphics, real-time dials and gauges, heat maps (Spakov&Miniotas, 2015). The visualization results like charts and bars are also interactive and they can be changed with a click of button. The data visualization is a well-developed domain where accomplished designers and data scientists have worked to build combination of the excellent visualization for data interpretation. It can be said that data visualization is not only creative but also decoding the data to the viewer is meaningful. In other words, connecting the gap between the actual data and logical inference is possible only by data visualization. A data designer uses his imagination to build the representation of the data which can easily be comprehended by the audience. All the combinations of data and its illustrations have the above mentioned sole purpose.

What Is Data Visualization?

Data visualization is the process of extracting the meaningful information from vast amount of data and then showing them in pictorial representation form for better understanding of the end users (Chen et al., 2007). Data visualization is science of filtering and isolating the data and then visualizing in different representation techniques.

The product of data visualization to the viewer may look as information moving from point A to point B. The data visualization process does not only involve designing the reports and charts but presenting it in a way that spectator can interpret the with least amount of effort.

Applications of Data Visualization

Data visualization is useful in areas of science and technologies. The data visualization can be broadly found in five areas:

1. Medical Science is an important area (Bajura, Fuchs,& Ohbuchi, 1992) where the data visualization is widely used for reporting patient's health data.
2. Corporate business analysis uses data visualization (Jou, Campbell, & Ballantyne, 2006) which helps in increasing the profit and acquiring new client and consumers.
3. The trend analysis in share market involves the data visualization (Shaw et. al., 2001) and other similar techniques.
4. Sports industry uses the data visualization for score display in more meaningful manner to viewer and also analyzing the data for performance improvement of players (Segel, et. al.,2010).

Data visualization uses various data dimensions for the graphical representation. Data dimensions may be described as the various information sets which can visually decode an illustration. Let us consider an example of grades of students in all subjects of his first semester. Data dimensions will be grades and names of subjects. These data dimensions can be illustrated through a simple line chart having two axes i.e. grades and names of subjects on x-axis and y-axis respectively. Similarly, illustration with different data dimensions can be constructed for the purpose of data visualization.

Business Intelligence

Business intelligence (BI) is process of storing, analyzing and finally visualizing data which is mainly data and technology driven. It is a set of complex tools and applications having a range of functions like data capture, data storage, data processing and data visualization. Data visualization is the final step of business intelligence and it uses reports, dashboards and charts to show the analyzed data in a comprehendible form.

Decision Support System

Decision support system (DSS) is a software which helps the decision maker in better understanding of the business data with graphs and charts. The decision support system uses the past recorded data. The system is nourished with data set in the algorithm. The algorithm makes the prediction for the future based on the historical data.

Steps of Data Visualization

The aim of any visualization is to furnish the thought concerning the data. The goal is perceived about actual visualization and sometime even before the actual data has been analyzed and represented. Visualization is just like any software artifact or message where the objective is to communicate the visualized data to end user. For example, the visualization of retail sales of range of products has the aim of showing the most sold products to spectators. The most sold product may be depicted using line, bar, heat chart. The format to chosen is the discretion of data designing and visualization team. They explore various pro and cons of each visualization technique suitable for presentation using the data and the team also considers the market trends. The visualization team then sets a goal, picks appropriate tool and technique and subsequently the data is visualized.

Data visualization and its goal fascination is multi-step process which involves the problem definition, schema design, pre-processing, analysis and visualization. These steps are discussed in the below headings.

Define the Problem

The problem statement is identified and recorded in the files. For example, the problem statement in the case of most popular and good products for e-commerce website will depend on the purchase of the product, its review and rating. So, the system should identify the most sold, positively reviewed and rated product in decreasing order. The result of this problem statement will provide the most popular and good products in sequence manner.

Design Schema for Data Requirement

The parameters required for data visualization is marked using the problem statement and passed to sequence algorithm which is discussed in the next step. The data set contains large number of parameters but only selected parameters are required for data analysis. The identification of the parameters which are required is analyzed. The result is termed as a high level schema. This schema is used for the extraction of required data from large data sets.

Pre-Processed Data: Extracting Relevant Features

The pre-processing of the data involves the extraction of relevant data using marked field in the dataset and designed schema. The designed schema is used for identification of the parameters and filtration of actual data. For example, the data set of scores in Olympic 2016 are for all the sports events but if you want to visualize the swimming related events only, then you have to design the schema for swimming related events and filter the data set.

Performing Analytics Over Data and Mapping Dataset Features

Analytics of data with already mapped data set filters is performed which yields the required results. The actual data processing is applied in this step. The filtered data is provided as an input to the algorithm to process. The algorithm constructs the desired data set based on the input. In the end, desired data set is stored on disk.

Visualizing Data: Graphs and Charts

This step involves the data visualization using various graphs and charts techniques. Graphs and charts are available in various packages of R. Thus visualization can be changed by using these R packages. The processed data which is stored on the disk is provided as an input to plot function of the visualization package. This data is associated and clustered as per representation requirement.

Advantages of Data Visualization

The advantages of data visualization are:

1. Better understanding of the data and its pattern: User can understand the flow of data like increasing sales. The line chart representation of the sales report will reveal the sales growth to the manager of the sales division of any organization.
2. Relevance of the hidden data like trends: The data may contain some unseen patterns which can be identified with data visualization. For example, the data of any stock in share market may increase at a particular period of time. This period can be identified using the data visualization.
3. Encapsulation and abstraction of data for layman audience: The data sets are of very large size and are not understandable by everyone like non-technical audience which is a part of top management. So, the data visualization helps them in understanding the data in an uncomplicated way.
4. Envisage the data based on visualization: The data visualization builds sort of period outlines for the users which they can link using their experience.

R LANGUAGE

R language is a programming language which is actually clubbed with packages. It is used for data processing and visualization. It is multi-functional language which provides the functions like data manipulation, computation and visualization. It can store the figures; performs computation on them with the objective of putting together as ideal set.

It has following features to support operations on data:

1. R has integral function for data handling like declaration and definition and it also supports in-memory storage of data.
2. It supports operations on collection of data like set and matrix.
3. Many tools are available for data analysis using R.
4. Visual representation produced using R can be displayed on the screen as well as can be printed.
5. 'S' programming language is available online to support function of R in more simplified manner.
6. Large numbers of packages are available in repository for various functionalities of data processing with R language.

R supports the graphical illustration function for data analysis which can also be exported to external files in various formats. R can be thought as an environment which supports end to end requirements of data analytics. It can be used to rapidly develop any analysis. It has large collection of packages which are available in its Comprehensive R Archive Repository (CRAN). R has limitation of single piece of data analysis as it does not directly support Big Data Analytics yet.

Getting Started With R

Any large scale modern statistics calculation is difficult without R environment. Most of the research and industrial analytics makes use of R language for their needs of computation and visualization. R has more than 25 packages built with R standard installation and more packages can be added using CRAN, provided online repository at URL "www.cran.r-project.org". (Team, R. C., 2013.).This standard installation is termed as "standard" package.

Installation Steps of R

If one wants to make use of R, then he has to install R environment on his system. The installation of R software involves multiple steps and these steps are discussed in this section with respect to Windows Operating System. R installation is also available for Mac OS X and Linux operating systems.

Download the R Software Setup

The steps mentioned below can be followed for downloading the software setup.

1. Firstly, open the URL "http://ftp.heanet.ie/mirrors/cran.r-project.org" in the browser and in the "Download and Install R" section, left click on "Download R for Windows" link.
2. Under section "R for Windows", left click on "base" link on the screen.
3. Click the link "Download R X.X.X for Windows" where X is for the latest version of R software.

Install the Setup of R Software

Installation guidance is provided in following points.

1. Double click on the downloaded setup icon "R-X.X.X-win.exe".
2. Select the appropriate language for installation. Note by default language is English.
3. Follow the instructions of the installation steps and use Next Button to step forward.
4. On completion of the instructions, you can use the "Finish" button.

Launch the R Software

The steps of opening R software in Windows Operation System are as follows:

1. If "R" icon is present on the desktop, then double click "R" icon.
2. Window screen is open on screen which looks similar to Figure 1.
3. At the top, menu bar along with the respective icons like open, save are provided. Also, a sub window called R Console is available to the user.

Reading Data With R

This section will provide guidelines for importing the data from Excel file. Most of the researchers gather and store the data in Excel as it is easy and uncomplicated to them. The Excel file is one of most popular spreadsheet softwares provided by Microsoft as part of their Office suite.

Figure 1. Screenshot of R Console (Captured by authors on Windows 8.1 platform)

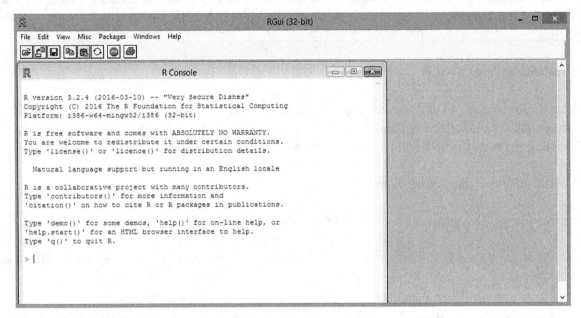

Excel file can be imported into R data store and for this purpose R has gdata package. Gdata package reads the Excel spreadsheets and load the data in R. It only requires Perl runtime environment to be installed in the system. It involves multiple steps and they are summarized in below points as commands to be entered in R console.

1. Load the gdata package using library() function of R package
   a. >library(gdata)
2. Use help() for documentation
   a. >help(sample.xls)
3. Use read.xls() function of gdata package to read the Excel file
   a. >sampleData = read.xls("sampleData.xls")

The commands of Rare used for the reading of data in Excel format. Similarly, the data in "csv" format can be read by R.

R Studio as an IDE (Integrated Development Environment)

RStudio is a user interactive software which simplifies the R programming. It supports multiple operating systems like Mac OS, Windows XP and Linux.

It is widely used as an Integrated Development Environment (IDE) for R tool by the users from different backgrounds of science. RStudio is developed using the C++ programming language and Qt framework. RStudio project was started in December 2010 and its first beta version was released in February 2011 as version 0.92.

What Is the Need to Use RStudio?

R mainly works through the command line interface which makes it difficult to use. For this purpose, an IDE like RStudio is used with R. The use of IDE is not unique to R but other languages like Java also use the IDE for simplification. RStudio is multi-featured IDE having console, code editor and shortcut key combinations. It can auto format the code and highlight the keywords which are used in R script. Object browser is available which is displayed as part of the workspace. This browser shows the variable defined by user and thus can be used quickly to identify the variable and its value. Object editor is a part of object browser that helps in checking and editing of objects. It has plot management screen present at bottom right corner of the window.

When the big and complex problem statements are involved with R programming, it is difficult to work and synchronize all the work. (Racine, 2012). Thus, it requires a simplified user interface for programming. RStudio is free and open source tool for R and it can be used even by enterprise level users. It was developed with a goal to encourage the users to become productive in usage of R tool.

RStudio Editions

The RStudio is provided in two editions and these editions are RStudio Desktop and RStudio Server. Both these editions are used for different requirements of the user.

1. **RStudio Desktop Edition:** RStudio Desktop Edition is available for local machine in a standalone mode of use of R. It can be used for all major platforms like Windows 7, Mac OS X and Ubuntu Linux.
2. **RStudio Server Edition:** RStudio Server Edition allows the user to access the functionality from remote location with the help of web browser like internet explorer. In this edition, R and RStudio server is installed on Linux based machine.

Installation Steps of RStudio

Follow the steps mentioned in the below points to install the RStudio in Windows based environment.

1. Open URLhttps://www.rstudio.com/products/rstudio/download/ in the browser.
2. Download the setup as per Operating System i.e. Windows OS.
3. Double click the setup downloaded from the website.
4. Follow the instructions of the setup for installation.
5. After the setup is finished, open the RStudio by using the shortcut icon by double clicking on the Desktop.
6. RStudio window which is looking similar to Figure 2 should appear on the screen.
7. Similarly, the RStudio can be installed on Linux and Mac OS X platforms.

The RStudio should automatically detect the R version installed on same machine and no extra setting of software is required by the user.

Figure 2. Showing screenshot of the RStudio running on Windows 8 platform (Captured by authors)

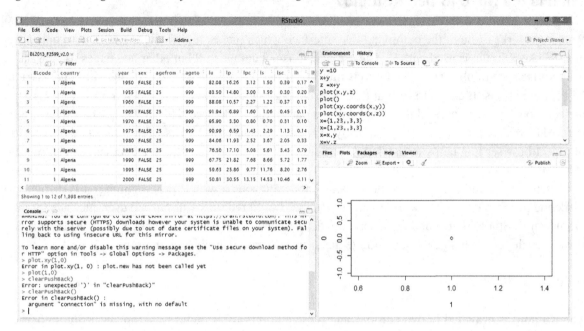

RStudio Functions and Features

RStudio provides many functions to the user like automatic integration of R by detecting the version of R on installed system. If a user has multiple R versions installed, he can choose the version manually from Options panel accessible by menu bar options "Tools". In Options panel, many other settings of R can be changed like initial working directory, workspace.

RStudio provides the facility of saving workspace in file with extension ".RData". When the user tries to exit the RStudio, it asks to save the workspace by default. It also restores workspace at the startup of RStudio from earlier saved workspace file. Like R, RStudio has various packages which can be installed by downloading them from Comprehensive R Archive Network (CRAN) mirror.

R + HADOOP: STATISTICAL ANALYSIS OF BIG DATA

R has many predefined functions as part of various packages for statistical analysis which are ideal tools for processing the statistical data. At the same time, Hadoop is one of the most popular frameworks for Big Data. In this section, we discuss the methodology and software for integrating the R and Hadoop software for the statistical analysis of Big Data.

What Is the Need to Integrate R and Hadoop

Despite having a vast array of functions for statistical data, R cannot be directly used on Big Data. To resolve these issues, some integration method or tool with supported framework of Big Data needs to be used. (Prajapati, V, 2013). Some of other limitations of R that creates hurdles in using R with Big Data are listed as below.

1. RAM available to R system is restricted to single computational platform and cannot be increased beyond a certain upper limit. Further, this creates boundary on data frame that can be loaded in R.
2. No parallel processing is available in R system to process massive amounts of data.
3. No mechanism of independently using R with Big Data to exploit horizontal scalability of computational systems in a network.

Ways to Integrate R and Hadoop

The integration of R and Hadoop can be achieved by using both open source and commercial tools available in the market. There are three major methodologies or tools for integration of R and Hadoop. These three tools are RHadoop, Hadoop streaming and RHIPE. (Prajapati, V, 2013; Oancea, B., 2014)

Figure 3. Major tools for integrating R and Hadoop (Designed by the authors)

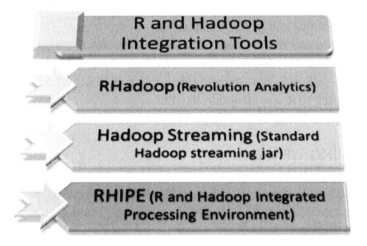

RHadoop

RHadoop is a software for integrating the R and Hadoop system which is developed by Revolution Analytics. It is developed using the C++ and Java language and can be used with native R. RHadoop comes with 3 major packages and these packages are rmr, rhbase and rhdfs. (Analytics, R., 2015).

1. **rmr:** The "rmr" package provides interface for running map and reduce jobs on the Hadoop streaming using the R script. The "rmr2" is the latest version for rmr package. It interacts with mapper and reducer processes of Hadoop MapReduce computational programming model.
2. **rhbase:** The "rhbase" package interfaces the read and writes data operation with the HBase tables. It is mainly used with HBase software. It makes use of HBase third party gateway for communication with the HBase.

3. **rhdfs:** The "rhdfs" package facilitates file manipulation capabilities directly on Hadoop distributed file system (HDFS). It supports the access, read and write operations on HDFS from R system.

Hadoop Streaming

Hadoop streaming is available as a part of Hadoop distribution package as jar file. The Hadoop package contains a jar file which is shipped along with the framework. This jar file can be used for communication between R and Hadoop. Hadoop streaming is discussed in detail in section 3 of this chapter.

RHIPE

RHIPE is considered to be the first attempt to integrate R and Hadoop. It was developed as part of PhD thesis project at Purdue University, USA in 2012. RHIPE stands for R and Hadoop Integrated Processing Environment. It is used for integration of R and Hadoop system. RHIPE was considered as a breakthrough in the field of data science. Saptarshi Guha developed RHIPE as part of his PhD thesis at Purdue University. Integration of R with Hadoop allows R to utilize parallel computation engine of later technology.

The GitHub, a group coding website has RHIPE coding group (RHIPE, 2011a) present and from here one can download the latest version of RHIPE. The latest discussion on RHIPE is present on RHIPE group (RHIPE, 2011b) host on Google discussion group.

RHIPE works on divide and rule concept. The large data sets are divided into smaller subsets of data using the R script. These smaller subsets of data create R objects. The R commands under RHIPE communicate with Hadoop. Subsequent analytics are performed through computation by Hadoop. The output data is retrieved back to R system within RHIPE.

HADOOP STREAMING WITH R

In the last section, various integration tools for R and Hadoop were studied. Now, the Hadoop Streaming which is one of the integration tools is studied in depth. The Hadoop streaming is utility provided along with the Hadoop package.

Hadoop streaming is intermediary software connecting the Hadoop and R platforms. It facilitates the user to create the Map and Reduce jobs with R scripts as mapper and reducer. It is part of Hadoop distribution package as jar file present in the"$HADOOP_HOME" classpath as shown in Figure 4. Sample code for Hadoop streaming is provided in the below section.

```
$HADOOP_HOME/bin/hadoop jar $HADOOP_HOME/hadoop-streaming.jar \
-input sampleInputDir \
-output sampleOutputDir\
-mapper sampleMap \
-reducer sampleReduce
```

Figure 4. Screenshot of Hadoop-streaming jar file as part of Hadoop package (Captured by authors on Ubuntu 14.04)

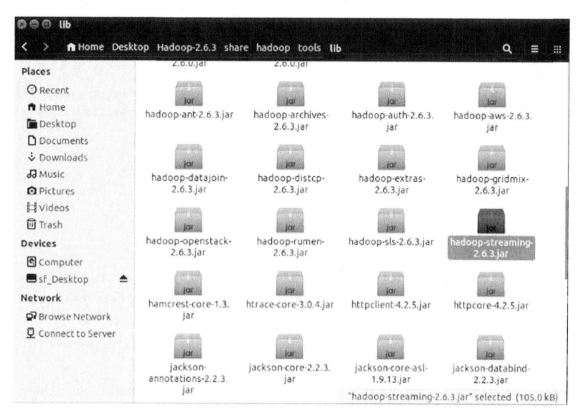

Here, four parameters are passed to Hadoop streaming utility. First parameter is input directory with option "input' for raw data path, second parameter is output directory with option "output" for storage of process information path. Third and fourth parameters are Mapper executable and Reducer executable respectively.

Working of Hadoop Streaming

Hadoop streaming as discussed in earlier section is an intermediate software which provides facility of creating map and reduce jobs in R and executing them in the Hadoop clusters. For the purpose of streaming, Hadoop streaming uses standard input stream or stdin and standard output stream or stdout.

As each map job is executed on the Hadoop cluster then the separate process called mapper is started and this mapper task is fed with input lines of code as stdin of the mapper process. In parallel, the mapper processes the output data which is fed through the stdout of the mapper. Output data is key/value pairs format by default which can be accessed by stdout stream of the mapper process and the key/value pairs are separated by tab characters. If there is no tab character, then complete set of data is single key only with value storing null.

Similarly, the reduce job is bundled with reducer process as in the case of map job and here also separate reducer processes are executed for each reduce job. With the execution of reducer tasks, the raw key/value pairs from mapper process are provided as input in stdin stream and reducer logic is applied on the input pairs generating the desired output key/value pairs which are available by stdout stream. The output key/value pairs are also separated by tab character and similar constrain also apply as discussed in input key/value pairs of no tab character.

Thus, the discussed mechanism is used for Map-Reduce framework communication with R using streaming of Hadoop-streaming utility.

For the purpose of getting familiar with Hadoop streaming jar, some sample mappers are provided with Hadoop package. One of these sample mappers is "IdentityMapper" and usage code in provided as below.

```
$HADOOP_HOME/bin/hadoop jar $HADOOP_HOME/hadoop-streaming.jar \
-input identityInputDirs \
-output identityOutputDir \
-mapper org.apache.hadoop.mapred.lib.IdentityMapper \
-reducer /bin/wc
```

Here, the mapper is provided as "org.apache.hadoop.mapred.lib.IdentityMapper". The "IdentityMapper" is simple mapper which converts the raw data to key/value pairs as input and directly write the data to the output key/value pairs without applying any logic.

Features of R Packages

R package has vast array of packages which can be used for Big Data Analytics and machine learning which can be downloaded from CRAN (Comprehensive R Archive Network) repository (www.cran.r-project.org). Some of these packages are discussed as below.

1. **"Misc Functions of the Department of Statistics, Probability Theory Group" Package:** It provides functions for latent class analysis, fuzzy cluster, Naive Bayes classifier and shortest path computation. It was earlier known as "E1071" package.
2. **"rpart" Package:** It contains functions which can be used for recursive partition and regression. Their functions are based on the 1984 book by "Breiman, Friedman, Olshen and Stone". (Therneau, Atkinson & Ripley, 2010).
3. **"igraph" Package:** Network Analysis functions are available in this package. It is useful in graph based data analysis where nodes and edges are present.

EXPLORING THE ENGINEERING OF HADOOP STREAMING COMMAND WITH RSTUDIO

The MapReduce application is composed of two components i.e. Mapper code and Reducer code. Mapper code is related to map phase of any MapReduce job and an R script file with ".R" extension is used for this purpose. The job of mapper is to convert the raw data into key/value pairs and forward to reducer for applying the logic on them. For example, a raw data separated by new line character about student and their marks in Computer Science are taken as input and total marks as output. The input key/value pairs will be student/marks pairs and the output will be "total_key/total-marks" pair. Reducer can be written in R script as given below.

```
# Type of the script
#! /usr/bin/envRscript
# Stop the warning messages to be echo
options(warn=-1)
# Initialize the standard input stream
inputStream<- file("stdin","r")
```

In each line two fields composed of student roll no and marks are provided which are separated by comma.

```
# Loop to read all lines
while(length(line <- readLines(inputStream, n=1,warn=FALSE))>0){
#Splitting the string separated by comma
fields<- unlist(strsplit(line,","))
#Extract the student ID and marks from fields
studentID<- as.character(fields[1])
marks<- as.character(fields[2])
# Display student ID and marks using standard output stream
print(paste(studentID,marks,sep="\t"),stdout())
}
# Close the input stream
close(inputStream)
```

Mapper process generates the key/value pairs and makes them available by standard output stream which can be consumed by reducer process to provide aggregated key/value pairs to the user.

Similarly, a reducer can be implemented using R script for above example. In this R script of reduce function, the key/value pairs from mapper process will be consumed and the aggregated total of marks will be generated.

```
# Type of the script
#! /usr/bin/envRscript
# Stop the warning messages to be echo
options(warn=-1)
#Define variable and set initial values
total.key<- "Total"
marks.value<- 0.0
# Create a standard input connection
inputStream<- file("stdin",open="r")
# Loop to read all lines
while(length(line <- readLines(inputStream, n=1,warn=FALSE))>0){
#Splitting the string separated by tab
```

```
fields<- strspit(line,"\t")
#Capturing value from fields
value <- as.character(fields[[1]][2])
marks.value = marks.value+ value
}
#Print the output on standard output stream
print(list(total.key,marks.value),stdout())
#Closing connection
close(inputStream)
```

Above code in R script can be executed in R system for above example. The standard input and output stream will be used for data exchange by system. More complex logics can be developed by referring this example.

Handing Multi-Formal Data on Hadoop Environment

As we have discussed the R script writing with the help of example, running the same script in Hadoop system will now be focused on. The Hadoop-streaming jar utility shall be used for the purpose to execute the R script on the Hadoop environment. The Hadoop streaming jar has been already discussed in details in Hadoop streaming section.

R script can be executed using two methods and these methods are mentioned as below.

1. From command line with CLA (Command Line Arguments)
2. From R/RStudio console

The Hadoop streaming utility combined with R script as arguments can be used in both methods. The details of execution of R script using command line is available in next section.

Command Line Arguments (CLA) for Hadoop Streaming

The command line usage of Hadoop streaming with help of R scripts as well as input and output directories path as command arguments will be discussed in this section. The Hadoop streaming jar file can be utilized by command line as mentioned below.

```
$ bin/hadoop{HADOOP_HOME}/hadoop-streaming-2.6.3.jar
-input /data/student_record.csv
-output /data/output
-file /usr/local/hadoop/data/stu_mapper.R
-mapper stu_mapper.R
-file /usr/local/hadoop/data/stu_reducer.R
-reducer stu_reducer.R
```

UNDERSTANDING THE HADOOP STREAMING: AN R PACKAGE

The Hadoop Streaming as an R package has been developed by D.S. Rosenberg (Rosenberg, 2012) and it can be downloaded from CRAN repository (https://cran.r-project.org/web/packages/HadoopStreaming/index.html).The version 0.2 of HadoopStreaming which had been published on 29 October, 2012 is referred in this chapter. This package is framework which allows user to write the map and reduce scripts for Hadoop streaming and it has also function of processing data in stream without involving the Hadoop. Note: HadoopStreaming package requires the "getopt" package as prerequisites.

1. Hadoop Streaming package in R environment has three main advantages of data capturing over direct data capturing using command line. These three advantages are described as below.
   a. **Chunk Based Data Capturing:** Small block of data called chunk are used for read and write operation of Hadoop streaming which allows users to process the data with comparative smaller memory.
   b. **Multi-Format Based Data Capturing:** The Hadoop streaming package supports multi-format data capturing. For example, the data can be comma, tab and semicolon separated.
   c. **Proven Software Based Data Capturing:** The Hadoop streaming is reliable software which supports many functions like read and write operations.

RStudio and HadoopStreaming Input Streams With Data Capturing Mechanism

RStudio and HadoopStreaming are used for effective data capturing and there are multiple reader functions available for same purpose. These readers are as follows:

1. hsTableReader
2. hsKeyValueReader
3. hsLineReader

The details about all the readers are provided in subsequent sections with the help of respective codes.

"hsTableReader" Function

The tabular data format is processed by hsTableReader and it has precondition of input connection to respective file. It captures each row at time of the table which means each row should have different keys to identify them. Sample commands of "hsTableReader" function are provided as below.

hsTableReader(file="filename.csv",cols='character',chunkSize=-1,FUN=print,
ignoreKey=FALSE,singleKey=TRUE,skip=1,sep=',',keyCol='Stu_ID',
carryMemLimit=512e6, carryMaxRow=Inf, stringsAsFactors=FALSE)

The arguments which have been used in hsTableReader function are discussed as follows:

- **file:** This argument is related to name of object, stream and file.
- **cols:** This argument is related to name of columns.

- **chunkSize:** This argument is related to reading of number of lines. The argument value "-1" denotes all lines.
- **FUN:** This argument is name of function that consumes the data.
- **ignoreKey:** This argument is key which have to ignored.
- **singleKey:** This argument denotes whether key is single or not. It has Boolean value i.e. TRUE and FALSE.
- **skip:** This argument is related to the number of rows that has to be skipped.
- **sep:** The argument is separate character for columns.
- **keyCol:** This argument specifies the key column name.
- **carryMemLimit:** This argument is for upper memory limit for a key.
- **carryMaxRow:** This argument is for upper rows limit for read from file.
- **stringsAsFactors:** This argument is for the acceptance of string as factors. It has two Boolean values TRUE and FALSE.

Let us consider an example for better understanding for syntax of hsTableReader function with installed and loaded HadoopStreaming library on R system. For loading the HadoopStreaming library, use **library("HadoopStreaming")** command.

- Create a variable "stu_records" with marks in English, Computer and Mathematics subjects separated by comma character as follows
  stu_records<- "Stu_ID1,58\nStu_ID1,86\nStu_ID1,66\nStu_ID2,88\n
  Stu_ID2,56\nStu_ID2,46\nStu_ID3,35\nStu_ID3,78\nStu_ID3,76\n"

Validate the variable values by using cat() function as follows
cat(stu_records)
The actual result of cat() function will look similar to Figure 5.
Create a variable named "cols" which creates a data list by executing command as follows
cols = list(key='',val=0)
Store the student records in the "con"
con<- textConnection(stu_records, open = "r")
Execute hsTableReaderfunction with "con", "cols" variables and having chunkSize 3 as follows
hsTableReader(con,cols,chunkSize=3,FUN=print,ignoreKey=TRUE,sep=',')

The result of hsTableReader function with student records should look similar to the Figure 6.

"hsKeyValueReader" Function

As "hsKeyValueReader" function name suggests, it reads the data in key/value pair and also supports chunkSize options for reading the data at a time. Sample command of "hsKeyValueReader" function is provided as below:

hsKeyValueReader(file="sample.csv",chunkSize=-1,skip=0,sep=",",FUN=function(key,value)
    cat(paste(key, value)))

Figure 5. Screenshot showing RStudio with student records data (Captured by authors)

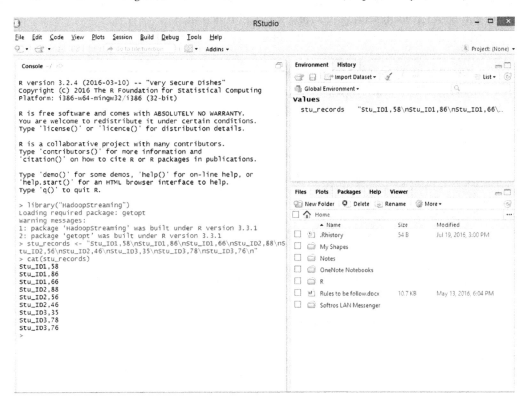

Figure 6. Screenshot showing the RStudio with hsTableReader command result (Captured by authors)

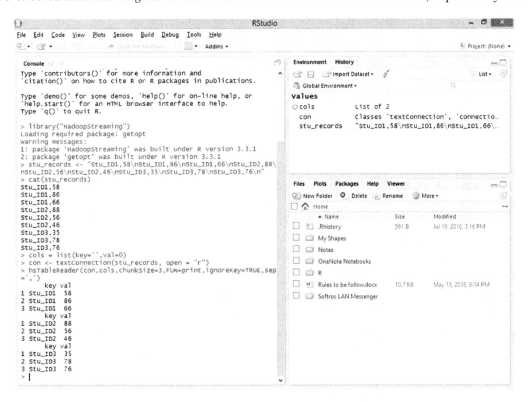

The arguments used in "hsKeyValueReader" function syntax have same meaning as in "hsTableReader" function and can be referred in section "hsTableReader" function.

Let us consider an example with "hsKeyValueReader" function as follows

```
stu_records<- "studID1,46\nstudID2,23\nstudID3,21\n"
con<- textConnection(stu_records, open = "r")
hsKeyValReader(con, chunkSize=1, sep=',', FUN=function(key,value) cat(paste(key, value,sep=':
    '),sep='\n'))
```

Figure 7. Screenshot showing the RStudio with hsKeyValueReader command result (Captured by authors)

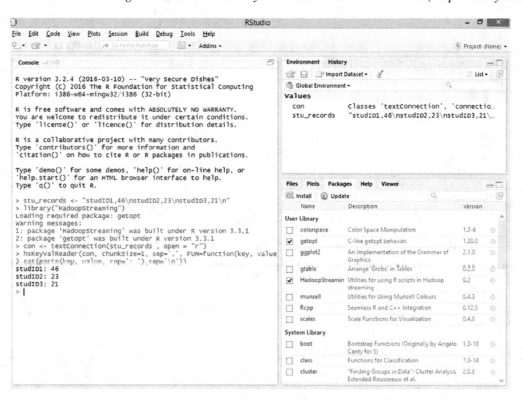

After executing the example of "hsKeyValueReader" function in RStudio, the result should be similar to Figure 7.

"hsLineReader" Function

"hsLineReader" function reads entire line as single set without any operation on the data. Here, chunk-Size denotes the number of lines to be read. The data processing based on streams involves capturing the required streams and thus it filters the stream of desired elements only. It is expected the filtered elements will also consume less memory in the system. Thus, the stream can be used in fixed length called "line" which is made up of "n" data items where n is usually a large number. Sample command of "hsLineReader" function is provided as below.

hsLineReader(file="sample.csv', chunkSize=3, skip=0, sep=',', FUN=func(line) cat(line, sep="\n"))

The arguments used in "hsLineReader" function syntax have same meaning as in "hsTableReader" function and can be referred in section "hsTableReader" function.

Let us consider an example with "hsLineReader" function as follows

sampleLines<- " Hello World!\n This line function is great."
con<- textConnection(sampleLines, open = "r")
hsLineReader(con, chunkSize=2,FUN=print)

After executing the example of "hsLineReader" function in RStudio, the result should be similar to Figure 8.

Figure 8. Screenshot showing the RStudio with hsLineReader command result (Captured by authors)

STATISTICAL DATA VISUALIZATION PROJECT USING HADOOP STREAMING COMMAND WITH R

In this section, the data visualization of statistical project using the technologies like R and Hadoop will be explored. The knowledge acquired from previous sections would be useful in understanding the key concept of this data visualization procedure.

Visualization of "WordCount" Example Using R and Hadoop

"WordCount" example is one of popular programs in the field of Big Data where the number of word occurrences is documented. (Kambatla et. al., 2009). The "India" country page of Wikipedia.org (free encyclopedia based website) for our data set requirement which is available under the "Creative Commons Attribution-ShareAlike License" will be used. This example has been used for single page for test for easier understanding and it can be expanded to entire level of data set with minimum modification. The version of "India" page published on "00:31, 20 July, 2016" having URL "https://en.wikipedia.org/w/index.php?title=India&oldid=730589461" had been used for the example. The data contains characteristics as mentioned below.

- **Number of Words:** 9,657
- **Number of Characters:** 64,176
- **Number of Sentences:** 192
- **Number of Paragraphs:** 200

The process of word counting involves converting the data key/value pair and combining the pairs to documents. These documents are sorted by the document and the next step is applied with the logic to process and store the data. It can be visualized as follows:

cat> input | cat | sort | cat > output

The word counting can be executed on Hadoop using R scripts as follows:

Step 1: Write the mapper R script named "wordCountMapper.R"

```
#!/usr/bin/envRscript
library('stringi')
inputStream<- file('stdin', open='r')
while(length(data<- readLines(con=inputStream, n=1024L))>0) {
lines<- unlist(stri_extract_all_words(data))
linesInTables<- table(lines)
word<- names(linesInTables)
wordCount<- as.integer(linesInTables)
cat(stri_paste(word, wordCount, sep='t'), sep='n')
}
```

Provide access permission using chmod command of Linux as follows:
chmod 755 wordCountMapper.R

Step 2: Write the reducer C++ program named "wordCountReducer.cpp"

```cpp
#include <iostream>
#include <string>
#include <cstdlib>
using namespace std;
int main()
{
string line;
string word = "";
int count = 0;
while(getline(cin,line))
{
size_t length = line.find_first_of("t");
if(length != string::npos)
{
string key = line.substr(0,length);
string value = line.substr(length);
intvaluei = atoi(value.c_str());
if(key != word)
{
if(word != "")
{
cout<< word <<"t"<< count <<endl;
}
else
{
word = key;
count = valuei;
}
}
else
{
count += valuei;
}
}
}
if(word != "") cout<< word <<"t"<< count <<endl;
return 0;
}
```

Compile C++ source file using g++ compile as follows:

```
$ g++ -O3 wordCountreducer.cpp -o wordCountReducer
```

Step 3: Run the hadoop streaming jar utility from Linux terminal as follows:

```
$ bin/hadoop jar /opt/hadoop/share/hadoop/tools/lib/hadoop-streaming-2.6.3.jar
-input /input/indiaPage.txt
```

```
-output /output
-mapper wordCountMapper.R
-reducer wordCountReducer
-file wordCountMapper.R
-file wordCountReducer
```

The output result will have top ten words by counting as in Table 1.

Table 1. Tabular form of top ten words along ranking based on word occurrences in the India page (Designed by the authors)

Rank	Word	Count
1	India	196
2	Indian	104
3	india's	36
4	South	33
5	Largest	27
6	Economic	26
7	World	26
8	States	25
9	Most	22
10	Also	22

These top ten data can visualize on RStudio using following commands as follows:

```
>data = read.table("/usr/home/User1/Desktop/output/WordCount.txt",header=TRUE)
>attach(data)
>stem(Count)
>plot(Word,Count)
```

Here, the commands of R used in visualization of word count example result are described as below.

- **read.table(): It** read the data from file and stores in data frame and each data is stored with corresponding lines.
- **attach():** It searches the data frame provided as an argument which helps in accessing the object of database by names only.
- **stem():** It helps in building the "x axis" values for stem-and-leaf plot.
- **plot():** It is used for generating graph of provided data sets on the screen.

The graph after the execution of above code will look similar as in Figure 9.

Figure 9. Graph plot of word count example (Captured by authors)

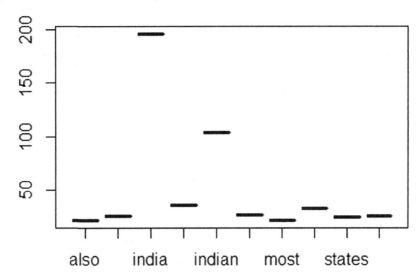

This word count example can be referred as a template for building other statistical visualization tools of Big Data using Hadoop streaming and RStudio.

SUMMARY

R programming language combined with Hadoop framework could be used as integrated solution for data visualization. This integration is simplified by the Hadoop streaming utility and RStudio.

Some of the points discussed in this chapter are listed below.

1. Data visualization is the process which involves pictorial representation such as charts and graphs of the records. It helps in getting the insight of pattern trend and make predictions.
2. R is programming language useful for data visualization. It has had multiple packages for visualization.
3. Hadoop is computational framework for Big Data storage and processing in a distributed environment. R and Hadoop can be combined to use best of both technologies.
4. Hadoop streaming is jar based utility that simplifies use of Hadoop MapReduce programming model from R scripts.
5. "HadoopStreaming" package is R package which has many readers helps in data exchange between R and Hadoop.
6. A statistical example was also studied whose result was visualized in RStudio and all data processing was realized on Hadoop MapReduce.

CONCLUSION

This chapter provides generic techniques and methodology involved in statistical visualization of Big Data through Hadoop framework in the context of R programming language. The reader is likely to have comprehended the concept of data visualization and the steps involved. The reader has been given a walkthrough of R and RStudio installation process on the Windows platform methods. The technological integration of R and Hadoop have been deliberated upon through an in-depth know how of Hadoop streaming package of R along with its readers using an appropriate demonstration case.

The chapter presents a sample statistical visualization through integration of the various concepts and techniques of R and Hadoop. The reader shall develop a better insight on the topic of data visualization using R and Hadoop systems and with an additional reading the reader shall be able to implement the visualization in various operational domains.

FUTURE RESEARCH WORK AND DIRECTIONS

Many sectors spanning from biological, astronomical and e-commerce apart from many emerging domains lay emphasis on Big Data. Further its analytics and visualizations are considered playing a pivotal role in information technology evolution. The field of Big Data, analytics and data visualization has grown many folds with the evolving technological developments. However, lots of problems have been encountered due to integration and seamless working. Big Data analytics and visualization renders great potential however many avenues are yet to be explored in the field of enhanced technology and techniques for capturing of relevant data, cleaning and editing of captured data, multi-dimensional storage and representation, Customization technologies to render end user data visualization options.

Future research directions would include development of algorithms, technologies, distributed processing concepts and architectural designs to speed up the analysis and result rendering time span. Improved decision making tools and techniques however needs reliable and timely information (Davenport, 2012; Schroeck et al., 2012; Shah et al., 2012). It has been argued that the biggest challenge is timely information delivery to respective authorities. (Kiron et al., 2014a). The manager in the decision making process are unable to point out the timely and reliable options (Barton, 2012) and this is a major bottleneck that needs to be overcome. These problem areas are being explored by experts, researchers and scholars. It is likely that next major research occurs in performance improvement and data reliability areas of Big Data.

ACKNOWLEDGMENT

We are grateful to Dr. Richard S. Segall and Neha Gupta for their cooperation over the few months of interaction, their suggestions have been valuable over the due course of chapter writing. We have learnt many finer details from them in the field of chapter writing.

We are indebted to our families for their moral support and inspiration. Our special thanks to the IGI Global for their excellent web platform. They also have endeavor of providing contemporary technical education and resources to their readers. We also acknowledge the construct advices of all those readers who contributed in the improvement of this chapter. We whole heartedly believe that the chapter shall address their learning needs in the given context.

REFERENCES

Bajura, M., Fuchs, H., & Ohbuchi, R. (1992). Merging virtual objects with the real world: Seeing ultrasound imagery within the patient. *ACM SIGGRAPH Computer Graphics*, *26*(2), 203-210. Retrieved on 02 September, 2016 from http://ieeexplore.ieee.org/document/6337722/

Chen, C. H., Härdle, W. K., & Unwin, A. (Eds.). (2007). *Handbook of data visualization*. Springer Science & Business Media. Retrieved on 02 September, 2016 from http://www.springer.com/us/book/9783540330363

Csardi, G., & Nepusz, T. (2006). The igraph software package for complex network research. *InterJournal. Complex Systems*, *1695*(5), 1–9.

Das, S., Sismanis, Y., Beyer, K. S., Gemulla, R., Haas, P. J., & McPherson, J. (2010). Ricardo: integrating R and Hadoop. In *Proceedings of the 2010 ACM SIGMOD International Conference on Management of Data* (pp. 987-998). ACM. Retrieved on 02 September, 2016 from http://dl.acm.org/citation.cfm?id=1807275

Guha, S. (2010). *Computing environment for the statistical analysis of large and complex data* (Doctoral dissertation). Purdue University. Retrieved on 02 September, 2016 from http://dl.acm.org/citation.cfm?id=2126096

Guha, S. (2010). *RHIPE-R and Hadoop Integrated Processing Environment*. Retrieved on August 20, 2016 from http://www.stat.purdue.edu/~sguha/rhipe/doc/html/

Holmes, A. (2012). *Hadoop in practice*. Manning Publications Company. Retrieved on 02 September, 2016 from http://dl.acm.org/citation.cfm?id=2543981

Jou, S. F., Campbell, D., & Ballantyne, I. (2006). *U.S. Patent No. 6,995,768*. Washington, DC: U.S. Patent and Trademark Office. Retrieved on 02 September, 2016 from http://www.google.co.in/patents/US6995768

Kambatla, K., Pathak, A., & Pucha, H. (2009). Towards Optimizing Hadoop Provisioning in the Cloud. *HotCloud, 9*, 12. Retrieved on 02 September, 2016 from https://www.usenix.org/legacy/events/hotcloud09/tech/full_papers/kambatla.pdf

McAfee, A., Brynjolfsson, E., Davenport, T. H., Patil, D. J., & Barton, D. (2012). Big data. The management revolution. *Harvard Business Review*, *90*(10), 61–67. PMID:23074865

Meyer, D., Dimitriadou, E., Hornik, K., Weingessel, A., & Leisch, F. (2015). *e1071: Misc Functions of the Department of Statistics, Probability Theory Group*. Retrieved on 02 September, 2016 from ftp://200.236.31.10/CRAN/web/packages/e1071/e1071.pdf

Naeem, F., Saeed, S., Irfan, M., & Kiran, T. (2015). Brief culturally adapted CBT for psychosis (CaCBTp): a randomized controlled trial from a low income country. *Schizophrenia Research*, *164*(1), 143-148. Retrieved on 02 September, 2016 from http://www.sciencedirect.com/science/article/pii/S0920996415001206

O'Malley, O. (2008). *Programming with Hadoop's Map/Reduce.* Yahoo! Apache Con EU 2008. Retrieved on 02 September, 2016 from http://docs.huihoo.com/apache/apachecon/eu2008/HadoopProgramming.pdf

Oancea, B., & Dragoescu, R. M. (2014). *Integrating R and Hadoop for big data analysis.* Retrieved on 02 September, 2016 from http://arxiv.org/abs/1407.4908

Prajapati, V. (2013). *Big data analytics with R and Hadoop.* Packt Publishing Ltd. Retrieved on 02 September, 2016 from https://www.packtpub.com/big-data-and-business-intelligence/big-data-analytics-r-and-hadoop

Racine, J. S. (2012). RStudio: A Platform-Independent IDE for R and Sweave. *Journal of Applied Econometrics, 27*(1), 167–172. - doi:10.1002/jae.1278

Reference index for {HadoopStreaming}. (n.d.). *HadoopStreaming: Utilities for using R scripts in Hadoop streaming.* Retrieved on August 20, 2016 from https://mran.microsoft.com/package/HadoopStreaming/

Rosenberg, D. S. (2012). *HadoopStreaming: Utilities for Using R Scripts in Hadoop Streaming.* R package version 0.2. Retrieved on August 20, 2016 from http://CRAN.R-project.org/package=HadoopStreaming

RStudio. (n.d.). In *Wikipedia.* Retrieved on August 20, 2016 from https://en.wikipedia.org/wiki/RStudio

Schroeck, M., Shockley, R., Smart, J., Romero-Morales, D., & Tufano, P. (2012). *Analytics: The real-world use of big data.* IBM Global Business Services. Retrieved on 02 September, 2016 from https://www.ibm.com/smarterplanet/global/files/se__sv_se__intelligence__Analytics_-_The_real-world_use_of_big_data.pdf

Segel, E., & Heer, J. (2010). Narrative visualization: Telling stories with data. *IEEE Transactions on Visualization and Computer Graphics, 16*(6), 1139–1148. doi:10.1109/TVCG.2010.179 PMID:20975152

Shah, N. H., & Tenenbaum, J. D. (2012). The coming age of data-driven medicine: Translational bio-informatics' next frontier. *Journal of the American Medical Informatics Association, 19*(e1), e2–e4. doi:10.1136/amiajnl-2012-000969 PMID:22718035

Shaw, M. J., Subramaniam, C., Tan, G. W., & Welge, M. E. (2001). Knowledge management and data mining for marketing. *Decision Support Systems, 31*(1), 127–137. doi:10.1016/S0167-9236(00)00123-8

Špakov, O., & Miniotas, D. (2015). Visualization of eye gaze data using heat maps. *Elektronika ir Elektrotechnika, 74*(2), 55–58.

Team, R. C. (2013). *R Foundation for Statistical Computing; Vienna: 2013.R: A language and environment for statistical computing.* Retrieved on 02 September, 2016 from http://cran.fiocruz.br/web/packages/dplR/vignettes/timeseries-dplR.pdf

Therneau, T. M., Atkinson, B., & Ripley, B. (2010). *rpart: Recursive Partitioning. R package* version 3.1–42. Retrieved on August 20, 2016 from http://CRAN. R-project.org/package= rpart.

Verma, C., & Pandey, R. (2016). An Implementation Approach of Big Data Computation by Mapping Java Classes to MapReduce. In *2016 IEEE INDIACom - 2016: Computing for Sustainable Global Development*. IEEE. Retrieved on 02 September, 2016 from http://bvicam.ac.in/news/INDIACom%20 2016%20Proceedings/Main/papers/838.pdf

Weston, S. (2014). *doParallel: Foreach parallel adaptor for the parallel package*. Revolution Analytics R package version, 1(8). Retrieved on 02 September, 2016 from https://cran.r-project.org/web/packages/ doParallel/index.html

ADDITIONAL READING

Begoli, E., & Horey, J. (2012).Design principles for effective knowledge discovery from big data. In *Software Architecture (WICSA) and European Conference on Software Architecture (ECSA), 2012 Joint Working IEEE/IFIP Conference on* (pp. 215-218). IEEE. Retrieved on 02 September, 2016 from http:// ieeexplore.ieee.org/document/6337722/

Berson, A., & Smith, S. J. (1997). Data warehousing, data mining, and OLAP. McGraw-Hill, Inc. Retrieved on 02 September, 2016 from http://dl.acm.org/citation.cfm?id=549950

Bollier, D., & Firestone, C. M. (2010). *The promise and peril of big data* Washington, DC: Aspen Institute, Communications and Society Program. (p. 1). Retrieved on 02 September, 2016 from http://23.66.85.199/ collateral/analyst-reports/10334-ar-promise-peril-of-big-data.pdf

Chen, C. P., & Zhang, C. Y. (2014). Data-intensive applications, challenges, techniques and technologies: A survey on Big Data. *Information Sciences*, *275*, 314–347. doi:10.1016/j.ins.2014.01.015

Chen, H., Chiang, R. H., & Storey, V. C. (2012). Business Intelligence and Analytics: From Big Data to Big Impact. *Management Information Systems Quarterly*, *36*(4), 1165–1188.

Cuzzocrea, A., Song, I. Y., & Davis, K. C. (2011).Analytics over large-scale multidimensional data: the big data revolution!In *Proceedings of the ACM 14th international workshop on Data Warehousing and OLAP* (pp. 101-104).ACM. Retrieved on 02 September, 2016 from http://dl.acm.org/citation. cfm?id=2064695

Fox, P., & Hendler, J. (2011). Changing the equation on scientific data visualization. *Science*, *331*(6018), 705–708. doi:10.1126cience.1197654 PMID:21311008

Frankel, F., & Reid, R. (2008). Big data: Distilling meaning from data. *Nature*, *455*(7209), 30–30. doi:10.1038/455030a

Gorban, A. N., Kégl, B., Wunsch, D. C., & Zinovyev, A. Y. (Eds.). (2008).*Principal manifolds for data visualization and dimension reduction* (Vol. 58, pp. 96-130). Berlin-Heidelberg: Springer. Retrieved on 02 September, 2016 from http://link.springer.com/book/10.1007/978-3-540-73750-6

Hinton, G. E., & Salakhutdinov, R. R. (2006). Reducing the dimensionality of data with neural networks. *Science*, *313*(5786), 504–507. doi:10.1126cience.1127647 PMID:16873662

Jacobs, A. (2009). The pathologies of big data. *Communications of the ACM, 52*(8), 36–44. doi:10.1145/1536616.1536632

Keim, D., Qu, H., & Ma, K.-L. (2013). Big-data visualization. *IEEE Computer Graphics and Applications, 33*(4), 20–21. doi:10.1109/MCG.2013.54 PMID:24921095

LaValle, S., Lesser, E., Shockley, R., Hopkins, M. S., & Kruschwitz, N. (2011). Big data, analytics and the path from insights to value. *MIT Sloan Management Review, 52*(2), 21.

Manovich, L. (2011). Trending: The promises and the challenges of big social data. *Debates in the Digital Humanities,* 2, 460-475. Retrieved on 02 September, 2016 from http://manovich.net/index.php/projects/trending-the-promises-and-the-challenges-of-big-social-data

Russom, P. (2011). Big data analytics. *TDWI Best Practices Report*, Fourth Quarter, 1-35. Retrieved on 02 September, 2016 from http://www.tableau.com/sites/default/files/whitepapers/tdwi_bpreport_q411_big_data_analytics_tableau.pdf

Sagiroglu, S., & Sinanc, D. (2013). Big data: A review. In *Collaboration Technologies and Systems (CTS), 2013 International Conference on (*pp. 42-47). IEEE Retrieved on 02 September, 2016 from http://ieeexplore.ieee.org/xpls/abs_all.jsp?arnumber=6567202

Steele, J., & Iliinsky, N. (2010). *Beautiful visualization: looking at data through the eyes of experts.*" O'Reilly Media, Inc.", USA Retrieved on 02 September, 2016 from http://shop.oreilly.com/product/0636920000617.do

Zikopoulos, P., & Eaton, C. (2011). *Understanding big data: Analytics for enterprise class Hadoop and streaming data.* McGraw-Hill Osborne Media. Retrieved on 02 September, 2016 from http://dl.acm.org/citation.cfm?id=2132803

KEY TERMS AND DEFINITIONS

chmod: It is UNIX command which used for changing the permission of files and directories. There are various code used with chmod. "chmod 755" is used for giving permission to everyone for read, write and execute the files and directories and this command code is commonly used in web server environment.

Chunk: Chunk or data chuck is standardized by Vangie Beal. Its details are available in RFC2960 SCTP regarding the Stream Control Transmission Protocol (SCTP) standards. It is used to define the measurement unit of SCTP packet.

Framework: Software Framework is set of general rules and functions which perform specific work. These frameworks act as a principle for engineers and users in the practice applications.

Hadoop Streaming: It is Hadoop package utility that helps in running the mapper and reducer functions from terminal using multiple programming languages.

Heat Maps: It is the illustration technique involving use of colors which mimic the hotness. The real geographical maps are also dual with colors coding in this procedure.

JAR: JAR is acronym for Java Archive. It is a package that includes many files and these files are mostly Java class files, images and metadata. It is used as libraries and executable files within the Java environment.

Network Analysis: The data analysis with related graphs and other linked data structured to specific output. It is generally done in planning, designing, traveling and marketing field related projects.

Real-Time Dials and Gauges: They are unique data visualization techniques used for displaying data load and flow speed. They mostly use JavaScript API for the animation purpose.

Statistical Analysis: It is branch of data analytics where sample sets are compiled to draw the mathematical conclusion using special software and tools.

Trend Analysis: It is a mathematical technique which is commonly used by trader in stock market to predict the future stock rate. It exploits the historic data from determining the stock performance.

Visualization: Illustration of data for purpose of getting insight of the unseen information is termed as visualization. It is extensively used in sports, medical science, education and management data interpretation.

This research was previously published in the Handbook of Research on Big Data Storage and Visualization Techniques; pages 549-577, copyright year 2018 by Engineering Science Reference (an imprint of IGI Global).

Chapter 36
Intelligent Information System for Academic Institutions:
Using Big Data Analytic Approach

Mamata Rath

C. V. Raman College of Engineering, India

ABSTRACT

Research and publication is considered an authenticated certificate of innovative work done by research-ers in various fields. In research, new scientific results may be assessed, corrected, and further built up by the scientific neighborhood only if they are available in published form. Guidelines on account-able research and publication are currently set to encourage and promote high ethical standards in the conduct of research and in biomedical publications. They address various aspects of the research and publishing including duties of editors and authorship determination. The chapter presents research and publication system using big data analytics and research data management techniques with a background of information systems and need of information in research data management.

INTRODUCTION

Research which is an essential section of advanced higher education system is experiencing a transfor-mation. Researchers crosswise over controls are progressively using electronic apparatuses to gather, break down, and sort out data. They are presently delivering, putting away, and spreading advanced data in substantially bigger volumes than the text.Vast amounts of conceived computerized data are being delivered in a wide assortment of structures at a quick rate in colleges and research institutes (Cox AM et.al, 2014).This "data storm" makes a need to create approaches, foundations and administrations in associations, with the target of helping researchers in making, gathering, controlling, breaking down, transporting, putting away and protecting datasets. This blast of conceived computerized research (data that are made in advanced shape) implies that the time of BIG DATA has arrived (Whyte A et.al, 2011). Alongside this computerized over-burden comes the developing requirement for astute and viable Re-search Data Management (RDM).

DOI: 10.4018/978-1-6684-3662-2.ch036

The proceeded with presence and access of this data is worry since the data isn't at present efficient and put away in libraries. Research is presently led in the computerized domain, with researchers producing and trading data among themselves (Whyte A et.al, 2011). Sharing research data and grant is of national significance because of the expanded spotlight on augmenting return on the administration's interest in research programs. Research funders are proactive and urge great practices and to accomplish more noteworthy quantifiable profit and incentive for the research supported, and in this manner require or command certain particular measures of data administration and sharing to be trailed by the researchers.

Research data administration (RDM) is about "the association of data, from its entrance to the research push through the spread and chronicling of profitable outcomes" (Whyte and Tedds, 2011).Cox and Pinfield(2014)mentioned that RDM comprises of various diverse exercises and procedures related with the data lifecycle, including the plan and formation of data, stockpiling, security, protection, recovery, sharing, and reuse, all considering specialized abilities, moral contemplations, lawful issues and administration systems. Data created as a feature of research take an extensive variety of structures, from insights and exploratory outcomes to talk with chronicles and transcripts (Borgman, 2012). Data could exist as physical records or documents on a researcher's PC or terabytes of data on shared servers.

INFORMATION IN RESEARCH

All people, organizations and, when all is said in done, all associations are constantly catching data, a considerable lot of which are of no essentialness to them by any means. Nonetheless, other data are accessible that would bear the cost of them their very own superior comprehension condition and of themselves. These data – what we know as data – empower them to settle on more precise choices. Hence, the appropriate measure of data at the ideal time is a key factor for each association. Organization administrators take choices, get ready designs and control their organization's exercises utilizing data that they can get either from formal sources or through casual stations, for example, eye to eye discussions, phone calls, social contacts, and so on. Chiefs are tested by an inexorably mind boggling and indeterminate condition. In these conditions, administrators ought to hypothetically have the capacity to characterize and acquire the sort of data they require. Notwithstanding, this isn't what occurs by and by; rather, the manner in which supervisors play out their work relies upon the accessible data that they approach. Most choices are in this manner made without total learning, either on the grounds that the data isn't accessible or on the grounds that entrance to it would be expensive.

All people, organizations and all associations are constantly communicating information, a significant number of which are of no hugeness to them by any means. Be that as it may, other information are accessible that would bear the cost of them a superior comprehension of their claim condition and of themselves. These information – what we know as information empower them to settle on more exact choices. Hence, the perfect measure of information at the ideal time is a key factor for each association. Organization chiefs take selection, get ready designs and control their organization's exercises utilizing information that they can acquire either from formal sources or through casual stations, for example, up close and personal discussions, phone calls, social contacts, and so forth. Supervisors are tested by an undeniably perplexing and indeterminate condition. In these conditions, supervisors ought to hypothetically be ready to characterize and get the sort of information they require. Be that as it may, this isn't what occurs practically speaking; rather, the manner in which administrators play out their work depends on the accessible information that they approach. Most choices are in this manner made without supreme learning, either on the grounds that the information isn't accessible or on the grounds that entrance to it would be exorbitant (Rath et.al, 2018).

In spite of the troubles in acquiring information, chiefs require applicable information on which to base their arranging, control and basic leadership capacities. In spite of the fact that the terms information and information are some of the time utilized unpredictably, they do have distinctive implications. Information are non-arbitrary images that speak to the estimations of properties or occasions. Subsequently, information are certainties, occasions and exchanges put away as indicated by a concurred code. Information are actualities gotten through perusing, perception, count, estimation, and so forth (Rath et.al, 2019). The sums and different points of interest on an association's solicitations, checks or pay slips, and so forth, are alluded to as information, for instance. Information are acquired consequently, the after effect of a standard methodology, for example, invoicing or estimation forms.

IMPORTANCE OF DATA & INFORMATION IN ORGANISATION

Firstly, we have to study why the data has to be processed. There are certain reasons for which the data is being processed. The data can have the features such as

- **Incomplete:** Lacking attribute values, containing attribute data.
- **Noisy:** Containing errors or outliers,
- **Inconsistent:** Containing discrepancies in code or names. The quality data should be available.

To obtain the required information from huge, incomplete, noisy and inconsistent set of data is the need of data processing.

The way toward contemplative and understanding data is the thing that enables the message to have distinctive implications for various individuals. This procedure likewise suggests that the data examined, outlined or prepared to deliver messages will just move toward becoming data if its beneficiary comprehends its importance. For data to be changed into data, there must be a consciousness of what the individual getting the message will utilize it for, his or her preparation, position in the association and commonality with the dialect and computations utilized in the message.

While all managers require data, they don't all need a similar sort of data. The sort of data required will rely upon a scope of elements: their level in the chain of command, the work they are doing, privacy, earnestness, and so on (Rath et.al, 2016). Without a doubt, the convenience of data is a disputable point, and what for one individual is data, for another is data. In an association, for instance, when data is exchanged starting with one authoritative level then onto the next its importance may change fundamentally, to such an extent that at one progressive level it is viewed as noteworthy data, while at another level it is just data (Menguzzato and Renau, 1991). Data is the beneficiary's information and cognizance of data. Data diminishes vulnerability and manages the beneficiary something he or she didn't know beforehand.

Data is one of many organization assets, nearby capital, crude materials and work, since no organization is reasonable without data. As to as a rare asset obliges us to think about the issue of data financial matters, at the end of the day, how to set up the essential connection between the estimation of data and its expense. The following section summarizes and reviews major and selected articles relating to various aspects of Research Data Management as per the following themes:

1. Need and Basics of Research Date Management
2. Big Data
3. Some existing Tools for Data management and Repositories

It has increasingly become a pressing issue in research organizations as they strive to assist researchers in addressing new public funding requirements surrounding data dissemination and preservation (Rath et.al, 2016). The trend of data-fuelled research has now become a global and across all sectors, creating the need to manage this vast data in a manner which can be used by other researchers and derive benefit.

Research Data Management is defined as the organization and description of data, from its entry to the research cycle through the dissemination and archiving of valuable results.(White, 2011)

Research DataServices (RDS) and Research Data Management (RDM) services are two umbrella phrases authors have used to describe data curation (Jones, Pryor, & Whyte 2013;Tenopir, Sandusky, Allard,&Birch2013).

Charles Bailey's (2012) *Research Data Curation Bibliography w*ith over 200 citations and growing, is comprehensive bibliography on the subject. However, other distinctive bibliographies include The Westra, et al. (2010) bibliography of *Selected Internet Resources on Digital Research Data Curation which* presents a thematically organized bibliography of the more important Internet based resources. Witt and Giarlo (2012) provide a description of another unique guide, *Databib: An Online Bibliography of Research Data Repositories. Databib* currently provides records on over 500 repositories worldwide and is an example of the growth and geographical breath in digital data repository services. Graham Pryor's *ManagingResearchData* (2012) also compiles important literature on this topic.

Although a variety of research data life cycle models exist, most generally contain variations on several common stages as follows:

*   Planning (potentially including creation of a formal data management plan, or DMP, to meet funder
*   requirements),
*   Data assortment or acquisition,
*   Data analysis or interpretation (including data visualization),
*   Data maintenance and curation, and
*   Data sharing

Many articles used the theme of life cycle management and long--term preservation of research data center as one of the primary reasons to preserve research data: so it may be shared and reused. A broad overview of the reasons for sharing (and not sharing) research data and an agenda for future research is provided by Christine Borgman (2012)

Federer (2016) states that the ways that scientific research are practiced have shifted fundamentally in the last several decades. Researchers of the 21st century often rely on large digital datasets, and sometimes they are using data that they themselves did not gather, but that they obtained from public sources for reuse.

Big Data describes innovative techniques and technologies to capture, store, distribute, manage and analyze datasets that traditional data management methods are unable to handle. The concept of "Big Data" was first defined by Laney in his research note. Laney described the characteristics of big data as which cannot be processed by traditional data management tools. Three Vs were first used to characterize the Big Data. With further study on big data, the "Three V's" have been expanded to "Five V's": volume, velocity, variety, veracity (integrity of data), value (usefulness of data) and complexity (degree of interconnection among data structures)

Gordon-Murname specifically addresses the rise in big data and in her article "Big Data: A Big Opportunity for Librarians." Gordon-Murname points out four key areas: (1) organization, (2) search and access of internal datasets, (3) awareness of external data sources, and (4) to serve as authorities on copyright and intellectual property issues for the management of research data.

Tools

Services specific to data management plans for grant-funded research may include consultations with grant writers, DMP training and workshops, and form-based tools for creating a DMP. Some libraries have begun to review larger sets of DMPs (Parham and Doty2012). Understanding researcher needs, and presenting services with measurable positive impacts on those needs are critical to the success of DMP services. The data curation profile provides a framework for determining data management practices and needs of researchers (Carlson, J., & Stowell-Bracke, M. (2013).

The DMP Online tool developed in the United Kingdom, and its relative, the DMP Tool developed by the California Digital Library and partners in the U.S., are employed by some libraries to walk grant-writers through the process of developing a data management plan for submission with a grant proposal. Sallans and Donnelly (2012) compare and contrast these two forms-based web resources. The DMP Tool links to data plan requirements published by the funding agency units, and local guidance materials can also be incorporated into the web pages.

SOURCES OF INFORMATION FOR RESEARCH

Data is a basic, key asset that can be gotten from various sources. In this segment, we recognize inward data identifying with the earth inside the organization, and data about its outer condition. A considerable lot of the data caught by data frameworks allude to the working of the association and are utilized to deliver inside data. This interior data gives administration information about how the organization is working and regardless of whether it is accomplishing its targets. Most inner data originates from the bookkeeping framework and factual examinations (deals, creation, and so on.). Other inner data sources, for example, studies and meetings with organization individuals give quantitative data on, for example, specialists' inspiration levels or different pointers that are not effectively measured.

Organization chiefs likewise require data on nature: deals volume of their most direct rivals, potential customer sections for the organization's product offerings, topographical conveyance of its investors, and so forth. An organization must be effective on the off chance that it adjusts to the requests of its outside condition. The earth is spoken to by various gatherings that change in their ability to impact the organization's satisfaction of its goals. Beneath, we distinguish these intrigue gatherings and the distinctive kinds of data about them that the organization requires:

- **Customers:** Advertising, deals, levels of fulfillment.
- **Distributors:** Advertising and coordinations (circulation).
- **Competitors:** Advertise infiltration, advancements, item quality.

- **Suppliers:** Exchange conditions.
- **Trade Associations:** Compensations and work soundness.
- **Shareholders:** Organization execution.
- **Financial Establishments:** Money related conditions and venture openings.
- **Government:** legitimate and political advancements.

The organization must be educated always about every one of these outside gatherings and, in the meantime, a portion of these gatherings (e.g., investors and the administration) should likewise get data from the organization.

Data on the earth can be gotten from the accompanying sources:

- Personal data sources, which give data through contact deals staff, clients, providers, wholesalers, investors, and so on.
- Impersonal data sources, which run from general productions (e.g., provides details regarding the momentum circumstance, bank and authority substance reports, particular diaries) to particular examinations (e.g., statistical surveying, sentiment considers, experts' reports).

Google Scholar: As a Case Study

Google Scholar is a freely available web internet searcher that files the full content or metadata of scholarly writing over a variety of distributing arrangements and orders. Discharged in beta in November 2004, the Google Scholar list incorporates most friend audited online scholastic diaries and books, meeting papers, theories and papers, preprints, abstracts, specialized reports, and other scholarly writing, including court feelings and licenses. While Google does not distribute the extent of Google Scholar's database, scientometric specialists assessed it to contain around 389 million records including articles, references and licenses making it the world's biggest scholastic internet searcher in January 2018. Beforehand, the size was evaluated at 160 million records as of May 2014. Prior measurable gauge distributed in PLOS ONE utilizing a Mark and recover strategy assessed around 80–90% inclusion of all articles distributed in English with a gauge of 100 million.[4] This gauge likewise decided what number of archives were freely accessible on the web.

Google Scholar is comparable in capacity to the freely accessible CiteSeerX and getCITED. It additionally takes after the membership based apparatuses, Elsevier's Scopus and Clarivate Analytics' Web of Science. Google Scholar has been condemned for not checking diaries and incorporating ruthless diaries in its record.

Google Scholar enables clients to look for advanced or physical duplicates of articles, regardless of whether on the web or in libraries. It lists full-content diary articles, specialized reports, preprints, postulations, books, and different records, including chosen Web pages that are esteemed to be 'scholarly. Because a significant number of Google Scholar's list items connect to business diary articles, the vast majority will have the capacity to get to just a dynamic and the reference subtleties of an article, and need to pay a charge to get to the whole article. The most important outcomes for the sought catchphrases will be recorded first, arranged by the creator's positioning, the quantity of references that are connected to it and their pertinence to other scholarly writing, and the positioning of the distribution that the diary shows up in.

Utilizing its "group " characteristic, it demonstrates the accessible connects to diary articles. In the 2005 adaptation, this component gave a connection to both membership get to forms of an article and to free full-content renditions of articles; for a large portion of 2006, it gave connections to just the distributers' variants. Since December 2006, it has given connects to both distributed forms and real open access storehouses, yet at the same time does not cover those posted on individual personnel web pages;[citation needed] access to such self-filed non-membership adaptations is currently given by a connection to Google, where one can discover such open access articles.

Through its "cited by" highlight, Google Scholar gives access to edited compositions of articles that have cited the article being seen. It is this element specifically that gives the reference ordering already just found in CiteSeer, Scopus, and Web of Science. Through its "Related articles" highlight, Google Scholar displays a rundown of firmly related articles, positioned fundamentally by how comparative these articles are to the first outcome, yet additionally considering the pertinence of each paper.

COMPONENTS OF INFORMATION SYSTEM

All frameworks can be separated into subsystems. Since the organization carries on as a framework, its distinctive components can be separated into subsystems. As indicated by the association hypothesis writing, the organization can be isolated into the accompanying frameworks: business, tasks, budgetary, work force, and data. The data framework is identified with the various frameworks and the earth. The reason for the organization's data framework is to accumulate the data it needs and, following fundamental changes, guarantee that it achieves the individuals from the organization who require it, regardless of whether for basic leadership, vital control, or for executing choices received by the organization (Menguzzato and Renau, 1991). A director's execution along these lines relies upon his or her abilities in misusing the data framework's abilities keeping in mind the end goal to get positive business results.

For the motivations behind this chapter we embrace the meaning of a data framework given by Andreu, Ricart and Valor (1991). As per these creators the data framework is a formal arrangement of procedures that, working from an accumulation of data organized depending to the organization's needs, assembles, forms and disperses the data important for the organization's tasks and for its relating administration and control exercises, consequently supporting, at any rate to a limited extent, the basic leadership forms vital for the organization to play out its business capacities in accordance with its technique.

This definition, thusly, just incorporates the formal data framework, which is the piece of the data framework that all the organization's individuals know about and know how to utilize. This does not imply that casual data frameworks are not vital, but rather essentially perceives the restriction that they are, by their extremely nature, more hard to study, plan and oversee, in any event from a strong and all encompassing perspective. Casual data frameworks are not the aftereffect of a planned procedure; rather they give chance data. We should not, notwithstanding, disregard the presence of casual data channels, and the speed and productivity with which they can work, on events spreading bits of gossip through the association more rapidly than data that takes after the standard channels.

The above definition alludes to the capacities and techniques of the organization; by this, we expect to transmit an organization's data framework must serve its business approach. At last, the data framework is just a single of the numerous components that the organization outlines and uses to accomplish its destinations, and all things considered, it must be expressly planned in accordance with these targets.

To finish this meaning of a data framework, we currently endeavor to clear up any disarray between data framework and PC framework. The PC framework comprises of an unpredictable interconnection of various equipment and programming parts, which are basically determinist, formal frameworks in that particular information dependably gives a similar yield. Data frameworks are social frameworks whose conduct is generally impacted by the goals, qualities and convictions of people and gatherings and by the execution of innovation. The manner in which a data framework acts isn't determinist and does not take after the portrayal of any formal algorithmic model.

BIG DATA AND RESEARCH DATA MANAGEMENT

Today it is generally centered around taking care of the data which is audited here as far as the most valuable approaches and classifications of data apparatuses to browse. Each time another capacity medium was invented, the measure of data open detonate in light of the fact that it could be effectively gotten to. They have been discovered in applications that create hundreds or thousands of solicitations in a second. Destinations where deals is done like Amazon or Flipcart; and the product that procedure terabytes or even petabytes of data. Continuous calculations done for deciding Twitter's drifting tweets.

Big data is a wonder that is portrayed by the fast extension of crude data. The test is identified with how an expansive degree of data is being bridled, and the open door is identified with how effectively it is utilized for breaking down the data from it. It is presently regular place to recognize big data solutions from traditional IT arrangements by thinking about the accompanying four measurements.

- **Volume:** Volume depicts the measure of data produced by associations or people. Big data solutions must oversee and process bigger measures of data.
- **Velocity:** Velocity portrays the recurrence at which data is created, caught and shared. Big data arrangements must process all the more quickly arriving data. By Velocity, they mean both the rate at which data arrive and the time in which it must be followed up on
- **Variety:** Big data arrangements must manage more sorts of data, both organized and unstructured in nature. By Variety, they typically mean heterogeneity of data composes, portrayal, and semantic interpretation
- **Veracity:** Big data arrangements must approve the rightness of the huge measure of quickly arriving data.

Today it is generally centered around taking care of this Big Data. The most valuable methodologies and classifications of data apparatuses are inspected to look over data stockroom to Business Intelligence (BI) now, we as a whole are experiencing startling development in organized and unstructured data is exceptionally colossal. The unstructured data can be from word, exceed expectations, PowerPoint records or PDF, HTML report, telecom data, satellite data etc.

As a matter of fact, in the wake of perusing the material on it, there is one more measurement one can consider, that is Complexity.

- **Complexity:** Organizations catch an assortment of data configurations and search over gigantic data sources in genuine time to examine and recognize designs inside the data. There are a few models, recognizing extortion for credit card clients, monetary patterns for speculation associations, anticipating power utilization for energy companies.

Big Data allows corporate and research organizations to do things not previously possible economically. It is used for:

- Analysis
- Business Trends

Research Data Management is a piece of the research procedure, and plans to make the research procedure as viable efficient as could be allowed, and meet desires and necessities of the college, research funders, and enactment.

Research data administration (or RDM) is a term which portrays the association, stockpiling, safeguarding, and sharing of data gathered and utilized in a research venture. It includes the administration of research data amid the lifetime of a research venture. It likewise includes choices about how data will be protected and shared after the task is finished. It concerns how a researcher:

- Creates data and plan for its utilization,
- Organizes, structure, and name data,
- Keeps – make it secure, give access, store and back it up,
- Finds data assets, and offer with partners and all the more comprehensively, distribute and get refered to.

Shielding research data from misfortune or incidental changes through great research data administration is especially critical while creating data that are special or arduous to get and reobtain the same. There are plentiful of reasons why research data administration is critical:

- Data, similar to diary articles and books, is an academic item.
- Data (particularly computerized data) is delicate and effortlessly lost.
- There are developing research data necessities forced by funders and distributers.
- Research data administration spares time and assets over the long haul.
- Good administration forestalls mistakes and expands the nature of your investigations.
- Well-oversaw and available data enables others to approve and duplicate discoveries.
- Research data administration encourages sharing of research data and, when shared, data can prompt important revelations by others outside of the first research group.

In this study, the big data concept is assumed to be extremely large amount of structured, semi structured or unstructured data continuously generated from diversified resources, which inundates business operation in real time and impacts on decision making through mining insightful information from rambling data. For research clarity, what constitutes big data include large structured datasets and unstructured data in the form of text(e.g. documents, natural languages), web data(e.g. web usage, web contents and web structure), social media data(e.g. virtual network), multimedia data(e.g. image, audio, video) and mobile data(viz. sensors. geographical location, application). The research community has developed standards and best practices to induce and improve the quality of data sharing with large data.

ASPECTS IN RESEARCH DATA MANAGEMENT

Emerging from analysis of various Research Data Management developments, a number of key components of an RDM programme have been identified. Following are the components describe the various activities, such as policy development and technology implementation, that together constitute concerted effort in a particular area.

- **Strategies**: defining the overarching vision for research data management within the institution and how it relates to the institutional mission and priorities, and outlining major developmental goals and principles which inform activity.
- **Policies**: specifying how the strategies are to be brought in operation through regular procedures, including not just an RDM policy but also a set of complementary policy frameworks covering issues such as intellectual property rights and openness that may be relevant.
- **Guidelines**: providing detail on how the policies will be implemented often written from the point of view of a particular user group (such as those within a particular disciplinary area) and defining specific activities, and roles and responsibilities.
- **Processes:** specifying and regulating activities within the research data life-cycle including research data management planning for individual projects, data processing, ingesting data into central systems, selecting data for preservation, etc, and involving the use of standards and standardised procedures wherever possible.
- **Technologies:** underpinning processes with technical implementations including data repositories and networking infrastructures allowing for storage and transport of data.
- **Services:** enabling end-user access to systems and providing support for research data life-cycle activities including supporting the creation of data management plans, providing skills training, and delivering helpdesk services. (Pinfield, Stephen, Andrew M. Cox, and Jen Smith,2014)

INSTITUTIONAL INFORMATION SYSTEM

A number of drivers for RDM developments have been identified at an institutional level:

1. **Storage:** There has to be immediate storage facilities for a wide variety of datasets at large scale for the future requirements of researchers which represents value for money and is convenient to use.
2. **Security:** The data must be kept confidential or sensitive, should be held securely with relevant authentication and authorisation mechanisms in place.
3. **Preservation:** The need for medium and long-term archiving of data with associated selection protocols and preservation activities along with a supporting technical infrastructure.
4. **Compliance:** There must be a need to fulfil the requirements and policies of other relevant agencies, and funders, as well as legal obligations, such as data protection, and industry good practice.
5. **Quality:** There is a need to maintain and enhance the quality of research activity in general in order to demonstrate the robustness of findings and enable results verification and reproducibility.
6. **Sharing:** The need to share data amongst targeted users and also to provide mechanisms and systems to enable open access to data where appropriate. There are few 'Influencing Factors' since they are

prevailing conditions which may affect an institutional RDM programme in a variety of complex ways including either facilitating or constraining action. Key Influencing Factors emerging from this research were culture, demand. Incentives. Policies, projects, skills and Governance. It has been observed that there are technical differences in areas such as metadata standards and interoperability protocols, but also in cultures around sharing and reuse. Nevertheless, despite the lack of detailed solutions discussed here, the importance of the issues of disciplinary differences should not be underestimated. In many respects, there is a discussion held on all of the other Influencing Factors.

THE PROPOSED LEARNING BASED SMART ANALYTICAL FRAMEWORK

Figure 1 presents a block diagram of smart methods used in research and publication process. There are multiple framework in smart applications that employ intelligent methods using big data analytics and IoT devices. As shown in the figure the review and selection rubric employs various mechanism starting from similarity checking to searching multiple databases such as DBLP and SCOPUS. DBLP formerly stood for DataBase systems and Logic Programming. As an acronym, it has been taken to arise for Digital Bibliography & Library Project; however, it is now favoured that the acronym be simply a name, hence the new title "The DBLP Computer Science Bibliography (https://en.wikipedia.org/wiki/DBLP). Mechanical advances enable more physical items to interface with the Internet and give their administrations on the Web as assets.

Figure 1. Proposed analytical framework for research paper evaluation

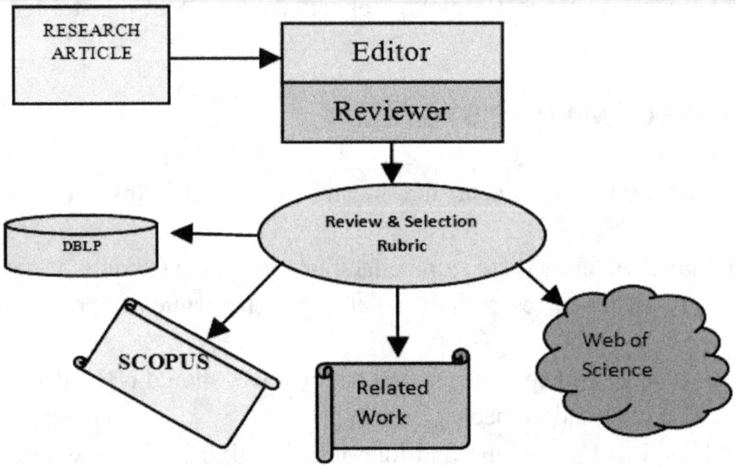

RESEARCH ASSESSMENT USING BIG DATA ANALYTICS

Web search tools are the way to completely use this developing Web of Things, as they connect clients and applications with assets required for their task. Building up these frameworks is a testing and various undertaking because of the decent variety of Web of Things assets that they work with. Every blend of assets in inquiry determination process requires an alternate sort of web search tool with its own particular specialized difficulties and use situations. Fig.2 depicts Factors determining quality of research work . This assorted variety entangles both the improvement of new frameworks and evaluate ment of the cutting edge. DBLP originally stood for DataBase systems and Logic Programming. As acronym, it has been taken to stand for Digital Bibliography & Library Project; however, it is now preferred that the acronym be simply a name, hence the new title "The DBLP Computer Science Bibliography (https://en.wikipedia.org/wiki/DBLP)

Figure 2. Factors determining quality of research work

Figure 2 demonstrates the parameters and important components that certifies good quality research. A digital object identifier (DOI) is a unique alphanumeric string assigned by a registration agency (the International DOI Foundation) to identify content and provide a persistent link to its location on the Internet. The publisher assigns a DOI when your article is published and made available electronically.

Citation Analysis- The procedure whereby the effect or "quality" of an article is evaluated by tallying the occasions different authors notice it in their work. Citation investigation invovles checking the occasions an article is cited by different attempts to gauge the effect of a publicaton or author. The caviat in any case, there is no single citation examination apparatuses that gathers all publications and their cited references. For an exhaustive investigation of the effect of an author or a publication, one needs to look in different databases to locate all conceivable cited references. Various assets are accessible at UIC that distinguish cited works including: Web of Science, Scopus, Google Scholar, and different databases with restricted citation data. To discover how much effect a specific article or author has had, by indicating which different authors cited the work inside their very own papers. The H-Index is one explicit technique using citation examination to decide a people affect.

Figure 3. Parameters of journal publication and details

Journal Publication Details									
Sl. No.	Year	Department	1st Author	2nd Author	3rd Author	Other Authors	Journal Type (National / Intl. Journal)	Journal Version (Print / E-journal)	Journal Category (Peer Review Journals / Non-Peer Review Journals)

An example of citation in Web of Science is given here. Web of Science gives citation checks to articles recorded inside it. It records more than 10,000 diaries in expressions of the human experience, humanities, sciences, and sociologies.

To discover the citation checks to your own articles - Enter the name of the author in the best inquiry box, Select Author starting from the drop menu on the right. To guarantee exactness for prevalent names, enter Univ Illinois in the center hunt box, at that point select "Address" from the field drop down menu on the right. (You may need to include the second pursuit box by clicking "include another field" before you enter the location) Tap on Search, a rundown of publications by that author name will show up. To one side of every citation, the occasions the article has been cited will show up. Tap the number alongside "times cited" to see the articles that have cited your article

Big data analytics expect to quickly remove learning capable data that aides in making forecasts, recognizing ongoing patterns, finding concealed data, and at last, settling on choices . Fig. 3 shows Parameters of journal publication and details. Data mining procedures are broadly conveyed for both issue particular techniques and summed up data analytics. Likewise, measurable and machine pick up ing techniques are used. The development of big data likewise changes analytics prerequisites. Despite the fact that the prerequisites for productive instruments lie in all parts of big data management, for example, catching, stockpiling, preprocessing, and investigation; for our dialog, big data analytics requires the same or speedier handling speed than conventional data analytics with least cost for high-volume, high-speed, and high-assortment data .

Plagiarism checkers are a compelling method to examine your papers for any warnings that may recommend plagiarism. This particular programming is accessible for the individuals who are not kidding about their scholarly or examine work. Plagiarism checker programming like WriteCheck is accessible on the web. Try not to take the risk of being blamed for plagiarism. There are some motivations to utilize a plagiarism software such as - a few people use Internet web crawlers to search for copied material, plagiarism programming can offer more sources, for example, vast databases that incorporate periodicals and books that may not be accessible on the web. A huge number of periodicals exist. Gigantic databases, for example, EBSCOhost and ProQuest contain such articles. Plagiarism checkers approach these databases.

Different arrangements are accessible for big data analytics, and progressions in creating and enhancing these arrangements are in effect persistently accomplished to make them appropriate for new big data patterns. Data mining assumes a vital part in analytics, and a large portion of the methods are produced utilizing data mining calculations as per a specific situation. Learning on accessible big data analytics alternatives is critical while assessing and picking a proper approach for basic leadership. In this segment, we show a few techniques that can be executed for a few big data contextual analyses. A portion of these analytics techniques are proficient for big IoT data analytics. Different and colossal size data sets contribute more in big data bits of knowledge. Be that as it may, this conviction isn't generally legitimate on the grounds that more data may have more ambiguities and variations from the norm.

Big data analytics techniques have been described here under characterization, grouping, affiliation run mining, and prediction classes. Every classification is a data mining capacity and includes numerous strategies and calculations to satisfy data extraction and investigation necessities. For instance, Bayesian network, support vector machine (SVM), and k-closest neighbor (KNN) offer grouping techniques. Additionally, parceling, various leveled grouping, and co-event are across the board in grouping. Affiliation govern mining and expectation involve noteworthy techniques. Order is a regulated learning approach that utilizations earlier information as preparing data to arrange data objects into groups. A predefined classification is doled out to a protest, and along these lines, the target of foreseeing a gathering or class for a question is accomplished. Discovering obscure or concealed examples is additionally trying for big IoT data. Besides, extricating significant data from extensive data sets to enhance basic leadership is a basic assignment. A Bayesian system is an order strategy that offers show interpretability.

Analysing data designs and making groups are effectively performed utilizing SVM, which is likewise classification approach for big data analytics. SVM uses factual learning hypothesis to break down data designs and make gatherings. A few appli-cations of SVM classification in big data analytics incorporate content classification, design coordinating, wellbeing diagnostics, and trade. Additionally, KNN is normally intended to give effective instruments for finding concealed examples from big data sets, with the end goal that recovered items are like the predefined classification. Utilizing cases hide ther enhance the KNN calculation for application in abnormality identification, high-dimensional data, and logical tests . Classification has different expansions while embracing countless insight and data mining systems. Therefore, classification is one of the across the board data digging systems for big data analytics.

Grouping is another data mining system utilized as a big data analytics strategy. In spite of classification, grouping utilizes an unsupervised learning approach and makes groupes for given articles in view of their unmistakable significant features . Gathering a substantial number of articles as groupes makes data control straightforward. The notable strategies utilized for grouping are progressive grouping and parceling. The progressive grouping approach continues joining little groupes of data articles to shape a various leveled tree and make agglomerative groupes. Disruptive groups are made in the contrary way by separating a solitary group that contains all data objects into littler suitable groupes.

Market investigation and business basic leadership are the most noteworthy utilizations of big data analytics. The procedure of association manage mining includes recognizing intriguing connections among various articles, occasions, or other enti-binds to dissect advertise patterns, purchaser purchasing conduct, and item request predictions. Association control mining centers around recognizing and making rules in light of the recurrence of events for numeric and non-numeric data. Data handling is performed in two behavior under association rules. In the first place, consecutive data handling utilizes priori-based calculations, for example, MSPS and LAPIN-SPAM, to recognize collaboration associations. Another significant data preparing approach under association lead is fleeting succession investigation, which utilizes calculations to examine occasion designs in consistent data.

Perceptive analytics utilize authentic data, which are known as preparing data, to decide the outcomes as patterns or conduct in data. SVM and fluffy rationale calculations are utilized to distinguish connections amongst free and ward factors and to get relapse bends for predictions, for example, for catastrophic events. Moreover, client purchasing predictions online networking patterns are dissected through prescient analytics. On account of big data analytics, preparing necessities are adjusted by the nature and volume of data. Quick data access and digging techniques for organized and unstructured data are real concerns identified with big data analytics. Moreover, data portrayal is a significant prerequisite in big data analytics. Time arrangement analysis lessens high dimensionality related with big data and offers portrayal for enhanced basic leadership.

CONCLUSION

Research and development is the procedure by which an organization attempts to acquire new information that it may use to make new innovation, items, administrations, or frameworks that it will either utilize or move. The objective frequently is to add to the organization's main concern. Various individuals consider pharmaceutical and innovation organizations when they hear "Research and development," yet different firms, including those that create shopper items, put time and assets into R&D also to some extent, the reuse of data as a consequence of data sharing distorts the classic distinction between primary and secondary data. Researchers will likely need assistance in learning how to access and utilize these datasets. It is been observed that, because of digitally archived research objects such as broadcasts and websites, new aspects have been added for data sharing. the amount of freely- and publicly-available research data continues to increase exponentially. This reflects the term "Data Deluge". In conclusion, research data management in context with library data could also be treated as big data without doubt due its property of large volume; high velocity and obvious variety. To sum up it can be said that to make big datasets more useful, visible and accessible. With new and powerful analytics of big data, such as information visualization tools, researchers can look at data in new ways and mine it for information they intend to have.

REFERENCES

Abadi, D., Agrawal, R., & Ailamaki, A. (2014). The Beckman reporton database research. *SIGMOD Record*, *43*(3), 61–70. doi:10.1145/2694428.2694441

Armour, F. (2012). *Introduction to big data*. Presentation at the symposium Big Data and Business Analytics: Defining a Framework, Center for IT and Global Economy, Kogod School of Business, American University, Washington, DC.

Borgman, C. L. (2012). The conundrum of sharing research data. *Journal of the American Society for Information Science and Technology*, *63*(6), 1059–1078p. doi:10.1002/asi.22634

Carlson, J., & Stowell-Bracke, M. (2013). Data management and sharing from the perspective of graduate students: An examination of the culture and practice at the water quality field station. portal. *Libraries and the Academy*, *13*(4), 343–361. doi:10.1353/pla.2013.0034

Charles, W. (2012). *Bailey J. Research Data Curation Bibliography*. Houston, TX: Charles W. Bailey, Jr. Available from http://digital-scholarship.org/rdcb/rdcb.htm

Codd, E. F. (1970). A relational model of data for large shared data banks. *Communications of the ACM*, *13*(6), 377–387. doi:10.1145/362384.362685

Cox, A. M., & Pinfield, S. (2014). Research data management and libraries: Current activities and future priorities. *J Librariansh Inf Sci*. Available: http://lis.sagepub.com/cgi/doi/10.1177/0961000613492542

Crosas, M. (n.d.). *Cloud Dataverse: A Data Repository Platform for the Cloud*. Available from https://openstack.cioreview.com/cxoinsight/cloud-dataverse-a-data-repository-platform-for-the-cloud-nid-24199-cid-120.html

Doty, J. (2012). *Survey of faculty practices and perspectives on research data management*. Retrieved from http://guides.main.library.emory.edu/datamgmt/survey

DuraCloud solutions. (n.d.). Retrieved from http://www.duracloud.org/solutions

Farid, M., Roatis, A., & Ilyas, I. F. (2016). CLAMS: bringing quality toData Lakes. In *Proceedings of the 2016 International Conference on Management of Data*. ACM.

Federer, L. (2016). Research data management in the age of big data: Roles and opportunities for librarians. *Information Services & Use, 36*, 35–43. DOI . doi:10.3233/ISU-160797

Godse, M., & Mulik, S. (2009). An approach for selecting Software-as-a-Service (SaaS) product. In *2013 IEEE Sixth International Conference on Cloud Computing* (pp. 155–158). Los Alamitos, CA: IEEE Computer Society. 10.1109/CLOUD.2009.74

Gordon-Murnane, L. (2012). Big Data: A Big Opportunity for Librarians. *Online (Bergheim), 36*(5), 34.

Hai, R., Geisler, S., & Quix, C. (2016). Constance: an intelligent Data Lake system. In *Proceedings of the 2016 International Conference on Management of Data*. ACM.

Halevy, A., Korn, F., & Noy, N. F. (2016). Goods: organizing Google'sdatasets. In *Proceedings of the 2016 International Conference on Management of Data*. ACM.

IBM Big Data & Analytics Hub. (2016). *The four V's of big data*. Available from http://www.ibmbigdatahub.com/infographic/four-vs-big-data-4V

Laney, D. (2001, February 6). *3-D data management: Controlling data volume, velocity and variety*. META Research Note.

Madduri, R. K., Dave, P., Sulakhe, D., Lacinski, L., Liu, B., & Foster, I. T. (2013). Experiences in building a next-generation sequencing analysis service using Galaxy, Globus Online and Amazon Web Service. In *Proceedings of the Conference on Extreme Science and Engineering Discovery Environment: Gateway to Discovery* (pp. 34:1–34:3). New York: ACM. 10.1145/2484762.2484827

Madera, L. A. (2016). The next information architecture evolution:the data lake wave. In *Proceedings of the 8ᵗʰInternational Conference on Management of Digital EcoSystems*. ACM.

Parham, S. W., Bodnar, J., & Fuchs, S. (2012). Supporting tomorrow's research: Assessing faculty data curation needs at Georgia Tech. *College & Research Libraries News, 73*(1), 10–13. doi:10.5860/crln.73.1.8686

Parker, Z., Poe, S., & Vrbsky, S. V. (2013). Comparing NoSQL MongoDB to an SQL DB. In *Proceedings of the 51st ACM Southeast Conference*. ACM. 10.1145/2498328.2500047

Pinfield, Cox, & Smith. (2014). Research data management and libraries: relationships, activities, drivers and influences. *PLoS One, 9*(12).

Pryor, G., Jones, S., & Whyte, A. (Eds.). (2013). *Delivering research data management services: Fundamentals of good practice*. London: Facet.

Rath. (2018). Effective Routing in Mobile Ad-hoc Networks With Power and End-to-End Delay Optimization: Well Matched With Modern Digital IoT Technology Attacks and Control in MANET. In *Advances in Data Communications and Networking for Digital Business Transformation*. IGI Global. Doi:10.4018/978-1-5225-5323-6.ch007

Rath, Pati, & Pattanayak. (2018). An Overview on Social Networking: Design, Issues, Emerging Trends, and Security. In *Social Network Analytics: Computational Research Methods and Techniques.* Academic Press.

Rath, M. (2017). Resource provision and QoS support with added security for client side applications in cloud computing. *International Journal of Information Technology, 9*(3), 1–8.

Rath, M. (2018). An Exhaustive Study and Analysis of Assorted Application and Challenges in Fog Computing and Emerging Ubiquitous Computing Technology. *International Journal of Applied Evolutionary Computation, 9*(2), 17-32. Retrieved from www.igi-global.com/ijaec

Rath, M. (2018). A Methodical Analysis of Application of Emerging Ubiquitous Computing Technology With Fog Computing and IoT in Diversified Fields and Challenges of Cloud Computing. *International Journal of Information Communication Technologies and Human Development, 10*(2).

Rath, M. (2018). An Analytical Study of Security and Challenging Issues in Social Networking as an Emerging Connected Technology (April 20, 2018). *Proceedings of 3rd International Conference on Internet of Things and Connected Technologies (ICIoTCT).* Available at https://ssrn.com/abstract=3166509

Rath, M., & Panda, M. R. (2017). MAQ system development in mobile ad-hoc networks using mobile agents. *IEEE 2nd International Conference on Contemporary Computing and Informatics (IC3I),* 794-798.

Rath, M., & Pati, B. (2017). *Load balanced routing scheme for MANETs with power and delay optimization. International Journal of Communication Network and Distributed Systems, 19.*

Rath, M., Pati, B., Panigrahi, C. R., & Sarkar, J. L. (2019). QTM: A QoS Task Monitoring System for Mobile Ad hoc Networks. In P. Sa, S. Bakshi, I. Hatzilygeroudis, & M. Sahoo (Eds.), *Recent Findings in Intelligent Computing Techniques. Advances in Intelligent Systems and Computing* (Vol. 707). Singapore: Springer. doi:10.1007/978-981-10-8639-7_57

Rath, M., Pati, B., Panigrahi, C. R., & Sarkar, J. L. (2019). QTM: A QoS Task Monitoring System for Mobile Ad hoc Networks. In P. Sa, S. Bakshi, I. Hatzilygeroudis, & M. Sahoo (Eds.), *Recent Findings in Intelligent Computing Techniques. Advances in Intelligent Systems and Computing* (Vol. 707). Singapore: Springer. doi:10.1007/978-981-10-8639-7_57

Rath, M., Pati, B., & Pattanayak, B. K. (2016). Inter-Layer Communication Based QoS Platform for Real Time Multimedia Applications in MANET. Wireless Communications, Signal Processing and Networking (IEEE WiSPNET), 613-617. doi:10.1109/WiSPNET.2016.7566203

Rath, M., Pati, B., & Pattanayak, B. K. (2017). Cross layer based QoS platform for multimedia transmission in MANET. *11th International Conference on Intelligent Systems and Control (ISCO),* 402-407. 10.1109/ISCO.2017.7856026

Rath, M., Pati, B., & Pattanayak, B. K. (2019). Relevance of Soft Computing Techniques in the Significant Management of Wireless Sensor Networks. In Soft Computing in Wireless Sensor Networks (pp. 86-106). New York: Chapman and Hall/CRC, Taylor & Francis Group.

Rath, M., & Pattanayak, B. (2017). MAQ:A Mobile Agent Based QoS Platform for MANETs. *International Journal of Business Data Communications and Networking, IGI Global*, *13*(1), 1–8. doi:10.4018/IJBDCN.2017010101

Rath, M., & Pattanayak, B. (2018). Technological improvement in modern health care applications using Internet of Things (IoT) and proposal of novel health care approach. *International Journal of Human Rights in Healthcare*.

Rath, M., & Pattanayak, B. (2018). Technological improvement in modern health care applications using Internet of Things (IoT) and proposal of novel health care approach. *International Journal of Human Rights in Healthcare*. doi:10.1108/IJHRH-01-2018-0007

Rath, M., & Pattanayak, B. K. (2014). A methodical survey on real time applications in MANETS: Focussing On Key Issues. *International Conference on, High Performance Computing and Applications (IEEE ICHPCA)*, 22-24. 10.1109/ICHPCA.2014.7045301

Rath, M., & Pattanayak, B. K. (2018). Monitoring of QoS in MANET Based Real Time Applications. Smart Innovation, Systems and Technologies, 84, 579-586. doi:10.1007/978-3-319-63645-0_64

Rath, M., & Pattanayak, B. K. (2018). SCICS: A Soft Computing Based Intelligent Communication System in VANET. Smart Secure Systems – IoT and Analytics Perspective. *Communications in Computer and Information Science*, *808*, 255–261. doi:10.1007/978-981-10-7635-0_19

Rath, M., & Pattanayak, B. K. (2019). Security Protocol with IDS Framework Using Mobile Agent in Robotic MANET. *International Journal of Information Security and Privacy*, *13*(1), 46–58. doi:10.4018/IJISP.2019010104

Rath, M., Pattanayak, B. K., & Pati, B. (2017). *Energetic Routing Protocol Design for Real-time Transmission in Mobile Ad hoc Network. In Computing and Network Sustainability, Lecture Notes in Networks and Systems* (Vol. 12). Singapore: Springer.

Riungu, L. M., Taipale, O., & Smolander, K. (2010). Research issues for software testing in the cloud. In *2010 IEEE Second International Conference on Cloud Computing Technology and Science (CloudCom)* (pp. 557–564). Indianapolis, IN: IEEE. 10.1109/CloudCom.2010.58

Rtah, M. (2018). Big Data and IoT-Allied Challenges Associated With Healthcare Applications in Smart and Automated Systems. *International Journal of Strategic Information Technology and Applications*, *9*(2). doi:10.4018/IJSITA.201804010

Rtah, M. (2018). Big Data and IoT-Allied Challenges Associated With Healthcare Applications in Smart and Automated Systems. *International Journal of Strategic Information Technology and Applications*, *9*(2). doi:10.4018/IJSITA.201804010

Sallans, A., & Donnelly, M. (2012). DMP Online and DMPTool: Different Strategies Towards a Shared Goal. *International Journal of Digital Curation*, *7*(2), 123–129. doi:10.2218/ijdc.v7i2.235

Sheng, J., Amankwah-Amoah, J., & Wang, X. (2017). A multidisciplinary perspective of big data in management research. *International Journal of Production Economics*, *191*, 97–112. doi:10.1016/j.ijpe.2017.06.006

Son, N. H. (2012). *Module on Data Preprocessing Techniques for Data Mining on Data Cleaning and Data Preprocessing*. Retrieved from http://elitepdf.com/

Tenopir, C., Sandusky, R. J., Allard, S., & Birch, B. (2014). Research data management services in academic research libraries and perceptions of librarians. *Library & Information Science Research*, *36*(2), 84–90. doi:10.1016/j.lisr.2013.11.003

Terrizzano, I., Schwarz, P., & Roth, M. (2015). Data wrangling: the challenging journey from the wild to the lake. *Proceedings of the 7th Biennial Conference on Innovative Data SystemsResearch (CIDR '15)*, 4–7.

UK Data Service. (2016). *Research data lifecycle*. Retrieved from https://www.ukdataservice.ac.uk/manage-data/lifecycle

University of California Digital Library. (2016). *DMPTool*. Available from https://dmptool.org/

University of Virginia Library Research Data Services. (2016). *Steps in the data life cycle*. Available from http://data.library.virginia.edu/data-management/lifecycle/

Vaidya, M. (2016). Handling critical issues of Big Data on cloud. In Managing Big Data in cloud computing environments. IGI Global. doi:10.4018/978-1-4666-9834-5.ch005

Vassiliadis, Simitsis, & Skiadopoulos. (2002). Conceptual modeling for ETL processes. In *Proceedings of the 5th ACM international workshop on Data Warehousing and OLAP*. ACM. 10.1145/583890.583893

Waddington, S. (2012). Kindura: Repository services for researchers based on hybrid clouds. *Journal of Digital Information, 13*(1).

Wang, C. (2016). Exposing library data with big data technology: A review. In *Computer and Information Science (ICIS), 2016 IEEE/ACIS 15th International Conference on*. IEEE. 10.1109/ICIS.2016.7550937

Westra, Ramirez, Parham, & Scaramozzino. (2010). Selected Internet Resources on Digital Research Data Curation. *Issues in Science and Technology Librarianship, 63*.

Whyte, A., & Tedds, J. (2011). *Making the case for research data management*. Edinburgh: Digital Curation Centre. Available http://www.dcc.ac.uk/webfm_send/487

This research was previously published in Interdisciplinary Approaches to Information Systems and Software Engineering; pages 207-232, copyright year 2019 by Engineering Science Reference (an imprint of IGI Global).

Chapter 37
Big Data and Digital Tools Applied to the Teaching:
Learning in Graduate Programs in Mexico

Jésica Alhelí Cortés Ruiz
https://orcid.org/0000-0002-5459-4874
Instituto Politécnico Nacional, Mexico

Rosa María Rivas García
https://orcid.org/0000-0002-8371-6068
Instituto Politécnico Nacional, Mexico

ABSTRACT

This chapter will focus on the characterization of big data and digital tools applied in postgraduate programs in Mexico. The new economic order demands from academic organizations more efficient ways in their production and transfer of teaching-learning in graduate programs in Mexico. In this chapter, an approach to big data technology and its influence on education explaining the main educational methods and new professional options derived from big data analytics is given. It discusses the technical, legal, and ethical aspects for the adoption and use of big data technology in educational institutions.

INTRODUCTION

The use of Big Data Technology in education has already begun to provide great benefits in terms of improving educational management, the development of new methods for teaching and learning, the creation of new careers and professional options for students, as well as in the exploitation and use of digital collections generated by educational institutions.

Thus, the Big Data Analytics is the current key resource to analyze, visualize, understand, and improve education. For this reason, this article is aimed at those responsible for guiding the course of this (academics, researchers, teachers and the general public), and it is intended to give an insight into the

DOI: 10.4018/978-1-6684-3662-2.ch037

current degree of advancement of this technology in education, as well as the facilities that exist for its instrumentation in educational institutions (Boyd, D., & Crawford, K., 2012).

The Big Data Technology allows the collection, storage, and preparation of large volumes of data to analyze or visualize the relationship between them. This includes data that are being generated in real time and that come from social networks, sensors, devices of various kinds or audio and video sources. In this way, it is possible to identify and predict in detail the causes or effects of complex events or processes (Lohr, S., 2012).

In the educational field, this technology has certainly started to offer great benefits. For example, in the improvement of educational management, the development of new methods for teaching and learning, the creation of new careers and professional opportunities, as well as the generation and storage of digital collections that constitute the product of years of academic, teaching and research activity (Gibson, D., & Ifenthaler, D., 2017).

Currently, it has transcended to a state in which new methods based on technology are needed to track students, improve their tutorials, obtain objective data from their evaluations, predict academic risks or simply understand the behavior of the students and the scholar groups. In this continuous change, teachers are more aware of the need to update themselves technologically in order to offer a more effective education adapted to the needs of the current school population.

For this reason, the method of observation in the classroom is no longer the most effective way to improve the educational process, but the big data analytics is the current key resource to understand and improve it. In the same way, digital collections, generated on a regular basis by educational institutions, must be integrated into the lake of data and thus improve its dissemination and exploitation, not only in the analytical processes of big data, but throughout society (Carrasco M., Sánchez C. & Carro A., 2015).

BIG DATA

Big Data (large data, large volumes of data or big data as recommended by the Fundeú BBVA Foundation) is the confluence of a multitude of technological trends that had been maturing since the first decade of the 21st century, and which were consolidated during the years 2011 to 2013, when they exploded and burst with great force in organizations and companies in particular, and in society in general: mobility, social networks, increase in broadband and reduction in the cost of internet connection, social media, internet of things, geo-location, and very significantly cloud computing.

On the other hand, Massive Data or Data Intelligence is a concept that refers to the treatment and analysis of huge repositories of data so disproportionately large that it is impossible to handle them with conventional database and analytical tools (Chen, H., Chiang, R. H., & Storey, V., 2012).

In fact, this technology deals with all activities related to systems that manipulate large data sets. The most common difficulties linked to the management of the latter are focused on the collection and storage, search, sharing, analysis and visualization of information. The tendency to manipulate huge amounts of data is due to the need, in many cases, of using such information in the creation of statistical reports and predictive models that can be used in many areas of human endeavor.

Furthermore, Big Data has been translated into personalized teaching and has focused on the constant improvement of learning methods, using one of the most important technological trends for analysis and information processes.

It is true that many people have heard the Big Data term, but what is it? What is it for? What are the benefits of its use within the educational field? When people talk about data and information, it is easy to understand the term if one thinks that it refers to everything that is created through a computer or a mobile and intelligent device, for example, when an email, document, spreadsheet or a publication in social networks is written (Mayer-Schönberger, V., & Cukier, K., 2013).

According to Chen, *et* al (2013), databases are sets of information in which different categories of a topic that people are interested in analyzing are managed; for example, the search for a concept on the Internet in which gender, author or publication are specified. So Big Data facilitates the management, analysis and processing of large amounts of data, and specific and very detailed information, which can be processed in various formats at an almost immediate speed, and is currently known as the seven V's: Volume, Velocity, Variety, Variability Veracity, Visualization and Value.

Also, Big Data analytics consists of collecting, storing, cleaning, organizing and preparing large amounts of data to analyze trends or relationships between them. Therefore, it is a complex task to try to manage them through a system of traditional databases, which by the way, are getting slower and slower. Hence the need to use different technologies and techniques to process lots of Big Data information in order to structure them in a way that makes sense and allows decisions to be made efficiently, regardless of the institutional corporate name (McAfee, A., Brynjolfsson, E., Davenport, T., Patil, D. & Barton, D., 2012).

BIG DATA IN HIGHER EDUCATION

The implementation of Big Data in higher education has many advantages; among them, an educational design tailored to the students is tangible. All the information that is collected from the analysis of courses taken by the students, the time they dedicate to them, the music they listen to, etc., is processed in an intelligent system that allows the design of customized classes, with a more personalized attention.

Through the Big Data Analysis, it is possible to have an innovation of the curricular design in real time, since the specialized packages in big data analysis offer the generation of immediate solutions, being able to identify the need to create new university careers, postgraduate courses and / or courses of continuous training.

In addition, the teacher is evaluated on different areas, including the teaching methodology, as well as the learning styles of the students. That is, what works and what does not is known, and improvements according to what students demand can be made. So a virtuous circle in the generation of digital content according to the learning experiences of each of them is entered.

However, an intelligent system such as Big Data cannot replace rational and human intelligence. This is where talent and creativity depend on educational figures for strategies and continuous improvement of teaching-learning processes. Big Data is the tool and the teacher the essence in the construction of knowledge.

Then, what implications does Big Data have? In virtual teaching, Big Data contributes to achieve a more personalized and focused teaching to improve the teaching-learning process as well as the different methods used.

In virtual education, the use of the internet, the cloud, live streaming, social networks and other technological tools present new ways of delivering, and at the same time increasing access to learning. With these interactions, a large amount of data is produced, which interpretation and analysis will allow the creation of personalized learning experiences.

These great data are produced or created by students while taking an online course or a training module. With Big Data, how to deliver content, improve student experiences and create an environment that develops their skills can even be innovated.

The big data applied in virtual teaching can contribute to:

- Adapt and improve delivery through personalization of the students' learning experience
- Standardize the presentation of content.
- Understand how students assimilate information and what learning needs attract them the most.
- Identify areas that need changes or modifications, such as time and content, among others.
- Identify the difficulties that students have during the course to provide opportunities to improve the results.
- Decrease dropout rates.
- Provide greater flexibility to the education system, adapting it to the learning needs of students in the 21st century.
- Data is received immediately, so changes can be quickly implemented to adjust the virtual teaching strategy.

Online education will continue to change in the coming years, and there is no doubt that many of the changes will be due to Big Data. Additionally, virtual education in higher education has become popular and its users are increasing day by day due to the fact that the flexibility that an online program offers represents an important attraction for students (Johnson, J., 2014).

STRATEGIES TO IMPROVE VIRTUAL TEACHING IN HIGHER EDUCATION

Higher Education, in its pretension to train citizens whose professional and academic preparation will serve them for life, assumes a challenge in its curricular dimensions: to offer students the digital competences that involve them as active agents for society and for the era to which they belong. In this investigation, to identify the digital competences of the students of the Master of Education, we will take the definition of Martín (2008, 155), for whom the digital competence is the ability of people to use properly the digital tools to identify, access, manage, integrate, evaluate, analyze and synthesize digital resources, build new knowledge expressed through multimedia resources, and communicate with others in any specific context of the lifetime.

Nowadays, to have digital capabilities, as well as to access information, has been constituted as a factor of wealth and well-being for the world; both of them are the main resources that support the complete inclusion of all sectors of the population, and specially in this case, the students, since their active incorporation to the benefits and advantages that offer the training, the information and communication, makes it possible for them to manage the tools necessary to participate fully in the development of societies. In this sense, those who do not have digital skills and abilities, take the risk of facing digital exclusion, which for the Low Incomes Tax Reform Group (2012) means the absence of a better use of technology, directly or indirectly, to improve the life and opportunities of all the citizens and the places where they live.

Additionally, when thinking about how to improve virtual teaching in higher education, many efforts and ideas are concentrated on content and design. Some studies indicate that although these aspects are very important, we must first pay attention to the students and how they feel when they start a virtual course. It is very easy to enroll in an online course but it is also very easy to leave it. If we want our students to be involved and motivated, we must pay attention to their experience when receiving the course (Picciano, A., 2012).

Familiarize Students with Online Teaching

One of the factors which determine that a student remains in an online course is that they feel comfortable with the system (the technology) that they will use. Several investigations have proven that a determining aspect for students to stay in the course and participate is their previous experience with technology. It is important that students receive an induction to the course.

Also, it must be short and very clear. It includes in detail how the system works, how to navigate through the course and do not forget to make it clear that they will have all the necessary support at any time. They should know that technology is the auxiliary to reach their goals but it is not the main thing, and that the technology to be used will be quite intuitive.

Likewise, include multiple examples and make sure everyone participates. Your presence must be very strong in order to reassure anxious students who have never studied online. Many courses or virtual courses offer a prior induction to start the course and many are still very shy and intimidated by the system to participate or pay attention to it.

Do not Allow Someone to Stay Without Participating

First, the communication is very important, many educators start the course thinking about the content and how to meet the objectives. But it is equally important to think about the students and the best way to communicate with them and feel their presence. It is not what you say and what you do, but it is how you say it. It is very important to maintain cordial communication at all times.

Secondly, online students tend to feel more isolated, and as they do not know the teacher personally, they may feel insecure about approaching and communicating. Offer your help through chat, sky, telephone, mail or any means they prefer in the schedule that you establish. Remember that written communication must be very clear and careful not to lend itself to misunderstandings. Sometimes, you should suggest your student that oral communication is the best way to clarify any doubt.

Also, every communication with your students improves or worsens the experience. Take every opportunity to strengthen the relationship. Be understanding and always try to offer solutions and support.

For example, studies show that virtual education in higher education is an option that many adults over 35 are taking, you must take into account that young people have grown up with the technology you use for your course and do not know another reality. However, adults over 35 have not had the same experience. For many of them, it is the first experience using this methodology, so you must be patient, understanding and offer the necessary support so that they feel comfortable and persevere.

Institutional Support

Students feel very anxious when working with technology. The system sometimes fails, the document did not go, the program does not work, the exam that was with a time limit was not recorded, etc. The technical and administrative problems can generate a lot of stress in the students and move them away from virtual teaching. Reflect and review that your institution has an efficient and quality customer support team.

Be flexible with your rules. Some are not negotiable, but most usually are. Think about how to support the student so that their experience is pleasant and helps them achieve their objectives.

Interactivity

When there is lack of interactivity or lack of commitment on the part of the student, incorporate videoconferences, chats and forums, social networks, augmented reality and virtual reality, and make it a priority to provide frequent and immediate feedback to your students.

Projects

Studies show that when students fail to understand the usefulness of online education, they are more likely to drop out or not get involved. It includes individual and group projects from which the result can be applied immediately to your personal or work experience; in this way, you will feel satisfied with your work and the time invested.

The ease of use of the system, the attractive and intuitive interface, and the quality of the content are of vital importance for a successful virtual course, but these aspects are usually the first ones to which attention is paid (Picciano, A., 2012).

EDUCATIONAL METHODS DERIVED FROM BIG DATA

Among the main educational methods derived from Big Data Analytics (which origins go back to the year 2003), and its integration with the new smart devices and web technology that are now being applied in the educational field, are:

- Adaptive learning
- Competency-based education
- Inverted classroom and combined learning (flipped classroom and blended learning)
- Gamification
- Mobile learning

These methods, which allow education to reach a larger student population and to satisfy the continuous demands of the students (each time they demand a more flexible and personalized training), are providing very promising results and have been changing the way in which students relate to each other and to their teachers and educational institutions. Below is a brief explanation of each one of them (Tulasi, B., 2013).

ADAPTIVE LEARNING

Adaptive learning is an educational method based on the modification of content and ways of teaching according to the particular needs of each student. For this, the lake of knowledge data, which will facilitate the analytical to create the tailored study plan, will be conformed by collecting information about the habits of learning, knowledge, weaknesses and strengths of each student. This method emphasizes areas in which students have more difficulties, in order to adapt them to their way and pace of learning and create a personalized, differentiated and adapted teaching path for each student.

Nowadays, there are different innovative technological platforms seeking to adapt the pace of study of certain subjects to the particular needs of each student. These platforms provide a unique learning which is totally coupled to the needs of students. An example is Knewton, which technology is able to identify the strengths and weaknesses of each student and, depending on these, offer the more appropriate materials.

COMPETENCY-BASED EDUCATION (CBE)

Competency-based education emerges as a formative conception for work. Its purpose is related to productivity, this in the sense of helping the graduates of the training programs to be quickly incorporated in a profitable work activity.

This educational method consists of adapting the learning process to the rhythm and the needs of each student. In this way, the students will only advance a certain subject when they master it with skill, regardless of the time they need to get it. In this sense, the students will be solely responsible to set their learning pace, which will significantly reduce their stress levels and will elevate their motivation towards study.

Although this procedure is not a new stream, the current education platforms based on competences, derived from the power of big data analytics under the learning metric. In fact, these enhance the independence of students and, at the same time, allow teachers to evaluate progress.

INVERTED CLASSROOM AND COMBINED LEARNING (FLIPPED CLASSROOM AND BLENDED LEARNING)

In recent years, advances in the development of web pages and the ease to perform digital audio and video content contributed to the growth of teaching methodologies based on the inverted classroom model and combined learning.

The inverted classroom (flipped classroom) is based on home study and class practice. In this sense, new information technologies allow the teachers to impart their content online by booking a class time for further training practice.

Combined learning or blended learning is also based on the combination of on-line and face-to-face training, but in a different way: some contents are taught in face-to face classes, while others are developed exclusively on the Internet.

A typical platform that uses these educational methods is Moodle. This is used in the main universities of the world and allows students to acquire distance knowledge, which they will then share with the teacher and their classmates through a virtual classroom. It should be noted that the knowledge bases that generate this type of platform serve to complement the data lakes of an educational institution and, therefore, facilitate the analytical of learning.

GAMIFICATION

You can define gamification as the use of game mechanics in environments of learning in order to enhance the motivation, concentration and effort of the students. It also constitutes a powerful strategy to influence and encourage groups of students. Its intention is to stimulate the teaching-learning process among members of a student community.

A correct implementation of the gamification allows the obtaining of a commitment, achieving that the students of a school participate in a dynamic and proactive way in actions that generally require an effort of will. The integration of game dynamics in learning environments is not new. In fact, the exponential growth of the use of video games aroused the interest of educational experts to decipher the keys that make these a medium so effective to teach.

An example of a platform implemented with this learning method is ClassDojo. This tool helps teachers improve learning in the classroom efficiently and in a fun way. In particular, it enriches specific behaviors and drives the active participation of students through the issuance of prizes in real time. Finally, this platform delivers follow-up reports to inform the progress of the students to both parents and teachers.

MOBILE LEARNING (MOBILE LEARNING)

Mobile devices have transformed everyday life and education has not been an exception. Nowadays, many universities, such as UNAM, are already beginning to use this technology to offer a friendlier and more effective education to their students.

Currently, these devices promote learning through educational content, such as electronic textbooks or interactive courses that help in the improvement of school performance. Also, they allow the application of evaluation or placement exams that streamline and simplify the evaluation process of students.

Among the main advantages that students have when using this learning method are:

- Have information in real time that allows students to download and review their files, as well as to share and contribute from anywhere they are.
- Attend their academic obligations.
- Feedback their learning between peers or with groups of students with similar interests.
- Interact with their teachers or other students simultaneously or not.
- Participate in distance courses.

Finally, these devices constitute one of the most important pillars to collect information from students and the educational processes they attend, thus increasing the possibilities of performing analytics with big data technology and identifying new areas of opportunity to improve education.

WHAT IS THE ANALYTIC OF LEARNING?

It involves the measurement, collection, analysis and presentation of data about students, their contexts and the interactions that are generated there, in order to understand the learning process that is being developed and optimize the environments in which it is produced.

In this case, the data lake for the analysis is made up of students' actions, for example, their academic activity (specifically through the realization and sending of exams or tasks by electronic means). Nevertheless, other activities that are not part of the student's work and which can encompass the websites they visit, their location, the works they consult, their online social activity, etc., are also retaken.

Once the data are extracted, they are analyzed, related and evaluated with the objective of being able to focus the teaching on the specific abilities of each student. The concept of learning analytics will look for a subsequent action to the results obtained, for example, to develop a new curriculum, to look for techniques to personalize and adapt education, as well as to predict and intervene about the abilities of the student with the aim of improving them.

The immediacy and effectiveness of learning analytics will serve to make the students know what their own difficulties are, so that their teachers understand more in depth the personal and group difficulties to teach. Nowadays, learning analytics is used to:

- Detect the weaknesses and strengths of education systems.
- Develop new curricula and educational methods.
- Improve the courses taught by educational institutions.
- Reflect on the achievements and behavior patterns of each student with respect to his peers or to the educational curriculum used.
- Predict in which specific areas students will need personalized support and attention.
- Help teachers and support staff in their interventions.
- Help teaching institutions in management and decision making.
- Adapt the evaluation processes and show the increasingly concrete and specific needs of the students.
- Design a training curricula more adjusted to the realities of the educational institutions.

NEW CAREERS AND CAREER OPTIONS DERIVED FROM BIG DATA ANALYTICS

Big data is also fostering the emergence of new careers and professional options, as those discussed below.

- Data scientist or big data consultant. This career is related to the fact that there is a growing need to have qualified professionals for the analysis and management of information. Basically, it is a trained person with a broad knowledge in mathematics and statistics, who dominates different languages of programming, computer science and analytics. The data scientist analyzes, interprets and communicates the new trends found in his research area and translates them to his company or institution so that it makes use of them and in this way, it can adapt its products or services and create new business or innovation opportunities that it finds advantageous.

- Expert in analytics of learning. This profession is related to the last advances in the field of education, such as the development of new environments, personalized learning and MOOC (Massive Online Open Courses). The functions of these professionals can be: counselor specialized in improving school performance, administrator of online platforms, specialist in student care, educational researcher or adviser, and counselor of managers and professors, etc. (West, D., 2012).
- Digital teachers. The majority of new jobs that will generate the digital economy in the coming years will be linked to education, especially digital teachers. Graduate training will also be in line with the demand of the labor market. Nowadays, there is a need for professionals who are capable of transferring educational content to the web. This type of professionals must have more extensive technology training and dominate other disciplines such as psychology, since they require managing the needs of students, who will become online users.
- Administrator of servers and storage systems. This professional will be responsible for managing all the information available in the information systems. Those who dedicate themselves to this should ensure that all the available information on the servers and mass storage systems is properly updated, protected, supported and available for online access. Also, they will be responsible for online security.
- Cyber-lawyer. He is the expert in computer crimes such as scams through the web, crimes in social networks, cyber-bullying, data protection and copyright, pornography, espionage, identity theft, phishing, etcetera.
- Internet of Things Developer. The Internet of Things (IoT) requires a new series of professionals capable of creating software that connects sensors with mobile devices and computer systems, or that links them directly with the data centers. Do not forget that a lot of information, which requires the big data, currently comes from different types of mobile devices and sensors housed in the facilities of companies and institutions (West, D., 2012).

TECHNICAL ASPECTS FOR THE ADOPTION AND USE OF BIG DATA TECHNOLOGY

One of the main limitations for the adoption of Big Data Technology in any institution is the economic resources, infrastructure and experienced human capital that are required for its instrumentation. However, today, there begin to appear relatively inexpensive alternatives to perform analytics with big data, among them BigQuery and some specialized tools that are designed to facilitate different aspects of this technology stand out.

BigQuery is a powerful big data analysis platform that can be used by all types of companies or organizations through an accessible rate. In this one, it is possible to store and analyze terabytes of data in seconds, taking advantage of the Google technology infrastructure.

The platform of BigQuery is relatively simple to use and allows developers and analysts to study the databases almost in real time. For this, it provides SQL consulting on information terabyte data sets, which yield results in a few seconds. These results can be stored in tables or exported for analysis or later visualization.

Technically, BigQuery can be used in three modes: from a browser web, through some command-line tool, or through making calls to its API13 REST14 using a wide variety of libraries such as Java, .NET or Python. It also supports a variety of third-party tools, both for visualization and for data loading.

Big data SQL implemented with the Google BigQuery platform takes advantage of the SQLstream Connector (technology for the extraction and processing of data from a geographical area in real time).

Amazon Inc., meanwhile, also offers a comprehensive set of computer services in the cloud called AWS (Amazone Web Services), which allows analytics with big data. This paid service offers technological solutions for each phase of the life cycle of a big data project (collection, transmission, storage, use of relational or NoSQL database manager, analysis and archiving).

WHAT ABOUT DATABASE MANAGEMENT SYSTEMS (DBMS) USED FOR BIG DATA?

Here are used basically two technologies, the SQL and the NoSQL. The first one contemplates all those high-level database managers which include a language of structured query or structured query language (SQL). These employ bases of relational data and are characterized because they support the handling of algebra and relational calculation that allows queries in order to retrieve information from the database, as well as making changes in it. This technology is widely used to treat structured information.

In contrast, NoSQL systems differ from relational databases in several important aspects, the most prominent is that they do not use SQL as the main language for consultations. Also, the data they store does not use fixed structures as tables, they also do not support operations to combine records of two or more tables in a relational database, or completely guarantee the atomicity, consistency, insulation and durability of the information. NoSQL systems are called sometimes "not just SQL" to highlight the fact that they can also support query type extended SQL languages.

Given this, why are both technologies used? The answer is simple: they complement each other. Modern relational databases have shown little efficiency in certain applications, for example, for the indexing of a large number of documents.

For this reason, they are more used in applications in which it is required to manage transactional data models. On the other hand, NoSQL technology allows the management of databases oriented to documents. Among the most popular applications of this technology are the handlers of MongoDB, MemcacheDB, CouchDB, Apache Cassandra and HBase, etc.

THE LEGAL AND ETHICAL ASPECTS OF THE USE OF BIG DATA IN EDUCATION

While it is true that the results obtained with big data technology can be surprising, their use also raises serious legal and ethical problems.

You have to remember that behind each number, of each piece of data, there is a person who should not be seen as a sum of patterns of behavior or habits of study, but as a human being who feels, who has rights and values his privacy.

You cannot, and you should not start collecting data about students and teachers or generate analytical reports about them without their consent. In this sense, legal advice is vital to the success of the project. Some of the aspects that should be considered are:

- The ownership of the data that is collected. This regularly comes from:
- The activity recorded by the students.
- The systems in which they interact.
- The student feedback mechanisms, such as their participation in surveys, suggestion portals and attention or advice of complementary services.
- The social networks.
- The data that needs to be shared among systems, organizations and actors involved.
- The principles of collection, conservation and exploitation of data by the educational institutions involved.
- The educational mission and the issues that remain hidden and cannot be easily seen in the learning management.
- The expectations of schools that decide to use the big data analytics.
- The motivation for the development of the analysis.

It is clear that the work of educational institutions in the field of big data should adhere to the legal framework to generate a safe and secure environment in which their communities feel comfortable. The data is the voice of the students and the educational institution they attend, and must be analyzed in order to extract knowledge with technology, but always in an ethical-legal framework that allows multiple reporting benefits.

Nowadays, there are certain legal mechanisms that allow protecting with existing laws many of the technological advances that have emerged, such as patents, trademarks, industrial designs, copyright, or contracts. However, there are many other situations in computer science which escape from the law or which the creators, developers or producers of them (including their own legislation) do not contemplate. The legislation has a long way to go to cover all the legal aspects that can be derived from big data analytics and, it should be aware that in practice, there are many other issues that are simply not going to be able to move quickly to reality. For this reason, each legislator should take advice from the computer specialists necessary to find real, valid and effective solutions to the situations presented by big data analytics (Zikopoulos, P., & Eaton, C., 2011).

DIGITAL TOOLS IN HIGHER EDUCATION

ICTs have immense potential to develop intelligence in students, but in most of the schools we are holding back their effectiveness in such a way that, not only are they not helping, but they are inhibiting them. Can you really talk about progress if you go over the traditional chalk board, to the white synthetic surface and then to the interactive digital board, when the only thing that is changing is the writing surface? Not possibly. Writing in a Text Processor is different from writing by hand, or is it simply easier? ICTs are a tool, not a solution (Thompson, 2010).

The changes are the meaning of life. We are in a historical period in which once again, the habits, customs and modes of production of people constantly change. An academic director of the Icesi University shares his experience from institutions and companies, in which he points out a clear tendency, summarizing the outstanding professional, not as the one who can retain the most amount of information, but the one who can handle large volumes of information in order to solve a problem. These new challenges proposed by the century of information, require tools and inputs that, along with the technological changes, facilitate the processes of knowledge construction.

The computer is a tool, not a tutor. With this phrase, Professor David Jonassen, from the University of Missouri, initiated a theory to which he called Mindtools (tools of the mind), in which he states that during the moment in which appropriate technology is used as an input for the construction of knowledge, higher order intellectual abilities are fostered, mainly in the analysis and creation of the information. Thus, it is not enough to switch to tactile platforms or equipped classrooms with the latest technological inputs, or to worry about being always at the forefront and counting with the most advanced programs, if they do not adapt; so that these new technologies are able to fulfill their function as instruments to solve problems, and not to become the solution.

Visual and spatial learning: There are several similar and related investigations to the problems raised in this project. Inspiration Software is the developer company of the Inspiration program, which allows the users to organize their ideas and concepts in conceptual maps in different ways. Through visual learning and on screens, they carried out an investigation in which they concluded that the process of developing and using graphic organizers has proven to increase the critical thinking or higher order intellectual abilities in students.

From a perspective of visual organizers, in the tools that help schematize the ideas in a visual plane with two or three dimensions, there are characteristics of the development of intellectual capacities of a higher order linked with skills in visual learning. You can find tools that point to the same direction in favor of the analysis or creation of information through visual learning systems. The sites and tools consulted manage to meet one of the many needs of the development of critical thinking, and some remain in digital representations of what conventional books offer, justifying interactivity in menus, buttons and navigation bars.

An example of this is:

- Conflict History (2012), which represents through a map and a line of time, the most important wars in the history of the world. It uses resources from visual learning, but does not invite the user to synthesize the information or contribute to the same.
- Resources such as Timetoast (2011) or X-timeline (Famento, 2009) invite the users to build their own timelines, with various themes and to take care of grouping them according to the suggested labels. These resources take into consideration what is handled (the theme to investigate) and when (the date), as well as being based within a visual space with the timeline. These tools do not allow a deepening of research topics, as the content is created by the users, and even though it can be shared, it cannot be complemented by someone else, who will have to make a new timeline - of the same theme - to complete the information.
- Edmodo (2012) allows users to create idea diagrams, to associate them and to visualize conceptual trees between users and share them, but it does not go beyond facilitating the visualization of ideas.

- Click2Map (2008) allows users to create custom maps on the Internet, and it is the only tool, different from Google Maps (but that uses its API), so that users can, through their created account, manage, create and easily publish their own maps, adding custom markers. This tool resembles to OTTO Line in the development of easy-to-create user accounts and maps.
- Tools for education (INTEL, 2009). This hardware developer company has created a series of technological inputs for teachers to enrich the experience in the classroom through the visual learning and the collaborative construction of knowledge. Its catalog of three tools covers areas of knowledge which range from language to mathematics, the humanities and the exact sciences. Its real strength is the ability to share content between students; it provides spatial learning tools, but only allows the analysis of a type of input in each tool; there is no clear evidence of integration of inputs from different types of learning.
- Timemap. Developed by Nick Rabinowitz (2011), it has the integration of maps and the timeline, which links the Google Maps tool and the system of lines of the Open Time SMILE Project of MIT (2011) in a single tool, created to facilitate the analysis of information through visual systems. Currently, it is the base technique in which OTTO Line works.
- GeoDia (LAITS / the University of Texas at Austin, 2011). It was developed under the principle of being a didactic, easy and intuitive tool which shows the facts and characteristics of the ancient civilizations of the Mediterranean. It has a map, the timeline and a window in which multimedia information that complements the facts listed is displayed.

CONCLUSION

Greater impetus should be given to the introduction of big data analytics and digital tools in higher education institutions. It is necessary to train human capital to perform big data analytics. Nowadays, there are greater technological facilities to adopt and use big data technology in higher education institutions. Digital collections, which are the product of years of academic activity, teaching and research, and which are generated on a regular basis by the educational institutions, must be incorporated into the lake of data for its use in the big data analytics processes. The use of big data technology poses serious legal and ethical problems that must be taken into account for their introduction in educational institutions.

CONTRIBUTION

Derived from the different conceptions and bibliography which describe the technological tools and big data that focus on the educational sphere, it is observed that the different models have a lot of applicability in different institutions, and can really be adapted to the sphere of higher education. For their development, it is necessary to promote and participate in research community circles, typical of the different sciences of knowledge that compromise big data as an axis of academic development which becomes a form of valuation of tangible assets, which focus on the generation of new knowledge in the higher education institutions of the new century.

REFERENCES

Boyd, D., & Crawford, K. (2012). Critical questions for big data: Provocations for a cultural, technological, and scholarly phenomenon. *Information Communication and Society*, *15*(5), 662–679. doi:10.108 0/1369118X.2012.678878

Carrasco M., Sánchez C. & Carro A. (2015). Digital skills in postgraduate students in education. *Lasallistan Research Magazine*, *12*(2).

Chen, H., Chiang, R. H., & Storey, V. C. (2012). Business intelligence and analytics: From big data to big impact. *Management Information Systems Quarterly*, *36*(4), 1165. doi:10.2307/41703503

Chen, J., Chen, Y., Du, X., Li, C., Lu, J., Zhao, S., & Zhou, X. (2013). Big data challenge: A data management perspective. *Frontiers of Computer Science*, *7*(2), 157–164. doi:10.100711704-013-3903-7

Gibson, D. C., & Ifenthaler, D. (2017). Preparing the next generation of education researchers for big data in higher education. In *Big data and learning analytics in higher education* (pp. 29–42). Cham: Springer. doi:10.1007/978-3-319-06520-5_4

Johnson, J. A. (2014). The ethics of big data in higher education. *International Review of Information Ethics*, *21*(21), 3–10.

Lohr, S. (2012). The age of big data. *New York Times, 11*(2012).

Mayer-Schönberger, V., & Cukier, K. (2013). *Big data: A revolution that will transform how we live, work, and think*. Houghton Mifflin Harcourt.

McAfee, A., Brynjolfsson, E., Davenport, T. H., Patil, D. J., & Barton, D. (2012). Big data: The management revolution. *Harvard Business Review*, *90*(10), 60–68. PMID:23074865

Picciano, A. G. (2012). The evolution of big data and learning analytics in American higher education. *Journal of Asynchronous Learning Networks*, *16*(3), 9–20.

Tulasi, B. (2013). Significance of Big Data and analytics in higher education. *International Journal of Computers and Applications*, *68*(14).

West, D. M. (2012). Big data for education: Data mining, data analytics, and web dashboards. *Governance studies at Brookings, 4*(1).

Zikopoulos, P., & Eaton, C. (2011). *Understanding big data: Analytics for enterprise class hadoop and streaming data*. McGraw-Hill Osborne Media.

KEY TERMS AND DEFINITIONS

Big Data: Is a recurring term when talking about technology and digitalization, its involvement in many areas of life begins to be relevant. Big Data refers to the management and analysis of huge volumes of data, which due to the magnitude of the information, exceed the capacity of data processing and should be treated in a special way.

Digital Tools: Software and platforms for teaching and learning that can be used with computers or mobile devices to work with text, images, audio, and video. Tools for language learning and teaching may include programs for editing digital materials (e.g., audio, video), and platforms for collaborating and sharing resources.

Postgraduate Programs: Encompass knowledge and a range of qualifications that require an undergraduate degree to be considered for entry, these include courses at a Postgraduate Diploma level all the way to a PhD. Postgraduate degrees are taken for a number of different reasons, such as to move into academia and research, to specialize a career path or to change track entirely.

This research was previously published in Management Training Programs in Higher Education for the Fourth Industrial Revolution; pages 1-21, copyright year 2020 by Information Science Reference (an imprint of IGI Global).

Chapter 38
From Business Intelligence to Big Data:
The Power of Analytics

Mouhib Alnoukari
Syrian Private University, Syria

ABSTRACT

Boundaries between business intelligence (BI), big data (BD), and big data analytics (BDA) are often unclear and ambiguous for companies. BD is a new research challenge; it is becoming a subject of growing importance. Notably, BD was one of the big buzzwords during the last decade. BDA can help executive managers to plan an organization's short-term and long-term goals. Furthermore, BI is considered as a kind of decision support system (DSS) that can help organizations achieving their goals, creating corporate value and improving organizational performance. This chapter provides a comprehensive view about the interrelationships between BI, BD, and BDA. Moreover, the chapter highlights the power of analytics that make them considered as one of the highly impact's organizational capability. Additionally, the chapter can help executive managers to decide the way to integrate BD initiatives as a tool, or as an industry, or as a corporate strategy transformation.

INTRODUCTION

We are in the middle of data explosion. According to Statistica (2020), the size of the digital universe in 2013 was estimated at about 50 zetabytes, it is expected to reach 175 zetabytes by 2025. The global market for software, hardware, and services for storing and analyzing big data is estimated to triple in size in the next five years (Statistica, 2020).

According to Forbes report, "The Global State of Enterprise Analytics, 2020", Cloud Computing, IoT, and Artificial Intelligence/Machine Learning will have the greatest impact on enterprises' analytics initiatives over the next five years. Across all enterprise executives globally, Big Data, 5G, and Security/ Privacy concerns are predicted to have the greatest impact (Columbus, 2019). Furthermore, advanced

DOI: 10.4018/978-1-6684-3662-2.ch038

and predictive analytics are dominating enterprises' analytics initiatives today, improved efficiency and productivity; achieving faster for more effective decision-making; and driving better financial performance are the top three benefits enterprises which are gaining from analytics (Columbus, 2019).

Going back to the 1990s, after the information warehousing quickly vanished, the BI era took over. This era introduced a way which is not only to reorganize data, but also to transform it into much cleaner and easier to follow. In this era, BI was pushed notably by the introduction of Data Warehousing (DW) and On-Line analytical Processing (OLAP) that provide a new category of data-driven DSS. OLAP tools provide users with the way to browse and summarize data in an efficient and dynamic way (Al-noukari, Alhawasli, Alnafea, & Zamreek, 2012). According to Ram, et al. (2016), BI is focusing mainly on structured and internal data. Therefore, many of valuable information embedded in the unstructured and external data remain hidden, which leads to an incomplete view and limited insights, thus biased decision-making.

Currently, the new technologies generate huge amount of data arriving from many sources including; computers, smartphones, tablets, sensors, social media, audios, videos, IoT, clickstreams, databases transactions, and so on (Walls & Barnard, 2020; Braganza, Brooks, Nepelski, Ali, & Moro, 2017; Fosso Wamba, Gunasekaran, Akter, Ren, Ji-fan, Dubey, & Childe, 2017). Wal-Mart generates about 2.5 petabytes per hour. Fiber optic cable, the most efficient media for data transfer, can transfer up to 100 gigabits per second. Wal-Mart, simply mean, produces more data than it could transfer to any another place (Brock & Khan, 2017).

Traditional tools are unable to store, manage and analyze such hug data. This situation leads to the creation of the new big data global phenomenon. In 1997, Michael Cox and David Ellsworth first used the word "Big Data" to explain data visualization and the challenges which would pose to computer systems (Wang, Kung and Byrd, 2018). BD moves away from traditional data management onto new methods focusing on data discovery, data integration and data exploitation within the context of "big" data. The word "big" does not only imply size, but rather the ability to produce insights, and manage complex types (Wang, Kung and Byrd, 2018). This leads to the adoption of famous BD three V's (Volume, Velocity, and Variety). The evolution of BD took place during the period from 2001 to 2008 when new tools and technologies were able to manage immense amount of data. 2009 was the year of the BD revolution where it was able to handle and manage unstructured data, in addition to the move from static environments into cloud-based environments (Wang, Kung and Byrd, 2018).

Another important challenge, BD technologies have to process BD in real-time (streaming processing). For example, the large hadrons collider (LHC) generates more raw data than the CERN computing grid can store; thus data has to be instantly analyzed, hence necessities the parallel and distributed computing (Brock & Khan, 2017).

Thus, in the light of this, the main goal of this study is to analyze recent literature of BD, and to find the relationship between BI, BD and BDA. Moreover, the study highlights the power of analytics that make them considered as one of the highly impact's organizational capability.

To achieve this goal, a conceptual literature review was adopted to find all the studies that relate BI with BD. Then, an analysis phase was required to find the interrelationship between both domains. Finally, the study helps managers to decide the way to adopt BD initiatives.

The remainder of this paper is organized as follows. The next section looks at the fundamentals of BI, BD, and BDA. Then a section discussing in details the relationships between BI, BD, and BDA. Thereafter, a section discusses big data analytics capability, and highlights the power of analysis in the current era. Then, the paper provides an overview about the current trends in BD initiatives adoption, with real examples and case studies. The final section ends this paper with some concluding remarks and future work.

BACKGROUND

Business Intelligence Overview

BI has received a widespread attention from scholars and professionals over the past three decades. BI has become an important technology to improve organizational performance (Alnoukari, Alhawasli, Alnafea, & Zamreek, 2012).

BI can be defined as a set of theories, methodologies, architectures, systems and technologies that support business decision making with valuable data, information and knowledge (Alnoukari, 2009; Sun, Zou, & Strang, 2015). Alnoukari et al. (2012) define BI as "The use of all organization's resources: data, applications, people and processes in order to increase its knowledge, implement and achieve its strategy, and adapt to the environment's dynamism". Jin & Kim (2018) consider BI as an information value chain gathering raw data that turned into useful information for better decision-making that in turn creates value and improves organizational performance.

BI main components include; tools for multidimensional data analysis (OLAP) and data mining, tools for data warehousing and DB management, tools for ETL, and tools for visualizations (Alnoukari, Alhawasli, Alnafea, & Zamreek, 2012; Sun, Zou, & Strang, 2015).

Arguably, BI can be seen as a DSS that includes the overall process of gathering huge data, extracting useful information, and providing analytical capabilities (Jin, & Kim, 2018). Other studies have been seen BI as an Information System to support decision-making (Sun, Zou, & Strang, 2015; Alnoukari, 2009), it consists of the following main steps; analysis, insight, action, and performance measurement (Sun, Zou, & Strang, 2015). Jin & Kim (2018) argue that the concept of BI has been growing according to the applications and technologies that support firm's to gather, store, analyze, and access data more effectively.

Self-service oriented BI architecture in an emergent BI approach that can empower casual users to perform custom analytics and to drive actionable information without having to involve BI specialist (Passlick, Lebek, & Breitner, 2017). Data lake implementation can be considered as a source for self-service BI (Llave, 2018).

Big Data Definition: From 3 V's To 7 V's

Literature refers to the three V's when trying to define BD. Many academics use this definition in the literature to date (e.g. Braganza, Brooks, Nepelski, Ali, & Moro, 2017). The three V's are volume, variety, and velocity. The main source of this exponentially increased data coming from the unstructured data of social networks, blogs, text messages, videos and audios (Braganza, Brooks, Nepelski, Ali, & Moro, 2017). Variety refers to the different types of data that can be manipulated using BD technologies (Faroukhi, El Alaoui, Gahi, & Amine, 2020). Structured, semi-structured, and unstructured data types are currently under BD process (Faroukhi, El Alaoui, Gahi, & Amine, 2020). Unstructured data is the challenge key that allows BD to overcome the main deficiencies of the traditional methods. Velocity refers to the speed at which data is generated and delivered (Faroukhi, El Alaoui, Gahi, & Amine, 2020).

Insights are close to the real time decision-making (Walls & Barnard, 2020). According to the three V's dimensions, BD was defined as; large volumes of extensively varied data that are generated, captured, and processed at high velocity (Walls & Barnard, 2020).

An additional two V's were embedded later to the set of BD definition. These are Value and Veracity. Value refers to the insights and benefits that can be gained from BD (Chen, Mao, & Liu, 2014; Erevelles, Fukawa, & Swayne, 2016; Faroukhi, El Alaoui, Gahi, & Amine, 2020). Veracity concerns to the anomalies and uncertainties in data, due to inconsistencies and incompleteness (Faroukhi, El Alaoui, Gahi, & Amine, 2020). The process of precluding bad data is therefore important to extract reliable insights (Faroukhi, El Alaoui, Gahi, & Amine, 2020). Based on the five V's definitions, Fosso Wamba et al. (2015) define BD as "a holistic approach to manage, process and analyze 5 V's (i.e., volume, variety, velocity, veracity and value) in order to create actionable insights for sustained value delivery, measuring performance and establishing competitive advantages.".

The five V's are lately extended to include Valence and Variability and became seven V's definition in order to provide the whole encompassing view of BD (Erevelles, Fukawa, & Swayne, 2016; Braganza, Brooks, Nepelski, Ali, & Moro, 2017). Valence refers to the connectedness of data collected, and Variability refers to constant and rapid changing of the data meaning (Braganza, Brooks, Nepelski, Ali, & Moro, 2017). With these all seven V's, BD is becoming a source of innovation and competitive advantage (Erevelles, Fukawa, & Swayne, 2016). Based on the seven V's definitions, we can update Fosso Wamba et al. (2015) BD definition as "a holistic approach to manage, process and analyze the 7 V's (i.e., volume, variety, velocity, veracity, value, valence, and variability) in order to create actionable insights for sustained value delivery, measuring performance, establishing competitive advantages, and becoming a source of innovation" (Figure 1).

Figure 1. Dimensions of Big Data

Big Data Analytics Fundamentals

BDA is considered as a disruptive technology that will reshape BI (Fan, Lau, & Zhao, 2015). Sun et al. (2015) considered BDA as an emerging science and technology involving the multidisciplinary state-of-art information and communication technology, statistics, operations research, machine learning, and decision sciences for BD (Sun, Zou, & Strang, 2015). Hence, it encompasses a wide range of mathematical, statistical and modeling techniques. From strategic perspectives, BDA differs from traditional data analytics in the way that it offers the possibilities to discover new opportunities, to offer the customer a high-value and innovative products and services (Davenport, 2014).

According to Sun et al. (2015), BDA can be defined as the process of collecting, organizing and analyzing BD to discover patterns, knowledge, and intelligence as well as other information within the BD. Fan et al. (2015) define BDA as the domain that uses data analytics to gain business insights that will lead firms to improve decision-making. Jin & Kim (2018) define BDA as the overall process of applying advanced analytics to identify patterns, trends, correlations, and other useful techniques. Al-Qirim et al. (2019) argue that BDA is the process of uncovering actionable knowledge patterns from BD. Polese et al. (2019) argue that BDA can enhance the comprehension of business opportunity, and gain better insight into customer behavior, and services/products effectiveness. Insights provided by BDA can improve the efficiency of the organizations' whole operations, as well as the strategy (Walls & Barnard, 2020; Holmlund, Van Vaerenbergh, Ciuchita, Ravald, Sarantopoulos, Villarroel-Ordenes, & Zaki, 2020). Moreover, Sadovskyi et al. (2014) argue that BDA adds additional characteristics to the conventional data analysis including; innovated technologies and skills that enable organizations to own deep analytical capabilities, and integration of wide range of data types from a large number of relatively unreliable data source in order to provide a meaningful and reliable source of business information. Aligned with this viewpoint, Fosso Wamba et al. (2017) and Holmlund et al. (2020) consider BDA as an innovative approach to deliver sustained value, and enable competitive advantage (Mikalef, Pappas, Giannakos, Krogstie, Lekakos, 2016). BDA allows firms to manage and analyze strategy through data lens (Fosso Wamba, Gunasekaran, Akter, Ren, Ji-fan, Dubey, & Childe, 2017; Shams, & Solima, 2019).

BDA has four different levels of analysis (Figure 2): descriptive, inquisitive (or diagnostic), predictive, and prescriptive (Holmlund, Van Vaerenbergh, Ciuchita, Ravald, Sarantopoulos, Villarroel-Ordenes, & Zaki, 2020; Sun, Zou, & Strang, 2015). After generating BDA, organizations are able to generate different insights including market, behavioral and attitudinal insights. Descriptive BDA is related to "What happened?" question answers. This kind of analytics helps describing the situation further analysis (Holmlund, Van Vaerenbergh, Ciuchita, Ravald, Sarantopoulos, Villarroel-Ordenes, & Zaki, 2020). Typical examples include descriptive statistics using charts, cross tabulation, or clustering graphs. Inquisitive DBA is related to "Why did things happen?" question answers (Holmlund, Van Vaerenbergh, Ciuchita, Ravald, Sarantopoulos, Villarroel-Ordenes, & Zaki, 2020). This kind of analytics helps validating research hypotheses, determining causation, and identifying variables to achieve desired results. Typical examples include statistical inference techniques or factor analysis (Holmlund, Van Vaerenbergh, Ciuchita, Ravald, Sarantopoulos, Villarroel-Ordenes, & Zaki, 2020). Predictive BDA is related to "What could happen?" question answers. This kind of analytics helps predicting future trends. Typical examples include forecasting models, classification models, or neural networks (Holmlund, Van Vaerenbergh, Ciuchita, Ravald, Sarantopoulos, Villarroel-Ordenes, & Zaki, 2020. Prescriptive BDA is related to "What should happen?" question answers. This kind of analytics helps providing quantifiable answers when solving a problem (Holmlund, Van Vaerenbergh, Ciuchita, Ravald, Sarantopoulos, Villarroel-Ordenes,

& Zaki, 2020). Typical examples include optimizations modeling, queuing modeling, or simulations. Building upon this tautology; BDA has been used successfully in many areas (Holmlund, Van Vaerenbergh, Ciuchita, Ravald, Sarantopoulos, Villarroel-Ordenes, & Zaki, 2020; Palem, 2014). Saidali et al. (2019) propose combining BDA and classical marketing analytics in order to gain valuable and real time insights, thus improve the marketing decision-making process. Different analytics have achieved great success including; usage based insurance, predictive maintenance, Epidemic outbreak detection, and sentiment analysis (Palem, 2014). Ram, et al. (2016) listed five main advantages when applying BDA; increasing data visibility, improving organizational performance, improving meeting customer's needs, revealing valuable insights, and revealing new business models, products and services. In their recent research, Faroukhi et al. (2020) propose a set of BDA tools that provide the ability to deal with various data status. DBA tools are categorized into three families; storage, processing, and visualization.

There is a strong relationship between BDA and strategic management (Şen, Körük, Serper, & Çalış Uslu, 2019; Mikalef, Pappas, Giannakos, Krogstie, Lekakos, 2016). BDA in the lens of strategic management are the capabilities required to gain organizational performance (Walls & Barnard, 2020). BDA provide the ability to show behavioral insights about customers (Suoniemi, Meyer-Waarden, & Munzel, 2017); these insights could be turned into strategic advantages (Şen, Körük, Serper, & Çalış Uslu, 2019). BDA can also improve the metrics used in decisional processes (Fosso Wamba, Gunasekaran, Akter, Ren, Ji-fan, Dubey, & Childe, 2017). Target Corporation is an example of how BDA can be used to track customers purchasing behaviors and predict future trends (Şen, Körük, Serper, & Çalış Uslu, 2019). A personalized purchasing recommendation program is another example (Şen, Körük, Serper, & Çalış Uslu, 2019). Furthermore, Şen et al. (2019) argue that BDA can be used in simulation modeling to gain insight knowledge about the simulated system, and determine the model parameters used in the simulation process.

Figure 2. Big Data Analytics Levels

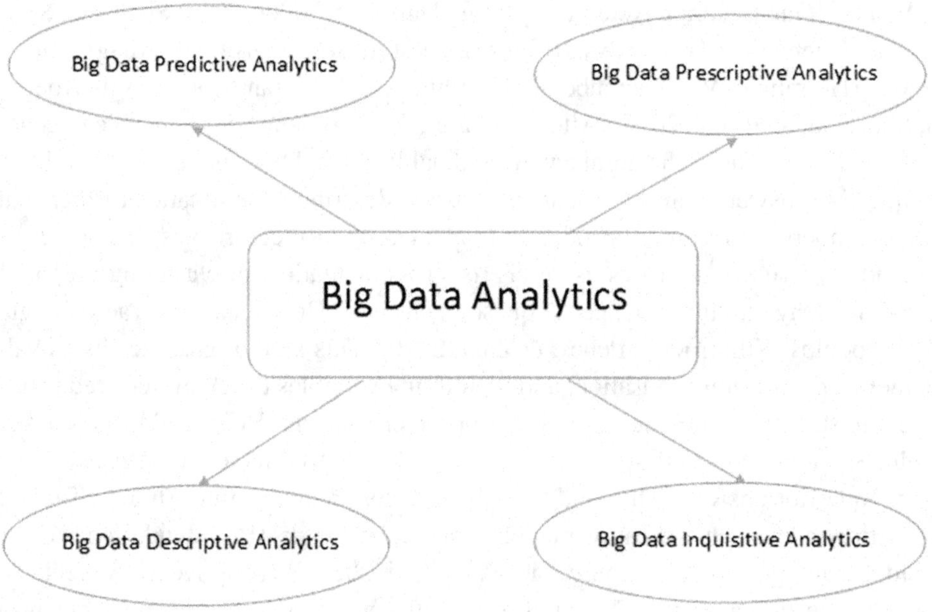

The Relationship between Business Intelligence, Big Data and Big Data analytics

Scholars argue that there is a close relationship between BI, BD & BDA because BI provides the methodological and technological capabilities for data analysis (e.g. Llave, 2018; Sun, Zou, & Strang, 2015). BI supports firm's decision making with valuable data, information, and knowledge (Alnoukari & Hanano, 2017), hence BDA can be seen as a part of BI (Sun, Zou, & Strang, 2015). In addition, both BI and BDA share some common tools supporting decision-making process. Furthermore, BI and BDA are common in emphasizing valuable data, information, and knowledge. Moreover, BI and BDA involve interactive visualization for data exploration and discovery. Even more, BI is currently based on four cutting-age technology pillars of cloud, mobile, big data, and social technologies; they are also supported effectively by BDA as a service and technology (Passlick, Lebek, & Breitner, 2017; Sun, Zou, & Strang, 2015). Sun et al. (2015) further argue that BDA is an essential tool for developing BI from at least technological and data viewpoints. From technological viewpoint, BDA is data-driven and business oriented techniques, hence; facilitates firm's decision-making and then improves BI. From data viewpoint, knowledge discovery is the core of BDA & BI systems (Sun, Zou, & Strang, 2015). Jin & Kim (2018) consider that BI's "raw data" have been expanded into "Big Data" due to the advanced technology capability. Hence, it is logical to consider that BI/BD/BDA are not independent concepts. Consequently, it is beneficial to integrate all of them into an integrated DSS incorporating all processes from data gathering to data analytics and insights to decision making (Jin, & Kim, 2018). Fan et al. (2015) argue that BDA supports marketing intelligence by providing the ability to monitor customer opinions toward a product, service, or company using social media mining techniques. Fan et al. (2015) further argue that customer opinion mining is a key factor for strategic marketing decision that can be based on multiple data sources including; social media, transactions, surveys, and sensors, can be applied to discover marketing intelligence (Fan, Lau, & Zhao, 2015). Analytical models based on single data source may provide limited insights that consequently lead to biased business decisions. Using multiple and heterogeneous data sources can provide a holistic view of the business and result in better decision-making (Fan, Lau, & Zhao, 2015). Fan et Al. (2015) conclude that big data and its applications on BI have great potential in generating business impacts. In the same vein, Kimble & Milolidakis (2015) argue that BI generated from BD could be in immense value. Sun et al. (2015) argue that due to the dramatic development of BD technologies, BI is currently facing new challenges and opportunities; that is how to use BDA to enhance BI becoming a big issue for organizational performance (Sun, Zou, & Strang, 2015).

However, other scholars highlight many of BI drawbacks when comparing with BD/BDA (e.g. Llave, 2018; Ram, Zhang, & Koronios, 2016; Marín-Ortega, Dmitriyevb, Abilovb, & Gómezb, 2014). During the 2000s, BI was becoming a strategic direction that was adopted by business and technology leaders. BI was based on technology-driven data analytics that extracts usable information (Faroukhi, El Alaoui, Gahi, & Amine, 2020; Marín-Ortega, Dmitriyevb, Abilovb, & Gómezb, 2014). These tools provide the decision-makers with the ability to use the analytical results delivered by the reports, dashboards, and data visualizations. However, BI focuses primarily on structured and internal enterprise data, overlooking valuable information embedded in unstructured and external data (Marín-Ortega, Dmitriyevb, Abilovb, & Gómezb, 2014). This could result in an incomplete view of the reality, and biased enterprise's decision-making (Llave, 2018; Ram, Zhang, & Koronios, 2016; Marín-Ortega, Dmitriyevb, Abilovb, & Gómezb, 2014). Scholars highlight some of BI implementation drawbacks (e.g. Marín-Ortega, Dmitriyevb, Abilovb, & Gómezb, 2014) such as the inability to focus on individual needs, lack of business context information that forces users to understand the semantics of data by themselves, poor alignment between business and IT, and high costs related to model time for new BI implementation. BI classical data analytics are unable to acquire valuable business insights (Saidali, Rahich, Tabaa, & Medouri, 2019). BD insights close the knowledge and time gaps of the traditional methods (Walls & Barnard, 2020). According to Marín-Ortega et al. (2014), data management is the most critical and stressing stage during BI development due to its time consuming. Most of the BI solution providers are focusing on the technological part of data management stage rather than the availability of all the required information (structured and unstructured) to build a good solution. In their recent research, Faroukhi et al. (2020) listed some of the differences between BI and BD/BDA such as; BI is based on File-Based or Object-Based storage models; whereas BD is based on Block-Based storage model. Additionally, BI is based on traditional database data model such as SQL databases and data warehouses. However, traditional databases cannot meet BD challenges, mainly storing and processing hug amount of unstructured data; hence, distributed storage and NoSQL databases are mainly adopted for BD data model (Faroukhi, El Alaoui, Gahi, & Amine, 2020). In the same vein, the hardware storage infrastructure for BI is mainly based on storage devices; whereas, BD requires additional storage infrastructure such as storage network infrastructure and storage virtualization. Furthermore, BD requires distributed processing infrastructure in order to be able to share data, calculations, and processing on over several interconnected nodes. However, traditional BI does not require such distributed processing infrastructure (Faroukhi, El Alaoui, Gahi, & Amine, 2020). Finally, and from analytical viewpoint, descriptive and predictive analyses were mainly developed by BI traditional systems; whereas, BD provides the ability to effectively develop and use additional analytics capabilities such as prescriptive and diagnostic analysis (Faroukhi, El Alaoui, Gahi, & Amine, 2020).

One of the suggested approaches is to fix the ETL (Extract, Transform, and Load) stage bottleneck (Marín-Ortega, Dmitriyevb, Abilovb, & Gómezb, 2014). In typical BI infrastructure, ETL stage starts extracting raw data from Operational Data Sources (ODS), then transforming the raw data into a normalized form, before loading the processed data into the data warehouse. Processing raw data during the transformation phase is critical. A DW typically consolidates a multitude different ODS with multiple schemas; therefore, the raw data must be normalized. In addition, the ODS may contain corrupted, erroneous, or missing data; therefore, the process of cleansing and consolidating data is required (Alnoukari, Alhawasli, Alnafea, & Zamreek, 2012). According to Marín-Ortega et al. (2014), ETL technologies have not been improved in scalability and performance at the same level with the DW technologies. Consequently, most of the BI infrastructures are facing serious bottleneck; data cannot be easily transformed and loaded into the DW in an acceptable time, whereas, the decision makers are looking for real time information. One of the suggested approaches to tackle the ETL serious bottleneck is to throw the transformation phase to the end of the ETL after the loading phase. Hence, ETL is becoming ELT. The main advantage of this switch is that ELT allows firstly extracting and loading data, then applying on-demand transformations according to business needs. In addition, ELT allows to apply and to re-apply data transformation in accordance to the changes in the environment. This provides ELT the flexibility needed to respond to the market changes. As a result, ELT addresses the issue related to design BI solutions in shorter time, as well as, provides the BI with the flexibility to reflect environmental changes. Passlick et al. (2017) proposed BI/BDA architecture model that support both traditional BI analytical reports, and BDA. The proposed architecture model integrates BI components with the BD ones. The data processing layer uses the classic ETL process, extended by the possibility to perform the BD EL(T) process. In addition, in the storage and analysis infrastructure layer, data integration can be done using the classic DW, as well as other BD technologies such as in-memory databases, or Hadoop clusters (Passlick, Lebek, & Breitner, 2017).

Another suggested approach is to integrate the Data Lakes with BI (Llave, 2018). Llave (2018) argues that Data Lakes has made it possible for BI to acquire data without caring of its structure. It is a huge capability to store inexhaustible amounts of raw data without performing any data transformation. Data transformation is considered as a bottleneck when using ETL process between the data sources and DW. Hence, it is similar to ELT, where the transformation is performed in the last step (Llave, 2018).

Data monetization is one of the concepts that has seen notable evolution starting BI era, until the BD era (Faroukhi, El Alaoui, Gahi, & Amine, 2020). Data monetization is a new concept that relies on using the data from organization to generate profit. Explicit data monetization is selling the data directly for cache, or sharing the data, whereas, implicit data monetization is an indirect way relying on that data to create value by enhancing own data-based products (Faroukhi, El Alaoui, Gahi, & Amine, 2020). During the BI era, data monetization was generally implicit, delivered by descriptive analytics. Production data was generally used for internal purpose. Thereafter, data monetization gain popularity and critical evolution during the BD era. Data monetization is becoming attractive in the era of BD (Faroukhi, El Alaoui, Gahi, & Amine, 2020). Data is integrated from external and internal sources that results in advanced analytical capabilities based on data-driven products and services. This allows for explicit monetization by selling data and provides the agility required for creating and monetizing knowledge. Faroukhi et al. (2020) argue that monetizing BD can be articulated based on the following business models directions; extracting customers-based activities data (data extractors), collecting and selling data (data providers), aggregating services (data aggregators), and providing technical platforms that enable processing, consuming and sharing data (technical platform providers). Monetizing BD provides firms with the ability to unlock value, and maximize the data-driven capability (Faroukhi, El Alaoui, Gahi, & Amine, 2020).

Big Data Analytics Capability: The Analytics Power

The complexity nature of BD stems from the difficulties in dealing with huge data sources, dealing with the complexity nature of the data itself, and the data processing to generate data insights (Al-Qirim, Rouibah, Serhani, Tarhini, Khalil, Maqableh, & Gergely, 2019). Data and information cannot, themselves, provide insights. Data insights could be generated by data transformation through analysis and interpretation, values are gained through the ability to drive actions (Holmlund, Van Vaerenbergh, Ciuchita, Ravald, Sarantopoulos, Villarroel-Ordenes, & Zaki, 2020). BD is one of the organization's resources that are necessary but not sufficient to create a Big Data Analytics Capability (BDAC), since many other firms are able to collect huge data from different resources (Gupta, & George, 2016). BD initiatives and BDAC can lead to improved organizational performance through value creation, better strategic decision-making, gains in competitive advantage, efficiency gains, improved marketing and increased innovation (Walls & Barnard, 2020). The term BDAC has been referred to in literature as the "next big thing in innovation", "fourth paradigm of science", "next frontier for innovation, competition, and productivity", "new paradigm of knowledge assets" and "next management revolution" because of the universal adoption of BDA technologies (Fosso Wamba, Gunasekaran, Akter, Ren, Ji-fan, Dubey, & Childe, 2017). In their recent research, Walls & Barnard (2020) adopt BDAC definition as "the holistic approach to managing, processing and analyzing huge volumes of incongruent data to determine actionable ideas and reactions to the data for sustained value and competitive advantage". BDAC refers to the organizational capabilities that can enable firms to analyze their huge data with nontraditional methods using BD tools and techniques; hence, producing insights that enable data-driven decision-making process (Dubey, Gunasekaran, & Childe, 2018). In the same vein, Akter et al. (2016) define BDAC as the competence to provide business insights using data management, technology, and talent capability to transform business into a competitive advantage and gain business value. Therefore, BDAC can be seen as an integration of the following three intertwined capabilities; big data analytics management capability, big data analytics infrastructure capability, and big data analytics talent capability (Walls & Barnard, 2020; Fosso Wamba, Gunasekaran, Akter, Ren, Ji-fan, Dubey, & Childe, 2017). Gupta, & George (2016) refer them as; tangible, human and intangible resources. Big data analytical management capability ensures the proper decision-making. It can be enhanced by improving the quality of planning, investment, coordination, and control (Walls & Barnard, 2020; Fosso Wamba, Gunasekaran, Akter, Ren, Ji-fan, Dubey, & Childe, 2017; Akter, Fosso Wamba, Gunasekaran, Dubey, & Childe, 2016). Big data analytical technology capability refers to the BDA platform flexibility that effectively enables the developing, deploying and supporting firm's resources. It can be improved by enhancing the performance of the BDA platforms in terms of connectivity, compatibility, and modularity (Walls & Barnard, 2020; Fosso Wamba, Gunasekaran, Akter, Ren, Ji-fan, Dubey, & Childe, 2017; Akter, Fosso Wamba, Gunasekaran, Dubey, & Childe, 2016). Big data analytical talent capability refers to the ability of an analytics professional to perform assigned tasks in the BD environment. Akter et al. (2016) argue that analysts should be competent in four important skills, technical knowledge (e.g., database management); technology management knowledge (e.g., visualization tools, and techniques management and deployment); business knowledge (e.g., understanding of short-term and long-term goals); and relational knowledge (e.g., cross-functional collaboration using information). Nocker & Sena (2019) argue that most organizations treat talent analytics as a capability, not as a resource, in order to contribute to value creation. This is in line with the Dynamic Capability Theory where talent analytics capabilities may include; learning capability, as organizational learning should support the implementation of talent analytics across the organization, coordinating capability between different organization sections so that talent analytics can create value, and technical capability for processing HR data.

Wang et al. (2018) listed some of the BDAC in the health care such as; analytical capability for patterns of care, unstructured data analytical capability, decision support capability, predictive capability, and traceability. Holmlund et al. (2020) classified customer experience insights as attitudinal/ psychographic, behavioral, and market insights. Attitudinal/ psychographic insights provide knowledge about satisfaction, advocacy, and valuable efforts by organizations. Behavioral insights help organizations with the knowledge about the behavioral aspect and consequences of customer experience. Market insights are extremely valuable as they are related to the knowledge about organizational performance in terms of the customer experience in relation with the marketplace.

Cloud computing and BD are complementary approaches (Lněnička, & Komárková, 2015). The marriage between cloud computing and BD derived Big data Analytics as a Service (BAaaS). BAaaS is an emergent service that provides individual, or organization, or information system, with the ability to share a wide range of analytical tools that can be available on the web or used by the smartphones. BAaaS is gaining popularity in recent years and many giant companies such as Microsoft, Amazon, and eBay adopted it (Sun, Zou, & Strang, 2015). Depeige & Doyencourt (2015) argue further that leveraging BDA to better manage and deliver knowledge services increases the benefits of Knowledge as a Service (KaaS) and its underlying processes offered in the cloud environment. KaaS can be considered as an on-demand knowledge store that has the ability to search, analyze and restructure its knowledge resources using cloud-computing environment (Depeige & Doyencourt, 2015). Furthermore, Depeige &

Doyencourt (2015) argue on the close relationship between BI/BD/BDA and Knowledge Management (KM). Depeige & Doyencourt (2015) highlight the evolution of BI analytics towards contextualized Knowledge Analytics (K-Analytics) that improve the capability to gain business value from data insights based on descriptive and predictive methods. Depeige & Doyencourt (2015) introduced actionable KaaS concept to induce valuable results.

Trends in Big Data Adoption

Amazon, Facebook, Google, Netflix, Dell, eBay, LinkedIn, Procter and Gamble, Target, Tesco, UPS, Walmart, and Zara are examples of organizations that have been successful at sustaining BDAC and setting the example (Walls & Barnard, 2020). The majority of these companies have born digital; they had a head step by digitizing all their operations. They have already adopted data-driven process as the source of the corporate strategy (Walls & Barnard, 2020).

However, this is not the case of the majority of the current organizations that trying to adopt BDA, and sustainably utilize BD to its full potential and benefits. Scholars argued the surveys' results showing how it is difficult for organizations to understand how to leverage BD insights in order to create value (Erevelles, Fukawa, Swayne 2016; Walls & Barnard, 2020). Even though an organization may extract BD insights successfully, there is no guarantee that they are able to utilize these insights effectively (Erevelles, Fukawa, Swayne 2016; Walls & Barnard, 2020). Even more many organizations could not understand how BDAC will affect their business performance and competitive advantages, and this explains Erevelles et al. (2016) findings that more than 50% of big data initiatives do not achieve their targets.

Mazzei, & Noble (2017) presented a BD maturity framework that highlights how BD can be used as an evolutionary strategic management tool, not only an IT tool that can use data as a source for corporate strategies. The framework is based on three tiers: big data as a tool, as an industry, and as a strategic tool. Scholars used Mazzei, & Noble (2017) BD framework in their studies; e.g. Walls & Barnard (2020) utilized it to identify the success factors of BDAC on organizational performance. Our study will use this framework to differentiate between the organizations adopting BD initiatives, and highlight how deeply BD technologies are used by different companies and integrated in their internal processes (Figure 3).

Big Data as a Tool

Many organizations currently use BD initiatives to improve their core functions performance using its analytics technology (Mazzei, & Noble, 2017). For example, Volvo Cars Company implemented a new automatic fault monitoring system. Using the data collected from the sensors installed inside vehicles. This data, combined with the data collected from the maintenance workshops, and the customer analysis results obtained from the social media data analysis, this device is able to provide a high quality advisor for its customers (Sadovskyi, Engel, Heininger, Böhm, & Krcmar, 2014). Ford Cars Company constantly provides information regarding relevant car parameters in real time to the driver. Ford's engineers can use this data to continuously improve the product or provide additional services, like location service to the next charging station (Bischof, Gabriel, Rabel, & Wilfinger, 2016). Starbucks, the famous coffee giant is using BDA with crowd sourcing to determine the success of any new location. It uses the information about the location, traffic, area demographic, and customer behavior to assess the location before opening any new store. Such analytics provides Starbucks with accurate estimation of the success rate of the new location (Satish & Yusof, 2017). Target proactively utilizes consumer insights from BDA to predict

Figure 3. Big Data Adoption Framework

consumer behavior. Target is able to estimate if a shopper woman is pregnant and her due date weeks before other competitors. The company is able due to predictive analysis to enhance adaptive capability to influence the customer's purchases towards baby items, and capturing sales before competitors (Erevelles, Fukawa, Swayne 2016). Southwest Airlines developed a BD application that extracts insights from customer's conversation records using a speech-analytics tool. Insights results are used to improve performance, and facilitate its dynamic capabilities (Erevelles, Fukawa, Swayne 2016). Los Angeles city is applying the demand-responsive pricing for parking application based on BDA. The goal is to reach a steadily high utilization of the parking spaces at all times, considering the data feed from parking sensors, the weather forecasts, holidays, etc. This BD based application helps them maximize parking utilization, with best pricing (El-Darwiche, Koch, Meer, Shehadi, & Tohme, 2014). United Healthcare, a large health insurance company, is using BD for its customer satisfaction application. The recorded voice files from customer calls to call center are transformed into text formats, and then analyzed to extract meaning from text using natural language processing. This analysis process is able to identify any customer's dissatisfaction (Davenport, 2014).

Big Data as an Industry

Organizations at this level are using BD for creating new ventures specialized in acquisition, storage and analysis of companies' huge data, construction of BD infrastructure, and development of all related software (Mazzei, & Noble, 2017). For example, Pivotal is using BD as an innovative industry. It provides "platform as a service" to allow clients to build their applications in its cloud (Mazzei, & Noble,

2020). Finning, a Caterpillar dealer, has transformed from a traditional repair service to a provider of support for customers' machines through predictive and prescriptive BDA. Customer experience insights enable Finning to track a machine's location, prevent premature failure, prolong service life, minimize downtime, increase operator efficiency, reduce the cost of repair, and recommend solutions (Holmlund, Van Vaerenbergh, Ciuchita, Ravald, Sarantopoulos, Villarroel-Ordenes, & Zaki, 2020). Netflix is a success story using BD sensing and seizing practices. Netflix created a new TV series, House of Cards, based on BDA that powerfully revealed viewers tastes such as favorites actors and actresses. This new innovative series brought Netflix millions as new revenues. This success showcase provides evidence supporting the relationship between market (customer) orientation and BD capability (Lin & Kunnathur, 2019; Akter, Fosso Wamba, Gunasekaran, Dubey, & Childe, 2016). Spotify, a streaming provider, created a personalized experience for each customer. Spotify capitalized on descriptive and predictive BDA to generate customer experience behavioral insights (i.e., knowledge on listening habits) and design highly personalized touchpoints. Spotify sent each customer a personalized email with information about their listening habits. These actions allowed Spotify to create personalized touchpoints in each customer's journey by generating custom playlists (Holmlund, Van Vaerenbergh, Ciuchita, Ravald, Sarantopoulos, Villarroel-Ordenes, & Zaki, 2020). Uber is the best showcase of the link between entrepreneurial orientation and BD capability. It is due to the entrepreneurial insights of Uber creators that helped them capturing the business value behind the real-time flow of digital data streams (Lin & Kunnathur, 2019).

Big Data as a Strategy

Organizations at this level reveal the new strategic thinking of using BD as a source of innovative business models of markets and products, and a driver of competitive strategy (Mazzei, & Noble, 2017). Inside these organizations, new leaders' innovative thinking concentrates on data flows rather than data stocks. They are able to create new ecosystems based on the data they accumulate and the increase of data flow. These learning organizations evolve dynamically; based on the uncovered trends in their data analysis. Organizations at this level have the ability to increase opportunities to diversify and expand into new markets (Walls & Barnard, 2020; Mazzei, & Noble, 2017; El-Darwiche, Koch, Meer, Shehadi, & Tohme, 2014). Amazon is an exceptional case where a company is using BD at all levels, as a tool, as an innovative industry, and as a corporate strategy (Mazzei, & Noble, 2020). Amazon is the best case showing a business model transformation based on Big-Data-Driven industry (Bischof, Gabriel, Rabel, & Wilfinger, 2016). Started as a traditional bookseller, it was evolved to one of the largest online traders. The company's platform was opened to other traders providing them access to their customer database and logistics network. Amazon is currently transformed its business model into a full service provider based mainly on BD (Mazzei, & Noble, 2020; Bischof, Gabriel, Rabel, & Wilfinger, 2016). Amazon restructures its distribution strategy in order to gain greater value through radical innovation. Amazon is able to predict when a customer will make a purchase, and start shipping products to nearest hub before the customer submits the order (Erevelles, Fukawa, Swayne 2016). Currently, 35% of purchases are generated from personalized purchase recommendations to customers based on BDA (Fosso Wamba, Gunasekaran, Akter, Ren, Ji-fan, Dubey, & Childe, 2017). Additionally, 30% of sales were newly generated from the new predictive technique called 'collaborative filtering' that generate "you might also want" prompt for each product bought or visited based on customer data (Akter, Fosso Wamba, Gunasekaran, Dubey, & Childe, 2016). Apple is another best showcase of a company using big data as a strategy (Mazzei, & Noble, 2017). Starting initially from a personal computer manufacturer, the company expanded its ecosystem data flows by collecting data in digital music, videos, telecommunications and other markets. Using BD as their corporate strategy, Apple was able to tackle and expand to new markets, including wearable, automobiles and mobile payment services. All of which are strategically integrated to the core company's platform (Mazzei, & Noble, 2017). John Deere, Agricultural equipment manufacturer, capitalized on BDA and equipped its machines with sensors that allowed customers to access and analyze their machine data, benchmarking it against other machines and combining it with historical data in real time and for free. Thus, John Deere introduced new touchpoint design that changed its customers' entire journey. Currently, myJohnDeere.com platform is opened to suppliers, retailers, and software developers. John Deere transitioned from a manufacturing business model to a platform-centric model, thus achieved innovation and revolutionized the agriculture industry (Holmlund, Van Vaerenbergh, Ciuchita, Ravald, Sarantopoulos, Villarroel-Ordenes, & Zaki, 2020).

FUTURE RESEARCH DIRECTIONS

Although BDA is a new research challenge, it is becoming a subject of growing importance. However, BD research has a relatively short history, starting in 2011 from only 38 studies listed in the Science Citation Index Expanded (SCIE), Social Science Citation Index (SSCI), Arts & Humanities Citation Index (AHCI), and Emerging Sources Citation Index (ESCI). The number of studies was increased to 3890 studies in 2017 (Jin, & Kim, 2018).

This paper outlines some avenues for future researches in the arena of BD; integration of BD with strategic management is an important research direction. A fundamental question remains: To what extent strategic management theories can be adopted to provide organizations with the ability to best adapt with BD initiatives. Big Data Maturity Model is another search direction, although different models were suggested, there is still a room for improvement, especially from best practices viewpoint.

CONCLUSION

BI was characterized by flexibility and adaptability in which traditional applications are not able to deal with. Traditional process modeling requires a lot of documentation and reports and this makes traditional methodology unable to fulfill the dynamic requirements of changes of our high-speed, high-change environment. BI main drawbacks was mainly related to data management issues, especially when dealing with huge data amount, and unstructured data types.

Technological development in data storage and processing make it possible to handle exponential increases in data volume in different type format. Hence, it was the cornerstone behind BD revolution. BD has become a source for innovation and competitive advantage by transforming decision making and leading to new strategic models. Decision-making process was redefined to incorporate the new strategic effects of BD & BDA concepts.

Borderlines between BI, BD and BDA still unclear for many companies. This paper provided a comprehensive view about all these concepts, the interrelationship between them, the new created organizational capabilities, and the different levels of BD adoption. Companies already integrated BI in their internal processes can extend their technological infrastructure and skills, and restructure their processes to gain value from BI/BD/BDA integration, improve their competitive advantages, and enhance organizational performance.

This paper concludes that analytics capability is the core power of BI/BD/BDA. BD (including BDA) is an extension of BI. It is worth noting that BD is more than a technology, and to be fully effective, it should be incorporated into corporate strategy. Arguably, BD affects organizational culture; it converts firms to become data and evidence-based organizations. Most notably, BD enables organizations to create entirely new innovative products, and new business models.

REFERENCES

Al-Qirim, N., Rouibah, K., Serhani, M. A., Tarhini, A., Khalil, A., Maqableh, M., & Gergely, M. (2019). The Strategic Adoption of Big Data in Organizations. In Z. Sun (Ed.), *Managerial Perspectives on Intelligent Big Data Analytics* (pp. 43–54). IGI Global. doi:10.4018/978-1-5225-7277-0.ch003

Alnoukari, M. (2009). Using Business Intelligence Solutions for Achieving Organization's Strategy: Arab International University Case Study. *Internetworking Indonesia Journal*, *1*(2), 11–15.

Alnoukari, M., Alhawasli, H., Alnafea, H. A., & Zamreek, A. (2012). Business Intelligence: Body of Knowledge. In Business Intelligence and Agile Methodologies for Knowledge-Based Organizations: Cross-Disciplinary Applications (pp. 1-13). IGI Global.

Alnoukari, M., & Hanano, A. (2017). Integration of business intelligence with corporate strategic management. *Journal of Intelligence Studies in Business*, *7*(2), 5–16. doi:10.37380/jisib.v7i2.235

Bischof, C., Gabriel, M., Rabel, B., & Wilfinger, D. (2016). Strategic Implications of BIG DATA – A Comprehensive View. *Proceedings of the Management International Conference (MIC 2016)*, 143–160.

Braganza, A., Brooks, L., Nepelski, D., Ali, M., & Moro, R. (2017). Resource management in big data initiatives: Processes and dynamic capabilities. *Journal of Business Research*, *70*, 328–337. doi:10.1016/j.jbusres.2016.08.006

Brock, V., & Khan, H. U. (2017). Big data analytics: Does organizational factor matters impact technology acceptance? *Journal of Big Data*, *4*(21), 1–28. doi:10.118640537-017-0081-8

Chen, M., Mao, S., & Liu, Y. (2014). Big data: A survey. *Mobile Networks and Applications*, *19*(2), 171–209. doi:10.100711036-013-0489-0

Columbus, L. (2019). *The Global State of Enterprise Analytics, 2020*. Retrieved May 9, 2020 from: https://www.forbes.com/sites/louiscolumbus/2019/10/21/the-global-state-of-enterprise-analytics-2020/#4966b9ba562d

Davenport, T. H. (2014). How strategists use 'big data' to support internal business decisions, discovery and production. *Strategy and Leadership*, *42*(4), 45–50. doi:10.1108/SL-05-2014-0034

Depeige, A., & Doyencourt, D. (2015). Actionable Knowledge As A Service (AKAAS): Leveraging big data analytics in cloud computing environments. *Journal of Big Data*, *2*(1), 12. doi:10.118640537-015-0023-2

Dubey, R., Gunasekaran, A., & Childe, S. J. (2018). *Big data analytics capability in supply chain agility: the moderating effect of organizational flexibility. In Management Decision.* Emerald. doi:10.1108/MD-01-2018-0119

El-Darwiche, B., Koch, V., Meer, D., Shehadi, R., & Tohme, W. (2014). *Big data maturity: An action plan for policymakers and executives.* Accessed April 25, 2020, https://www.strategyand.pwc.com/media/file/Strategyand_Big-data-maturity.pdf

Erevelles, S., Fukawa, N., & Swayne, L. (2016). Big Data consumer analytics and the transformation of marketing. *Journal of Business Research, 69*, 897-904.

Fan, S., Lau, R., & Zhao, J. A. (2015). Demystifying Big Data Analytics for Business Intelligence Through the Lens of Marketing Mix. *Big Data Research, 2*(1), 28–32. doi:10.1016/j.bdr.2015.02.006

Faroukhi, A. Z., El Alaoui, I., Gahi, Y., & Amine, A. (2020). Big data monetization throughout Big Data Value Chain: A comprehensive review. *Journal of Big Data, 7*(1), 3. doi:10.118640537-019-0281-5

Fosso Wamba, S., Akter, S., Edwards, A., Chopin, G., & Gnanzou, D. (2015). How 'big data' can make big impact: Findings from a systematic review and a longitudinal case study. *International Journal of Production Economics, 165*, 234–246. Advance online publication. doi:10.1016/j.ijpe.2014.12.031

Fosso Wamba, S., Gunasekaran, A., Akter, S., & Ren, S. (2017). Big data analytics and firm performance: Effects of dynamic capabilities. *Journal of Business Research, 70*, 356–365. doi:10.1016/j.jbusres.2016.08.009

Gupta, M., & George, J. F. (2016). Toward the development of a big data analytics capability. *Information & Management, 53*, 1049-1064.

Holmlund, M., Van Vaerenbergh, Y., Ciuchita, R., Ravald, A., Sarantopoulos, P., Villarroel-Ordenes, F., & Zaki, M. (2020). Customer Experience Management in the Age of Big Data Analytics: A Strategic Framework. *Journal of Business Research, 116*, 356–365. doi:10.1016/j.jbusres.2020.01.022

Jin, D. H., & Kim, H. J. (2018). Integrated Understanding of Big Data, Big Data Analysis, and Business Intelligence: A Case Study of Logistics. *Sustainability, 10*(10), 3778. doi:10.3390u10103778

Kimble, C., & Milolidakis, G. (2015). Big Data and Business Intelligence: Debunking the Myths. *Global Business and Organizational Excellence, 35*(1), 23–34. doi:10.1002/joe.21642

Lin, C., & Kunnathur, A. (2019). Strategic orientations, developmental culture, and big data capability. *Journal of Business Research, 105*, 49–60. doi:10.1016/j.jbusres.2019.07.016

Llave, M. R. (2018). Data lakes in business intelligence: Reporting from the trenches. *Procedia Computer Science, 138*, 516–524. doi:10.1016/j.procs.2018.10.071

Lněnička, M., & Komárková, J. (2015). The Impact of Cloud Computing and Open (Big) Data on the Enterprise Architecture Framework. *Proceedings of the 26th International Business Information Management Association Conference*, 1679-1683.

Marín-Ortega, P. M., Dmitriyevb, V., Abilovb, M., & Gómezb, J. M. (2014). ELTA: New Approach in Designing Business Intelligence Solutions in Era of Big Data. *Procedia Technology*, *16*, 667–674. doi:10.1016/j.protcy.2014.10.015

Mazzei, M. J., & Noble, D. (2017). Big data dreams: A framework for corporate strategy. BUSHOR-1369. *ScienceDirect*. Elsevier.

Mazzei, M. J., & Noble, D. (2020). Big Data and Strategy: Theoretical Foundations and New Opportunities. In *Strategy and Behaviors in the Digital Economy*. IntechOpen. https://www.intechopen.com/books/strategy-and-behaviors-in-the-digital-economy/big-data-and-strategy-theoretical-foundations-and-new-opportunities

Mikalef, P., Pappas, O. I., Giannakos, N. M., Krogstie, J., & Lekakos, G. (2016). Big Data and Strategy: A Research Framework. *Tenth Mediterranean Conference on Information Systems (MCIS)*, 1-9.

Nocker, M., & Sena, V. (2019). Big Data and Human Resources Management: The Rise of Talent Analytics. *Social Sciences*, *8*(10), 273. doi:10.3390ocsci8100273

Palem, G. (2014). Formulating an Executive Strategy for Big Data Analytics. *Technology Innovation Management Review*, *4*(3), 25–34. doi:10.22215/timreview/773

Passlick, J., Lebek, B., & Breitner, M. H. (2017). A Self-Service Supporting Business Intelligence and Big Data Analytics Architecture. In J. M. Leimeister & W. Brenner (Eds.), Proceedings der 13. Internationalen Tagung Wirtschaftsinformatik (WI 2017) (pp. 1126–1140). Academic Press.

Polese, F., Troisi, O., Grimaldi, M., & Romeo, E. (2019). A Big Data-Oriented Approach to Decision-Making: A Systematic Literature Review. *22nd International Conference Proceedings*, 472-496.

Ram, J., Zhang, C., & Koronios, A. (2016). The implications of Big Data analytics on Business Intelligence: A qualitative study in China. *Procedia Computer Science*, *87*, 221–226. doi:10.1016/j.procs.2016.05.152

Sadovskyi, O., Engel, T., Heininger, R., Böhm, M., & Krcmar, H. (2014). Analysis of Big Data enabled Business Models using a Value Chain Perspective. Proceedings of Multikonferenz Wirtschaftsinformatik (MKWI 2014), 1127–1137.

Saidali, J., Rahich, H., Tabaa, Y., & Medouri, A. (2019). The combination between Big Data and Marketing Strategies to gain valuable Business Insights for better Production Success. *Procedia Manufacturing*, *32*, 1017–1023. doi:10.1016/j.promfg.2019.02.316

Satish, L., & Yusof, N. (2017). A Review: Big Data Analytics for enhanced Customer Experiences with Crowd Sourcing. *Procedia Computer Science*, *116*, 274–283. doi:10.1016/j.procs.2017.10.058

Şen, E., Körük, E., Serper, N., & Çalış Uslu, B. (2019). Big Data Analytics and Simulation for Better Strategic Management. *Journal of Current Research on Engineering. Science and Technology*, *5*(2), 1–12.

Shams, S., & Solima, L. (2019). Big data management: Implications of dynamic capabilities and data incubator. *Management Decision*, *57*(8), 2113–2123. doi:10.1108/MD-07-2018-0846

Statistica. (2020). Retrieved May 9, 2020 from: https://www.statista.com/statistics/871513/worldwide-data-created/#statisticContainer

Sun, Z., Zou, H., & Strang, K. (2015). Big Data Analytics as a Service for Business Intelligence. *14th Conference on e-Business, e-Services and e-Society (I3E)*, 200-211. 10.1007/978-3-319-25013-7_16

Suoniemi, S., Meyer-Waarden, L., & Munzel, A. (2017). Big Data Resources, Marketing Capabilities, and Firm Performance. In *2017 Winter AMA Conference*. American Marketing Association.

Walls, C., & Barnard, B. (2020). Success Factors of Big Data to Achieve Organisational Performance: Qualitative Research. *Expert Journal of Business and Management*, 8(1), 17–56.

Wang, Y., Kung, L., & Byrd, T. A. (2018). Big data analytics: Understanding its capabilities and potential benefits for healthcare organizations. *Technological Forecasting and Social Change*, *126*, 3–13. doi:10.1016/j.techfore.2015.12.019

ADDITIONAL READING

Cecilia, A., Rusli, A., Rodziah, A., & Yusmadi, Y. J. (2016). Towards Developing Strategic Assessment Model for Big Data Implementation: A Systematic Literature Review. *Int. J. Advance Soft Compu. Appl*, *8*(3), 174–192.

Charles, V., & Gherman, T. (2013). Achieving Competitive Advantage Through Big Data. Strategic Implications. *Middle East Journal of Scientific Research*, *16*(8), 1069–1074.

Costa, J., Dantas, R., Santos, C., Medeiros, F., & Rebouças, S. (2018). The Impact of Big Data on SME's Strategic Management: A Study on a Small British Enterprise Specialized in Business Intelligence. *Journal of Management and Strategy*, *9*(4), 10–21. doi:10.5430/jms.v9n4p10

Court, D. (2015). *Getting big impact from big data*. McKinsey Global Institute. https://www.mckinsey.com/business-functions/business-technology/our-insights/getting-big-impact-from-big-data

Etzion, D., & Aragon-Correa, J. A. (2016). Big data, management, and sustainability: Strategic opportunities ahead. *Organization & Environment*, *29*(2), 3–10. doi:10.1177/1086026616650437

Zahra, S. A., & George, G. (2002). Absorptive capacity: A review, reconceptualization, and extension. *Academy of Management Review*, *27*(2), 185–203. doi:10.5465/amr.2002.6587995

KEY TERMS AND DEFINITIONS

Big Data (BD): Is a holistic approach to manage process and analyze the 7 V's (i.e., volume, variety, velocity, veracity, value, valence, and variability) in order to create actionable insights for sustained value delivery, measuring performance, establishing competitive advantages, and becoming a source of innovation.

Big Data Analytics (BDA): Is the process of collecting, organizing, and analyzing big data to discover patterns, knowledge, and intelligence as well as other information within the big data.

Big Data Analytics Capability (BDAC): Is the organizational capabilities that can enable firms to analyze their huge data with nontraditional methods using big data tools and techniques; hence, producing insights that enable data-driven decision-making process.

Business Intelligence (BI): Is an umbrella term that combines architectures, tools, databases, applications, practices, and methodologies. It is the process of transforming various types of business data into meaningful information that can help, decision makers at all levels, getting deeper insight of business.

Cloud Computing (CC): Is the result of evolutions of distributed computing technologies, enabled by advances in fast and low-cost network, commoditized faster hardware, practical high performance virtualization technologies, and maturing interactive web technologies.

Data Mining (DM): Is the process of discovering interesting information from the hidden data that can either be used for future prediction and/or intelligently summarizing the details of the data.

Data Warehouse (DW): Is a physical repository where relational data are specially organized to provide enterprise-wide, and cleansed data in a standardized format.

Knowledge Management (KM): Is the acquisition, storage, retrieval, application, generation, and review of the knowledge assets of an organization in a controlled way.

This research was previously published in Integration Challenges for Analytics, Business Intelligence, and Data Mining; pages 44-62, copyright year 2021 by Engineering Science Reference (an imprint of IGI Global).

Chapter 39
Big Data and Enterprise Applications

Ahmet Doğan
Osmaniye Korkut Ata University, Turkey

Emin Sertaç Arı
iD https://orcid.org/0000-0003-4453-5528
Osmaniye Korkut Ata University, Turkey

ABSTRACT

Today, a company continues its activities in a highly competitive environment regardless of the sector in which it operates. An important point has been emphasized in many developments by experienced managers and academics which have been released to the public. From marketing to finance, human resource management, auditing and planning, all business processes have entered an incredible innovative process. One of the topics in this process is big data. When cumulative data are not used, they cannot transcend being huge piles of garbage. However, it is not possible to analyze such large, complex, and dynamic data via conventional methods. At this point, the concept of big data has emerged. In this study, after the explanation and definition of the concept, a vast literature review was conducted in order to present the relationship of big data with IoT, big data-related topics, and academic researches on big data. Afterwards, real-life enterprise applications were exemplified from various industries.

INTRODUCTION

In his published book: *The Scholar and the Future of the Research Library*[1] in 1944, Fremont Rider; a librarian in Wesleyan University; estimated that the size of the U.S. university libraries were doubling every sixteen years and with this rate of growth, the Library of Yale University would have nearly 200 million volumes which would require more than 10 thousand kilometers of shelves, with around six thousand working staff by the year 2040 (Press, 2013).

DOI: 10.4018/978-1-6684-3662-2.ch039

In 1975 The Ministry of Posts and Telecommunications in Japan conducted a project called "Information Flow Census", in order to track the volume of information flowing in Japan. The study presented "amount of words" as the consolidative unit of measurement. The results found out that information supplied was increasing much faster than information demanded (Hilbert, 2012). Similarly, in 1981 The Hungarian Central Statistics Office started a research initiation to call on the information industries of the country (Hilbert, 2012).

Then in 1983 Pool published a paper; *Tracking the Flow of Information* (Pool, 1983) which explored the growth trends in communications media industry from 1960 to 1977. In the period of research, much of the growth observed in the information flow was because of the growth in broadcasting.

The quantity of data gradually became an important problem. In his very influencing study *Saving All the Bits* (Denning, 1990) Denning (1990) pointed out that the imperative to save all the data forced them into such a difficult situation that the rate and volume of information flow submerged their networks, storage infrastructures and information retrieval systems, just as the human comprehension capacity. So, some type of machines or methods should be developed in order to reduce the amount of data that must be saved, and the risk of losing hidden discoveries in a broad database could be reduced (Press, 2013).

By the penetration and the exponential growth of internet, the concerns on data processing became an important topic for all related stakeholders. In 1997, Lesk published a paper with the aim of calculating the volume of the current data and its future all over the world (Lesk, 1997); where correspondingly Cox and Ellsworth (1997) named the data processing concern as "the problem of big data" (Cox & Ellsworth, 1997). It was the first article in the ACM Digital Library which used the term "big data", although the quantity of the data was not comparable with the one, we deal with currently (Press, 2013).

The main purpose of the above-mentioned examples is to find an answer to the very head question: How do we deal with and benefit from that much, fast-growing and diverse data?

The human being has started to generate value from cumulative data which has become ginormous stacks just as producing energy from garbage mountains of municipal dump sites of cities, which pile up over years. In the recent decades, with the outbreak of data in all courses of all activities, humanity has faced a new global threat, which was called the "Information gap". Non-analyzed and irrational data could be expressed as "black information holes", which call many unexpected, poorly explained events (Zugurovsky & Zaychenko, 2019).

Communication has been one of the key aspects of humanity since ancient times. During last several decades we have witnessed considerable changes in communication and information technology (Sarma, Borah, & Dutta, 2016). Social networks generate huge volume of data at any time. Similarly, mobile devices generate data, like instant messages, voice calling, video conferencing, GPS. Also, sensor technologies like, satellites, GPS, radars generate huge data by measuring other sorts of data (Titimus, 2016). The consistent increase in the volume of data gathered by organizations because of the increase of data in social media, Internet of Things (IoT) and multimedia platforms. (Madakam, Ramaswamy, & Tripathi, 2015). The amount of generated data in everywhere, every day is really huge. It is important to analyze this huge volume of data in order to benefit from it. Hence, there is need for more complicated and smart computing techniques (Sarma, Borah, & Dutta, 2016). In data analysis field, conventional methods previously used to explore the data sets have become unable to cope with the recent data type and at this point the new concept has emerged: Big Data.

Even though having numerous definitions, big data can be qualified as *"the data that exceeds the processing capacity of conventional database systems"*. Chapman (2018) specifies the most important reasons of using big data as; time saving, better real-time analytics, modernized data storage methods, delivery of high-quality insights and support on better decision making (Chapman, 2018). The data is too big, moves too fast, or doesn't fit the structures of common database architectures. To gain value from this data, an alternative way must be chosen to process it (Dumbill, What is Big Data?, 2012). By having such unfamiliar behaviors, the new type of data should have various characteristics; named as 5V of big data by academics, researchers and field experts.

Next section of this chapter explores the characteristics of big data. Third section presents a vast literature review. The following section gives numerous real-world enterprise implication examples and the last section concludes the chapter.

THE CHARACTERISTICS OF BIG DATA

It has already been mentioned that big data exhibits different behaviors considering common data types. The fundamental features of big data were told as having large amounts, diverse datatypes and hi-speed dynamic structure. Even though the majority of the early big data research in the literature has determined the characteristics of this concept as 3V (Volume, Variety, Velocity) based on the fundamental features, current literature agrees on 5V (Volume, Variety, Velocity, Value, Veracity). Albeit some of recent field studies propose new V's (Validity, Variability, Visualization, Viscosity, Virality, etc.), they remain insufficient at building the concept. The characteristics of big data (5Vs of big data) are presented below.

- **Volume:** As its name suggest, big data is collection of a very large amount of data which should be handled properly (Sharma & Agarwal, 2018). The most interesting data for any organization to tap into today is social media data. Several additional applications are being developed; such as remote sense, environmental monitoring, traffic monitoring, remote monitoring, patient monitoring and stock control with radio frequency identification (RFID) (Kale, 2017). For data analysts the storage is a difficult task. This large volume of data should benefit to obtain accurate results (Desai, 2018). If companies can analyze that amount of data effectively to distinguish patterns and anomalies, businesses can begin to understand the data in new ways (Kale, 2017).
- **Variety:** Generally, it is not probable to find data in an ordered and ready-for-processing form. A common feature of big data systems is that the source data is diverse and doesn't fall into neat relational structures (Dumbill, Volume, Velocity, Variety: What You Need to Know About Big Data, 2012). Data comes in multiple formats as it ranges from e-mails to tweets and sensor data. There is no control over the format or the structure of the data. In traditional applications, the data sources were mainly transactions and judicial processing. The types of sources have expanded dramatically with various file extensions. Big data includes structured, semi-structured, and unstructured data in different proportions depending upon the context (Kale, 2017).
- **Velocity:** The *"de facto"* business model which has been adopted by the most of web-based companies; such as Amazon, Facebook, Google, etc.; operate on tracking the clicks and navigation behaviors of their customers, in order to develop personalized browsing and/or shopping experiences. In the clickthrough behavior of customer, there are millions of clicks gathered from them at every second, resulting in large amount of data. The dramatical increase in data means that the data should be analyzed more carefully. The faster the data increases, the faster the need for the data increases; therefore, the process shows increase as well (Özköse, Arı, & Gencer, 2015). Large volume of data might be supposed to result in performance decrease of computation. But

big persists its performance flawlessly to handle real-time data despite all challenges (Sharma & Agarwal, 2018).

- **Value:** The difficulty in producing large amounts of data is knowing how to find concrete value. The data value is usually deeply hidden in the collected dataset and can only be viewed by a discovery method that is specific to each data type. In fact, the actual value is based on the selection of the correct model to be followed for analysis as well as the correct data for each type of data. Fortunately, big data platforms offer many tools to find hidden connections between different cube-based platforms. (El Alaoui, Gahi, & Messoussi, 2019).

- **Veracity:** Veracity deals with trueness, trustworthiness, origin, etc. In such a large volume of data set, providing the veracity of complete data is a difficult task. There may be some dirty data as well (Sharma & Agarwal, 2018). Veracity has two fundamental features: the reliability of the source and the expediency of data. Many sources generate data that is uncertain, incomplete, and inaccurate; therefore, making its veracity suspicious (Kale, 2017).

Along with the intensive daily use in many sectors, the academy is also interested in providing both theoretical and technical contribution to big data. Several researches conducted in the literature are presented below.

BACKGROUND

In this section, after the explanation and definition of the concept of big data, a vast literature review is conducted on big data-related topics and academic researches on big data. In terms of being related to the concept of the book, the literature review was conducted in scope of the relationship of Big Data with Internet of Things (IoT). The researches studied within the content of this chapter are presented below.

Ahmed, et al. (2017) analyzed the relevant scientific literature by concentrating on the relationship between big data and internet of things (IoT). In this context, first of all, the latest developments and solutions on the IoT-based big data and its analytics were addressed. Then, the emphasis was placed on the big data processing and analytical platforms which could be used for a great deal of data produced by the IoT. These platforms were stated as apache Hadoop, 1010data, Cloudera data hub, SAP-Hana, Hortonworks etc. Afterwards, a taxonomy of big data and analytical solutions were created for the IoT systems. According to this taxonomy, the taxonomy of big data and its analytical solutions designed for the IoT systems were categorized with respect to certain properties. These properties were determined as big data sources, system components, big data enabling Technologies, functional elements and analytics type. In addition, the existing opportunities and difficulties were discussed for big data and its analytics in the IoT environment. Consequently, when the relationship between big data and IoT was investigated, it was highlighted by the authors that the available big data solutions in the IoT paradigm were still in their infancy and these difficulties needed to be overcome day by day.

Ge, et al. (2018) stressed that big data analytics turned into a more critical data analyzing tool within the IoT with the rapid developments in the internet of things over time, and they presented a conceptual framework by conducting a broad literature research in this field. In the study, a focus was set on big data technologies with the purpose of preventing the drawbacks of using Big data analytics differently in every IoT domain and enabling information-sharing and application integrity in IoT domains. 139 papers were reviewed within the scope of the literature research. The papers were classified according to

IoT domains, the big data techniques used in relation with these domains and the way these techniques were applied. In this context, firstly, eight IoT domains were determined. Within the scope of the papers reviewed, the distribution of the studies related to the determined IoT domains is as follows: healthcare papers have 25% (35 papers), energy 17% (24 papers), smart cities 13% (18 papers), agriculture 9% (13 papers), transportation 8% (11 papers), industry 7% (10 papers), military 6% (8 papers) and building automation 5% (20 papers). When this distribution is examined, it is possible to say that the IoT domain where big data technologies are mostly used is healthcare, and the domain where they are least used is building automation.

Rehman, et al. (2019) emphasized that large amounts of data were produced because of the prevalent use of sensors and IoT devices in industrial areas, however, major data procedures faced a lot of difficulties inside the lot due to the limitation of the factors such as network and storage resources. Even though there are many studies conducted in this field, very few studies have been reported to exactly reflect these two paradigms. In this context, the literature was reviewed, and studies were examined within the framework of a certain taxonomy. According to this taxonomy, they approached the big data analytics in the IoT under six categories as data sources, analytics tools, analytics techniques, Requirements, industrial analytics applications and analytics types. Besides, they tried to detect the applications of the big data analytics in the IoT by including the structure and the purpose of the problem, solution method, data set, limitations and potential solutions. Within the context of the studies reviewed, it was concluded that performing big data analytics in IoT systems was still in its infancy, it was necessary to create some procedures and standards for the applications of big data analytics on IoT systems and a great effort was required to adapt the current processes to these new developments.

In their study, Babar and Arif (2017) suggested an approach of a smart city architecture based on big data and internet of things analytics. The suggested approach was realized at three stages. At stage 1, various data were collected regarding city services. At stage 2, data calculation, normalization, filtering, processing and data analysis were executed in respect of the data collected. At stage 3, some rules were formed as a result of the algorithm of the method and application was started within the framework of the rules established. The suggested system was tested with the Hadoop Ecosystem. Accordingly, it was concluded that the suggested system could make contribution to the development of the current smart city architectures and it was effective in terms of efficiency.

Din and Paul (2019) proposed a new approach related to the health sector as the smart health monitoring and management system by making use of big data and internet of things technologies. The model is comprised of three layers as data production and pre-processing, Hadoop processing layer and data application layer. Moreover, the proposed system was supported with an architecture including both online and offline data; the proposed model was practiced with the data obtained from the health sector and it was concluded that its performance was at the desired level.

In their study, Côrte-Real et al. (in press) tried to assess the European and American companies' perception of big data analytics and Internet of things (IoT) technologies by relying on the strategic management perspective. In this context, a survey was applied on a total of 618 European and American companies for assessing whether these technologies provided a competitive advantage. Accordingly, it was concluded that these technologies would provide businesses with a great competitive advantage as long as the data quality is high.

In their study, Yao, et al. (2019) put forward the approach of a deep learning model for detecting the gallbladder stones with the big data obtained from the internet of things in medical field. It was revealed that the medical IoT could enable data flow for researchers who conduct studies in this field by benefiting from large data sources such as large ultrasonographic images, computed tomography, magnetic resonance etc. Furthermore, it was observed that medical IoT data were also used in this study. As a result of the study, it was discovered that the proposed model could help with detecting and treating the cases of gallbladder stones and efficiency was high.

Babar, et al. (2019) suggested large data analytics based on the Internet of Things and smart city architecture for the urban data management system. The suggested architecture has two different modules. These modules are stated as Big Data loading and Big Data processing. In the discussed method, the analyses were performed with Hadoop. It was emphasized with the experimental results that the method proposed for the urban data management system was much more efficiency when the manual and traditional data loading and the suggested solution architecture were compared.

Jan, et al. (2019) proposed a smart transportation system model with the big data and internet of things approach. The proposed model was carried out at 4 stages: stage 1 - data collection, stage 2 - communication, stage 3 - data processing, stage 4 - application. Analyses were conducted through the Hadoop Ecosystem in the system discussed. The suggested system was tested with real transportation data sets from various sources. As a result, it was emphasized that the suggested system provided very realistic results and could generally be used in the solution of transportation network problems.

In their study, Gu, et al. (2017) researched the potential of big data and internet of things applications to solve the problems of Waste Electrical and Electronic Equipment (WEEE) management. Accordingly, it was found in the analyses of IoT and big data technologies for the aforementioned field that they could produce some difficulties as well as important opportunities. These difficulties and opportunities were approached from an economic, technological and practical perspective. Scenarios created within the context of the proposed framework for the application of IoT and big data technologies in the WEEE management were tested with real-life problems. Consequently, it was specified that using the IoT and big data technologies together made a positive contribution to the WEEE management problems. Finally, another purpose of the paper was stated as providing the researchers who were interested in this field with a new vision in terms of IoT and big data.

In their study, Babar and Arif (2018) proposed a model based on the analysis of energy harvesting, which means storage of the energy interrupted in the systems that were unable to be fed by energy continuously, for health monitoring sensors, and big data analytics in the health sector. Accordingly, first of all, a comprehensive conceptual framework was established in relation with energy harvesting area for health monitoring sensors and data processing and decision-making for health services. The suggested approach was realized at three stages: stage 1 - energy harvesting and data production, stage 2 - data pre-processing, stage 3 - data processing and application. In the discussed method, the analyses were performed with Hadoop. The proposed model stressed the significance and effectiveness of big data and IoT technologies in health services.

It was also expressed that the model set forth in the study would make important contributions to the field of smart health.

Kho et al. (2018) conducted a study on examining the large amounts of RFID data with big data analytics in an IoT-enabled production workshop. A method consisting of the combination of gradient descent and clustering methods algorithms was used to perform this analysis. As a result, it was discovered that predictions could be made for the future of production with the big data obtained from the production site and efficiency could be increased substantially.

Sun, et al. (2016) made an applied research on the internet of things and big data analytics for Smart and Connected Communities (SSC), which developed within the context of smart city applications. The application was executed in the city of Trento in Italy. The aim of the application is to re-enliven the city, make the city more livable and ease the transportation of the city by establishing smart and connected communities. In line with this purpose, the TreSight technology, which combines IoT and big data analytics, was used for smart tourism and sustainable cultural heritage in the application conducted in Trento. According to the results, the proposed system was reported to be successfully applicable to problems complying with the smart city concept.

Chen, et al. (2014) made broad conceptual research related to big data covering the past of big data, cloud computing, internet of things, data centers, big data technologies such as Hadoop, requirements of big data, obstacles of big data and big data applications. Thus, the most important data analysis sources in big data applications were specified as data analysis, text data analysis, web data analysis, multimedia data analysis, network data analysis and mobile data analysis. The most important areas of big data application were determined as application of IoT based big data, application of online social network-oriented big data, applications of healthcare and medical big data, collective intelligence and smart grid. Finally, authors state that big data is a field quite open to research and development despite the significant difficulties experienced by big data and researchers are needed for contributing to the development of this field.

Hashem, et al. (2016) presented an applied study on the role of big data in a smart city. In this context, they firstly touched upon the developing communication technologies such as RFID, WSN, Wi-Fi, Ultra-wideband, ZigBee, and Bluetooth, 4G LTE, LTE-A, and 5GT, Network function virtualization. Then, they concentrated on what big data applications could be performed in a city according to the smart cities concept. It was stated that big data smart city applications could be performed in areas such as smart grid, smart healthcare, smart transportation and smart governance. Finally, big data was applied in Stockholm, Helsinki and Copenhagen. According to the results, it was revealed that big data has a key role in the analysis of the increasing data by the increasing connection of devices to networks via the internet of things technology in urban cities. A business model and architecture were also proposed for managing data in smart cities. Consequently, despite various difficulties in this area, it was emphasized that these difficulties might also bring about an opportunity for new studies.

Zheng, et al. (2016) set forth a conceptual study on making use of the big data technology for social transportation. Accordingly, they discussed how data could be obtained for social transportation, how the transportation data should be analyzed, how traffic and transportation analytics should be carried out in social transportation in addition to crowdsourcing in social transportation. Regarding social transportation, the CPSS-based transportation 5.0 system was examined, and it is expressed that this system could be very useful in terms of auditing and controlling the traffic in both physical and cyber areas. Finally, opinions and suggestions were presented with respect to the future of social transportation in the technological sense.

Jaradat, et al. (2015) executed a conceptual study on the management of big data for smart sensor networks and smart grid. Accordingly, it was stated that smart sensor networks could provide numerous opportunities in smart grid applications such as demand-oriented energy management and integration of renewable energy generators. Moreover, it was mentioned that smart sensor grids would be preferred in the future because of their cost advantages. It was stressed that the relationship between smart sensor networks and smart grids and big data was very strong as huge data are produced in these networks and grids. However, it is stated that efficient management of the data is still difficult although big data is a very significant technology. In this paper, proposals and applications for the future of smart grids and internet of things technologies were discussed. It was also mentioned what methods need to be used to make use of the big data technology and for manage the big data produced by the sensor and counters in IoT during application processes. Finally, it was stated that smart power grids and IoT technology became more popular every passing day and we should benefit from them to the full extent in order to make our daily lives smarter and easier.

In their study, Rathore et al. (2016) proposed an integrated IoT-based approach for smart city development and city planning by using big data analytics. The proposed model was carried out at 4 stages: 1 - data production and collection from IoT sources, 2- coordination of the communication between base stations, Internet etc. 3 - use of Hadoop 4 - use and application of data through analysis. The system was tested in terms of efficiency of the performance considering the processing time and throughput. As a result of the tests, it was concluded that the proposed system was more efficient than the existing systems and it could be applied successfully in the studies that could be conducted on the smart city concept.

Nobre and Tavares, (2017) reviewed the big data and internet of things studies on circular economy (CE), which means industrial economy based on zero pollution and zero waste generation, through literature analysis. In this context, they examined 70 of many documents which were published between 2006-2015 with the help of R statistics software. Accordingly, it was found that Brazil and Russia, which have high rates of greenhouse gas emissions, were not interested in this field so much while China and USA were discovered as countries with the highest publications and interest in this field. It is thought that the results can be useful for researchers and institutions that are interested in this field.

Kumari, et al. (2018) examined the existing situation resulting from the increase in the data obtained from multimedia devices with the development of the internet of things technology and suggested a model for this field. Besides, they developed a comprehensive taxonomy for reviewing a significant amount of multimedia data named as Multimedia big data. It can be said that this suggested approach related to multi-media big data aims at researching the difficulties in this field such as scalability, accessibility, reliability, heterogeneity and quality of service and proposing solutions. The suggested model was implemented on intelligent transport systems in India.

In their study, Elhoseny et al. (2018) proposed an integrated new approach on the basis of the internet of things and cloud computing for managing the big data appearing in health service applications. As the solution method in the suggested model, genetic algorithm, particle swarm optimizer and parallel particle swarm optimization methods were used. It has been discovered that this new approach exhibits a performance 50% better than the models available and also increases the system efficiency by 5.2% as a result of the application with real data.

In their study, Firouzi et al. (2018) evaluated the importance, architecture, applications and analysis of the field called "smart healthcare" in the health system with the new technologies which have been developed in recent years (big data, internet of things). According to the results, the components of the IoT systems of the health sector were specified as device layer, fog layer and cloud layer. In the study, an example was presented to draw attention to the importance of the IoT-based big data analytics. Hence, IoT expenditures in the health market of North America were 50 billion Dollars in 2012, but 150 billion Dollars in 2019. In 2022, this value is expected to be 300 billion Dollars. According to these findings, it is possible to say that IoT-based big data analytics will become popular worldwide day by day and turn into an essential element for many sectors such as the health sector.

BIG DATA SOLUTIONS IN THE REAL WORLD

Despite being a brand-new concept, big data analytics have widely been used and led to outstanding outputs in many industries recently. It is worth mentioning in which sectors and for what purposes big data is used before moving to the real-life application examples in various sectors. The main sectors in which big data is commonly used can be specified as media and entertainment, finance, transportation, healthcare, education, retail, manufacturing and government services. The usage purposes and application forms of big data in related sectors can be listed as follows.

Media and Entertainment

Emerging technologies have always been the leading contributor of the media and entertainment industries. The main business problems which drive media companies consider big data solutions are the need to cut the costs of operating and at the same time the need to make money from various platforms and products (Lippel, 2015). Big data in the media and entertainment industry helps businesses in many ways. It discovers customer behaviors, delivers personalized scope helps drive digital transformation as well. Therefore, big data pulls the strings to ensure profitability for media and entertainment companies (Quantzing, 2019). By executing big data management systems which include conventional warehouses and new age data storages, broader types of data can be analyzed to ensure that the business can become more active (Oracle, 2015). Certain ways big data make contribution to the industry are presented below:

- Nowadays, the traditional way of developing media content has been replaced by numerous media services such as pay-per-view, live broadcasting and much more. In the content delivery process, media distributors and providers collect vast amounts of user data. Big data in the media and entertainment industry helps consumers seek comprehensive understanding of their behavior and preferences. (Quantzing, 2019). By adopting predictive big data analytics, media and entertainment suppliers can easily foresee the interests and needs; thus, develop applications and launch special offers for their customers / subscribers.
- Finding out the reason of unsubscribing of subscribers to mailing lists has been the sixty-four-thousand-dollar question for years. In contrast to conventional processes, big data has enabled to learn why customers subscribe and unsubscribe; and which content they enjoy and dislike. Therefore, media and entertainment companies create the best promotional to attract and keep customers (Maropost, 2019).
- In a traditional advertising, the provider put random content in front of the target customer and wish / wait for they like what they watch (Anderson, 2018). In recent years, the advertising sector has shifted their traditional advertising activities to a new media, using new ways / tools of marketing. Search engine and social media advertisement is done more accurately with the support of big data. Since it made it easy to understand the trends of customers, it's more fruitful for entertainment industry to develop more personalized content for them. Efficient ad leads to an increase in rates of return (A.K., 2018).
- The customer gained strength by virtue of big data which ease the complexities of on-demand viewing. Advanced analytics are used to generate exact forecasts about users' actions from various sources. This could be helpful in determining right type of content for user (A.K., 2018). By virtue of big data, content providers are able to optimize the scheduling of their media streams.

Banking, Finance & Insurance

The banking, finance and insurance sector has congenitally been an intensively data-driven industry, with financial institutes managing considerable amount of customer data and using data analytics through financial activities. The insurance sector is based on data analysis to understand and effectively assess risk. Insurance appraisers and professionals depend on the analysis of data to carry out their businesses (Hussain & Prieto, 2016).

- In consideration of storing all the details of a customer under name or account number, the details by just a click can be found, however this is just a basic use.
- Big data helps in fraud detection to find abuse of all financial products by keeping account of customer statistics, hence triggering a warning when any unusual activity is detected (Chapman, 2018).
- Big data also helps credit checks go faster by analyzing customer credit reports, spending habits, social media profiles and credit card payment rates, just in seconds (Razin, 2015).

Transportation

Owing to the growth of big data, it has been used in a variety of ways to make transport more fruitful and easier. Below are some of the areas where big data contributes to transport:

- In route planning; big data can be used to comprehend and determine the requirements of users on different routes and in multiple transport modes and then use it to reduce waiting times (IntelliPaat, 2019). Big data collects information such as GPS location, traffic cameras, weather conditions, and then provides appropriate information as requested by the user. (Chapman, 2018).
- Congestion management and traffic control is another field of interest for big data. Real-time forecast of jam and traffic patterns is possible by means of big data. For example, people use Google Maps to locate the most suitable routes (IntelliPaat, 2019).
- Using the real-time processing of big data and predictive analysis to identify turbulent areas results in reduction in accident rates and increase in the safety of road and traffic (IntelliPaat, 2019).
- Big data also offers favorable solutions for logistics and supply chain management processes that provide huge time and money savings by virtue of its real time route optimization, strategic network planning, operational capacity planning, service improvement, risk evaluation, address verification and environmental intelligence contributions.

Healthcare

The ability to enhance the standard of living, to provide customized treatment exercises and to discover the developments in the field of medicine, makes the healthcare industry an ideal beneficiary of big data. In healthcare, the aim of the use of big data differs. The utilizers of this sector use big data in a more patient-centric way, rather than using with a purpose of increasing profits or finding new product opportunities. (Pickell, 2019). With the extensive use of wearables and IoT technologies and integration of machine / deep learning algorithms, the contribution of big data to healthcare sector is forecasted to be far greater. Several exciting ways in which the healthcare industry has begun to leverage big data to improve patient outcomes are mentioned as follows:

- Big data improves patient outcomes because it helps doctors and other medical professionals be more efficient and accurate with their diagnoses and treatments. With the improved data analyzing methods big data provides, doctors can hope to find solutions to treat rare and serious conditions that would otherwise seem incurable because research can progress at a faster pace (Turea, 2019).
- Many consumers are interested in smart devices that record every step, heart rate and sleep habits. A chronic insomnia and an increasing heart rate may indicate future risk of heart disease. Patients are directly involved in monitoring their own health and incentives from health insurers can push them to lead a healthy lifestyle. (Lebied, 12 Examples of Big Data Analytics In Healthcare That Can Save People, 2018).
- By the effective use of big data, notable reductions in prescription errors have achieved, outcomes improved, lives saved.
- The use of electronic health records is the most common utilization area of big data in medicine. Patients have their own digital records including their information like age, gender, anamnesis, allergies, test results etc. All records are shared via information systems for related parties (Lebied, 12 Examples of Big Data Analytics In Healthcare That Can Save People, 2018).

Education

Education industry streams with enormous amounts of data related to students, faculty, courses, results, and so on. Field experts have started to make use of big data throughout all stages of education process.

- Big data helps educational institutions understand the specific requirements of students by syncretizing conventional and online learning methods. This allows educators keep track of the improvement of the students and reorganize their teaching-learning process (Pickell, 2019).
- By virtue of the personalized and dynamic learning environments and schedules, students can be improved using the data collected about the learning history of each. This enhances the overall results (IntelliPaat, 2019).
- New improvements in grading systems also have been presented as a result of a suitable analysis of student data (IntelliPaat, 2019).
- Suitable analysis of every student's records gives clear insights on each student's performance, strength, weakness, field of interest, etc. It also helps in career planning of the students in near future. The customized applications of big data provide a solution to one of the biggest problems in the education system; "the one-size-fits-all" perspective (IntelliPaat, 2019).

Retail

The retail sector is highly dependent on the collection of internal and external data. To be successful, retailers must have the ability to extract the right information out of real-time data collections (Zillner, ve diğerleri, 2016). In today's hyper-connected digital world, we all have a digital footprint and almost everything we do online can be tracked, measured and used to predict consumer trends. (Lebied, The Impact of Big Data on The Retail Sector: Examples And Use-Cases, 2018). The retailers - either offline or online - adopt data-first strategy towards understanding the buying behavior of their customers, attach them to products and launch strategies for increased profits (Virmani, 2018). Big data offers broad information about the target market and it changes the philosophy of the retail world strikingly (Lebied, The Impact of Big Data on The Retail Sector: Examples And Use-Cases, 2018). It is now being applied at every stage of the retail process as follows:

- Many retailers; especially the ones who have multiple locations; suffer from inventory management. The organization of the needs of each store is a complicated task and without data, it's a gamble. To cope with the problem, retailers use predictive analytics. Data-driven inventory management take numerous factors into account; including current inventory, future needs, promotion activities, pricing strategy, etc. (Paiva, 2018).

- Within the trend prediction support of big data analytics, retailers recently have a great deal of tools available to them in order to work out what will be this season's "must have" items, regardless of the product category. Trend forecasting algorithms scan social media posts and web browsing behaviors to work out what causes an excitement and purchase data is analyzed to see what marketing campaign will be launched. Brands and marketers are interested in "sentiment analysis", using miscellaneous machine learning algorithms to determine the context when a product is discussed, and the related data is used to predict what the best seller products in a category are probable to be (Marr, Big Data: A Game Changer In The Retail Sector, 2015).

- Similarly, recommendation generation (market basket analysis) based on the customers' purchase history and demand forecast that involve demographic data and economic indicators build a clear picture of spending habits of the related market.

- Another use of big data in retail industry is price optimization. The price should not be too low that the retailer lose money, but not too high where the customer abandon purchase. Predictive price analytics with considering product pricing, consumer interest, inventory, competitor pricing and margins to optimize the price for each product. (Paiva, 2018).

- It is also possible to value customers with support of big data analytics. All customers are worthy, but some worth more than others. Big data gives ideas on customer behavior and spending patterns to identify the most precious customers. Once knowing who they are, the marketing team can target them with special offers and personalized strategies.

Manufacturing

Most of the industrial manufacturing firms have complex manufacturing processes, often with complex relationships across the supply chain with retailers and suppliers (Kurtz & Shockley, 2013). In the core of the process they generate big amounts of data. Many manufacturing organizations are looking for ways of taking advantage of the data generated, in order to improve their quality of manufacturing; reduce their costs by improving defect tracking and forecasting abilities to optimize supply chains, thus leading overall efficiency (Oracle, 2015). Several scopes of big data in manufacturing industry are scrutinized below.

- By taking advantage of big data solutions production optimization and efficiency enhancement can be achieved. Machine logs contain data on asset performance. IoT also adds a new dimension with connected devices and sensors. This data potentially has great value for manufacturers. (Consoli, 2018).

- In the commodity-intensive manufacturing industry, equipment failure and periodical mainte- nance are regular tasks (Capgemini, 2018). Big data helps predict equipment failure. With this data, manufacturers can maximize equipment runtime and provide maintenance more cost effec- tively (Oracle, 2018).
- Sustainable product quality is a core issue for manufacturers. Most of the manufacturers already have the data needed in order to enhance product quality and reduce costs. Big data can be used for this purpose. Notable savings can be made with predictive analytics. One of the costliest processes in manufacturing industry is quality tests. The number of the tests required can be significantly reduced with the use of pattern recognition and predictive analytics to determine the number and type of tests needed indeed, instead of trying all tests on all items.
- As being another costly process resulting from minor mistakes in the production stage can easily get the costs of warranties and recalls go out of control. With the support of big data, it is pos- sible to avoid or foresee warranty / recall issues, which leads saving significant amounts of money (Bodi, 2018).

Telecommunication

Telecommunications companies provide network equipment such as routers, switches, and gateways for wired and wireless networks. They are used by carriers to provide voice calls, text, internet data, TV, video conferencing, music, etc. services. This equipment, which requires big data solutions to calculate and deliver the capacity to manage, generates a lot of data. (Insight Lake, 2017). With the dramatic evolve- ment of all smart mobile devices, communications service providers need to swiftly process, store and deduce insights from such volume of data across networks. Big data analytics help them increase profit- ability with optimization of their services, customer experience and security issues (McDonald, 2017).

- Firstly, fraud detection is an important activity in which big data analytics is intensively used for telecommunication industry, as for other several industries. The most common fraud cases in the industry are illegal access, authorization issues, fake profiles, cloning, behavioral issues, etc.
- Another important activity is the network optimization and predictive analytics. In order to maxi- mize their revenue and manage irregular traffic, telecom companies strictly plan their network capacities on a regular basis. To develop the capacity planning they collect data, perform traffic data analysis and forecast usage which results in efficient outcomes by taking advantage of big data analytics (Insight Lake, 2017).
- Gaining new customer is a challenging task. Customer retention requires a lot of effort as well. Smart data platforms enable immediate handling of satisfaction-related issues and churn preven- tion (Active Wizards, 2019).
- With the integration of IoT technologies, telecom firms find an opportunity for enrichment of incoming events, anomaly detection, correlation of all event and executive actions (Insight Lake, 2017).

Government Services

The public sector is increasingly aware of the potential value of big data-driven innovation via progresses in productivity and efficacy. Governments produce and get great quantities of data by means of their activities, such as tax collection, salary payment or social security processes. (Zillner, ve diğerleri, 2016).

- With big data tools, governments can minimize tax and social security frauds. Algorithms used for pattern detection are suitable to notice real-time suspicious transactions. (Chapman, 2018).
- As well as fraud detection, governments can use big data analytics to fight against other crimes. Big data provides more elucidated risk assessment, improved ease of discovering information, great cooperation across offices, awareness of potential criminal intelligence and criminality and new lines of inquiry for investigation (Amit, 2019).
- IoT plays an important role in the use of big data in government sector. For example, data from traffic sensors can be mapped to time and other metrics to determine traffic patterns as part of planning to ease traffic jam. Government and scientific agencies also are using satellite telemetry and weather sensors to track weather patterns and assess global warming (Ingram, 2017). The public sector has been making use of sensor-measured applications for several physical phenomena like environmental pollution, usage levels of waste containers, location of municipal vehicles or detection of unusual behavior; as well as traffic volumes for quite some time (Munné, 2016).

After addressing the main purposes of big data usage for several industries, it's worth telling of real-life big data applications from a wide range of sectors, from telecommunication to energy.

REAL-LIFE BIG DATA APPLICATIONS

Airbnb

Airbnb brings various accommodation opportunities to the travelers in 34.000 cities all around the world since 2008. The core business of the company; which has over 1.5 million records and 50 million visitors; is to bring a large number of guests with the accommodation suppliers together.

As a big data analytics strategy, they focus their attention on registering new householders around popular locations or optimize pricing for the use of global real estate network during high tide seasons through the data gathered from the comments online. Moreover, by dint of Aerosolve®; a machine learning platform developed by Airbnb data team; the householders are able to determine the best price for their services. This platform analyzes the photos submitted by the hosts (records with comfortable bedroom photos find more favor than those with stylish living room photos) and automatically divides cities into micro-neighborhoods (Badger, 2015). Thanks to Airpal, another user-friendly application, not only data analysis oriented; all employees have access to and use company information effectively.

In reaction to those data practices, both technical and non-technical persons within the organization want to check the data analytics prior to making their decisions.

Amazon

If not the creator, as being the heaviest user of recommendation algorithm, Amazon could be called the most effective practitioner of big data analytics. Already in 2003, which was an early time of its technology, they used similarity methods from collaborative filtering. From that time Amazon increasingly has evolved its recommender engine and today they bring to perfection. (Smith, 2019).

Amazon also uses big data to monitor, track and secure its 1.5 billion items in its retail stores operating all around the world (Datafloq, 2019).

Amazon makes billions of dollars and dramatically increases the number of its customers every year by means of big data analytics focused on customer profile.

Apixio

Apixio, a California-based IT company, was founded in 2009 with the vision of extracting clinical information from digital medical records and making them accessible to improve healthcare decision-making.

Being aware of the fact that the biggest problem in the data analysis in health sector is that the data is unstructured (from the handwritten notes of the doctors to the social security records) rather than reaching the data; the organization makes valuable patient-based and disease-based inferences by using various instruments ranging from Optical Character Recognition (OCR) technology to machine learning algorithms. Such practices generate various outcomes from cost reduction to exact diagnoses and right decisions (Marr, Why We Need More Big Data Doctors, 2015).

Apple

Tech giant Apple is officially the most valuable brand in the world (Badenhausen, 2019). Known for its iconic product designs and user-friendly interfaces, the company has taken considerable steps towards becoming a "big data company" in recent years.

Sounds received through Siri, which have been used for years, are compared with millions of other voices using cloud-based big data analysis methods to optimize the system's ability to recognize audio patterns.

Moreover, by the corporate cooperation with IBM, it is now possible for iPhone and Apple Watch users to share real-time health data with related data center or healthcare organization (Campbell, 2015).

CERN

Scientists from around the world since 2008 have been using the world's largest and most powerful particle accelerator; The Large Hadron Collider (LHC), to create conditions similar to the Big Bang and to gain a better understanding of our universe (Louie, 2016).

LHC's sensors record hundreds of millions of collisions between particles, some of which provide 99.9% of the speed of light when accelerating around the collider. Obviously, this generates large amounts of data - only the LHC generates about 30 petabytes of information per year (Marr, CERN: Understanding the universe with Big Data, 2016).

Using reliability and simulation tools built into the Oracle Big Data Discovery platform, the CERN Openlab Team can associate breakdown conditions related to electricity consumption, power conversion, water use and cryogenic. CERN can determine which investment combinations in infrastructure and technical systems will yield the most beneficial results for physics research (Louie, 2016).

Facebook

Facebook's main business strategy is to understand who its users are and to show customized ads on the timeline of Facebook users by understanding their behavior, interests, and geographic locations.

Facebook collects astonishing amount of data. While it cannot sell data directly, it may sell its research results to stakeholders as long as it is anonymous. More importantly, in this case, Facebook's own advertising platform allows marketers to maximize their campaign activities indirectly by using big data analysis (Hyde, 2017).

Another innovative feature of Facebook is the face recognition function. The tool used for face recognition is DeepFace, a deep learning application which learns by recognizing people's faces in photos. This is an advanced image recognition tool because it recognizes whether a person in two different photos is the same (Bibrainia, 2019).

In recent years, Facebook has acquired Instagram and WhatsApp and boomed its data sources.

Lotus F1 Team

Velocity is one of the characteristics that define big data, and there are a few areas where velocity is more vital for than motorsports. In all categories of motorsports, teams and race organizers use more sophisticated, data-driven strategies than ever before.

Formula 1 has always used the most advanced technology. Telemeters have been used since the 1980s to transmit live data from cars to the pit lane technical team. Therefore, data analysis is very important for this field. Teams save time and money. Most importantly, it helps to reduce very important milliseconds during lap times.

The collected data is used to make real-time adjustments and match it to the drive's performance.

Big data has also been used for simulations recently. The importance of simulations has increased, especially with the International Automobile Federation (FIA) limiting the practical and test-driving time of drivers to level the playing field for teams; especially with lower budgets. The most important element of a simulation system that will perfectly represent the real world is that the data flow is accurate and reliable (Marr, Big Data in Practice, 2016).

In 2013, the Lotus F1 team replaced its data warehouse provider with a faster system that allowed them to transfer 2000 statistics per lap. They consider this change as the main reason for the improvement in the performance of the team's young pilot Marlon Stöckinger.

Formula 1 followers also produce a lot of data. For example, during the 2014 US Grand Prix, spectators sent about 2.5 terabytes of data to mobile networks with photos and tweets they posted on social media.

Nest

The Internet of Things (IoT) has been a popular concept for some time and has begun to bring results in recent years. As computers became smaller, more powerful and integrated with objects, almost everything has become digitally communicated with each other. The idea of smart home emerged with the spread of this technology.

Nest is a company which hit the headlines with the advent of smart home technology. Its products (smart thermostat, smoke detector, security camera, etc.) are in thousands of homes. In 2013, it was purchased by Google (Olson, 2014).

Nest thermostat monitors the users' behavior and "learns" the most efficient strategy to keep the home at the optimized temperature. In order to carry out an effective strategy, the system employs correct data with applicable algorithms.

According to Nest's reports, on average the products saved 10% to 12% on heating and 15% on cooling in 2016 (Nest, 2017).

Netflix

Today Netflix is a media-services provider and production company with over 150 million subscribers watching over 150 million hours of TV programs and movies in more than 190 countries every day.

Essentially, a short tour through the pages of Netflix; especially job postings, it is clear how much they attach importance to data and data analysis. From personalization analysis to messaging analysis, from content analysis to device analysis, almost every step is taken in consideration of data (Netflix, 2019). Although big data is used extensively in all Netflix activities, the core business is to predict what customers will enjoy watching. The most important infrastructure of recommendation system is big data analysis (Amatriain & Basilico, 2012).

The broadcasting story of *House of Cards* on Netflix is also the result of a big data analysis. Netflix took action to get the broadcasting rights of the series when the data center inferred from the customer data, which showed that the contents directed by David Fincher and performed by Kevin Spacey got high credit (Carr, 2013).

The company increases the number of subscribers every year by means of the "blockbuster" contents - based on data analytics - it produces continuously, such as *House of Cards*, *Narcos* and *Orange is the New Black*.

Royal Bank of Scotland

Recently, the Royal Bank of Scotland; one of the businesses which is conscious of the vital importance of data analysis; announced an investment of £ 100 million in data analysis technology and named its first initiative "personology" emphasizing a focus on customers rather than financial products. Afterwards, the concept was adopted as a business philosophy for a highly personalized integrated management throughout the organization (Marr, Big Data in Practice, 2016). This approach has resulted in significant improvements in the response and engagement of bank customers.

Spotify

Spotify, the largest on-request music provider, uses big data, artificial and machine learning algorithms to deliver personalized music experience (Rpark, 2018).

They unveiled the first music streaming analysis tool, also known as "Publishing Analytics". It provides music broadcasting companies with daily broadcast statistics for recordings such as data on songwriters and how many albums they've sold since their first album (Delgado, 2018).

Spotify offers algorithmically designed playlists, including music that the user already knows and music that the user will not be aware of. Because Spotify has a lot of data on users' listening habits, it can also create playlists based on different weather conditions (Rpark, 2018).

Twitter

Twitter, announced as a micro blogging platform in 2006, has become one of the most extensively used social networks today. Twitter provides insights into people's relationships with each other, their political stance, what they buy, where they eat; in short, almost every aspect of their lives. This platform is like gold mine for those who know how to take advantage.

By the year 2014, Twitter formed a global partnership with IBM; referring to their broad experience on data analytics; to make use of such a "gold mine" more effectively (IBM, 2014). In a nutshell, IBM creates value from the data Twitter collects when users tweet, hundreds of thousands of tweets are sent to IBM for real time analysis using the Firehose API. Other companies have access to Twitter data that are used to get their own data-based insights through IBM's tools.

Uber

Uber's whole business model is based on the massive working principle of big data: a person who has a car and wants to help someone who wants to go somewhere offers help.

Uber records and tracks data for each journey of its users and uses this information to identify the request, allocate resources, and determine fees. Uber has a large driver database in all cities where it operates, so that when a passenger requests a vehicle, he can instantly match it to the nearest driver.

They have developed their own algorithms that track traffic conditions and travel times in real time. Thus, prices can be adjusted accordingly if there is a change in the demand for the vehicle or if the journey takes longer due to traffic conditions. The company also applied for patents for this big data-based pricing method, which is called "Surge Pricing" (Uber, 2019).

By virtue of the company's Uber Pool service, users can share the cost of the journey by finding people traveling on similar trips at similar times.

Uber has data at the heart of every business it does. The Uber case points to the long-term development of a data-driven business model rather than short-term results.

UPS:

Probably the world's most extensive operations research project; ORION (On-Road Integrated Optimization and Navigation) was announced by UPS; which analyzes the real-time data coming from the vehicles of the fleet, including the directions, speeds, drive-train performances, etc. in order to reconfigure the drivers' pick-ups and drop-offs and eventually optimize the route of a huge transportation network. The company also works on a same project to optimize the efficiency of their aircraft flights (Davenport, 2014).

US Government

Managing the world's leading economic power and over 300 million inhabitants undoubtedly requires enormous effort and resources. The federal government is responsible for almost everything in the lives of citizens; including national security, economic security, health, enforcement of laws, disaster prevention, food production, education.

The Washington Post called Barack Obama the "Big Data President," who invested $ 200 million in data analysis and security to provide the public with as much data as possible (Scola, 2013). During this period, the US government initiated several data-driven strategies in a number of departments and departments, each related to its area of responsibility.

As education is becoming more and more online, institutions responsible for determining education policy can gain more insight into how the population learns and assess the level of education and skills among people in a particular geographic area. All of these allow for more efficient planning and resource allocation.

Social media analyzes in the field of health care are used by the Centers for Disease Control and Prevention (CDC) to monitor the spread of outbreaks and other public health threats.

In addition, the Ministry of Agriculture provides research and scientific analysis on agriculture and food production based on big data collected in fields and farms. Through genetic records, studies have been conducted to identify bulls; which fertilize the most milk-productive cows; resulted in significant increases in milk production throughout the country.

Similarly, CIA used predictive data algorithms in its work to fight against international and domestic terrorism and financial fraud.

US Women's Cycling Team

Sports and data analysis are very close. Sky Christopherson, the champion cyclist in the 35+ age category, worked with the 2012 US Women's Cycling Team. Using a range of advanced data collection and monitoring techniques, Christopherson recorded all areas affecting athletes' performance, including diet, sleep patterns, environment and training intensity. In this way, the patterns related to the performance of the athletes were determined and necessary arrangements were made in the training programs (Taylor, 2015).

Analyzes called "Individual Optimal Zones" led to very interesting results. For example, when the cyclist Jenny Reed slept at a low temperature the night before, it was understood that she performed much better in practice and was given a water-cooled bed to keep her body at a certain temperature during the night (Marr, Big Data in Practice, 2016). By dint of personalized interventions, the team won a silver medal at the Olympics.

Walmart

As being world's largest retailer; with more than 2 million employees and 20 thousand stores in 28 countries; it is not surprising that Walmart has already understood the value of data analysis.

Data analysts, who analyzed the data as a whole just before Hurricane Sandy hit the United States in 2004, found unexpected insights. Expected bad weather led to an increase in sales of strawberry Pop Tarts in some locations as well as sales of flashlight and emergency equipment. Since then, in 2015 Walmart has expanded its big data and analytics department, creating the largest private data cloud in the world to provide 2.5 petabytes of data processing per hour.

Walmart combined all data and retail work in its "Data Café". It's a place where the merchant teams and business leaders see all the data in real time and come up with real time solutions (Becker, 2015). This is seen as the key to improving the company's performance. The average time between detection and resolution of a problem is reduced from approximately two to three weeks to about 20 minutes owing to the Walmart Data Café system.

Another initiative is the Walmart Social Genome Project, which tracks public social media interviews and tries to predict which products people will buy based on these conversations (Marr, Big Data, Walmart And The Future Of Retail, 2015).

Xbox

The gaming industry makes use of big data to attract customers, make more money from ads, and optimize the gaming experience.

Microsoft and Xbox Live Platform use an algorithm called TrueSkill, which extends the Elo Rating system to a wider range of players for better game matches. TrueSkill has been used to rank and match players in many different games, from Halo 3 to Forza Motorsport 7 (Minka, 2016).

CONCLUSION

In today's world, which is proceeding its development and formation, technology hungrily continues to be an indispensable part of life. The widespread use of the internet and the exponential rise in the number of connected devices have led to the creation of another world beyond the world we live. This second world, which is called the digital world, has been intertwined with the real-life day by day.

With the digital world, the digitalization process has generated a massive data. One of the most important concepts that the digital world has brought to our lives in recent years, especially with Industry 4.0, is big data. Considering and applying big data analytics in many industries results in increase in capabilities of efficiency and decision making.

The main reason why big data has become so important and emphasized is the understanding of the importance of data created during the practices that are spread through the use of internet and similar technologies, as well as the services provided and rendered by various countries, communities and institutions. These organizations have realized that by processing big data, they can produce information that can be of great benefit. As a result, huge investments are made in big data.

Along with big data, major changes have happened not only in the field of technology, but also in our thinking and perception, research methods and many other areas. Institutions, organizations and individuals cannot be excluded from these changes.

This chapter emphasized the concept of big data and its characteristics, referred the studies carried out in the academy, mentioned the usage areas on the basis of sectors and gave examples of real-life applications on the basis of firms. Many other aspects-especially the future and outcomes of the use of big data could - and will - be discussed in both academy and industry over the short haul.

REFERENCES

Active Wizards. (2019). *Top 10 Data Science Use Cases in Telecom*. KDnuggets. Retrieved from https://www.kdnuggets.com/2019/02/top-10-data-science-use-cases-telecom.html

Ahmed, E., Yaqoob, I., Hashem, I. A., Khan, I., Ahmed, A. I., Imran, M., & Vasilakos, A. V. (2017). The role of big data analytics in Internet of Things. *Computer Networks*, *129*, 459–471. doi:10.1016/j. comnet.2017.06.013

A.K. (2018). *Popular Big Data Applications In Media And Entertainment Industry*. AeonLearning Pvt. Ltd. Retrieved from https://acadgild.com/blog/big-data-applications-in-media

Amatriain, X., & Basilico, J. (2012). *Netflix Recommendations: Beyond the 5 stars (Part 1)*. Netflix. Retrieved from https://medium.com/netflix-techblog/netflix-recommendations-beyond-the-5-stars-part-1-55838468f429

Amit. (2019). *Big data in the public sector: five ways the government is using data science*. AnalyticsJobs. Retrieved from https://www.analyticsjobs.in/big-data/five-ways-the-government-is-using-data-science/

Anderson, A. (2018). *This Is How Big Data Is Changing the Media & Entertainment Industry – Are You Ready?* Retrieved from http://www.netnewsledger.com/2018/07/10/this-is-how-big-data-is-changing-the-media-entertainment-industry-are-you-ready/

Babar, M., & Arif, F. (2017). Smart urban planning using Big Data analytics to contend with the. *Future Generation Computer Systems*, *77*, 65–76. doi:10.1016/j.future.2017.07.029

Babar, M., Arif, F., Jan, M. A., Tan, Z., & Khan, F. (2019). Urban data management system: Towards Big Data analytics for Internet of Things based smart urban environment using customized Hadoop. *Future Generation Computer Systems*, *96*, 398–409. doi:10.1016/j.future.2019.02.035

Babar, M., Rahman, A., Arif, F., & Jeon, G. (2018). Energy-harvesting based on internet of things and big data analytics for smart health monitoring. *Sustainable Computing: Informatics and Systems*, *20*, 155–164.

Badenhausen, K. (2019). *The World's Most Valuable Brands 2019: Apple On Top At $206 Billion*. Forbes. Retrieved from https://www.forbes.com/sites/kurtbadenhausen/2019/05/22/the-worlds-most-valuable-brands-2019-apple-on-top-at-206-billion/#42b7c38d37c2

Badger, E. (2015). WiFi, hot tubs and big data: How Airbnb determines the price of a home. *The Washington Post*. Retrieved from https://www.washingtonpost.com/news/wonk/wp/2015/08/27/wifi-hot-tubs-and-big-data-how-airbnb-determines-the-price-of-a-home/

Becker, D. (2015). *When Data Met Retail: A #lovedata story*. LinkedIn Corporation. Retrieved from https://www.linkedin.com/pulse/when-data-met-retail-lovedata-story-david-becker/

Bibrainia. (2019). *How Big Data Can Be Used in Facebook*. Bibrainia. Retrieved from https://www.bibrainia.com/how-facebook-is-using-big-data

Bodi, K. (2018). *10 big data use cases in manufacturing*. Actify Inc. Retrieved from https://www.actify.com/industry-topics/10-big-data-use-cases-manufacturing/

Campbell, M. (2015). *Apple, IBM to take partnership into education with app for teachers*. Quiller Media, Inc. Retrieved from https://appleinsider.com/articles/15/06/19/apple-ibm-to-take-partnership-into-education-with-predictive-modeling-app

Capgemini. (2018). *Big data potential to eradicate challenges in the manufacturing industry*. Capgemini. Retrieved from https://www.capgemini.com/2018/11/big-data-potential-to-eradicate-challenges-in-the-manufacturing-industry/#

Carr, D. (2013). *Giving Viewers What They Want*. The New York Times Company. Retrieved from https://www.nytimes.com/2013/02/25/business/media/for-house-of-cards-using-big-data-to-guarantee-its-popularity.html

Chapman, R. (2018). *7 Big Data Examples with Analytics & Applications in Real Life*. Retrieved from https://limeproxies.com/blog/big-data-examples-in-real-life/

Chen, M., Mao, S., & Liu, Y. (2014). Big Data: A Survey. *Mobile Networks and Applications*, *19*(2), 171–209. doi:10.100711036-013-0489-0

Consoli, R. (2018). *Using Big Data Analytics To Improve Production*. Advantage Business Marketing. Retrieved from https://www.manufacturing.net/article/2018/05/using-big-data-analytics-improve-production

Côrte-Real, N., Ruivo, P., & Oliveira, T. (in press). Leveraging internet of things and big data analytics initiatives in European and American firms: Is data quality a way to extract business value? *Information & Management*.

Cox, M., & Ellsworth, D. (1997). Application-Controlled Demand Paging for Out-of-Core Visualization. *Proceedings of the 8th IEEE Visualization '97 Conference*. Retrieved from https://www.evl.uic.edu/cavern/rg/20040525_renambot/Viz/parallel_volviz/paging_outofcore_viz97.pdf

Datafloq. (2019). *How Amazon Is Leveraging Big Data*. Datafloq. Retrieved from https://datafloq.com/read/amazon-leveraging-big-data/517

Davenport, T. H. (2014). *Big data at work*. Harvard Business Review Press. doi:10.15358/9783800648153

Delgado, R. (2018). *How big data has changed the music industry*. The Innovation Enterprise Ltd. Retrieved from https://channels.theinnovationenterprise.com/articles/how-big-data-has-changed-the-music-industry

Denning, P. (1990). Saving All the Bits. *American Scientist*, *78*, 402–405.

Desai, P. (2018). A survey on big data applications and challenges. *Proceedings of the 2nd International Conference on Inventive Communication and Computational Technologies (ICICCT 2018)*, 737-740. 10.1109/ICICCT.2018.8472999

Din, S., & Paul, A. (2019). Erratum to ''Smart health monitoring and management system:Toward autonomous wearable sensing for Internet of Things using big data analytics. *Future Generation Computer Systems*, *91*, 611–619. doi:10.1016/j.future.2017.12.059

Dumbill, E. (2012). *Volume, Velocity, Variety: What You Need to Know About Big Data*. O'Reilly Media. Retrieved from https://www.forbes.com/sites/oreillymedia/2012/01/19/volume-velocity-variety-what-you-need-to-know-about-big-data/#2314accd1b6d

Dumbill, E. (2012). *What is Big Data? Big Data Now*. Sebastopol, CA: O'Reilly Media, Inc.

El Alaoui, I., Gahi, Y., & Messoussi, R. (2019). Full Consideration of Big Data Characteristics in Sentiment Analysis Context. *2019 IEEE 4th International Conference on Cloud Computing and Big Data Analysis (ICCCBDA)*.

Elhoseny, M., Abdelaziz, A., Salama, A. S., Riad, A., Muhammad, K., & Sangaiah, A. K. (2018). A hybrid model of Internet of Things and cloud computing to manage big data in health services applications. *Future Generation Computer Systems*, *86*, 1383–1394. doi:10.1016/j.future.2018.03.005

Firouzi, F., Rahmani, A. M., Mankodiya, K., Badaroglu, M., Merrett, G., Wong, P., & Farahani, B. (2018). Internet-of-Things and big data for smarter healthcare: From device to architecture, applications and analytics. *Future Generation Computer Systems*, *78*, 583–586. doi:10.1016/j.future.2017.09.016

Ge, M., Bangui, H., & Buhnova, B. (2018). Big Data for Internet of Things: A Survey. *Future Generation Computer Systems*, *87*, 601–614. doi:10.1016/j.future.2018.04.053

Gu, F., Ma, B., Guo, J., Summers, P. A., & Hall, P. (2017). Internet of things and Big Data as potential solutions to the problems in waste electrical and electronic equipment management: An exploratory study. *Waste Management*, 434–448.

Hashem, I. A., Chang, V., Anuar, N. B., Adewole, K., Yaqoob, I., Gani, A., ... Chiroma, H. (2016). The role of big data in smart city. *International Journal of Information Management*, *36*(5), 748–758. doi:10.1016/j.ijinfomgt.2016.05.002

Hilbert, M. (2012). How to Measure "How Much Information"? Theoretical, Methodological, and Statistical Challenges for the Social Sciences. *International Journal of Communication*, *6*, 1042–1055.

Hussain, K., & Prieto, E. (2016). Big Data in the Finance and Insurance Sectors. In *New Horizons for a Data Driven Economy* (p. 209). Springer Open.

Hyde, E. (2017). *How big data is affecting social media metrics and Facebook ad strategies*. SmartData Collective. Retrieved from https://www.smartdatacollective.com/how-big-data-affecting-social-media-metrics-and-facebook-ad-strategies/

IBM. (2014). *Twitter and IBM Form Global Partnership to Transform Enterprise Decisions*. IBM. Retrieved from https://www.03.ibm.com/press/us/en/pressrelease/45265.wss

Ingram. (2017). *Four big data use cases in the public sector*. Ingram Micro. Retrieved from https://imaginenext.ingrammicro.com/data-center/four-big-data-use-cases-in-the-public-sector

Insight Lake. (2017). *Big Data Use Cases*. Insight Lake. Retrieved from http://www.insightlake.com/telecommunications.html

IntelliPaat. (2019). *7 Big Data Examples: Applications of Big Data in Real Life*. IntelliPaat. Retrieved from https://intellipaat.com/blog/7-big-data-examples-application-of-big-data-in-real-life/

Jan, B., Farman, H., Khan, M., Talha, M., & Din, I. (2019). Designing a Smart Transportation System: An Internet of Things and Big Data Approach. *IEEE Wireless Communications*, *26*(4), 73–79. doi:10.1109/MWC.2019.1800512

Jaradat, M., Jarrah, M., Bousselham, A., Jararweh, Y., & Al-Ayyoub, M. (2015). The Internet of Energy: Smart Sensor Networks and Big Data Management for Smart Grid. *Procedia Computer Science*, *56*, 592–597. doi:10.1016/j.procs.2015.07.250

Kale, V. (2017). *Big Data Computing. In Creating Smart Enterprises: Leveraging Cloud, Big Data, Web, Social Media, Mobile and IoT Technologies* (p. 174). Boca Raton, FL: CRC Press, Taylor & Francis Group. doi:10.1201/9781315152455

Kho, D. D., & Seungmin Lee, R. Y. (2018). Big Data Analytics for Processing Time Analysis in an IoT-enabled manufacturing Shop Floor. *Procedia Manufacturing*, *26*, 1411–1420. doi:10.1016/j.promfg.2018.07.107

Kumari, A., Tanwar, S., Tyagi, S., Kumar, N., Maasberg, M., & Choo, K.-K. R. (2018). Multimedia big data computing and Internet of Things applications: A taxonomy and process model. *Journal of Network and Computer Applications*, *124*, 169–195. doi:10.1016/j.jnca.2018.09.014

Kurtz, J., & Shockley, R. (2013). *Analytics: The real-world use of big data in manufacturing*. IBM Institute for Business Value.

Lebied, M. (2018). *12 Examples of Big Data Analytics In Healthcare That Can Save People*. datapine. Retrieved from The datapine Blog: https://www.datapine.com/blog/big-data-examples-in-healthcare/

Lebied, M. (2018). *The Impact of Big Data on The Retail Sector: Examples And Use-Cases*. datapine. Retrieved from The datapine Blog: https://www.datapine.com/blog/big-data-in-retail-examples/

Lesk, M. (1997). *How Much Information Is There In the World?* Retrieved from http://www.lesk.com/mlesk/ksg97/ksg.html

Lippel, H. (2015). Big Data in the Media and Entertainment Sectors. In *New Horizons for a Data Driven Economy* (p. 245). Springer Open. doi:10.1007/978-3-319-21569-3

Louie, S. (2016). *CERN Tests Data Exploration Using Big Data, Analytics, And The Cloud*. Forbes Media LLC. Retrieved from https://www.forbes.com/sites/oracle/2016/09/12/cern-tests-data-exploration-using-big-data-analytics-and-the-cloud/#61b78f465123

Madakam, S., Ramaswamy, R., & Tripathi, S. (2015). Internet of Things (IoT): A Literature Review. *Journal of Computer and Communications*, *3*(5), 164–173. doi:10.4236/jcc.2015.35021

Maropost. (2019). *5 Ways Big Data Plays a Major Role in the Media and Entertainment Industry*. Maropost. Retrieved from https://www.maropost.com/blog/5-ways-big-data-plays-a-major-role-in-the-media-and-entertainment-industry/

Marr, B. (2015a). *Big Data, Walmart And The Future Of Retail*. Linkedin Corporation. Retrieved from https://www.linkedin.com/pulse/big-data-walmart-future-retail-bernard-marr/

Marr, B. (2015b). *Big Data: A Game Changer In The Retail Sector*. Forbes Media LLC. Retrieved from https://www.forbes.com/sites/bernardmarr/2015/11/10/big-data-a-game-changer-in-the-retail-sector/#3caa67f29f37

Marr, B. (2015c). *Why We Need More Big Data Doctors*. SmartData Collective. Retrieved from http://www.smartdatacollective.com/why-we-need-more-big-data-doctors/

Marr, B. (2016a). *Big Data in Practice*. Wiley. doi:10.1002/9781119278825

Marr, B. (2016b). *CERN: Understanding the universe with Big Data*. 123 Internet Group. Retrieved from https://www.bernardmarr.com/default.asp?contentID=697

McDonald, C. (2017). *Big Data Opportunities for Telecommunications*. MapR Technologies. Retrieved from https://mapr.com/blog/big-data-opportunities-telecommunications/

Minka, T. (2016). *TrueSkill Ranking System*. Microsoft. Retrieved from https://www.microsoft.com/en-us/research/project/trueskill-ranking-system/

Munné, R. (2016). Big Data in the Public Sector. In *New Horizons for a Data Driven Economy* (p. 196). Springer Open. doi:10.1007/978-3-319-21569-3

Nest. (2017). *Real Savings*. Nest Labs. Retrieved from https://nest.com/thermostats/real-savings/

Netflix. (2019). *The Netflix Tech Blog*. Netflix. Retrieved from https://medium.com/netflix-techblog

Nobre, G. C., & Tavares, E. (2017). Scientific literature analysis on big data and internet of things applications on circular economy: A bibliometric study. *Scientometrics*, *111*(1), 463–492. doi:10.100711192-017-2281-6

Olson, P. (2014). *Nest Gives Google Its Next Big Data Play: Energy*. Forbes. Retrieved from https://www.forbes.com/sites/parmyolson/2014/01/13/nest-gives-google-its-next-big-data-play-energy/#1dc8b82720ff

Oracle. (2015). Improving Manufacturing Performance with Big Data Architect's Guide and Reference Architecture Introduction. *Oracle Enterprise Architecture Whitepaper*, 1. Retrieved from http://www.oracle.com/us/technologies/big-data/big-data-manufacturing-2511058.pdf

Oracle. (2015). Improving Media & Entertainment Performance with Big Data. *Oracle Enterprise Architecture Whitepapers*, 4. Retrieved from http://www.oracle.com/us/technologies/big-data/big-data-media-2398958.pdf

Oracle. (2018). *Big Data Use Cases*. Oracle. Retrieved from https://www.oracle.com/big-data/guide/big-data-use-cases.html

Özköse, H., Arı, E., & Gencer, C. (2015). Yesterday, Today and Tomorrow of Big Data. *Procedia: Social and Behavioral Sciences*, *195*, 1042–1050. doi:10.1016/j.sbspro.2015.06.147

Paiva, L. (2018). *The Future of Retail: How Big Data, AI, and IoT are Creating Change*. BairesDev. Retrieved from https://www.bairesdev.com/blog/the-future-of-retail/

Pickell, D. (2019). *6 Real-World Examples of Industries Using Big Data*. G2 Crowd. Retrieved from https://learn.g2.com/big-data-examples

Pool, I. (1983). Tracking the Flow of Information. *Science*, *221*(4611), 609–613. doi:10.1126cience.221.4611.609 PMID:17787717

Press, G. (2013). *A Very Short History Of Big Data*. Retrieved from https://www.forbes.com/sites/gilpress/2013/05/09/a-very-short-history-of-big-data/#4ee5e17c65a1

Quantzing. (2019). *How is Big Data Analytics Transforming the Media and Entertainment Landscape?* Retrieved from https://www.businesswire.com/news/home/20190718005037/en/Big-Data-Analytics-Transforming-Media-Entertainment-Landscape

Rathore, M. M., Ahmad, A., Paul, A., & Rho, S. (2016). Urban planning and building smart cities based on the Internet of Things using Big Data analytics. *Computer Networks*, *101*, 63–80. doi:10.1016/j.comnet.2015.12.023

Razin, E. (2015). *Big Buzz About Big Data: 5 Ways Big Data Is Changing Finance*. Retrieved from https://www.forbes.com/sites/elyrazin/2015/12/03/big-buzz-about-big-data-5-ways-big-data-is-changing-finance/#2872822c376a

Rehman, M. H., Yaqoob, I., Salah, K., Imran, M., Jayaraman, P. P., & Perera, C. (2019). The role of big data analytics in industrial Internet of Things. *Future Generation Computer Systems*, *99*, 247–259. doi:10.1016/j.future.2019.04.020

Rpark. (2018). *Spotify may know you better than you realize*. Harvard Business School Digital Initiative. Retrieved from https://digital.hbs.edu/platform-digit/submission/spotify-may-know-you-better-than-you-realize/#

Sarma, H., Borah, S., & Dutta, N. (2016). Advances in Communication, Cloud and Big Data. In *Proceedings of 2nd National Conference on CCB 2016*. Sikkim, India: Springer Nature Singapore. doi:10.1007/978-981-10-8911-4

Scola, N. (2013). *Obama, the 'big data' president*. The Washington Post. Retrieved from https://www.washingtonpost.com/opinions/obama-the-big-data-president/2013/06/14/1d71fe2e-d391-11e2-b05f-3ea3f0e7bb5a_story.html

Sharma, N., & Agarwal, M. (2018). Real-Time Big Data Analysis Architecture and Application. In *Data Science and Big Data Analytics* (p. 314). Singapore: Springer. doi:10.1007/978-981-10-7641-1

Smith, C. (2019). *150 Amazing Amazon Statistics, Facts and History*. Retrieved from https://expandedramblings.com/index.php/amazon-statistics/

Sun, Y., & Song, H., Jara, A. J., & Bie, R. (2016). Internet of Things and Big Data Analytics for Smart and Connected Communities. *IEEE Access: Practical Innovations, Open Solutions*, 4.

Taylor, T. (2015). *How the U.S. women's cycling team transformed itself with technology*. Sports Illustrated. Retrieved from https://www.si.com/edge/2015/05/14/personal-gold-documentary-us-womens-cycling-team

Titimus, P. M. (2016). *Big Data Analytics in the Higher Education: Need of the Future. In Advances in Communication, Cloud and Big Data* (p. 23). Springer Nature Singapore. doi:10.1007/978-981-10-8911-4

Turea, M. (2019). *Ultimate Guide To Big Data In Healthcare*. Retrieved from https://healthcareweekly.com/big-data-in-healthcare/

Uber. (2019). *How surge pricing works*. Uber Technologies, Inc. Retrieved from https://www.uber.com/us/en/drive/partner-app/how-surge-works/

Virmani, A. (2018). *How Big Data is Transforming Retail Industry*. Simplilearn Solutions. Retrieved from https://www.simplilearn.com/big-data-transforming-retail-industry-article

Yao, C., Wu, S., Liu, Z., & Li, P. (2019). A deep learning model for predicting chemical composition of gallstones with big data in medical Internet of Things. *Future Generation Computer Systems*, *94*, 140–147. doi:10.1016/j.future.2018.11.011

Zheng, X., Chen, W., Wang, P., Shen, D., Chen, S., Wang, X., & Yang, L. (2016). Big Data for Social Transportation. *IEEE Transactions on Intelligent Transportation Systems*, *17*(3), 620–630. doi:10.1109/TITS.2015.2480157

Zillner, S., Becker, T., Munne, R., Hussain, K., Rusitschka, S., Lippel, H., . . . Ojo, A. (2016). Big Data-Driven Innovation in Industrial Sectors. In *New Horizons for a Data Driven Economy* (p. 175). Springer Open. doi:10.1007/978-3-319-21569-3

Zugurovsky, M., & Zaychenko, Y. (2019). *Big Data: Conceptual Analysis and Applications*. Springer International Publishing. doi:10.1007/978-3-030-14298-8

ENDNOTE

[1] Rider, Fremont (1944); "The Scholar and the Future of the Research Library. A Problem and Its Solution."; New York: Hadham Press.

This research was previously published in Internet of Things (IoT) Applications for Enterprise Productivity; pages 185-218, copyright year 2020 by Business Science Reference (an imprint of IGI Global).

Chapter 40
A Service–Oriented Foundation for Big Data

Zhaohao Sun

https://orcid.org/0000-0003-0780-3271

Papua New Guinea University of Technology, Papua New Guinea

ABSTRACT

This paper provides a service-oriented foundation for big data. The foundation has two parts. Part 1 reveals 10 big characteristics of big data. Part 2 presents a service-oriented framework for big data. The framework has fundamental, technological, and socio-economic levels. The fundamental level has four big fundamental characteristics of big data: big volume, big velocity, big variety, and big veracity. The technological level consists of three big technological characteristics of big data: Big intelligence, big analytics, big infrastructure. The socioeconomic level has three big socioeconomic characteristics of big data: big service, big value, and big market. The article looks at each level of the proposed framework from a service-oriented perspective. The multi-level framework will help organizations and researchers understand how the 10 big characteristics relate to big opportunities, big challenges, and big impacts arising from big data. The proposed approach in this paper might facilitate the research and development of big data, big data analytics, business intelligence, and business analytics.

1. INTRODUCTION

Big data has become one of the most important frontiers for innovation, research and development in computing (Kumar B., 2015; McKinsey, 2014; Manyika, Chui, & Bughin, 2011) (Sun, Strang, & Li, 2018), industry and business (Chen & Zhang, 2014) (Sun Z., 2019). Big data has become a strategic asset for organizations, industries, enterprises, businesses, and individuals as well as national security. Big data has also been a key enabler of exploring business insights and economics of services. These have drawn an unprecedented interest in industries, universities, governments and organizations (Gartner, 2020) (Sun, Strang, & Li, 2018). Big data and its emerging technologies including big data analytics and intelligent analytics (Coronel & Morris, 2015; Tableau, 2020) have been not only making big changes in the way the business operate but also making traditional business analytics bring about new

DOI: 10.4018/978-1-6684-3662-2.ch040

big opportunities for academia and enterprises (Sun, Strang, & Yearwood, 2014; Manyika, Chui, & Bughin, 2011). Big data analytics and intelligent analytics has big market and investment opportunities (Sun Z., 2019). For example, International Data Corporation (IDC) forecasts that big data and business analytics (BDA) revenue will be $274.3 billion by 2022 with a five-year compound annual growth rate (CAGR) of 13.2% from 2018 to 2022 (IDC, 2019). However, some fundamental issues are still open for comprehending big data. For example:

- Why is big important for big data?
- What are the characteristics of big data?
- How do we understand the relationships among the characteristics of big data?

This article will address these three issues. It addresses the first issue taking into account a mathematical thinking. To address the second issue, different from the existing literature on big data (Borne, 2014; Gandomi & Haider, 2015; McAfee & Brynjolfsson, 2012), this article identifies and reveals 10 Bigs as the ten big characteristics of big data based on our early research (Sun, Strang, & Li, 2018). The 10 Bigs include big volume, big velocity, big variety, big veracity, big intelligence, big analytics, big infrastructure, big service, big value, and big market. Then this article presents a service-oriented framework through exploring the interrelationships among these 10 Bigs. This framework reveals that the 4 Bigs are fundamental characteristics of big data; another 3 Bigs are technological characteristics of big data; the remaining 3 Bigs are socioeconomic characteristics of big data.

The remainder of this article is organized as follows. Section 2 overviews the characteristics of big data from an evolutionary Perspective. Section 3 looks at why big is important in a big data world. Section 4 identifies and reveals 10 Bigs as the ten big characteristics of big data. Section 5 presents a service-oriented framework and looks at service providers, brokers and requestors for fundamental, technological, socioeconomic level of the framework respectively. The final sections discuss the related work, implications, and end this paper with some concluding remarks and future work.

2. CHARACTERISTICS OF BIG DATA: AN EVOLUTIONARY PERSPECTIVE

This section looks at the characteristics of big data from an evolutionary perspective.

The characteristics of big data have been scattered in a significant number of publications. From an evolutionary perspective, Doug Laney of the META Group (now Gartner) uses 3 Ds: data volume, data velocity, and data variety to represent the characteristics of data in e-commerce in 2001. These 3 Ds should be controlled in data management using novel techniques (Laney, 2001). Late these 3 Ds have been changed into 3 Vs (volume, velocity, and variety) which have been explained as three characteristics of big data (Tsai, Lai, Chao, & Vasilakos, 2015; McAfee & Brynjolfsson, 2012; Gandomi & Haider, 2015). These 3 Vs have been extended first to 4 Vs as four characteristics of big data by adding veracity (Sathi, 2013; IBM, 2015), and then to 5 Vs as five characteristics of big data (volume, variety, velocity, veracity, value) (DataCom, 2015; Wang, 2012), finally to 10 Vs by adding another 5 Vs: validity, variability, venue, vocabulary and vagueness (Borne, 2014).

With the development of big data as a computing, big data computing, more Vs might be proposed to extend these 10 Vs, because case based reasoning (CBR) researchers have extended the R model of CBR from 4 Rs, 5 Rs (Sun & Finnie, 2004; 2010) to 11 Rs (Bridge, 2005). To our knowledge, however, these studies are a kind of linear thinking, because, from 3 Vs we can have 4 Vs, and then, mathematically, we can have infinite Vs (at least a big number) for understanding data and big data, and the above-mentioned Vs are used to characterize data rather than big data. The importance of Big has been deeply minded in a big data world. In this sense, the inception of big data does not belong to Laney (2001), because he has not used the concept of big data at that time. Frankly speaking, the researchers prefer to use esoteric concept rather than popular word to represent what they have done in their research, "big" is not a word in any jargon. The existing literature on big data still prefers to Vs. The core of big data is "Big". Then incorporating "big" with data becomes more important for business, industry, and government. It is necessary to characterize "big" of the big data.

The above discussion motivates us to change 3 Ds (Laney, 2001) to 3 Bigs rather than 3 Vs (McAfee & Brynjolfsson, 2012) for big volume, big variety, big velocity as the three "big" characteristics of big data. Then, this article extends 3 Bigs to 10 Bigs to examine ten big characteristics of big data and their interrelationships, as shown in Figure 1. In Figure 1, level 1 illustrates what most researchers have done as discussed above, whereas level 2 illustrates what we delve into the following sections.

Figure 1. An evolutionary perspective to characteristics of big data

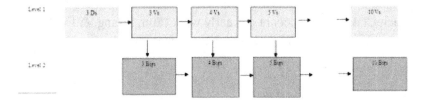

3. WHY BIG IS IMPORTANT IN A BIG DATA WORLD?

This section first reviews two definitions of big data. It then looks at why big is important in a big data world.

McKinsey defines big data as "the datasets whose size is beyond the ability of typical database software tools to capture, store, manage, and analyze". (Manyika, Chui, & Bughin, 2011). This definition makes McKinsey, a global consulting group, as one of the most important players usher big data in the important frontier for innovation, competition, and productivity.

Gartner, another global consulting company, defines big data as the "high-volume, high-velocity and high-variety information assets that demand cost-effective, innovative forms of information processing for enhanced insight and decision making" (Gartner, 2020). This definition has been most-frequently used in both business communities and academia communities for research and development of big data because of its marketing feature (Techopedia, 2018). This definition implies that big data is data with high-volume, high-velocity and high-variety, where 3 highs can be considered as three characteristics of data or big data. This infers that big data can be defined as data with n characteristics, where n is an integer. Currently, Gartner uses $n = 3$ (with 3 highs), IBM uses $n = 4$ (IBM, 2015). Borne uses $n = 10$ (with Vs) (Borne, 2014).

Now a fundamental question arises: Why big is important in a big data world? In what follows, we address this question.

A decade ago and even after 2012, researchers did not like "big" but use "large-scale" (Tsai, Lai, Chao, & Vasilakos, 2015), "complex" (Tsai, Lai, Chao, & Vasilakos, 2015; Pence, 2015), "massive amount of data, "humongous data" (Kumar, 2015)", "huge", "tremendous amount of data" (Hu & Kaabouch, 2014), "very large", "vast amounts of data" (Jovanovič, Štimec, & Vladušič, 2015), "large-scale data" (Halevy, Norvig, & Pereira, 2009), "enormous amount of data" (Kumar, 2015), "high volume" (Gartner, 2020) as well as Web-scale data to represent the size or volume of data. We can see "big" is the smallest metric, and least jargon related concept for measuring volume or size in terms of "large-scale", "complex", and "very large", etc., like the greatest common factor in elementary mathematics so that everyone can accept "big" and have a big space for thinking about "big volume" of data. It is only "big" of data that makes everyone draw big attention to data, big data, because everyone can engage in data and big data; everyone can understand "big" well based on his or her background knowledge although not everyone can imagine how big the 100 Zettabytes (ZB) of data is.

4. TEN BIG CHARACTERISTICS OF BIG DATA

This section identifies and examines ten big characteristics of big data with an example for each. They are illustrated in Figure 2. In what follows, this article does not go into big volume, big velocity, big variety and big veracity, taking into account our early work (Sun, Strang, & Li, 2018). Instead, it looks at big analytics, big intelligence, big infrastructure, big service, big value, and big market in some detail.

Figure 2. Ten big characteristics of big data

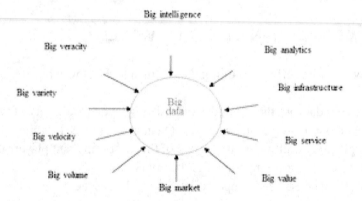

4.1. Big Analytics

Big analytics is a brief representation of big data analytics or big data based analytics or big data-driven analytics (Minelli, Chambers, & Dhiraj, 2013). Big analytics can be defined as the science and technology of collecting, organizing and analyzing big data to discover, visualize and interpret patterns, knowledge, and intelligence from big data for supporting decision making (Sun, Strang, & Li, 2018). Big analytics is an emerging science and technology involving the multidisciplinary state-of-art information and communication technology (ICT), mathematics, operations research (OR), machine learning (ML), data sciences, and decision sciences for big data (Sun, Strang, & Yearwood, 2014; Chen & Zhang, 2014). The main components of big analytics include big descriptive analytics, big predictive analytics and big prescriptive analytics (Minelli, Chambers, & Dhiraj, 2013) (Sun, Strang, & Li, 2018):

1. Big descriptive analytics is descriptive analytics for big data (Delena & Demirkanb, 2013; Kantardzic, 2011) (Sun, Strang, & Li, 2018). It addresses the problems such as what happened, and when, as well as what is happening. For example, web analytics for pay-per-click or email marketing data belongs to big data descriptive analytics (Cramer, 2014);
2. Big data predicative analytics is predicative analytics for big data (Sun, Strang, & Li, 2018), which focuses on forecasting trends by addressing the problems such as what will happen, what's going to happen, what is likely to happen and why it will happen (Delena & Demirkanb, 2013) (Howson, Richardson, Sallam, & Kronz, 2019). For example, big data predicative analytics can be used to predict where might be the next attack target of terrorists (Sun, Sun, & Strang, 2018);
3. Big data prescriptive analytics is prescriptive analytics for big data (Sun, Sun, & Strang, 2018), which addresses the problems such as what we should do, why we should do it, and what should happen with the best outcome under uncertainty (Minelli, Chambers, & Dhiraj, 2013, p. 5). For example, big data prescriptive analytics can be used to provide an optimal marketing strategy for an e-commerce company (Sun, Strang, & Li, 2018).

Big analytics or big data analytics (BA) has been drawing increasing attention in academia of computing, mathematics, operations research, decision sciences, business, management and industry of healthcare, medical science (Sun, Sun, & Strang, 2018). Big analytics including augmented analytics platforms represent mainstream market for data and analytics leaders in the areas of Business intelligence (BI), data science and machine learning (Howson, Richardson, Sallam, & Kronz, 2019).

4.2. Big Intelligence

Intelligence is not only a lasting topic for computer science, artificial intelligence (AI) and intelligence computing, but also an exciting topic for industries, organizations and businesses (Sun, Sun, & Strang, 2018). AI has facilitated the development of intelligent services, intelligent manufacturing, and intelligent systems (Russell & Norvig, 2010) and intelligent analytics (Sun Z., 2019). BI has promoted the improvement of competitiveness of business and marketing performance, and supported management decision making of organisations, and produced the billion level enterprises such as Google and Facebook (Sabherwal & Becerra-Fernandez, 2011). Generally speaking, big intelligence includes BI, organisational intelligence, marketing intelligence (Chen, Chiang, & Storey, 2012), mobile intelligence, cloud intelligence, social networking intelligence, networking intelligence, Web intelligence, and enterprise intelligence.

In the big data world, big intelligence particularly refers to big data intelligence and big data analytics intelligence (Sun & Wang, 2017). They are about automating intelligence in general and human intelligence for processing big data and optimizing data analytics in specific as well as human intelligence for business and management (Sun, Strang, & Li, 2018) (Sun & Finnie, 2004; 2010). Big data intelligence is big data-driven intelligence. It can be defined as a set of methods, technologies, systems and tools that can imitate the human intelligence related to big data management and processing (Sun, Strang, & Li, 2018). For example, intelligent methods for searching big data, visualizing knowledge discovery from big data belong to big data intelligence. Big data analytics intelligence (BAI) can be defined as a set of methods, systems and tools that can imitate the human intelligence related to big data analytics (Sun, Sun, & Strang, 2018).

Big intelligence has drawn increasing attention with the development of BI and big data analytics. Big intelligence can be developed as an important part of big data computing (Wang, 2012). Big analytics intelligence incorporating data analytics intelligence with big data intelligence has become most important part for enhancing BI and big intelligence (Sun, Sun, & Strang, 2018). Global free WIFI (Payton, 2015) is a big intelligence, because it meets the big expectation from billions of people (Sun, Sun, & Strang, 2018) (Sun, Strang, & Li, 2018).

4.3. Big Infrastructure

Infrastructure refers to structures, systems, and facilities serving a country, city, or area, including the services and facilities necessary for its economy to function (Wikipedia, 2020). Big infrastructure, abbreviated from big data infrastructure, refers to all the structures, technologies, systems, platforms, facilities, management, governance and control serving the big data management and processing in a country, city or beyond (Goes, 2014). Big data processing includes ingesting, storing, analyzing, modelling, mining big data, and discovering, visualizing, simulating, and reporting knowledge (Sathi, 2013). Currently, Apache Hadoop ecosystem has been considered as a part of big infrastructure for processing big data (Kumar, 2015; Goes, 2014). To some extent, big infrastructure is a decisive factor for the utility of big data with applications, reflecting the level of national big data research and development, just as traffic infrastructure and network infrastructure as the criteria for the standards of social advancement.

Although the price of the elements of computing machinery such as storage, memory, processing, bandwidth has been declining (McAfee & Brynjolfsson, 2012), big infrastructure is still a big characteristic to differentiate developing countries from developed ones. This is the reason why Chinese government launched big data infrastructure as a national development strategy in its 13th National Development Planning (2016-2020) (State Council, China, 2016).

The cloud infrastructure is a kind of big infrastructure (Erl, Mahmood, & Puttini, 2013). 5G wireless network infrastructure (for short, 5G) is also a big infrastructure in the big data world, facing fierce competition in the international communication and networking market. 5G revenue will nearly double between 2019 and 2020 and will reach $4.2 billion in 2020 (Goasduff, 2019).

4.4. Big Service

Services are playing a pivotal role in nations, organizations, businesses, individuals, service computing, and cloud computing (Erl, Mahmood, & Puttini, 2013). Web services have been changing people's work, life and thinking with the healthy development service-centered society (Sun & Yearwood, 20014). Big services are big data driven services or big data based services or big data as a service (Sun, Strang, & Li, 2018). The big in big service implicates that it can provide big data based services to at least hundreds of millions people, if not billions. For example, big data infrastructure services, cloud services, mobile services, big analytics services (Sun, Sun, & Strang, 2016), social networking services provided by Facebook and WeChat are examples of big services for billions of people in the world.

In the big data age, everyone is enjoying the big services in terms of living, studying, working, moving and socializing. For example, when one drives from one city to a corner of another city, the GPS navigation services can guide the car to arrive at the destination optimally and easily. The automation of driving (Vardi, 2016) based on big data will make everyone enjoy wonderful driving service from one place to a corner of another city easily, safely and optimally even if he can sleep in the car, enjoy the chat using WeChat (www.wechat.com) in the car, watch movies in the car, until his car arrives at the destination and tells him "You have reached your destination, my darling".

Big services, the web of services (Sun & Yearwood, 20014) and the Internet of services are interchangeably (Sun, Strang, & Li, 2018). The Internet of services (IoS) is a big service covering all the services on the Internet based on big data, as an important part of the Internet of things (IoT). For example, online storage service is a kind of big services (Huang, Smith, & Sun, 2014). Big services are an emerging frontier for innovations, competences and improving business performance of governments, organizations, and enterprises (Sun, Strang, & Li, 2018).

4.5. Big Value

Oracle introduced value as a defining characteristic of big data (Gandomi & Haider, 2015). Big value indicates the importance and context of the big data (Vajjhala, Strang, & Sun, 2015). It characterizes the big business value, ROI, and potential of big data to transform an organization to have more competitiveness in the global market (Borne, 2014) (Sun, Strang, & Li, 2018). Big data has extremely big business value for increasing productivity, efficiency and revenues, lowering costs and reducing risk in businesses and management (Chen & Zhang, 2014; Loshin, 2013) (Wang, 2012). For example, big data has brought big value for Microsoft, Amazon, Apple, Alphabet, and Facebook, as well as Alibaba and Tencent, and made them become the top 8 companies in the world, based on market cap (Desjardins, 2019). Big data also has big value for scientific breakthrough that has given and will give us a big number of opportunities to make great progresses in many fields. For example, many medical studies based on big data could find better solutions to cure chronic diseases like diabetes and hypertension (Minelli, Chambers, & Dhiraj, 2013). When writing this part, we are facing the coronavirus pandemic worldwide, how to use big data and intelligent analytics to fight coronavirus successfully is a desperate issue for medical scientists, computing developers and governments in the world (Shah & Shah, 2020). More generally, organizations are utilizing advanced analytics platform to gain big value from big data in order to grow faster than their competitors and seize new opportunities in the global market of big data and analytics (Kumara & al, 2015) (Howson, Richardson, Sallam, & Kronz, 2019). For example, Governments use big data analytics to gain insight into citizen activities and requirements (Koorn & al, 2015).

Big value also implies that big data brings big social value and big cultural value. The big social value means that big data has been revolutionizing the society in terms of working, living and thinking (Mayer-Schoenberger & Cukier, 2013). For example, learning heavily relies on teachings, books, libraries, schools, and so on in the past centuries whereas in the digital age, learning could be based on search online, online learning, learning as a search (LaaS), one can learn using LaaS whenever and wherever s/he is.

Big cultural value means that big data has significantly impacted the cultural activities of human beings. For example, Twitter, Facebook, and WeChat have made everyone know what happen at every corner of the globe instantly. They also make everyone share the different cultures globally due to semi-automated translation from one language to another through the Google translator.

4.6. Big Market

In the big data world, big market refers to big data driven market. Big market consists of markets of big data technologies, systems, tools and services. According to IDC's research, big data and business analytics (BDA) revenues will maintain a five-year compound annual growth rate (CAGR) of 13.2% throughout 2018-2022, and worldwide BDA revenue will be $274.3 billion By 2022 (Kumar M., 2019).

The big market of big data attracts the CEOs of big companies to make big decisions for developing big data and related technologies, systems, tools and services. For example, more and more executives put big data and advanced analytics as the strategic priorities in both strategy and spending in order to compete in the era of big data and advanced analytics (Howson, Richardson, Sallam, & Kronz, 2019) (Brown, Gandhi, & Herring, 2019).

Based on the above-examined ten (10) big characteristics of big data, the definition of big data provided by Gartner (2020) can be updated as "the information assets with 10 big characteristics that demand cost-effective, innovative forms of information processing for enhanced hindsight, insight, foresight and decision making, where 10 characteristics are big volume, big velocity, big variety, big veracity, big analytics, big intelligence, big infrastructure, big service, big value, and big market". These 10 big characteristics of big data form the foundation of big data as a service (Techopedia, 2018).

5. A SERVICE-ORIENTED FRAMEWORK OF BIG DATA WITH BIG CHARACTERISTICS

This section proposes a service-oriented framework based on the above mentioned 10 big characteristics of big data. It looks at each level of the proposed framework from a service-oriented perspective (Papazoglou & Georgakopoulos, 2003).

The service-oriented framework is illustrated in Figure 3. This framework covers the 10 Bigs along with their interrelationships to one another. The framework consists of three levels: a fundamental, technological, and socio-economical level. At the fundamental level, there are 4 Bigs: Big volume, big velocity, big variety, and big veracity (Sun, Strang, & Li, 2018). They are four fundamental characteristics of big data (Sun, Sun, & Strang, 2016).

Gartner's definition of big data, mentioned as above, can also be simplified as "big volume, big velocity, big variety, and big veracity data assets that demand cost-effective, innovative forms of information processing for enhanced insight and decision making" (Gartner, 2020). Here "bigs" have replaced the "highs" in the Gartner's definition. Integrating the above two definitions, this framework defines big data as a set of datasets, each of them satisfies that:

1. It has big volume, big velocity, big variety and big veracity;
2. It is beyond the ability of typical ICT systems or tools to capture, store, manage, and analyse;
3. It demands cost-effective, innovative technologies of data processing for enhanced insight and decision making.

This definition of big data covers the four fundamental characteristics of big data.

The main services providers on this level include data scientists, and cloud services providers including Amazon, Google, Facebook and Tableau (Howson, Sallam, & Richa, 2018). The main service

Figure 3. A service-oriented framework based on 10 Bigs

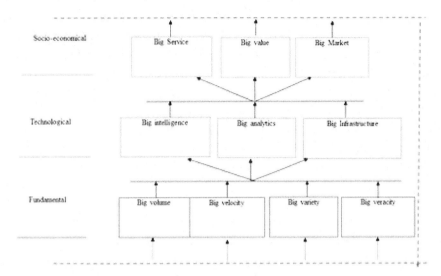

requestors on this level include everyone who can access the Internet. The main service brokers on this level include big consulting groups like McKinsey, Gartner and IDC as well as public media (Sun, Sun, & Strang, 2016) (Sun, Strang, & Li, 2018).

Computing scientists are working on big intelligence, big analytics, and big infrastructure to meet the challenges of big data with these four fundamental characteristics using ICT technologies, systems, and tools. This requires transforming from the fundamental level to the technological level.

At the technological level, there are three (3) Bigs: Big intelligence, big analytics, and big infrastructure. They are three technological characteristics of big data. These 3 Bigs provide smart solutions and technologies to meet the challenges arising from the 4 Bigs at the fundamental level. The smart solutions and technologies include MapReduce, NoSQL (Not only SQL) technology, MPP (Massively Parallel Processing), In-Memory database technologies (Bakshi, 2014; Tableau, 2020), augmented analytics (Howson, Sallam, & Richa, 2018), and intelligent analytics (Sun Z., 2019), to name a few. Apache Spark is a popular big data analytics platform for a number of enterprises (Tableau, 2020; Reddy, 2014). Spark provides dramatically increased large-scale data processing compared to Hadoop, and a NoSQL database for big data management (Coronel & Morris, 2015; Reddy, 2014). Apache Spark has provided Goldman Sachs with excellent big data analytics services (Tableau, 2020).

The main service providers on this level include Google, Amazon, Tableau (Tableau, 2020; Chen & Zhang, 2014), Microsoft and Salesforce (Howson, Richardson, Sallam, & Kronz, 2019) and other digital technology-driven companies and computing scientists. Big analytics service providers include developers, vendors, systems or software and other intermediaries that can provide big analytics services (Sun, Sun, & Strang, 2018). For example, Tableau as a software developer has been provisioning decentralized analytics and agile, centralized BI services (Tableau, 2020) (Howson, Richardson, Sallam, & Kronz, 2019). Amazon, Google and Microsoft, and Baidu are examples of big analytics services providers on the cloud (Sun, Strang, & Li, 2018).

The main service requestors on this level include everyone who can access the Internet. Big analytics service requestors include organizations, governments and all level business decision makers such as CEOs, CIOs and CFOs as well as managers. More generally, big analytics service requestors include people who like to acquire information based on analytical reports provided by big data analytics service provider (Sun, Strang, & Yearwood, 2014). Therefore, a person with smartphone receiving analytics services such as GPS information and sleeping analytics is also a big data analytics service requestor (Delena & Demirkanb, 2013) (Sun, Strang, & Li, 2018).

The main service brokers on this level are all the entities that facilitate the development of big intelligence, big analytics and big infrastructure, which include popular presses, traditional media and social media, consulting companies, scholars and university students, and so on (Sun, Strang, & Yearwood, 2014). Big consulting groups like McKinsey, Gartner and IDC as well as all the big data intermediaries (Mayer-Schoenberger & Cukier, 2013) have played an important role as brokers on this level (Sun, Strang, & Li, 2018).

At the socioeconomic level, there are 3 Bigs: Big service, big value, and big market. They are three big socioeconomic characteristics of big data. The socioeconomic consequence of dramatic development of big intelligence, big analytics and big infrastructure brings about big service, big value (Manyika, Chui, & Bughin, 2011), and big market (IDC, 2015; Tableau, 2020) to the society in a big data world. Clearly, big service, big value, and big market are interdependent on and complementary to each other closely. Big value from big data brings big market (IDC, 2015) (Kumar M., 2019), big market from big data brings about big services and big services bring about big value and big market, vice versa. All these statements have been proved and will be justified repeatedly in the big data world (McAfee & Brynjolfsson, 2012) (Manyika, Chui, & Bughin, 2011) (Minelli, Chambers, & Dhiraj, 2013) (Kumar M., 2019). The main service providers on this level include big global industries such as manufacturing, healthcare, finance and insurance, social networking and all the companies related to Industry 4.0 (GTAI, 2014), China Manufacturing 2025 (State Council, China, 2016) and so on. The main service requestors on this level include everyone in the big data age. The main service brokers on this level include big consulting groups like McKinsey, Gartner and IDC and public media as well as the big data intermediaries (Mayer-Schoenberger & Cukier, 2013) (Sun, Strang, & Li, 2018).

It should be noted that the arrows with dash line represent that big service, big value and big market will bring big impacts on the 4 big fundamental characteristics of big data at the bottom level (Sun, Strang, & Li, 2018). For example, it will increase the big volume of data from PB level to ZB level with big pace. It will improve the big velocity of big data in the cloud. It leads to bigger variety and veracity of big data. One the other side, the arrows with dash line and other arrows form a cycle from and to big volume, big velocity, big variety and big veracity via big service, big value and big market. This cycle reflects the close interrelationships among the 10 big characteristics of big data.

6. DISCUSSION AND IMPLICATIONS

We have mentioned a number of scholarly researches on big data and its characteristics. In what follows, we will focus on related work and discussion on characteristics of big data. We also look at theoretical, technical and social implications of this research and future research directions.

6.1. Discussion

Data volume, variety and velocity were not introduced as the three characteristics of big data in 2001 but as a part of data management for e-commerce (Laney, 2001). This implies that new characteristics of big data should be introduced in order to reflect the fast development of data since then. This has motivated the authors to delve into 10 big characteristics (10 Bigs) of big data. The introduction of 10 Bigs of big data has also been motivated by Table 1.

In Table 1, Google Scholar is used to search each of 10 Bigs, and the researched results are listed in each cell of the second column with parentheses. For example, there are about 26,400 results from searching for "big market", and about 18,600 results from searching for "big value" (on 7-8 April 2020). This means that 1. The 10 bigs for revealing big characteristics of big data are reasonable. 2. "big veracity" is the least popular, whereas big volume, big service, big value and big market are the most popular term in a big data world. This basically conforms to the current state of art research and development of big data.

Table 1. Backgrounds of 10 big characteristics of big data based on Google Scholar search

No.	10 Bigs of Big Data (Google scholar x)	Remarks	References/Sources
1	Big volume (16,500)	Gartner uses high volume. There are no universal benchmarks for Big volume.	(Laney, 2001), (Manyika, Chui, & Bughin, 2011), (Tsai, Lai, Chao, & Vasilakos, 2015), (Gandomi & Haider, 2015), (Gartner, 2020)
2	Big velocity (1,080)	Gartner uses high velocity.	(Laney, 2001), (Manyika, Chui, & Bughin, 2011), (Gandomi & Haider, 2015), (Gartner, 2020), (Tsai, Lai, Chao, & Vasilakos, 2015)
3	Big variety (13,800)	Gartner uses high variety.	(Laney, 2001), (Manyika, Chui, & Bughin, 2011), (Gandomi & Haider, 2015), (Gartner, 2020), (Tsai, Lai, Chao, & Vasilakos, 2015)
4	Big veracity (31)	IBM uses veracity	(IBM, 2015), (Sathi, 2013), (Gandomi & Haider, 2015)
5	Big intelligence (292)	Bifet states that big data needs big intelligence	(Sun, Sun, & Strang, 2016) (Bifet, 2013) (Sun, Strang, & Li, 2018)
6	Big analytics (1,720)	Minelli et al uses big analytics for big data analytics	(Sun, Sun, & Strang, 2016), (Minelli, Chambers, & Dhiraj, 2013) (Holsapple, Lee-Post, & Pakath, 2014), (Chen, Chiang, & Storey, 2012), (Sun, Strang, & Li, 2018)
7	Big Infrastructure (4,400)	Kumar and Goes discuss big infrastructure. China is expediting the development of national big infrastructure	(Kumar, 2015; Goes, 2014; State Council, China, 2016), (Sun, Strang, & Li, 2018)
8	Big Service (2,480)	Sun uses big services for big data, service and intelligence	(Sun & Yearwood, 20014); (Sun, Strang, & Li, 2018)
9	Big value (18,600)	big data has big value	(Manyika, Chui, & Bughin, 2011); (Borne, 2014), (Gandomi & Haider, 2015), (Sun, Strang, & Li, 2018)
10	Big market (26,400)	IDC implies that big market arising from big data	(IDC, 2015), (Manyika, Chui, & Bughin, 2011), (Sun, Strang, & Li, 2018)

Borne (2014) extends well-known 5 Vs (McAfee & Brynjolfsson, 2012; IBM, 2015; Gandomi & Haider, 2015) to 10 Vs of big data: volume, variety, velocity, veracity, value, validity, variability, venue, vocabulary and vagueness. However, he emphasized the 10 Vs as ten challenges of big data, and did not examine the interrelationships among these mentioned Vs. This article identifies and reveals the 10 Bigs as 10 big characteristics of big data and discusses their interrelationships through three levels: fundamental, technological, socio-economic level. It looks at each level from a service-oriented perspective by providing service providers, brokers and requestors to it (Papazoglou & Georgakopoulos, 2003).

The 10 Bigs have not yet been wholly addressed although each of them have mentioned in literature (see Table 1), for example, at the time of writing, big infrastructure, big service, big market, and big intelligence have not been formally introduced in the community of big data. To our knowledge, we are the first authors to identify these 10 Bigs as the big ten characteristics of big data (Sun, Strang, & Li, 2018).

Different from the 10 Vs of Borne (2014), we merge vagueness into veracity, because vagueness is related to uncertainty, ambiguity, incompleteness and fuzziness (Zadeh, 1965). The big veracity of big data aims to eliminate the vagueness using big data technology. Similarly, validity related to data quality, governance of data (Borne, 2014) can also be merged to veracity. Venue and variability of data (Borne, 2014) have been merged into big variety. Further, we do not use some of other Vs mentioned by (Borne, 2014), even if some Vs can be considered as characteristics of big data, but they are not big characteristics of big data, for example, vocabulary mentioned in (Borne, 2014) describing the data's structure, syntax, content, and provenance is a basic concept, data vocabulary, in database systems (Coronel & Morris, 2015).

If one likes to put more Bigs to characterize big data, then big variability and big complexity are two additional big characteristics, because SAS has introduced variability and complexity as defining attributes of big data (Gandomi & Haider, 2015). Further, big opportunity (Jovanovič, Štimec, & Vladušič, 2015), big challenge (Tableau, 2020; Mayer-Schoenberger & Cukier, 2013; Chen & Zhang, 2014) and big impact (Mayer-Schoenberger & Cukier, 2013) are also good choices for addition, because all these three have been closely associated with the discussion of big data and their research and development, although we have not put them into the 10 Bigs (Sun, Strang, & Li, 2018). Big data brings forth big challenges for our thinking, work, life, industry and society (Minelli, Chambers, & Dhiraj, 2013) and technologies (Chen & Zhang, 2014). Big data brings about big challenges to strategic decision making and organizational intelligence (Morabito, 2015). Big data also brings about new challenges to data quality management (Sathi, 2013), taking into account control over the management of external data.

Big Data as a Service (BDaaS) has drawn increasing attention in the academia and industries. For example, Xinhua, et al, define BDaaS, and propose a user experience-oriented BDaaS architecture (Xinhua & Han, 2013). This architecture supports for unstructured data and provides a wide variety of services such as analysis and visualization services, different from the existing data services architectures. Swami and Sahoo propose a service delivery model for BDaaS and claims that their model achieves quicker deployment than other models (Swami & Sahoo, 2016). To our knowledge, there are no research into DBaaS deeply. However, a service-oriented framework of big data proposed in this research is the first attempt to delve into BDaaS, which emphasizes that BDaaS will play an central role in big intelligence and big market, and big analytics as a service, big intelligence as a service, big infrastructure as a service will play a significant role in the age of big data and big data analytics taking into account service providers, brokers, and requestors at fundamental, technological and socio-economic level, discussed in Section 5.

6.2. Theoretical, Technical and Managerial Implications

There are at least theoretical, technological and industrial applications of this research. The theoretical implication of this research is that ten big characteristics of big data will provide a theoretical foundation for big data with applications. For example, the definition of big data proposed by Gartner (2020) has been updated in this research based on the mentioned big characteristics. It provides a novel way for understanding big data with applications.

The technical implication of this research is that the proposed service-oriented framework of big data can attract more researchers and practitioners to undertake the research and development of systems and applications based the principle of big data as a service for various business services, public services and social services. The proposed approach in this paper might facilitate research and development of big data, big data analytics, business intelligence, and business analytics.

The industry implication of this research is that the proposed 10 bigs and proposed service-oriented framework of big data can help development of big data industry including big service industry, big intelligence industry and big market industry to gain big business value in the near future. It can also facilitate the 10 bigs of big data and proposed service-oriented framework of big data for supporting decision making and intelligent management of organizations and businesses. The proposed service-oriented framework of big data will help organizations and researchers better understand how 10 Bigs relate to big opportunities, big challenges and big impacts arising from big data.

6.3. Limitations and Future Research Directions

There are at least three limitations of this research. The first limitation of this research is that it should use more different research methods to verify the soundness of the proposed 10 Bigs as ten characteristics of big data. The second limitation of this research is that it should consider the relationships among the providers and requestors not only on each of the mentioned three levels, but also between levels, for example, from level 1 to level 2 or from level 2 to level 3, or reversely. The third limitation of this research is that it should consider implementation issues of service-oriented framework for big data.

Therefore, three important future directions from this research are as follows. The first future research direction is to use more different methods to analyse the ten characteristics of big data with real-world applications and use these ten big characteristics as the elements of big data to develop big data systems, intelligent analytics systems and then provide big analytics as a service and big intelligence as a service for individuals and organizations. The second future research direction is to delve into the relationships among the providers and requestors mentioned in the service-oriented framework for big data. The third future research direction is to present an extended service-oriented framework for big data through reviewing more technologies of AI, big data, and data science.

7. CONCLUSION

The core of big data is "big". How to understand "big" becomes a fundamental issue for research and development of big data with applications. It is critical for developing big data as a computing, an industry and a society.

There are at least two main contributions of this research. The first is a theoretical contribution, which provides a service-oriented foundation for big data. This can also be considered as a unified foundation of big data as a service. It identifies and reveals the 10 big characteristics of big data and discusses their interrelationships through three levels: fundamental, technological, socio-economic level. The second is a practical contribution, which proposes a service-oriented framework of big data as a realization of big data as a service. It looks at each level from a service-oriented perspective by looking at service providers, brokers and requestors to it.

The research demonstrates that the proposed 10 Bigs of big data cover the fundamental, technological, and socio-economic characteristics of big data. The 10 Bigs have basically covered the research and development of big data and its social impacts on society, economy, and human being's work and life based on the literature review. The research also discusses the interrelationships among these 10 Bigs as a part of the service-oriented framework. The benefit of this service-oriented foundation is its novel 10 Bigs of big data for researchers and practitioners to improve their comprehending of big data. Another benefit is its service-oriented framework for researchers and practitioners to explore big opportunities and challenges at fundamental and technological levels and for organisations and businessmen to meet the big socioeconomic impacts at the socio-economic level of the framework.

10 Bigs of big data have been challenging existing sciences, technologies, methods and techniques in many fields. Big data has become a hot research area spanning the fields of computer science to that of engineering, applied mathematics, optimization, healthcare, business, government, and telecommunications (McAfee & Brynjolfsson, 2012) (Sun Z., 2019). This article takes an important step toward building a service-oriented foundation not only for big data but also for big data as a computing, science, and technology as well as for the development of big data as an industry and economy.

In the future work, besides what we mentioned in the future research directions, we will use the 10 Bigs as 10 elements of big data to examine the impacts of big data, big analytics, and big intelligence on business, management, marketing, industry and governance as well as society. We will also explore the applications of the service-oriented framework in cloud services, and the Internet of things as well as the Internet of services through providing real-world cases. We will also look at big intelligence-driven approach for big data management and processing.

ACKNOWLEDGMENT

The authors would like to thank the anonymous reviewers for their valuable suggestions and erudite comments on the paper.

REFERENCES

Bakshi, K. (2014). Technologies for Big Data. In W.-C. Hu (Ed.), Big Data Management, Technologies, and Applications (pp. 1-22). IGI-Global. doi:10.4018/978-1-4666-4699-5.ch001

Bifet, A. (2013). Mining Big Data in Real Time. *Informatica (Vilnius)*, *37*, 15–20.

Borne, K. (2014, April). *Top 10 Big Data Challenges – A Serious Look at 10 Big Data V's.* Retrieved from https://www.mapr.com/blog/top-10-big-data-challenges-%E2%80%93-serious-look-10-big-data-v%E2%80%99s

Bridge, D. (2005). The Virtue of Reward: Performance, Reinforcement and Discovery: Invited talk. *International Conference on Case-Based Reasoning (ICCBR).*

Brown, S., Gandhi, D., & Herring, L. (2019, 9). *The analytics academy: Bridging the gap between human and artificial intelligence.* Retrieved 4 8, 2020, from McKinsey: https://www.mckinsey.com/business-functions/mckinsey-analytics/our-insights/the-analytics-academy-bridging-the-gap-between-human-and-artificial-intelligence

Chen, C. P., & Zhang, C.-Y. (2014). Data-intensive applications, challenges, techniques and technologies: A survey on Big Data. *Information Sciences, 275,* 314–347. doi:10.1016/j.ins.2014.01.015

Chen, H., Chiang, R., & Storey, V. (2012, December). Business intelligence and analytics: From big data to big imppact. *Management Information Systems Quarterly, 36*(4), 1165–1188. doi:10.2307/41703503

Coronel, C., & Morris, S. (2015). *Database Systems: Design, Implementation, and Management* (11th ed.). Cengage Learning.

Cramer, C. (2014, May 19). *How Descriptive Analytics Are Changing Marketing.* Retrieved 7 6, 2015, from http://www.miprofs.com/wp/descriptive-analytics-changing-marketing/

DataCom. (2015). *DataCom 2015 International Conference on Big Data Intelligence and Computing.* Retrieved from WikiCFP: http://www.wikicfp.com/cfp/servlet/event.showcfp?eventid=46304&copyownerid=22598

Delena, D., & Demirkanb, H. (2013). Data, information and analytics as services. *Decision Support Systems, 55*(1), 359–363. doi:10.1016/j.dss.2012.05.044

Desjardins, J. (2019). *A Visual History of the Largest Companies by Market Cap (1999-Today).* Retrieved 4 8, 2020, from Visual Capitalist: https://www.visualcapitalist.com/a-visual-history-of-the-largest-companies-by-market-cap-1999-today/

Erl, T., Mahmood, Z., & Puttini, R. (2013). *Cloud Computing: Concepts, Technology & Architecture.* Pearson.

Gandomi, A., & Haider, M. (2015). Beyond the hype: Big data concepts, methods, and analytics. *International Journal of Information Management, 35*(2), 137–144. doi:10.1016/j.ijinfomgt.2014.10.007

Gartner. (2020). *Big data.* Retrieved from Gartner IT Glossary: https://www.gartner.com/en/information-technology/glossary/big-data

Goasduff, L. (2019). *Gartner Forecasts Worldwide 5G Network Infrastructure Revenue to Reach $4.2 Billion in 2020.* Retrieved April 8, 2020, from Gartner: https://www.gartner.com/en/newsroom/press-releases/2019-08-22-gartner-forecasts-worldwide-5g-network-infrastructure

Goes, P. B. (2014). Big Data and IS Research. *Management Information Systems Quarterly, 38*(3).

GTAI. (2014). *Industrie 4.0 Smart Manufacturing for the Future.* Retrieved 8 13, 2016, from Germany Trade & Invest: https://www.gtai.de/GTAI/Content/EN/Invest/_SharedDocs/Downloads/GTAI/Brochures/Industries/industrie4.0-smart-manufacturing-for-the-future-en.pdf

Halevy, A., Norvig, P., & Pereira, F. (2009). The Unreasonable Effectiveness of Data. *IEEE Intelligent Systems, 24*(May), 8–12. doi:10.1109/MIS.2009.36

Holsapple, C., Lee-Post, A., & Pakath, R. (2014). A unified foundation for business analytics. *Decision Support Systems, 64*, 130–141. doi:10.1016/j.dss.2014.05.013

Howson, C., Richardson, J., Sallam, R., & Kronz, A. (2019). *Magic Quadrant for Analytics and Business Intelligence Platforms.* Retrieved 7 7, 2019, from Gartner: https://cadran-analytics.nl/wp-content/uploads/2019/02/2019-Gartner-Magic-Quadrant-for-Analytics-and-Business-Intelligence-Platforms.pdf

Howson, C., Sallam, R. L., & Richa, J. L. (2018, Feb 26). *Magic Quadrant for Analytics and Business Intelligence Platforms.* Retrieved Aug 16, 2018, from Gartner: www.gartner.com

Hu, W. C., & Kaabouch, N. (2014). *Big data management, technologies, and applications.* IGI Global. doi:10.4018/978-1-4666-4699-5

Huang, C., Smith, P., & Sun, Z. (2014). Securing network for cloud services. In Z. Sun, & J. Yearwood (Eds.), Demand Driven Wen Services. IGI-Global.

IBM. (2015). *The Four V's of Big Data.* Retrieved from IBM: https://www.ibmbigdatahub.com/infographic/four-vs-bigdata

IDC. (2015). *Big Data & Analytics.* Retrieved 3 28, 2020, from https://www.idc.com/prodserv/4Pillars/bigdata

IDC. (2019). *IDC Forecasts Revenues for Big Data and Business Analytics Solutions will Reach $189.1 Billion This Year with Double-Digit Annual Growth Through 2022.* Retrieved 1 23, 2020, from IDC: https://www.idc.com/getdoc.jsp?containerId=prUS44998419

Jovanovič, U., Štimec, A., Vladušič, D., Papa, G., & Šilc, J. (2015). Big data analytics: A critical review and some future directions. *International Journal of Business Intelligence and Data Mining, 10*(4), 337–355. doi:10.1504/IJBIDM.2015.072211

Kantardzic, M. (2011). *Data Mining: Concepts, Models, Methods, and Algorithms.* Wiley & IEEE Press. doi:10.1002/9781118029145

Koorn, R., & al, e. (2015). Big Data Analytics & Privacy: How To Resolve This Paradox? *Compact, 4*, 1–10.

Kumar, B. (2015). An encyclopedic overview of 'big data' analytics. *International Journal of Applied Engineering Research, 10*(3), 5681–5705.

Kumar, M. (2019). *IDC Forecasts Revenues for Big Data and Business Analytics Solutions.* Retrieved 4 7, 2020, from IDC: https://www.idc.com/getdoc.jsp?containerId=prUS44998419

Kumara, B. T. (2015). Ontology-Based Workflow Generation for Intelligent Big Data Analytics. In *2015 IEEE International Conference on Web Services, ICWS 2015, 27 June 2015 to 2 July* (pp. 495-502). New York: IEEE. 10.1109/ICWS.2015.72

Laney, D. (2001). *3D data management: controlling data volume, velocity, and variety, META Group, Tech. Rep.* Retrieved 10 27, 2015, from http://blogs.gartner.com/doug-laney/files/2012/01/ad949-3D-Data-Management-Controlling-Data-Volume-Velocity-and-Variety.pdf

Loshin, D. (2013). *Big Data Analytics: From Strategic Planning to Enterprise Integration woth Tools, Techniques, NoSQL and Graph.* Elsevier.

Manyika, J., Chui, M., & Bughin, J. E. (2011, May). *Big data: The next frontier for innovation, competition, and productivity.* Retrieved from McKinsey Global Institute: https://www.mckinsey.com/business-functions/business-technology/our-insights/big-data-the-next-frontier-for-innovation

Mayer-Schoenberger, V., & Cukier, K. (2013). *Big Data: A Revolution that Will Transform How We Live, Work, and Think.* Houghton Mifflin Harcourt Publishing Company.

McAfee, A., & Brynjolfsson, E. (2012). Big data: The management revolution. *Harvard Business Review*, 61–68.

McKinsey. (2014). *The digital tipping point: McKinsey Global Survey results.* Retrieved 7 1, 2014, from Insights & Publications: https://pdfslide.net/documents/the-digital-tipping-point-mckinsey-global-survey-results.html

Minelli, M., Chambers, M., & Dhiraj, A. (2013). *Big Data, Big Analytics: Emerging Business Intelligence and Analytic Trends for Today's Businesses* (Chinese Edition 2014). Wiley & Sons. doi:10.1002/9781118562260

Morabito, V. (2015). *Big Data and Analytics: Strategic and Organizational Impacts.* Springer. doi:10.1007/978-3-319-10665-6

Papazoglou, M. P., & Georgakopoulos, D. (2003). Service-orented computing. *Communications of the ACM, 46*(10), 25–28. doi:10.1145/944217.944233

Parker, S., & Hira, A. T. (2015). *Australia Reaches a Tipping Point for Big Data Adoption, Says IDC Australia.* Retrieved from IDC: https://www.idc.com/getdoc.jsp?containerId=prAU25707715

Payton, M. (2015). *Google wants to bring free wifi to the world and its starting now.* Retrieved 8 12, 2016, from Metro.co.uk: https://metro.co.uk/2015/06/25/google-wants-to-bring-free-wifi-to-the-world-and-its-starting-now-5265352/

Pence, H. E. (2015). What is big data and why is it important? *Journal of Educational Technology Systems, 43*(2), 159–171. doi:10.2190/ET.43.2.d

Reddy, C. K. (2014). A survey of platforms for big data analytics. *Journal of Big Data (Springer), 1*(8), 1–20.

Russell, S., & Norvig, P. (2010). *Artificial Intelligence: A Modern Approach* (3rd ed.). Prentice Hall.

Sabherwal, R., & Becerra-Fernandez, I. (2011). *Business Intelligence: Practices, Technologies, and Management*. Wiley & Sons.

Sathi, A. (2013). Big data analytics: Disruptive technologies for changing the game. Boise, ID: MC Press, IBM Corporation.

Shah, J., & Shah, N. (2020, April 6). Fighting Coronavirus with Big Data. *Harvard Business Review*.

State Council China. (2016). *Made in China 2025*. Retrieved 8 13, 2016, from https://baike.baidu.com/item/%E4%B8%AD%E5%9B%BD%E5%88%B6%E9%80%A02025

Sun, Z. (2019). *Managerial Perspectives on Intelligent Big Data Analytics*. IGI-Global. doi:10.4018/978-1-5225-7277-0

Sun, Z., & Finnie, G. (2010). Intelligent Techniques in E-Commerce: A Case-based Reasoning Perspective. Berlin: Springer-Verlag.

Sun, Z., Strang, K., & Li, R. (2018). Big data with ten big characteristics. In *Proceedings of 2018 The 2nd Intl Conf. on Big Data Research (ICBDR 2018)* (pp. 56-61). Weihai, China: ACM.

Sun, Z., Strang, K., & Yearwood, J. (2014). *Analytics service oriented architecture for enterprise information systems. In Proceedings of iiWAS2014, CONFENIS 2014*. ACM. doi:10.1145/2684200.2684358

Sun, Z., Sun, L., & Strang, K. (2016). Big data analytics services for enhancing usiness Intelligence. *Journal of Computer Information Systems*. Advance online publication. doi:10.1080/08874417.2016.1220239

Sun, Z., Sun, L., & Strang, K. (2018). Big Data Analytics Services for Enhancing Business Intelligence. *Journal of Computer Information Systems*, *58*(2), 162–169. doi:10.1080/08874417.2016.1220239

Sun, Z., & Wang, P. (2017). Big Data, Analytics and Intelligence: An Editorial Perspective. *Journal of New Mathematics and Natural Computation*, *13*(2), 75–81. doi:10.1142/S179300571702001X

Sun, Z., & Yearwood, J. (2014). A theoretical foundation of demand-driven web services. In Z. Sun, & J. Yearwood (Eds.), Demand-Driven Web Services: Theory, Technologies, and Applications (pp. 1-25). IGI-Global.

Swami, D., & Sahoo, B. (2016). Service Delivery Model for Big Data as a Service. *International Journal of Data Mining and Knowledge Engineering, 8*. Retrieved from https://www.researchgate.net/publication/305040380_SERVICE_DELIVERY_MODEL_FOR_BIG_DATA_AS_A_SERVICE

Tableau. (2020). *Top 8 Trends for 2016: Big Data*. Retrieved from www.tableau.com/Big-Data

Techopedia. (2018). *Big Data as a Service (BDaaS)*. Retrieved 4 2, 2020, from Techopedia: https://www.techopedia.com/definition/29399/big-data-as-a-service-bdaas

Tsai, C., Lai, C., Chao, H., & Vasilakos, A. (2015). Big data analytics: A survey. *Journal of Big Data*, *2*(1), 31–62. doi:10.118640537-015-0030-3

Vajjhala, N., Strang, K., & Sun, Z. (2015). Statistical modeling and visualizing of open big data using a terrorism case study. In *The International Conference on Open and Big Data (OBD 2015)*, (pp. 489-496). Rome: IEEE Press. 10.1109/FiCloud.2015.15

Vardi, M. Y. (2016). The Moral Imperative of Artificial Intelligence. *Communications of the ACM*, *59*(5), 5. doi:10.1145/2903530

Wang, F.-Y. (2012). A big-data perspective on AI: Newton, Merton, and Analytics Intelligence. *IEEE Intelligent Systems*, *27*(Sept/Oct), 2–4. doi:10.1109/MIS.2012.91

Wikipedia. (2020, April). *Infrastructure*. Retrieved 4 8, 2020, from Wikipedia: https://en.wikipedia.org/wiki/Infrastructure

Xinhua, E., & Han, J. (2013). Big Data-as-a-Service: Definition and architecture. In *15th IEEE International Conference on Communication Technology*. IEEE.

Zadeh, L. A. (1965). Fuzzy sets. *Information and Control*, *8*(3), 338–353. doi:10.1016/S0019-9958(65)90241-X

This research was previously published in the International Journal of Systems and Service-Oriented Engineering (IJSSOE), 10(1); pages 1-17, copyright year 2020 by IGI Publishing (an imprint of IGI Global).

Chapter 41

Customer Analytics Capabilities in the Big Data Spectrum:
A Systematic Approach to Achieve Sustainable Firm Performance

Md Afnan Hossain
University of Wollongong, Australia

Shahriar Akter
https://orcid.org/0000-0002-2050-9985
School of Management and Marketing, University of Wollongong, Australia

Venkata Yanamandram
University of Wollongong, Australia

ABSTRACT

Customer analytics plays a vital role in generating insights from big data to improve service innovation, product development, personalization, and managerial decision-making; yet, no academic study has investigated customer analytics capability through which it is possible to achieve sustainable business growth. To close this gap, this chapter explores the constructs of the customer analytics capability by drawing on a systematic review of the literature in the big data spectrum. The chapter's interpretive framework portrays a definitional aspect of customer analytics, the importance of customer analytics, and customer analytics capability constructs. The study proposes a customer analytics capability model, which consists of four principal constructs and some important sub-constructs. The chapter briefly discusses the challenges and future research direction for developing the customer analytics capability model in the data rich competitive business environment.

DOI: 10.4018/978-1-6684-3662-2.ch041

INTRODUCTION

"Big Data" continuously challenges firms, creating an exhilarating leading edge of prospect in the last couple of years. Contemporary firms are taking initiatives to adopt analytics for gaining a superior advantage in the rapidly changing data-rich business environment (Popovič et al., 2016; Nam et al., 2018). The worldwide market in business intelligence and analytics is estimated to be worth $200 billion by 2020 (IDC, 2016), with many industry experts predicting that the customer analytics capability of a firm would enhance the overall firm's performance in the big data environment (Germann et al., 2014). France and Ghose (2018) refer to customer analytics as to the advanced technology that able to solve the customer-centric challenges by analyzing the massive amount of marketing data. A large stream of research focuses on the benefit of customer analytics (e.g., Verhoef et al., 2010; Erevelles et al., 2015; Braun and Garriga, 2018), with relatively little or no attention been devoted to understanding the firm's capacity building of customer analytics in the data-rich environment. Therefore, this chapter seeks to answer the following question.

RQ: What are the dimensions of customer analytics capability to gain sustainable firm performance?

To answer this research question, firstly, we portray the definitional aspects of customer analytics, including discussing the difference between customer and marketing analytics. Secondly, we highlight the importance of customer analytics, and we articulate the findings of a systematic literature review and propose a set of customer analytics capability constructs.

In addressing the research question, this chapter makes two contributions to customer analytics research. Firstly, it offers a theoretical framework of capability dimensions of customer analytics. Secondly, managers can get a clear idea of the customer analytics capability that will lead to attaining sustainable firm performance in the competitive business environment. Following an extensive literature review, we propose a model of customer analytics capability that gives direction to achieve sustainable business growth. Finally, we present a brief discussion on the challenges and a path for future research in this particular area.

LITERATURE REVIEW

Customer Analytics in Big Data Environment

Customer analytics is a robust procedure to manage today's ever-changing customers in the data-rich environment (Sun et al., 2014). Magill (2015) argues that customer analytics is no longer just an exility; it is a necessity to create the superior customer experience, triggering firms to perform large-scale customer analytics to gain profound insights into customers and the entire market.

In defining customer analytics, one stream has reflected on value creation and strategy-centric analysis. For example, verhoef et al. (2010) enlightened that the application of customer analytics in the data-rich environment helps managers to implement a cross-selling strategy through analyzing individual customer's purchasing pattern over the various product categories. Indeed, an analytically mature organization is strategically ahead to gain a competitive advantage (Ransbotham & Kiron, 2018). In another study, Germann et al. (2013) mentioned a firm's actual performance, and management's decision-making shape well when managers strategically applied analytics.

Another stream of research defines customer analytics from the viewpoint of discovering new opportunities. For example, Surma (2011) explained the scope of data mining for customer intelligence in four areas. Firstly, customization on portable devices and the convergence of media, secondly analysis of internet user behavior, thirdly correlation between physical location and customer behavior, and finally develop an advanced system can all converse with customers inconvincible ways that provide opportunities for a firm to attain competitive differentiation. In a similar stratum, Wedel & Kannan (2016) explained that the extensive development of media, channels, digital gadgets, and programming applications (analytics) has given firms incredible opportunities to use information to enhance experiences, deliver enormous value to customers, increment their happiness, and pull out the value in return. Braun & Garriga (2018) pointed out that improvements to customer journey experiences and driving product or service design can be achieved through customer journey analytics.

Table 1 presents the concepts of customer analytics and how they have been defined in the literature.

Table 1. Definitional views of customer analytics

Study	Definitions
Davenport and Harris (2007a)	Customer analytics refers to the use of quantitative data analysis statistically through various models to make managerial decisions and actions.
Kayande et al. (2009)	Customer analytics refers to customers' data interpretation mechanism to make a superior decision.
Verhoef et al. (2010)	Customer analytics is used to manage and understand a significant amount of customers' data by applying a descriptive and predictive model.
Agarwal and Weill (2012)	Customer analytics helps to understand customer needs, make an emotional connection, and improve business process.
Germann et al. (2014)	Customer analytics is the technique used to seek endless opportunities to generate discovery and to support repetitive decisions.
Erevelles et al. (2015)	Customer analytics is the technological advancement that helps to capture customer's observable fact in the real-time from the data-rich environment.
Dhaoui et al. (2017)	Customer analytics focuses on technological advancement to get customer's best insight, such as Lexicon text mining software to analyze the consumer's sentiment.
France and Ghose (2018)	Customer-centric analytics in marketing is the technological advancement that able to solve the customer-centric challenges by analyzing the massive amount of marketing data.
Braun and Garriga (2018)	Customer analytics in big data refers to the quantitative fact-based analysis throughout the consumer's life cycle.

Positioning of Customer Analytics

Customer analytics is a sub-dimension of marketing analytics. Customer is the king in marketing, and a company's sustainable long-term existence depends on customers lifetime value. Marketing analytics is the technological advancement that focuses on the collection, coordination, management, and analysis of every marketing touchpoint data to confirm higher marketing return on investment (Wedel & Kannan 2016). Prior research in the big data spectrum has uncovered the critical relationship between the investigation of technology-based analytics and their considerable advantages (Braun & Garriga 2018; Dhaoui et al. 2017; Erevelles et al. 2015). However, McAfee et al. (2012) and Ross et al. (2013) suggested business firm should focus on more exclusive assets in addition to technology, and that will help to develop firm's analytics capability infrastructure in the data-rich environment. Marketers always manage customers. A firm needs a few assets to reap benefits from the massive volume of customer data and information; although, a number of firms rarely determine how they could build and embed customer analytics inside their firms. The adequacy and ability of the customer's value creation can be enhanced through the mix of analytics models and algorithm development (Erevelles et al., 2015). A strategic fit model that analyze voluminous data helps to identify demographic and other vital factors of the customers, allowing firms product innovation, favorable pricing, meaningful promotion, and to set up the right place or online space for distributing products for the ultimate target customers (Verhoef et al. 2016). More precisely, customer analytics refers to the processes and technologies that give organizations insightful customers information which is necessary to deliver relevant and timely offers; further, as the resolution for all marketing activities, customer analytics comprises techniques such as predictive modeling, data visualization, information management, and segmentation (Germann et al., 2014).

THE IMPORTANCE OF CUSTOMER ANALYTICS

It has been observed that now there is a higher pressure than before on attaining an enterprise view of the customer systematically with the accessibility of enormous amount of data (structured and unstructured) from both the internal and external sources of the firm (Sun et al. 2014; Wedel & Kannan 2016). Such pressure triggers firms to perform large-scale customer analytics to gain more profound customers insights. Kayande et al. (2009) and Germann et al. (2014) advocate that a firm benefits from customer analytics if they possess three main characteristics. Firstly, the customer's data available are voluminous within the firm. Secondly, the existence of an analytics-based method and finally, analytics-based techniques are used to support the repetitive decision. Fieldler et al. (2013) considered a Wal-mart example to show the relationship between voluminous data and customer analytics effectiveness. Wal-mart successfully discovered through scanner data that hurricane warnings significantly increase sales of particular products such as Pop-Tarts. Kumar & Petersen et al., (2012) also refer to the analytic based method such as customer relationship management (CRM) and Customer lifetime value (CLV) metrics to maximize the firm's profitability. Analytics also helps to take the repetitive decisions on customer's product or service. For example, Kannan et al. (2009) found that the National Academies Press (NAP) of the USA that made many of the same decisions repeatedly, built a pricing model through analytics-based customer understanding. In another example, a German mail-order company made profits after introducing a dynamic multilevel response modeling system that answered when, how often and to whom should the company mail its catalogs (Elsner et al., 2004). Similarly, Erevelles et al., (2015) focussed on customer analytics and the strategic transformation of firms, where researchers bring up an example of Southwest airlines which introduced speech analytic software to gain superior competitive advantage through extracting customer insights.

Despite the potential benefits of analytics in data-rich environments, some firms are yet to introduce such mechanisms properly (Mithas et al., 2013). To be competitive in the marketplace, firms require the right process of generating and storing customer activities' records as big data, ensure the technical capability of extracting insights from big data, and adequately manage ideas to enhance dynamic capability (Erevelles et al., 2015). Hence, to embed customer analytics as an integral part of a firm's culture and its business routine, the firm's top management team must adequately support it. (Germann et al.,

2013). The techniques of customer analytics have rapidly transformed over the past ten years, from text analytics to audio Analytics, then video analytics, web analytics, social media analytics, behavior analytics, predictive analytics, journey analytics, and to most recently, cognitive analytics (Magill, 2016).

RESEARCH APPROACH

The study embraced a rigorous systematic literature review applying the guidelines of Ngai and Wat (2002), Benedettini and Neely (2012), and Akter and Fosso Wamba (2016) to answer the research question: What are the dimensions of customer analytics capability to gain sustainable firm performance? Relevant studies of big data analytics capability, marketing analytics, and IT capability are also considered along with customer analytics literature; because customer analytics is emerging in the big data spectrum and information technologies are involved with the process. We considered the time frame of searching for academic papers from 2006 (January) to 2018 (November). We have selected the year 2006 as the lowest boundary because the first seminal paper "competing on analytics" by Davenport was published in Harvard Business Review in 2006 (cited>1000 times). We considered five well-recognized databases (Scopus, Web of Knowledge, ABI/Inform Complete, Business Source Complete, and Science Direct). The searches were limited to the abstract, title, and keywords field. A total of 107 papers were critically reviewed. As we aimed to identify the primary and secondary customer analytics capability dimensions, we considered the 25 most relevant articles (see Table 2).

CUSTOMER ANALYTICS CAPABILITY DIMENSIONS

We propose the following customer analytics capability dimensions based on the above mentioned systematic literature review process and its findings.

Customer Analytics Management Capability

The concept of customer analytics management capability in the data-rich environment refers to a technological unit's ability to process and manage customer-centric routine works (such as CRM, with methods that help acquisition, retention, satisfaction, and improvement of customer's lifetime value) in a structured manner, based on the firm's requirements and priorities. According to Kim et al. (2012), planning, coordination, controlling, and investment decision making for technology are the elemental building blocks of analytics management capability. Thus, firstly customer analytics management capability should start with the appropriate planning process, which helps to improve a firm's performance through big data-based models, and identifies new business opportunities (Barton & Court, 2012). Secondly, a firm's unique strategic position depends on the proper investment decision on analytics, and which helps to build up the funding model of the enterprise to balance costs of investment (Makadok, 2001; McKeen & Smith, 2015). Thirdly, the concept of coordination in the context of information technology represents a type of routine that forms the cross-functional harmonization of analytics initiatives through instruments such as task forces, direct contacts, and gatherings of interdepartmental teams (Karimi et al., 2001). Finally, managers must make sure that the analytics controlling tasks are prearranged, and information technology related procedures are executed efficiently following other tools (Kim et al., 2012).

Customer Analytics Technology/Infrastructure Capability

Resource-based theory (RBT) views that resources are rare, valuable, non-replaceable, and static. Firms with the proper technology capabilities are arguably ahead of the competitors in terms of providing superior value to the customers (Morris 2006). Firms need to attain IT capability urgently to deal with the changing business surroundings (Johnson & Lederer 2005; Fink & Neumann 2009). A customer-centric technological ability such as Relational Database Management System (RDBMS) is capable of storing and handling structured data (e.g., customer's orders, customer's inventory management data, and financial transactions) (Storey & Song, 2017). However, eighty percent (80%) of a firm's data exists in an unstructured format (Gupta & George, 2016). To benefit from customer analytics capability, a firm has to urgently change the traditional RDMS into new-fangled technological tools such as a Java-based software Hadoop that process parallel to massive unstructured data (Bagheri & Shaltooki, 2015). Firms require some other technological tools apart from Hadoop to process, store, visualize, and analyze the large volume of data (Kaisler et al., 2013). Moreover, to gain the competitive advantage in the data-rich environment, firms must ensure the technological advancement to connect the cross-functional data, maintain compatibility in multiple platforms and assure modularity to build the advanced model (Akter et al., 2016). The concept of customer analytics infrastructure in big data environment refers to the technological capability to connect various data points from remote places, generate well-matched (Compatible) data sharing through channels, and develop multiple models to engage in the changing environment (Cosic et al., 2012). Thus, the first infrastructure capability is to ensure the connectivity among the different customer-centric data, which consequently helps to build more critical management of customer relationship. For instance, banks often improve customer services by analyzing ATM transaction data, social media comments, and online queries in the data-rich environment (Barton & Court, 2012). The second component is compatibility that helps to synchronize overlapping data and to fix missing information for real-time decision making. For example, Amazon uses cloud technologies for rapid data analysis, collaboration, and trial suggested that connectivity and compatibility make it possible to embed information system within organizations, and such capability facilitates and develops the firm's overall technological skills. Besides, Akter et al., (2016) refer modularity as another essential component of analytics capability, allowing firms to remove or modify features as required. Similarly, Zhang et al., (2009) pointed out that the modularity facilitates IT to be reorganized and amplified when it needs changes; so the modularity progresses technology capabilities, taps business opportunities, and improves firm's performance.

Customer Analytics Personnel Expertise Capability

Personnel expertise capability refers to the ability (e.g., skills or knowledge) of analytics personnel to execute, given customer centric responsibilities in the data-rich environment. This 'know-how' knowledge counts as capabilities and generates a firm's competitive advantage (Gupta & George, 2016). Studies highlight that an analytics professional must be proficient in four discrete talent sets. Firstly, technical knowledge (e.g., proper management of databases and networking) refers to the understanding of mechanical fundamentals, including programming languages and equipped systems. Secondly, technology management knowledge (e.g., technique management, use of imagery tools, and operations) refers to the experience on specific resource management in the data-rich environment to attain a firm's desired goal. Thirdly, business knowledge (e.g., awareness of business units and goals) refers to the understanding of the business environment and a range of business tasks. Finally, relational learning (e.g., collaboration with business functions) refers to the capability of analytics personnel to interact and communicate with the group of people from various business functions (Melville et al., 2004; Ravichandran et al., 2005; Bhatt & Grover 2005; Aral & Weill, 2007; Kim et al., 2011; Akter et al., 2016).

Table 2. Dimensions of customer analytics (CA) capability

Constructs	Exemplary Studies	Key Findings
1. CA *Management Capability* • Planning • Decision making • Coordination • Control	LaValle, (2011); Ross et al., (2013); Kim et al., (2012); Barton & Court, (2012); McKeen & Smith, (2015)	Managers must systematically perform analytics planning process. Management must take their analytics investment decision appropriately. The capability of the coordination is required among the analysts and support staffs, and the ability of customer analytics controlling should be executed efficiently.
2. CA *Technology/ Infrastructure Capability* • Connectivity • Compatibility • Modularity	Morris, (2006); Davenport & Harris, (2007b); Fink & Neumann, (2009); Zhang et al., (2009); Barton & Court, (2012); Gupta & George, (2016); Akter et al., (2016); Storey & Song, (2017)	Customer analytics infrastructure capability is to ensure the connectivity among the different customer-centric data which consequently helps to build a more significant management of customer relationship and compatibility helps to synchronize overlapping data and to fix missing information for real-time decision making, and Modularity is also merely allowing firms for removal or modification of features to, or from, the model.
3. CA *Personnel Expertise Capability* • Technical • Technological • Business • Relational	Aral & Weill, (2007); Kim et al., (2011); Kim et al., (2012); Gupta & George, (2016)	The ability of analytics professionals to execute customer-centric responsibilities in the data-rich environment. This 'know-how' knowledge count as capabilities and generate a firm's competitive advantage. Personnel expertise should know technical elements, including operational systems, programming languages, and database management systems.
4. CA *4P Mix- Modeling Capability* • Incorporation • Allocation • Assessment	Keller & Lehmann (2006); Srinivasan et al. (2010); Fischer et al. (2011); Hui et al, (2013); Hanssens et al. (2014); Andrews et al., (2015); Wedel & Kannan, (2016); Verhoef et al., (2016)	Advanced customer-centric models are required to incorporate big data such as VAR model (combining 4P and attitudinal metrics) improve sales prediction and recommendation for customer-centric marketing mix allocation.

Customer Analytics 4P Mix Modeling Capability

The effectiveness and capability of customers' value creation can be improved through the 4P mix, with models (models help to measure and improve the performance of firm's marketing mix) and algorithms (Wedel & Kannan, 2016). Appropriate modeling to analyze big data helps to identify demographic factors, competitor's offerings and overall market trends which allow firms to improve the product, favorable price, meaningful promotion, and to set up adequate distribution channels (Verhoef et al., 2016; Wedel & Kannan, 2016). However, conventionally, marketing mix models aim to set up the marketing budget, based on the sales and marketing expenditure. In fact, this process is not sufficient, and eventually, managers are more concerned about the firm's marketing actions, performance, and consumer attitude matrix (Keller & Lehmann 2006). Likewise, Srinivasan et al. (2010) developed a consumer mindset metrics, to improve marketing activities and a sales response. To predict and explain customer choices more rigorously, Godes & Mayzlin (2004) showed the measurement process of word of mouth (WOM); Chevalier and Mayzlin, (2006) discussed the idea of online reviews; and Moe (2003) suggested click streams data. In the model of 4P mix stratum, Hanssens et al. (2014) also developed the concept of consumer mindset metrics and attitudinal metrics in Vector Autoregressive (VAR) models to track down the firm's sales performance and recommendations for marketing mix allocation. Albers (2012) presented plans for developing decision aids for optimal marketing mix allocation, although, a most favorable distribution of resources requires a vigilant study of how expenses should be circulated across segments. Fischer et al. (2011) recommended a heuristic approach to decipher the marketing mix budget allocation problem for multi-segment countries firms. Hui et al., (2013) and Andrews et al. (2015) emphasized on quasi and natural experiments that enable the investigators to assess the causal effect of marketing variables which helps to attain firm's better performance. Thus, although the causality assessment in the marketing mix model has received extensive attention in academia, industry managers have not exposed their concern in the analytics capability aspect yet. Thus, the recommendation is to develop a 4P mix modeling capability to allocate marketing resources and assess the overall marketing variables effect.

Figure 1. Customer analytics capability dimensions and sustainable firm performance model

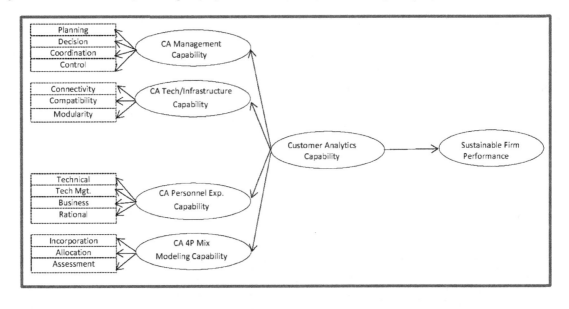

CUSTOMER ANALYTICS CAPABILITY AND
SUSTAINABLE FIRM PERFORMANCE

Previous researchers investigated the importance of analytics capability in the big data environment and performance of a firm (e.g., Akter et al., 2016). While much research has reported the benefits of customer analytics (e.g., Verhoef et al., 2010; Erevelles et al., 2015), relatively little or no attention has been committed to understanding the customer analytics capability and firm's performance. Our study presumes that if a firm satisfies the needs of the customers through the customer analytics, and consequently, if the firm achieves the customer analytics capability by fulfilling the above dimensions, that would create a long term positive effect on the firm's profitability. A company can generate more customer lifetime value, and subsequently, would likely sustain excellent performance.

FUTURE RESEARCH, CHALLENGES, AND OPPORTUNITIES

There are challenges for the managers of firms to personalize the product, especially for the individual customer. Managers' ability to introduce and use the advanced algorithm to process heterogeneity in the behaviors of individual consumers are essential to secure customer lifetime value (Wedel & Kannan, 2016). According to Sonnier (2014) and Buhalis and Amaranggana, (2015) managers can introduce personalization analytics in the firm level not only for developing product or services but also for setting up the price, promotion and distribution channels for the target customers. Furthermore, in the competitive market environment, customers' expectation is raising to get a seamless experience in all the channels. Thus, firms need to achieve the channel integration analytics capability where they will be able to assemble and integrate to deploy data technology resources in the offline and online channels to meet the customers' expectations. Channel integration can be formed appropriately through inside-out capabilities (analytical and technical skills), outside-in capabilities (market responsiveness) and spanning capabilities (change management after combining inside-out and outside-in capabilities) (Hosseini et al., 2017). Furthermore, privacy and security is also a challenge for the firm. Customers expect secure transaction and want to get an assurance from the firm level regarding the highest level of privacy (Miller & Tucker 2011). Thus, firms need to address this issue seriously and must have achieved the capability of data protection in term of privacy and security issue.

With the ongoing development of analytics for big data, many firms can detect the entire path of customers purchase across channels and multiple devices to improve explanations and predictions on the customer's future purchase pattern. These provide further opportunities to consider the specific content that should be personalized and also helps to make the tailored contents for individual customers using individual-level insights.

CONCLUSION AND IMPLICATIONS

This chapter has reviewed the concept of customer analytics and more importantly, has addressed the customer analytics capability dimensions in the key domains of management capability, technology/infrastructure capability, personnel expertise capability, and 4p mix modeling capability. Table 2 summarizes the aspects of customer analytics capability, and that would be expected to work at the interface of econometrics, statistics, and marketing to attain sustainable business growth. Analysts must have in-depth knowledge on customer-centric activities, programming and in contemporary marketing. The analyst of the firm must work as intermediaries between the marketing manager and decision makers. Internal marketing would be necessary to build up the capacity of customer analytics. Through the process, firms can generate value for the ultimate customer, and in return, can capture the value again from the customer, and that will lead to achieving the sustainable highest level of performance.

Managers and analysts need proper training and also required to play a vital role within the organization to carry out customer analytics tools. Firms need to invest in developing skillful, talented employees, and analytics models to gain a sustainable competitive advantage. Therefore, practitioners can benefit from specialized training and can use their skills within the organization to achieve sustainable business growth.

REFERENCES

Agarwal, R., & Weill, P. (2012). The benefits of combining data with empathy. *MIT Sloan Management Review*, *54*(1), 35–41.

Akter, S., & Wamba, S. F. (2016). Big data analytics in E-commerce: A systematic review and agenda for future research. *Electronic Markets*, *26*(2), 173–194. doi:10.100712525-016-0219-0

Akter, S., Wamba, S. F., Gunasekaran, A., Dubey, R., & Childe, S. J. (2016). How to improve firm performance using big data analytics capability and business strategy alignment? *International Journal of Production Economics*, *182*, 113–131. doi:10.1016/j.ijpe.2016.08.018

Albers, S. (2012). Optimizable and implementable aggregate response modeling for marketing decision support. *International Journal of Research in Marketing*, *29*(2), 111–122. doi:10.1016/j.ijresmar.2012.03.001

Andrews, M., Luo, X., Fang, Z., & Ghose, A. (2015). Mobile ad effectiveness: Hyper-contextual targeting with crowdedness. *Marketing Science*, *35*(2), 218–233. doi:10.1287/mksc.2015.0905

Aral, S., & Weill, P. (2007). IT assets, organizational capabilities, and firm performance: How resource allocations and organizational differences explain performance variation. *Organization Science*, *18*(5), 763–780. doi:10.1287/orsc.1070.0306

Bagheri, H., & Shaltooki, A. A. (2015). Big data: Challenges, opportunities and Cloud based solutions. *Iranian Journal of Electrical and Computer Engineering*, *5*(2), 340.

Barton, D., & Court, D. (2012). Making advanced analytics work for you. *Harvard Business Review*, *90*(10), 78–83. PMID:23074867

Benedettini, O. & Neely, A. (2012, June). Complexity in services: an interpretative framework. In *23rd Annual Conference of the Production and Operations Management Society (POMS)* (pp. 1-11). Academic Press.

Bhatt, G. D., & Grover, V. (2005). Types of information technology capabilities and their role in competitive advantage: An empirical study. *Journal of Management Information Systems*, *22*(2), 253–277. doi:10.1080/07421222.2005.11045844

Braun, A. & Garriga, G. (2018). Consumer journey analytics in the context of data privacy and ethics. Digital Marketplaces Unleashed, 663-674. Springer, Berlin, Germany.

Buhalis, D., & Amaranggana, A. (2015). Smart tourism destinations enhancing tourism experience through personalisation of services. In *Information and communication technologies in tourism* (pp. 377–389). Cham, Switzerland: Springer.

Chevalier, J. A., & Mayzlin, D. (2006). The effect of word of mouth on sales: Online book reviews. *JMR, Journal of Marketing Research, 43*(3), 345–354. doi:10.1509/jmkr.43.3.345

Cosic, R., Shanks, G., & Maynard, S. (2012, January). Towards a business analytics capability maturity model. In *ACIS 2012: Location, Location, Location: Proceedings of the 23rd Australasian Conference on Information Systems 2012* (pp. 1-11). ACIS.

Davenport, T. H., & Harris, J. G. (2007a). The dark side of customer analytics. *Harvard Business Review, 85*(5), 37.

Davenport, T. H., & Harris, J. G. (2007b). *Competing on analytics: The new science of winning.* Harvard Business Press.

Dhaoui, C., Webster, C. M., & Tan, L. P. (2017). Social media sentiment analysis: Lexicon versus machine learning. *Journal of Consumer Marketing, 34*(6), 480–488. doi:10.1108/JCM-03-2017-2141

Elsner, R., Krafft, M., & Huchzermeier, A. (2004). Optimizing Rhenania's direct marketing business through dynamic multilevel modeling (DMLM) in a multicatalog-brand environment. *Marketing Science, 23*(2), 192–206. doi:10.1287/mksc.1040.0063

Erevelles, S., Fukawa, N., & Swayne, L. (2015). Big data consumer analytics and the transformation of marketing. *Journal of Business Research, 69*(2), 897–904. doi:10.1016/j.jbusres.2015.07.001

Fiedler, L., Germann, F., Kraus, M., & Perrey, J. (2013). KoenigKunde – Kapital Kundenwissen. *Akzente, 3,* 24–29.

Fink, L., & Neumann, S. (2009). Exploring the perceived business value of the flexibility enabled by information technology infrastructure. *Information & Management, 46*(2), 90–99. doi:10.1016/j.im.2008.11.007

Fischer, M., Albers, S., Wagner, N., & Frie, M. (2011). Practice prize winner—Dynamic marketing budget allocation across countries, products, and marketing activities. *Marketing Science, 30*(4), 568–585. doi:10.1287/mksc.1100.0627

France, S. L. & Ghose, S. (2018). Marketing analytics: Methods, practice, implementation, and links to other fields. *arXiv preprint arXiv:1801.09185.*

Germann, F., Lilien, G. L., Fiedler, L., & Kraus, M. (2014). Do retailers benefit from deploying customer analytics? *Journal of Retailing, 90*(4), 587–593. doi:10.1016/j.jretai.2014.08.002

Germann, F., Lilien, G. L., & Rangaswamy, A. (2013). Performance implications of deploying marketing analytics. *International Journal of Research in Marketing, 30*(2), 114–128. doi:10.1016/j.ijresmar.2012.10.001

Godes, D., & Mayzlin, D. (2004). Using online conversations to study word-of-mouth communication. *Marketing Science, 23*(4), 545–560. doi:10.1287/mksc.1040.0071

Gupta, M., & George, J. F. (2016). Toward the development of a big data analytics capability. *Information & Management, 53*(8), 1049–1064. doi:10.1016/j.im.2016.07.004

Hambrick, D. C., & Mason, P. A. (1984). Upper echelons: The organization as a reflection of its top managers. *Academy of Management Review*, *9*(2), 193–206. doi:10.5465/amr.1984.4277628

Hanssens, D. M., Pauwels, K. H., Srinivasan, S., Vanhuele, M., & Yildirim, G. (2014). Consumer attitude metrics for guiding marketing mix decisions. *Marketing Science*, *33*(4), 534–550. doi:10.1287/mksc.2013.0841

Hosseini, S., Röglinger, M., & Schmied, F. (2017). Omni-channel retail capabilities: an information systems perspective.

Hui, S. K., Inman, J. J., Huang, Y., & Suher, J. (2013). The effect of in-store travel distance on unplanned spending: Applications to mobile promotion strategies. *Journal of Marketing*, *77*(2), 1–16. doi:10.1509/jm.11.0436

IDC. (2016). IDC's worldwide semiannual big data and analytics spending guide.

Johnson, A. M., & Lederer, A. L. (2005). The effect of communication frequency and channel richness on the convergence between chief executive and chief information officers. *Journal of Management Information Systems*, *22*(2), 227–252. doi:10.1080/07421222.2005.11045842

Kaisler, S., Armour, F., Espinosa, J. A., & Money, W. (2013). Big data: Issues and challenges moving forward. In *Proceedings 2013 46th Hawaii International Conference on System Sciences (HICSS)*, (pp. 995-1004). IEEE.

Kannan, P. K., Pope, B. K., & Jain, S. (2009). Practice prize winner—Pricing digital content product lines: A model and application for the National Academies Press. *Marketing Science*, *28*(4), 620–636. doi:10.1287/mksc.1080.0481

Karimi, J., Somers, T. M., & Gupta, Y. P. (2001). Impact of information technology management practices on customer service. *Journal of Management Information Systems*, *17*(4), 125–158. doi:10.1080/07421222.2001.11045661

Kayande, U., De Bruyn, A., Lilien, G. L., Rangaswamy, A., & Van Bruggen, G. H. (2009). How incorporating feedback mechanisms in a DSS affects DSS evaluations. *Information Systems Research*, *20*(4), 527–546. doi:10.1287/isre.1080.0198

Keller, K. L., & Lehmann, D. R. (2006). Brands and branding: Research findings and future priorities. *Marketing Science*, *25*(6), 740–759. doi:10.1287/mksc.1050.0153

Kim, G., Shin, B., Kim, K. K., & Lee, H. G. (2011). IT capabilities, process-oriented dynamic capabilities, and firm financial performance. *Journal of the Association for Information Systems*, *12*(7), 487–517. doi:10.17705/1jais.00270

Kim, G., Shin, B., & Kwon, O. (2012). Investigating the value of sociomaterialism in conceptualizing IT capability of a firm. *Journal of Management Information Systems*, *29*(3), 327–362. doi:10.2753/MIS0742-1222290310

Kumar, V., & Petersen, J. A. (2012). *Statistical methods in customer relationship management*. West Sussex, UK: John Wiley & Sons. doi:10.1002/9781118349212

LaValle, S., Lesser, E., Shockley, R., Hopkins, M. S., & Kruschwitz, N. (2011). Big data, analytics and the path from insights to value. *MIT Sloan Management Review, 52*(2), 21.

Magill, E. (2015). *Harnessing the power of customer analytics at IBM Amplify 2015.* IBM Watson Customer Engagement. Retrieved from https://www.ibm.com/blogs/watson-customer-engagement/2015/05/01/harnessing-the-power-of-customer-analytics-at-ibm-amplify-2015/

Magill, E. (2016). *The customer analytics evolution: A path to cognitive.* IBM Watson Customer Engagement. Retrieved from https://www.ibm.com/blogs/watson-customer-engagement/2016/06/17/the-customer-analytics-evolution-a-path-to-cognitive/)

Makadok, R. (2001). Toward a synthesis of the resource-based and dynamic-capability views of rent creation. *Strategic Management Journal, 22*(5), 387–401. doi:10.1002mj.158

McAfee, A., Brynjolfsson, E. T. H., Patil, D. J., & Barton, D. (2012). Big data: The management revolution. *Harvard Business Review, 90*(10), 60–68. PMID:23074865

McKeen, J. D. & Smith, H. A. (2015). IT strategy: Issues and practices. Pearson Higher Ed.

Melville, N., Kraemer, K., & Gurbaxani, V. (2004). Information technology and organizational performance: An integrative model of IT business value. *Management Information Systems Quarterly, 28*(2), 283–322. doi:10.2307/25148636

Miller, A., & Tucker, C. (2011). Encryption and data security. *Journal of Policy Analysis and Management, 30*(3), 534–556. doi:10.1002/pam.20590 PMID:21774164

Mithas, S., Lee, M. R., Earley, S., Murugesan, S., & Djavanshir, R. (2013). Leveraging big data and business analytics. *IT Professional, 15*(6), 18–20. doi:10.1109/MITP.2013.95

Moe, W. W. (2003). Buying, searching, or browsing: Differentiating between online shoppers using in-store navigational clickstream. *Journal of Consumer Psychology, 13*(1-2), 29–39. doi:10.1207/S15327663JCP13-1&2_03

Morris, A. K. (2006). Assessing pre-service teachers' skills for analyzing teaching. *Journal of Mathematics Teacher Education, 9*(5), 471–505. doi:10.100710857-006-9015-7

Nam, D., Lee, J., & Lee, H. (2018). Business analytics use in CRM: A nomological net from IT competence to CRM performance. *International Journal of Information Management.*

Ngai, E. W., & Wat, F. K. T. (2002). A literature review and classification of electronic commerce research. *Information & Management, 39*(5), 415–429. doi:10.1016/S0378-7206(01)00107-0

Popovič, A., Hackney, R., Tassabehji, R., & Castelli, M. (2016). The impact of big data analytics on firms' high value business performance. *Information Systems Frontiers,* 1–14.

Ransbotham, S. & Kiron, D. (2018). Using analytics to improve customer engagement. *MIT Sloan Management Review, Research report,* 1-20

Ravichandran, T., Lertwongsatien, C., & Lertwongsatien, C. (2005). Effect of information systems resources and capabilities on firm performance: A resource-based perspective. *Journal of Management Information Systems, 21*(4), 237–276. doi:10.1080/07421222.2005.11045820

Ross, J. W., Beath, C. M., & Quaadgras, A. (2013). You may not need big data after all. *Harvard Business Review*, *91*(12), 90–98. PMID:23593770

Sonnier, G. P. (2014). The market value for product attribute improvements under price personalization. *International Journal of Research in Marketing*, *31*(2), 168–177. doi:10.1016/j.ijresmar.2013.09.002

Srinivasan, S., Vanhuele, M., & Pauwels, K. (2010). Mind-set metrics in market response models: An integrative approach. *JMR, Journal of Marketing Research*, *47*(4), 672–684. doi:10.1509/jmkr.47.4.672

Storey, V. C., & Song, I. Y. (2017). Big data technologies and Management: What conceptual modeling can do. *Data & Knowledge Engineering*, *108*, 50–67. doi:10.1016/j.datak.2017.01.001

Sun, N., Morris, J. G., Xu, J., Zhu, X., & Xie, M. (2014). iCARE: A framework for big data-based banking customer analytics. *IBM Journal of Research and Development*, *58*(5/6), 4–1. doi:10.1147/JRD.2014.2337118

Surma, J. (2011). *Business intelligence: Making decisions through data analytics: Customer Intelligence.* New York, NY: Business Expert Press.

Verhoef, P. C., Kooge, E., & Walk, N. (2016). *Creating value with big data analytics: Making smarter marketing decisions.* Routledge. doi:10.4324/9781315734750

Verhoef, P. C., Venkatesan, R., McAlister, L., Malthouse, E. C., Krafft, M., & Ganesan, S. (2010). CRM in data-rich multichannel retailing environments: A review and future research directions. *Journal of Interactive Marketing*, *24*(2), 121–137. doi:10.1016/j.intmar.2010.02.009

Wedel, M., & Kannan, P. K. (2016). Marketing analytics for data-rich environments. *Journal of Marketing*, *80*(6), 97–121. doi:10.1509/jm.15.0413

Zhang, J., Li, H., & Ziegelmayer, J. L. (2009). Resource or capability? A dissection of SMEs' IT infrastructure flexibility and its relationship with IT responsiveness. *Journal of Computer Information Systems*, *50*(1), 46–53.

This research was previously published in Technological Innovations for Sustainability and Business Growth; pages 1-17, copyright year 2020 by Business Science Reference (an imprint of IGI Global).

Chapter 42

Social Media Big Data Analytics for Demand Forecasting:
Development and Case Implementation of an Innovative Framework

Rehan Iftikhar
Maynooth University, Maynooth, Ireland

Mohammad Saud Khan
Victoria University of Wellington, New Zealand

ABSTRACT

Social media big data offers insights that can be used to make predictions of products' future demand and add value to the supply chain performance. The paper presents a framework for improvement of demand forecasting in a supply chain using social media data from Twitter and Facebook. The proposed framework uses sentiment, trend, and word analysis results from social media big data in an extended Bass emotion model along with predictive modelling on historical sales data to predict product demand. The forecasting framework is validated through a case study in a retail supply chain. It is concluded that the proposed framework for forecasting has a positive effect on improving accuracy of demand forecasting in a supply chain.

INTRODUCTION

Big data represents a tremendous opportunity for companies, as it can help to make better decisions in an operational, tactical and strategic level (Schroeck, Shockley, Smart, Romero-Morales, & Tufano, 2012), with direct impact on business profitability (Waller & Fawcett, 2013). The ability to draw insights from different types of data creates huge value for a firm (Dijcks, 2013; Kiron & Shockley, 2015). Big data presents a far greater opportunity than what is being utilized. Only 0.5% of big data is being utilized and analysed while there is potential for so much more (Guess, 2015). Bearing in mind this huge potential,

DOI: 10.4018/978-1-6684-3662-2.ch042

literature providing empirical evidence of the business value added by big data analytics in a supply chain remains little and even poor (Wamba, 2017).

All supply chain operations and activities are set in motion by the final customers' demand (Syntetos et al., 2016). Demand forecasting is used as a basis to make supply chain strategy (Marshall, Dockendorff, & Ibáñez, 2013) and forecasting weaknesses is one of the main reasons for supply chain failures (Zadeh, Sepehri, & Farvaresh, 2014). Demand Forecasting can be improved significantly by using big data (Chao, 2015), especially the big data from social media (Arias, Arratia, & Xuriguera, 2014). With an increase in social media activity, there has been an emergence of academic and industrial research that taps into these social media data sources. However, the utilization of these data sources remain at an early stage and outcomes are often mixed (Yu, Duan, & Cao, 2013).

Companies face a challenge in forecasting with regards to analysing their historical data in the same breath as big data from social media (Papanagnou & Matthews-Amune, 2017). There has been an increased focus from supply chain practitioners to leverage effects from unstructured big data such as social media data, but there is very little support in terms of empirical evidence (Syntetos et al., 2016). Integration of social media analytics and supply chain management is needed to comprehensively establish 'what can be actually done' in the field of forecasting with the help of analytics. There is a paucity of predictive frameworks for forecasting using social media big data. This paper aims to bridge the gap between traditional forecasting techniques and big data analytics utilization and contributes towards a forecasting platform using social media big data as well as historical sales data.

This work presents a framework to utilize social media big data in Bass-Emotion Model introduced by Fan, Che, & Chen (2017). The proposed framework uses the results of sentiment analysis on Facebook and Twitter for demand forecasting. This work provides empirical evidence on the usage of social media big data for demand forecasting in supply chain management (Choi, 2018; Schaer, Kourentzes, & Fildes, 2018). It is one of the first studies that incorporates word analysis, topic modelling and sentiment analysis to provide social media data parameters to the Bass- Emotion model.

LITERTATURE REVIEW

Big Data Analytics in Supply Chain Management

Diverse, massive and complex data on different domains of business and technology which cannot be efficiently addressed by the traditional technologies, skills, and infrastructure is referred to as big data. Most big data researchers and practitioners in general agree on three dimensions that characterize big data: volume, velocity and variety (Zikopoulos & Eaton, 2011). Big data analytics in supply chain management can be described as applying analytical techniques on big data to facilitate optimization and decision making in a supply chain (Souza, 2014). The use of big data analytics can help us understand 'what has happened, what is happening at the moment, what will happen and why things happen' (Feki & Wamba, 2016 p.1127). Three distinct analytics approaches for answering these questions have been classified as descriptive, predictive, and prescriptive analytics (Hahn & Packowski, 2015). The most valued use of big data analytics in a supply chain is the ability it provides to analysts in predicting a reaction or an event by detecting changes based on current or historical data (Sanders, 2014). The utilization of current data, is very effective in improving a supply chain which is seeing a start in its use now in industry. Amazon has patented 'Anticipatory Shipping' which predicts based on an analysis of previous orders and other factors such as customers' shopping trend to anticipate that when and by whom a certain product will be bought and ship it in advance and deliver it instantly after the order has been placed (Kopalle, 2014). Another example is that of DHL. DHL is implementing big data analytics to re-route their vehicles and re-define the delivery/picking sequence to save significant time; additionally, DHL has also developed 'MyWays': a crowd-based platform that assigns the parcels to daily commuters, students and taxi drivers by their geo-location and usual routes which in turn improves the efficiency of the last-mile delivery (Jeske, Grüner, & WeiB, 2013).

Most important aspect which hinders maximum utilization of big data is the lack of analytical techniques and applications which could be used to convert the unstructured data from various sources to business intelligence for the user (Sanders, 2014). This calls for more practical applications and techniques to be introduced which use big data analytics for improving decision making in supply chain management. To cater for this call, this paper introduces a framework which utilizes social media big data to update the demand forecast while also using information from the related product's sale. The proposed framework will generate direct implications to supply chain practitioners who are keen to utilize customers' opinions for improving their demand forecasting.

Social Media Analytics

Social Media is defined as "a conversational, distributed mode of content generation, dissemination, and communication among communities" (Zeng et al., 2010 p. 13). Social Media is an effective sensor when it comes to receiving signals from potential customers. Social media data contains emotions, opinions, and preferences which makes it potentially useful as a market sensing platform but with social media data being qualitative, unstructured and subjective form of big data, it calls for a different analytics approach from traditional approach used in big data (Wong, Chan, & Lacka, 2017). Descriptive analytics, network analytics and content analytics have been identified as three major type of analytics which can be used to create value from social media data (Chae, 2015). As the concern of this study is analysis of the text on Twitter and Facebook, content analytics will be used. Three main dimensions have been identified in the content analytics domain through which social media data can be used to create value for a supply chain forecasting in the proposed framework which are sentiment analysis, word analysis and topic modelling.

Sentiment Analysis

Analysing people's opinion, sentiment, evaluation, attitude, judgment and emotions towards tangible or intangible objects, issues or attributes, such as, product, service, organizations, individuals, events, topics is known as Sentiment Analysis (Liu, 2012). Twitter and Facebook are a very tempting source for sentiment analysis due to the variety, velocity and volume (3vs of big data) of the available content. But informal style of posts and tweets, length of tweets, the resulting use of special symbols in posts makes it challenging to extract high performance result from analysis on these sources. Appraisal theory (Scherer, 2005) describes a way to extract sentiment from text. Arnold and Plutchik (1964) introduced the basic concept of the theory. The theory lays basis for structured sentiment extraction that is based on appraisal expression, a basic grammatical unit by which an opinion is expressed . Korenek and Šimko (2014) utilized appraisal theory to analyse microblogs using sentiment analysis and categorize sentiments as positive, negative and neutral. The sentiments have been categorized in the proposed framework utilizing concepts from appraisal theory. Various organizations from different sectors have used sentiment analysis for gathering information, predicting market response, election results, product innovation, improving customer service, stock forecasting and supply chain management as shown in Table 1. Machine learning, lexicon based, statistical and rule based approaches are the most widely used methods for sentiment analysis (Medhat et al., 2014) but n-gram analysis and artificial neural networks methods have also been used (Ghiassi, Skinner, & Zimbra, 2013). Fan et al. (2017) used Naïve Bayes (NB) algorithm for sentiment analysis on online reviews for use in product forecasting. NB algorithm is better suited to classifications where text is treated independently. Cui et al. (2017) used Support Vector Machine (SVM) for classifying text from social media for event detection. In the proposed framework, both NB and SVM algorithm are used but different from all it is being applied on social media data from Twitter and Facebook and is used in conjunction with trend and word analysis results.

Table 1. Studies based on sentiment analysis

Research Topic	Previous work with description
Stock Forecasting	Arias et al. (2013) and Bollen et al. (2011) have used social media analytics for stock forecasting using twitter information. Srivastava et al. (2016) and (Zhang, Xu, & Xue, 2017) used sentiment analysis and transaction data to predict market trends for stock market customers. Ren, Wu and Liu (2018) used SVM with sentiment analysis to predict market movements.
Brand management	Ghiassi et al. (2013) have used sentiment analysis from twitter data for brand management employing techniques such as n-gram analysis and artificial neural networks.
Election results	Oliveira, Bermejo and dos Santos (2017) compared results from sentiment analysis on social media data to traditional opinion surveys and found it 1 to 8% more accurate for predicting election results. Giglietto (2012) used likes on Facebook pages to the study the predictive power of Facebook to forecast Italian elections in 2011.
Product Innovation	KIA motors and The Royal Bank of Canada, have used sentiment analysis to innovate new products (Kite, 2011).
Supply Chain Management	Singh et al. (2017) presented a framework for improving supply chain management in food industry using sentiment analysis. Swain and Cao (2017) explored the sharing of information by supply chain members on social media and by using sentiment analysis gauged its association with supply chain performance.
Box Office Forecasting	Asur and Huberman (2010) presented a study to use data from Twitter for Box Office forecasting using sentiment analysis.
Customer Service	Bank of America used sentiment analysis to recognize key issues facing their customers by collecting and analysing texts from different social media sources (Purcell, 2011). Malhotra et al. (2012) used sentiment analysis to implement improved marketing methods using Twitter.

Topic Modelling

Social media sources provide huge amount of information every day and with proper tools an understanding of the trends of that information for actionable insights can be developed. Topic Modelling is typically used to uncover industry data across a certain topic or domain (Kwak, Lee, Park, & Moon, 2010), such as product demands, consumer insights, and service quality of an industry. It can help business managers or decision makers to predict the future behaviours or trends of a community based on a relevant set of data. Lansley and Longley (2016) demonstrates a way to use Twitter information to analyse and present geographical trends using Latent Dirichlet Allocation (LDA). Blei, Ng and Jordan (2003) describes LDA as an unsupervised model which is used to find possible topics from collections of text.

Word Analysis

Word analysis of social media data encompasses term frequency analysis, word cloud formation and clustering (Chae, 2015). Term frequency is used to identify key words and phrases from the dataset by use of algorithms such as n-gram. N-gram combines adjacent words of length 'n' from the given dataset to capture the language structure from statistical point of view. Word cloud is a visually appealing method to get an overview of the text (Heimerl et al., 2014). Word analysis have been used frequently in literature for text summarization (Kuo, Hentrich, Good, & Wilkinson, 2007), opinion mining (Wu et al., 2010) and text visualization (Stasko, Görg, Liu, & Singhal, 2007), patent analysis (Koch et al., 2011) and investigative analysis (Stasko et al., 2007). In the proposed framework, word analysis is used to get an overview of the text being used for the selected keywords and to identify related words to add to the search.

Social Media Analytics in Supply Chain

Getting accurate information from extremely noisy data such as social media data, is a big challenge and as is unifying all social media data and making sense of it, which hinders wide use of social media analytics. Table 2 lists the major studies which have used social media big data in supply chain management. In the last few years, there has been a growing interest in utilizing value from social media data in supply chain management as evident from Table 2. But there is still a lack of accurate models for supply chain management which utilize social media data. One of the reason is that with extremely noisy sources such a social media getting the external casual factors right is a big challenge. Making sense of all the casual data (particularly social media) poses a big question for supply chain practitioners and software developers and requires further research (Syntetos et al.,2016). The framework proposed in this paper tries to address this issue.

FRAMEWORK

The authors have developed a framework for extracting maximum benefits out of social media in terms of product forecasting. Three main dimensions were identified from the literature and experimentation through which social media data can be used to create value in demand forecasting which are sentiment analysis, word analysis and topic modelling. The framework utilizes these dimension for using social media analytics to improve demand forecasting. The framework consists of data collection and preprocessing, sentiment extraction and building of forecasting model as shown in Figure 1.

Data Collection and Preprocessing

Data is collected and preprocessed using following methods in the given order.

Table 2. Use of social media analytics in supply chain

Research Topic	Previous work with description	Used Feature
Supply Chain Forecasting	(Chong, Li, Ngai, Ch'ng, & Lee, 2016) conducted a study using neural network and sentiment analysis to see effect of online user generated contents on product sales.	Three-layered neural network Sentiment Analysis
	Choi (2016) analytically explored the impact of positive sentiment on social media on market demand of fashion retailers.	Word Analysis
	Beheshti-Kashi (2015) explored whether microblogging websites such as Twitter can be used for predicting fashion trends.	Trend Analysis
	Boldt et al., (2016) tested utilization of Facebook data for predicting sales of Nike Products and the effects of events on activity on Nike's Facebook pages.	Event Study
Supply Chain Management	Chae (2015) developed a framework to study usefulness of twitter information in supply chain management.	Descriptive Analytics Content Analytics Network Analytics
	Sianipar and Yudoko (2014) concluded in their work that social media integration with a supply chain can be helpful to improve collaboration among supply chains and to increase the agile response of a supply chain.	Content Analysis
	Singh et al. (2017) presented a framework for improving supply chain management in food industry using sentiment analysis	Sentiment Analysis

Keywords Identification

The first step is to identify the initial keywords to be provided by the user. Keywords are used to harvest public data from Facebook and Twitter which are selected after input from the user. N-gram is then applied.

API Streaming

The process of getting data from Twitter and Facebook is the next step and it starts authentication from Twitter and Facebook APIs and establishing a connection. After the authentication, data can be captured using different platforms such as R and Python.

Data Cleaning

The Twitter and Facebook data extracted contains a lot of details (tweets, posts, number of comments, coordinates, embedded URLs, hashtags, retweet count, number of follower, username, location). This data is then transformed using data parsing, data cleansing and noise cancellation to get only relevant data for analysis. All those SMDs (Social Media datasets) collected from Facebook and Twitter are to be neglected which contained less than three words as they didn't represent the customer comments in focus. SMDs from users with 2000 plus posts or tweets are also discarded. If a user is tweeting or posting on the same subject with high frequency those will also be discarded to prevent bias as the results which include these are skewed by the company's marketing campaign. Beheshti-Kashi, Karimi, Thoben, Lütjen, & Teucke (2015) had similar results in their study when they found URLs linked of such tweets and posts to eBay shops. In the final step of data cleansing, the pre-processing of the collected data is

Figure 1. Overview of the demand forecasting framework using social media big data

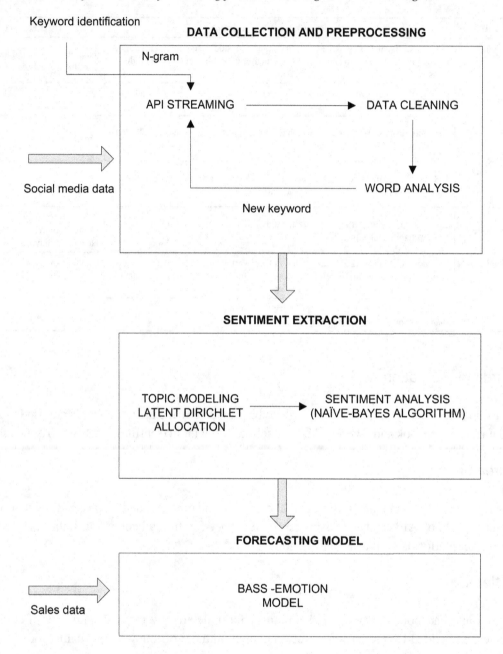

done which is mainly cleaning the data. This includes removing URL links, symbols, punctuation and spaces to transform cases.

Word Analysis

Word analysis of social media data encompasses term frequency analysis, word cloud formation and clustering (Chae, 2015). Term frequency is used to identify key words and phrases from the dataset by use of algorithms such as n-gram. In the proposed framework, n-grams that occur with frequency above the selected threshold are selected. This step involves identifying keywords for the products using word analysis. It is then later compared to quantitative result from the sentimental analysis obtained by rating positive and negative words being used. Bounding Boxes and restricting region approach is used which helps in extracting more useful data from the API (Singh et al., 2017). Specific keywords and exact regions are used to make sure of the accuracy of the data.

Sentiment Extraction

In the second major part of the framwork topic modelling is performed to form different groups of text extraced from Facebook and Twitter in terms of product type, colour and brand.

Topic Modelling

LDA is used in the proposed framework to identify topics related to a product and then perform sentiment analysis on the groups. It is described as an unsupervised model which is used to find possible topics from text collections (Blei et al., 2003). LDA is applied using R and the library 'topicmodels'.

Sentiment Analysis

Liu (2012) provides an English Lexicon of about 6800 words which has been amended and used for the purpose of Sentiment Analysis . NB method (Yu et al., 2013) is used for polarity classification with the aim of obtaining a sentiment index for each SMD. Three categories of sentiment are positive, negative and neutral. The value of W_{tk} is calculated using the NB and SVM method. 'R' is the software used in this study. NB is applied using 'E1071' library in R and SVM using 'caret' package in R. 'Caret' package has in built algorithms for different machine learning algorithms including decision tree, K-Nearest Neighbours(KNN) and SVM. In this instance, the authors are using only SVM from caret package.

The sentiment index in time period t, W_t, is calculated by $W_t = \sum_h (W_{tk} \times c)$ where value of 'c' is

from 1 to -1 depending on the category of W_{tk} i.e. sentiment value of the SMD(positive, negative, neutral) and h is the number of SMDs.

Forecasting Model

In this framework, the Bass Emotion Model (Fan et al., 2017) is extended to include sentiment analysis results from SMDs collected in the first step. In the Bass model (Bass, 2004), potential buyers are classified as innovators and imitators, and then the general form of the Bass model is as follows.

$$S(t) = m \frac{1 - e^{-(p+q)t}}{1 + \frac{q}{p} \times e^{-(p+q)t}}$$

where S(t) is the cumulative sales by the end of time period t. p refers to the coefficient of innovation, q refers to the coefficient of imitation, and m refers to the total number of potential adopters. m and p are calculated using historical sales data. q is related to the sentiment and can be perceived as a function of the social media sentiment $q=f(W_t)$. From the SMDs, if positive sentiment is obtained it means that social media users are talking positively about the product and it gives a potential increase in adopters q and vice versa. The function is described as

$$q = \frac{q^m q^0}{q^0 + \left(q^m - q^0\right)e^{-\gamma W_t}}$$

where q denotes the effect of word of mouth via social media. q^0 refers to the minimum of q, q^m refers to the maximum of q. Υ is a constant that represents the slope of the sales curve. Υ is calculated using historical product data.

CASE STUDY

The study was conducted at an apparel retail company. Focal company's business model is buying and selling apparel products. The suppliers are from different countries encapsulating Far East, South Asia and Europe. Clothes are imported from these countries as well as bought from the local market and then sold to more than 60 countries throughout the world. The complete supply chain is huge spanning four continents. The focal apparel retail company was chosen because of importance of customer-oriented content in apparel industry and because of the focal company's significant presence on social media.

It is difficult to coordinate longer apparel supply chains, so it becomes really important to have very accurate demand forecasting (Syntetos et al., 2016). Traditional forecasting methods like time series data don't work particularly will in an apparel industry as designs and items of one season are typically replaced next season by new collections and trends, and therefore, companies often face a lack of historical sales data (Thomassey, 2010). Moreover, demand in the industry is significantly influenced by additional factors such as the economic situation, events or changing weather conditions (Thomassey, 2014). Many practitioners have been using univariate method (Au et al., 2008) for supply chain forecasting in apparel industry which utilizes historical sales data and it is assumed that the underlying variation of data is constant. For instance, Wong and Guo (2010) utilized one-step-ahead sales data to predict the sales of medium-priced fashion products in Mainland China. Au et al. (2008) used previous time series data to predict the sales of T-shirt and jeans from several shops with the use of neural networks. The sales of products in apparel industry are volatile, often influenced by changing trends and weather conditions and events. So, for the forecasting purposes, it is not right to hypothesize that the trend of time series sales data is unchanged. To cope with this, researchers integrate other influencing factors as the inputs of forecasting models besides the historical time series data, which is known as multivariate forecasting. Beheshti-Kashi (2015) has presented current fashion forecasting approaches in the industry and academia. Most successful techniques surveyed were Extreme machine learning(Sun, Choi, Au, & Yu, 2008), evolutionary neural network (ENN) (Au et al., 2008; Wong & Guo, 2010), Thomassey and

Happiette fuzzy inference systems (Thomassey, Happiette, & Castelain, 2005) and hybrid intelligent sales forecasting model (Aburto & Weber, 2007).

Most of the forecasting models discussed above give reliable results for middle and long-term forecasting. But due to a very competitive market and short selling span accurate and customer centric and short-term forecasting is necessary. With the advent of information technology and affordable information systems, most companies (big and small) have developed or implemented information systems from which they get sales reports, graphs and even forecasts. With the advent of social media data, this is not enough to be competitive. Data gathered by the companies needs to add the information circulating on social media, which could deliver another type of insight for forecasting and result in the increased competitiveness especially for creative industry such as apparel industry with the involvement of potential customers in style design, colour preference and judging trends, and scope for new products (Banica & Hagiu, 2016).

Short term forecasting methods have not been explored as much (N. Liu, Ren, Choi, Hui, & Ng, 2013). Short term forecasting is very important in the apparel industry because of the ever-changing trends and short selling times. For this purpose, Beheshti (2015) suggested adding social media to the discussion of fashion forecasting and Syntetos et al. (2016) predicted that future of supply chain forecasting will include predictive analytics based on social media data. For an apparel supply chain, there can be multiple topics of interest which are being discussed in social media. The authors try to utilize these topics to make this data viable using the proposed framework for supply chain forecasting in apparel industry.

For the implementation of the framework, company sales and social media data i.e. Twitter and Facebook data was collected. This data was collected for a period of six weeks. Data collection for this study began in July 2016 and data was collected till August 15, 2016. Beheshti-Kashi (2015) did a study for exploration of trends using twitter and found out it hard to present the finding in quantitative form. To cater for this issue, the authors expanded the study by analysing specificities and increased the amount of data collection by including both Facebook and Twitter so results could be presented in quantitative form. The period of six weeks was chosen with the insights from the user, which in this case is the supply chain manager of the focal company. 'Shorts' were selected as the product to be used for the study. For collection of data from social media i.e. Twitter and Facebook, APIs were used and the related SMDs was analysed. Only those SMDs were selected which were either brand related, product type related, or a fashion trend related. Data was collected every 7 days as twitter allowed tweets to be collected which were 7-8 days old. SMDs were extracted for brand and products. Hashtags and texts for the brands sold by the focal company were analysed. The total number of tweets analysed were 1,208,650. For the category product type shorts were chosen as they were the most selling item as the data was collected in summers. SMDs were collected against different type of shorts as shown in Table 3 and for different brands as shown in Table 4. As this data of brands was analysed there were a lot of data which wasn't related to the brand or products of the focal company. One such example was #next being used for election campaign in United States. After extraction of text, it was used to form word clouds which can be helpful in manual inspection of the data gathered as the viewer can get a general idea about the kind of words being used and this can later be used for cross checking the results obtained by sentimental analysis to make sure no anomaly has occurred during the process. Word Clouds were formed before and after processing and cleaning of data to investigate manually the dataset being used for sentiment extraction. Figure 2 displays a word cloud for keyword 'nike' before data cleaning process. The noise in this dataset is evident as there are words from different languages and some completely unrelated words. Figure 3 displays the word cloud after data cleaning which removes all the unrelated SMDs.

Figure 2. Word cloud for brand 'Nike'

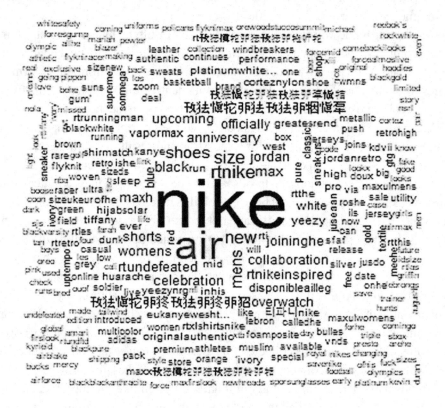

Figure 3. Word cloud after data cleaning

Table 3. Keywords used for SMDs extraction for 'shorts'

Shorts#nike	Shorts#green	Shorts#swimming	zara#swimmingshorts
Shorts#adidas	Shorts#navy	Shorts#running	zara#runningshorts
Shorts#reebok	Shorts #jersey	nike#jerseyshorts	zarablack#jerseyshort
Shorts#next	Shorts #cargo	nike #cargoshorts	zarablack#cargoshorts
Shorts#blue	Shorts#jorts	nike #jorts	zarablack#jorts
Shorts#black	Shorts#fleece	nike #fleeceshorts	zarablack#fleeceshort
Shorts#grey	Shorts#gym	nike #gymshorts	zarablack#gymshorts
Shorts#swimming	nike#swimmingshort	Shorts#swimming	adidas#swimmingshor
Shorts#running	nike#runningshorts	Shorts#running	puma#runningshorts
nike#jerseyshorts	nikeblack#jerseyshor	adidas#jerseyshorts	nikeblack#jerseyshort
nike#cargoshorts	nextblack#cargoshor	adidas#cargoshorts	pumablack#cargoshts
nike #jorts	nike black#jorts	adidas #jorts	nike black#jorts
nike #fleeceshorts	nikeblack#fleeceshor	adidas#fleeceshorts	nikeblack#fleeceshort
adidasShorts#ru	nike#runningshorts	adidasShorts#runni	puma#runningshorts
next#jerseyshorts	nikeblack#jerseyshorts	adidas#jerseyshorts	pumablack#jerseyshorts
next #cargoshorts	nextblack#cargoshors	adidas#cargoshorts	pumblack#cargoshorts
next #jorts	nike black#jorts	adidas #jorts	puma black#jorts
next #fleeceshorts	nikeblack#fleeceshorts	adidas#fleeceshorts	pumablack#fleeceshorts
next #gymshorts	nikeblack#gymshorts	adidas #gymshorts	pumablack#gymshorts

Table 4. Number of Brands and Product Related SMDs for week 1

Brand	# of SMDs	Product Type	# of SMDs
Zara	12,456	#jerseyshorts	651
Nike	29,435	#cargoshorts	543
Adidas	36,792	#jorts	189
NEXT	71,234	#gymshorts	984
BHS	61,281	#swimmingshorts	429
Puma	23,124	#runningshorts	183

For a period of 6 weeks, the SMDs were analysed and then compared to the sales period for that period as well as next 6 weeks. Table 5 shows the sentiment analysis score for different product categories after application of SVM and then calculation of parameter q. Analysis of sentiment score show that the amount of sales had a co relation with the sentiment around that particular brand or colour. There was no co relation found when sentiment analysis was done for the product type which could be attributed to the noise in the data as single word or single product search was susceptible to much more noise than a search using words for multiple characteristics. Multiple character searches with positive sentiment lead to an increase in sale and the negative sentiment lead to a decrease. Analysing the tweets and Facebook comments for running shorts and running a sentiment analysis on it using SVM and NB methods. Comparison of the results of these models have been shown in Table 7.

Table 5. Product type with sentiment analysis score

Product Type	Sales	Number of SMDs	Sentiment Analysis Score	Product Type	Sales	Number of SMDs	Sentiment Analysis Score
Nike Jersey Shorts	1120	651	0.23	Adidas Jersey Shorts	983	156	0.64
Nike Cargo Shorts	2832	543	0.12	Adidas Cargo Shorts	811	531	0.12
Nike Denim Shorts	563	189	0.70	Adidas Denim Shorts	641	145	0.53
Nike Fleece Shorts	212	84	0.34	Adidas Fleece Shorts	1212	821	0.31
Nike Gym Shorts	984	984	0.05	Adidas Gym Shorts	1944	547	0.43
Nike Swimming Shorts	1367	429	0.76	Adidas Swimming Shorts	937	122	0.53

Table 6. Comparison of forecasted and actual values for Bass Model and proposed Emotion Enhanced Model

Forecasting week	1	2	3	4	5	6
Actual value	712.3409	817.6867	921.2260	843.5641	926.7657	923.9208
Forecasted value (Bass Model)	704.5435	810.4631	927.0904	841.5382	922.7238	918.6123
Forecasted value (Proposed Model)	708.6674	816.5294	923.1996	844.2350	926.8046	922.7927

Table 7. Comparison of SVM and NB Methods

Product Brand	Algorithm	Accuracy
Nike	NB	67.21
	SVM	69.24
Adidas	NB	67.46
	SVM	75.12
Puma	NB	65.24
	SVM	71.81
BHS	NB	69.42
	SVM	78.10
Next	NB	63.41
	SVM	63.51
Zara	NB	75.87
	SVM	75.11

The results from sentiment analysis were then used in Bass Emotion model to predict the sales. The parameters m,p and γ for Bass- Emotion model were calculated using historical sales data and q was calculated using sentiment analysis from SMDs. Parameters calculated are represented in Table 8. All these parameters were calculated using R. Table 6 shows the forecasting accuracy of the proposed emotion enhanced model which is a significant improvement on the forecasting accuracy of original Bass Model. Figure 4 displays the forecasted values using proposed model compared to actual values.

Table 8. Parameter for bass model

Parameter	Results
m	887.0306
p	0.023777
q^0	0.090407
q^m	0.093113
γ	0.170784

Figure 4. Results of Forecasting Model of Emotion Enhanced Model

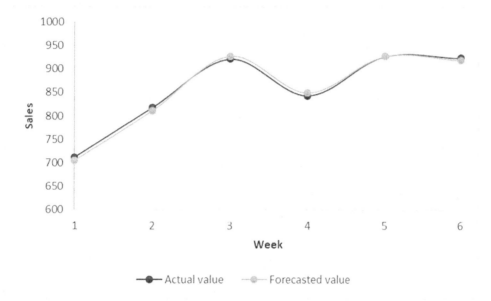

CONCLUSION

This paper introduced a framework that provides a way of utilizing social media big data in Bass-Emotion Model for demand forecasting using results from sentiment analysis on Facebook and Twitter data. As social media data is very noisy, it is difficult to make accurate predictions from social media data about products in general but if the products are broken down and multiple characteristics search is applied then the information which is collected can be converted as a demand forecasting and market or trend sensing tool. The major factor in extracting value from the social media is to apply multiple data cleaning techniques in conjunction with one another, so the data subjected to later analysis gives reliable results as described in the framework presented in the paper. More than 1200,000 tweets, posts and comments from Facebook and Twitter were analysed in the case study. The study showed that social media big data is extremely useful for apparel industry and can be very effective if used to support demand forecasting. With proper modelling and implementation of right techniques, social media big data has the potential to help forecast with accuracy. Results from this study shows a co relation between customers opinion on Facebook and Twitter to actual sales. The framework presented in this study can be further verified and improved with the help of case studies to make it a reliable mechanism for using social media big data in demand forecasting.

As this a relatively new research area, there is a considerable need for enhancing our understanding social media data in supply chain contexts. One area which needs urgent work, is developing detailed, practical guidelines, which can help companies in designing industry applications, using Facebook, Twitter and other social media platforms, for diverse supply chain activities, including new product development, stake holder engagement, supply chain risk management, and market sensing. Further research is needed in the implementation of this framework on other industries and using cloud-based systems. Moreover, sentiment extraction could be improved by including other social media platforms including YouTube, google trends and Instagram. Sentiment analysis can be implemented on videos and pictures posted instead of limiting it only to the text. This could further improve the results as it will take into consideration users from other platforms as well, painting a more accurate picture of customers sentiment.

REFERENCES

Aburto, L., & Weber, R. (2007). Improved supply chain management based on hybrid demand forecasts. *Applied Soft Computing*. doi:10.1016/j.asoc.2005.06.001

Arias, M., Arratia, A., & Xuriguera, R. (2014). Forecasting with Twitter Data. *ACM Transactions on Intelligent Systems and Technology*. doi:10.1145/2542182.2542190

Arnold, M. B., & Plutchik, R. (1964). The Emotions: Facts, Theories and a New Model. *The American Journal of Psychology*. doi:10.2307/1421040

Asur, S., & Huberman, B. A. (2010). Predicting the Future with Social Media. *Journal of Interactive Marketing*. doi:10.1007/978-1-4419-7142-5

Au, K. F., Choi, T. M., & Yu, Y. (2008). Fashion retail forecasting by evolutionary neural networks. *International Journal of Production Economics*. doi:10.1016/j.ijpe.2007.06.013

Banica, L., & Hagiu, A. (2016). Using big data analytics to improve decision-making in apparel supply chains. In Information Systems for the Fashion and Apparel Industry. doi:10.1016/B978-0-08-100571-2.00004-X

Bass, F. M. (2004). A New Product Growth for Model Consumer Durables. *Management Science*. doi:10.1287/mnsc.1040.0264

Beheshti-kashi, S. (2015). *Twitter and Fashion Forecasting : An Exploration of Tweets regarding Trend Identification for Fashion Forecasting*. Academic Press.

Beheshti-Kashi, S., Karimi, H. R., Thoben, K.-D., Lütjen, M., & Teucke, M. (2015). A survey on retail sales forecasting and prediction in fashion markets. *Systems Science & Control Engineering: An Open Access Journal*. doi:10.1080/21642583.2014.999389

Blei, D. M., Ng, A. Y., & Jordan, M. I. (2003). Latent Dirichlet Allocation. *Journal of Machine Learning Research*. doi:10.1162/jmlr.2003.3.4-5.993

Boldt, L. C., Vinayagamoorthy, V., Winder, F., Schnittger, M., Ekran, M., Mukkamala, R. R., & Vatrapu, R. (2016). Forecasting Nike's sales using Facebook data. In *Proceedings - 2016 IEEE International Conference on Big Data, Big Data 2016*. IEEE. 10.1109/BigData.2016.7840881

Bollen, J., Mao, H., & Zeng, X. (2011). Twitter mood predicts the stock market. *Journal of Computational Science*. doi:10.1016/j.jocs.2010.12.007

Chae, B. (2015). Insights from hashtag #supplychain and Twitter analytics: Considering Twitter and Twitter data for supply chain practice and research. *International Journal of Production Economics*. doi:10.1016/j.ijpe.2014.12.037

Chao, L. (2015). *Big Data Brings Relief to Allergy Medicine Supply Chains - WSJ*. Retrieved September 18, 2017, from https://www.wsj.com/articles/big-data-brings-relief-to-allergy-medicine-supply-chains-1432679948

Choi, T.-M. (2016). *Incorporating social media observations and bounded rationality into fashion quick response supply chains in the big data era*. doi:10.1016/j.tre.2016.11.006

Choi, T. M. (2018). Incorporating social media observations and bounded rationality into fashion quick response supply chains in the big data era. *Transportation Research Part E, Logistics and Transportation Review*. doi:10.1016/j.tre.2016.11.006

Chong, A. Y. L., Li, B., Ngai, E. W. T., Ch'ng, E., & Lee, F. (2016). Predicting online product sales via online reviews, sentiments, and promotion strategies: A big data architecture and neural network approach. *International Journal of Operations & Production Management*. doi:10.1108/JFM-03-2013-0017

Cui, W., Wang, P., Du, Y., Chen, X., Guo, D., Li, J., & Zhou, Y. (2017). An algorithm for event detection based on social media data. *Neurocomputing*. doi:10.1016/j.neucom.2016.09.127

Dijcks, J.-P. (2013). *Oracle : Big Data for the Enterprise. Academic Press*.

Fan, Z.-P., Che, Y.-J., & Chen, Z.-Y. (2017). Product sales forecasting using online reviews and historical sales data: A method combining the Bass model and sentiment analysis. *Journal of Business Research*. doi:10.1016/j.jbusres.2017.01.010

Feki, M., & Wamba, S. F. (2016). Big Data Analytics-enabled Supply Chain Transformation : A Literature Review. *49th Hawaii International Conference on System Sciences*, 1123–1132. https://doi.org/10.1109/HICSS.2016.142

Fosso Wamba, S. (2017). Big data analytics and business process innovation. *Business Process Management Journal*. doi:10.1108/BPMJ-02-2017-0046

Ghiassi, M., Skinner, J., & Zimbra, D. (2013). Twitter brand sentiment analysis: A hybrid system using n-gram analysis and dynamic artificial neural network. *Expert Systems with Applications*. doi:10.1016/j.eswa.2013.05.057

Guess, A. R. (2015). *Only 0.5% of All Data is Currently Analyzed - DATAVERSITY*. Retrieved September 4, 2017, from http://www.dataversity.net/only-0-5-of-all-data-is-currently-analyzed/

Hahn, G. J., & Packowski, J. (2015). A perspective on applications of in-memory analytics in supply chain management. *Decision Support Systems*, *76*, 45–52. doi:10.1016/j.dss.2015.01.003

Heimerl, F., Lohmann, S., Lange, S., & Ertl, T. (2014). Word cloud explorer: Text analytics based on word clouds. *Proceedings of the Annual Hawaii International Conference on System Sciences*, 1833–1842. 10.1109/HICSS.2014.231

Jeske, M., Grüner, M., & Wei, B. F. (2013). *Big data in logistics: A DHL perspective on how to move beyond the hype*. DHL Customer Solutions & Innovation.

Khalil Zadeh, N., Sepehri, M. M., & Farvaresh, H. (2014). Intelligent sales prediction for pharmaceutical distribution companies: A data mining based approach. *Mathematical Problems in Engineering*. doi:10.1155/2014/420310

Kiron, D., & Shockley, R. (2015). Creating business value with analytics. *MIT Sloan Management Review*.

Koch, S., Bosch, H., Giereth, M., & Ertl, T. (2011). Iterative integration of visual insights during scalable patent search and analysis. *IEEE Transactions on Visualization and Computer Graphics*. doi:10.1109/TVCG.2010.85

Kopalle, P. (2014). *Why Amazon's Anticipatory Shipping Is Pure Genius*. Retrieved September 4, 2017, from https://www.forbes.com/sites/onmarketing/2014/01/28/why-amazons-anticipatory-shipping-is-pure-genius/#5056b0bf4605

Korenek, P., & Šimko, M. (2014). Sentiment analysis on microblog utilizing appraisal theory. *World Wide Web (Bussum)*. doi:10.100711280-013-0247-z

Kuo, B. Y.-L., Hentrich, T., & Good, B. M., & Wilkinson, M. D. (2007). Tag clouds for summarizing web search results. *Proceedings of the 16th International Conference on World Wide Web - WWW '07*. 10.1145/1242572.1242766

Kwak, H., Lee, C., Park, H., & Moon, S. (2010). *What is Twitter, a Social Network or a News Media?* Network. doi:10.1145/1772690.1772751

Lansley, G., & Longley, P. A. (2016). The geography of Twitter topics in London. *Computers, Environment and Urban Systems*. doi:10.1016/j.compenvurbsys.2016.04.002

Liu, B. (2012). *Sentiment Analysis and Opinion Mining*. Morgan & Claypool Publishers. doi:10.2200/S00416ED1V01Y201204HLT016

Liu, N., Ren, S., Choi, T. M., Hui, C. L., & Ng, S. F. (2013). Sales forecasting for fashion retailing service industry: A review. *Mathematical Problems in Engineering*. doi:10.1155/2013/738675

Malhotra, A., Kubowicz, C., & See, A. (2012). How to Get Your Messages Retweeted. *MIT Sloan Management Review*. https://doi.org/1532-9194

Marshall, P., Dockendorff, M., & Ibáñez, S. (2013). A forecasting system for movie attendance. *Journal of Business Research*, *66*(10), 1800–1806.

Medhat, W., Hassan, A., & Korashy, H. (2014). Sentiment analysis algorithms and applications: A survey. *Ain Shams Engineering Journal*. doi:10.1016/j.asej.2014.04.011

Oliveira, D. J. S., Bermejo, P. H. de S., & dos Santos, P. A. (2017). Can social media reveal the preferences of voters? A comparison between sentiment analysis and traditional opinion polls. *Journal of Information Technology & Politics*. doi:10.1080/19331681.2016.1214094

Papanagnou, C. I., & Matthews-Amune, O. (2017). Coping with demand volatility in retail pharmacies with the aid of big data exploration. *Computers & Operations Research*.

Ren, R., Wu, D. D., & Liu, T. (2018). Forecasting Stock Market Movement Direction Using Sentiment Analysis and Support Vector Machine. *IEEE Systems Journal*.

Sanders, N. R. (2014). *Big data driven supply chain management: A framework for implementing analytics and turning information into intelligence*. Pearson Education.

Schaer, O., Kourentzes, N., & Fildes, R. (2018). Demand forecasting with user-generated online information. *International Journal of Forecasting*.

Scherer, K. R. (2005). Appraisal Theory. In Handbook of Cognition and Emotion. https://doi.org/doi:10.1002/0470013494.ch30

Schroeck, M., Shockley, R., Smart, J., Romero-Morales, D., & Tufano, P. (2012). *Analytics: The real-world use of big data*. IBM Global Business Services Saïd Business School at the University of Oxford.

Sianipar, C. P. M., & Yudoko, G. (2014). Social media: Toward an integrated human collaboration in supply-chain management. WIT Transactions on Information and Communication Technologies. doi:10.2495/Intelsys130221

Singh, A., Shukla, N., & Mishra, N. (2017). Social media data analytics to improve supply chain management in food industries. *Transportation Research Part E: Logistics and Transportation Review*. https://doi.org/https://doi.org/10.1016/j.tre.2017.05.008

Souza, G. C. (2014). Supply chain analytics. *Business Horizons*. doi:10.1016/j.bushor.2014.06.004

Stasko, J., Görg, C., Liu, Z., & Singhal, K. (2007). Jigsaw: Supporting investigative analysis through interactive visualization. *VAST IEEE Symposium on Visual Analytics Science and Technology 2007, Proceedings*. https://doi.org/10.1109/VAST.2007.4389006

Sun, Z.-L., Choi, T.-M., Au, K.-F., & Yu, Y. (2008). Sales forecasting using extreme learning machine with applications in fashion retailing. *Decision Support Systems*. doi:10.1016/j.dss.2008.07.009

Swain, A. K., & Cao, R. Q. (2017). Using sentiment analysis to improve supply chain intelligence. *Information Systems Frontiers*. doi:10.100710796-017-9762-2

Syntetos, A. A., Babai, Z., Boylan, J. E., Kolassa, S., & Nikolopoulos, K. (2016). Supply chain forecasting: Theory, practice, their gap and the future. *European Journal of Operational Research*. doi:10.1016/j.ejor.2015.11.010

Thomassey, S. (2010). Sales forecasts in clothing industry: The key success factor of the supply chain management. *International Journal of Production Economics*. doi:10.1016/j.ijpe.2010.07.018

Thomassey, S. (2014). Sales Forecasting in Apparel and Fashion Industry. *Intelligent Fashion Forecasting Systems: Models and Applications*. doi:10.1007/978-3-642-39869-8

Thomassey, S., Happiette, M., & Castelain, J. M. (2005). A global forecasting support system adapted to textile distribution. *International Journal of Production Economics*. doi:10.1016/j.ijpe.2004.03.001

Waller, M. A., & Fawcett, S. E. (2013). Data Science, Predictive Analytics, and Big Data: A Revolution That Will Transform Supply Chain Design and Management. *Journal of Business Logistics*, *34*(2), 77–84. doi:10.1111/jbl.12010

Wang, G., Gunasekaran, A., Ngai, E. W. T., & Papadopoulos, T. (2016). Big data analytics in logistics and supply chain management: Certain investigations for research and applications. *International Journal of Production Economics*. doi:10.1016/j.ijpe.2016.03.014

Wong, T. C., Chan, H. K., & Lacka, E. (2017). An ANN-based approach of interpreting user-generated comments from social media. *Applied Soft Computing*. doi:10.1016/j.asoc.2016.09.011

Wong, W. K., & Guo, Z. X. (2010). A hybrid intelligent model for medium-term sales forecasting in fashion retail supply chains using extreme learning machine and harmony search algorithm. *International Journal of Production Economics*. doi:10.1016/j.ijpe.2010.07.008

Wu, Y., Wei, F., Liu, S., Au, N., Cui, W., Zhou, H., & Qu, H. (2010). OpinionSeer: Interactive visualization of hotel customer feedback. *IEEE Transactions on Visualization and Computer Graphics*. doi:10.1109/TVCG.2010.183

Yu, Y., Duan, W., & Cao, Q. (2013). The impact of social and conventional media on firm equity value: A sentiment analysis approach. *Decision Support Systems*. doi:10.1016/j.dss.2012.12.028

Zeng, D., Chen, H. C. H., Lusch, R., & Li, S.-H. (2010). Social Media Analytics and Intelligence. *IEEE Intelligent Systems*.

Zhang, G., Xu, L., & Xue, Y. (2017). Model and forecast stock market behavior integrating investor sentiment analysis and transaction data. *Cluster Computing*. doi:10.100710586-017-0803-x

Zikopoulos, P., & Eaton, C. (2011). *Understanding big data: Analytics for enterprise class hadoop and streaming data*. McGraw-Hill Osborne Media.

This research was previously published in the Journal of Global Information Management (JGIM), 28(1); pages 103-120, copyright year 2020 by IGI Publishing (an imprint of IGI Global).

Chapter 43

Using Big Data Analytics to Forecast Trade Volumes in Global Supply Chain Management

Murat Ozemre
Yasar University, Turkey

Ozgur Kabadurmus
 https://orcid.org/0000-0002-1974-7134
Yasar University, Turkey

ABSTRACT

As the supply chains become more global, the operations (such as procurement, production, warehousing, sales, and forecasting) must be managed with consideration of the global factors. International trade is one of these factors affecting the global supply chain operations. Estimating the future trade volumes of certain products for specific markets can help companies to adjust their own global supply chain operations and strategies. However, in today's competitive and complex global supply chain environments, making accurate forecasts has become significantly difficult. In this chapter, the authors present a novel big data analytics methodology to accurately forecast international trade volumes between countries for specific products. The methodology uses various open data sources and employs random forest and artificial neural networks. To demonstrate the effectiveness of their proposed methodology, the authors present a case study of forecasting the export volume of refrigerators and freezers from Turkey to United Kingdom. The results showed that the proposed methodology provides effective forecasts.

DOI: 10.4018/978-1-6684-3662-2.ch043

INTRODUCTION

With the rise of globalization, supply chains operations became more complex and therefore harder to manage. Nowadays, the companies not only interact with the companies within their supply chains and but also interact with outside supply chains. They also constantly compete with global supply chains. This fierce global competition increases the importance of the effective management of supply chain operations. Many supply chain operations, such as production, procurement, sales, warehousing, and forecasting, cannot be effectively designed with considering only local parameters. Today's supply chains are interconnected with global companies and supply chains, and this requires to think globally when designing and managing supply chain operations. Thus, the supply chain operations must be designed and managed with the global parameters and the effective management of global supply chain operations has become very important.

To effectively design logistics activities, the availability of accurate forecast data is crucial. For example, the effective resource allocation of a company for the distribution of its goods depends on the sales forecast data. Similarly, the quality of the sales forecast affects the performance of production scheduling and resource utilization. A good inventory management practice can help to achieve an agile response to the customer demand, however, it depends on the accurate forecast data. All these company level forecast related issues are important, but the requirement of a good forecast becomes more significant for the design of supply chain operations. In supply chain management, accurate forecasts help to streamline the operations. For example, data sharing with the other echelons of the supply chain can lead to better forecasts and help reducing bullwhip effect, which may lead to increased inventories, poor customer service levels, poor resource allocation, and wrong logistics decisions (Kabadurmus, Erdogan, & Tasgetiren, 2017). Therefore, an effective forecasting practice can reduce the inventory levels without affecting the service level and improve supply chain performance.

Forecasting in global supply chain operations is more challenging than the forecasting in local supply chains due to the complexity of the global supply chain networks. For exporters (or importers), predicting export (or import) volumes are also important since their entire supply chain operations depend on the forecasted exports. The prediction of total export volume of a country to a specific country may help to adjust their marketing strategies. If the exporting company can foresee that the total export volume would increase in the future, they can increase their production by adjusting their own supply chain operations. If they can predict that the export volume to a specific country to be reduced in the near future, they can search for alternative markets to sell their products and reshape their global supply chain operations without hindering the progress of supply chain strategies. Therefore, being able to make accurate forecasts is very important. However, in today's global and complex trade environment, forecasting has become even more difficult.

In the last fifteen years, the total exports in the world increased by more than 30 percent in value (Piezas-Jerbi & Wardyn, 2017). The major contribution to this increase has been the export of Asian countries, mainly China. However, with the increased competition, new country policies and recent trade wars, the international trade volumes can be significantly affected and accurate forecasting can become harder. In this dynamic world trade environment, the traditional forecasting tools cannot yield satisfactory results. However, with the consideration of the big data, accurate forecasts can be achieved.

For the last 20 years, the amount of data has increased significantly because of wide internet access, digitalization, and globalization. According to Chen, Mao & Liu (2014), the amount of data generated in two days in 2011 is equal to the amount of data from the start of the civilization to 2003. Today's supply chains depend on the data to design supply chain operations for reducing the cost and increasing performance (Hazen et al., 2014). In this context, "Big Data" has been one of the major topics in supply chain research. The main characteristics of big data are Volume, Variety, Velocity, Veracity and Value (Nguyen et al., 2018). The size of the data determines the volume. The different types and sources of the data indicate the variety of data. The velocity of the data is determined by the frequency of data. Therefore, only the amount of data does not refer to big data. Along with high volume, high variety and high velocity, veracity must be taken into account in Big Data Analytics (BDA) (Addo-Tenkorang & Helo, 2016). The value of the data is also significant and it can affect the impact of the Big Data Analytics. However, according to a survey performed by LaValle et al. (2011), the quality of the data is one of the main problems in Big Data Analytics applications. Big Data Analytics combines mathematical, statistical, computer science, and social sciences (Hazen et al., 2014). Machine learning, statistics, data mining, pattern recognition, optimization methods and visualization are the main tools of Big Data Analytics (Davenport & Dyché, 2013).

The most widely acknowledged big data benefits are the increased operational efficiency, better decision making, higher visibility, improved customer service and experience (Chen & Zhang, 2014; Russom, 2011; Schoenherr & Speier-Pero, 2015). Although Big Data Analytics can help reducing costs, being more agile and achieving higher service levels (Nguyen et al., 2018), according to Wang et al. (2016), less than 20% of companies adapted BDA in their supply chains due to people, culture or process related challenges (Chen & Zhang, 2014; Hu et al., 2014; Russom, 2011; Schoenherr & Speier-Pero, 2015; Villars, Olofson, & Eastwood, 2011).

Trade is one dimension of the global supply chain management that affects the operations and the performance of the supply chain. With the increased availability of wide data sources, exporters and importers can assess the progress of the trade volumes between countries and adjust their global supply chain operations accordingly. An accurate estimate of trade volumes can be achieved by simultaneously considering the market, product and time-related factors. Different countries (markets) can be compared for different products to assess different trade opportunities. Time is also important because the forecast accuracy depends on the chosen forecast horizon (e.g., monthly, quarterly or yearly). All these three aspects can be combined with the available wide data sources using Big Data Analytics to accurately forecast trade volumes between countries.

In this chapter, we present a novel methodology using Big Data Analytics to forecast the trade volumes between countries. To demonstrate our proposed methodology, the case of forecasting the export volume of refrigerators and freezers of Turkey to United Kingdom is presented. This product group is one of the main export products of Turkey, and United Kingdom is one of the main importers. Within this main product group, three different sub-product groups are tested to validate the effectiveness of our methodology and the results are discussed. Our study provides a non-parametric forecasting method using machine learning algorithms. Two different machine learning algorithms, Random Forest (RF) and Artificial Neural Networks (ANN) have been applied to forecast the export volumes. Different than the other models in the literature, our proposed Big Data Analytics approach employs more variety in data sources and machine learning features. To predict global trade data, our model employs an extensive amount of data. The results showed that our methodology provides effective forecasting for export volumes.

The rest of this chapter is organized as follows. Background Section summarizes the literature on the forecasting of trade products. In the next section, the problem is defined in more detail and the case study is given. The method to forecast international trade by using big data is presented in Methodology Section. Solutions Section reports the results of the study in detail. Conclusions and future work are summarized in the last section.

BACKGROUND

Supply chain management has been seen as a tool for gaining competitive advantage and according to Global Supply Chain Forum, one of the key processes of supply chain management is demand management (Barbosa et al., 2018). Forecasting international bilateral trade is a critical element of effective decision making for business and even for policy makers. In recent years, various forecasting models were applied for trade forecasting that uses extrapolation, time-series and economic models, agent-based computational economics models, and machine learning (Nummelin & Hänninen, 2016). There are two mainstream research approaches, parametric and nonparametric approaches, were used in trade forecasting models. AutoRegressive Integrated Moving Average (ARIMA), Exponential Smoothing, Vector Auto Regression (VAR) and their variations are the widely used parametric time series models. To forecast U.S. merchandise exports, Dale & Bailey (1982) used Box Jenkins method. Veenstra & Haralambides (2001) studied Vector Auto Regression (VAR) to forecast the seaborne trade flow of crude oil, iron ore, grain and coal products. Seasonality in Pakistan's Merchandise Exports and Imports was studied by Akhtar (2003) by using univariate ARIMA. Again, ARIMA was used to explain spice import-export and production behaviors of India and China by Sahu & Mishra (2013). Khan (2011) studied to forecast Bangladesh's total import by using ARIMA, Holt-Winter and VAR techniques. Kargbo (2007) forecasted South Africa's agricultural exports and imports by using ARIMA, VAR, Engle-Granger (EG) single-equation and vector error-correction models (VECM). Emang et al. (2010) worked on univariate time series models to forecast Peninsular Malaysia's export demand for molding and chipboard volume.

Difficulties in managing structural interdependencies and the need for parametric assumptions and estimated elasticities make the usage of parametric models harder. In addition to the difficulties of applying parametric models, easier use of machine learning tools and increased accessibility of data sources are supportive reasons to use non-parametric models. There are some studies compare parametric and non-parametric models in trade forecasting. For example, Co & Boosarawongse (2007) compared Artificial Neural Network (ANN) model with parametric models for the forecasts of Thailand's rice export. Their study applied to four different types of rice products. To compare the models, exponential smoothing and ARIMA techniques were taken as parametric models and ANN was taken as the non-parametric model. They showed that ANN yielded the best forecast results. In a similar study, Pakravan, Kelashemi, & Alipour (2011) studied the forecasting of Iran's rice import by using ANN. Singular Spectrum Analysis is used by Silva & Hassani (2015) to forecast the trade of the United States before, during and after the recession of 2008. To analyze and forecast global bilateral trade flows of sawn wood, Nummelin & Hänninen (2016) studied various machine learning models. Support vector machines (SVM), random forests, ANN and their variations were used in their study. Similar to our model, the model build by Nummelin & Hänninen (2016) uses not only export volumes but also other economic indicators, such as exchange rates and Gross Domestic Product (GDP), however, their model includes a very limited number of factors. Shibasaki & Watanabe (2012) forecasted cargo flow in Asia-Pacific Economic Cooperation (APEC) region by using relations between economic growth, trade, and logistics demand models. Sokolov-Mladenović et al. (2016) forecasted economic growth by using ANN which is based on trade, import, and export parameters. Using the same relationship, our model takes economic growth as an input to forecast international trade but uses more input factors. Gupta & Kashyap (2015) used ANN to forecast inflation in G-7 countries where our model takes inflation as one of the input factors to predict import and export volumes.

MAIN FOCUS OF THE CHAPTER

The first research question that we address in this study is "How can we use open data sources in bilateral trade forecasting?". The next question is "Which factors are affecting the bilateral trade forecasting?". The third one is "How can we achieve accurate forecast results in the selected machine learning method?". These are the main research questions we address in this study. To answer these questions, we used our proposed forecasting methodology to forecast trade volumes. However, the product and the country pair (exporting and importing) should be selected first to conduct the analyses.

In international bilateral trade, there are three important aspects for evaluating current and future business situations. The first point is the representation of the market. A single country, geographical region (West Africa, Far East, etc.) or a group of countries with a common point of agreement (EU, OECD, etc.) can be considered as the market. The next aspect is the level of detail of the product definition. The third one is the forecast horizon, which may vary from a month to years. Product level of detail is handled according to Harmonized Commodity Description and Coding System (HS)[1] levels. HS is an international coding system for the classification of products. The products are represented as six-digit codes in HS. The first two digits of an HS code represents the main chapter of goods (e.g., "84" is "Machinery"). The next two digits represent the grouping within that chapter. For example, "84.18" code "Refrigerator and freezers" group in machinery chapter. The last two digits identify a specific product in that group. For example, "84.18.10" represents "Refrigerators and freezers fitted with separate external doors".

For our study, Chapter 84 (Machinery) is selected because it is closely related to the end-customer behavior. Also, according to Turkey's export volumes (see Table 1), Chapter 84 (Machinery) is the second biggest export chapter to the World after Chapter 87 (Vehicles). Within Chapter 84, the product group of refrigerators and freezers (HS=84.18) is the biggest product group according to the export volumes. To be more product specific, three different product types are selected in HS=84.18 group. According to trade volumes in 2016, these three product types are top three exported products from Turkey in that product group. The three product groups selected in our study are listed below:

- **84.18.10:** Refrigerators and freezers; combined refrigerator-freezers, fitted with separate external doors, electric or other
- **84.18.40:** Freezers; of the upright type, not exceeding 900l capacity
- **84.18.50:** Furniture incorporating refrigerating or freezing equipment; for storage and display

As seen in Table 2, United Kingdom is the biggest importer in HS=84.18 product group from Turkey in 2016. Due to these reasons, for our Bilateral Trade Forecasting case presented in this chapter, Turkey and United Kingdom are selected as the source (exporting) and target (importing) countries, respectively.

Table 1. Turkey's export volumes according to HS Codes (Thousand USD)

HS Code			Product Label	2015	2016	2017	2018
87			Vehicles other than railway or tramway rolling stock, and parts and accessories thereof	17,463,564	19,801,974	23,940,852	26,759,684
84			Machinery, mechanical appliances, nuclear reactors, boilers; parts thereof	12,333,803	12,339,237	13,825,494	15,831,703
	8418		Refrigerators, freezers and other refrigerating or freezing equipment, electric or other; heat . . .	1,721,260	1,740,073	1,802,257	1,970,693
		841810	Refrigerators and freezers; combined refrigerator-freezers, fitted with separate external doors, electric or other	711,584	884,550	916,703	992,722
		841850	Furniture incorporating refrigerating or freezing equipment; for storage and display	231,983	241,678	259,520	295,578
		841840	Freezers; of the upright type, not exceeding 900l capacity	184,068	197,103	202,870	220,714

Table 2. Turkey's export partners in HS 84.18 product group (Thousand USD)

Country	2015	2016	2017	2018
United Kingdom	222,308	212,341	200,071	224,844
Germany	188,426	202,314	211,439	220,487
United States of America	101,850	108,716	128,181	171,648
France	131,387	118,826	105,107	124,153
Italy	81,251	98,137	121,638	106,398

METHODOLOGY

Big Data Analytics can be seen as data manufacturing and it is similar to traditional manufacturing (Hazen et al., 2014) because raw data are converted into forecasted data like converting raw materials into physical products. Our study is based on CRISP-DM (CRoss Industry Standard Process for Data Mining) which was used by Wirth & Hipp (2000). To forecast trade volumes between countries, we used all the steps of CRISP-DM (business understanding, data understanding, data preparation, modeling and evaluation). In Figure 1, the followed CRISP-DM process is given.

As the first step, business understanding is crucial. In this step, the dynamics and potentially influential factors for bilateral trade are identified. After doing a literature survey and conducting appropriate research, the candidate factors are identified. These factors come from various domains, such as trade, economy, business and politics. Since our aim is to forecast the bilateral trade volume, there are some constraints for determining factors. In this study, we included more than 10 years of data, to have enough training and test sets. The data set is examined according to intrinsic data dimensions (Wigan & Clarke, 2013). Intrinsic dimensions are accuracy, timeliness, consistency, completeness and frequency. The first concern is the accuracy and our 10 years of data are reachable from reliable open data sources. The next one is timeliness, and the start and end dates of our data are around 2007 and 2017, respectively. Completeness is the next dimension, and it means that data do not have any missing points during that

Figure 1. CRISP-DM (CRoss Industry Standard Process for Data Mining) process

period. Consistency dimension is the expectancy to be on the same unit or at least convertible to the same unit. As the frequency dimension, the monthly period is selected in our model and data served in monthly periods are preferred. After passing all these intrinsic data dimension constraints, the features used in the forecast models are determined.

The features are the factors affecting the trade volume and summarized in Table 3. These factors can be grouped into two main groups: (1) product-specific trade information, and (2) country or global conditions related features. The components affecting bilateral trade are mainly supply and demand factors of the related countries (Ayankoya, Calitz, & Greyling, 2016; Kangas & Baudin, 2003; Nummelin & Hänninen, 2016). To model the demand for a specific product in a target country (in our study, United Kingdom), the trade volumes of the top five exporters to the target country are considered. To model the supply from the source country (in our study, Turkey), the trade volumes of the top five target countries that the source country exports are taken into account. As the last product specific factor, the unit value of the traded product is included in the model. Country or global factors are product independent data. These factors are divided into the political environment, business environment (Bovi & Cerqueti, 2016), economic environment (Keck, Raubold, & Truppia, 2010; Sokolov-Mladenović et al., 2016) and trade environment-related factors. Business environment is represented by adding Business Confidence and Consumer Confidence Indicators. With the inclusion of Economic Political Uncertainty Index, political factors are covered. Economic factors are GDP, Exchange Rates, Composite leading Indicators, Consumer and Producer Price Indices. World Trade Volume and World Economic Political Uncertainty indices are included as global trade parameters. To obtain these data, four different open data sources are used (see Source column of Table 3).

Table 3. The features used in the proposed big data analytics trade forecasting model

Group	Feature	Source
Trade Information	• Supply Capacity of the Source Country for each Product: Export volume of top five importing countries from Turkey (the countries for each product are given in Table 5) • Total Supply Capacity of the Source Country for each Product: Turkey's export volume to the World • Demand Capacity of the Target Country for each Product: Import Volume of top five exporting countries to United Kingdom Turkey (countries for each product are given in Table 5)	International Trade Center
	• Unit Value of each Product from Source Country (Turkey) to Target Country (United Kingdom)	
Political Environment	• Economic Policy Uncertainties of Source and Target Countries, and the World: EPU [a]	Economic Politic Uncertainty
Business Environment	• Business Confidence Indicators of Source and Target Countries: BCI • Consumer Confidence Indicators of Source and Target Countries: CCI	OECD
Economic Environment	• Composite Leading Indicators of Source and Target Countries: CLI	OECD
	• GDPs of Source and Target Countries: GDP	
	• Producer Price Indices of Source and Target Countries: PPI	
	• Consumer Price Indices of Source and Target Countries: CPI	
	• Exchange Rate of Local Currencies of Source and Target Countries to USD: TRY and GBP	
Trade Environment	• Total World Trade Volume	CPB World Trade Monitor

[a] EPU of Turkey is not included in the study, since there is no available data for Turkey

According to CRISP-DM methodology, the next step is data understanding. There are two different trade data reporting the trade volumes. These are export data reported by exporter country and import data reported by the importer country. These two data do not fully match with each other due to the differences in export and import data keeping procedures of the countries. In this study, to be consistent, the trade data based on data reported by the exporter countries are used.

After data understanding step, data preparation step is applied. In this step, data sets from different sources are formatted to be on the same basis and joined according to their dates. In addition, multiple entries are cleaned. Time windowing is done by shifting the data points one through eight months. After time windowing, the dependent variable data sets and independent variable data sets are prepared for each product to determine the forecast horizon. All data combinations are created to find the best set of dependent variables from past trade data. These combinations are based on monthly data as listed in Table 4. For example, 2 months ahead forecast horizon of two input month combinations uses the data of two and three months ago.

In the modeling step, common machine learning methods can be applied. Random Forests, Artificial Neural Networks, Decision Trees, Support Vector Machines, or Association Rule Analysis are some of the algorithms in order to derive knowledge from data reflecting conditions, processes and patterns (Stahlbock & Voß, 2010). Our data set contains monthly input data and can be classified as a multivariate time series. Because of their learning ability from complex relationships from these multivariate data (Mishra, Mishra, & Santra, 2016), Random Forests and Artificial Neural Networks are selected as forecasting methods herein.

Table 4. Forecast horizon and input month combinations

Input month combinations	Forecast Horizon					
	1 month ahead	2 months ahead	3 months ahead	4 months ahead	5 months ahead	6 months ahead
Single	Only -1	Only -2	Only -3	Only -4	Only -5	Only -6
Two	-1 and -2	-2 and -3	-3 and -4	-4 and -5	-5 and -6	-6 and -7
Three	-1, -2 and -3	-2, -3 and -4	-3, -4 and -5	-4, -5 and -6	-5, -6 and -7	-6, -7 and -8

Random Forest (RF)

Decision Tree is a widely used machine learning method for both classification and regression. Random Forest Model is based on ensemble learning by different Decision Trees. This ensemble learning approach was first developed by Breiman (2001). A prediction by using a single decision tree mainly depends on the formation of the training set. It can cause overfitting problem in the train set and low-quality results in the test set. To avoid this overfitting due to the single dimension of randomness in a single decision tree, random forest algorithm trains each tree with a random subset of the complete data set. Including the second dimension of randomness by using random subsets, Random Forest algorithm has the ability to reach high stability and robustness. This property allows using the best features among a random subset of candidate features. Therefore, Random Forest is used not only in forecasting but also in the feature selection processes. In Random Forest method, after creating a large number of trees, the best descriptive combination is selected within that trees (Breiman, 2001). Figure 2 summarizes this procedure used in Random Forest algorithms.

Figure 2. The procedure of random forest algorithm

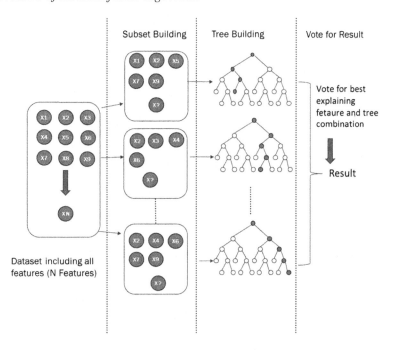

Artificial Neural Networks (ANN)

For the last two decades, Artificial Neural Networks have been used in various application areas (Tkáč & Verner, 2016). The ANN's first application is dated back to 1964 with a weather forecast model (Zhang, Patuwo, & Hu, 1998). Since neural networks have become a mature technique, it has a wide range of applications including forecasting, credit scoring, financial analysis, customer metrics to fraud analysis (Chen & Zhang, 2014; Tkáč & Verner, 2016). In the ANN, there are computational structures that are designed to mimic biological central nervous system (Nummelin & Hänninen, 2016; Zhang et al., 1998). ANN is based on the idea of accumulation of knowledge during training sessions. Due to the generalization ability coming from the knowledge accumulation attribute, the ANN can be used in any function approximation problem (Iebeling & Milton, 1996). The important benefits of the ANN, such as the efficiency, robustness and adaptability, make it a valuable tool for pattern recognition, classification and forecasting. There are various types of Neural Network topologies. Multi-layer Perceptron (MLP), Recurrent Neural Networks (RNN), Convolutional Neural Networks (CNN) and Long Short-Term Memory (LSTM) are some of the well-known ANN topologies (Øyen, 2018). In this study, MLP with the feedforward type selected, because it is one of the most widely used topologies in forecasting and it has low resource requirements. MLP topology consists of three layers: the input layer, hidden layer and output layer. The task of the input layer is to transfer raw input data to the network. The number of nodes in the input layer depends on the number of features used in the model. The next element in the network is the hidden layer, which consists of multiple layers and many nodes within them. After the hidden layer, the output layer is located. The final solution is produced in the output layer. Figure 3 shows a Multi-Layer Perceptron topology with three inputs, hidden layers (with two layers) and a single output. Note that each node in MLP is fed from the nodes of the previous layers and they are fully connected.

Figure 3. A Multi-Layer Perceptron topology with three inputs, two hidden layers and a single output

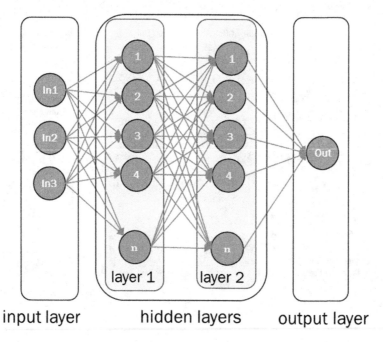

Each node has four components: input, weight, bias, and activation functions. The input of each node is generated by the outputs of the previous layer nodes. Weight is the transformation factor of each input. Bias is a general factor in each node. A linear transformation applied to input values using weight and bias as shown in Figure 4. The summation passes through an activation function, which decides how much of the information from this sum is the resulting output for that node. Non-linearity of ANN is provided by this activation function, which can be can be various types, such as logistics sigmoid or hyperbolic tangent (Øyen, 2018).

Figure 4. Mathematical model for a single node

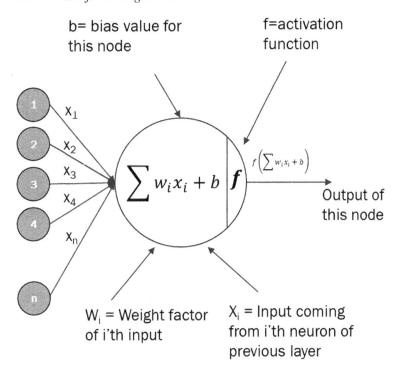

While training the MLP, the calculations are bi-directional. In the first move, the train data set passes through the entire network and results in an output. This move is called the forward directional calculation move. This output is the network's prediction results. Prediction results of train set and real values of train set are compared to find necessary adjustments. After calculation the difference between the predicted and real values, backpropagation step starts in the reverse direction. In this backward move, various types of solver methods are used to optimize weights and biases in each node. The solvers continue to optimize weights with these back and forth moves until the convergence achieved or a certain number of iterations is reached.

All machine-learning methods use two types of parameters. Some of them are determined before the training process and some of them are calculated during the training process. Parameters set before the training process are called as hyperparameters. Each model has a different hyperparameter sets. For Random Forest, maximum features, minimum samples leaf, and maximum leaf nodes are some of the hyperparameters. The hyperparameters of Random Forest are explained in the next section (see Table 9).

Solver type, activation function type and the maximum number of iterations are some hyperparameters of MLP. These hyperparameters are explained in the next section (see Table 11) in detail. To achieve more robust and successful results, convenient hyperparameter values should be found by applying a tuning process instead of using the default parameter values of the algorithms. In the tuning process, high R^2 scores and robustness are aimed. The evaluation of the results is the final step of CRISP-DM and is presented in the following section including the detailed preliminary analysis on data preparation and the process of hyperparameter tuning.

SOLUTIONS AND RECOMMENDATIONS

As explained in Main Focus Section in detail, our model is built to forecast the trade volumes of three types of products from Turkey to United Kingdom. The data set used in the forecasting model is combined from different open data sources that are given in the "Source" column of Table 3. The resulting data set is from 2006 April to 2018 March with 144 monthly data points. To give an insight about data series, time series plot with moving average and moving standard deviation values for products 841810, 841840 and 841850 are given in Figure 5, Figure 6 and Figure 7, respectively.

Figure 5. Time series plot for export product 841810 from Turkey to United Kingdom

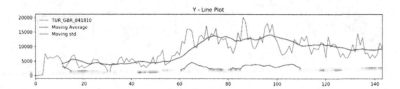

Figure 6. Time series plot for export product 841840 from Turkey to United Kingdom

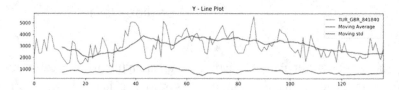

Figure 7. Time series plot for export product 841850 from Turkey to United Kingdom

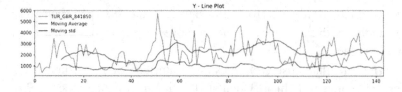

The top five importers and exporters are determined based on Turkey's yearly exports and United Kingdom's total import volumes in 2016. The list of importer and exporter countries given in Table 5.

Table 5. The top five importers from Turkey and exporters to United Kingdom for each product in 2016

Product HS Code	The top five importing countries from Turkey (Sorted by the largest trade volume to the lowest)	The top five exporting countries to United Kingdom (Sorted by the largest trade volume to the lowest)
841810	Germany, United Kingdom, Italy, France, United States	China, Turkey, Poland, Korea, Republic of, Italy
841840	United Kingdom, United States, France, Germany, Sweden	Turkey, China, Germany, Hungary Netherlands
841850	United Kingdom, Germany, Iraq, Saudi Arabia, Netherlands	Italy, China, Turkey, Austria, Czech Republic

The main process of our proposed Big Data Analytics methodology is presented in Figure 8. For all products, there are 28 features in both random forest and neural network models. The specific features to be used in the model depend on the preliminary study. This preliminary step analyzes the effects of the input month combinations, feature selection and dependent variable transformation decisions on the forecast quality. Without preliminary analysis model, the model forecasts one month ahead using the previous month's data and all other features without transforming the dependent variable. As the first step, the data of each feature is scaled according to min-max normalization since each feature in our data set has different ranges. After the scaling step, the data split into training and test sets. The training set is 80 percent of the entire data set with 115 observations and test set is the remaining 20 percent with 28 observations. Data stratification is applied to ensure the presence of each month to be included train and test sets. Therefore, the accumulation of certain months in test or training sets is prevented. Training is held by using train data. If no tuning process is applied to the models, then both model takes default values for hyperparameters. The hyperparameters of Random Forest and Artificial Neural Networks are specific to the method and affect the quality of the results. Trained models are tested with the test data to see the performance of the model. Since all data are scaled (including dependent variable) inverse scaling should be applied to see the real behavior of the output. Both models were implemented by using "scikit-learn" open source libraries for Python on a Windows PC. Python libraries of "MLPRegressor" and "RandomForestRegressor" were used for Neural Network and Random Forest implementations, respectively.

During the data preparation, a preliminary search process is conducted with three aspects to achieve successful results on forecasting. After checking these three aspects, the tuning process is started. The first aspect is to decide on which month or month combinations of the past trade data should be taken as input factors in the forecasting model. The month combinations are given in the first column of Table 6. Note that, Table 6 only reports the summary of the important results since extensive analyses were conducted with different combinations. The second aspect is the feature selection threshold, which defines the percentage of the features to be included in the model according to their feature selection scores. The searched options are 50 percent, 75 percent, and 100 percent. In this case, 50 percent means that only half of the features are included in the model according to their feature ranks and the remaining ones are omitted. To calculate each feature's rank two methods are combined. The third aspect is to determine the usage of the dependent variable. In this aspect, three options are searched: (1) same (no transformation), (2) transformed with logarithm and (3) transformed with square root. With all these

Figure 8. The proposed big data analytics process followed in this study

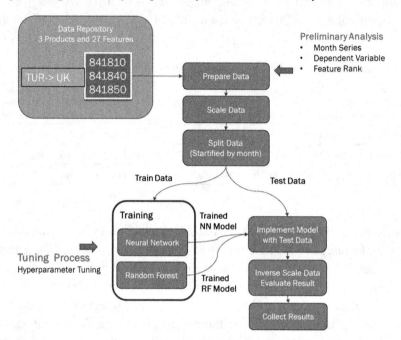

aspects and their combinations, 162 different data sets are trained. The results of this preliminary search with 162 combinations (with 10 random seed each) are presented in Table 6. According to these results, the dependent variable without any transformation, with 50 percent of the most important features and with the past trade data of 6 and 7 months yield the best result (R^2 of 0.859) for product 841810.

Repeating this process for the other products gives the best combinations for all products as shown in Table 7. The results indicate that the products 841840 and 841850 have the best forecast horizon of four months, while the product 841810 has the best forecast horizon of six months. For all products, the feature selection with 50 percent of the most important features achieved the best results. According to the results, two months of past data for products 841810 and 841850, while single month past data for product 841840 are used in the model. For all products, using the dependent variable as it is (without transformation) yielded the best results.

After this preliminary search, the top 10 features used in forecasting models are listed in Table 8 where the data labels are standardized for easy understanding. For example, TUR_GBR_841810-3 stands for: Source country is Turkey, Target Country is the United Kingdom, the product is 84.18.10 and the export values are shifted three months back. For all product types, Consumer Confidence Indicator plays an important role. Supply Capacity of the Source Country and Demand Capacity of the Target Country are common for all products. Consumer Price Index is a dominant feature for product 841810 whereas it does not appear in the other products. Note that the other features are product type dependent, which demonstrates the importance of our preliminary analysis.

Then, the hyperparameters are tuned for both Random Forest and Artificial Neural Networks algorithms according to the process is summarized in Figure 9.

Table 6. The R^2 results of the preliminary analysis for product 841810

Dependent Variable		same			sqrt			log		
Selected Features		50	75	100	50	75	100	50	75	100
Past Trade Data (Months)	-1	0.789	0.780	0.775	0.765	0.757	0.752	0.735	0.738	0.741
	-1 and -2	0.780	0.767	0.775	0.767	0.754	0.751	0.745	0.742	0.740
	-1, -2 and -3	0.773	0.770	0.767	0.776	0.762	0.761	0.767	0.760	0.754
	-2	0.772	0.765	0.768	0.759	0.756	0.753	0.739	0.743	0.738
	-2 and -3	0.759	0.764	0.768	0.771	0.773	0.770	0.776	0.763	0.761
	-2, -3 and -4	0.773	0.774	0.773	0.780	0.774	0.777	0.772	0.767	0.768
	-3	0.757	0.777	0.765	0.793	0.786	0.783	0.787	0.777	0.772
	-3 and -4	0.783	0.780	0.776	0.786	0.789	0.787	0.788	0.786	0.780
	-3, -4 and -5	0.817	0.810	0.803	0.811	0.800	0.803	0.793	0.786	0.782
	-4	0.781	0.789	0.789	0.772	0.788	0.786	0.767	0.763	0.771
	-4 and -5	0.826	0.813	0.813	0.796	0.804	0.797	0.775	0.770	0.775
	-4, -5 and -6	0.830	0.821	0.816	0.830	0.817	0.818	0.805	0.802	0.801
	-5	0.827	0.816	0.815	0.782	0.802	0.793	0.766	0.757	0.765
	-5 and -6	0.828	0.819	0.817	0.831	0.824	0.822	0.811	0.800	0.801
	-5, -6 and -7	0.858	0.852	0.845	0.847	0.839	0.839	0.811	0.812	0.818
	-6	0.814	0.814	0.806	0.829	0.826	0.819	0.788	0.805	0.803
	-6 and -7	0.859	0.843	0.835	0.841	0.833	0.835	0.806	0.810	0.807
	-6, -7 and -8	0.823	0.816	0.810	0.831	0.814	0.807	0.792	0.785	0.783

The hyperparameters of the Random Forest algorithm are explained in Table 9. Upon completing the tuning process for each product, hyperparameter values were obtained as in Table 10. Only one parameter value is common for all products, therefore applying the tuning process and using the appropriate parameters are very important to achieve good quality results.

The hyperparameters of the Artificial Neural Network algorithm are explained in Table 11. Similar to the tuning process of the Random Forest model, the hyperparameter values of the Artificial Neural Network models for each product are fixed as in Table 12. Only two parameter values, "solver" and "activation", are common for all products. Again, this shows the importance of the tuning process.

Table 7. Preliminary analysis results to determine best input combination for each product

Product HS Code	Past Trade Data (Months)	Transformation of the Dependent Variable (same, log, sqrt)	Percentage of Selected Feature (50%, 75%, 100%)
841810	-6 and -7	same	50
841840	-4	same	50
841850	-4 and -5	same	50

Table 8. The top ten feature list for each product

Rankings of the features	Product HS Code		
	841810	**841840**	**841850**
1.	CCI_TUR-6 [a]	TUR_FRA_841840-4	TUR_World_841850-4
2.	CPI_TUR-7	CCI_GBR-4	TUR_IRQ_841850-4
3.	CCI_TUR-7	GDP_GBR-4	CCI_TUR-4
4.	CPI_GBR-6	NLD_GBR_841840-4	CLI_TUR-4
5.	CPI_TUR-6	TUR_DEU_841840-4	World-4
6.	CPI_GBR-7	HUN_GBR_841840-4	BCI_TUR-4
7.	TUR_FRA_841810-6	EPU_World-4	BCI_GBR-4
8.	TUR_ITA_841810-6	TRY-4	ITA_GBR_841850-5
9.	TUR_DEU_841810-6	GBP-4	CCI_TUR-5
10.	POL_GBR_841810-7	TUR_GBR_841840_UV-4	CHZ_GBR_841850-4

[a]CCI refers to Consumer Confidence index, TUR indicates Turkey, and -6 means six months ago. The other variables in this table are coded similarly.

Figure 9. Tuning process for random forest and artificial neural network algorithms

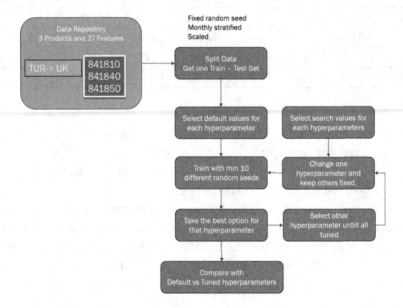

To demonstrate the efficiency of the tuning process, Figure 10 compares the R^2 values of the Random Forest model between tuned hyperparameter values and default (not tuned) hyperparameter values for all products. The cases of tuned and default values are repeated with 10 different random number seeds for each product. As seen from Figure 10, the tuning process yielded significantly higher R^2 values and more robust results in the Random Forest model. The same results are observed in the Artificial Neural Network model as well. Therefore, the tuning process is an essential step to increase forecast accuracy.

Table 9. The hyperparameters of the random forest model

Hyperparameter	Description
Maximum Features	It refers to the number of variables randomly sampled as candidates at each individual decision tree. Four different parameters (10,"log2","sqrt" and "auto"). The default value is 10.
Minimum Sample Leaf	It represents the minimum number of samples in newly created leaves. Five different parameters (which 1, 2, 5, 20 and 30) are selected in tuning. The default minimum sample leaf is 5.
Maximum Leaf Nodes	It refers to the maximum number of terminal node trees that a forest can have. Five different parameters (2, 5, 10, 100, 200 and 300) are selected in tuning. The default maximum leaf node is 100.
Minimum Weight Fraction For Leaf	It stands for the threshold value for minimum weighted fraction of the sum total of all input weights in newly created leaves. Five different parameters (0.00001, 0.0001, 0.001, 0.01 and 0.1) are selected in tuning. The default minimum weight fraction for leaf is 0.00001.
Minimum Impurity Decrease	It refers to the threshold value for the impurity decrease achieved by node split. Three different parameters (0.000001, 0.00001, 0.001 and 0.01) are selected in tuning. The default impurity decrease is 0.001.
Number Of Estimators	It represents the number of trees created in the forest by the algorithm. Seven different parameters (100, 200, 500, 1000, 5000, 10000 and 20000) are selected in tuning. The default estimator is 200.
Random State	It is the random number used while training. Since each training session is held with different random seed, random state is excluded from tuned hyperparameter set.

Table 10. Tuned values for hyperparameters of the random forest model for all products

Product HS Code	Maximum Features	Minimum Sample Leaf	Maximum Leaf Nodes	Minimum Weight Fraction For Leaf	Minimum Impurity Decrease	Number Of Estimators
841810	auto	1	300	0,0001	0,000001	1000
841840	10	5	100	0,0001	0,000001	5000
841850	10	2	10	0,00001	0,001	1000

Table 11. The hyperparameters of the neural network model

Hyperparameter name	Description
Solver	It is the solver method used for weight optimization in network. There are three options ("lbfgs", "sgd" and "adam") in library for this parameter which. The default solver is "adam".
Activation	It refers to the activation function type used in layers. There are four options ("identity", "logistic", "tanh" and "relu") in the library and the default activation function is "relu".
Alpha	It denotes the regularization parameter by giving penalty to the system. Three different parameters (0.001, 0.00001 and 0.0000001) are selected in tuning. The default alpha is 0.001.
Maximum Number Of Iterations	It refers to the solver continue to optimize weights until to reach this number of iterations. Four different parameters (1000, 10000, 50000 and 100000) are selected in tuning. The default maximum iteration is 200.
Hidden Layer Size	It represents the topology of the network in hidden layer. It has two dimensions, the number of layers and the number of neurons on each layer. The default is (30, 30) and it means two hidden layers with 30 neurons each. 5 different hidden layer size option is determined for tuning which, (10, 10), (30, 30), (100, 100), (30, 30, 30) and (30, 100, 30).
Learning Rate	It changes the weight optimization learning rate strategy. There are three options in library for this parameter which are 'constant', 'invscaling' and 'adaptive'. This parameter works only where the solver is 'sgd'. Since our set has small number of observations, 'lbfgs' perform better than the other solvers. Therefore, this hyperparameter omitted from tuning process.
Random State	It denotes the random number used during training. Since each training session is held with different random seed, random state is excluded from tuned hyperparameter set.

Table 12. Tuned values for hyperparameters of the neural network model for all products

Product HS Code	Solver	Activation	Alpha	Maximum Number Of Iterations	Hidden Layer Size
841810	lbfgs	identity	0,0000001	100000	(30, 30, 30)
841840	lbfgs	identity	0,0000001	10000	(10, 10)
841850	lbfgs	identity	0,00001	10000	(30, 30)

Figure 10. Before tuning and after tuning R^2 results of the Random Forest for all products

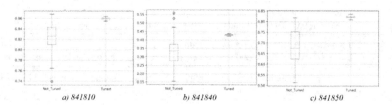

For all products, Random Forest and Artificial Neural Network algorithms were compared according to R^2 values. As shown in Figure 11, Random Forest gives better R^2 values than Neural Network models for all product types. Note that, Figure 11 presents the median R^2 values with the tuned hyperparameters for both algorithms. Among three product types, Product 841810 gives the best result with 0.86 R^2 value and 841840 gives the lowest R^2 value.

Figure 11. The median R^2 values of random forest and artificial neural network models for all products

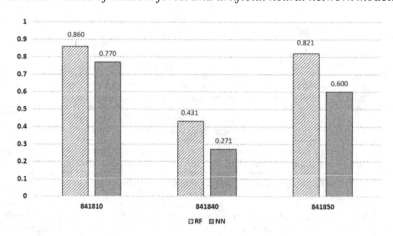

The scatter plots presented in Figure 12 show the actual and predicted values of train and test data in the Random Forest model. In this figure, the blue dots represent the train data and the red ones represent the test data. Note that, R^2 values given in Figure 11 are calculated for the test data. Figure 13, Figure 14 and Figure 15 show the forecasts of all products with the Random Forest model.

Figure 12. Scatter plots for the train and test data prediction of the random forest model for all products

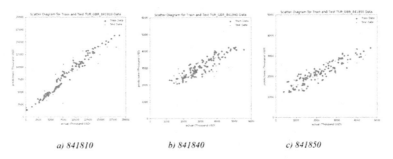

a) 841810   *b) 841840*   *c) 841850*

Figure 13. Line plot of all data set for product 841810 from Turkey to United Kingdom

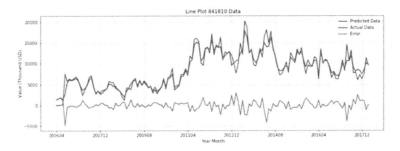

Figure 14. Line plot of all data set for product 841840 from Turkey to United Kingdom

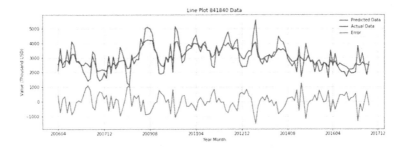

Figure 15. Line plot of all data set for product 841850 from Turkey to United Kingdom

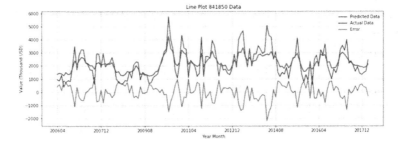

During the tuning and training processes, the main goal is to increase the R^2 value of the test set. However, R^2 value for the train set can decrease while increasing R^2 value for the test set. For example, Table 13 shows the R^2 value changes in the Random Forest model with the tuning and training processes for 841810 product because this product type has the most dramatic results. According to these results, although the train set achieves high R^2 value, the test set has significantly lower R^2 value. This indicates a possible overfitting problem of the train set. Also, the default hyperparameter values yield higher R^2 values than the tuned parameters for the train set, however, higher test R^2 values are achieved by the tuned hyperparameters. Therefore, lower R^2 values in the train set do not necessarily indicate lower R^2 values in the test set. Similar results were observed with the other products, however, their R^2 values are significantly higher and overfitting does not seem to be a problem. In addition, overfitting is not a significant issue for 841810 product because it has acceptable R^2 values (0.446). The same tests were conducted with the Artificial Neural Network model and the same observations were made.

Table 13. R^2 value changes in the Random Forest model with the tuning and training processes for 841810 product

	R^2 for Test Set	R^2 for Train Set	R^2 for All Data Set
Trained with default hyperparameters	0.42	0.958	0.87
Trained with tuned hyperparameters	0.446	0.807	0.752

CONCLUSION AND FUTURE RESEARCH DIRECTIONS

Today's supply chain operations have become more complex due to globalization. Therefore, many supply chain operations, such as production, procurement, sales, warehousing, and forecasting, should be designed with considering global factors. Among these factors, international trade significantly affects the performance of the global supply chain operations. Forecasting the future trade volumes of specific products between countries can help companies to adapt to new trade environments and make their supply chain decisions accordingly. However, with the increased complexity of the global supply chain networks and global trade between countries, forecasting has become harder. Using Big Data Analytics, accurate forecasts can be achieved.

In this chapter, we presented a new Big Data Analytics methodology to forecast trade volumes of specific products between the two countries. In this methodology, various open data sources are used to forecast trade volumes. As the main forecasting algorithm, Random Forest and Artificial Neural Networks are used. A case study, forecasting the export volume of refrigerators and freezers from Turkey to United Kingdom is presented to demonstrate our proposed methodology. In this case study, 28 different factors are considered and the data (ranged from 2006 April to 2018 March) of each factor are obtained from various online data sources (OECD, International Trade Center, etc.). We demonstrated the effectiveness of our methodology on three sub-product of the main product type. The results showed that our methodology provides an accurate forecast on the export volumes. According to the results, both Random Forest and Artificial Neural Networks provide robust results. However, Random Forest performs better than the Artificial Neural Network to forecast demand export volumes.

Using feature selection, the important factors to forecast international trade volumes are also identified with our study. For all product types, Consumer Confidence Indicator has been seen as a dominant feature. Features related to Turkey's supply capacity and United Kingdom's demand capacity are also significant for all products types. The other features are product type specific and it shows the importance of the feature selection in the forecasting accuracy. Instead of using all features obtained from the data sources, using 50 percent of the features improves the forecasting accuracy for all products. Therefore, feature selection procedure improves the results for all products. The best forecast results are achieved by using different forecast horizons. Best forecast horizon for products 841840 and 841850 is four months and for product 841810 is six months. The reason for this difference may be the different market dynamics and seasonality structures of these products. The overfitting problem is mostly avoided by using hyperparameter tuning process. Therefore, this shows that the tuning process is a necessary step in machine learning methods and it helps to find better and more robust results.

For future work, our methodology can be tested on other export products for different countries. Differentiating significant factors affecting the forecast accuracy of different product groups is another possible extension of this work. In this study, Random Forest and Artificial Neural Networks are used. However, other machine learning methods, for example, Long Short Term Memory, can be employed to improve the forecast quality. Another research direction would be applying this methodology to other forecast areas in global supply chain management.

REFERENCES

Addo-Tenkorang, R., & Helo, P. T. (2016). Big data applications in operations/supply-chain management: A literature review. *Computers & Industrial Engineering*, *101*, 528–543. doi:10.1016/j.cie.2016.09.023

Akhtar, S. (2003). Is there seasonality in Pakistan's merchandise exports and imports? The univariate modelling approach. *Pakistan Development Review*, *42*(1), 59–75. doi:10.30541/v42i1pp.59-75

Ayankoya, K., Calitz, A. P., & Greyling, J. H. (2016). Real-Time grain commodities price predictions in South Africa: A big data and neural networks approach. *Agrekon*, *55*(4), 483–508. doi:10.1080/03031853.2016.1243060

Barbosa, M. W., Vicente, A. C., Ladeira, M. B., & de Oliveira, M. P. V. (2018). Managing supply chain resources with Big Data Analytics: A systematic review. *International Journal of Logistics Research and Applications*, *21*(3), 177–200. doi:10.1080/13675567.2017.1369501

Bovi, M., & Cerqueti, R. (2016). Forecasting macroeconomic fundamentals in economic crises. *Annals of Operations Research*, *247*(2), 451–469. doi:10.100710479-015-1879-4

Breiman, L. (2001). Random forests. *Machine Learning*, *45*(1), 5–32. doi:10.1023/A:1010933404324

Chen, C. P., & Zhang, C.-Y. (2014). Data-intensive applications, challenges, techniques and technologies: A survey on Big Data. *Information Sciences*, *275*, 314–347. doi:10.1016/j.ins.2014.01.015

Chen, M., Mao, S., & Liu, Y. (2014). Big data: A survey. *Mobile Networks and Applications*, *19*(2), 171–209. doi:10.100711036-013-0489-0

Co, H. C., & Boosarawongse, R. (2007). Forecasting Thailand's rice export: Statistical techniques vs. artificial neural networks. *Computers & Industrial Engineering*, *53*(4), 610–627. doi:10.1016/j.cie.2007.06.005

Dale, C., & Bailey, V. B. (1982). A box-jenkins model for forecasting U.S. merchandise exports. *Journal of International Business Studies*, *13*(1), 101–108. doi:10.1057/palgrave.jibs.8490542

Davenport, T. H., & Dyché, J. (2013). Big data in big companies. International Institute for Analytics.

Emang, D., Shitan, M., Abd. Ghani, A. N., & Noor, K. M. (2010). Forecasting with univariate time series models: A case of export demand for peninsular Malaysia's moulding and chipboard. *Journal of Sustainable Development*, *3*(3), 157–161. doi:10.5539/jsd.v3n3p157

Gupta, S., & Kashyap, S. (2015). Forecasting inflation in G-7 countries: An application of artificial neural network. *Foresight*, *17*(1), 63–73. doi:10.1108/FS-09-2013-0045

Hazen, B. T., Boone, C. A., Ezell, J. D., & Jones-Farmer, L. A. (2014). Data quality for data science, predictive analytics, and big data in supply chain management: An introduction to the problem and suggestions for research and applications. *International Journal of Production Economics*, *154*, 72–80. doi:10.1016/j.ijpe.2014.04.018

Hu, H. A. N., Wen, Y., Chua, T., & Li, X. (2014). Toward scalable systems for big data analytics: A technology tutorial. *IEEE Access: Practical Innovations, Open Solutions*, *2*, 652–687. doi:10.1109/ACCESS.2014.2332453

Iebeling, K., & Milton, B. (1996). Designing a neural network for forecasting financial and economic time series. *Neurocomputing*, *10*(3), 215–236. doi:10.1016/0925-2312(95)00039-9

Kabadurmus, O., Erdogan, M. S., & Tasgetiren, M. F. (2017). Design of multi-product multi-period two-echelon supply chain network to minimize bullwhip effect through differential evolution. *2017 IEEE Congress on Evolutionary Computation (CEC)*, 789–796. 10.1109/CEC.2017.7969390

Kangas, K., & Baudin, A. (2003). *Modelling and projections of forest products demand, supply and trade in Europe*. UN.

Kargbo, J. M. (2007). Forecasting agricultural exports and imports in South Africa. *Applied Economics*, *39*(16), 2069–2084. doi:10.1080/00036840600707183

Keck, A., Raubold, A., & Truppia, A. (2010). Forecasting international trade: A time series approach. *OECD Journal: Journal of Business Cycle Measurement and Analysis*, *2009*(2), 157–176.

Khan, T. (2011). Identifying an appropriate forecasting model for forecasting total import of Bangladesh. *Statistics in Transition New Series*, *12*(1), 179–192.

LaValle, S., Lesser, E., & Shockley, R., Hopkins, M. S., & Kruschwitz, N. (2011). Big data, analytics and the path from insights to value. *MIT Sloan Management Review*, *52*(2), 20–32.

Mishra, S., Mishra, D., & Santra, G. H. (2016). Applications of machine learning techniques in agricultural crop production: A review paper. *Indian Journal of Science and Technology*, *9*(38), 1–14. doi:10.17485/ijst/2016/v9i38/95032

Nguyen, T., Zhou, L., Spiegler, V., Ieromonachou, P., & Lin, Y. (2018). Big data analytics in supply chain management: A state-of-the-art literature review. *Computers & Operations Research*, *98*, 254–264. doi:10.1016/j.cor.2017.07.004

Nummelin, T., & Hänninen, R. (2016). Model for international trade of sawnwood using machine learning models. *Natural Resources and Bioeconomy Studies, 74*.

Øyen, S. (2018). *Forecasting Multivariate Time Series Data Using Neural Networks* (Unpublished Master's thesis). Norwegian University of Science and Technology, Norway.

Pakravan, M. R., Kelashemi, M. K., & Alipour, H. R. (2011). Forecasting Iran's rice imports trend during 2009-2013. *International Journal of Agricultural Management and Development*, *1*, 39–44.

Piezas-Jerbi, N., & Wardyn, S. (2017). Trends in world trade: Introduction. *World Trade Statistical Review*, 4–6.

Russom, P. (2011). Big data analytics. *TDWI Best Practices Report*, *19*(4), 1–34.

Sahu, P. K., & Mishra, P. (2013). Modelling and forecasting production behaviour and import-export of total spices in two most populous countries of the world. *Journal of Agricultural Research*, *51*(1), 81–97.

Schoenherr, T., & Speier-Pero, C. (2015). Data science, predictive analytics, and big data in supply chain management: Current state and future potential. *Journal of Business Logistics*, *36*(1), 120–132. doi:10.1111/jbl.12082

Shibasaki, R., & Watanabe, T. (2012). Future forecast of trade amount and international cargo flow in the APEC Region: An application of trade-logistics forecasting model. *Asian Transport Studies*, *2*(2), 194–208.

Silva, E. S., & Hassani, H. (2015). On the use of singular spectrum analysis for forecasting U.S. trade before, during and after the 2008 recession. *Inter Economics*, *141*, 34–49. doi:10.1016/j.inteco.2014.11.003

Sokolov-Mladenović, S., Milovančević, M., Mladenović, I., & Alizamir, M. (2016). Economic growth forecasting by artificial neural network with extreme learning machine based on trade, import and export parameters. *Computers in Human Behavior*, *65*, 43–45. doi:10.1016/j.chb.2016.08.014

Stahlbock, R., & Voß, S. (2010). Improving empty container logistics – Can it avoid a collapse in container transportation ? *Liber Amicorum In Memoriam Jo Van Nunen*, 217–224.

Tkáč, M., & Verner, R. (2016). Artificial neural networks in business: Two decades of research. *Applied Soft Computing*, *38*, 788–804. doi:10.1016/j.asoc.2015.09.040

Veenstra, A. W., & Haralambides, H. E. (2001). Multivariate autoregressive models for forecasting seaborne trade flows. *Transportation Research Part E, Logistics and Transportation Review*, *37*(4), 311–319. doi:10.1016/S1366-5545(00)00020-X

Villars, R. L., Olofson, C. W., & Eastwood, M. (2011). Big Data: What it is and why you should care. *IDC Analyze the Future*, 1–14.

Wang, C., Li, X., Zhou, X., Wang, A., & Nedjah, N. (2016). Soft computing in big data intelligent transportation systems. *Applied Soft Computing*, *38*, 1099–1108. doi:10.1016/j.asoc.2015.06.006

Wigan, M. R., & Clarke, R. (2013). Big data's big unintended consequences. *Computer*, *46*(6), 46–53. doi:10.1109/MC.2013.195

Wirth, R., & Hipp, J. (2000). CRISP-DM: Towards a standard process model for data mining. *Proceedings of the Fourth International Conference on the Practical Application of Knowledge Discovery and Data Mining*, 29–39.

Zhang, G., Patuwo, B. E., & Hu, M. Y. (1998). Forecasting with artificial neural networks: The state of the art. *International Journal of Forecasting*, *14*(1), 35–62. doi:10.1016/S0169-2070(97)00044-7

ENDNOTE

[1]   https://unstats.un.org/unsd/tradekb/Knowledgebase/50018/

This research was previously published in Managing Operations Throughout Global Supply Chains; pages 70-99, copyright year 2019 by Business Science Reference (an imprint of IGI Global).

Chapter 44

Efficient Big Data–Based Storage and Processing Model in Internet of Things for Improving Accuracy Fault Detection in Industrial Processes

Mamoon Rashid

(iD) https://orcid.org/0000-0002-8302-4571

School of Computer Science and Engineering, Lovely Professional University, India

Harjeet Singh

(iD) https://orcid.org/0000-0003-3575-4673

Department of Computer Science, Mata Gujri College, Fatehgarh Sahib, India

Vishal Goyal

Department of Computer Science, Punjabi University, India

Nazir Ahmad

Department of Information Systems, Community College, King Khalid University, Saudi Arabia

Neeraj Mogla

Nike Inc. Global Headquarters, USA

ABSTRACT

As the lot of data is getting generated and captured in Internet of Things (IoT)—based industrial devices which is real time and unstructured in nature. The IoT technology—based sensors are the effective solution for monitoring these industrial processes in an efficient way. However, the real—time data storage and its processing in IoT applications is still a big challenge. This chapter proposes a new big data pipeline solution for storing and processing IoT sensor data. The proposed big data processing platform uses Apache Flume for efficiently collecting and transferring large amounts of IoT data from Cloud—based server into Hadoop Distributed File System for storage of IoT—based sensor data. Apache Storm is to be used for processing this real—time data. Next, the authors propose the use of hybrid prediction model of Density-based spatial clustering of applications with noise (DBSCAN) to remove sensor data outliers and provide better accuracy fault detection in IoT Industrial processes by using Support Vector Machine (SVM) machine learning classification technique.

DOI: 10.4018/978-1-6684-3662-2.ch044

1. CHAPTER OUTLINE

This chapter is structured around the concepts of efficient storage of sensor IoT based data and its processing in Big Data pipeline. Further the inclusion of novel prediction model will help to improve fault detection in IoT Industrial processes. In today's scenario we have to consider the big source of data generation as well as the plausible suitable platform of such huge data analysis. Therefore, the associated challenges are also included in this chapter.

1.1 Introduction to Big Data and IoT

Big Data Analytics along with Internet of Things (IoT) finds its use in areas of Smart Cities, Healthcare, Agriculture and Industrial Automation Units. The challenge of large amount of data generation in IoT devices is fulfilled by Big Data technologies in terms of its storage and processing (Chen et al., 2016). The advanced IoT devices and their applications have given rise to voluminous data in different varieties (Mavromoustakis et al., 2016). On the other side, Big Data technologies have discovered new kind of opportunities for developing IoT based systems (Rashid et al., 2013). Therefore, IoT based Systems and Big Data technologies integration will create new challenges in terms of storage and processing which needs to be addressed by the researchers (Singh et al., 2015).

1.1.1 Types of Big Data

The classification of Big Data is mostly given in terms of structure of data. The structure of data depends usually on its organization. Based on this, Big Data is classified into structured, unstructured and semi-structured data (Oussous et al., 2018). These types are explained below:

- **Structured Data:** Structured data is having fixed format and is easily stored, processed and accessed. Structured data is always following particular order as in row and column format and always results into ordered output. This data is easy to process as the format of data is always known in advance. All traditional databases containing data in row column format belong to this category.
- **Unstructured Data:** Unstructured data is usually huge data which is not in organized manner. This kind of data remains usually unknown and poses numerous challenges while processing for valuable insights as output. Moreover, this data is not having any kind of order and is raw in nature. Data in the form of images, audio, video and sensor-based data belong to this category.
- **Semi-Structured Data:** This kind of data usually contains both the forms but remain undefined. Usually this kind of data is not organized inherently at the beginning, but it can be turned into structure form while taking its analysis. Representation of data in terms of XML files belong to this category.

The different types of Big Data are shown in Figure 1.

Figure 1. Different types of big data

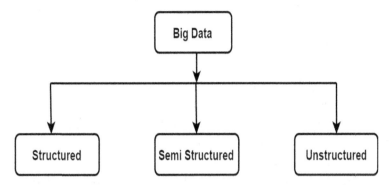

1.1.2 Characteristics of Big Data

The research work on Big Data reveals the following characteristics in terms of its storage and processing (Kapil et al., 2016).

- **Volume:** It is related to amount of data which is getting stored in Big Data file systems. Size of data is one important aspect of Big Data and based on its volume, one can decide whether this data can turn Big Data or not. Volume is the amount of data which is collected and stored in Big Data storage units (Oguntimilehin et al., 2014).
- **Velocity:** It refers to the speed of data which is arriving for its storage or the rate at which data is getting generated from various sources. These days a lot of data is getting generated at high velocities from various sources like Social Media, Sensors, Industrial Units, Weather Forecasting and Mobile devices. The nature of all such remains continuous and come at higher velocities (Kaisler et al., 2013).
- **Variety:** The nature of Big Data remains both structured and unstructured and thus gives it the characteristic of being heterogeneous. Variable data usually consist of data in the form of emails, images, audio and videos. It is always a challenge to analyze the data of these forms (Reddi et al., 2013).
- **Variability:** The nature of Big Data is sometimes decided by the inconsistency of data as well. It is always challenge to process data effectively which is inconsistent in nature (Owais et al., 2016).

1.1.3 Advantages of Big Data Processing

- **Improvement in Business Intelligence:** The organizations which are using Big Data platforms access social media like Twitter, Facebook by using various Application Programming Interfaces (API) and get enough insights to fine tune their strategies for the betterment of organization.
- **Improvement in Customer Services:** Big Data technologies resulted in new kind of feedback systems for customers which are far better than traditional systems for getting feedback. The use of Natural Language Processing makes it possible on top of Big Data Platforms for efficient evaluation of Customer responses.

- **Improvement in Operational Efficiency:** Big Data platforms are used for the identification of significant data which is required for its processing and are quite productive in data warehouses.

1.1.4 Architecture of IoT

The internet of Things is defined as Internet of Everything which is dynamic network of machines capable of interacting with each other (Lee et al., 2015). The essence of Internet of Things is realized when communication is taking place in connecting devices and its integration with customer support systems, business analytics and business intelligence applications. The stage wise architecture of IoT is given by (Boyes, 2018). The various things are inputted to stage of architecture where the presence of sensors remain in wired or wireless manner. The Internet Gateways and Data Acquisition Systems are used in next stage for data aggregation and its control. The pre-processing and various analytics are performed in next stage for which services in terms Data Centre or cloud is to be used. The whole process is explained in IoT architecture given in Figure 2.

Figure 2. Stage- Wise Architecture of IoT

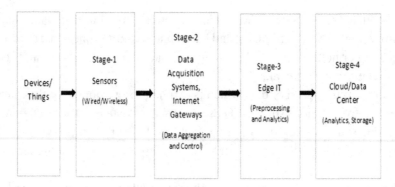

1.1.5 Standards of IoT for Industrial Applications

There is no clear line for classifying IoT Standards, however the major standard Protocols in use are based on IOT Data Link Protocols (Salman et al., 2017). Physical layer and MAC layer protocols are mostly used by various IoT standards.

- **IEEE 802.15.4**: This standard is used in MAC layer and specifies source and destination addresses, headers, format of frames, identification in communication between the nodes. Low cost communication and high reliability is enabled in IoT by the use channel hopping and synchronization in terms of time.
- **IEEE 802.11ah:** This kind of standard is used in traditional networking as Wi-Fi for IoT applications. This standard is used for friendly communication of power in sensors and supports lower overhead. This standard covers features of Synchronization Frame, Shorter MAC Frames and Efficient Bidirectional Packet Exchange.

- **WirelessHART:** This standard works on MAC layer and uses time division multiple access. This standard is more secure and reliable than other standards as it uses efficient algorithms for encryption purposes.
- **Z-Wave:** This standard works on MAC layer and was designed specifically for automation of homes. This standard works on Master Slave Configuration where the master sends small messages to slaves and is used for point to point short distances.
- **ZigBee:** This standard is common one and is used for communication in Health Care Systems and Remote Controls. This standard is meant for medium level communications.
- **DASH7:** This standard is used on MAC layer and is used in RFID devices. This standard supports master slave architecture and is very suitable for IoT applications and is designed for IPv6 addressing.
- **HomePlug:** This standard is MAC based and is used in smart grid applications. The beauty of this standard lies in its power saving mode where it allows nodes to sleep when not required and wakes them only whenever required.

2. RELATIONSHIP BETWEEN INTERNET OF THINGS AND BIG DATA

Internet of Things (IoT) is a conversion of range of things into smart objects like refrigerators, vehicles or any electric and electronic gadgets. In IoT, sensors and computer-based chips are used for gathering data in case of those devices which cannot be linked to the internet (Riggins et al., 2015). Whenever this gathered data from smart devices demonstrate volume, velocity and variety, then the role of Big Data comes into picture along with IoT. Usually the data acquired via various sensors remains quite voluminous and carries data in terms both structured and unstructured form. The challenge of velocity in Big Data is the speed of data at which it is getting processed and always shows its presence in terms of IoT based data. Variety is the data in different forms and is one of form in IoT based data. The major challenge in IoT is the way to handle large volumes of data which is getting generated from IoT devices. Big Data Tools are having the capacity to handle this IoT based data with its continuous streaming nature of information. Internet of Things and Big Data is cohesively related as IoT based data is usually raw in nature and it is Big Data Analytics tools which are extracting information from this raw data to get valuable insights to bring smartness in IoT systems. However, the scale for conducting data in IoT is completely different and analytics platform should take care of exact solutions for extracting accurate data. The relation between Big Data and Internet of Things is outlined by (Ahmed et al., 2017). The sketch of IoT environment in terms of IoT Infrastructure is shown in Figure 3.

There are various kinds of application domains like agriculture, shipping and logistics organizations which are making use of Big Data and Internet of Things together for offering insights and analysis. In agriculture, the crop fields are connected to monitoring systems for observing moisture levels in fields and later this data is provided to agriculture farmers for timely information. The shipping organizations are using sensor data and Big Data Analytics for improving efficiency in terms of delivery of various vehicles to maintain their mileage and speeds.

Figure 3. Broader View of IoT Ecosystem

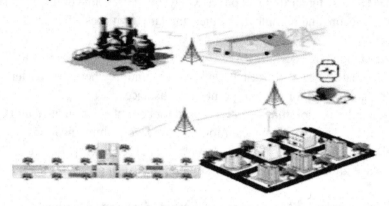

3. ARCHITECTURE OF APACHE FLUME AND STORM

Apache Flume is Big Data tool which is used for ingesting data on Hadoop Distributed File System (HDFS) for storage purpose (Hoffman et al., 2015). This tool is quite beneficial when one needs to collect and transport huge amount of real time streaming data from various sources like social media and sensors in the form of temperature, pressure and humidity. Apache Flume is scalable tool when it comes to large streaming of real data and anytime if the read rate of data from any generator exceeds the rate of writing, this tool provides flow for maintaining the read and write rates steadily (Makeshwar et al., 2015). The basic architecture of Apache Flume is given in Figure 4.

Figure 4. Architecture of Apache Flume for Storage of Real Time Data

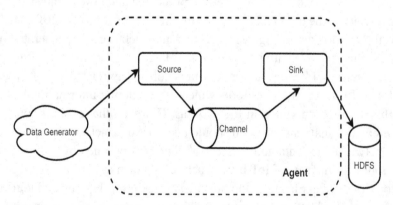

The major components used in Apache Flume architecture are events, agents and clients.

- **Flume Events:** Event is the fundamental unit of data which moves inside Flume pipeline between data source and Hadoop Distributed File System for final storage. Flume Events are data units which are carried out from source to destination with various kinds of headers associated with the data.

- **Flume Agents:** Flume Agents are responsible for the carriage of data from source to sink and receive data from clients. Apache Flume makes use of multiple agents for data transfer purposes until it reaches to final destination. Every Flume Agent internally contains three sub components in the form of Source, Channel and Sink. The source is used for receiving data from the data generator and transfers this received data to one of channels in medium. The channel is component which transfers the events received from source and acts as transient buffer until these events are taken by sink. The sink is used for storing the data in file systems like HDFS or HBase.
- **Flume Clients:** Client is the component which generates data in the form of events and then transfers this data to agents for transporting to HDFS environment.

Apache Storm is the real time data processing engine which accepts large volumes of data from various kinds of sources and analyses without storing any actual data (Iqbal et al. 2015). Apache Storm consists of Spouts and Bolts. Initially the data is retrieved from various data sources using Spout which passes this data to various Bolts which perform various operations on this data in the form of analyses and filtration which are later sent for view to end users. The architecture of Apache Storm is given in Figure 5.

Figure 5. Apache Storm Architecture for Real Time Processing of Data

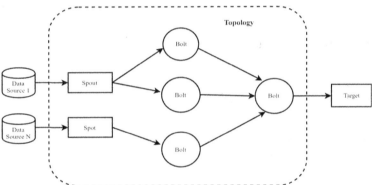

Combination of Spouts and Bolts form the topology in Apache Storm and data flow operation takes place in the form of tuples. Data flow in Apache Storm is unidirectional where the data is retrieved by spouts from data sources which are then sent to one or more bolts in one-way direction and remains flowing among blots until the data is finally published to end user (Nivash et al., 2014).

4. DATA ANALYTICS FOR IOT USING BIG DATA ANALYTICS

The need of Big Data Platforms and Analytics environment in Internet of Things have increased many folds in last few years and provide valuable benefits and improvement in processes of decision making. Therefore the requirements and demands of Big Data Analytics Platforms in Internet of Things have increased for better analytics in its data processing. The inclusion of Big Data Pipelines in Internet of Things have completely changed the way for storing and analyzing the data. The bigger amounts of data generated by various sensor devices can be effectively processed by Big Data Analytics for the extraction of meaningful insights. This section of chapter outlines key requirements required by Internet of Things environment for processing data in Big Data Analytics Platform.

- **Connectivity:** Better connectivity is one of the important requirement in IoT environment for Big Data Analytics on large amounts of machine generated sensor data (Ahmed, E. et al. 2017). Reliable connectivity is a way for connecting infrastructures with high performance with various kinds of objects for enabling services of Internet of Things.
- **Streaming Analytics:** This kind of data analytics is another key requirement in IoT environments and deals with real time data in motion. Data streams which are real time in nature are analyzed for the detection of critical situations. Big Data Analytics platforms require data on the fly and process it in the form of data streams (Tönjes et al., 2014).
- **Storage:** Another key requirement in IoT based Big Data Platforms is the storage of huge amounts of data generated by various IoT objects on some commodity storage units with low latency factors in its analytics. M2M communication protocols are widely used in most Internet of Things services for handling large streams and provide benefits of cloud systems in terms of distributed storage (Suciu et al., 2015).
- **Quality of Services:** The requirement in IoT based Big Data Platforms is the quality of Services in mobile devices and IoT sensors in terms of resource management. The Quality of Service must be quite efficient in IoT based network where efficient data transfer is required from various devices and objects to Big Data platforms (Jin et al., 2012).

5. BIG DATA PIPELINE FOR IOT DATA STORAGE AND PROCESSING

This section of the chapter provides the novel outline of Big Data Pipeline for processing IoT sensor data keeping various requirements into consideration.

5.1 Proposed Big Data Pipeline for processing IoT Sensor Data

The proposed model takes care of storage of IoT based sensor data and then processes it on the Big Data Real Time Engine and later uses hybrid prediction model for detecting faults in industrial assemblies. The hybrid prediction model for fault detection is discussed in the next section. The idea is to connect IoT based sensors to the industrial assembly pipelines for sensing the data. The temperature, accelerometer and humidity sensors are used for capturing data from assemblies. The IoT sensor-based data is transmitted to the cloud server which is later stored in Big Data storage unit of Hadoop Distributed File System in terms of large volumes. The outliers in stored sensor data are filtered with the help of clustering method of Density-based spatial clustering of applications with noise (DBSCAN) where from the fault predictions are taken by applying machine learning classification technique of Support Vector Machine (SVM). The data in HDFS is processed on real time basis with the help of Apache Storm. The structure of proposed pipeline for storage and processing of IoT data is given in Figure 6.

Figure 6. Proposed Big Data Pipeline for Storage and Processing IoT Data

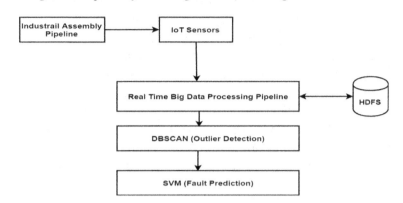

5.2 Hybrid Prediction Model for Fault Detection

Outlier detection is done with the help of Density-based spatial clustering of applications with noise (DBSCAN) for given dataset (Ester et al., 1996). After the removal of outliers from sensor data, Support Vector Machine (SVM) is used for the prediction of faults. A classification model is trained in terms of SVM classifier for predicting faults in terms of events are taking place normally or abnormally due to halts.

5.2.1 Step Procedure of DBSCAN Algorithm

For given dataset of T, DBSCAN will work on two parameters. ε (eps) and minPts. ε is the measure of distance between two assumed points of 'p' and 'q' for checking the density reachability from neighbors. minPts are the minimum number of points which are required to form the cluster.

Step 1: Any point (P) is assumed as starting point which has not been visited before.
Step 2: Select neighbors of this arbitrary starting point (P) on the basis of distance with ε.
Step 3: If density of neighbors is achieved for the point (P), then it is marked as visited and clustering begins. Otherwise it is marked as noise.
Step 4: If P is in cluster, then ε in its neighborhood is in cluster as well.
Step 5: Repeat Step 2 for all ε neighborhood points until all points in cluster are taken.
Step 6: New point which is unvisited and marked as clustering point or noise.
Step 7: Repeat Step 2 to Step 6 until all points are visited and marked.

5.2.2 Features of DBSCAN Algorithm

1. DBSCAN is a clustering algorithm which is not relying on specifying the number of clusters for a given data.
2. DBSCAN algorithm is very robust for outliers and have tendency to filter them out.
3. DBSCAN algorithm is quite useful in finding patterns and predicting trends where data is complex and hard to find manually.
4. DBSCAN algorithm has a tendency to produce variable number of clusters depending on the size of input.

Support Vector Machine (SVM) is one of the popular classification machine learning algorithm which effectively segregates classes within a hyper-plane (Evgeniou et al., 2001). Hyper-plane in n-dimensional plane is n-1 dimensional subsets in space which divides it into parts that are disconnected. SVM classifier makes the prediction decisions of classifying with a wider boundary between the classes.

The data from IoT sensors is stored on Hadoop Distributed File System (HDFS) with faulty data as well. The collected dataset is labelled with attributes of normal and faulty for classification purposes. Once the outliers in data DBSCAN, the refined data is finally inputted to SVM classifier for the detection of faults in data. The achieved results are compared with Logistic Regression, Naïve Bayes and Random Forest. The proposed model of DBSCAN+SVM showed increase in detection rate of faults in comparison to existing state-of-art. The performance of hybrid prediction model in terms of various performance measures is shown in Table 1.

Table 1. Comparison of prediction models for fault detections

Model	Accuracy (%)	Precision	Recall
Logistic Regression	96.91	0.979	0.978
Naïve Bayes	93.50	0.939	0.936
Random Forest	98.05	0.985	0.984
SVM	97.35	0.928	0.926
DBSCAN+ SVM	98.85	0.990	0.987

Proposed model is evaluated for performance in terms Logistic Regression, Naïve Bayes, Random Forest and SVM classifiers and the results achieved for hybrid prediction model of DBSCAN +SVM are better than other classifiers. The comparison performance accuracy is plotted in Figure 7.

Figure 7. Comparison of accuracy for various classifiers

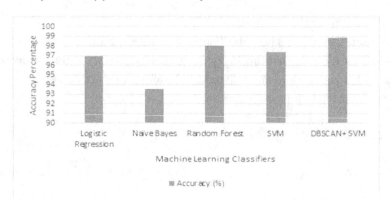

Proposed model is evaluated for precision in terms Logistic Regression, Naïve Bayes, Random Forest and SVM classifiers and the results achieved for hybrid prediction model of DBSCAN +SVM are better than other classifiers. The comparison performance measure for precision is plotted in Figure 8.

Figure 8. Comparison of precision for various classifiers

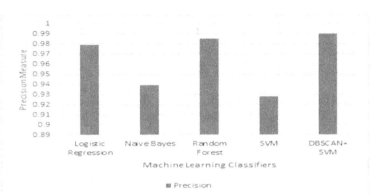

Proposed model is evaluated for recall in terms Logistic Regression, Naïve Bayes, Random Forest and SVM classifiers and the results achieved for hybrid prediction model of DBSCAN +SVM are better than other classifiers. The comparison performance measure in terms of recall is plotted in Figure 9.

Figure 9. Comparison of recall for various classifiers

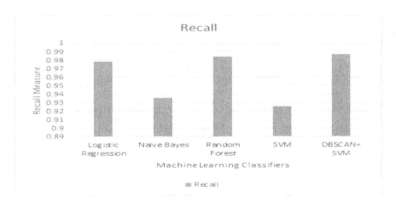

6. CONCLUSIONS AND FUTURE DIRECTIONS

In this research, the authors have tried to solve the challenge of real time processing of sensor-based data and fault detection of industrial assembly data. The IoT based sensor data is stored on Hadoop Distributed File System (HDFS) which is processed with Apache Storm on Big Data processing pipeline. The outliers in stored data were removed with the help of Density-based spatial clustering of applications with noise (DBSCAN) and then faults in industrial processes were detected using Support Vector Means classifier. The results suggest that this hybrid prediction model is scalable for data processing of IoT based sensor data and detections in faults are much better than traditional models. However, there is still room of improvement for this model in terms of its training for multi-fault system where the data to be trained is of complex type.

REFERENCES

Ahmed, E., Imran, M., Guizani, M., Rayes, A., Lloret, J., Han, G., & Guibene, W. (2017). Enabling mobile and wireless technologies for smart cities. *IEEE Communications Magazine*, *55*(1), 74–75. doi:10.1109/MCOM.2017.7823341

Ahmed, E., Yaqoob, I., Hashem, I. A. T., Khan, I., Ahmed, A. I. A., Imran, M., & Vasilakos, A. V. (2017). The role of big data analytics in Internet of Things. *Computer Networks*, *129*, 459–471. doi:10.1016/j.comnet.2017.06.013

Boyes, H., Hallaq, B., Cunningham, J., & Watson, T. (2018). The industrial internet of things (IIoT): An analysis framework. *Computers in Industry*, *101*, 1–12. doi:10.1016/j.compind.2018.04.015

Chen, Z., Chen, S., & Feng, X. (2016, October). A design of distributed storage and processing system for internet of vehicles. In *Proceedings 2016 8th International Conference on Wireless Communications & Signal Processing (WCSP)* (pp. 1-5). IEEE. 10.1109/WCSP.2016.7752671

Ester, M., Kriegel, H. P., Sander, J., & Xu, X. (1996, August). A density-based algorithm for discovering clusters in large spatial databases with noise. *Proceedings of International Conference on Knowledge Discovery & Data Mining (KDD)*, *96*(34), 226–231.

Evgeniou, T. & Pontil, M. (2001). Workshop on support vector machines: Theory and applications.

Hoffman, S. (2015). Apache flume: Distributed log collection for hadoop. Birmingham, UK: Packt Publishing.

Hsu, C. W., Chang, C. C., & Lin, C. J. (2003). A practical guide to support vector classification.

Iqbal, M. H., & Soomro, T. R. (2015). Big data analysis: Apache storm perspective. *International Journal of Computer Trends and Technology*, *19*(1), 9–14. doi:10.14445/22312803/IJCTT-V19P103

Jin, J., Gubbi, J., Luo, T., & Palaniswami, M. (2012, October). Network architecture and QoS issues in the internet of things for a smart city. In *2012 International Symposium on Communications and Information Technologies (ISCIT),* (pp. 956-961). IEEE. 10.1109/ISCIT.2012.6381043

Kaisler, S., Armour, F., Espinosa, J. A., & Money, W. (2013, January). Big data: Issues and challenges moving forward. In *Proceedings 2013 46th Hawaii International Conference on System Sciences* (pp. 995-1004). IEEE.

Kapil, G., Agrawal, A., & Khan, R. A. (2016, October). A study of big data characteristics. In *Proceedings 2016 International Conference on Communication and Electronics Systems (ICCES)* (pp. 1-4). IEEE.

Lee, I., & Lee, K. (2015). The Internet of Things (IoT): Applications, investments, and challenges for enterprises. *Business Horizons*, *58*(4), 431–440. doi:10.1016/j.bushor.2015.03.008

Makeshwar, P. B., Kalra, A., Rajput, N. S., & Singh, K. P. (2015, February). Computational scalability with Apache Flume and Mahout for large scale round the clock analysis of sensor network data. In *Proceedings 2015 National Conference on Recent Advances in Electronics & Computer Engineering (RAECE)* (pp. 306-311). IEEE. 10.1109/RAECE.2015.7510212

Mavromoustakis, C. X., Mastorakis, G., & Batalla, J. M. (Eds.). (2016). *Internet of Things (IoT) in 5G mobile technologies* (Vol. 8). Springer. doi:10.1007/978-3-319-30913-2

Nivash, J. P., Raj, E. D., Babu, L. D., Nirmala, M., & Kumar, V. M. (2014, July). Analysis on enhancing storm to efficiently process big data in real time. In *Proceedings Fifth International Conference on Computing, Communications and Networking Technologies (ICCCNT)* (pp. 1-5). IEEE. 10.1109/ICCCNT.2014.7093076

Oguntimilehin, A., & Ademola, E. O. (2014). A review of big data management, benefits and challenges. *A Review of Big Data Management, Benefits and Challenges*, 5(6), 1–7.

Oussous, A., Benjelloun, F. Z., Lahcen, A. A., & Belfkih, S. (2018). Big Data technologies: A survey. *Journal of King Saud University-Computer and Information Sciences*, 30(4), 431–448. doi:10.1016/j.jksuci.2017.06.001

Owais, S. S., & Hussein, N. S. (2016). Extract five categories CPIVW from the 9V's characteristics of the Big Data. *International Journal of Advanced Computer Science and Applications*, 7(3), 254–258.

Rashid, M., & Chawla, R. (2013). Securing data storage by extending role-based access control. *International Journal of Cloud Applications and Computing*, 3(4), 28–37. doi:10.4018/ijcac.2013100103

Reddi, K. K., & Indira, D. (2013). Different technique to transfer Big Data: Survey. *Int. Journal of Engineering Research and Applications*, 3(6), 708–711.

Riggins, F. J. & Wamba, S. F. (2015, January). Research directions on the adoption, usage, and impact of the internet of things through the use of big data analytics. In *2015 48th Hawaii International Conference on System Sciences (HICSS)*, (pp. 1531-1540). IEEE. 10.1109/HICSS.2015.186

Salman, T. & Jain, R. (2017). A survey of protocols and standards for internet of things. *Advanced Computing and Communications*, 1(1).

Singh, P., & Rashid, E. (2015). Smart home automation deployment on third party cloud using internet of things. *Journal of Bioinformatics and Intelligent Control*, 4(1), 31–34. doi:10.1166/jbic.2015.1113

Suciu, G., Suciu, V., Martian, A., Craciunescu, R., Vulpe, A., Marcu, I., & Fratu, O. (2015). Big data, internet of things and cloud convergence–an architecture for secure e-health applications. *Journal of Medical Systems*, 39(11), 141. doi:10.100710916-015-0327-y PMID:26345453

Tönjes, R., Barnaghi, P., Ali, M., Mileo, A., Hauswirth, M., Ganz, F., & Puiu, D. (2014, June). Real time IoT stream processing and large-scale data analytics for smart city applications. In *poster session, European Conference on Networks and Communications*. sn.

This research was previously published in Security and Privacy Issues in Sensor Networks and IoT; pages 215-230, copyright year 2020 by Information Science Reference (an imprint of IGI Global).

Chapter 45
Application of Big Data in Digital Epidemiology

Sameena Naaz

iD https://orcid.org/0000-0003-0080-5063

Jamia Hamdard, India

Farheen Siddiqui

Jamia Hamdard, India

ABSTRACT

Epidemiology is the study of dynamics of health and disease in human population. It aims to identify the occurrence, pattern, and etiology of human diseases so that the causes of these diseases can be understood, which in turn will help in preventing their spread. In traditional epidemiology, the data is collected by various public health agencies through various means. Many times, the actual figures vary a lot from the one reported. Sometimes this difference is due to human errors, but most of the time, it is due to intentional underreporting. Big data techniques can be used to analyze this huge amount of data so as to extract useful information from it. The electronic health data is so large and complex that it cannot be processed using traditional software and hardware. It is also not possible to manage this data using traditional data management tools. This data is huge in terms of volume as well as diversity and the speed at which it is being generated. The ability to combine and analyze these different sources of data has huge impact on epidemic tracking.

INTRODCUTION

The power of technology in this era is so huge that anyone can track your whereabouts just by using your cellphone location. They can even predict where you can be at some later point of time by using various analytics. This information may be used by a security agency for nabbing the criminals. But not only this! There is a Swedish project by the name of Flowminder which tracks the movement of population during any natural disaster and can use it for the sake of relief and rescue.

DOI: 10.4018/978-1-6684-3662-2.ch045

This is just one of the examples of a project in the field of digital epidemiology. Epidemiology is a field which deals with the study and analysis of various patterns, their reasons and how they affect the health and disease in any geographical area or a defined population. Traditionally the data has been collected from various sources by different agencies and it is analyzed using tools to get some insight into the reasons for the spread of diseases. The new field of digital epidemiology relies on collecting the data using digital techniques such as getting data from various social networking sites and then using computational methods to measure health and the spread of disease. Governments of various countries are supporting projects which use big data for digital epidemiology. Air quality data is being captured by environmental scientists from the polluted areas and then it is compared with the health status of the people living in those areas. This can give an insight into the correlation between the environmental hazards and the diseases present there. Information on sexual and social networks are gathered by Epidemiologists which helps them predict the signs of spread of diseases so that early warning signs can be issued.

Big data analytics helps in predictive modeling in healthcare sector which provide faster, better and more targeted results in digital epidemiology which helps to develop better vaccines faster. It also helps in analysis of disease patters which helps track disease outbreaks which results in faster disaster management.

The study of distribution and changes of health and disease in human population is Epidemiology. It identifies the incidence, distribution and etiology of human diseases in order to understand their causes in a better manner which in turn will help in preventing them from spreading (Green, Freedman & Gordis, 2000). Traditionally, the data was collected by various public health agencies which used to go to the hospitals, doctors and the effected people to get first-hand information. Latest work in this area is to get the data from online sources. People search for different types of information on the internet. The pattern of search in any particular area can give us some insight on their health issues. This has become possible due to increase in use of electronic devices and modern communication techniques (Eysenbach, 2009). Due to the huge size of this data various big data analytics tools are used to process it and get useful information.

The electronic health data set is so large that it cannot be managed by traditional software and hardware. The traditional data base management system also fails to manage such huge amount of data (Zenger, 2012). It is not only huge in volume but is also very diverse and extremely fast changing. These are the main reasons why we need big data techniques to handle them.

BIG DATA IN HEALTH CARE

Epidemic tracking has gone through a huge change as it can combine and analyze various sources of data. Big data initiative in the health care sector is being supported by governments of many countries. Some of the instances are: The government of Denmark is providing anonymously health as well as hospitalization data for carrying out research in the field of Big Data (Szlezak et al., 2014). They have a program which helps in better care of patients with diabetes and heart diseases by employing data analytics on the medical data available (IBM, 2013).

Swedish government is also trying to help research in Big Data analytics. Huge amount of data from lab results, healthcare centers and from ambulances carrying critically ill people or accident cases can be merged for the analytics purposes. A lot of research is going on for developing tools and techniques which can support decision making. One important area of research is the analysis of structured and unstructured data to study the effect of various drugs (Network, T.S.B.D.A., 2013).

A project on review of Big Data privacy was undertaken by the US government in January 2014. The recommendations of this work can be found in Podesta et al. (2014) and PCAST (2014). There is a World Health Organization project by the name of "Be He@lthy Be mobile" which uses the mobile devices and various wireless technologies for the study of health care. The study in the field of health care which uses mobile devices and latest communication technologies come under the domain of mHealth. A project in this domain by the name of mDiabetics is helping countries in their tryst to control, manage and prevent non-communicable diseases such as cancer, diabetes and heart disease (WHO, 2014).

The dynamics of spread of any communicable disease depends a lot on human movement. We can get the information about a person's location using mobile phone data. This data could be collected using the the mobile phone tower location used when a person makes a call. With the latest advancements in the mobile technology now all the smart phones have Global Positioning System (GPS). A person's location can be tracked using their GPS location also (Cattuto et al., 2010). All this helps in the study of mobility of human's and its influence on spread of diseases (Gonzalez, Hidalgo & Barabasi, 2008). Other wearable devices also help in tracking the social behavior (Pentland & Pentland, 2008) of a person, the work which was previously done using large-scale surveys and self reporting (Mossong et al., 2008). The self reported data and the measurements taken from social media compliment each other and helps in getting better understanding and accurate description of infectious disease dynamics. The study of disease dynamics involves collection of data from a large number of individuals, refine this data as per our requirement and then to decide upon the parameters that will be used for large scale computer simulation. In the traditional method modeling was done using population aggregates, but now with the advent of technology it is possible to use data collected from large number of individuals. This helps us in getting more variety in the data which is collected and hence better results can be achieved. Realistic models of human mobility have been developed using mobile phone (Gonzalez, Hidalgo & Barabasi, 2008). It has also been used to predict the rate at which drug resistance has increased (Lynch & Roper, 2011), to study the chances of malaria eradication (Tatem et al., 2009), and to monitor population movements in near real-time during cholera outbreak in Haiti (Bengtsson et al., 2011). Data obtained for close proximity interactions among individuals using wireless sensor network technology can be used to develop models which can help in targeted immunization strategies (Salathe et al., 2010). This method is different from the static representation of contact networks (Stehle et al., 2011) and yields better results. Worldwide spread of new emerging infectious diseases such as H1N1 can be studied using large-scale mobility (Balcam et al., 2009; Merler et al., 2011).

BioMosaic is a tool developed by Centers for Disease Control (CDC), USA and World Health Organization (WHO) to track the Ebola virus outbreak. Big Data was used to track the movement of people across US borders. BioMosaic is a tool that combined together the health data of people, population trend and movement data and used it for prediction of spread of Ebola. It has also been used for many other epidemics in the area of forecasting, targeting, testing, intervention and surveillance. CDC has also developed a new software tool, the Epi Info viral hemorrhagic fever (VHF) which helps in identifying people who are exposed to the virus faster in much lesser time as compared to the traditional reporting methods.

Researcher's and epidemiologists at Boston Children's Hospital have developed a website by the name of HealthMap which is used for disease-monitoring using big data analytics. The site collects real time data from various sources including social media, chat rooms, online news, travel sites, official records etc. and aggregates and analyses this data. The result of this analysis is used for early detection and real-time surveillance on latest health hazards.

Huge amount of data gets generated on social networking sites during outbreak of any disease. This happens as patients as well as people who are living in areas affected by these diseases share their symptoms, look for hospitals and clinics and search for various medicines on the apps. Therefore, social media plays an important role in supplying huge amount of data which can be analyzed to identify outbreaks and predict the regions where the disease can spread later on, so that preventive measures can be taken. In both the flu and Ebola epidemics data analysis was done in this manner.

Google Flu Trends is a service provided by Google which accumulates data related to influenza in 25 different countries. This web site collects data from Google search queries and aggregates it in order to predict flu activity. Google.org first launched this project in 2008 to predict outbreak of flu (Khoury & Wei, 2015). There is another project by the name of flu-prediction (Khoury & Ioannidis, 2014) launched by the institute of Cognitive Science, Osnabrück which combines social media data such as data from twitter with data from Centers for Disease Control (CDC) to develop structural models that predict the temporal and spatial spreading of the disease (Lauer, 2012)).

An ecological niche model using geographically weighted regression has been developed in Lpoeset al (2014) for prediction of H1N1 influenza in Vellore. This model based on geographically weighted regression helped in identifying high risk areas so that proper prevention steps could be implemented there. Big Data will have huge impact on the future of epidemiologic research as it collects data from a large section of population. Some of these implications have been discussed in Mooney, Westreich, and El-Sayed (2015).

National Center for Disease Control (NCDC) collects data from various Indian states through Integrated Disease Surveillance Project (IDSP). The aim of this project is to collect, compile, analyze and use data on several target diseases for surveillance so that fast response can be provided for preventing and controlling the spread these diseases in the masses. Data is collected by Syndromic Surveillance which is done by the health worker, Presumptive Surveillance which is done by the Medical Officer and Laboratory Surveillance. The health workers collect data on the water quality also. The data is collected on a weekly basis which helps to identify disease trends and seasonal outbreaks. There are Rapid Response Teams (RRT) to diagnose and control sudden outbreak of diseases. Data is collected from Major Hospitals and Infectious Disease Hospitals and is analyzed by respective State/District Surveillance Units. The status of this weekly surveillance data is further analyzed by a committee of Epidemiologists from IDSP and experts from NCDC.

There are many diseases which occur due to high level of air pollution. Some of them include Asthma and Chronic Obstructive Pulmonary Disease (COPD). In order to keep a check on these diseases air quality is being monitored by environmental scientists from the polluted areas. The data gathered from here is matched with the health care data sets to get an insight into respiratory diseases. Epidemiologists also gather information from social and sexual networks and analyze them to predict the spread of disease and create early warnings.

IMPORTANCE OF DIGITAL EPIDEMIOLOGY

The world has become a small place now. Due to easy accessibility to various places across the globe it has become very easy to travel from one corner to another. This results in ease of transmission of diseases also and so the threat of global epidemics has increased exponentially. Traditionally, data is collected manually and is analyzed to develop methods for prevention of disease outbreaks. But the response time in this manual setup is too high for a global population which keeps moving at a fast pace. Due to this the epidemics also spread from one region to another at a speed unimaginable a century ago. The viruses have also become resistant to antibiotics and this is also a major threat because traditional preventative measures are no more effective. Due to all this we need to have a new approach to disease control.

Big Data collects large sets of data from various sources such as field work, research and open web and analyzes it to develop methods to combat epidemics.

Massive data which consists of data obtained from syndromic surveillance indicators (non-medical in nature) and data from lab results and electronic health records (medical in nature) are accessed and analyzed in computational epidemiology. These two kinds of data are combined to construct flexible and dynamic system which operates in real time to provide early warnings to combat spread of diseases.

Future prediction of epidemic is difficult in India as the various factors responsible for the spread of these diseases is unmanageably scattered. Communicable as well as chronic diseases hit a large population of our country every year. The government is not able to use the available data on time due to lack of resources and such huge spread and therefore it is not possible for the Government Bodies to issue any health advisories in time. We are also not able to develop proper vaccinations and medicines to control the epidemic.

USE OF DIGITAL EPIDEMIOLOGY TO PREVENT OUTBREAK OF DENGUE IN INDIA

Dengue resurged in India at the onset of monsoon last year (2016), to put many lives at risk. Directorate of National Vector Borne Disease Control Programme (NVBDCP) is the agency which is responsible for the preventing and controlling the vector borne diseases such as Malaria, Kala azar, Dengue, Japanese Encephalitis and Chikungunya in India. According to this agency a large number of cases of Malaria, Dengue and Chikungunya occured due to heavy rainfall in many regions of the country, especially in Delhi, resulting in serious health threat.

Dengue is currently considered as the most important mosquito-borne viral disease globally (Murray, Quam & Wilder-Smith, 2013). It causes a huge amount of disease and socioeconomic burden on subtropical and tropical areas of the world (Guzman & Kouri, 2002; Gubler, 2011). Dengue is one of the major arboviral disease which has affected over 50% of the world population and approximately 50% countries in the world are dengue endemic (Gibler, 2002, 2011; WHO, 2012a, 2012b, 2013; Ferreira, 2012). There are several factors for such high rate of dengue infections and it's predicted growth. This includes evolution of news viruses, change in climatic conditions and societal factors such as population growth, rapid urbanization as well as global trade and travel (Wilder-Smith & Gubler, 2008; Astrom et al., 2012).

As no vaccine or antiviral therapy has been developed so far for dengue, so the only method to control it is through early detection and symptomatic treatment (WHO, 2009). The WHO Global Strategy for Dengue Prevention and Control, 2012–2020, talks about the necessity for better estimation of the real burden of dengue across the globe due to the current under-represented number (WHO, 2012b). Surveillance and reporting is very important for controlling dengue efficiently. Political, financial as well as research priorities will change once the impact of dengue gets quantified. This will also help in better decision making and modeling (Gubler, 2011, 2012; Shepard, Undurraga & Halasa, 2013; Bhatt et al., 2013; Beatty et al., 2010).

There has been a substantial change in the epidemiology of dengue fever in India in the past few decades. This change has occurred in terms of geographical location where it spread, severity of outbreak and the type of strain. The first reported case of dengue fever in India is from 1946 (Karamchandani, 1946). After that there were not much cases of the disease reported for the next 18 years. The first reported epidemic of dengue is from the Eastern Coast of India (Carey et al., 1966; Ramakrishnan et al., 1964; Sarkar et al., 1964; Chaudhuri, Saha & Chaudhuri, 1965; Krishnamurthy, Kasturi & Chittipantulu, 1965; Paul et al., 1965) and it occurred in the year 1963-1964. From there it spread northwards and reached Delhi in 1967 (Balaya et al., 1969)] and Kanpur in 1968 (Chaturvedi et al., 1970; Chaturvedi et al., 1970). During the same period, it also spread in the south India (Meyers et al., 1968; Ghosh, 1968) and gradually the whole country was involved. After this epidemic outbreak Dengue became endemic/ hyperendemic with all four serotypes of DV.

Good amount of work has been done on traditional epidemiology in India. Digital epidemiology has great potential to predict the future trends of spread of diseases. Methods and strategies are being developed by researchers to use digital epidemiology for monitoring and surveillance of infectious diseases. There is a need to integrate these new methods with traditional practices keeping in mind the ethical concerns about privacy.

Work on digital epidemiology for various diseases has been reported in literature, but not work has been found in the Indian sub-continent. We know that the use of social media has increased many folds in our country during the last few years. Data for research in the field of digital epidemiology can be taken from social media such as Twitter feeds (Bian et al., 2012), status updates on Facebook and other platforms, blogs (Raghupathi & Ragupathi, 2013) and web sites. Apart from these online sources of data less patient-specific data such as data available from emergency care services, data from news feeds, articles in journals of medical science etc. can all be collected in an offline mode.

APPLICATION OF BIG DATA ANALYTICS FOR DENGUE EPIDEMIOLOGY

Three main characteristics of big data that is volume, velocity and variety exist in the healthcare data (IBM, n.d.). Huge amount of health data is being generated with each passing day resulting in an tremendous volume of data. Various sources of existing healthcare data include radiology images, personal medical records, electronic submissions from Food and Drug Administration (FDA), population data, human genetics and genomic data etc. Latest technologies such as 3D imaging and genomics and biometric sensors are also generating huge volume of data.

This huge amount of data needs to be captured using some techniques for further processing in order to extract useful information. Storage of such large volume of data in another issue related to it's use in digital epidemiology. Fortunately, virtualization and cloud computing is a tool which helps us to achieve all of these (Feldman, Martin & Skotnes, 2012). The data is being created and assembled at a very fast speed in real-time and hence the velocity of the data is also quite high. There are many new challenges due to the constant flow of new data at an unprecedented rate. Tools and techniques need to be developed which can retrieve, analyze, compare and make decisions based on such fast-changing data. Analysis of such huge amount of data which has got high velocity by considering data from various sources results in the third characteristic of big data which is variety (IHTT, 2013).

With continuously changing volume, velocity and variety of health data new analytics techniques have to be developed to accommodate them. The data that was collected from electronic health records was structured in nature. But the data from digital media is unstructured in nature. Due to this variety in healthcare data: structured, unstructured and semi structured the field of digital epidemiology is both interesting and challenging.

BIG DATA ARCHITECTURAL FRAMEWORK (BDAF)

A big data analytics project in healthcare uses the same conceptual framework as any other traditional health informatics project or analytics project in any other domain. It only differs in where and how the processing is carried out. If big data is not involved, then any business intelligence tool can be used on a standalone system or a laptop for the processing of data. On the other hand, when the data is very huge it is broken down and the processing takes place simultaneously across multiple nodes. Hence, we can say that data analysis in big data uses the concept of distributed processing which has been there for decades. In the healthcare domain the available data is analyzed to gain insight which can be used for a better more informed health decision. Furthermore, we have many open source platforms such as Hadoop/MapReduce, which can be accessed over the cloud, which have been of great help for use of big data analytics in healthcare.

Although the models and algorithms used in big data analytics are similar to the one used in traditional analytics but they are not as user friendly and transparent as the later. The main reason for this is that they have evolved in an ad hoc manner mostly as an open-source development tool and platform. Although having these tools available as open source has its own advantages but it lacks support and user friendliness which a vendor provided tool possesses. The available tools are programming intensive, more complex and require a whole lot of skills.

The architectural framework of big data to be used in the healthcare domain is discussed below. The conceptual architecture of big data analytics shown in figure 1 highlights the major challenges in relation to the Big Data properties and technologies. The proposed BDAF consists of the following 4 components which together address different aspects of Big Data definition.

Data Sources

The health data that is available to us could be structured, semi-structured or unstructured. The data that can be stored and analyzed with the help of machine to extract useful information are structured data. Structured data is obtained from legacy applications, ERP and from external feeds. Semi-structured as well as unstructured data is obtained from Web Logs, Network/Application Logs, Social Media, Chat Transcripts, Emails, readings from instruments and the electronic health data. Office medical records, handwritten prescriptions, admission and discharge summary etc. also provide unstructured data.

Latest advancements in technology has resulted in many more sources of structured as well as unstructured data. These include data from fitness devices, social media records, genetics and other sources. There is a need for technological advancements which can help in capturing, storing and organizing this enormous amount of data to extract useful information.

Figure 1. Conceptual architecture of big data analytics

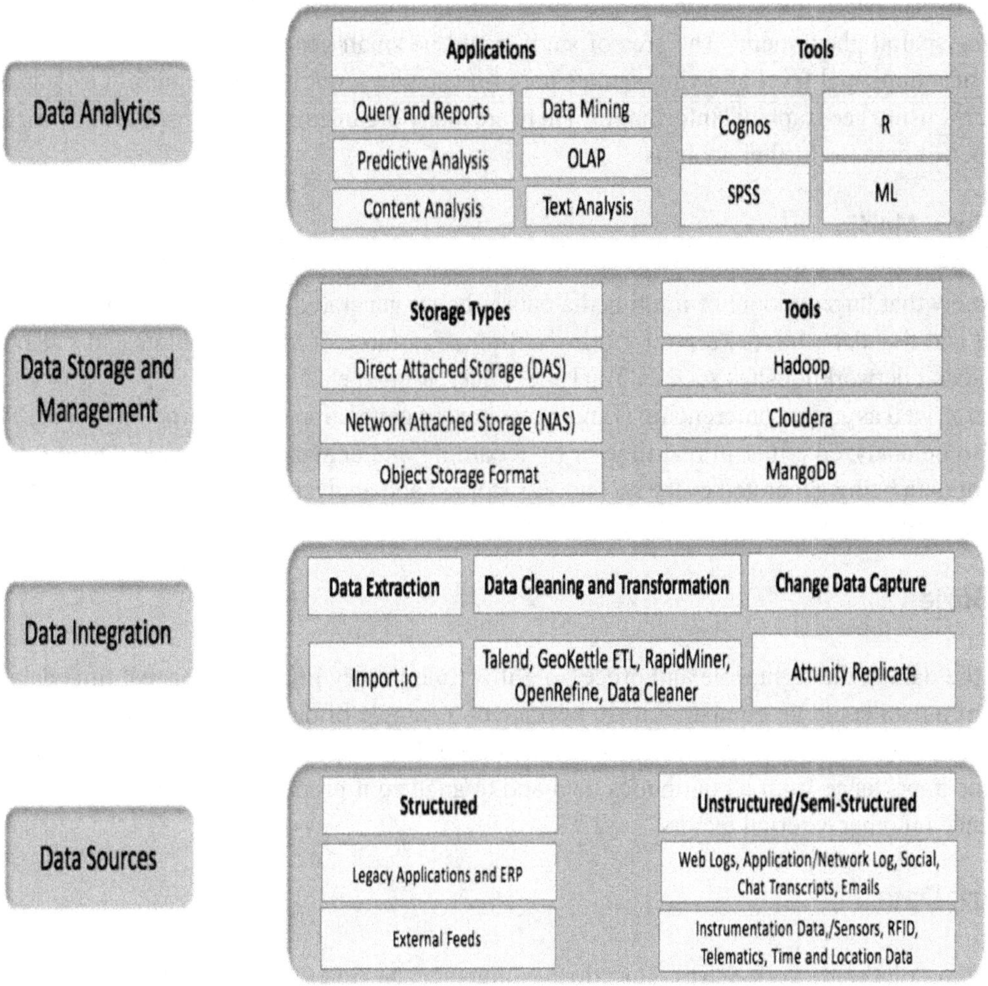

Data Analytics	**Applications**		**Tools**	
	Query and Reports	Data Mining	Cognos	R
	Predictive Analysis	OLAP	SPSS	ML
	Content Analysis	Text Analysis		

Data Storage and Management	**Storage Types**	**Tools**
	Direct Attached Storage (DAS)	Hadoop
	Network Attached Storage (NAS)	Cloudera
	Object Storage Format	MangoDB

Data Integration	**Data Extraction**	**Data Cleaning and Transformation**	**Change Data Capture**
	Import.io	Talend, GeoKettle ETL, RapidMiner, OpenRefine, Data Cleaner	Attunity Replicate

Data Sources	**Structured**	**Unstructured/Semi-Structured**
	Legacy Applications and ERP	Web Logs, Application/Network Log, Social, Chat Transcripts, Emails
	External Feeds	Instrumentation Data,/Sensors, RFID, Telematics, Time and Location Data

Tools need to be developed which can combine the traditional data with new types of data both at an individual level as well as at population level. This is the strength of big data.

Apart from the medical data being generated there are other types of data which also directly or indirectly play an important role in Epidemiological study. Some of them are:

Geographic Data

Huge amount of data related physical landscapes such as roads, buildings, lakes etc. are available today from Geographic Information Systems. This information may include address of a person, work place information, routes taken by the person for commuting or may be the personal information of the person. Although people are worried about the safety of all their personal data but still they are willing to share such information. All this has resulted in new application areas and innovations both for the general public as well as for the governments.

Geostatistics is the branch of statistics which deals with the spatiotemporal and spatial datasets. In this field interpolation methods are used to build statistical models which are used for estimating and simulating spatial phenomena. The area of study could be small geographical area such as municipal level or sub-municipal level allowing studies on a fine spatial level. The geodata for Geostatistics can be collected using geographical information There are many organizations and institutions which collect these types of data for further analysis.

Real Time Media

We all know that huge amount of multimedia data is being generated in real-time which includes both recorded and live data. Users keep on sharing unlimited number of audio, pictures and video through various social networking sites such as YouTube, Flickr, Vimeo etc.

Video as well as audio conferencing is another source of generation of huge amount of data. This data could also be analyzed either in real time or by recording and analyzing it later on. Due to such huge amount of data being generated every second, it's storage and analysis requires technological advancements at a very fast pace.

Time Series

Getting the data at the right time and processing it is time is very important for real time data. Single reading of a data could be compared to an average of a sample of data or an individual data could be compared to another individual value at a different time. It is important to identify a discrete value of interest or importance from a continuous data and to analyze it properly to get the actual context and dependence on other external factors.

Network Data

Data from very large networks have connections within them and interesting information can be extracted from the structure of this connectivity. Some of the networks in this category includes biological networks (e.g. gene regulatory and metabolic nets), communication networks and social networks.

Data Integration

The data from various sources has to be pooled for the purpose of big data analytics. The data which is collected from various sources is in a 'raw' form and has to be processed or transformed. There are various methods to do this. One method is to combine service- oriented architecture with web services (middleware) (Ragupathi & Kesh, 2007). In this approach the data remains as it is in its raw form and services are used to call, extract and process the data. A different approach could be to use data warehousing in which the data from different sources is aggregated and then processed. But the drawback of this approach is that we cannot get the data in real- time. The steps of extract, transform, and load (ETL) are used here to collect data from diverse sources which is then pre-processed before being processed further. One example of a tool that can be used to extract data is Import.in. Similarly, we have various tools for data cleansing and transformation such as Talend, GeoKettle ETL, RapidMiner, OpenRefine, Data Cleaner etc.

The concept of Change Data Transfer (CDC) can be used to make the data truly "real time". This is achieved by making the data being analyzed complete and up-to-date and the analytic databases providing interactive query capabilities. The data which is being analyzed is obtained from a number of heterogeneous databases which have their set of challenges in integrating this data. The database where the data is processed is deployed on the cloud, so that also has it's own constraints.

Attunity Replicate is a tool that can be used to apply change data capture (CDC) to Big Data analytics. ETL is a batch-oriented method for data integration but CDC methods update the target analytic databases only if some change is detected in the source database.

Data Storage and Management

There are various technologies that can be used to store huge amount of data that has to be processed. Three technologies that have been discussed in this chapter are direct attached storage (DAS), network attached storage (NAS) and object storage format. In Direct Attached Storage there is direct connection between various hard disk drives (HDDs) and the servers. This approach is in accordance with the fundamental principle of Hadoop which is to move the processing to a location where the data lives, taking advantage of disk locality to optimize performance. Disk locality is the core concept used in Hadoop and virtually every description of Hadoop starts with it. But, DAS can be used only if the number of servers is limited. This type of storage is less scalable, expandable and upgradeable. Network Attached Storage (NAS) on the other hand, is a storage device that supports a network. It has a direct connection with the network, through a switch or hub via TCP/IP protocols. In NAS computation and storage takes place at different places. Here storage is shared across a number of servers by shipping data over the network in form of various files. Because NAS heavily depends on the network, so it is slower than DAS but the burden of input/output is lesser in NAS server as compared to DAS server. The third storage format is the object storage that can handle very large numbers of files. If there are very large number of files then traditional tree-like file systems become unmanageable. Object-based storage gives each file a unique identifier indexes the data with its location. Object storage systems can scale to capacity as high as billions of files, so it is the best option for companies that want to use big data to their advantage. The object storage technology is far less mature than DAS and NAS and is still evolving. Various tools are used for data management which are discussed in the next section.

Data Analytics

Some of the applications of data analytics are queries and reports, predictive analysis, content analysis, text analysis, OLAP and data mining. The main concept in all these applications is visualization. A variety of tools and techniques have been developed to analyze and visualize big data in healthcare.

TOOLS AND TECHNIQUES FOR BIG DATA ANALYSIS

Platforms

Hadoop

Hadoop (Apache platform) is an open-source platform for distributed processing of big data. It was developed in the beginning to aggregate web search indexes. It belongs to the class "NoSQL" technologies. Other tools in this class are CouchDB and MongoDB which aggregate data in unique ways. Extremely large amount of data can be processed using Hadoop. It allocates partitioned data sets to various servers (nodes), each of which solves different portions of the bigger problem and then combines them to get the final result (Borkar, Carey & Chen, 2012; Ohlhorst, 2012; Zikopoulos et al., 2013; Dean & Ghemawat, 2008). Hadoop works as a data organizer as well as an analytics tool. It has the potential harness huge amount of data which was difficult to manage and analyze till now. Hadoop can handle all the three types of data: structured, semi-structured and unstructured. But the problem with Hadoop is that although it is open source it is difficult to install, configure and administer and not many individuals with Hadoop skills are available in the market. In spite of all these associated problems companies are interested in Hadoop Distributed File System (HDFS) because it can manage and process extremes of big data for warehousing, integration and analytics at a low cost. Hadoop along with various other products layered above HDFS gives a highly scalable and high-performance platform for a wide range of applications which are data-intensive. There are many additional tools and platforms that support the Hadoop distributed platform (Zikopoulos et al., 2013; Dean & Ghemawat, 2008).

MapReduce (Singh & Reddy, 2014) is an execution engine which uses parallel processing for executing hand coded routines written in a variety of programming languages such as Java, R or Pig. MapReduce executes these routines for accessing huge file and repositories of data being managed by an HDFS cluster. By deploying MapReduce as a layer on top of HDFS we are able to obtain a high-performance analytic application which can handle huge data collections.

MapReduce breaks the entire job into two parts which are known as mappers and reducers (Lee et al., 2012). The data is read from the HDFS by the mappers, they process the data and generate some intermediate results for the reducers. Reducers use the results generated by the mappers, aggregate them and then generate the final output which finally is again written to HDFS. Several mappers and reducers run in parallel across different nodes in the cluster. A good description of MapReduce for parallel data processing is given in Deepak (2016). In 2013, Apache created YARN framework (also called MapReduce 2.0) from MapReduce. The basic MapReduce algorithm remains the same here but other processing algorithms including the ones that run interactively can be changed.

NoSQL DBMSs A NoSQL database manages data which is not relational in nature, so it need not support SQL. But the data here may be structured based on some other schema like records or value pair or may have no fixed schema. Various storage strategies may be used in NoSQL such as document stores, wide-column stores, key-value stores and graph databases (Chen & Zhang, 2014). The Hadoop family includes many other tools such as Cassandra, Hive, HBase Pig etc. some of which are discussed later on.

Spark

Spark is a paradigm developed at the University of California, Berkeley for big data processing. It overcomes the limitation of disk I/O in Hadoop (Lee et al., 2012) and hence improves the performance. The main advantage of Spark is that it can perform in-memory computations. The data can be cached in memory and in this manner, it eliminates the disk overhead problem in Hadoop for iterative tasks. Scala, Python and Java are all supported by Spark and it has been found to be 100 times faster than Hadoop MapReduce when the data can fit in the memory, and up to 10 times faster when it is on the disk. Spark can run on the YARN manager of Hadoop and can take data from HDFS

Storm

Storm (Kelly, 2013) is an open source real-time computation system which is distributed and fault-tolerant in nature. It has the power to process limitless stream of data. It differs from Hadoop as it works in real time whereas Hadoop is for batch processing. It is easy to set up Storm as compared to Hadoop and it also guarantees all the data will be processed. Some of the application areas where we can use Storm are on-line machine learning, real-time analytics, distributed RPC, ETL etc. Twitter uses Storm it to help generate its trending topics.

Drill

Apache Drill is another another platform for interactive analysis of Big Data (Malviya, Ughani & Soni, 2016). Apache Drill allows super fast ad hoc querying of giant data sets for interactive analysis and it is similar to Google's Dremel. The beauty of drill is that it can extract data from traditional databases as well as data sources such as HBase, Cassandra, MongoDB, etc. It is an excellent tool to scan petabytes of data and trillions of records in seconds and can exploit nested data. Drill is more flexible in the sense that it supports various query languages, data formats and data sources.

Statistical Languages

R

R is a freely available statistical programming language which is becoming rapidly popular as a software for data analysis, statistics and visualization. The main reasons for it's popularity are that it is cheap, powerful and works well with Hadoop. In fact, R is replacing SAS and SPSS and is preferred by the best statisticians, data scientists and analysts. Due to it's popularity we have R libraries for virtually all types of applications and this makes it even more popular as the analysts need not write new code for accessing data for their application.

Big data in cloud computing can be analyzed using R tool frame work (Mukhopadhyay et al., 2014). First thing is to identify the challenges associated with analyzing big data. Powerful business decisions are made by data scientist and business leader uses R today. The RFramework is very flexible and is available as open source. R consists of various packages that are used for analysis of data. The R Framework consists of Deploy R server, Deploy R repository and Deploy R API's. The analyst can write the scripts using R and can also upload data in files of different formats. RFramework can also be linked with other languages such as java and .NET.

Data Mining

Data mining is the term used for discovering new, interesting, and useful patterns from large data sets and applying algorithms for the extraction of hidden information. It builds an efficient predictive or descriptive model which can be used to generate new useful data (Asay, 2014). Different types of software packages can be used for data mining. Generally, Sophisticated search operations are performed in data mining which return targeted specific results. We can say that data mining is a handler that tries to dig out beneficial results from big data which is our asset.

Mahout

This Apache project is a machine learning and data mining library that is used to recognize patterns in data. It generates freely distributed machine learning algorithms which are scalable. Four data science use cases supported by Mahout are: clustering (grouping related documents together), classification (learning to match documents to categories), collaborative filtering (matching users to probable favorites) and frequent pattern matching (identifying items that typically fall into groups together).

Mahout is implemented on top of Hadoop and uses the MapReduce paradigm. It provides data science tools to find meaningful patterns from the big data sets stored on the Hadoop Distributed File System (HDFS).

Weka

Weka was developed at the University of Waikato and is a machine learning library consisting of a number of algorithms and tools for data analysis and predictive modeling. It is Java based and is capable of carrying out the various tasks of data preprocessing, clustering, classification, regression, visualization etc. which are a part of data mining.

RapidMiner

This is a stand-alone application for analysis of data. It is also used for integration with other products. RapidMiner uses Rapid-I scripting language or the R language of statistical modeling and it's learning methods are similar to that of Weka. It is written in Java and can run on multiple platform and operating system. RapidMiner can be used for machine learning, data mining, text mining and predictive analytics.

Databases / Data Warehousing

We know that we prefer NoSQL databases in big data and they are classified into the following four types each suited to different kinds of tasks:

- Document databases (or stores)
- Key-Value stores

- Wide-Column (or Distributed Column) stores
- Graph databases.

Cassandra

This is Apache's database management system which can handle huge amounts of data from various servers. It has the features of both key-value stores and distributed stores and is highly available, scalable and fault tolerant. It is also very efficient at handling bottlenecks and single points of failure. It is good for data critical applications as the data is replicated at multiple nodes using peer to peer replication.

Cassandra is being used in Facebook to power the Inbox Search feature. It is also working for eBay, Twitter, Netflix, Reddit and many more.

HBase

HBase, like Cassandra is a column-oriented key-value store (Datafloq, n.d.), built on Hadoop and is designed to support billions of messages per day. It provides a record based storage layer which helps in fast and random reads and writes to data. HBase is massively scalable, provides high throughput and low latency I/O. Because HBase is tightly integrated with the Hadoop ecosystem, so SQL queries can be used to get data for users and applications. Tools such as Apache Hive, Apache Phoenix and Cloudera Impala can be used for this purpose. It can also get data by faceted free-text search using Cloudera Search. HBase is written in Java and is modeled after Google's BigTable.

MongoDB

MongoDB is a document-oriented database which is cross-platform and is the most popular NoSQL database. The main reason for popularity of MangoDB is that it is very easy to learn (Datafloq, n.d.). It has a balanced approach that can be used for a wide variety of applications. It has the feature of horizontal scalability and can easily work with the diverse data sets due to its flexible data model. MangoDB is being used in Shutterfly's photo platform, Forbes's storage system, eBay's search suggestion and MetLife's "The Wall."

OrientDB

OrientDB is again a NoSQL DBMS which is also written in Java. It is very flexible as it is schema-less, it provides the complexity of the graph model where document records are directly related and is object oriented in nature. It can also function in schema-full and hybrid mode and is very fast.

CouchDB

CouchDB is Apache's NoSQL database which is extremely web-friendly as it uses the following components: It uses JSON for documents, JavaScript for MapReduce queries and HTTP for an API. CouchDB works well with data that does not change very frequently.

Data Aggregation

The data which is processed using big data techniques is scattered over various sources. The process of transforming this scattered data into a single source is data aggregation. The output of the aggregator is smaller than the input because the data from various sources gets combined. This makes the processing task simpler and also reduces the network traffic and increases the performance.

Sqoop

Sqoop (Spidlen et al., 2013) is an Apache product that moves bulk data between Hadoop and structured data stores. It uses MapReduce for importing and exporting data among HDFS, Hive and HBase which provides fault tolerance as well as parallel operation. Sqoop-based connector is used by Microsoft to transfer data from its SQL server databases into Hadoop.

Flume

Flume (Spidlen et al., 2013) is also an Apache product which moves data between applications and Hadoop. It can collect, aggregate and move huge amount of data log. It has a simple fault tolerant architecture based on streaming data flows which can be used for online analytic applications.

Chukwa

Chukwa (Spidlen et al., 2013) is an application built on top of MapReduce framework and Hadoop Distributed File System. It is capable of monitoring, analyzing and displaying results and is very robust and scalable.

Big Data Tools for Healthcare

Some projects specific to the use of big data in healthcare are discussed below:

GenePattern

This is a genomic analysis platform developed at the Broad Institute which has a number of free tools for gene expression analysis, SNP analysis, proteomics, RNA-sequence analysis and flow cytometry.

SpatioTemporal Epidemiological Modeler (STEM)

This is a project developed by IBM and Eclipse foundation which helps enables scientists and public health officials in creating models of emerging infectious diseases as they develop so that there spread could be controlled. IBM along with researchers from University of California, San Francisco and Johns Hopkins University developed this project to create models for spread of dengue and malaria.

This model can predict future spread pattern of the diseases by taking into account the environmental characteristics like temperature, soil conditions and precipitation. STEM helps in correlating all this data with the data of the disease and forecasts the region where the disease could spread next.

CHALLENGES ASSOCIATED WITH USE OF BIG DATA IN HEALTHCARE

There are many challenges associated with analysis of healthcare data using big data concepts. Two main challenges are the technical expertise needed and non-availability of robust and integrated security.

Expertise

Specialized skill sets are needed to process the huge amount of medical data available. But the IT experts in the hospital are only familiar with the SQL programming language and traditional data processing using RDBMS. They are not ready the learn the complexities associated with big data processing. Hence most of the work is carried out only at the research level.

Data scientists who are experts in manipulating the big data environment are employed by organizations to extract the information from it. There are very few experts available with these skill sets and are also very expensive. There is a huge demand for these data scientists specially in the banking and e-business domain.

But the situation is ought to change with the development of new tools which will help people with less-specialized skillsets to work easily with big data. Tools are being developed which can use SQL for querying. Once this happens big data can be used in a big way in the health care sector.

Polybase is a tool developed by Microsoft which uses an extended SQL syntax to query both SQL relational databases and Hadoop Distributed File System (HDFS) systems. Impala is another tool which enables the use of SQL over a Hadoop database. Use of these types of tools will help the big data analytics in healthcare in a great way.

Security

The security and privacy of patient data is of utmost importance in the healthcare sector. Health Insurance Portability and Accountability Act of 1996 (HIPAA) is an act developed in United States that provides data security and privacy provisions for safeguarding medical history of patients. HIPAA compliance is non-negotiable in healthcare. But integrated methods to manage security in big data are still not available. Till the patient information is shared only with a small group of data scientists, it is not a big issue. But once this information has to be shared by a large group of people security becomes the most important concern.

Steps have to be taken by healthcare organizations today to make the patient data secure. We know that big data runs on an open source technology with a lot of inconsistencies with regard to everything including security. The choice of big data vendors for organizations is very crucial to avoid security issues in the future.

Healthcare organizations should go for well supported, commercial software's to implement big data instead of starting with a new Apache distribution which does not consider the security aspect. Cloud-based solution like Azure HDInsight can also be used as a startup option. Cloudera is an example of a well supported secure distribution. This company has created a Hadoop environment which supports authentication, authorization, auditing and data protection. It is a Payment Card Industry (PCI) compliant environment. Other commercially available tools are also trying to ensure that they provide services which are HIPAA complaint so that they can be used in the healthcare industry.

REFERENCES

Asay, M. (2014, November 19). *MongoDB, Cassandra, and HBase -- the three NoSQL databases to watch*. Retrieved from http://www.infoworld.com

Astrom, C., Rocklov, J., Hales, S., Beguin, A., Louis, V., & Sauerborn, R. (2012). Potential distribution of dengue fever under scenarios of climate change and economic development. *EcoHealth*, *9*(4), 448–454. doi:10.100710393-012-0808-0 PMID:23408100

Balaya, S., Paul, S. D., D'Lima, L. V., & Pavri, K. M. (1969). Investigations on an outbreak of dengue in Delhi in 1967. *The Indian Journal of Medical Research*, *57*, 767–774. PMID:5805380

Balcan, D., Hu, H., Goncalves, B., Bajardi, P., Poletto, C., Ramasco, J. J., ... Vespignani, A. (2009). Seasonal transmission potential and activity peaks of the new influenza A(H1N1): A Monte Carlo likelihood analysis based on human mobility. *BMC Medicine*, *7*(1), 45. doi:10.1186/1741-7015-7-45 PMID:19744314

Beatty, M. E., Stone, A., Fitzsimons, D. W., Hanna, J. N., Lam, S. K., Vong, S., ... Margolis, H. S. (2010). Best practices in dengue surveillance: A report from the Asia-Paci c and Americas Dengue Prevention Boards. *PLoS Neglected Tropical Diseases*, *4*(11), e890. doi:10.1371/journal.pntd.0000890 PMID:21103381

Bengtsson, L., Lu, X., Thorson, A., Garfield, R., & von Schreeb, J. (2011). Improved response to disasters and outbreaks by tracking population movements with mobile phone network data: A post-earthquake geospatial study in Haiti. *PLoS Medicine*, *8*(8), e1001083. doi:10.1371/journal.pmed.1001083 PMID:21918643

Bhatt, S., Gething, P. W., Brady, O. J., Messina, J. P., Farlow, A. W., Moyes, C. L., ... Hay, S. I. (2013). The global distribution and burden of dengue. *Nature*, *496*(7446), 504–507. doi:10.1038/nature12060 PMID:23563266

Bian, J., Topaloglu, U., Yu, F., & Yu, F. (2012). *Towards Large-scale Twitter Mining for Drug-related Adverse Events*. Maui, HI: SHB. doi:10.1145/2389707.2389713

Borkar, V. R., Carey, M. J., & Chen, L. (2012). Big data platforms: What's next? *ACM Crossroads*, *19*(1), 44–49. doi:10.1145/2331042.2331057

Carey, D. E., Myers, R. M., Reuben, R., & Rodrigues, F. M. (1966). Studies on dengue in Vellore, South India. *The American Journal of Tropical Medicine and Hygiene*, *15*(4), 580–587. doi:10.4269/ajtmh.1966.15.580 PMID:5949559

Cattuto, C., Van den Broeck, W., Barrat, A., Colizza, V., Pinton, J.-F., & Vespignani, A. (2010). Dynamics of Person-to-Person Interactions from Distributed RFID Sensor Networks. *PLoS One*, *5*(7), e11596. doi:10.1371/journal.pone.0011596 PMID:20657651

Chaturvedi, U. C., Kapoor, A. K., Mathur, A., Chandra, D., Khan, A. M., & Mehrotra, R. M. L. (1970). A clinical and epidemiological study of an epidemic of febrile illness with haemorrhagic manifestations which occurred at Kanpur, India in 1968. *Bulletin of the World Health Organization*, *43*, 281–287. PMID:4249614

Chaturvedi, U. C., Mathur, A., Kapoor, A. K., Mehrotra, N. K., & Mehrotra, R. M. L. (1970). Virological study of an epidemic of febrile illness with haemorrhagic manifestations at Kanpur, India, during 1968. *Bulletin of the World Health Organization, 43*, 289–293. PMID:5312525

Chaudhuri, R. N., Saha, T. K., & Chaudhuri, A. D. (1965). Dengue-like fever in Calcutta: Further preliminary observations. *Bulletin of the Calcutta School of Tropical Medicine, 13*, 2–3. PMID:14281058

Datafloq. (n.d.). Retrieved from https://datafloq.com/big-data-open-source-tools/os-data-aggregation/

Dean, J., & Ghemawat, S. (2008). MapReduce: Simplified data processing on large clusters. *Communications of the ACM, 51*(1), 107–113. doi:10.1145/1327452.1327492

Deepak. (2016). *A Critical Comparison of NOSQL Databases in the Context of Acid and Base*. Culminating Projects in Information Assurance. Paper 8.

Eysenbach, G. (2009). Infodemiology and infoveillance: Framework for an emerging set of public health informatics methods to analyze search, communication and publication behavior on the Internet. *Journal of Medical Internet Research, 11*(1), e11. doi:10.2196/jmir.1157 PMID:19329408

Feldman, B., Martin, E. M., & Skotnes, T. (2012). *Big Data in Healthcare Hype and Hope*. Retrieved from http://www.west-info.eu/files/big-data-in- healthcare.pdf

Ferreira, G. L. (2012). Global dengue epidemiology trends. *Revista do Instituto de Medicina Tropical de São Paulo, 54*(Suppl 18), S5–S6. doi:10.1590/S0036-46652012000700003 PMID:23011450

Ghosh, B. N. (1968). A study on the epidemic of dengue-like fever in Pondicherry (1964-65 and 1965-66). *Journal of the Indian Medical Association, 51*, 261–264. PMID:5706900

Gonzalez, M. C., Hidalgo, C. A., & Barabasi, A.-L. (2008). Understanding individual human mobility patterns. *Nature, 453*(7196), 779–782. doi:10.1038/nature06958 PMID:18528393

Green, M. D., Freedman, D. M., & Gordis, L. (2000). *Reference guide on epidemiology. Reference manual on scientific evidence*. Available: http://www.fjc.gov/public/pdf.nsf/lookup/sciman06.pdf/$file/sciman06.pdf

Gubler, D. J. (2002). The global emergence/resurgence of arboviral diseases as public health problems. *Archives of Medical Research, 33*(4), 330–342. doi:10.1016/S0188-4409(02)00378-8 PMID:12234522

Gubler, D. J. (2011). Dengue, Urbanization and Globalization: The Unholy Trinity of the 21(st) Century. *Tropical Medicine and Health, 39*(Suppl 4), 3–11. doi:10.2149/tmh.2011-S05 PMID:22500131

Gubler, D. J. (2012). The economic burden of dengue. *The American Journal of Tropical Medicine and Hygiene, 86*(5), 743–744. doi:10.4269/ajtmh.2012.12-0157 PMID:22556068

Guzman, M. G., & Kouri, G. (2002). Dengue: An update. *The Lancet Infectious Diseases, 2*(1), 33–42. doi:10.1016/S1473-3099(01)00171-2 PMID:11892494

IBM. (2013). *Southern Denmark Tackles Heart Disease with IBM Big Data Analytics Program*. Press Release.

IBM. (n.d.). *Big data and information management*. Retrieved from http://www-01.ibm.com/soft ware/data/bigdata/

IHTT. (2013). *Transforming Health Care through Big Data Strategies for leveraging big data in the health care industry*. Retrieved from http://ihealthtran.com/ wordpress/2013/03/iht%C2%B2-releases-big-data-research-report- download-today/

Karamchandani, P. V. (1946). Dengue group of fevers in India. *Lancet, 1*(6386), 92–93. doi:10.1016/S0140-6736(46)91229-9 PMID:21011278

Kelly, J. (2013). *Apache drill brings sql-like, ad hoc query capabilities to big data*. Retrieved from http://wikibon.org/wiki/v/Apache-Drill-Brings-SQL-Like-Ad-Hoc-Query-Capabilities-to-Big-Data

Khoury, M. J., & Ioannidis, J. P. (2014). Big data meets public health. *Science, 3466213*(6213), 1054–1055. doi:10.1126cience.aaa2709 PMID:25430753

Khoury, M. J., & Wei, G. (2015). The future of epidemiology in the era of precision medicine: cancer, cardiovascular disease, and beyond [Web log post]. Retrieved from http://epi.grants.cancer.gov/blog/archive/2015/08-11.html

Krishnamurthy, K., Kasturi, T. E., & Chittipantulu, G. (1965). Clinical and pathological studies of an outbreak of dengue-like illness in Visakhapatnam. *The Indian Journal of Medical Research, 53*, 800–812. PMID:5830412

Lauer, M. S. (2012). Time for a creative transformation of epidemiology in the United States. *Journal of the American Medical Association, 30817*(17), 1804–1805. doi:10.1001/jama.2012.14838 PMID:23117782

Lee, K.-H., Lee, Y.-J., Choi, H., Chung, Y. D., & Moon, B. (2012). Parallel data processing with MapReduce: A survey. *SIGMOD Record, 40*(4), 11–20. doi:10.1145/2094114.2094118

Lopez, D., Gunasekaran, M., & Murugan, B. S. (2014) Spatial Big Data Analytics of Influenza Epidemic in Vellore, India. *Proceedings: IEEE International Conference on Big Data. IEEE International Conference on Big Data*, 19–24.

Lynch, C., & Roper, C. (2011). The transit phase of migration: Circulation of malaria and its multi-drug-resistant forms in Africa. *PLoS Medicine, 8*(5), e1001040. doi:10.1371/journal.pmed.1001040 PMID:21655316

Malviya, A., Udhani, A., & Soni, S. (2016). R-tool: Data analytic framework for big data. *Symposium on Colossal Data Analysis and Networking (CDAN)*. 10.1109/CDAN.2016.7570960

Merler, S., Ajelli, M., Pugliese, A., & Ferguson, N. M. (2011). Determinants of the spa- tiotemporal dynamics of the 2009 H1N1 pandemic in Europe: Implications for real- time modelling. *PLoS Computational Biology, 7*(9), e1002205. doi:10.1371/journal.pcbi.1002205 PMID:21980281

Mooney, S. J., Westreich, D. J., & El-Sayed, A. M. (2015). Epidemiology in the Era of Big Data. *Epidemiology (Cambridge, Mass.), 26*(3), 390–394. doi:10.1097/EDE.0000000000000274 PMID:25756221

Mossong, J., Hens, N., Jit, M., Beutels, P., Auranen, K., & Mikolajczak, R. (2008). Social contacts and mixing patterns relevant to the spread of infectious diseases. *PLoS Medicine, 5*(3), e74. doi:10.1371/journal.pmed.0050074 PMID:18366252

Mukhopadhyay, A., Maulik, U., Bandyopadhyay, S., & Coello, C. A. C. (2014). A survey of multiobjective evolutionary algorithms for data mining: Part I. *IEEE Transactions on Evolutionary Computation, 18*(1), 4–19. doi:10.1109/TEVC.2013.2290086

Murray, N.E.A., Quam, M.B., & Wilder-Smith, A. (2013). Epidemiology of dengue: past, present and future prospects. *Clinical Epidemiology, 5*, 299–309.

Myers, R. M., Carey, D. E., Banerjee, K., Reuben, R., & Ramamurti, D. V. (1968). Recovery of dengue type 3 virus from human serum and *Aedes aegypti* in South India. *The Indian Journal of Medical Research, 56*, 781–787. PMID:5680412

Network, T. S. B. D. A. (2013). *Big Data Analytics A Research and Innovation Agenda for Sweden*. The Swedish Big Data Analytics Network Sweden.

Ohlhorst, F. (2012). *Big Data Analytics: Turning Big Data into Big Money*. John Wiley & Sons. doi:10.1002/9781119205005

Paul, S. D., Dandawate, C. N., Banerjee, K., & Krishnamurthy, K. (1965). Virological and serological studies on an outbreak of dengue-like illness in Visakhapatnam, Andhra Pradesh. *The Indian Journal of Medical Research, 53*, 777–789. PMID:5830410

PCAST. (2014). P.s.C.o.A.o.S.a.T., Big Data and Privacy: a Technological Perspective. Washington, DC: White House.

Pentland, A., & Pentland, S. (2008). *Honest signals: how they shape our world*. Cambridge, MA: MIT Press.

Philip Chen, C. L., & Zhang, C.-Y. (2014). Data-intensive applications, challenges, techniques and technologies: A survey on Big Data. *Inform. Sci., 275*, 314–347. doi:10.1016/j.ins.2014.01.015

Podesta, J., Pritzker, P., Moniz, E. J., Holdren, J., & Zients, J. (2014). *Big data: seizing opportunities, preserving values*. Executive Office of the President. Report. Retrieved from: https://obamawhitehouse.archives.gov/sites/default/files/docs/big_data_privacy_report_may_1_2014.pdf

Raghupathi, W., & Kesh, S. (2007). Interoperable electronic health records design: towards a service-oriented architecture. *e-Service Journal, 5*, 39–57.

Raghupathi, W., & Raghupathi, V. (2013). *An Overview of Health Analytics*. Working paper.

Ramakrishanan, S. P., Gelfand, H. M., Bose, P. N., Sehgal, P. N., & Mukharjee, R. N. (1964). The epidemic of acute haemorrhagic fever, Calcutta, 163: Epidemiological inquiry. *The Indian Journal of Medical Research, 52*, 633–650. PMID:14195504

Salathe, M., Kazandjieva, M., Lee, J. W., Levis, P., Feldman, M. W., & Jones, J. H. (2010). A high- resolution human contact network for infectious disease transmission. *Proceedings of the National Academy of Sciences of the United States of America, 107*(51), 22020–22025. doi:10.1073/pnas.1009094108 PMID:21149721

Sarkar, J. K., Pavri, K. M., Chatterjee, S. N., Chakravarty, S. K., & Aanderson, C. R. (1964). Virological and serological studies of cases of haemorrhagic fever in Calcutta. *The Indian Journal of Medical Research, 52*, 684–691. PMID:14195508

Shepard, D. S., Undurraga, E. A., & Halasa, Y. A. (2013). Economic and disease burden of dengue in Southeast Asia. *PLoS Neglected Tropical Diseases*, *7*(2), e2055. doi:10.1371/journal.pntd.0002055 PMID:23437406

Singh & Reddy. (2014). A survey on platforms for big data analytics. *Journal of Big Data*, *1*, 8. PMID:26191487

Spidlen, Barsky, Breuer, Carr, Nazaire, Hill, ... Qian. (2013). GenePattern flow cytometry suite. *Source Code for Biology and Medicine*, *8*(1), 14. doi:10.1186/1751-0473-8-14

Stehle, J., Voirin, N., Barrat, A., Cattuto, C., Colizza, V., Isella, L., ... Vanhems, P. (2011). Simulation of an SEIR infectious disease model on the dynamic contact network of conference attendees. *BMC Medicine*, *9*(1), 87. doi:10.1186/1741-7015-9-87 PMID:21771290

Szlezak, N., Evers, M., Wang, J., & Perez, L. (2014). The role of big data and advanced analytics in drug discovery, development, and commercialization. *Nature*, *95*(5), 492–495. PMID:24642713

Tatem, A. J., Qiu, Y., Smith, D. L., Sabot, O., Ali, A. S., & Moonen, B. (2009). The use of mobile phone data for the estimation of the travel patterns and imported Plasmodium falciparum rates among Zanzibar residents. *Malaria Journal*, *8*(1), 287. doi:10.1186/1475-2875-8-287 PMID:20003266

WHO. (2009). *Dengue: Guidelines for Diagnosis, Treatment, Prevention and Control*. Geneva: World Health Organization.

WHO. (2012a). *Dengue and severe dengue: Fact Sheet No 117*. Geneva: World Health Organization (WHO). Available from: http://www.who.int/mediacentre/factsheets/ fs117/en/index.html

WHO. (2012b). *Global Strategy for Dengue Prevention and Control, 2012–2020*. Geneva: WHO Press.

WHO. (2013). *TDR Global Alert and Repsonse Dengue/Dengue Haemorrhagic Fever* Geneva: World Health Organization (WHO). Available from: http://www.who. int/csr/disease/dengue/en/index.html

WHO. (2014). Mobile phones help people with diabetes to manage fasting and feasting during Ramadan. *Features 2014*.

Wilder-Smith, A., & Gubler, D. J. (2008). Geographic expansion of dengue: The impact of international travel. *The Medical Clinics of North America*, *92*(6), 1377–1390. doi:10.1016/j.mcna.2008.07.002 PMID:19061757

Zenger, B. (2012). Can Big Data Solve Healthcare's Big Problems? *HealthByte*. Retrieved from: http://www.equityhealthcare.com/docstor/EH%20Blog%20on%20Analytics.pdf

Zikopoulos, P.C., DeRoos, D., Parasuraman, K., Deutsch, T., Corrigan, D., & Giles, J. (2013). *Harness the Power of Big Data*. McGraw-Hill.

This research was previously published in Intelligent Systems for Healthcare Management and Delivery; pages 285-305, copyright year 2019 by Medical Information Science Reference (an imprint of IGI Global).

Chapter 46
Big Data Analytics Using Apache Hive to Analyze Health Data

Pavani Konagala

Vaagdevi College of Engineering, India

ABSTRACT

A large volume of data is stored electronically. It is very difficult to measure the total volume of that data. This large amount of data is coming from various sources such as stock exchange, which may generate terabytes of data every day, Facebook, which may take about one petabyte of storage, and internet archives, which may store up to two petabytes of data, etc. So, it is very difficult to manage that data using relational database management systems. With the massive data, reading and writing from and into the drive takes more time. So, the storage and analysis of this massive data has become a big problem. Big data gives the solution for these problems. It specifies the methods to store and analyze the large data sets. This chapter specifies a brief study of big data techniques to analyze these types of data. It includes a wide study of Hadoop characteristics, Hadoop architecture, advantages of big data and big data eco system. Further, this chapter includes a comprehensive study of Apache Hive for executing health-related data and deaths data of U.S. government.

INTRODUCTION

In today's life, web is playing an important role. A large amount of data is available online. These data are getting generated from various sources such as twitter, face book, cell phone GPS data, healthcare etc. Big data analytics (Chen et al, 2014) is the process of collecting and analysing large complex data sets containing a variety of data types to find customer preferences and other useful information. The processing of such data is difficult using traditional data processing applications. Therefore, to manage and process these types of data requires a new set of frameworks. Hadoop is an open software project for structuring Big Data and for making this data useful for analytics purposes. The creator of this software is Doug Cutting. He is an employee at Yahoo for the Nutch search engine project. He named it after seeing his son's toy elephant. The symbol for Hadoop is a yellow elephant. Hadoop serves as a core

DOI: 10.4018/978-1-6684-3662-2.ch046

platform to enable the processing of large data sets over cluster of servers. These servers are designed to be scalable with high degree of fault tolerance.

- **Seven V's of Big Data Analytics:** The Big Data (Sagiroglu et al, 2013) is broken into seven dimensions: Volume, Variety, Velocity, Veracity, Visualisation, Variability and Value.
  - ○ **Volume:** Volume is the amount of data. The volume of data stored in an organisation has grown from megabytes to petabytes. The big volume represents Big Data.
  - ○ **Variety:** Variety refers to the many sources and types of data such as structural, semi structural and un structural.
  - ○ **Velocity:** It deals with the speed at which data flows from different sources such as social media sites, mobile device, business process, networks and human interaction etc. This velocity of data should be handled to make valuable business decisions.
  - ○ **Veracity:** It is virtually worthless, if the data set being analysed is incomplete and inaccurate. This may happen due to the collection of data set from various sources with different formats, with noise and errors. Large amount of time may be involved to clean up this noisy data rather than analysing it.
  - ○ **Visualisation:** Once the data set is processed it should be presented in readable format. Visualisation may contain many parameters and variables which cannot be represented using normal graphical formats or spread sheets. Even three-dimensional visualisations also may not help. So, the visualisation has become a new challenge of Big Data Analytics. AT & T has announced a new package called Nanocubes for visualisation.
  - ○ **Variability:** Variability refers to the data set whose meaning and interpretations changes constantly. These changes occur depending on the context. Particularly this is true with Natural Language Processing. A single word may have different meanings. Over time new meanings may be created in place of old one. Interpreting them is essential in the applications like social media analytics. Therefore, the boundless variability of Big Data presents a unique challenge for Data scientists.
  - ○ **Value:** There is a high potential value for Big Data Analytics. In the applications such as US health care system, Big Data Analytics have reduced the spending to 12-17 percent. The Big Data offers not only new and effective methods of selling but also new products to meet previously undetected market demands. Many industries use Big Data for reducing the cost of their organisations and their customers.

Although the popular 3 V's (Volume, Velocity, and Variety) of Big Data Analytics are intrinsic but the other V's (Variability, Veracity, Value and Visualisation) are also important attributes. All of them are useful to analyse and benefit from Big Data Analytics.

- **Hadoop Advantages:** The characteristics or advantages of Hadoop which makes it best solution to handle the data is as listed below.
- **Scalability:** Depending on amount of client data more systems are added to store any amount of data. i.e. Hadoop can scale up incrementally.
- **Flexibility:** Hadoop can store any variety of data i.e. structured and un structured data or semi structured data.
- **Cost Effective:** Hadoop is an open source and can be downloaded freely.

- **Fault Tolerance:** By using the facility of Replication factor the data can replicated or duplicated on two, three or more systems. If one system crashes also the data is available on other system.
- **High Performance:** Hadoop provides high performance in presence of failures also.

COMPONENTS OF HADOOP

HDFS (Hadoop File System) (Patnaik, 2013) and MAP REDUCE are the two core components of Hadoop (Dhawan et al, 2013). Hadoop provides reliable shared storage by Hadoop File System and analysis by Map Reduce.

- **HDFS:** Hadoop Distributed File System is a file system which is used for storing large data sets in a default block of size of 64 MB in distributed manner. Hadoop creates a cluster of computer machines. Each cluster can be built within expensive computer machines. Hadoop coordinates work among the cluster of machines. In case of failure, Hadoop operates continually by shifting the work to remaining machines in the cluster. HDFS stores the data on the cluster in form of 64 MB (by default) or 128 MB blocks each. And each block is replicated 3 times by default. This replication factor may be incremented depending on the requirement.

Components of HDFS

As shown in the figure 1, the main components of HDFS are Name Node, Data Node and Secondary Name Node. Name Node works as a master of the system. It manages and maintains the blocks which are present on Data Node. However Data Nodes serve as slaves which are deployed on each machine and provide actual storage. It also processes the read and write requests of the clients. Secondary Name Node works as a backup for Name Node metadata. It connects to Name Node every hour. If Name Node fails, Secondary Name Node sends metadata back to Name Node so that it can be built again. Name Nodes meta data contains list of files, list of blocks for each file, list of Data Node for each block and file attributes such as access time, replication factor etc.

- **MapReduce:** MapReduce (Pandey, 2016) is created by Google and works as a programming framework for distributed computing. It is based on divide and conquer method to solve complicated Big Data problems into small units of work and process them parallel. In other words, we can say that the data set is reduced into smaller subset where analytics can be applied. Basically, there are two main functions of Map Reduce. They are listed below.
- **Map:** This function splits up the input data into multiple jobs and executes them in parallel. It takes key/value pairs as input and generates an intermediate set of key/value pairs.
- **Reduce:** This function receives the mapped intermediate values and key then produces the final result.
- **Job Tracker and Task Tracker:** A Job Tracker node is assigned to each Map Reduce. It distributes mapper and reducer functions to available Task Trackers and monitors the result. i.e. it schedules and manages jobs. However, a Task Tracker executes map and reduce functions on each cluster node and then result is communicated back to the Job Tracker. The high-level architecture of Map Reduce is shown in the Figure 2.

Figure 1. Components of Hadoop File System.

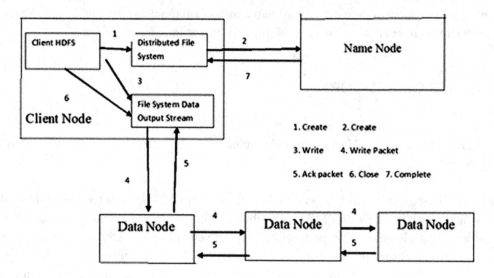

Figure 2. High level architecture of MapReduce

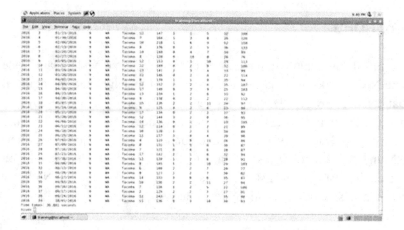

HADOOP ECO SYSTEM

Many technologies are built on the top of Hadoop to increase its efficiency and performance. These sets of technologies along with the Hadoop are known as Hadoop Eco System (Bhradwaj et al, 2015; Garg et al, 2016; Urmila et al, 2016) This Hadoop Eco System is represented in the figure 3 which consists of following technologies.

- **Apache Pig:** It was developed by Yahoo for creating and executing MapReduce (Harshawardhan et al, 2014; Dhyani et al, 2014) jobs on very large data sets. Then it was moved to Apache Software Foundation and known as Apache pig. The language used for this platform is known as pig Latin. It is an alternative to java for writing MapReduce programs. Pig scripts take 5% of the time compared to writing MapReduce programs. Similar to actual pig that can digest almost any type of food, Apache pig can handle any type of data. Using pig, overall development and testing time is reduced as we have to write only fewer lines of codes.

Figure 3. Hadoop Eco System.

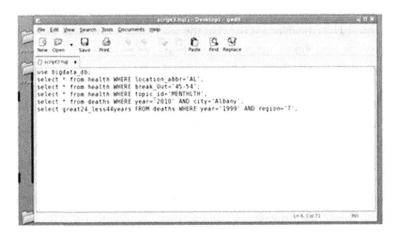

- **Sqoop:** It is similar to an ETL (Extract, Transfer and Load) tool which is used to transfer bulk data between Apache Hadoop and structured data stores such as Relational Database servers and vice versa. It facilitates bidirectional exchange of data between relational databases and HDFS. With Sqoop the contents of table are imported to HDFS which further may be used as MapReduce jobs and can be exported from HDFS to Relational databases.
- **Hbase:** In Hadoop, the data is accessed in a sequential manner only. That is, even for a simplest job, entire data set has to be searched. So, a new solution is needed to access data in random manner. Applications such as Hbase, MongoDB, Dynamo and couchDB are some of databases that store large amount of data and allows data access in random manner. Hbase is an open source, horizontally scalable which built on top of Hadoop. It is a column-oriented database. It provides quick and fast random access of large amount of structured data set.
- **Zookeeper:** Apache Zookeeper is an open source project to provide centralized infrastructure. This centralised infrastructure helps to synchronize across the Hadoop cluster. The architecture of Zookeeper has hierarchical name space architecture. Each node in the Zookeeper architecture is called as Znode. These Znodes can be updated by any node in the cluster. These changes are informed to Znode by any node in the cluster. Zookeeper was designed to store Metadata such as status information, configuration, location information etc.
- **Flume:** Flume is used in social media analytics. It is a reliable, distributed and available service to collect, aggregate large amounts of data sets efficiently. It is used for moving large amount of streaming data sets into Hadoop Distributed File System. This application is built on the top of Hadoop. The stream data may be generated from various sources such as sensor, machine data, logs, face book, twitter or any other social media. The data model for flume consists of source, sink, channel and agent. Through source the stream data enters into the Flume. Sink is used to de-

liver the data to the destination. However, channel will act as a medium between source and sink. Agent is the Java Virtual Machine which creates an environment to run Flume.

- **Solr:** Like Flume, Solr is also used in social media analytics. Flume is used to stream web data where as Solr is used to store this web data. This can be done by indexing via XML, JSON, CSV, python, Ruby or binary. Queries are executed and results are received inform of XML, JSON, CSV, python, Ruby or binary. It is reliable, scalable and fault tolerant.

- **Hue:** Hadoop User Experience (HUE) is an open source project which provides a web user interface or Graphical User Interface (GUI) for the users. As it provides web GUI, users can easily interact with Apache Hadoop to increase productivity.

- **Oozie:** It is a scheduling tool which is a part of Hue. Oozie is a java web application used to schedule Hadoop jobs. There are two basic types of Oozie Jobs. They are Oozie Workflow and Oozie scheduler. After creating the job it is submitted to work flow with all the inputs. After submitting the job through work flow it comes to scheduler. The Scheduler will schedule the jobs. Oozie can be accessed through hue.

- **Impala:** Impala is a flavour of Cloudera and it is 20 to 100 times faster than Hive for retrieval of the data. It is a distributed SQL engine. Clients can connect to Impala through JDBC or ODBC and authentication is done using Kerberos. Once job is submitted to Job Tracker, job is executed by Impala server. There are three key components of Cloudera Impala. They are Impala shell, Impalad, Impala-state-store. Impala shell is used to start the shell script and queries are executed here. On each Hadoop data node, Impalad runs which plans and executes the queries sent from Impala shell. The location information about all the running Impalad instances is stored by Impala-state-store.

- **Tableau:** Tableau transforms the data into interactive visualisations called dashboards. It is fast and easy tool for analysing the data. It is also used for Visualisation and information sharing. Hadoop is one of the data sources for Tableau. That is, it can connect to any flavours of Hadoop, corporate Data Warehouse, Microsoft Excel or web-based data.

- **Yarn:** Apache Hadoop Yarn is a cluster management tool which is redesigned as resource manager. Two separate daemons are created for the functionalities of resource management and job scheduling/monitoring. Yarn has two basic components: a global Resource Manager (RM) and a per-application Application Master (AM). Scheduler and Applications Manager are the two components of Resource Manager. Scheduler allocates the resources to various running applications. However, Application Manager accepts job submissions and executes the application specific application Master and provides the service for restarting the Application Master container on failure.

- **Spark:** Apache spark is an open source cluster computing framework. It provides up to 100 times faster performance compared to Map reduce. Map Reduce is suitable for batch processing whereas spark is suitable for batch processing and real time processing. Spark provides machine learning algorithms which allow programs to load and query data repeatedly. The core components of spark are: Spark Core and Resilient Distributed Datasets, Spark SQL, Spark Streaming, MLib and GraphX.

- **Apache HIVE:** It is developed by Face book initially then it was taken by Apache software and named as Apache Hive (Singh et al, 2015). Hive provides a platform to develop scripts similar to SQL. The developers can write the queries in Hive using Hive Query Language. It is an open source and scalable query language. It analyses large datasets stored in Hadoop's HDFS. The architecture of Hive is represented in the figure 4. The main components of Hive architecture are Meta store, Driver, Compiler, Optimizer, Executer and command line interface and user interface. Meta data about each table is stored in Meta store. This Meta data may store information such as schema and location of table etc. It helps the driver to keep track of the data sets distributed over network. Driver receives the HIVE query statements and executes them by creating sessions. It also monitors the life cycle and progress of the execution and stores the necessary meta data generated during the execution of query statement. The driver contains three parts compiler, optimizer and executor. Compiler converts the Hive query to an Abstract Syntax Tree (AST). Then this AST is converted into Directed Acyclic Graph (DAG). However, an Optimizer performs various transformations such as converting a pipeline of joins by a single join etc to get an optimized DAG. After compilation and optimization, the executer executes the tasks according to the DAG by interacting with the job tracker.

Command Line Interface (CLI) and User Interface (UI) are used to allow an external user to interact with HIVE by submitting queries. The process status is also monitored here. Like JDBC and ODBC servers, a Thrift server also allows the external clients to interact with HIVE (Lakavath et al, 2014).

HIVE provides a query language called Hive Query Language (HQL) which is similar to Structured Query Language (SQL). HIVE Query Language supports commands such as select, project, join, aggregate, union all and sub queries. HIVE supports Data Definition Language (DDL) statements to create tables. Then the data can be loaded from external sources into Hive tables using load command. Two different types of tables can be created by using HIVE. They are Managed tables and External tables. The data in managed tables are managed by HIVE whereas the data in External tables are managed outside HIVE. That means when a file is loaded into a managed table, the file is moved to data warehouse by HIVE. So, when the table is dropped, both the data and metadata are deleted. However, when a file is loaded into external table, no files are moved. So, when the table is dropped only metadata is deleted and the data is left alone. External tables are useful when more than one schema is used on the same data and to share the data between HIVE and other Hadoop applications.

Figure 4. Hive Architecture or components of Hive.

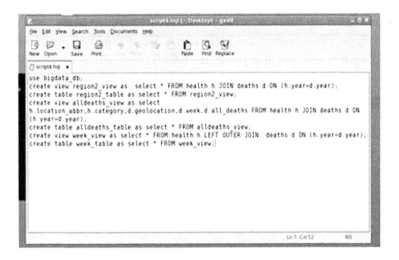

While creating the table the data can be partitioned based on the value of column (Frank et al, 2013). This partitioned data is used effectively for applying filters than unpartitioned data. In addition to primitive data types such as integer, float, double and string HIVE also supports associative arrays, lists and structures. To speed up the queries HIVE provides the concept of bucketing. Bucketing splits the data by a particular column. The benefit of bucketing is that, it imposes extra structure on table which can be used to speed up the queries. It improves performance when sampling the data. Number of buckets used can be specified using CLUSTERED BY clause. If the bucket to be sorted, then the command SORTED BY is used.

Hive also supports SQL join statements but supports only equi-joins. It supports inner joins, left outer joins, right outer joins, full outer joins, left semi joins, Map-side joins and Cartesian product joins. Currently Hive is not supporting update and delete of rows in existing tables.

EXPERIMENTAL RESULTS

This section highlights a case study which is based on Health & Human Services. The goal was a big data solution for predictive analysis of Health & Human Services. The challenge was to design a data warehouse to consolidate Health & Human Service data. In this work pre-configured Cloudera Hadoop 4.3.0 ("Index of Documents, n.d.; Rathbone, 2013) with virtual machine10 is used. The data set used for the experiments is collected from U.S. Department of Health & Human Services. This data set gives the Health Related Quality of Life (HRQOL) of people. This data set is collected from Behavioural Risk Factor Surveillance System (BRFSS). This data can be used to evaluate the public health programs introduced by U.S. government. This data is collected from non-institutionalized adults, 18 years old or older. The other data set used for the experiments is on Deaths in 122 U.S. cities. This data set contains the cause of death by age group. Also, the place and week of the death was included in the data set. The size of the data set "Behavioural Risk Factor Data: Health-Related Quality of Life (HRQOL)" is 32,228 KB with 1,26,466 rows whereas the size of the data set "Deaths in 122 U.S. cities - 1962-2016. 122 Cities Mortality Reporting System" is 17,146 KB with 3,46,344 rows. Figure 5 shows the organisation of this section to describe the implementation of Health data case study.

Hive scripts are executed to create tables for two data sets and to load them to Hive. Then two more scripts have written to join these two data sets and to create views. Figures 6 to 14 shows the screen shots of experiments conducted on the data sets using Hive Query Language (hql).

The above case study provides an overview of the utilisation of Big Data Technologies as an emerging discipline in health & human services. It explores the health condition of US citizens. It also calculates death rates per year.

Figure 5. Flowchart to implement Health data case study

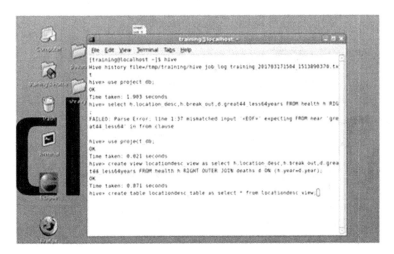

Figure 6. Creation of health database

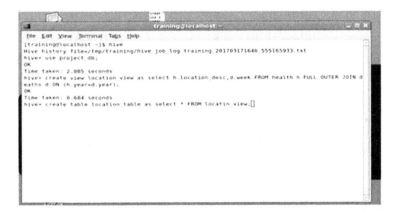

Figure 7. Description of health database.

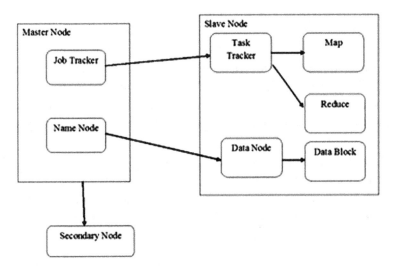

Figure 8. Contents of health database table.

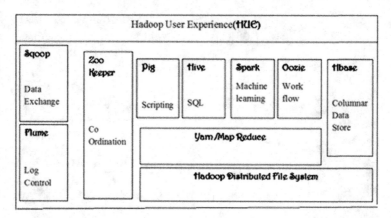

Figure 9. Creation of deaths database

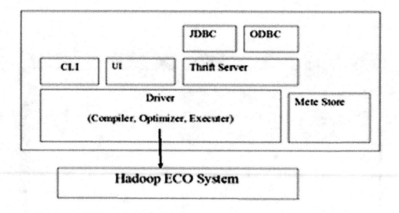

ISSUES OF BIG DATA TECHNOLOGIES

Storage, Processing and Management are the three issues which are to be addressed in dealing with big data.

- **Storage Issue:** If the data size is more, the system takes longer time to transfer data from storage node to processing node than the time required to process it. To solve this issue, transmit only the resulting data by processing the data in a place i.e. bring the code to the data.
- **Processing Issue:** If the data size is more, the system may take longer time to process it. One solution for this is to use new analytical and parallel algorithms in order to provide processing of data within acceptable time limits.
- **Management Issue:** Managing data is a difficult problem in big data analytics. Because the data may be in different formats such as documents, drawings, pictures, audio and video recordings etc. Further metadata to describe about the data may be in adequate. Till now there is no open source, platform independent solution exists to solve the above problem (Jason, 2018). There is a need to find a perfect solution in big data analytics for the same problem.

Figure 10. Contents of deaths database table.

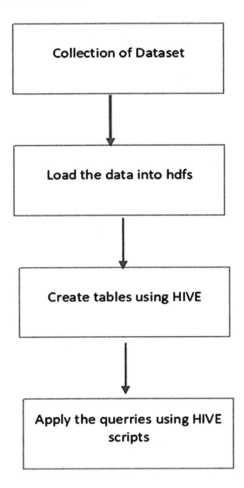

Figure 11. Hive script to display the contents of health and deaths table.

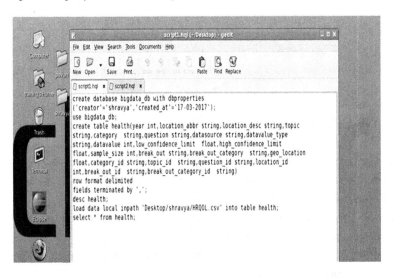

Figure 12. Hive script to create the view and join.

Figure 13. Hive script on right outer join.

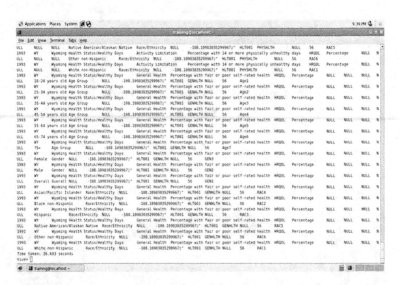

CHALLENGES OF BIG DATA TECHNOLOGIES

- **Privacy and Security:** The major challenge of big data is the privacy and security. The personal information of a person, such as cause of death in the Death database, may be sensitive and the person might not want any other person to know about them.

- **Fault Tolerance:** Fault Tolerance is another challenge of big data. In case of failure the damage should be in the acceptable limits. It is very difficult to achieve 100 percent fault tolerant system. However, a method should be employed to reduce the failure to an acceptable limit. One method is to divide the task into sub tasks and compute these sub tasks on different nodes.

Figure 14. Hive script on full outer join.

CONCLUSION

Big Data analytics has become most promising research area over the globe. Also, it is generating new opportunities and new challenges for business across each industry. The challenge is to integrate data from social media and other unstructured data into traditional Business Environment. Apache Hadoop provides a cost-effective solution for this challenge.

This paper describes characteristics of Big Data along with 7Vs, Volume, Variety, Velocity, Veracity, Visualisation, Variability and Value of it. Also, this paper described the Hadoop Eco system which can be used to process structured, semi structured and un structured data sets. Hive is used to load the dataset of about 1 lakh thirty thousand rows within 36 seconds. The concepts such as Join and Views are also applied to integrate the two data sets. From the results we can conclude that HIVE can be used effectively on large data sets for analysis. Also, for the developers who are good in SQL language, Hive provides an easy platform for analysis. Further this work may be extended by implementing a new and emerging Big Data tools to improve the performance of Hadoop.

REFERENCES

Bhradwaj, A. (2015). Big Data emerging Technologies: A case Study with Analyzing Twitter Data using Apache Hive. In *RAECS UIET Punjab University Chandigarh*. IEEE.

Chen, M., Mao, S., & Liu, Y. (2014). Big data: A survey. Mobile Networks and Applications, 9(2), 171-209. doi:10.100711036-013-0489-0

Dhawan & Rathee. (2013). Big Data Analytics using Hadoop Components like Pig and Hive. In *American International Journal of Research in Science* (pp. 88–93). Technology, Engineering & Mathematics.

Dhyani, B., & Barthwal, A. (2014). Big Data Analytics using Hadoop. *International Journal of Computers and Applications*, *108*(12), 1–59. doi:10.5120/18960-0288

(2016). Dr. Urmila R. Pol: Big Data Analysis: Comparison of Hadoop MapReduce, pig and Hive, International Journal of Innovative Research in Science. *Engineering and Technology, 5*(6), 9687–9693.

Garg, R., & Agarwal, H. (2016). Big Data Analytics Recommendation Solutions for Crop Disease using Hive and Hadoop Platform. *Indian Journal of Science and Technology, 9*(32), ●●●. doi:10.17485/ijst/2016/v9i32/100728

Harshawardhan, Bhosale, Devendra, & Gadekar. (2014). A Review Paper on Big Data and Hadoop. *International Journal of Scientific and Research Publications, 4*.

Index of Documents. (n.d.). Apache Hadoop. Retrieved from https://hadoop.apache.org/docs/

JASON. (2008). Data Analysis Challenges. The Mitre Corporation, JSR-08-142.

Lakavath, S. (2014). *A Big Data Hadoop Architecture for Online Analysis*. Academic Press.

Matthew Rathbone Blog. (2013). *A Beginners Guide to Hadoops*. Accessed May 3rd 2018: http://blog.mattherwrathbone.com/2013/04/17/what-is-hadoop.html

Pandey, P., Kumar, M., & Srivastav, P. (2016). Classification Techniques for Big Data: A Survey. *IEEE International Conference on Computing for Sustainable Global Development*, 3625-3629.

Patnaik, L. M. (2014). Bid Data Analytics: An Approach using Hadoop Distributed File System. International Journal of Engineering and Innovative Technology, 3, 239-243.

Sagiroglu, S., & Sinanc, D. (2013). Big data: A review. *IEEE International Conference on Collaboration Technologies and System (CTS)*, 42-47.

Singh, J., & Singhla, V. (2015). Big Data:Tools and Technologies in Big Data. *International Journal of Computers and Applications*.

Stephen, K., & Frank, A. J. (2013). Big data: Issues and challenges moving forward. *IEEE International Conference on System Science*.

This research was previously published in Nature-Inspired Algorithms for Big Data Frameworks; pages 358-372, copyright year 2019 by Engineering Science Reference (an imprint of IGI Global).

Index

B

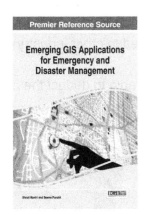
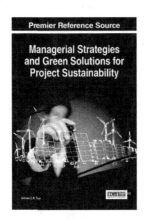

IGI Global's Transformative Open Access (OA) Model:
How to Turn Your University Library's Database Acquisitions Into a Source of OA Funding

Well in advance of Plan S, IGI Global unveiled their OA Fee Waiver (Read & Publish) Initiative. Under this initiative, librarians who invest in IGI Global's InfoSci-Books and/or InfoSci-Journals databases will be able to subsidize their patrons' OA article processing charges (APCs) when their work is submitted and accepted (after the peer review process) into an IGI Global journal.

How Does it Work?

Step 1: **Library Invests in the InfoSci-Databases:** A library perpetually purchases or subscribes to the InfoSci-Books, InfoSci-Journals, or discipline/subject databases.

Step 2: **IGI Global Matches the Library Investment with OA Subsidies Fund:** IGI Global provides a fund to go towards subsidizing the OA APCs for the library's patrons.

Step 3: **Patron of the Library is Accepted into IGI Global Journal (After Peer Review):** When a patron's paper is accepted into an IGI Global journal, they option to have their paper published under a traditional publishing model or as OA.

Step 4: **IGI Global Will Deduct APC Cost from OA Subsidies Fund:** If the author decides to publish under OA, the OA APC fee will be deducted from the OA subsidies fund.

Step 5: **Author's Work Becomes Freely Available:** The patron's work will be freely available under CC BY copyright license, enabling them to share it freely with the academic community.

Note: This fund will be offered on an annual basis and will renew as the subscription is renewed for each year thereafter. IGI Global will manage the fund and award the APC waivers unless the librarian has a preference as to how the funds should be managed.

Hear From the Experts on This Initiative:

"I'm very happy to have been able to make one of my recent research contributions *freely available* along with having access to the *valuable resources* found within IGI Global's InfoSci-Journals database."

– **Prof. Stuart Palmer,**
Deakin University, Australia

"Receiving the support from IGI Global's OA Fee Waiver Initiative *encourages me to continue my research work without any hesitation*."

– **Prof. Wenlong Liu,** College of Economics and Management at Nanjing University of Aeronautics & Astronautics, China

Printed in the United States
by Baker & Taylor Publisher Services